THE WAR ON POVERTY

THE WAR ON POVERTY

A New Grassroots History,

1964–1980

EDITED BY

ANNELISE ORLECK AND

LISA GAYLE HAZIRJIAN

The University of Georgia Press
Athens and London

© 2011 by the University of Georgia Press

Athens, Georgia 30602

www.ugapress.org

All rights reserved

Set in 10/14 Minion Pro by Graphic Composition, Inc.

Printed and bound by Thomson-Shore

The paper in this book meets the guidelines for
permanence and durability of the Committee on
Production Guidelines for Book Longevity of the
Council on Library Resources.

Printed in the United States of America

15   14   13   12   11   P   5   4   3   2   1

Library of Congress Cataloging-in-Publication Data

The war on poverty : a new grassroots history, 1964–1980 / edited by Annelise Orleck and Lisa
Gayle Hazirjian.

  p.   cm.

Includes index.

ISBN-13: 978-0-8203-3101-0 (hbk. : alk. paper)

ISBN-10: 0-8203-3101-5 (hbk. : alk. paper)

ISBN-13: 978-0-8203-3949-8 (pbk. : alk. paper)

ISBN-10: 0-8203-3949-0 (pbk. : alk. paper)

1. Poverty—Government policy—United States—History—20th century. 2. Economic
assistance, Domestic—United States—History—20th century. 3. Poor—Political activity—
United States—History—20th century. 4. Community development—United States—
History—20th century. 5. Public welfare—United States—History—20th century. I. Orleck,
Annelise. II. Hazirjian, Lisa Gayle, 1968–

HC110.P63W37 2011

362.5′561097309045—dc22

2011012914

British Library Cataloging-in-Publication Data available

In memory of Adina Back, historian, community organizer, and fierce mother-activist.

CONTENTS

THE WAR ON POVERTY

ANNELISE ORLECK

Introduction

The War on Poverty from the Grass Roots Up

On a blistering Las Vegas day in 1972, a desolate, dangerous corner of the city's black West Side came to life. Sweating, skinny teens carried load after load of garbage out of an abandoned hotel while their mothers, arms laden with cleaning supplies, set to work making the long-abandoned interior habitable again. Over the next few months, poor African American women and men armed with hammers and saws and carrying two-by-fours and rolls of wallpaper transformed a crumbling shell dating to the days of segregation into a thriving community and social service center.

Long an eyesore, a symbol of the flight of capital and of the government's lack of interest in the poor, the old Cove Hotel would soon become home to one of the nation's most successful free pediatric clinics, a medical and nutrition center for pregnant and nursing mothers, free breakfast and lunch programs, community anticrime projects, a food stamp distribution office, a day care center, parenting courses, a community newspaper, and a public swimming pool. All of these programs were funded at least in part by government antipoverty dollars and were run by the poor themselves. The women who created the Operation Life center soon opened their neighborhood's first library and performance center. They mounted voter registration drives; attended county, state, and national political party conventions; and ran electoral candidates who called this desperately poor neighborhood home. A sign hanging over the doorway to the clinic summed up this local movement's efforts and ethos: "In the Poverty Community, Of the Poverty Community, For the Poverty Community."[1]

That spirit—the fierce, proud energy with which a group of poor families reclaimed and revitalized a long-impoverished community—was ubiquitous between 1964 and 1980, the era that President Lyndon Baines Johnson ushered in on January 8, 1964, when he declared America's War on Poverty. That initiative galvanized poor people across the United States. It bubbled up from community meetings in coal-mining hollows and among councils of elders on Indian reservations. It animated late-night fireside discussions in the camps where Mexican migrant workers lived. This book captures the spirit that animated the War on Poverty from the bottom up. It is a story of how the poorest of the poor, despite daunting obstacles, transformed themselves into effective political actors who insisted on being heard.

These antipoverty activities swept up large numbers of African Americans, building on the accomplishments and the disappointments of the civil rights movement. The Economic Opportunity Act of 1964, with its call for "maximum feasible participation" by the poor, grew out of the mass civil rights mobilizations in the 1950s and early 1960s that, with blood and sacrifice, had won basic political rights for African Americans across the South. With more than half of all black Americans still living in poverty, waging a struggle for economic justice was the logical next step. In an age of intensifying racial nationalism, the soaring rhetoric of a president who promised to end poverty in our time raised the hopes of poor black city- and country-dwellers, inspired and ignited by visions of community control and economic self-sufficiency. African Americans responded with clear social blueprints for revitalizing their communities as well as with a willingness to perform the hard work necessary to make it happen.

They were not alone. Poor people across the nation mobilized in the name of participatory democracy and greater community control: rural whites in Appalachia, Cherokee Indians in Oklahoma, Puerto Ricans in the Bronx, migrant Mexican farmworkers in Wisconsin, and Chinese immigrants in overcrowded Chinatowns from New York to California. This book chronicles the largely untold histories of these community crusades: how people built enduring social programs based on LBJ's vision of a greater, more just society.

The master legislator from Texas was not the sort of president to present his policies in muted shades of gray. "I have called for a national war on poverty," he announced from the porch of a house inhabited by an out-of-work white coal miner in Inez, Kentucky, on April 24, 1964. "Our objective: Total victory." During that winter and spring, President Johnson traveled the country drumming up support for his antipoverty crusade. He consciously sought to appeal to white voters. A White House–produced film of his Appalachian tour highlights cheering, nearly all-white crowds.[2]

However, when Johnson stood in the stadium at the University of Michigan in May 1964 to lay out his vision of a "Great Society," he did not shy away from acknowledging that the effort formed part of a struggle for racial justice. He evoked a future of "abundance and liberty for all" Americans, "an end to poverty and racial injustice. . . . But that is just the beginning." Johnson called on his fellow citizens to help him create a society that "serves not only the needs of the body and the demands of commerce but the desire for beauty and the hunger for community."[3]

If Johnson's rhetoric now sounds inflated, he spoke during a very different time—after a decade in which hundreds of thousands of men, women, and children had put their bodies on the line to end a century of legal segregation; less than a year after a quarter of a million marchers had listened to Martin Luther King Jr.'s "I Have a Dream" speech; just a few months after a charismatic young president with a flair for high-flown speech had been murdered. Moreover, this vision of change was being articulated not by a political neophyte but by a man dubbed "Master of the Senate," a legendary legislative tactician and political pragmatist. Over the next two years, Johnson would shepherd through Congress a body of legislation more ambitious than that of any other modern president except for his mentor and role model, Franklin D. Roosevelt.

Within months of his call for a Great Society, Johnson pushed through Congress two bills that put the federal government in the business of defending rights and opening up opportunities for all Americans: the Civil Rights Act of 1964 and the Economic Opportunity Act. The Food Stamp Act, which also passed that summer, gave the government responsibility for feeding the hungry. By 1966, Johnson had spearheaded passage of the Voting Rights Act, the Elementary and Secondary Education Act, Social Security amendments establishing Medicare and Medicaid, bills creating the Department of Housing and Urban Development and the Department of Transportation, and legislation overhauling the nation's immigration and higher education systems. He drove creation of a national network of preschools for poor children, federally designated wilderness areas, and a national Teacher Corps and Public Health Service. In just two years, Johnson and Congress fundamentally and permanently transformed the structure and function of the federal government.

But Johnson's missteps in deepening U.S. military involvement in Vietnam enraged and alienated precisely the constituencies he had hoped to win over through his Great Society programs and doomed his chances for reelection. In 1968, Johnson announced that he would not run again for the presidency. He left Washington a broken man, with the nation torn apart. Johnson's presidency is widely seen as both the high-water mark of mid-twentieth-century American liberalism—filled with optimistic faith in government's capacity to redress inequities of rights and resources—and the rock on which that faith foundered.

The unfinished War on Poverty is similarly seen as both the most ambitious and the most disastrous of Johnson's Great Society programs. Yet we have only begun honestly to examine its complex legacy. The top-down view of the War on Poverty has been written many times over, by historians and politicians from across the political spectrum. As seen from the alabaster buildings of Washington, D.C., the antipoverty crusade's failures can seem glaring and its successes insignificant. But to truly understand its impact on American cities and rural areas, on men and women, on children and the elderly, on blacks, whites, Latinos, Native Americans, and Asian Americans, requires looking from the bottom up.

This book takes a fresh look from a largely ignored perspective: that of the men and women in impoverished communities across America who made the War on Poverty work and whose contributions endure. It chronicles the internecine divisions and disagreements that sometimes short-circuited these efforts. It describes the campaigns of terror waged against activists in the South who challenged the long-established political and social order. And it evokes the crushing disappointment so many people felt when they realized that the president and Congress would let them run only so far with their dreams and that local authorities—mayors, city council members, governors, police chiefs—had no intention of relinquishing their power over the poor or their control over the distribution of federal dollars. In many parts of the country, entrenched politicians perverted the spirit of the federal poverty program, turning it into yet another mechanism to enhance their hold on power or to line their pockets. Their actions are an uncomfortable but essential part of this history.

Despite those setbacks, the War on Poverty years were extraordinary—in the upsurge of grassroots organizing, in democratic activism by people so poor and disfranchised that they had never before been politically engaged, in community-created and -run service institutions. This book captures that mood on the ground, offering snapshots of that time.

Poor black and white mothers, Native Americans and Chicanas, in Memphis, Los Angeles, and rural Mississippi and Oklahoma went door to door to survey living conditions, to assess nutritional needs, to register voters, to seek the input of the nation's poorest families about what they wanted and needed to improve their lives. Poor black men and women in Baltimore formed self-help housing cooperatives to identify and repair violations of the housing code. Community activists in Durham, North Carolina, in the Mississippi Delta, and in Los Angeles opened health clinics run for and by the poor. Idealistic young participants in the Volunteers in Service to America (VISTA) program helped the poor resist evictions and fight mortgage swindlers. White Appalachian residents protested strip mining and the conditions that made black lung disease endemic in their communities. Chinese immigrants in overcrowded, underserved neighborhoods created community development corporations to build homes and provide social services.

By taking readers behind the front lines of the innumerable battles fought on the ground during the War on Poverty, the exhilaration of small victories, the frustrating conflicts between competing constituencies, the grueling day-to-day work of community action, and the violence of the repression that antipoverty activists encountered, the essays in this volume convey the spirit and the complexity of a remarkable period in this nation's history. The authors also raise questions about the continuing relevance of that period and its struggles as we seek to address poverty in our own time.

AMERICA DISCOVERS "POVERTY IN OUR MIDST"

Many Americans have forgotten—or never knew—the dire conditions that gave rise to the War on Poverty. At the end of the prosperous 1950s, 22 percent of Americans—more than forty million people—lived in daily, grinding poverty.[4] Their lives and concerns were little seen or thought of before the civil rights era. Then, as television cameras entered some of the poorest parts of the nation, reporters chronicling the protests of youthful activists lingered to capture images of the America these activists had come to change. Scenes of unimaginable deprivation—of rickets and swollen bellies, of cardboard-patched shacks and backyard outhouses—were beamed into millions of middle-class American homes. In 1962, sociologist Michael Harrington's myth-shattering study of poverty in the United States, *The Other America*, became the talk of John F. Kennedy's Washington and of a nation previously convinced of its own widely enjoyed abundance. "Tens of millions of Americans," Harrington wrote, "are, at this very moment maimed in body and spirit, existing at levels beneath those necessary for human decency . . . without adequate housing and education and medical care."[5]

JFK made fighting poverty a focus of his domestic agenda. And though he did not live long enough to develop this idea into a concrete set of initiatives, he laid some of the earliest foundations for what would become the War on Poverty through education and job training programs aimed at reducing juvenile delinquency.[6] After Kennedy's death, Johnson picked up the gauntlet, declaring "unconditional war on poverty" in January 1964. Calling it a national disgrace, Johnson vowed to "end poverty in our time." Over the next few months, Johnson and a task force of experts worked out the particulars of what would become the Economic Opportunity Act, the legislative centerpiece of the antipoverty campaign. His efforts represented more than a token gesture, Johnson insisted when he introduced the bill to Congress and the American people in March 1964. He proposed a "total commitment by this President, and this Congress, and this nation, to pursue victory over the most ancient of mankind's enemies."[7]

Of course, Johnson's War on Poverty did not end poverty either in his time or in ours. Few observers imagined that he really expected to eradicate need in America. Ample evidence shows, however, that Johnson intended the War on Poverty and his larger Great Society package of more than one hundred social welfare, education, and health care reforms to lift millions of the poorest Americans out of squalor, hunger, illiteracy, and disease. On that score, Johnson succeeded. By 1974, the number of Americans living in poverty had been cut in half. Child poverty rates had dropped from 27 percent to 14 percent. Programs created during Johnson's years in office brought food aid to tens of millions of hungry Americans, medical care to communities that had previously had none, and new housing to crumbling neighborhoods. In the 1970s, Presidents Richard Nixon and Jimmy Carter attempted to distance themselves from the expanding welfare state built by Johnson, but both men initiated federal programs that built on the Great Society—among them Nixon's Comprehensive Employment and Training Act (CETA) public jobs program and Carter's Youth Employment Training Program, the two most expansive public jobs programs since the Great Depression.[8]

Still, the War on Poverty's popularity began to ebb almost as soon as Johnson declared the initiative. Urban riots, conservative criticism, and complaints by local officials in Johnson's own party that the government was stirring the pot of subversion gradually eroded white support for the program. The War on

Poverty came to end, at least rhetorically, with the election of Ronald Reagan as president in 1980. "Government is not the solution to our problem," Reagan famously said in his first Inaugural Address. "Government is the problem."[9]

An increasingly suspicious and disenchanted American electorate knew what they had voted for. As governor of California, Reagan had slashed student aid and cash assistance for the poor. As a candidate for president, he capitalized on white, middle-class worries about the growth and direction of the War on Poverty, explicitly rejecting the social welfare priorities that had guided Republican as well as Democratic presidents since Franklin Delano Roosevelt. Reagan excoriated Johnson for vastly expanding government bureaucracy and blamed poverty programs for encouraging dependency. During his first term, Reagan made sharp cuts in a range of Great Society programs, repealing the Economic Opportunity Act and ending CETA. These cuts had immediate impact. By 1983, 16 percent of Americans were again living below the federal poverty line, an increase of 5 percent.[10]

Yet the Reagan Revolution never fully shredded the safety net put in place by the War on Poverty, as evidenced by the fact that national poverty rates have never again approached pre-1964 levels. Federal measures initially written into law during the War on Poverty years have kept hundreds of millions of Americans afloat. Most of the programs enacted as part of the War on Poverty continue to function, even if in changed form. These programs have not reached as many Americans as they might, in part because large sectors of Congress and the American electorate accepted Reagan's arguments about the failures of "big government." Still, even Reagan ultimately approved increased allocations for federal nutrition, health care, housing, education, and cash assistance programs, and Republicans as well as Democrats have resisted attempts to cut those programs. Medicare, the most sweeping and successful social welfare measure of the Johnson years, has become so inviolable that members of both parties compete to cast themselves as its fiercest defenders.[11]

Why, then, is the public view of the War on Poverty so negative? If the social welfare initiatives of the Johnson years have pulled several generations of Americans out of destitution and engendered strong loyalties among key constituents, such as the politically emboldened elderly, why do so many Americans see Lyndon Johnson's War on Poverty as an outright failure? In large part, the answer is that from the outset, the War on Poverty faced attacks from both the left and the right. Progressives argued that the proposed antipoverty programs were too stingy, while conservatives countered that these efforts were subversive and costly. These criticisms have continued to echo in mass media and in the halls of government from Johnson's day to our own.

Poverty and the poor remain with us. But so does the federal social safety net that limits how far this country's poor can fall. Federal poverty programs initially passed between 1964 and 1980—nutrition aid; medical care for seniors, children, and the poor; housing, social service, and educational assistance— have become so enshrined in our political culture that it is now nearly impossible to kill them. Yet as the Tea Party's ascendancy vividly illustrates, America's simmering hostility toward Great Society programs in general and the War on Poverty in particular continue to animate U.S. political discourse.

The essays in this book explore those conflicts and ambivalences as well as other issues: How did federal poverty programs come into being? Did they unleash unrealistic hopes and consequently intensify societal tensions? Did they challenge local power structures or in any way alter the operations of Washington, D.C.? The politics and legacies of mid-twentieth-century federal poverty programs are complex and conflicted. Not surprisingly, then, the authors in this volume offer some very different interpretations of the origins of these programs, their effects, and how well they worked for poor people. Some of the essays that follow tell uplifting success stories; others trace the course of agonizing failures. Despite our differences, the contributors to this volume share some fundamental assumptions. First is that there were many and complex reasons why the federal poverty program did not deliver economic justice to regions where people struggled mightily to get it. This is, however, primarily a political study: The essays in this book explore the powerful political forces constraining the War on Poverty but do not adequately address similarly powerful and important economic forces, such as the collapse of U.S. industry or the outsourcing of jobs in a globalizing economy. Other scholars will have to undertake those important lines of economic analysis.

Second, all of the essays in this volume are based on the assumption that despite innumerable failings—most importantly inadequate funding, insufficient attention to job creation, and near-total blindness to the vital role played by sex oppression in keeping so many women and children poor—the War on Poverty succeeded in some crucial ways. Expanded medical insurance, income support, and jobs programs helped reduce overall poverty rates. Food aid and community health centers brought improved nutrition and health care to the nation's poorest communities, extending life expectancy. And the call from Washington in 1964 for "maximum feasible participation" by the poor sparked two decades of community activism and political struggle across the United States, engaging and empowering people who had rarely before been heard in American politics. Those achievements are significant.

Few Americans today know much about the history of federal poverty programs or about the struggles to create, control, and sustain them. The essays in this book fill some of those gaps in knowledge and open up fresh discussion about the effectiveness of government efforts to fight poverty. Thirty years after Reagan declared government the problem rather than the solution, many Americans have difficulty imagining a moment when there was widespread feeling that fighting poverty was a national imperative. The essays that follow take readers back to that time.

WHAT WAS THE WAR ON POVERTY?

In August 1964, Congress passed the Economic Opportunity Act, which poured $947 million into job training, youth employment, adult education, rural economic development, services for migrant farm workers, Legal Services, and VISTA, a domestic version of the Peace Corps that paid small stipends to volunteers to bring much-needed services to impoverished U.S. communities. A new federal Office of Economic Opportunity (OEO) was created to coordinate these and other federal poverty programs.

The new law, drafted over several months by a presidentially appointed committee serving under former Peace Corps director Sargent Shriver, called for a dramatic change in the relationship between the federal government and the nation's poorest citizens. The measure's introduction declared, "It is the policy of the United States to eliminate the paradox of poverty in the midst of plenty in this nation by opening, to everyone, the opportunity for education and training, the opportunity to work, and the opportunity to live in decency and dignity."[12]

While this philosophical shift was notable, the Economic Opportunity Act was not as radical as it seemed at first blush. The product of months of heated negotiations and political compromises, it represented Johnson advisers' varied and conflicting views about what role the federal government should play in trying to lift millions of Americans out of poverty. Aware of cost concerns and potential political fallout, Johnson and Congress had focused mostly on job training and service delivery. Such programs were not as expensive as large-scale job creation and did not threaten local politicians, economic elites, or social welfare agencies.

Still, the Economic Opportunity Act committed federal government power and resources to increase opportunities for all Americans, opening up doors for the previously excluded and disfranchised to organize and participate in local politics. That approach was a prescription for widespread conflict, as many members of Congress and state government officials understood. Debate over the bill centered on questions of states' rights, and the final version included Republican amendments allowing governors to veto federal funding to community projects that they simply could not abide.[13]

Those amendments did not, however, change the bill's use of a language of opportunity. This reflected the philosophical as well as the strategic orientation of the bill's framers. Richard Boone, one of Kennedy's key antipoverty advisers, was deeply influenced by the work of sociologists Lloyd Ohlin and Richard Cloward, who had first presented the notion of "opportunity theory" in 1960 as a strategy for combating youth gangs in urban centers. Ohlin and Cloward argued that poverty, juvenile delinquency, and urban unrest stemmed from a lack of opportunity that could be remedied by redirecting young people's energy away from criminal activities and toward projects to enhance community life. Ohlin and Cloward's ideas were first funded through President Kennedy's initiative to stem juvenile delinquency and were tested by Mobilization for Youth, an experimental social service agency on Manhattan's Lower East Side. Authors of the Economic Opportunity Act drew on this program as they shaped the most controversial part of the bill: the Community Action Program.[14]

The Economic Opportunity Act funded more than a thousand community action agencies (CAAs) across the United States with the goal of fostering bottom-up revitalization of the country's poorest areas. Boone lobbied for inclusion of what would become the most famous mandate in the bill. Federally funded CAAs would have to strive for and demonstrate "the maximum feasible participation of residents of the areas and groups served." CAAs would not emulate charitable agencies; instead, they would engage the poor directly in the work of fighting poverty. In so doing, the poverty program would provide, as Johnson put it, "a hand up, not a handout."[15]

Shriver and Johnson saw "maximum feasible participation" as a means of ensuring that African Americans, particularly in the South, would not be excluded. However, many people in the Johnson administration, in Congress, and in local government clearly saw this provision's radical potential for disrupting power relations. "The poor," wrote Fred O'R. Hayes, who would become director of the Community Action Program, "need to emerge in the American community as a major political factor capable of pressing their needs upon the political officials and the bureaucracies of the community." This, he wrote with pleased anticipation, would constitute a kind of "revolution." That is precisely what had many local politicians worried.[16]

A sort of revolution did begin very quickly after passage of the Economic Opportunity Act. In decaying, inner-city neighborhoods, Rust Belt towns, backwoods hollows, and Indian reservations, grassroots activists, elected officials, and social welfare professionals feverishly conceived and submitted proposals to the OEO for "community action" projects. Channeling federal stipends and grants, poor men and women rehabilitated abandoned buildings and opened clinics, preschools, and community centers. Residents cleaned up neighborhood parks, planted community gardens, and renovated and reopened public swimming pools. They published community newspapers, chased drug dealers out of neighborhoods, and kept them away with resident-run anticrime patrols. Help came from idealistic young teachers, doctors, nurses, lawyers, and college students, many paid through one of the new programs the Economic Opportunity Act had created. But local activists also took on new roles as administrators, learning to run community-based institutions.[17]

Perhaps most challenging to existing power structures, poor people began to educate themselves about their rights, under federal law, to income support, medical care, and social services and about how government works. With the help of the Legal Services program and of college-educated VISTA volunteers, poor people learned not only about newly created programs such as Medicaid but also about New Deal–era programs such as Aid to Families with Dependent Children. In the process, millions of poor people became politicized.

Poor people went from conducting surveys about neighborhood needs to fielding candidates who promised to address those needs and registering voters to try to elect those candidates. In many poor communities, residents ran for (and sometimes won) elected office. This political awakening paralleled events in the 1930s, when previously disfranchised Americans—workers, homemakers, young people, the elderly—began to petition the federal government as organized interest groups. Similarly, passage of the Economic Opportunity Act gave poor people hope that the federal government might ally with them against such oppressive forces as employers, politicians, landlords, and welfare and housing officials.

America's poor did not blindly and immediately embrace the federal government in the summer of 1964. Many people at first remained doubtful about both the Johnson administration's motives and its strategies.[18] Still, people found themselves drawn in, if not by faith then by visions of what they could do with an infusion of federal money.

Previously apolitical poor mothers became swept up by the idea that they could do the heavy lifting in transforming and revitalizing their communities. Paid by Community Action Program funds, poor black women in Memphis scoured their neighborhoods documenting the conditions that led to devastatingly high infant mortality rates. They then made common cause with medical professionals, together opening clinics and lobbying successfully for the creation of the Special Supplemental Nutrition Program for Women, Infants, and Children (WIC), which offered improved health care and nutrition for poor babies and mothers across the country. Poor black and white mothers in the Southeast, Puerto Ricans in the Bronx, and Chicanas in the West organized for better health care, housing, and education for their children. Politicizing welfare mothers was not part of Johnson's or Shriver's social blueprint. Few local politicians or social welfare professionals considered it an appropriate use of federal funds. But in an era when the language of civil and citizenship rights was on nearly everyone's tongue and when a sitting U.S. president insisted that poor people deserved a slice of the pie, unintended consequences were inevitable.[19]

Some veteran community activists also bought into the poverty program. Though they did not trust LBJ, they gambled that the rhetoric of maximum feasible participation could further a genuinely radical vision of community control. In this they drew on the work of veteran organizer Saul Alinsky, who in *Reveille for Radicals* (1946) had offered a model for building local "people's organizations" that would "precipitate the social crisis by action—by using power." Houston's OEO head, William Ballew, explicitly and openly applied Alinsky's ideas. In San Antonio, grassroots organizations using Alinsky's methods ran federally funded community projects that lasted well beyond the Johnson years.[20]

Even self-proclaimed revolutionaries who suspected that the idea of maximum feasible participation was little more than a ruse by the Johnson administration to quell urban unrest were lured by the promise of federal dollars flowing into resource-starved communities. In Baltimore, Black Power leaders fought for War on Poverty monies to develop community-run housing projects. In Milwaukee, Chicano activists sought funding through the Economic Opportunity Act's migrant worker provisions, not simply to deliver services but also to empower and politicize Tejano farm laborers (Texans of Mexican descent). In New York's Chinatown, community organizers who had not long before been preaching communist revolution began to seek federal grants to fund construction of desperately needed affordable housing.[21]

Though the War on Poverty has usually been seen as an urban program, its reach extended deep into what one Alabama organizer called "the rurals," enabling a former sharecropper living outside Selma to challenge a powerful minister who insisted that illiterate country people could not run their own poverty programs. It reached into the coal-scarred hills of Mill Creek, Kentucky, where poor rural whites organized against corruption in schools and hiring, against strip mining and the labor conditions that gave rise to black lung disease. It walked from town to town in the backwoods of Bolivar County, Mississippi, with the country folk who tried to figure out the best strategies for fighting hunger, disease, and poverty. It took hold in Tallulah, Louisiana, despite death threats and Klan bombings aimed at preschool children and their teachers. In many ways, rural organizing took something extra—a willingness to walk miles, the fortitude and courage to stand up to terror.[22]

But mass migration from some of those rural hinterlands to the cities had set the stage for the creative, explosive urban politics of the 1960s. Historians have argued that the great exodus that brought nearly twenty million migrants from the poverty-stricken South to northern and western cities between 1900 and 1970 paved the way for the upsurge of protest and participatory democracy. By the time federal antipoverty funds started flowing, millions of poor people were living in densely populated urban neighborhoods in cities such as New York, Los Angeles, Houston, Milwaukee, Memphis, Durham, and San Antonio, where organizing could be done on foot and gathering a crowd was easy. Migrants who flocked to cities seeking economic opportunity were fascinated and inspired by the cross-fertilization of political ideas they found there. Living in public housing projects also fostered activism, as once-isolated rural migrants came into contact for the first time with government social service programs and their representatives and in the process learned how government works.[23]

But the move to the inner city also had its costs. As early as the summer of 1964, while the particulars of the poverty program were still being debated, frustration with police misconduct, joblessness, and the slow pace of change sparked violent urban uprisings across the nation. Chicago was still smoldering on August 20, 1964, the day that Johnson signed the Economic Opportunity Act, and the "long, hot summer" brought chaos and street warfare to New York, Jersey City, and Philadelphia, among other cities. Los Angeles's 1965

Watts Riots, in which thirty-four people died and more than one thousand were injured during six days of unrest, left perhaps the greatest imprint on the national psyche.

These spontaneous revolts left wide swaths of destruction, devastating what little commerce was left in decaying inner-city neighborhoods and riveting the attention of media, politicians, and an increasingly nervous white middle class. Though these eruptions had their roots in poverty and racism, inadequate housing, poor schools, and lack of jobs, many Americans came to associate the violence with the poverty programs that had been created to offer the poor a way out.

President Johnson sensed that his legacy was in danger. On August 15, 1965, after order had been restored in Watts, he told the nation that his poverty program was the best answer to the violence. "It is not enough simply to decry disorder," he said. "We must also strike at the unjust conditions from which disorder largely flows. . . . Aimless violence finds fertile ground among men imprisoned by the shadowed walls of hatred, coming of age in the poverty of slums, facing their future without education or skills and with little hope of rewarding work. We must not only be relentless in condemning violence, but also in taking the necessary steps to prevent violence."[24] The president's words, however, could do little to change the fact that just one year after passage of the Economic Opportunity Act, a war on the War on Poverty had begun.

"MAXIMUM FEASIBLE MISUNDERSTANDING": POVERTY WARS ON THE GROUND

During the summer of 1964 and in the turbulent summers that followed, urban machine Democrats and southern Dixiecrats who had loyally delivered votes to Lyndon Johnson complained bitterly about federal dollars being channeled to community activists believed to be fomenting riots on the government's dime, lighting matches in cities that were highly flammable.[25] If LBJ envisioned community action, neighborhood youth corps, and job training programs as riot control, local elected officials argued that such programs simply fueled the fires of urban discontent. "The question," Alabama's Selma Times-Journal declared in 1966, "is whether Sargent Shriver has any business helping to shake up anybody else's city hall. . . . The question is also whether, in the name of local flexibility, Mr. Shriver should help impose federally financed revolutionary movements that could become, given enough money, local quasi-governments."[26]

Early in 1965, Johnson received a letter from the mayor of Baltimore, Theodore McKeldin, expressing anger about the Community Action Program and letting the president know that the mayors of Philadelphia, St. Louis, and Cleveland shared this view. Poor residents of Baltimore were equally frustrated with the city's management of the program. By the end of that year, Vice President Hubert Humphrey, Johnson's liaison to the cities, had attended a special session in Miami where he heard several mayors complain about community action. Humphrey apparently came to agree that the program was a problem.[27]

President Johnson backed away quickly from the promise of community control. He had never been comfortable with the activist vision of Shriver's more progressive staff and never intended federal dollars to fund attempts to destabilize local government. "What you need is three camps in Gainesville, Georgia [to] take these kids and prepare them where they won't stay on relief all their life," the president said to Georgia congressman Phil Landrum in 1964. When Landrum urged Johnson to scrap the program entirely, Johnson did not demur, saying, "To hell with Community Action." And when Johnson adviser Bill Moyers argued that the program was central to the War on Poverty, Johnson replied simply, "I don't think so."[28]

From 1964 to 1968, as many of America's inner cities burned, an increasingly anxious Johnson tried to quiet voices of outrage from within his own party, urging Democratic mayors and city council members to take control of the poverty program in their cities. For their part, Republicans jumped on this tension within the Democratic Party. In 1966, the Republican National Committee issued a wholesale condemnation of the Community Action Program, *The War on Poverty: An American Tragedy.*[29]

Resistance to the Community Action Program was particularly rife among city council members, housing and school boards, and mayors and governors. Because the program allowed community organizations to bypass local bureaucracies and appeal directly to the federal OEO for antipoverty dollars, pitched battles erupted from California to Mississippi between 1964 and 1967. In the Old South, these struggles pitted dyed-in-the-wool segregationist politicians against some of the same civil rights activists they had been fighting for the past ten years.

The War on Poverty has usually been seen as distinct from the southern civil rights movement, but the two historic movements were inextricably tied together. The Economic Opportunity Act passed Congress in the same month that the bodies of civil rights workers Andrew Goodman, Michael Schwerner, and James Chaney were found in an earthen dam in Neshoba County, Mississippi,

alongside the fairgrounds where Mississippi's Democratic politicians traditionally began their campaigns. The veteran organizers who worked in rural Mississippi at the Tufts-Delta Health Center and the Child Development Group of
Mississippi (CDGM) understood all too well the challenge that their programs
posed to still-entrenched segregationist officials. So did antipoverty activists
across the river in Tallulah, Louisiana, where a terrifying campaign of violence
was waged against Head Start preschools.[30]

Democratic senators and governors across the South blasted grassroots projects funded through the War on Poverty, livid at the idea that taxpayer dollars were being used to fund projects sponsored by civil rights activists. These
public condemnations were reinforced on the ground by Ku Klux Klan violence and by threats of violence against the staffs of OEO-funded children's programs, health clinics, and community centers. In Mississippi and Louisiana
Delta towns, these threats were all too credible, given the region's long history
of white supremacist violence.

Often, as in the case of the CDGM, the harassment took other forms. Threatening to wield their considerable political power to defeat President Johnson's
next request for Vietnam War funding, Mississippi's Democratic senators,
James Eastland and John Stennis, convinced Shriver to investigate CDGM preschools on trumped-up charges of fraud. These highly publicized investigations
ultimately led to a withdrawal of OEO funds from the flourishing program. The
tactic of charging and investigating local antipoverty agencies for fraud would
be used again and again to defund successful grassroots antipoverty organizations from the 1970s into the twenty-first century.[31]

But like their northern and western counterparts, many southern mayors
and governors soon realized that instead of resisting federal poverty programs,
it would be smarter to establish CAAs and use them to win federal funding away
from grassroots groups. Selma mayor Joe Smitherman divided black activists by
appointing middle-class black leaders to a biracial antipoverty board, convincing OEO officials to fund his program rather than an initiative created by the
rural poor. Then, like mayors in so many cities at that time, he channeled federal antipoverty funds into patronage appointments that tightened his hold on
power by enriching his friends and cronies. Honest city and state officials also
tinkered with local poverty boards, stacking them with economic power brokers. In Houston, oil magnate George H. W. Bush was appointed to the county
economic opportunity board in its early years. Such practices heightened mistrust of the federal poverty program in poor communities.[32]

That mistrust grew when Congress in 1967 passed the Quie and Green Amendments, giving local officials the power to designate which community organizations were eligible for federal monies. Elected officials would now comprise a third of the local poverty boards and could fill another third of the seats with welfare professionals and representatives of the private sector. Residents of "target areas" were guaranteed the remaining seats, a proviso that in some places increased their representation and voice in local poverty programs. Still, elected officials were now empowered to appoint people to those seats, a very different road to political representation than the democratic elections that many community groups had previously employed.

Local politicians in Baltimore, Houston, Selma, and elsewhere moved quickly to take advantage of these new opportunities to control the War on Poverty. Understanding the racial sensitivities of the era and of the Johnson administration, white city and county officials looked for black, Mexican, Indian, and Chinese leaders with whom they felt they could work and appointed them to CAAs in place of more militant grassroots activists and then sold these appointees to OEO officials in Washington as true community representatives. The OEO tended to accept such arguments. If mayors could get together biracial boards, particularly in Selma and other locales that had so recently been bathed in blood over the issue of black voting, the OEO was content.[33]

As local governments played favorites with desperately needed funds, intra-racial conflicts flared up in many communities. In Deep South states, competition for control of federal antipoverty dollars exacerbated long-existing tensions between poor black farm workers and more educated and affluent black town dwellers, who saw themselves as the natural leaders and representatives of their race. Rifts also opened up in Oklahoma between those trying to fund "traditional" Indian-run institutions and those who insisted that the Indian poor must integrate into multiracial poverty programs. In Johnson's home state, Texas, angry conflicts erupted between Mexican Americans of different generations. While older Latino politicians espoused the benefits of allying with Johnson's Democratic machine, younger activists distrusted the idea of integration, championing a politics of Chicano control.[34]

In Asian American communities, War on Poverty funds helped fuel the rise of a new breed of 1970s political leader, young, educated, and able to penetrate the inner circles of city governments. This new style and strategy dramatically distanced the new leaders from the insular fiefdoms of Six Companies and other immigrant societies that had long controlled politics, patronage, and social services in America's Chinatowns. A New York City group, Asian Americans for Equality, illustrates how the War on Poverty brought Chinese activists into positions of influence in municipal governments. But it also led to intense conflicts between old and new forms of authority in Chinatown— between college-educated and working-class Chinese, between American-born Chinese and newly arrived immigrants.[35]

The War on Poverty also exacerbated tensions among ethnic groups competing for limited resources. In Los Angeles, battles over community control of federal poverty dollars pitted blacks against Mexican Americans. In rural Texas, Mexican American activists protested when leadership positions in OEO offices went to African Americans. In Oklahoma, Indian tribal chiefs resented an Indian-run, federally funded group, Oklahomans for Indian Opportunity, because the chiefs felt that its poverty programs infringed on their autonomy. At the same time, Oklahomans for Indian Opportunity resisted demands that Indians integrate into multiracial community programs run by whites and members of other minority groups. White CAA heads complained to Washington about discrimination against white people.

President Nixon's OEO chief, Donald Rumsfeld, and his second-in-command, Dick Cheney, stepped in to resolve the impasse. In 1970, the agency enacted the Oklahoma Plan, allowing state government officials to control all antipoverty programs. Congress had explicitly refused to legislate such state control, Indian antipoverty activists complained, but a new, more conservative OEO sheriff was now in charge. Nixon was not averse to using federal resources to fight poverty, but grassroots control of federal poverty programs had become anathema in Washington.[36]

MOTHERIST POLITICS AND COMMUNITY ACTION

The fact that far more women than men were involved in community action programs worried Nixon-era OEO administrators. One official complained in 1970 that every community action program he knew was "dominated by women and preachers." Rather than celebrating this success at mobilizing poor mothers in unprecedented numbers, Nixon's OEO staff considered it a failure that their programs appealed primarily to women. Johnson's staff had been little better on gender: from the early 1960s into the late 1970s, federal poverty policy was bedeviled by the notion that women were secondary economic players and by the belief that the primary purpose of poverty programs was to transform poor men into wage-earning heads of household.[37]

From the perspective of poor mothers, the War on Poverty offered something very different. Many of them had been drawn to activism by the belief that good mothers have a right and an obligation to demand that government agencies provide improved services for children. That belief seemed to be reinforced by the fact so many of the War on Poverty programs were aimed at children—the WIC program and clinics, Early Periodic Screening and Diagnostic Testing for children, Head Start preschools, public school breakfast and lunch programs, among others. Job training programs geared toward male wage-earners were of no use to the increasingly large numbers of women who were the primary or sole breadwinners for their households. They wanted government programs geared toward women. To antipoverty officials of Johnson's generation, these requests simply made no sense.

Women consequently found alternative routes to paid work through the War on Poverty. They protested to gain access to new medical care, food assistance, and educational programs for themselves and their children. With the help of the Legal Services staff in their communities, they learned that many of the other new programs included allocations to hire poor people in a variety of positions. Growing increasingly sophisticated in their activism and their understanding of government programs, they pushed for federally funded jobs as Head Start teachers, school lunch aides, health outreach workers, community organizers, and screeners at local clinics. These jobs furthered the women's political education. And over time they began to argue that mothers should have control of programs affecting their children. As the mothers of West Las Vegas put it, "We can do it and do it better!"[38]

Motherist politics created some fresh and unlikely coalitions. In Durham's Edgemont neighborhood, working-class black and white mothers joined together, if only temporarily, thereby shattering Jim Crow taboos. At first they circled each other warily, organized separately, and even came at different times to the health clinic they had fought so hard to bring to their community. But as that clinic and an integrated school were threatened with extinction, the women came to see their commonalities. Similar dynamics unfolded in the Bronx, where Puerto Rican and African American mothers, tired of the poor schooling their children were getting and tired of being told that children were failing because their parents did not value education, banded together to fight back. In these cases, women of different racial and ethnic backgrounds initially found themselves united by their shared commitment to bringing improved services to their children but increasingly came to see how prejudice damaged and divided the poor. Black and Chicana women in Los Angeles came to the same conclusion, though they did so less easily.[39]

Across the country, untold numbers of poor mothers became politicized during the 1960s and 1970s in pursuit of better food, schools, and health care for their children. Unwilling to remain passive clients of social welfare and health professionals, they came to see themselves as the true experts on poverty and to believe that they could run poverty and community health and education programs more effectively than the supposed experts. This was the promise of maximum feasible participation fulfilled.

In the process, women who had never graduated from high school learned to navigate byzantine city, state, and federal agencies and skillfully to play officials from different branches and levels of government against one another. These women lobbied policymakers in municipal governments, in state capitals, and in Washington, D.C. And when states dragged their heels, refusing to accept and implement new federal antipoverty programs such as food stamps, free breakfast and lunch programs, WIC, and Early Periodic Screening and Diagnostic Testing, poor mothers not only protested in the streets but also sued—and won—in federal court.[40]

Many people both at the time and now have perceived as profound and game-changing the idea that poor, uneducated mothers could have such a sweeping impact on nationwide policy. Yet many community organizers derided this situation as counterrevolutionary—piecemeal, temporary, and apolitical. Radical activists in Durham, Baltimore, Houston, and other places argued that women's focus on service delivery undermined community action. In their view, improved service provision was just a way of buying off poor people. The only permanent way out of poverty was for the poor to demand power, to overhaul the entire American system, to create revolution. This difference of opinion often put male organizers at odds with women in their communities. In some very concrete ways, both perspectives have proven correct.[41]

Many poor women energized by the War on Poverty were less interested in overturning the system than in becoming voices for change from within it. Community activists such as Evelina Antonetty of United Bronx Parents and Unita Blackwell of the CDGM worked to empower poor mothers locally but also to apply their insights and life experiences to larger policy questions. Antonetty and Blackwell were primarily concerned with education, while other activists focused on hunger, health care issues, and job development for poor mothers of color.[42]

Graciela Olivarez, a Mexican American feminist and civil rights activist, was one of those voices. She was one of the few War on Poverty officials who raised consciousness about women's concerns. But it was an uphill struggle. A rarity in the male-dominated world of the OEO, Olivarez was the office's Arizona director during the program's early years. President Johnson appointed her to the national OEO Advisory Board, where she brought much-needed attention to the needs of poor Hispanic women. She left Washington to become an attorney but was drawn back in the late 1970s when Jimmy Carter appointed her director of the Community Services Administration (the successor to the OEO), a position in which she worked to broaden the number of woman-run community organizations funded through community economic development grants. One of these groups, the Chicana Service Action Center, continues to provide health services, job training, and education to poor Latinas in East Los Angeles in the present day.[43]

Other mother-organizers politicized during the War on Poverty lobbied Congress and the Department of Labor to develop jobs programs to help poor women break into traditionally male fields. Ruby Duncan, leader of the Las Vegas antipoverty movement, helped draft portions of the second Comprehensive Education and Training Act and the Youth Employment Training Act, both passed in the late 1970s and both of which set aside funding to train poor mothers for jobs in the construction trades. More than a decade after Johnson declared war on poverty, federal policymakers were finally beginning to address issues of women's poverty and underemployment. Even as that shift was occurring, however, a national uprising against "big government" was gathering steam. Many community institutions first funded through War on Poverty programs came under siege. Community-run programs were defunded, and federal support shifted to agencies run by more highly educated and less political professionals.[44]

Nevertheless, many women galvanized by the War on Poverty remained active for decades in the areas of education, health care, housing, and political representation. San Antonio activist Beatrice Cortez argued that community organizing represented an extension of women's organic roles rather than a radical departure from them: According to Cortez, "Women have community ties. We knew that to make things happen in a community, you have to talk to people. It was a matter of tapping our networks." Many women organizers have continued to tap into that community spirit well into the twenty-first century. As Mississippi Head Start activist Unita Blackwell noted in 2003 the "spirit of community" enabled her to keep working for more than four decades. It "uplifted" her and reminded her "of the original spirit of CDGM and the movement—open, communal, and full of faith that progress is possible."[45]

CULTURES OF POVERTY

The War on Poverty, with its "faith that progress is possible," was both driven and limited by the twentieth century's most powerful and influential explanatory framework for poverty: the idea that the poor remain poor because they are mired in a "culture of poverty"—pathological behavior patterns that reproduce poverty in each generation. This concept was popularized in the 1930s studies of black southern migrants by social psychologist John Dollard and sociologist E. Franklin Frazier but really caught fire in the mid-1950s, when anthropologist Oscar Lewis published books on Puerto Rican and Mexican poverty that shaped a generation of social work professionals. Then, in 1965, the Labor Department's Daniel Patrick Moynihan gave the culture of poverty a new twist in his report on *The Negro Family*, arguing that one kind of "pathological" behavior, black women's economic independence, had stunted the black male wage earner. His report had a profound impact on the early evolution of poverty programs.[46]

Architects of the War on Poverty saw community action and community economic development as tools to end this multigenerational transmission of poverty. Some Washington, D.C., planners described War on Poverty programs as "human reclamation" or "human renewal," comparable to land reclamation and urban renewal programs. Johnson characteristically put things more bluntly: "I'm going to take tax-eaters and make taxpayers out of them. And I'm going to stop these damn riots. . . . All these young people have nothing to do. . . . I'm going to put 150,000 of them to work. . . . Teach them some discipline and when to get up, and how to work all day, and in two years, I'll have them trained where they can at least drive a truck instead of sit around a pool room."[47]

More than a few elected officials and social service professionals shared Johnson's belief that poverty could be solved by getting poor men out of the pool hall. They doubted the capacity of people damaged by a culture of poverty to envision or run successful community programs. The prejudices stoked by culture-of-poverty arguments fueled opponents' suspicions about fraud and ineptitude in community-based organizations, convincing local prosecutors that they should investigate and even indict group leaders. Such investigations did not frequently produce real evidence of criminality but nevertheless resulted in the dismantling of many organizations and the defunding of others in the 1970s and 1980s.

Culture-of-poverty arguments affected how school officials responded to Puerto Rican families' complaints about their children's education. That discourse predominated in Memphis, too, during the early 1960s. Investigating frighteningly high African American infant mortality rates, city health officials blamed eating habits, drinking, and sexual mores rather than poverty, malnutrition, and lack of health care.[48]

Culture-of-poverty arguments were also used in relation to white Appalachian residents and Native Americans. Seeking to identify the causes of rural poverty, both academics and on-the-ground reformers blamed deep-rooted cultural practices that sustained community in places such as Mill Creek, Kentucky, and Oklahoma Indian country. They saw local people as traditionalists who clung to antimodern ways of living with a stubbornness and tenacity that made them seem unsuited to shape and run successful community programs. Rural dwellers were thus seen through the same lens of prejudice that continues to taint policymakers' views of any organization run by poor people.

In all of these ways, the War on Poverty has had legacies both negative and positive. It improved the lives of poor people across the country even as it left many communities languishing. It dramatically expanded political participation in the United States but left the structures of power and repression largely intact. Poor women and men challenged the policies and the incumbencies of politicians and public officials. Parents challenged curricula, teaching methods, and the authority of school principals and district superintendents. Poor people registered to vote, ran for office, and in some cases became successful politicians. They opened clinics and preschools where there had been none before, training and hiring other impoverished people to deliver services. They built housing, revitalized crumbling neighborhoods, and incubated small businesses in stretches of cities and rural outposts that had until recently been empty and hopeless. From the beginning, those positive changes wrought by the War on Poverty have been obscured by popular stereotypes about the poor.

That successes did not happen in every locale where War on Poverty funds spurred community organizing is not surprising. That these successes did not last in many places where they took root is disappointing but not hard to understand. The miracle is that in many inner-city neighborhoods and isolated rural pockets of poverty, federal antipoverty programs brought positive and lasting change. Such instances, along with the failures, the conflicts, and the complexities of the War on Poverty, are worth studying and remembering. That is the purpose of this book.

Most of the contributors to this volume began our research in isolation. In time, we heard of each other's work. We began coming together to speak to each other in seminars and on conference panels and to read each other's manuscripts. Out of these conversations and our individual research as well as the important work of other historians, there has emerged a vibrant new literature about the War on Poverty that enables readers to examine its influences, conflicts, and legacies. The authors in this collection have published books and articles that examine civil rights and antipoverty organizing in New Orleans, Selma, Durham, Memphis, Baltimore, Milwaukee, Los Angeles, San Antonio, and New York City as well as rural Appalachia, Mississippi, and Oklahoma. This book is the first time these scholars appear in a single volume. It is also the first book that examines the War on Poverty with attention both to its varied local contexts and to the national themes and trends that transcend region and locale.[49]

Notes

1. For the full story of this community-based antipoverty movement, see Annelise Orleck, *Storming Caesars Palace: How Black Mothers Fought Their Own War on Poverty* (Boston: Beacon, 2005).

2. Diana Nelson Jones, "Appalachia's War: The Poorest of the Poor Struggle Back," *Pittsburgh Post Gazette*, November 26, 2000; "LBJ Wraps up His Poverty Tour of the Appalachian States," Lyndon Baines Johnson Library (hereafter LBJL), www.lbjlib.utexas .edu/johnson/lbjforkids/pov_media.shtm.

3. Lyndon B. Johnson, Remarks at the University of Michigan, May 22, 1964, http:// www.lbjlib.utexas.edu/johnson/archives.hom/speeches.hom/640522.asp; "LBJ Wraps up His Poverty Tour."

4. "Number in Poverty and Poverty Rate, 1959–2008," in U.S. Census Bureau, *Income, Poverty and Health Insurance Coverage in the United States, 2008* (Washington, D.C.: U.S. Census Bureau, 2009).

5. Sasha Torres, *Black, White, and in Color: Television and Black Civil Rights* (Prince-

ton: Princeton University Press, 2003); Michael Harrington, *The Other America: Poverty in the United States* (New York: Macmillan, 1962), 2.

6. C. M. Brauer, *John F. Kennedy and the Second Reconstruction* (New York: Columbia University Press, 1977), 265–68.

7. Lyndon Baines Johnson, State of the Union Address, January 8, 1964, http://www .lbjlib.utexas.edu; "'Proposal for a Nationwide War on the Sources of Poverty,' Lyndon B. Johnson's Special Message to Congress, March 16, 1964," in *Public Papers of U.S. Presidents: Lyndon B. Johnson, 1963–1964* (Washington, D.C.: U.S. Government Printing Office, 1965), 1:375–80.

8. "Number in Poverty." Scholars have extensively debated the exact numbers and percentages, with some consensus that poverty rates have averaged about 13 percent since the 1970s (National Poverty Center, Gerald Ford School of Public Policy, University of Michigan, "Poverty in the United States," http://www.npc.umich.edu/poverty).

9. Ronald Reagan, "Presidential Addresses," in *A Tide of Discontent: The 1980 Elections and Their Meaning*, ed. E. Sandoz and C. Crabb Jr. (Washington, D.C.: Congressional Quarterly Press, 1981). For a lucid summary of Reagan's cuts in social welfare and social insurance programs, see John O'Connor, "U.S. Social Welfare Policy: The Reagan Record and Legacy," *Journal of Social Policy* 27:1 (January 1998): 37–61.

10. "Number in Poverty."

11. Robert Rector, "How Not to Be Poor," *National Review*, October 13, 2005.

12. Public Law 88–452, the Economic Opportunity Act of 1964. For details on the politics of drafting the Economic Opportunity Act, see McKee, this volume.

13. Economic Opportunity Act of 1964, S. Rep. No. 1458 (1964), *U.S. Code Congressional and Administrative News*, 88th Cong., 2nd sess., 1964, 2900–2989.

14. Richard Cloward and Lloyd Ohlin, *Delinquency and Opportunity: A Theory of Delinquent Gangs* (New York: Free Press, 1960). See also Mobilization for Youth Papers, 1958–70, Rare Book and Manuscript Library, Columbia University, New York. Mobilization for Youth, a social service agency founded in 1957, was funded as part of JFK's juvenile delinquency initiative in 1961.

15. Public Law 88–452, The Economic Opportunity Act of 1964; Joseph Califano Jr., "What Was Really Great about the Great Society," *Washington Monthly*, October 1999.

16. F. O'R. Hayes, "The Role of Indigenous Organizations in Community Action Programs," 3, May 4, 1964, Office Files of White House Aides: Fred Bohen, Box 2, "OEO Material," LBJL; Jack Conway Oral History Interview I, 18–19, 24–25, August 13, 1980, by Michael L. Gillette, LBJL.

17. David M. Austin, "Resident Participation: Political Mobilization or Organizational Co-Optation?," *Public Administration Review* 32 (September 1972): 409–20.

18. For examples of this skepticism, see Williams, Phelps, Clayson, Bauman, all in this volume.

19. See Green, Greene, Back, all in this volume.

20. See Phelps, this volume; Clayson, this volume. See also Saul Alinsky, *Reveille for Radicals* (Chicago: University of Chicago Press, 1946), 29–30, 208.

21. See Williams, Rodriguez, Tani, all in this volume.

22. See Kiffmeyer, Cobb, Ashmore, Jordan, de Jong, Germany, all in this volume.

23. James T. Patterson, *America's Struggle against Poverty, 1900–1980* (Cambridge: Harvard University Press, 1981); James N. Gregory, *The Southern Diaspora: How the Great Migrations of Black and White Southerners Transformed America* (Chapel Hill: University of North Carolina Press, 2005). Patterson calls the mass movement of the nation's poor from rural areas to the cities one of the most important phenomena in American history (80). See also Back, this volume; Williams, this volume; Rhonda Williams, *The Politics of Public Housing: Black Women's Struggles against Urban Inequality* (New York: Oxford University Press, 2005).

24. Lyndon Baines Johnson, "Statement Following the Restoration of Order in Los Angeles," August 15, 1965, http:/www.lbj100.org/otd/august.

25. The title of this section comes from Daniel Patrick Moynihan, *Maximum Feasible Misunderstanding: Community Action in the War on Poverty* (New York: Free Press, 1969).

26. *Selma Times-Journal*, March 10, 1966, in Ashmore, this volume.

27. Nicholas Lemann, "The Unfinished War," *Atlantic Monthly*, December 1988, http://www.theatlantic.com/past/politics/poverty/lemunfi.htm. See also Williams, this volume.

28. Lyndon Baines Johnson to Phil Landrum, May 14, 1964, in *The Presidential Recordings: Lyndon B. Johnson*, vol. 6: *Toward the Great Society, April 14, 1964*, ed. Guian A. McKee (New York: Norton, 2005), 709–10. See also McKee, this volume.

29. See McKee, this volume; *The War on Poverty: An American Tragedy* (Washington, D.C.: Republican National Committee, 1966).

30. See Jordan, de Jong, Germany, all in this volume.

31. See Jordan, Germany, this volume. See also Diana Vernazza, "Who Killed the Child Development Group of Mississippi?" (undergraduate honors thesis, Dartmouth College, 2001).

32. See Ashmore, Phelps, this volume.

33. See Ashmore, Phelps, de Jong, Cobb, and Clayson, all in this volume.

34. See Ashmore, de Jong, Cobb, and Clayson, all in this volume.

35. See Tani, this volume.

36. See Bauman and Clayson, this volume.

37. *CDCs: New Hope for the Inner City* (New York: Twentieth Century Fund Task Force on Community Development Corporations, 1971), 42.

38. Orleck, *Storming Caesars Palace*, 208.

39. See Greene, Green, Back, and Bauman, all in this volume. For sustained treat-

ments of motherist politics in the War on Poverty, see Nancy A. Naples, *Grassroots Warriors: Activist Mothering, Community Work, and the War on Poverty* (New York: Routledge, 1998); Orleck, *Storming Caesars Palace*. See also Alexis Jetter, Annelise Orleck, and Diana Taylor, eds., *The Politics of Motherhood: Activist Voices from Left to Right* (Hanover, N.H.: University Press of New England, 1997).

40. See Back, Green, Greene, Bauman, Clayson, all in this volume. See also Orleck, *Storming Caesars Palace*, chaps. 7–8.

41. See Greene, Phelps, Williams, all in this volume. See also Richard Cloward and Frances Fox Piven, *The Politics of Turmoil: Poverty, Race and the Urban Crisis* (New York: Pantheon, 1974). The idea that the greatest weapon the poor had to influence policy was "publicly visible disruption" was put forward by these two authors in "A Strategy to End Poverty," *Nation*, May 2, 1966.

42. See Jordan, Back, this volume.

43. See Bauman, this volume.

44. Orleck, *Storming Caesars Palace*, chaps. 8–9.

45. Vicki Ruíz, "Communities Organized for Public Service," in *Latinas in the United States: A Historical Encyclopedia*, ed. Vicki Ruíz and Virginia Sánchez Korrol (Bloomington: Indiana University Press, 2006), 1:170; Unita Blackwell and Jo Anne Prichard Morris, *Barefootin': Life Lessons from the Road to Freedom* (New York: Crown, 2006), 156.

46. Back, this volume; Oscar Lewis, *Five Families* (New York: Basic Books, 1959); Oscar Lewis, *The Children of Sánchez: Autobiography of a Mexican Family* (New York: Random House, 1961); Oscar Lewis, *La Vida: A Puerto Rican Family in the Culture of Poverty—San Juan and New York* (New York: Random House, 1966); Daniel Patrick Moynihan, *The Negro Family: A Case for National Action* (Washington, D.C.: Office of Policy Planning and Research, U.S. Department of Labor, 1965); E. Franklin Frazier, *The Negro Family in the United States* (Chicago: University of Chicago Press, 1939); John Dollard, *Caste and Class in a Southern Town* (New York: Doubleday, 1937).

47. Lyndon Baines Johnson, July 29, 1964, Tape WH6407.18, Citation 4407, in *Presidential Recordings of Lyndon B. Johnson Digital Edition*, ed. David B. Coleman, Kent B. Germany, Guian A. McKee, and Mark J. Selverstone, War on Poverty Series (Charlottesville: University of Virginia Press, 2010). See also Williams, this volume.

48. See Green, this volume.

49. Susan Youngblood Ashmore, *Carry It On: The War on Poverty and the Civil Rights Movement in Alabama, 1964–1972* (Athens: University of Georgia Press, 2008); Robert Bauman, *Race and the War on Poverty: From Watts to East L.A.* (Norman: University of Oklahoma Press, 2008); William Clayson, *Freedom Is Not Enough: The War on Poverty and the Civil Rights Movement in Texas* (Austin: University of Texas Press, 2010); Kent Germany, *New Orleans after the Promises: Poverty, Citizenship, and the Search for the Great Society* (Athens: University of Georgia Press, 2008); Christina Greene, *Our*

Separate Ways: Women and the Black Freedom Movement in Durham, North Carolina (Chapel Hill: University of North Carolina Press, 2005); Laurie Green, *Battling the Plantation Mentality: Memphis and the Black Freedom Struggle* (Chapel Hill: University of North Carolina Press, 2007); Thomas Kiffmeyer, *Reformers to Radicals: Appalachian Volunteers and the War on Poverty in Kentucky* (Lexington: University Press of Kentucky, 2008); Guian McKee, *The Problem of Jobs: Liberalism, Race, and Deindustrialization in Philadelphia* (Chicago: University of Chicago Press, 2008); Marc Rodriguez, *Mexican Americanism: The Tejano Diaspora and Ethnic Politics in Texas and Wisconsin after 1950* (Chapel Hill: University of North Carolina Press, forthcoming); Williams, *Politics of Public Housing.*

PART ONE

Battles over Community Action

GUIAN A. MCKEE

"This Government Is with Us"

Lyndon Johnson and the Grassroots War
on Poverty

On a summer morning in late June 1967, President Lyndon Baines Johnson
set out to visit the ghetto. On his way to Texas for a long weekend at his
ranch, Johnson made a side trip to Philadelphia, where he toured the headquarters of the Opportunities Industrialization Centers (OIC). A community-based
job training program, OIC had been founded three years earlier by a group of
African American ministers led by the Reverend Leon H. Sullivan. Its origins
lay in a consumer boycott that the ministers had organized in the early 1960s
against Philadelphia-area companies that discriminated against blacks. Since
1964, OIC had received federal War on Poverty funding channeled through Philadelphia's Community Action Program. The program had grown into the city's
largest and most successful antipoverty program and had undertaken a national
expansion project—mostly funded by the Office of Economic Opportunity and
other federal agencies—that would reach 130 cities by the mid-1970s.[1]

The Philadelphia visit resulted from Johnson's realization in early 1967 that
his usual sources of advice on urban problems—"all these reports from the bureaucracy and the experts"—could not provide the insight he needed into on-
the-ground conditions in northern cities. In an attempt to gain insight into the
grassroots, Johnson quietly sent young aides such as Sherwin Markman, James
Gaither, and Thomas Cronin on missions into the inner cities, where they met
informally with community leaders and activists.[2] Markman met with Sullivan
during his Philadelphia "ghetto tour." In a memo to the president following the
trip, Markman described OIC "as the pride of Philadelphia's poverty unit" and
"the Nation's outstanding ghetto project." He also suggested that Johnson associate himself with OIC through a "spontaneous" but well-publicized visit.[3]

At the time of his OIC visit, Johnson was beleaguered by the Vietnam War and congressional hostility, and he would later recall the event as "one of the memorable days, a day of hope and progress."[4] In his speech that morning, Johnson argued that the problems of poverty could still be solved: "I know you have made me feel that we—all 200 million of us—are going to make it." Sullivan spoke as well, boldly claiming that "this government is with us, [the Office of Economic Opportunity] is with us, Brother Sargent Shriver is with us, the Department of Labor is with us, the Department of Health, Education and Welfare is with us, the Department of Commerce is with us. All of them have combined their resources for the first time in American history to help a program created from the community."[5] Sullivan omitted any reference to Johnson's support of the program. Although likely unintentional, this oversight nonetheless suggests several historical questions: Exactly how did Lyndon Johnson view the social movements of the 1960s, and in particular, those that worked with War on Poverty programs? Did programs such as OIC, let alone more radical grassroots efforts, have the president's support? Was Johnson in fact with them? These questions raise core issues about the nature of policy formation, the relationship between the grassroots and federal policy elites, and the interaction of political, policy, and social history.

Historians are currently exploring how community activists transformed the War on Poverty for their own purposes but have paid little attention to how federal policymakers, particularly President Johnson, responded to such grassroots activity. In part, this inattention reflects an irony of U.S. political history, an irony that has made it surprisingly difficult to establish definitively Johnson's specific personal views on many subjects. While American presidents are uniquely powerful in their capacity to shape public policy and public political discourse, they are often nearly totally silent in the archival records of their administrations. Researchers using the collections of the Johnson Presidential Library, for example, find the perspectives of presidential aides, assistants, members of Congress, and outside advisers but face a distinct void when they attempt to assess the views of Johnson himself. Direct traces of the president's thought appear only occasionally, most often as brief handwritten notes or a set of initials scrawled across the bottom of a memo written by someone else.

This essay fills part of this gap by establishing Johnson's reaction to the grassroots War on Poverty through a relatively new and largely unanalyzed source, the telephone conversations that Johnson secretly recorded throughout his presidency. During his time in office, President Johnson recorded 296 conversations that addressed the War on Poverty in some way. While these conversations varied greatly in depth and specific topic, three interrelated themes emerge that extend or challenge the existing historiography of the War on Poverty. First, the conversations graphically illustrate Johnson's personal conception of what the War on Poverty should be, particularly in the months during which his administration planned the program and lobbied Congress for passage of its core legislative framework, the Economic Opportunity Act (EOA). Second, the recordings demonstrate that the Community Action Program, which provided the primary opportunity for grassroots War on Poverty activism, was initially misunderstood by Johnson, never won his full support, and eventually became a target of his outright hostility. Third, the tapes show that Johnson distrusted direct grassroots action and feared that it would undermine political support for the War on Poverty and potentially weaken his presidency and his chances for reelection. The source of Johnson's opposition lay in his views about the appropriate roles of policymakers and citizens in implementing policy as well as in his general conception of American liberalism.[6]

COMMUNITY ACTION AND TWENTIETH-CENTURY LIBERALISM

These insights into presidential ideology and presidential policy positions reveal that LBJ and community action activists stood on opposite sides of a powerful emerging division within twentieth-century liberalism. Johnson's approach to the War on Poverty represented an effort to update the older ethos of a New Deal liberalism that he saw as emphasizing the obligations of citizens to aid one another through the mediating and socially ameliorative institutions of government as well as to contribute, primarily through work, to the greater good of society. Johnson's version of this liberalism emphasized issues of quality of life and economic opportunity. However, his acceptance of a tax-cut-based "commercial" Keynesianism that focused on macroeconomic growth limited his ability to think about the War on Poverty in a way that related issues of economic structure—such as unequal access to jobs—to problems of race, class, and power. In particular, Johnson rejected social democratic ideas about economic planning that had animated the left flanks of the New Deal, which was part of the reason he opposed proposals for public job programs suggested by secretary of labor Willard Wirtz.[7]

Ironically, the antipoverty planners who developed the Community Action Program similarly had little willingness to pursue underlying questions of economic structure, but their liberalism emphasized the failures and exclusions of the older liberalism and sought redress for those left out of the New Deal paradigm. The New Deal had eased the suffering of Americans during the Great Depression and had created at least a partial guarantee of security for specific categories of Americans, particularly the elderly.

Constrained, however, by the political and legislative power of influential southern congressmen, the New Deal had also produced a two-tiered system of social insurance. The first tier, which consisted primarily of Social Security and unemployment insurance, derived legitimacy from its tight connection to employment and was largely limited to white, male, middle-class wage earners and their dependents. These programs initially excluded domestic and agricultural workers, employment sectors that included nearly two-thirds of employed African Americans and 85 percent of African American women.[8] The second social policy tier, made up of Aid to Dependent Children and a few other direct aid programs, suffered from stigmatization because of its status as "welfare" and its increasing association with poor, female, and minority Americans. This pattern would be repeated in housing policy, veterans' benefits, and, in the 1960s, health care policy. Highly racialized and deeply gendered in its basic nature, this two-tiered system was the policy world in which Lyndon Johnson received his political education and in which he rose to power as well as the paradigm that community action sought to challenge.

The advocates of community action emphasized community empowerment, grassroots participation and democratization, and attainment of rights and resources for identifiable groups marginalized by this racialized welfare state. Through community action, they sought to empower poor communities by allowing them to plan and implement local antipoverty programs according to residents' perceptions of community needs. Backed by the power of the federal government and radicalized by the legislation's requirement that it facilitate the "maximum feasible participation" of the poor, community action in theory allowed the poor to challenge and potentially even restructure local governmental and social service institutions to better serve the interests of poor communities. This development marked one of a number of dividing points during the 1960s between the two liberalisms. It belonged quite distinctly to the newer liberalism yet was unwittingly sponsored by a president who saw in it comfortable but misleading echoes of the older liberalism that he sought to modernize. In certain areas, such as civil rights, Johnson transcended this rift and at least briefly linked the two liberalisms; in the War on Poverty, however, community action brought the liberalism of rights, empowerment, and protest to the field of political organization and mobilization, an arena in which Johnson's existing interests and commitments were so strong that reconciliation proved impossible.[9]

Although discussions about a federal attack on poverty had begun in 1963 as part of an effort to develop themes for President John F. Kennedy's expected reelection bid, the concept had made little progress by the time of his assassination. Johnson nonetheless endorsed the idea immediately after taking office. He told Council of Economic Advisers chair Walter Heller, "That's my kind of program."[10]

Community action quickly emerged as the core component of what still remained a highly theoretical initiative. The strategy derived from two cutting-edge ideas about the causes of poverty: Lloyd Ohlin and Richard Cloward's "opportunity theory" ideas, which held that youth gang members and possibly entire poor communities pursued deviant behaviors because society denied them opportunities to achieve conventional social and economic aspirations, and the "cycle of poverty" thesis, which posited that poverty could be passed across generations through the cultural traits of poor families. Building on these ideas, supporters of community action believed that poverty could be addressed by involving poor communities in planning services and programs to meet their own needs. The approach implicitly suggested that the persistence of poverty could best be explained by individual and cultural characteristics rather than by the larger structures of the economy and society. An antipoverty campaign, therefore, could avoid the costly and politically difficult project of reorganizing such structures and could focus instead on the seemingly more tractable problems of reforming the culture of the poor and reorganizing local institutions such as welfare agencies, charities, and school systems.[11]

In February 1964, Johnson appointed JFK's brother-in-law, Sargent Shriver, who had organized the widely hailed Peace Corps program, to head a new task force that would draft authorizing legislation for the recently declared War on Poverty. Shriver immediately expressed doubts about community action's viability, at least in the short term, and with Johnson's support, the task force added a range of programs favored by the cabinet departments. These programs included the Job Corps, a residential job training and remedial education effort for high school dropouts; the Neighborhood Youth Corps, a local work program for teenagers; Volunteers in Service to America (VISTA); and a work-study program for high school and college students. Shriver believed that the Job Corps in particular would provide the kind of immediate success needed to galvanize support for the War on Poverty. Community action, he thought, would take more time to develop. Still, community action remained as Title II of the bill.[12]

During this planning period, advocates generally thought of the measure as a means of generating better coordination of existing federal programs and local social services through input from both poor and nonpoor citizens. Local governments, most observers assumed, would remain firmly in control. Early in the process of drafting the bill, task force member Richard Boone insisted on the insertion of a requirement that community action provide for the "maximum feasible participation of residents of the areas and groups served." Boone and others on the task force, including Shriver, appear to have seen the phrase as simply a way to ensure that African Americans would not be completely excluded from the program. Planners also believed that community action would facilitate alliances between community members and local governments against hidebound private social agencies and unresponsive federal bureaucrats but did not think that activists would use community action against City Hall.[13]

During the spring of 1964, however, task force members assigned to community action recognized the potential power of maximum feasible participation. Enjoying considerable autonomy in developing the program, their goals became bolder. In May, one wrote that "an effective anti-poverty program must change these institutions and programs but it can be done only through a revolution. The poor need to emerge in the American community as a major political factor capable of pressing their needs upon the political officials and the bureaucracies of the community."[14] Community action, in this view, would provide a means of making right the limitations of New Deal liberalism as well as returning to the people some of the functions assumed by the modern administrative state.

Although little noticed at the time—maximum feasible participation received only passing mention in congressional hearings and debates about the EOA—the phrase would provide the basis for much of the grassroots mobilization around the War on Poverty. In some cases, these activities would include aggressive challenges to the prerogatives and powers of local governments. There is no evidence that President Johnson recognized, much less considered, the implications of maximum feasible participation and what it might mean either for community action itself or for the War on Poverty as a whole.

JOHNSON'S CONCEPTION OF THE WAR ON POVERTY

Recordings from the early months of Johnson's presidency reveal significant uncertainty about the War on Poverty's policy content. Yet they also show a relatively consistent core ideological position on the part of the president, a position characterized by both a deep-seated belief in the responsibility and capacity of an activist state to help the underprivileged, and an equally strong insistence that individuals should use the resources offered by that state to achieve a position of self-reliance from which they could contribute back to the nation.

On the morning of the 1964 State of the Union address, in which he would declare "unconditional war on poverty," Johnson emphasized the importance of work and self-help as he explained the antipoverty effort to former secretary of the treasury Robert Anderson: "What we're trying to do—instead of people getting something for nothing, we're going to try to fit them where they can take care of themselves. . . . We want to get them where they can carry their own weight."[15] This emphasis on work and on resolving poverty by enabling individual self-reliance would recur throughout Johnson's effort to promote the War on Poverty.

Speaking to Georgia senator Richard Russell on June 11, 1964, Johnson portrayed the initiative as a strategy to address the unemployment that persisted despite the macroeconomic growth generated by the tax cut passed earlier in the year. He also argued that the programmatic content of the War on Poverty would consist largely of existing but reorganized federal programs:

PRESIDENT JOHNSON: The tax bill has just worked out wonderfully.

RUSSELL: We're in a boom period [unclear]—

PRESIDENT JOHNSON: The married people, only 2.6 percent of the married people are unemployed; 97.4 got jobs. There's 16 percent of these youngsters, and I'll have all them employed when I give them a job where they can stay in high school, give them a job where they can stay in college, and give them a job at one of these camps, and I'll cover that 16 percent when I get my other program. . . .

RUSSELL: Well, a lot of that's not firm unemployment at all.

PRESIDENT JOHNSON: No, it's kids that are dropping out of school and then they're going on a [welfare] roll. But I'll take care of that with my poverty [program], just by organizing it all. We've got the money in these various departments: Labor and HEW [Health, Education, and Welfare] and

Justice. Justice has got a juvenile delinquency program; Labor's got a re-training program; HEW's got an education program. I'm going to put all of them in one and put one top administrator and really get some results, go in and clear up these damn [welfare] rolls. And I'll do it with only 300 million [dollars] more than was in the budget anyway, last year.

PRESIDENT JOHNSON: Well, I was down in Kentucky the other day. We've got fifty kids there that are teaching beauty culture, how to fix [his daughter] Lynda's hair, and they're all going out and get jobs at fifty dollars, sixty dollars a week in another three months. They've been at it now for about a year. I had fifty auto mechanics in the same building, and those kids from all over the mountain, they're teaching them how to tear down a differential and put it back together, and they'll get jobs. Now, that's what we ought to do instead of paying out four billion [dollars] a year on relief, for nothing. They don't have to work. To hell with this employment compensation relief.[16]

In this and other conversations, Johnson shows no evidence of having as-similated ideas such as opportunity theory, with its emphasis on the imbal-ance between individual aspirations and opportunities and on the power rela-tions embedded in local institutions. Instead, he viewed poverty primarily as a problem of male unemployment (despite the beauty parlor reference) caused by a lack of skills. Through work-study programs and especially the Job Corps, he would provide directionless young men with the training necessary to ob-tain respectable employment and bring them into fully realized American manhood. Masculinized and work-oriented, this approach to the War on Pov-erty shared opportunity theory's emphasis on removing barriers, but it did so through attention to individual improvement rather than community organ-ization. It also ignored opportunity theory's challenge to existing social and political institutions.

Yet neither Johnson nor the advocates of opportunity theory seriously inter-rogated the relationship between poverty and structural features of the econ-omy. Where could jobs be found, who had access to them, and how much did they pay? Nor did they question whether permanent jobs would be available for people who completed War on Poverty training programs or how empow-erment might be sustained for those who participated in the community mobi-lization efforts. In particular, Johnson's focus on work revealed a crucial contra-diction. Throughout the War on Poverty planning process, Wirtz had lobbied aggressively for a public jobs program, an idea that Heller and Shriver resisted and that Johnson ultimately rejected with an "absolute blank stare" at a February cabinet meeting.[17]

Johnson and these key advisers wanted to avoid the expense of direct job creation. He doubted the Labor Department's ability to administer such a program and above all accepted the Keynesian position that macroeconomic growth policy could generate enough jobs to employ all who possessed the necessary skills. From such a position, work and self-reliance depended on the individual, aided as necessary by the state, with little attention to the wider community, to local politics, or to possible economic imbalances between inner cities and suburbs, between growing and declining regions of the country, between racial groups, or between men and women.[18]

In addition, Johnson's focus on the obligation to assist fellow citizens was often balanced by a harsher emphasis on citizens' reciprocal obligations.[19] The president expounded on this view in a July 29, 1964, conversation with the influential chair of the House Appropriations Committee, George Mahon of Texas, during the run-up to the House vote on the EOA:

PRESIDENT JOHNSON: I want you to take a good look now and help me on my poverty [bill]. That's what the Republicans want to beat, that one bill, and I'm going to take tax-eaters and make taxpayers out of them and I'm going to stop these damn riots. I've gotten every one of these cities—all these young people have nothing to do, sitting around, and I got them all to agree today to no more demonstrations and they're asking please, put these people to work, and I'm going to put 150,000 of them to work in ninety days' time on useful hardworking projects. Teach them some discipline and when to get up, and how to work all day, and in two years, I'll have them trained where they can at least drive a truck instead of sit around a pool room.

PRESIDENT JOHNSON: This is one I just can't lose. . . . I'm making them work for it. I want to take tax-eaters . . . and make taxpayers out of them. And all they're doing is sitting around on the porch now. Every home I've gone into has had an old eighteen-, nineteen-year-old boy that's been turned back from the army, and all he's doing is sitting there with a relief check. I want to take him and work [the] hell out of him, and . . . I'll work a good many of them right in your Lubbock and show them how to do it, and they'll be bragging on it more than they are the Peace Corps. And the conservatives will be leading the way, because my NYA [National Youth Administration] produced the governor of Texas [John Connally]. That's where I got him.[20]

Few of Johnson's turns of phrase better captured his view of the program's purpose than the idea of turning "tax-eaters" into "taxpayers," and no example better captured this transformative capacity than that of Governor Connally and the New Deal's NYA, which had provided work-study jobs for high school and college students as well as work experience projects for unemployed young people. Johnson had first come to national notice as Texas director of the NYA under President Franklin Delano Roosevelt, and the experience had shaped Johnson's expectation of how federal programs might interact with state and local governments.

The NYA played a central role in Johnson's understanding of the War on Poverty and especially community action. The president later recalled that when Heller first presented the community action concept to him at a Christmas 1963 meeting at his ranch, he called Jesse Kellam, who had worked with him on the Texas NYA, "to join in our ranch discussions, because my thoughts kept going back to those NYA days."[21] Heller remembered that Johnson "made very clear that it had to have some hard, bedrock content, and he kept referring time and again to his NYA . . . experience in the thirties. He liked the idea of learning while doing."[22] The most obvious connection lay in how his time with the NYA embedded in Johnson a belief in the value in putting young people, especially young men, to work. Much of this belief involved a sense that government could remasculinize men who had been excluded from customary social and economic roles and prepare them for community and family leadership. This gendered sensibility pervaded many aspects of the Great Society.[23]

Johnson saw the War on Poverty in the same way, anticipating that its programs would focus the energies of underemployed young men. On July 24, 1964, Johnson explained his views to Georgia governor Carl Sanders:

PRESIDENT JOHNSON: I'll tell you what you can produce out of that. . . . You think these are the ragtags. And we thought NYA was. I don't know whether you were old enough to help in the NYA or not. But John Connally—John Connally's an NYA boy, governor of the state. He worked [for] fifteen dollars a month. And you'll find that a good many of these people that you take in there and give them a job for a couple of years wind up being the leaders in your state.[24]

Johnson's view of the War on Poverty thus emphasized both the potential for state-supported uplift and the need to maintain order by directing male energies into productive channels.

Just as important, the NYA also shaped how Johnson understood the concept of local participation in community action. More than almost any other New Deal program, the NYA had granted extensive discretion to Johnson and other state administrators. Far less centralized and far less a part of the emerging administrative state than the rest of the New Deal, it had succeeded, particularly as Johnson had experienced it. This experience, in turn, defined Johnson's vision of community action: as replicating the structure of the NYA by finding energetic state and local administrators of the kind he had once been and providing them with resources and the authority to innovate in service delivery, skills training, and perhaps infrastructure construction.

The NYA, though, had not allowed for direct enrollee involvement in program administration. Instead, it had provided for meaningful participation in the administrative state by local and state officials, and Johnson thought that community action would replicate this approach.[25] Johnson explained this concept of community action to Chicago mayor Richard Daley on January 20, 1964:

PRESIDENT JOHNSON: What I wish you'd do [is] I wish you'd get your local people together through local initiative and let us cooperate and establish the coordinating mechanisms, the planning and developing, what you think ought to be done for it there in Chicago. Then [when] we get this money, we can drop a hunk of it in there and do it.

DALEY: [Unclear.] That'll be great.

PRESIDENT JOHNSON: But get your planning and development people busy right now to see what you do for the crummiest place in town, the lowest, the bottom thing, and see what we can do about it. We'll get our dough, and then you can have your plan ready, and we'll move.[26]

The principle of direct participation by the poor had apparently not yet entered the president's consciousness. Instead, Johnson envisioned the antipoverty effort as an as-yet-unspecified combination of federally supported job and education programs that would be implemented through local planning and service coordination efforts.

The rising discontent in the nation's inner cities also began to impose itself on President Johnson's NYA-inspired thinking about the War on Poverty. In particular, the brief reference to riots in the conversation with Mahon marked the emergence of another recurring theme in Johnson's discussions of the program. A day earlier, while speaking with AFL-CIO president George Meany, Johnson argued that simply by providing jobs, the War on Poverty would address the primary cause of the revolts that had recently broken out in Harlem: "Now, Dick Daley tells me he's got one hundred thousand folks out there that are on his [welfare] rolls just waiting. Where all this Harlem stuff comes from is they've got no jobs; they can't do anything. They're just raising hell. And we'll— Shriver will put them to work right quick."[27] The idea that urban revolts could be prevented by the Job Corps or Neighborhood Youth Corps became a frequent Johnson refrain during the late summer of 1964. On August 31, Johnson again emphasized the connection in a call to his friend, Wesley West:

PRESIDENT JOHNSON: I'm going to take a bunch of these young, strapping boys out of these damn rioting squads that they're engaged in and put them out and put them to work. Feed them and clothe them and try to get them where they can get in the army.

WEST: Yes.

PRESIDENT JOHNSON: Particularly a lot of your Negro youths. They've got nothing to do, and they can't get a job. You know, it's hard to believe what you see in a good many of these places. If you had the same population density in New York that you've got in Harlem, you could put the whole United States in three boroughs.

WEST: That's what they tell me.

PRESIDENT JOHNSON: People living that way—the bottom is just going to blow off the tea kettle. It's just got to. We've got to get them out and put them to work some way. There's 16 percent of our young people unemployed. That's where all of our crime rate's coming from, you see—these damn youngsters. . . . So we've got to put them to work, and we're going to do it. Make them—scrub them up, get some tapeworms out of their bellies. Get them to where they can get up at six o'clock in the morning, and work all day. Then we can get them to where they can serve. One out of every two that come into us now in the draft are being turned back—not fit physically or mentally. We think we can clean them up this way and shoot them on in there. Maybe even teach them to be a truck driver or something.[28]

Johnson's formulation of the problem thus produced a peculiar transformation of liberalism in which job training followed by military enlistment became a method to absorb surplus minority labor, remasculinize the seemingly lost young men of the inner city, and prevent riots. Long-term employment remained an afterthought. Yet with Wirtz's jobs plan rejected, the War on Poverty would embrace little of the New Deal's broader conception of labor and economic rights. The absence of a structural conception of rights drastically constrained War on Poverty's reach and ambition at the federal level, as Johnson's liberalism relied solely on Keynesian macroeconomic policy (and later, military spending) to generate jobs. While the War on Poverty might prepare the underprivileged for work, it would not guarantee them a job.

The concern with draftee rejection in the West conversation should be viewed less in terms of the not-yet-escalated conflict in Vietnam than in the context of Johnson's failure to comprehend fully how poverty issues had become intertwined with race in the urban North, particularly in relation to police brutality, restrictive local governments, and demands for economic and political self-determination in inner-city communities. This disconnect also appeared in a conversation between Johnson and Philadelphia Democratic city committee chair Francis Smith:

PRESIDENT JOHNSON: Are you having any disturbances in Philadelphia?

SMITH: We had a shooting yesterday of a young sixteen-year-old boy by a policeman that was no good.

PRESIDENT JOHNSON: Mmm.

SMITH: But they've kept calm about it. And I'm hopeful that nothing breaks out today and will be handled in an orderly fashion. Now, we did have disturbances, and, of course, the Chester thing was right at our backdoor.

PRESIDENT JOHNSON: Mm-hmm.

SMITH: But . . . we've had sensible people. Now, I had a meeting yesterday with fifteen of the outstanding Negroes, and they speak just as vigorously as you or I do about retaining order.

PRESIDENT JOHNSON: Mm-hmm.

SMITH: And using intelligence and getting their people registered. They want to voice it through the ballot box, and that's what I want them to do.

PRESIDENT JOHNSON: Did . . . what—did the policeman just lose his head?

SMITH: [sadly] Yeah. Quick . . .

PRESIDENT JOHNSON: Mmm.

SMITH: . . . quick with the revolver.

PRESIDENT JOHNSON: Kill him?

SMITH: Yeah. Right through the chest. Right through the heart.

PRESIDENT JOHNSON: What was the boy doing?

SMITH: Uh, larceny, robbery. Sixteen-year-old, unarmed. It's just a terrible thing.

PRESIDENT JOHNSON: Did he threaten him or anything?

SMITH: No. He hollered to him to stop, and the boy ran and he fired. Killed him.

PRESIDENT JOHNSON: Mmm, mmm. Frank, have you got any influence— any of your friends, or associates—with any of these Republicans in the House of Representatives?[29]

Although Johnson expressed interest and concern about the shooting, his final response was that Smith should help him find the Republican votes necessary to pass the antipoverty program, which would provide temporary jobs and training for young people otherwise likely to be shot by reckless police officers. The exchange demonstrates Johnson's almost mechanistic approach to policymaking. For Johnson, the solution to the inner cities' multilayered racial, housing, political, and economic problems lay in the passage of a bill that would aid restless and misdirected young men. This programmatic liberalism overvalued legislation, assuming that provision of an appropriate program would meet the immediate needs and at least begin to resolve the underlying difficulties.

In Johnson's formulation, poverty and urban unrest alike rested on the issue of jobs and skills, which could be solved by programs modeled on the New Deal's Civilian Conservation Corps (CCC) and NYA. Johnson expressed this perspective, along with his belief that community action should be run by local and state governments, in a bitter conversation with his special assistant, Bill Moyers, just before the final House vote on the bill:

PRESIDENT JOHNSON: I'm going to rewrite your poverty program. You-all, you boys got together and wrote this stuff, and I thought we were just going to have [another] NYA. As I understood it—do you know what I think about the poverty program, what I thought we were going to do?

MOYERS: What?

PRESIDENT JOHNSON: I thought we were going to have CCC camps.

MOYERS: We've got that.

PRESIDENT JOHNSON: And I thought we were going to have community action [programs] where a city or county or a school district or some gov-

Figure 1. Lyndon Johnson with Bill Moyers, September 8, 1966. Photo by Yoichi R. Okamoto. Lyndon Baines Johnson Library and Museum.

ernmental agency could sponsor a project—state highway department sponsor it—and we'd pay the labor and a very limited amount of materials on it but make them put up most of the materials and a good deal of supervision and so forth just like we used to have.

MOYERS: We've got that.

PRESIDENT JOHNSON: I thought that we'd say to a high school boy that was about to drop out, "We'll let you work for the library or sweep the floors or work in the shrubs or pick the rocks, and we'll pay you enough so [you] can stay in school."

MOYERS: We've got that.

PRESIDENT JOHNSON: I thought you'd let a college boy do the same thing.

MOYERS: We've got that.

PRESIDENT JOHNSON: And college girl. Now, I never heard of any liberal outfits that's where you could subsidize anybody. I think I'm against that. I
just—if you-all want to do it in the Peace Corps, then that's your private
thing and that's Kennedy. But my Johnson program: I'm against subsidiz-
ing any private organization. Now, if we had a hundred billion, we might
need to, but with all the governmental agencies in this country, I'd a whole
lot rather Dick Daley do it than the Urban League. . . . And he's got heads
of departments and he's got experienced people that are handling hundreds of millions of dollars. In every one of these places, I'd make them
come in [and] sponsor these projects. And I just think it makes us wide
open, and I don't want anybody to get any grants.[30]

Johnson's vision of community action consisted of "heads of departments
and . . . experienced people" in local and state agencies lending their expertise
to the management of federally supported antipoverty programs. The Urban
League, much less radical organizations run by the poor themselves, would
have little to do with the president's program. His version of community action
would ensure the maximum feasible participation not of the poor but of innovative local and state bureaucrats. In contrast, the antipoverty planners who had
developed community action saw it as a tool for community self-determination
that would allow the poor to challenge the prerogatives of precisely the "heads
of departments" whom the president assumed would run the initiative. Conflict was inevitable.

JOHNSON, COMMUNITY ACTION, AND THE CONSTRAINTS OF POLITICS

The extent of the gap between the president's priorities and those of community action advocates became clear in a May 14, 1964, conversation between
Johnson and Phil Landrum, a Georgia congressman and the floor leader for
the EOA in the House. Throughout the spring, a group of Catholic Democratic
congressmen from northern cities had threatened to block the bill in the House
Education and Labor Committee unless the community action provisions were
rewritten to include direct funding for programs in Catholic schools.[31] At the

time, many southerners still deeply distrusted the Catholic Church, and the possibility that parochial schools might receive federal funding in any form had repeatedly generated heated controversies during the 1950s and early 1960s. In this case, rumors that the poverty bill would provide such funds had again produced a backlash among southern Democrats.

During the conversation with Landrum, a furious President Johnson indicated that his primary interest lay in the Job Corps camps of Title I rather than in the community action provisions of Title II:

> PRESIDENT JOHNSON: Well, my judgment would be, if you could, we don't have to get everything in one year. If we don't get anything but a work camp, we're all right.
>
> LANDRUM: Mm-hmm . . . yeah. Well, that's the truth, if you—
>
> PRESIDENT JOHNSON: And if I had to, if I had to, and the Catholics made an issue, I'd just lay it right in their lap. With the Republicans, say, "All right, you vote it out," and let them vote it out.
>
> LANDRUM: Well, here's what we can do: we can justify this nine hundred million dollars with the first title of this bill.
>
> PRESIDENT JOHNSON: Yeah, that's right.
>
> PRESIDENT JOHNSON: That's what we're going to have. What you need is three camps in Gainesville, Georgia, [to] take these kids and prepare them where they won't stay on relief all their life.
>
> LANDRUM: That's right. . . . [T]hat's exactly right. Now, this community action thing . . .
>
> PRESIDENT JOHNSON: To hell with community action.
>
> LANDRUM: . . . could be junked entirely.
>
> PRESIDENT JOHNSON: To hell with community action.[32]

A few hours later, Moyers gently tried to rebuff a similar presidential suggestion by asserting the significance of community action to the entire War on Poverty program. Johnson quietly replied, "Well, I don't think so."[33]

While less dramatic than the presidential damnation of community action in the Landrum call, conversations recorded during the days preceding passage of the EOA in early August 1964 offer additional evidence about Johnson's motivations. As the House engaged in a final debate on the bill, southern Democrats offered an amendment that granted state governors a veto over any community action program in their state. The governor's veto represented an explicit concession to states' rights, albeit one that the administration did not anticipate would be used with any frequency.[34]

When Johnson, his advisers, and House Democratic leaders discussed the amendment on August 4, Moyers warned that an expanded governor's veto would have negative consequences in other policy areas: "They've been trying for a number of years to get the governor to have a veto power on a program that [the federal government runs] in the state, particularly in the cities. If they succeed in setting a precedent in the poverty program . . . they'll start trying to do this on every federal program that goes to the states." Landrum, who had recommended that the amendment be accepted, countered that a substitute Republican bill would almost certainly offer a broadened governor's veto and asked, "How are we going to hold these southern boys that are a little bit trembly about the thing anyway? And say we do hold them and beat down the substitute, and then the Republicans want to put that in a motion to recommit. We're going to run into a problem of keeping these southern boys, and they'll use that as an excuse to vote against it."[35]

The consequences of the amendment, Landrum maintained, would be limited. Less than an hour later, Speaker of the House John McCormack, from Massachusetts, concurred:

MCCORMACK: What the hell, it doesn't hurt the cause any; it just . . . if a state don't want it, let them go without it! And if it's more money for other places. A governor would have a hell of a job vetoing anything.

PRESIDENT JOHNSON: Well, they're afraid of your people, John. You take the northerners, and I'll go along with it if you'll tell [New York representative] Jim Delaney and the northerners not to [object]. I don't want them to think I sold them out.[36]

Johnson's interest thus lay not in the content of the amendment and its implications for control over community action but in maintaining the coalition of northern and southern Democrats necessary for passage of the bill. The governor's veto would soon set the stage for numerous pitched battles over poverty programs, especially in the southern states, but that development was beyond the scope of Johnson's concern at that moment.[37]

On August 5, as he lobbied uncommitted southern Democrats, Johnson deployed the governor's veto as evidence of his commitment to local governmental discretion. In a conversation with Virginia congressman Porter Hardy, Johnson offered assurances that the governor's veto, along with the president's oversight, would block any circumvention of local government; for supporters of community action, such circumvention had been exactly the point:

PRESIDENT JOHNSON: [Landrum] said some of the southern boys were upset about the states' rights angle. I told him to write an amendment that would take care of them and leave it up to the governor, where he could veto any project that they wanted to develop.

First of all, we can't have any unless they initiate it, unless it's started in the state. But if some school superintendent or some mayor had one that he didn't like, the governor could veto it, and we'd have to submit them to him before we could put them into operation—give him thirty days. My governor [Connally] said that would take care of any of their problem. I thought that would help us with the southerners and—

HARDY: I think it'll help some, but I don't believe it will provide the answer. Now, I talked—I talked about this thing at some length with Sarge Shriver the other day, and I told him some of the things that were particularly bothering some of us in the South. I don't know whether there's much that can be done about one or two aspects of it.

But anyway, I'm trying to find—trying to find answers, and I hope it's so that I can go along with it, but I don't mind telling you I'm—I just don't know what to do with it. I've had a lot of resistance from in my own district to it, and a good bit of it comes from the official family down there and . . .

PRESIDENT JOHNSON: What is their objection, Porter? What can we do to—

HARDY: Well, I don't know what you can do about it, but some of the city people say that this proposal to contract direct with private organizations would completely bypass the local governmental organizations. And they are really very much concerned about that aspect of it.

PRESIDENT JOHNSON: Well . . . suppose I told you this: that I won't let them contract with any private organization in your district you don't approve of.

HARDY: Well, that might help them some, but . . .

PRESIDENT JOHNSON: [W]hat I can do is this: I can lay down the law to Sargent Shriver that in—what's the number of your district in Virginia?

Figure 2. President Lyndon Johnson on the telephone
at the White House, April 5, 1968. Photo by Yoichi R.
Okamoto. Lyndon Baines Johnson Library and Museum.

HARDY: Mine's the Second District, but now, you know—
PRESIDENT JOHNSON: Now, wait just a minute. That there's no—whatever
objections you've got to it—that there's no project started in the Second
District with any private organization that hasn't got your initial on it,
or mine.[38]

Johnson's willingness to offer such compromises indicates that the principle
of community control could be readily sacrificed to keep the varied factions of
the Democratic Party happy, loyal, and ready both to pass the bill and to reelect
the president.[39]

Taken together, Johnson's early conversations about community action indicate that at best, he tolerated its inclusion because of his largely imagined assumption that it would replicate the NYA and other New Deal programs. In contrast, some scholars have argued that Johnson and his aides saw community action as a way to reconcile the older New Deal liberalism with the group-rights-based liberalism emerging from the conjuncture of the civil rights movement and the New Left.[40] Some of Shriver's task force members may well have viewed the program this way, and it might be possible to see Johnson as at least a potential advocate for such a form of community action if any of the recorded 1964 conversations showed that he had expressed support for or even interest in the concept. In all of the conversations recorded as the War on Poverty moved from planning to implementation, however, no such examples exist.

THE REALITY OF COMMUNITY ACTION

The implementation of the War on Poverty only reemphasized the tension between Johnson's vision and the reality of the legislation that Congress had passed. Community action, in particular, brought such strains to the fore. The program quickly generated explosive conflicts between mayors and activists in communities around the United States. During this period, Johnson began to record his telephone conversations with far less frequency. The existing conversations nevertheless offer significant insights into the president's perspective on grassroots social movements and particularly into his desire to contain or restructure the Community Action Program while sustaining the wider War on Poverty.

Evidence for this view exists among traditional sources as well as in the recordings. In a September 1965 memo to Johnson, budget director Charles Schultze outlined growing resistance to community action among mayors who feared that such programs would be "setting up a competing political organization in their own backyards." Schultze noted that community action had begun with the legitimate goal of engaging "the poor themselves in the anti-poverty program." The concept of involvement, however, had received what he saw as "the wrong emphasis from the start." Maximum feasible participation, he argued, should simply have meant hiring the poor for staff jobs with the programs, recruiting volunteers from the affected communities, and surveying the poor about their needs and problems; it should not have involved elections for community action planning boards or "organizing the poor to speak up with a louder voice." In particular, challenging City Hall had no place in the program:

mayors might tolerate conflict between community action programs and social welfare bureaucracies, "but they won't stand for what appears, to them at least, as the Federal creation of competing political groups in their own cities." The Community Action Program, Schultze concluded, should not "be in the business of organizing the poor politically." In a handwritten note at the end of the memo, Johnson stated his position in stark terms: "O.K. I agree. L."[41]

Johnson's recorded conversations about the operation of community action expand significantly on his views. The first substantive recorded presidential comment on community action's problems occurred on August 18, 1965, just after the Watts Riots and in the midst of a reauthorization fight for the EOA. Late that afternoon, Johnson had a brief conversation in which he expressed his frustration with the program: "I think somebody ought to veto these damn fool community action [programs]. Don't you put any money in community action. Just cut it down. Hear that? Just cut that down—I'm tired of these political organizations going out and trying to run a [unclear]."[42] The passage not only captures Johnson's anger and frustration but also suggests a president weighing the value of a politically troublesome program toward which he had little commitment.

While Johnson on occasion expressed interest in community action as a means of checking urban unrest, this limited support quickly dissipated in the face of more immediate political imperatives or of direct challenges from activists. One such attack came just before Christmas 1965, when antipoverty activists from a controversial community action program in Syracuse, New York, staged a protest outside the gates of Johnson's Texas ranch.[43] On the morning of December 24, Johnson discussed the incident with Daley:

PRESIDENT JOHNSON: I got your poverty group from Syracuse down here giving me hell—

DALEY: Oh yeah?

PRESIDENT JOHNSON:—because the mayor turned them down and they came over and invaded my house yesterday and got arrested.

DALEY: My God.

PRESIDENT JOHNSON: We got FBI says one of them is a strong communist sympathizer.

DALEY: Yeah. . . . Well, they're trying to pressure you, Mr. President. [Unclear] pressure. And they're trying to snatch your control of this country, control of everything, just under this program. And the fact is and the truth of the matter is that they've never had such a fine program in the history of our country. And what I keep saying is, "Lord, God, let's get together, let's co-operate." What difference does it make who gets credit as long as we get jobs and get the people out of slums and blight and get education. But many of these people throughout the country are not concerned with the solution; they're concerned with the agitation of the problem. And this is all over the country, and they've seen an opportunity to snatch it—a popular issue, but one that you and I could have known doesn't bear the right of logic, and that is: only the poor can control these programs. Well, that's ridiculous.

PRESIDENT JOHNSON: That's a good—

DALEY: . . . It'd be the same thing as saying . . . that only the soldier could control the army, that you are not entitled to generals, to scientists, to the great experts, to the fine educated and dedicated—

In part, the president's quiet acquiescence to Daley's dismissal of community action may have reflected a desire to avoid challenging a mayor whose support and organizational acumen Johnson still badly needed. In 1965, however, a mainstream politician such as Daley had no immediate alternatives to Johnson for national leadership of the Democratic Party. Had Johnson wanted to defend an activist version of community action, he could have done so.

A brief June 2, 1966, exchange between Johnson and Georgia's Russell supports this interpretation. Following discussions of the budget and inflation, the two men agreed in their evaluation of the Community Action Program:

PRESIDENT JOHNSON: This Community Action Program, poverty, is a wasteful thing, they ought to cut it out. It's a dangerous thing, too, these folks are liable to—

RUSSELL: It's terrible. . . . It is terrible, and the way they handle it is just like that they got a gift from on high and then [there is] no accounting for it.

PRESIDENT JOHNSON: What do you think about the election? How many seats do you think I'm going to lose in the House?

RUSSELL: In the House? About twenty-eight.[44]

The conjunction of concerns about community action with fears about the midterm elections provides a key framework for assessing community action's problematic political nature. Just as Johnson did not fully comprehend the local context of urban poverty, race relations, and unrest, the advocates of community action in Shriver's poverty task force had underestimated how efforts to unsettle local power relations would reverberate through national politics.

The Vietnam War and its resulting budgetary pressures as well as the antiwar movement also shaped Johnson's views of the War on Poverty and the grassroots. In late December 1966, with Shriver contemplating resigning as Office of Economic Opportunity (OEO) director, Johnson expounded on his views regarding the budgetary constraints on the War on Poverty, the consequences of street protests, and his difficulties with Robert F. Kennedy and other liberal senators who actively supported an expanded poverty program. Johnson's observations suggest a deep discomfort with the new liberalism and even more with radicalism:

> PRESIDENT JOHNSON: Whatever figure I give in the budget I will fight for it as I did last year, but I cannot keep [Shriver] from being the victim of Bobby [Kennedy], and [Senator Abraham] Ribicoff, and [Senator] Joe Clark, and [Senator Wayne] Morse. And I cannot keep him from being [the] victim of the Commies who were out here yesterday. [They] said give the money to poverty not Vietnam, and I think that's hurting poverty more than anything in the world, is that these Commies are parading . . . and these kids, long-hairs, . . . saying, you know, that they want poverty instead of Vietnam, and the Nigras, and I think that's what the people regard as the Great Society. . . . [I]n my judgment, the bigger request I make for poverty, the more danger it is being killed.[45]

This comment shows that while participatory, grassroots democracy formed an organizing principle for community action and thus offered a potential connection between the old liberalism and the social movements of the 1960s, Johnson's views should not be blurred with those of his aides and his task forces, much less those of policymakers at OEO. Such a unitary view of the executive branch vastly underestimates the relative autonomy of officials in executive agencies and task forces as well as the discretion and creativity of activists in communities around the country. Whether they worked in unison or at cross-purposes, such historical actors could reshape public policy in ways that the president could not fully control.

LIBERALISM AND THE GRASSROOTS

The 1967 congressional battle over reauthorization of the EOA poses particular problems for interpretations that view Johnson as an architect of participatory democracy through community action. During the reauthorization struggle, the administration fought to preserve the War on Poverty as a whole but largely abandoned the maximum feasible participation principle. Although community action survived as a formal War on Poverty program, the Green Amendment to the reauthorization bill significantly undermined the core concept, giving local governments formal control over community action programs.[46] The recordings shed little light on Johnson's views about the Green Amendment but suggest that between 1964 and 1966, Johnson had moved from disinterest not to support of participatory community action but to active hostility toward this key dimension of his own War on Poverty. In addition, the administration's 1967 legislative proposal included amendments to the EOA that banned "partisan political activity" by community action agencies and instituted new requirements "for representation of local public agencies on community action boards."[47] Although the Green Amendment imposed even greater restrictions on community action, it merely pushed Johnson further in a direction toward which he was already headed.

Conversations from early 1968 reveal that even after passage of the Green Amendment, Johnson continued to express hostility regarding community action and those whom he associated with it. Shortly after accepting Shriver's resignation in February 1968, Johnson indicated to secretary of state Dean Rusk that Daley opposed Shriver's possible bid for the Illinois governorship, largely because of the OEO's efforts to engage the "gangsters" of the inner city:

> PRESIDENT JOHNSON: Well, Daley is not going to have anything to do with [Shriver. He] says that Shriver's rather unpopular, and the downstaters, that they would murder Shriver and murder me. And he said there's gangs. . . . [The] gangsters he's got on the payroll out there just ruined him with the good people of Chicago. They're in jail, and we send them checks every two weeks and stuff like that.[48]

This assessment of antipoverty efforts in Chicago was crude, and LBJ's invocation of "gangsters" and "the good people of Chicago" bore clear racial connotations, but his comments demonstrated that the Green Amendment had done nothing to lessen his opposition to federally sponsored grassroots mobilization. On March 23, 1968, Johnson made his views clear to Daley, urging the mayor to assert total control over the antipoverty program in Chicago. Older, community-based projects could be discarded:

PRESIDENT JOHNSON: You've got to get your best planners, and we've got to
take things like you've brought in there, and your housing and your poverty. I've got a new poverty man now [new OEO director Bertrand Hard-
ing], and I'm going to tell him [to] come sit down with your people, and
you take charge of this goddamn thing. Let's get all these, let's handle
these, let's just sidestep them, let's start some new projects, and let their
old ones kind of wither a little, transfer them, and let's get completely in
charge. And I'm going to tell [Harding] that I want him to sit down and
work with your people.[49]

The president may even have associated community action with his despised
rival, Robert F. Kennedy. As attorney general, Kennedy had chaired a presidential juvenile delinquency committee that contributed significantly to antipoverty planners' embrace of the community action concept. As senator, he had
defended the program and pushed for an expansion of the overall War on Poverty. Some of Johnson's anger at Kennedy overflowed in an April 1968 conversation with special assistant Joseph Califano in which the president explored possible linkages between the senator and community action. LBJ concluded that
in conjunction with television, Kennedy and community action bore near total
responsibility for the urban riots of the previous years, primarily through the
funding (real and imagined) of African American activists:

PRESIDENT JOHNSON: Bobby Kennedy and Ribicoff plus community action
have brought riots on this country. Solely. I don't think it's the poverty
causes at all because they've had a hell of a lot more poverty, [a] lot more
unemployment, [a] lot more other things. It's the leadership that's brought
this on. And I think number one is Bobby Kennedy and Ribicoff, number
two is Sargent Shriver and his poverty, number three is television. That's
my judgment. Now do you think I'm wrong?
CALIFANO: I, uh, I think the Kennedy-Ribicoff hearings and what . . . both
those guys have said have really been very inflammatory. I'm not sure
community action has been as bad as . . .
PRESIDENT JOHNSON: I think . . . well, I'm sure that by God, they [unclear]
every bit of it, and they've got somebody in every one of these things. The
Rap Browns and the Martin Luther Kings and the [Floyd] McKissicks and
all of them are products of community action. That's where they get the
money. We finance all of them, Joe.[50]

Whatever he might write in his postpresidential memoirs, whatever his aides and speechwriters might offer as evidence of his visionary qualities, Lyndon Johnson never embraced a grassroots version of community action.[51] Instead, he consistently viewed the activist form of community action as a threat to his authority and that of his allies and as a source of succor for his enemies. The evidence in the White House recordings points exclusively toward this conclusion, and nothing in the written archival record that can be directly traced to Johnson contradicts it.

This assessment suggests a broader set of conclusions about the Johnson presidency, the War on Poverty, and the 1960s. The Johnson recordings depict a president operating from an updated New Deal perspective and seeking to address poverty through mostly male-oriented work-training and work-study programs that would serve a broadly conceived common good by helping underprivileged Americans left behind by economic growth and to a lesser extent discrimination. The reciprocal obligations of those Americans to learn, to work, and to become "taxpayers" rather than "tax-eaters" formed a core of this conception. The president assumed that local participation would consist primarily of efforts at innovation by energetic state and local administrators that resembled his work during his tenure with the Texas NYA. Civil rights had been integrated into this vision only as far as the recognition that the legacy of discrimination meant that African Americans would constitute many of the underprivileged who would participate in the programs.

When Sargent Shriver's poverty task force included community action in the EOA, however, Johnson encountered a new and far more unruly liberalism that focused on attacking inequities of power in American society and on rectifying the consequences of those inequities. This new liberalism and its more radical movement-based relations emphasized the rights and interests of aggrieved groups, justifying this move on the previous exclusions of minorities, women, and other groups from the liberal commons.

Community action brought this conflict to the heart of Johnson's domestic legislation. On the one hand was an older liberalism built on a broad social justice concept that emphasized economic inequity and the creation of opportunity; on the other was a new liberalism motivated by the failures of the older liberalism on issues of race and gender in particular but also, and often in closely related form, on issues of place, on concerns about inner cities and isolated rural communities that remained untouched by post–World War II prosperity and that lacked the control over local institutions necessary to remake their situations. This new liberalism based its conception of social justice on challenging and restructuring existing political, organizational, and institutional relationships for the benefit of particular groups—especially minorities—that had often been excluded from the benefits of the New Deal state. The rift between these two liberalisms remained broad, rooted in the real limitations of the old and the sweeping but sometimes naive ambitions of the new. For all the very real policy accomplishments of his presidency, Johnson would not prove able to comprehend, much less reconcile, the fissures that community action and grassroots activism helped to reveal in twentieth-century American liberalism.

Notes

1. For an extended analysis of the OIC program, see Guian A. McKee, *The Problem of Jobs: Liberalism, Race, and Deindustrialization in Philadelphia* (Chicago: University of Chicago Press, 2008).

2. Transcript, Sherwin J. Markman Oral History Interview I, May 21, 1969, by Dorothy Pierce McSweeney, Lyndon B. Johnson Library, Austin, Texas (hereafter, LBJL), 24–33; Sherwin J. Markman, "Memorandum for the President," March 14, 1967, White House Central Files, Ex WE 9, Box 28, Folder "March 1–23, 1967," LBJL.

3. Sherwin J. Markman, "Memorandum for the President," May 9, 1967, 5–6, White House Central Files, Ex WE 9, Box 29, Folder "April 20–May 10, 1967," LBJL; Robert J. Donovan, "G.M.'s Black Director on 'Opening Doors,'" *Washington Post*, May 27, 1972.

4. Lyndon Baines Johnson, *The Vantage Point: Perspectives of the Presidency, 1963–1969* (New York: Holt, Rinehart, and Winston, 1971), 85.

5. Opportunities Industrialization Center, Inc., "The President Visits OIC," 1967, Opportunities Industrialization Centers of America Records, Accession 688, Box 24, Folder: Regional/Local OIC Newsletters, Annual Reports, and Program Descriptions, Temple University Urban Archives, Philadelphia.

6. Other scholars have noted Johnson's disinterest in the community action concept, but the recordings make the disjuncture between the president's ideas and those of the antipoverty planners starkly evident. See, for example, Allen J. Matusow, *The Unraveling of America: A History of Liberalism in the 1960s* (New York: Harper and Row, 1984), 123–25.

7. Margaret Weir, "The Federal Government and Unemployment: The Frustration of Policy Innovation from the New Deal to the Great Society," in *The Politics of Social Policy in the United States*, ed. Margaret Weir, Ann Shola Orloff, and Theda Skocpol (Prince-

ton: Princeton University Press, 1988), 149–97; Michael L. Gillette, *Launching the War on Poverty: An Oral History* (New York: Twayne, 1996), 89–90.

8. Alice Kessler-Harris, *In Pursuit of Equity: Women, Men, and the Quest for Economic Citizenship in Twentieth-Century America* (New York: Oxford University Press, 2001), 131; Ira Katznelson, *When Affirmative Action Was White: An Untold History of Racial Inequality in Twentieth-Century America* (New York: Norton, 2005), 43.

9. James T. Patterson, *Grand Expectations: The United States, 1945–1974* (New York: Oxford University Press, 1996), 524–92; Michael Tomasky, "Party in Search of a Notion," *American Prospect*, May 2006, 20–28.

10. Walter Heller Oral History Interview I, February 29, 1970, by David McComb, LBJL, 20.

11. James L. Sundquist, *Politics and Policy: The Eisenhower, Kennedy, and Johnson Years* (Washington, D.C.: Brookings, 1968), 115–25; Matusow, *Unraveling of America*, 107–20; Noel A. Cazenave, *Impossible Democracy: The Unlikely Success of the War on Poverty Community Action Programs* (Albany: State University of New York Press, 2007), 19–63.

12. William Cannon Oral History Interview I, 11–15, May 21, 1982, by Michael L. Gillette, LBJL; "Poverty and Urban Policy: Conference Transcript of 1973 Group Discussion of the Kennedy Administration Urban Poverty Programs and Policies," Brandeis University, June 16–17, 1973, in *The JFK Presidential Oral History Collection*, Part 1 (Frederick, Md.: University Publications of America, 1988), 126–28, 144–51, 172–80, 234–39.

13. "Poverty and Urban Policy," 243–49, 254–55; Adam Yarmolinsky Oral History Interview I, 9–11, July 13, 1970, by Paige Mulhollan, LBJL; Adam Yarmolinsky Oral History Interview III, 15–17, October 22, 1980, by Michael L. Gillette, LBJL; Cannon, Oral History Interview I, 3–11; Sundquist, *Politics and Policy*, 138–42. Boone had become involved in delinquency and antigang projects as a police captain in Chicago and had served on Attorney General Robert Kennedy's juvenile delinquency committee.

14. F. O'R. Hayes, "The Role of Indigenous Organizations in Community Action Programs," 3, May 4, 1964, Office Files of White House Aides: Fred Bohen, Box 2, "OEO Material," LBJL; "Poverty and Urban Policy," 230; Jack Conway Oral History Interview I, August 13, 1980, by Michael L. Gillette, LBJL, 18–19, 24–25.

15. Lyndon Johnson to Kermit Gordon and Robert Anderson, January 8, 1964, in *The Presidential Recordings: Lyndon B. Johnson*, vol. 3, *The Kennedy Assassination and the Transfer of Power, January 1964*, ed. Kent B. Germany and Robert David Johnson (New York: Norton, 2005), 275.

16. Lyndon Johnson to Richard Russell, June 11, 1964, Tape WH6406.05, Citations 3680 and 3681, in The Presidential Recordings: Lyndon B. Johnson, vol. 7, Mississippi Burning and the Passage of the Civil Rights Act: June 1964–July 4, 1964, ed. Guian A. McKee (New York: Norton , 2011).

17. "Poverty and Urban Policy," 287. See also Adam Yarmolinsky Oral History Interview II, 4–5, October 22, 1980, by Michael L. Gillette, LBJL.

18. Judith Russell, *Economics, Bureaucracy, and Race: How Keynesians Misguided the War on Poverty* (New York: Columbia University Press, 2004); James T. Patterson, *America's Struggle against Poverty, 1900–1994* (Cambridge: Harvard University Press, 1994), 141.

19. For an exceptionally racialized example of this tendency, see Lyndon Johnson to Walker Stone, January 6, 1964, in *Presidential Recordings*, 3:179.

20. George Mahon to Johnson, July 29, 1964, Tape WH6407.18, Citation 4407, in *Presidential Recordings of Lyndon B. Johnson Digital Edition*, ed. David B. Coleman, Kent B. Germany, Guian A. McKee, and Mark J. Selverstone, War on Poverty Series (Charlottesville: University of Virginia Press, 2010).

21. Johnson, *Vantage Point*, 72.

22. Heller Oral History Interview I, 27.

23. Michael B. Katz, *The Undeserving Poor: From the War on Poverty to the War on Welfare* (New York: Pantheon, 1989), 24–29; Eileen Boris, "Contested Rights: The Great Society between Home and Work," in *The Great Society and the High Tide of Liberalism*, ed. Sidney Milkis and Jerome Mileur (Amherst: University of Massachusetts Press, 2005), 115–44.

24. Lyndon Johnson to Carl Sanders, July 24, 1964, Tape WH6407.14, Citation 4328, in *Presidential Recordings of Lyndon B. Johnson Digital Edition*.

25. W. Sherman Birdwell Oral History Interview, 3–19, April 1965, by Eric F. Goldman, LBJL; Randall B. Woods, *LBJ: Architect of American Ambition* (New York: Free Press, 2006), 106–15.

26. Lyndon Johnson to Richard Daley, January 20, 1964, in *Presidential Recordings*, 3:651.

27. Lyndon Johnson to George Meany, July 28, 1964, Tape WH6407.15, Citation 4360, in *Presidential Recordings of Lyndon B. Johnson Digital Edition*.

28. Johnson to Dick [*sic*] West, August 31, 1964, Tape WH6408.43, Citation 5279, in *Presidential Recordings of Lyndon B. Johnson Digital Edition*; Gillette, *Launching*, 98.

29. Lyndon Johnson to Francis Smith, July 30, 1964, Tape WH6407.19, Citation 4418, in *Presidential Recordings of Lyndon B. Johnson Digital Edition*.

30. Lyndon Johnson to Bill Moyers, August 7, 1964, Tape WH6408.12, Citation 4817, in *Presidential Recordings of Lyndon B. Johnson Digital Edition*. Moyers conveyed this information at least to Shriver's chief deputy, Adam Yarmolinsky ("Poverty and Urban Policy," 249–50).

31. Guian McKee, "Prelude to Faith-Based Initiatives?: The Johnson Presidential Recordings and the Debate over Parochial Schools in the War on Poverty," *Miller Center Report* 19:1 (Winter 2003): 21–27.

32. Lyndon Johnson to Phil Landrum, May 14, 1964, in *The Presidential Recordings: Lyndon B. Johnson*, vol. 6, *Toward the Great Society, April 14, 1964*, ed. Guian A. McKee (New York: Norton, 2005), 709–10.

33. Moyers told Johnson that community action "is a vital part of the poverty program. . . . Shriver thinks it's as important as the camps, because if you ever prove that a community can get together and solve its problems, you're half-way on home" (Bill Moyers to Lyndon Johnson, May 14, 1964, Tape WH6405.07, Citation 3456, in *Presidential Recordings*, 6:716).

34. Gillette, *Launching*, 130; OEO, "The Office of Economic Opportunity during the Administration of President Lyndon B. Johnson, November 1963–January 1969," 167–68, 1969, Folder: "Volume I, Part II; Narrative History (1 of 3)," Box 1, Special Files, Administrative Histories, LBJL.

35. Lyndon Johnson to Phil Landrum, August 4,.1964, Tape WH6408.05, Citations 4660 and 4661, in *Presidential Recordings of Lyndon B. Johnson Digital Edition*.

36. Lyndon Johnson to John McCormack, August 4, 1964, Tape WH6408.05, Citation 4667, in ibid.

37. See also Lyndon Johnson to Bill Moyers, August 4, 1964, Tape WH6408.05, Citation 4672, in ibid.

38. Lyndon Johnson to Porter Hardy, August 5, 1964, Tape WH6408.08, Citation 4752, Recordings of Telephone Conversations—White House Series, Recordings and Transcripts of Conversations and Meetings, LBJL.

39. In 1965, Congress gave Shriver authority to override the governor's veto on some War on Poverty programs, including community action (OEO, "Office of Economic Opportunity," 168–71).

40. Jill Quadagno, *The Color of Welfare: How Racism Undermined the War on Poverty* (New York: Oxford University Press, 1994), 31; James A. Morone, *The Democratic Wish: Popular Participation and the Limits of American Government*, rev. ed. (New Haven: Yale University Press, 1998), 218–49; Sidney M. Milkis, "Lyndon Johnson, the Great Society, and the 'Twilight' of the Modern Presidency," in *Great Society*, ed. Milkis and Mileur, 6–13, 31; Jerome M. Mileur, "The Great Society and the Demise of New Deal Liberalism," in *Great Society*, ed. Milkis and Mileur, 438.

41. Charles Schultze, "Memorandum for the President; Subject: Poverty Program; Opposition from the Mayors," 1–4, September 18, 1965, Office Files of Bill Moyers, Box 56, "Office of Economic Opportunity, 1 of 2," LBJL.

42. Lyndon Johnson to Dwight Eisenhower, August 18, 1965, Tape WH6508.05, Citation 8555, Recordings of Telephone Conversations—White House Series, Recordings and Transcripts of Conversations and Meetings, LBJL.

43. Eve Edstrom, "Civil War Develops in Antipoverty Leadership," *Washington Post*, December 16, 1965; Eve Edstrom, "Poverty War Group Fails to See LBJ," *Washington Post*,

December 22, 1965; "4 Protestors Arrested near Johnson Ranch," *Washington Post*, December 24, 1965; OEO, "Office of Economic Opportunity," 86A–91.

44. Johnson to Richard Russell, June 2, 1966, Tape WH6606.01, Citation 10205, Recordings of Telephone Conversations—White House Series, Recordings and Transcripts of Conversations and Meetings, LBJL.

45. Lyndon Johnson to Bill Moyers, December 26, 1966, Tape WH66612.11, Citation 11206, Recordings of Telephone Conversations—White House Series, Recordings and Transcripts of Conversations and Meetings, LBJL.

46. *Congressional Quarterly Almanac*, 90th Cong., 1st sess., 1967, (Washington, D.C.: Congressional Quarterly Service, 1968), 23:1075–81; OEO, "Office of Economic Opportunity," 598–604.

47. Lyndon Baines Johnson, "Special Message to the Congress: America's Unfinished Business, Urban and Rural Poverty, March 14th, 1967," *Public Papers of the Presidents of the United States: Lyndon B. Johnson, 1967* (Washington, D.C.: U.S. Government Printing Office, 1968), 1:334–35; "It's Official," *New Republic*, March 25, 1967, 6.

48. Lyndon Johnson to Dean Rusk, February 19, 1968, Tape WH6802.02, Citation 12721, Recordings of Telephone Conversations—White House Series, Recordings and Transcripts of Conversations and Meetings, LBJL.

49. Lyndon Johnson to Richard Daley, March 23, 1968, Tape WH6803.03, Citation 12835, in ibid.

50. Lyndon Johnson to Joseph Califano, April 27, 1968, Tape WH6804.03, Citation 12938, in ibid.

51. Johnson, *Vantage Point*, 74; Richard N. Goodwin, *Remembering America: A Voice from the Sixties* (Boston: Little, Brown, 1988), 268–78, 285–87.

RHONDA Y. WILLIAMS

"To Challenge the Status Quo by Any Means"

Community Action and Representational Politics in 1960s Baltimore

Proclaiming his desire to fulfill each citizen's "basic hopes, ones all too often circumscribed by poverty and race"—hopes for "a fair chance," "fair play from the law," "a full-time job on full-time pay," "a decent home for his family in a decent community," "a good school for his children with good teachers," and "security when faced with sickness or unemployment or old age"—President Lyndon Baines Johnson challenged Congress during his State of the Union address on January 8, 1964, to deliver a historic session. "Let this session of Congress be known as the session which did more for civil rights than the last hundred sessions combined . . . as the session which declared all-out war on human poverty and unemployment in these United States." In grandiose language, Johnson positioned poverty as "a national problem, requiring improved national organization and support," but he also asserted that it was a battle that could not be won solely in Washington. If the "attack" was to be effective, it had to be waged "in every private home, in every public office, from the courthouse to the White House," "organized at the State and the local level," and "supported and directed by State and local efforts."[1]

To produce a "Great Society" that "rests on abundance and liberty for all," the Johnson administration launched programs to provide education, job training, employment, medical care, and housing. The most controversial component of this idea, the 1964 Economic Opportunity Act, created the Office of Economic Opportunity (OEO) and the Community Action Program, which mandated "maximum feasible participation" of the poor. Almost immediately, the War on Poverty instigated political tensions and urban struggles. Far from embracing "new concepts of cooperation, a creative federalism, between the National Capital and the leaders of local communities," as Johnson had imagined, many local authorities recoiled both at the thought of federal meddling in local affairs and at the creation of policies and programs that poor people and their representatives could use to challenge entrenched authority.[2]

For all of these reasons, the War on Poverty and community action provoked apprehension and obduracy among local officials even as it generated hope (no matter how fleeting) among civic leaders, grassroots activists, and "disadvantaged people"—those economically underprivileged persons identified as the War on Poverty's proposed beneficiaries. Johnson's articulated unconditional war and the availability of federal dollars spurred the development of antipoverty plans that both engaged the question of how to break the poverty cycle and legitimized the idea (though with tremendous conflict) "that the people who know poverty best—the poor—can come up with the answer."[3] The essence of the program was enough to engender fear and, perhaps inevitably, led to collisions between local authorities and grassroots organizers throughout the country.

Such collision sites in Baltimore provide a means of exploring the relationships among federal government programs, municipal politics, and poor people's engagement. Poor people and their allies deployed representational politics as well as grassroots protest as weapons in the struggle over the War on Poverty. This narrative has elements not only of political engagement and possibility that emerged from dissension over what a war on poverty should look like and who should control it but also of frustration and thwarted opportunities. More specifically, War on Poverty initiatives and black activists' claims to power sharing reveal the skirmishes won and lost and expose the pressure points where welfare paternalism clashed with activist visions of racial and working-class democracy.

These activist visions included democratizing urban institutions through representation. While political participation is not a panacea for structural inequalities or an automatic leveler of hierarchies, access to decision making, policy development, and program creation provided potential routes for securing help for self and community, power sharing, and broader social transformation. Politicized by the war on poverty and taking hold of its rhetoric, black poor people and their allies challenged those who sought to broker their exclusion. Baltimore's Self-Help Housing program, which sought simultaneously to target unemployment and substandard housing, is one example of such a struggle.

Addressing a major concern of residents, the housing program sought to provide jobs in neighborhoods with chronic underemployment, positioned poor people as experts on substandard housing and its hazards, and legitimized tenants as those with the most right to hold landlords accountable.

A PLAN FOR ACTION

The Community Action Program officially arrived in Baltimore in 1965. When Johnson first announced the War on Poverty, Baltimore's primarily white civic and municipal leaders were already in the final stages of a two-year effort to develop "A Plan for Action" to address the social problems of the city's poor people. Instead of "bricks and mortar," the target of urban renewal, the city's plan focused on "human renewal," or providing new and better-coordinated services aimed at rehabilitating the poor—two of the three objectives of community action. (The third was "promoting institutional change in the interest of the poor.")[4] Within the first few months of 1965, Baltimore officials had submitted this plan to the OEO, created a community action agency (CAA), and appointed an eleven-member policymaking board that included the mayor, comptroller, and city council president—but no poor people.

The absence of the poor or their representatives on the policymaking board was not surprising, nor was the fact that this omission generated conflict. Months before Baltimore established its CAA, activists in the city's black communities had begun criticizing the planning process. As early as December 1964, the Baltimore chapter of the National Association for the Advancement of Colored People (NAACP) charged that developers of the city's plan for action had not consulted black leaders, social workers, or civil rights or neighborhood organizations. The NAACP did not specifically advocate for the inclusion of poor people as an overlooked constituency, however, but called for a racial politics of representation that subsumed economic distinctions.

In February 1965, members of Baltimore's Union for Jobs or Income Now (U-JOIN), a newly established equal rights and economic justice organization led by Philadelphia native Walter Lively, mobilized in anticipation of the city council's imminent approval of the Plan for Action. The organization and its members wanted a local antipoverty plan that helped solve problems with "unemployment, bad housing, and just plain money" and that allowed poor people some say in "what should be done about poverty."[5] This meant more than including black representation without regard to economic status or seeking the advice of poor people. It meant establishing avenues of representation that included poor people in the process, addressing poor people's issues, and, if necessary, promoting strident social action. Such social action was neither intended by the developers of Baltimore's Plan for Action nor desired by the federal Community Action Program.

To convey residents' and grassroots activists' concerns, U-JOIN presented a petition, signed by more than eight hundred people, asking for five improvements to the antipoverty plan. Petitioners wanted "greater participation in the decision making structure of the Plan for the poor," the creation of programs dealing "simultaneously with the problems of unemployment and housing by putting jobless area residents to work rehabilitating sub-standard housing," the development of consumer and recreational facilities to be managed by the poor, "a food stamp program for all low-income residents of Baltimore," and a $1.25/hour guaranteed minimum wage for War on Poverty employees.[6] These efforts to change the plan met with resistance, and the city council ultimately ignored the demands, passing the antipoverty plan without change.[7]

The Plan for Action primarily envisioned poor people as recipients of better, more efficiently delivered services. As far as developers of the Baltimore plan were concerned, the mandate for maximum feasible participation by the poor themselves need be little more than an official willingness to "learn directly from a representative group of low-income residents" about their "perceptions of their own problems" and ideas for ameliorating those problems.[8] It did not mean following through on those ideas. The plan also mentioned "helping residents to organize into small self-help groups for group-action purposes," but the underlying goal was advantageously to position civic and municipal officials to coordinate and deliver services such as libraries, maternal and child health programs, youth character-building efforts, Legal Services, job training, and education. Many city officials saw attacking poverty as using bureaucratic expertise to rehabilitate the poor, thereby reflecting the human reclamation and welfare paternalism emphases of some War on Poverty planners. Seen in this way, government programs were not entitlements but useful state interventions for "improving" the poor and by extension their circumstances. It represented a politically palatable, uncontroversial approach to antipoverty efforts.

These reformist visions would soon collide with the democratic expectations of low-income Baltimore residents and their allies, to whom representational politics meant opportunities for inclusion as well as for altering inequitable and unfair systems. Many poor people accepted services without expecting more, but for others, the concept of maximum feasible participation fueled expectations of political engagement, an understandable view in an era ripe with liberation struggles. Equally important, battles over maximum feasible participation also revealed the asymmetrical power of the status quo, municipal officials' desire to control War on Poverty programs, their obstinacy and belief in patronage politics, and their low views of the poor.

Poor people's assertions of their needs and expectations clashed with municipal officials' attempts to protect their authority. City council members thwarted progressive reforms that challenged established racial, political, and economic interests. Poor people's claims to expertise about poverty chipped away at the influence of paternalistic social welfare practices and municipal control, sparking city officials' resistance and antipathy to community-level governance. This almost reflexive defense of white middle-class political privilege occurred even when CAA officials, some of them African American, harbored a genuine desire to include poor people and their advocates in policymaking roles. Such staunch opposition by entrenched power structures was a problem in many other cities as well and constituted a major reason why many poor people and community activists harbored negative feelings toward municipally controlled wars on poverty. The problems of community action were many—rival expectations, competing desires for power, and limited resources—yet at the root of these problems lay not simply stories of failure but complex narratives of conflict and social change that convey the voices and antipoverty struggles of the poor.

VOICES FOR THE POOR

Baltimore city council officials and civic leaders had envisioned the CAA coordinating resources, sensitizing institutions to the needs of poor people, and spurring self-sufficiency primarily through remediation and rehabilitation of the poor. At the neighborhood level, however, different visions and expectations emerged. Cadres of community action organizers, grassroots activists, and neighborhood residents argued that fighting a real war on poverty required listening to the voices of poor people. In the Baltimore program's initial days, community action staff held neighborhood meetings to explain their human renewal plan and ferret out the concerns of poor people. At these meetings, the city's first CAA executive director, Dr. Melvin J. Humphrey, acknowledged the poor people's voices. In so doing, he likely raised their expectations and municipal officials' apprehensions. A former economics professor at the historically black Morgan State College and a special consultant with OEO in Washington, D.C., prior to his Baltimore appointment, Humphrey asserted, "We have to find out in more detail what these people want. Then we will have to work with these people to provide it. There will be no more planning from the top [down]. The poor want to be involved in planning these programs." Humphrey also maintained, "The thing we must remember . . . is that this program is the poor's program. We are working for them. A lot of people don't realize it and won't accept it, but the poor will call every shot in the game, and when they speak to us, we had better listen."[9]

Members of U-JOIN again questioned the lack of poor people's voices on the community action policymaking board. U-JOIN was affiliated with Students for a Democratic Society (SDS) through its Emergency Rehabilitation Assistance Project (ERAP). SDS, a leftist student organization committed to fostering participatory democracy, had started ERAP in northern cities and now moved south, hoping to build an "interracial movement" by galvanizing poor people at the grass roots around issues such as housing, schools, medical care, and food insecurity.[10] In Baltimore, U-JOIN activists sought greater influence for poor people, who were also deemed experts who should have formal representation on policy boards, including that of the Community Action Program. Poor people's absence from the initial community action policymaking board meant that they had not been able to shape or vote on antipoverty measures now being managed by City Hall and social welfare bureaucrats.

As these battles over community action and the city's antipoverty plan unfolded, the first two neighborhood centers opened in East Baltimore, one in the old Northeastern Police Station on Ashland Avenue. Neighborhood centers were run by local counselors, who applied for their jobs through the municipal Civil Service Commission, and by assistants chosen from among neighborhood residents. As CAA employees, neighborhood counselors went door to door to get to know residents, held meetings to publicize the centers' services, advised residents "on problems individually and in groups, and help[ed] them come together in organizations to deal with community problems and issues."[11] Gaining residents' confidence or broad participation would not be easy. A combination of distrust, exploitation, apathy, fear, and lack of time complicated mobilizing efforts in Baltimore, as in other cities. Over the years, neighborhood workers would consistently identify as one of their "toughest problem[s] . . . getting to meet the poor face to face."[12] Yet while widespread involvement of the poor might have been a struggle, some poor people became engaged.

At the neighborhood center on Ashland Avenue, the community action counselor met some residents who wanted the horse stables in their neighborhood removed. One of those residents was Catherine Johnson, a "soft-voiced woman with a pleasant smile," mother of four, and private nurse whose husband was a truck driver. Johnson later became one of the first five neighborhood residents nominated to represent poor people on the community action board, but only after she was politicized through a successful campaign to close the stable and in grassroots protests challenging municipal authorities. The neighborhood center thus provided not only a resource for residents who sought help but also a base for mobilizing and politicizing them. "A lot of people don't know how to get to the problem," said Johnson. "I didn't. I didn't know how to get down to make things happen." With the help of staff at the neighborhood center, she and others became "more conscious of the community's problems" and "more steamed up."[13]

From the beginning, Baltimore's Community Action Program experienced criticism as well as internal conflicts that led to the program's instability. Humphrey resigned as the agency's executive director just three months after taking the job. Without going into specifics, he suggested that program inefficiencies (such as teenage workers for the Neighborhood Youth Corps who were not paid for a month) and discord with the community action board, particularly chair Morton Macht, had been at fault. Humphrey nevertheless believed that "under the able guidance of a wise Community Action Commission, [the program] will move toward final victory against poverty." He ended his resignation letter, "God protect the anti-poverty program and give courage and wisdom to those who will direct the attack."[14]

After learning of Humphrey's resignation, the Anti-Poverty Action Committee (APAC), a loose coalition of grassroots civil rights groups led by housing activist A. Eugene Chase, sought audiences with municipal officials. Low-income Baltimore residents had come to trust Humphrey, and his departure motivated them to mobilize. APAC asked Mayor Theodore McKeldin to refuse Humphrey's resignation, but it had already been accepted. APAC then asked to meet with Macht, a man deeply distrusted by the black community. Madeline Murphy, a black former community action board member, described Macht as a "developer of segregated housing." U-JOIN leaders dubbed him a "wealthy construction boss" who cared little about disadvantaged Baltimoreans. Macht repeatedly refused to meet with neighborhood residents and activists about the Community Action Program. In July 1965, frustrated by his response, APAC called for Macht's "immediate dismissal." Politicized citizens, they insisted, will not "tolerate attempts by anyone, and least of all by a man in Mr. Macht's position, to obstruct the desires of the masses of Baltimore's poor." A month later, at a three-hour meeting in an East Baltimore school auditorium with the CAA's two white associate directors, APAC leaders slammed the local antipoverty program as "an extension of welfare paternalism."[15]

In the midst of these grassroots struggles to gain access to and influence the policymaking process, Parren J. Mitchell replaced Humphrey as the agency's executive director. Mitchell's blend of civil rights and social welfare experience shaped how he envisioned poor people. A member of a well-respected Baltimore civil rights family, Mitchell was a trained social worker and was serving as executive secretary of the Maryland Interracial Commission at the time of his appointment. When he accepted the executive director position, Mitchell emphasized "focus[ing] every bit of our energy" on strengthening families "weakened by generations of urban poverty." His ideas clearly reflected the social welfare emphasis that fueled the federal government's concern with improving the poor, particularly the focus on poverty as a result of "broken" and "disintegrating" black families. But Mitchell also stressed the need for a "three pronged alliance" between labor, civil rights, and poor people to "eliminate poverty in this country." Mitchell argued that "every other group, except the poor, ha[s] a lobby. . . . Who really speaks for the poor?" According to Mitchell, "only the poor can speak for themselves with any understanding or effectiveness."[16]

Mitchell's support of poor people's political participation, along with grassroots protests that called attention to their absence, opened the way for their representation on policymaking boards. In February 1966, the first poor people's representatives, all of them black and all from East Baltimore, were officially nominated by neighborhood committees and block clubs for appointment to the community action board. In addition to Johnson, the group included Beatrice Reid and Leander Douglass. When a reporter for the *Baltimore Evening Sun* asked them, "Would you call yourself poor?" Johnson responded, "I don't know what these people consider poor. . . . I live on what I make and what my husband makes and in winter he don't work but two or three days a week. Sometimes we live on $40 a week. I guess I am poor."[17]

Reid had lived in the neighborhood for thirty years, owned a three-story home, and volunteered at the Ashland Avenue neighborhood center as well as at her church. She answered, "Well, I don't consider myself poor, by no means. . . . We're not asking for no help." But, Reid added, many other people needed assistance. Douglass was a fifty-one-year-old taxi driver, married with six children, and living in public housing. His wife, Gloria, volunteered as an assistant in a CAA neighborhood center.[18]

While poor people might have won their first skirmish to gain formal representation, the CAA board remained top-heavy and therefore, in grassroots leaders' estimation, still not fully capable of addressing the "basic economic and social problems of the poor."[19] Refusing to give up their fight for control of the community action board, U-JOIN activists attended a January 1967 city council meeting where they threatened to "take to the streets," using protest politics to try to leverage greater representation. Such threats of disruption were taken seriously, especially since Washington, D.C., officials had sold their poverty program to the public and to local politicians as an answer to the rising turmoil in the nation's poor communities. Hoping to keep peace, the board expanded its membership to twenty-one, including ten poor people's representatives. Poor people remained shy of a majority, but they had more equitable representation in the city's poverty policymaking process than had ever before been the case.

Although poor people could not control the community action board, their representatives became vocal advocates, particularly regarding the agency's future direction, its leadership, and its programs. Such sustained pressure by the poor highlights the democratic possibilities of the War on Poverty. But the history of the poverty wars in Baltimore also reveals the limitations of government-sponsored change. In the face of intensifying demands to share power and equitably distribute resources, city officials became adept at making compromises that, even while expanding representation of the poor and raising public awareness of inequalities, preserved existing municipal authority structures.

SELF-HELP HOUSING

The Self-Help Housing program, one of the first OEO-funded projects in Baltimore designed by residents of the action area, emerged in this fraught political context. While battles still raged over Humphrey's resignation and poor people's participation on the community action board, the agency initiated a new kind of housing project, designed by poor people in conjunction with urban renewal and housing officials in 1965. Not surprisingly, controversy quickly emerged.

Battles for control of the Self-Help Housing program, like those that raged over representation on the community action board, highlight the tensions among municipal officials, white and black political appointees, grassroots activists, and low-income residents politicized by the War on Poverty. These battles also expose the friction between social service delivery programs and low-income citizens' efforts at self-determination and between state-controlled mechanisms for reducing poverty and the racial and economic justice agendas of 1960s activists. At the center of all these debates were the malleable concepts of self-help and self-sufficiency. In an era of increased rights and power struggles, "self-help" and "self-sufficiency" not only meant providing black working-class people with services aimed to rehabilitate them or their neighborhoods but also legitimated residents' search for representation, control over neighborhood resources, and attempts to achieve economic independence.

Under the aegis of the CAA, neighborhood residents in 1966 formed the Neighborhood Housing Action Committee, with Leander Douglass as its head. Over the next eight months, the committee developed the Self-Help Housing and Environmental Improvement Program to tackle unsanitary and unsafe housing conditions. The Self-Help Housing collaborative proposed training low-income residents as housing and sanitation inspectors, targeting landlords lax on maintenance and repairs, mandating landlord-tenant mediation to prevent residents from being evicted, and operating a maintenance and sanitation service to help correct violations. This model of self-help and self-sufficiency highlighted residential control of the program. It allowed tenants to police landlords who profited from the substandard housing conditions. It also offered the poor paths to municipal jobs at a time when most of the city's poor people held menial, low-wage jobs. Finally, the program would train residents in skills that would enable them to fix their own residences, thereby preserving their homes and neighborhoods. Instead of following a municipal service model, Self-Help Housing addressed the concerns that low-income residents had raised when the city's poverty plan was first outlined—unemployment, substandard housing, and exploitation.

Some city officials immediately objected both to the program and the planning process. In March 1966, Edgar Ewing, the black assistant director of the Baltimore Urban Renewal and Housing Agency (BURHA) Neighborhood Rehabilitation program, objected to the idea of neighborhood residents developing their own housing plan. CAA staff and members of the city's Health and Welfare Council countered that letting residents develop a program, which BURHA and other municipal agencies could then review, would allay residents' fears "that they were being bypassed and that their interest would not be safeguarded." Ewing felt otherwise. He believed in soliciting residents' ideas and affording them opportunities for "meaningful participation." However, he believed that developing and operating a housing inspection and maintenance program required experts and that allowing residents to conceptualize the plan without BURHA input would only build "frustration into the neighborhood because substantial changes to their work more than likely will have to be made, if not completely redone."[20]

Similar battles arose across the country as stakeholders disputed whether the Economic Opportunity Act's mandate for "maximum feasible participation" meant that policymakers should consider the poor experts on poverty who could offer ideas for improving their communities, as many politicized poor people believed. Some CAA staff accepted that view. One CAA associate director in Baltimore argued in 1965 that "the only expert about poverty is someone who has managed to live and survive in the inner city."[21] But numerous municipal officials and social service professionals and some community action staff and board members believed that being poor did not qualify people to devise solutions or control resources.

Baltimore city council member Reuben Caplan, a Democrat and a part of the council's conservative bloc, challenged poor people's leadership of Self-Help Housing, asking how "people who haven't yet proved they can earn a living" could have the expertise and skill to administer such a program.[22] Heated disagreements regarding who had expertise and could make the best use of federal funds gripped antipoverty and neighborhood revitalization programs around the United States and eventually would help doom numerous community-based projects. Poor people's perceived lack of economic self-sufficiency, lack of property, and inability to pay taxes were used as arguments against their demands for self-determination.

In the case of Self-Help Housing, even sympathetic city council members were swayed by landlord and property owner complaints as well as concerns that the CAA was moving beyond its service-delivery role. They feared that under Mitchell, the agency was transmogrifying into a political organization that facilitated citizen protest against established authorities. Convening a closed session, council members devised amendments to the program granting municipal authorities control of Self-Help Housing. The amendments called for the proposed program to lower salary projections for employees, hire workers through the municipal Department of Public Works and civil service, and increase tenants' responsibilities. When Mitchell told the city council that he was "virtually certain" that the city council amendment removing control over hiring from the Neighborhood Housing Action Committee and giving it to municipal officials would be rejected by federal antipoverty officials, Democrat John A. Pica replied, "Well, that's tough, 'cause then you ain't got a program."[23]

The Neighborhood Housing Action Committee flatly rejected the proposed amendments. "We feel that it is an insult to the poor of Baltimore," committee members wrote to the city council, "to be asked to subject our program to possible political patronage. . . . This is fundamentally opposed to our basic philosophy of hiring neighborhood people to improve the neighborhood by using persuasion, education and their personal relationships in working with their neighbors."[24]

According to the Self-Help Housing proposal, jobs as sanitation aides and corpsmen would go to unemployed men in the inner city. The aides would educate community members and serve on mediation panels. The corpsmen would complete approved repairs. Like so many early War on Poverty programs, Self-Help Housing gendered its jobs programs as male. By focusing on job provision for black men, Self-Help Housing advocates upheld traditional expectations of the male breadwinner as the foundation of a strong black community. The program also positioned black men as the appropriate brokers between families and landlords—between community members and housing authorities. Finally, the proposal reified construction and sanitation jobs as male work. As the 1960s wore on, the almost exclusively male focus of OEO job training programs generated protest by poor women, although whether such protests arose in Baltimore is not clear.

Supporters of community-controlled Self-Help Housing organized a February 6, 1967, rally at which two hundred inner-city residents and civil rights, antipoverty, and religious leaders gathered on the War Memorial Plaza in front of City Hall and listened to speakers and held signs bearing such slogans as, "A Rat Is a Hell of a Roommate" and "Show the Nation That We're Not Backwards." Just days earlier, Mitchell had received official word from the regional director of the mid-Atlantic OEO office that the federal government would reject the program if the hiring amendment stayed in place since it would exclude most poor residents. After the rally and after learning of the federal government's position, city council members dropped the hiring amendment and endorsed the program. Three hundred area residents and supporters who had squeezed into the council chamber and balcony greeted the news with applause and cheers.[25]

In a move that rattled the status quo but cheered poor people and their allies, Self-Help Housing hired APAC's Chase as its executive director and appointed U-JOIN's Lively to its board of directors. Some city council members argued that Chase lacked the requisite education and experience to serve as director and objected to Lively's civil rights activities.[26] Wrote one reporter for the *Baltimore Afro-American*, "To say Mr. Lively is controversial would be a delicate understanding. The mention of his name is enough to make certain City Fathers go rigid."[27]

The Self-Help Housing program held its opening ceremony on September 1, 1967. City council president Thomas D'Alesandro III touted the program as "the first of its kind in the country," emanating not "from City Hall down into the streets" but "from the people." In its first year, the program served fifteen thousand families. Mitchell later explained that the program generated such success and popularity because planners had looked "at why that neighborhood went down, and we went for the cause. Landlords hated us. And some members of city council couldn't stand us. But that's what I meant [to do]: to challenge the status quo by any means."[28]

The battle over who should control Self-Help Housing exposes the ways that race and class shaped municipal politics and authority in the era of the federal War on Poverty. In contesting entrenched interests, poor people, grassroots activists, and progressive anti-poverty officials sought federal intervention. In the case of the community action board appointments and the Self-Help Housing program, federal regulations and financial resources supported grassroots activists against entrenched local authorities' desires. Just as revealing, the story of Self-Help Housing also spotlights the blending of civil rights tactics and community mobilization with Black Power principles of politicization, self-determination, and economic justice.

PLANNING THE QUIET REVOLUTION

Collisions over representation on policymaking boards and control over local programs were not the only flash points. Questions of philosophical bent also provoked intense debates. In November 1967, Parren Mitchell and community action board members representing poor people argued that community organizing and "social change" should be the program's "accent," "rather than just service delivery to the poor."[29]

An internal community action board report, "Planning the Quiet Revolution," maintained that community action alone would not address the under-lying problems causing poverty—structural inequality, unequal status, and po-litical disfranchisement as a result of a "breakdown" in the "democratic process." Emphasizing the importance of open political engagement, the report's authors endorsed Black Power as a legitimate route for transforming economic margin-alization and attacking inequality, arguing that "this power can only be achieved in the black ghetto through struggle and concrete victories."[30] Such rhetoric, as well as the relationships forged between CAA leaders and black grassroots and militant activists such as Self-Help Housing's Chase and U-JOIN's Lively, alarmed the city council and its allies on the community action board.

By 1968, numerous CAA officials, particularly those supportive of black lib-eration struggles, backed citizens' mobilizations and protests at the city and neighborhood levels. This emphasis on community organization, which con-trasted with the liberal state's emphasis on service delivery and rehabilitation, would contribute to greater dissension and eventually turnover among CAA leaders. Three of the agency's top administrators resigned, including Mitchell and the two associate directors, Richard W. Bateman and Stanley Mazer. The same year, the city council refused to pass the agency's proposed budget, anger-ing a subset of community action board members, the majority of them poor people's representatives. Members of this group, including Reid, resigned in protest. Without their involvement, the CAA was not in compliance with federal guidelines mandating at least one-third representation for the poor on com-munity action boards. Local news media then decried entrenched politicians' stranglehold on local poverty programs.

On July 3, 1968, the resigning board members prepared a position paper in which they upheld their right to protest. They also enumerated what they saw as the goals of the War on Poverty: economic justice, democratic representa-tion, and the transformation of dysfunctional institutions. In their view, the federal government had established the Community Action Program "to at last, remove the shameful spectre of poverty from this, the most affluent society the world has ever known." And the local agency's board was supposed to provide people at the grassroots with "the well earned right to work within the frame-work of a policy-making body, rather than vainly protest without." The docu-ment's authors contended that with the "steady reduction in the effectiveness of the program—its philosophies and funds—by vested interests, political ma-chines and outright bigots," the hope for "effective social change" had become "a farce, a false dream and millions of light years away from reality."[31] Poor people and their advocates had become increasingly disgusted with local elites' resistance to their attempts to represent fully and make decisions on behalf of their communities. This political wariness and weariness, along with local machinations and federal policy shifts, would ultimately compel some poor people to abandon or avoid government-generated antipoverty efforts.

D'Alesandro, now serving as the city's mayor, moved quickly to put out the political fire. He refused to accept the board members' resignations and affirmed his commitment to the Community Action Program, calling it "an essential part of City Government." D'Alesandro blamed the minimal increase in funding for neighborhood development projects on federal government cutbacks and argued that the only way to counteract the wavering government commitment to fighting poverty was to maintain strong local action agencies. City government cannot "be responsive or meaningful," he concluded, "unless citizens . . . are prepared to serve and to continue the good fight in the face of adversity." Two weeks later, the board members who had tendered their resignations returned to their positions, but not before holding a press conference at City Hall. They insisted that their "drastic and dramatic action" reflected "a deliberate sense of highest civic responsibility." They called for the city council, business community, fellow community action board members, "and all men of good will to join us in making a new commitment to keep the hope element alive within our impoverished brothers and sisters in Baltimore."[32]

But the drama was far from over. In the wake of Mitchell's resignation, the community action board chose as the new executive director Walter P. Carter, an activist who irked conservative members of the City Council, though he had D'Alesandro's support. Carter had protested race-based hiring discrimination, participated in Freedom Rides across the South during the summer of 1961, served as Maryland's coordinator for the March on Washington, engaged in battles for open housing, and supported welfare rights activism.[33] Carter's refusal to bow to municipal power brokers had earned him the title "Mr. Civil Rights." At the time, Carter was the Model Cities Agency's chief community organizer in Baltimore and, therefore, according to D'Alesandro, the right person to build connections among poor people at the grassroots, the Community Action Program, and Model Cities. But not everyone agreed. Viewing Carter "as a symbol of Negro rebellion," the city council rejected Carter by a vote of ten to eight.[34]

Carter's rejection despite the overwhelming support of the mayor and community action board members allied with poor people "symbolized white racism to local Negro leaders." In this case, the battle over who would best represent black and poor people's agendas as the new executive director ignited yet another political powder keg. This time, local activists called into question the efficacy of democratic participation, positioned municipal authorities as duplicitous, and painted poor people and their allies as the true voices of inclusion and change. Most of the same board members resigned again because, they believed, the city council's rejection of Carter "has deprived us of that essential *foundation* of any future program, namely, a competent dedicated courageous man with integrity." Local community action members also publicly accused unsupportive city council members of waging a "secretive assault on the anti-poverty program and the people it serves." Even a *Baltimore Evening Sun* editorial called the city council's action a "conservative backlash slap at the Community Action Commission" and a "capricious and wrong rejection" that resembled a "calculated rebuff to Negroes and the poor."[35] Nevertheless, the vote stood.

The poor people's representatives had hoped that their resignations would educate the public about the political logjams that jeopardized poor people's interests. Moreover, their absence again threatened the stability and federal compliance of the city's Community Action Program. The federal government did not support social action against or the political dethroning of established municipal authorities, but it did expect poor people to serve on advisory boards and hold jobs in community action neighborhood centers and programs. While poor people and their representatives had serious concerns about the influence of the city council's "conservative" faction, in the end, all but two of those who had resigned rejoined the community action board.[36] As representatives of the poor, they still were not ready to relinquish their hope for change or seats at the policymaking table.

The community action board began searching for another executive director, with the effort headed by a new black board chair, Clarence Blount, who was expected "to restore harmony." With the political wounds of the tempest surrounding Carter still fresh and neighborhood representatives on the board feeling wary, they questioned the commitment of prospective directors to poor people. Community resident Mary Sollers wanted to know what the new candidates for the director job "had in mind . . . for the people." She stressed the "importance of having a director interested in planning programs that will reach out into the areas of the City where the people need help. If we don't obtain such a person as our director, the program will be back in the first stage from whence it started." Resident Marvey Smothers reminded the agency board that it "should be mindful that when we are recommending people to lead the poor that the poor will remember these decisions." He continued. "They may not have the power. . . . We know about the strength downtown, [but] people who represent neighborhoods are also leaders. . . . We must learn to listen to leaders regardless of their status, economic conditions, etc."[37]

Three black men were nominated for the director position. Frank J. Ellis, a Baltimore native, had served as a director for a private urban renewal agency in Wilmington, Delaware. A proponent of fiscal conservatism and service distribution rather than protest, community organizing, or neighborhood control, Ellis was the least progressive of the nominees. The second candidate, Lenwood Ivey, had worked for the Baltimore CAA since 1965 and was among the city's first community action neighborhood development supervisors. The final candidate, Harry Smith, was a member of the city's Civil Service Commission Board. The city council appointed Ellis, who vowed to create "an agency with a different personality."[38]

Within four months of his appointment, Ellis had closed four of the thirty-three neighborhood centers without a public announcement or any discussion at community action board meetings. Within six months, disagreement, which "had been cherished" at the CAA, had given way to "restraint and quiet." According to the *Baltimore Sun*'s Stephen J. Lynton, who reported on social welfare issues, "Gone, apparently, are the days of protest, abrupt challenge to established modes, expansion and rash hopes." Also gone were some aggrieved board members, two associate directors, and Mitchell, who had staged demonstrations outside City Hall and "denounced the government for having failed to show a 'gut commitment' to ending poverty."[39]

In the midst of this shift toward fiscal and administrative conservatism, Self-Help Housing was audited in early 1969 and was found to have made financial missteps that jeopardized its ongoing independence. Adopting a strategy that would be deployed throughout the country over the next twenty years, city officials argued that poor people lacked the ability or education to manage public funds. Two audits, one conducted by a private company and the other by the city, claimed that Self-Help Housing had mismanaged $20,000 of its $311,139 budget for the preceding year. The city auditor, Daniel Paul, suggested that the community action board suspend funding to Self-Help Housing until "adequate qualified personnel" could be appointed to run the program. Self-Help Housing employees understood the need to prevent financial improprieties and inefficiencies but argued that this relatively small mistake should not result in the city taking over the program.[40]

The battle for control over the neighborhood program exposed how municipal officials challenged poor black people's visions of self-determination. At one of numerous community action board meetings convened to discuss the fate of the program, the Self-Help Housing board chair, Douglass, avowed that the staff had made fiscal errors but argued that "people who have been given something to work with for the first time, to determine how they will live or how things will be taken care of around them, by themselves will make errors. Mankind himself has made progress through trial and error." The bookkeeping errors revealed mathematical mistakes and money spent on electric typewriters, rental cars, furniture, and office improvements. There was no evidence that anyone had bought personal items or taken vacations with the organization's funds. Municipal officials believed, however, that Self-Help Housing was spending money not simply wrongly but with "no sense of value." Douglass acknowledged that some money might have been "spent nonchalantly" but claimed that it had been spent to make the office more comfortable and professional. He asked, "How would you feel if you came out of a house all broken down and went to a place for help where it is broken down?"[41]

Speaking specifically about administrative needs, Douglass also argued that the city and the CAA had ignored Self-Help Housing's requests for assistance in keeping track of finances. At the agency's board meeting in the auditorium of Flag House Courts, an East Baltimore public housing complex, Douglass maintained that Self-Help Housing would gladly accept the agency's assistance and was even willing to submit to a monthly audit. But the director, board members, and employees did not want to relinquish control of their neighborhood business to municipal authorities. Douglass then asked, "When are people who are not in power or in the power structure going to be allowed the freedom of executing and solving some of their problems?"[42]

Despite a motion by poor people's representatives to keep Self-Help Housing "with no changes," the CAA took temporary control of the program and placed its director, Chase, on leave. Self-Help Housing workers again protested, picketing the CAA office the following afternoon. Dean Pappas, a white Self-Help Housing adviser, stormed out of the meeting where Chase's suspension was announced and argued that the takeover masked the true power issues: "The real issue is that A. Eugene Chase is a black man who will not be compromised in his attempts to better the lot of his people." Equally important, Pappas believed, was Self-Help's effective challenge of "those in our society . . . who would preserve the status quo. . . . The real issue is that Self-Help Housing, the only people's program, has seriously challenged entrenched power groups like land-lords and city hall bureaucracies." Pappas resigned in protest, declaring, "As a white person who is unequivocally dedicated to the struggle of black Ameri-cans, and all other oppressed and exploited Americans, for dignity and social justice, I cannot in good conscience be part of this process."[43]

In May 1969, the CAA "officially discharged" Chase, set up internal personnel and financial systems, and returned Self-Help Housing to a reconstituted board of directors. As far as Chase was concerned, the temporary takeover and his dismissal were only a "subterfuge to have City Council interference." He main-tained that most of the opposition to his stewardship "came from landlords who were persuaded or forced to repair their property for the first time in twenty years." Chase accused city comptroller Hyman Pressman of "systematically ap-plying white power structure fiscal policies to discredit the successful efforts of black militant administrators who are slowly correcting the causes of poverty. He has no concept of the important values of resident-run programs." For its part, the CAA, explained that Chase had been terminated as a result of fears that the city council would not renew Self-Help Housing's contract if he remained the leader, even with the other adjustments and safeguards in place. Pappas de-scribed the conflict as involving "two symbols: the militant but dignified black man—Mr. Chase—and the 'safe' Mr. Ellis. The white power structure is using one to eclipse the other."[44]

The CAA could not seem to escape criticism or turmoil, although it con-tinued to deliver services and had relative moments of calm. In January 1969, Gilmer Blankespoor, the mid-Atlantic regional OEO administrator, complained that Baltimore's Community Action Program was "more rigidly controlled by the city government than any other anti-poverty agency in the country." In more cities than not, however, city and state elites attempted to control com-munity action agencies and limit their potential to mobilize the poor. Blank-espoor expressed concern about the high staff vacancy rate, low morale, and an "embarrassing" $600,000 surplus resulting from delays in the implementation of programs that had yet to be approved by the city council. Blankespoor pro-posed a 20 percent budget cut for the 1969–70 fiscal year because of the past surpluses.[45] Amid this federal critique and the Self-Help Housing controversy, Ellis was indicted for embezzling $8,500 from an emergency riot fund set up in the aftermath of Martin Luther King Jr.'s April 1968 assassination.

In an exclusive interview with the city's black newspaper, the *Baltimore Afro-American*, Ellis acknowledged that he had written personal checks on the emergency riot fund in other people's names and had them countersign the checks, but he contended that he had done so to provide people with emergency help. Ellis explained that he wanted to show the poor that he cared about them, "that a $20,000 per year man could stop what he was doing long enough personally to help someone in emergency distress," thereby proving that he was not an "Administration man." After Mitchell's resignation and the council's rejection of Carter, Ellis believed, "many people in the community felt that because of the apparent ease with which I was approved by Council that I had no real feeling for people and would just be the pawn of Big Interest."[46]

Officials in the city auditor's office did not believe Ellis's story and accused him of using the money for himself. In an ironic twist, Ellis now found himself echoing Chase's language when he was fired as the director of Self-Help Housing by Ellis: "That is why I say I believe a concerted effort is being made by some persons in high places to degrade and discredit black leadership." Six months after the grand jury indicted him, Ellis resigned, and Ivey took over as executive director. Self-Help Housing continued operating at least until 1971, maintaining its efforts to improve inner-city residents' housing and awareness about deteriorating neighborhoods.[47]

CONCLUSION

Although the War on Poverty definitely was short on resources in Baltimore and nationwide, it had concrete democratizing effects. Federal regulations requiring at least minimal representation of the poor in community action agencies legitimized demands that focused on economics and the democratic process as central to equality and empowerment. Community action fueled primarily black grassroots activism in many urban locales. Black neighborhood activists and their leaders challenged the old political boss system in Baltimore and in other cities where urban machines controlled patronage and representation. These grassroots representatives demanded improved service delivery to black communities and insisted that local people could envision and run better programs than could middle-class experts. The struggles of black poor people for their militant and democratic brands of self-determination and justice, while not always successful, set the tone and, in Mitchell's words, provided the context "for new leadership to emerge."[48]

Some local black leaders who worked with the Community Action Program ultimately won election to city or federal office. Clarence Blount, the principal of black Dunbar High School, became chair of the Community Action Commission in 1968. He had never before held political office before, but by 1973 he was a state senator. Mitchell eventually became Baltimore's first black U.S. congressman. Mitchell recognized community action's importance to his political career: "Not that the agency was used as a political instrument but rather it gave an opportunity to be seen and heard and to have some impact, and this facilitated the whole political process."[49] Still, this empowerment went only so far. Neither poor people who were part of this struggle nor their most militant advocates rose to high elected or appointed office. Both Lively and Carter remained grassroots activists and died young.

The resources available for the Community Action Program and its neighborhood centers and projects were clearly meager. Ivey described the Community Action Program as "just a drop in the bucket. Our program is probably dealing with one-tenth of one percent of the poor. . . . The program never was set up so that you could touch more than a fraction of the people."[50] However, poor people and their allies pushed the War on Poverty and the Community Action Program farther than Johnson or local elites had ever intended. While there was to be no revolution, quiet or otherwise, neighborhoods, boardrooms, city halls, and the streets became sites where entrenched political authorities collided with grassroots demands for racial and economic justice. These collisions revealed both the possibilities and shortcomings of 1960s state programs. They also reveal the complexities and difficulties of direct political action.

Black people's efforts to seek representation and to democratize urban institutions—their grassroots initiatives to secure better services, housing, and jobs and to challenge the overweening power of municipal authorities—often involved highly visible, vocal public protests. These protests at first helped to open up the democratic process to the poor. But they also solidified in the public's mind the belief that the War on Poverty, Community Action Program, and battles for racial democracy were inextricably linked. Black-run neighborhood antipoverty programs consequently were especially vulnerable when the nation's political winds began to shift. In the 1970s and 1980s, as Presidents Richard Nixon and Ronald Reagan reorganized federal poverty programs under what they called the "new federalism," the relatively little money that had gone directly to neighborhood organizations and grassroots groups was rechanneled to state and municipal authorities. Antipoverty efforts would continue, but citizen participation was no longer required.

Notes

I thank Lisa Hazirjian, who invited my participation in the War on Poverty and Grassroots Struggles for Racial and Economic Justice Conference at the Miller Center of Public Affairs at the University of Virginia in November 2007 as well as in this essay collection. Johanna Fernandez, Kali N. Gross, Lisa Hazirjian, Thomas F. Jackson, Premilla Nadasen, Yohuru Williams, and fellow War on Poverty conference participants provided invaluable feedback on initial versions of this essay. Finally, I especially thank Annelise Orleck, whose intellectual engagement, keen suggestions, and consistent encouragement immeasurably improved this essay.

1. Lyndon Baines Johnson, "State of the Union Address," January 8, 1964, http://www.presidency.ucsb.edu/ws/index.php?pid=26787.

2. Lyndon Baines Johnson, "Remarks at the University of Michigan," May 22, 1964, http://www.presidency.ucsb.edu/ws/index.php?pid=26262.

3. "Local War on Poverty Needs Poor's Help," *Baltimore Evening Sun* (hereafter *BES*), June 1, 1965, Box 145, Folder "June 1965," Commission on Government Efficiency and Economy Collection VI, University of Baltimore Archives, Baltimore, Maryland (hereafter UBA).

4. Allen J. Matusow, *The Unraveling of America: A History of Liberalism in the 1960s* (New York: Harper and Row, 1984), 294.

5. Kim Moody, "City Council's 'War on the Poor,'" *Jobs Now* 1:2 (February 8, 1965), Series 2B, Box 22, Folder 12, "Students for a Democratic Society, Baltimore Newsletters and Leaflets," Manuscript Collection 177, Wisconsin Historical Society, Madison.

6. Ibid.

7. Ibid.

8. Edgar Ewing to Richard Steiner, March 7, 1966, Box 2, "BURHA—I," Folder "March 15, 1966," UBA.

9. "Local War on Poverty Needs Poor's Help," *BES*, June 1, 1965, Box 145 (Poverty), Folder "June 1965," CGEE VI, UBA.

10. During the summer of 1964, SDS-ERAP opened ten offices, including the one in Baltimore. See Jennifer Frost, *"An Interracial Movement of the Poor": Community Organizing and the New Left in the 1960s* (New York: New York University Press, 2001).

11. Ray Abrams Jr., "More to Be Added: Two Programs Completed in War on Poverty," *Baltimore News Post*, February 7, 1966.

12. Rea Murdock, "Poor Stay away from Center That Is Anxious to Help," *Baltimore News American*, November 21, 1966.

13. Carl Schoettler, "Voices for the Poor: They Know Poverty—They Live with It," *BES*, February 17, 1966; Stephen J. Lynton, "Anti-Poverty 'Self-Help' at Issue," *Baltimore Morning Sun* (hereafter *BMS*), January 20, 1969.

14. Peter Marudas, "Dr. Humphrey Quits City Anti-Poverty Program Post," *BES*, June 29, 1965; Charles V. Flowers, "Dr. Humphrey Quits as Director of City Anti-Poverty Setup," *BMS*, June 30, 1965.

15. Marudas, "Dr. Humphrey Quits"; Madeline Murphy, interview by Nick Kotz, 1973, Series III: Equality Series, Nick Kotz Papers (unprocessed), Wisconsin Historical Society, Madison; "Action Unit Urges Macht's Dismissal," *Baltimore News American*, July 25, 1965, Folder July 1965, Box 145 (Poverty), CGEE VI, UBA.

16. Arnold R. Isaacs, "Family Integrity Viewed as Vital," *Baltimore Sunday Sun*, August 29, 1965; David C. Goeller, "Labor Urged to Aid Poor," *BMS*, February 11, 1966; Ray Abrams Jr., "War on Poverty—1st Anniversary: Nixon Criticism Dismays the CAC," *Baltimore News Post*, February 6, 1966.

17. Schoettler, "Voices for the Poor"; Lynton, "Anti-Poverty 'Self-Help.'"

18. Schoettler, "Voices for the Poor"; Lynton, "Anti-Poverty 'Self-Help.'"

19. "What Is U-JOIN?" U-JOIN Pamphlet, ca. 1965, Maryland Vertical Files, Folder "Union for Jobs or Income Now," Enoch Pratt Free Library, Baltimore; James D. Dilts, "Organization Man for the Other America," *BES*, June 16, 1968.

20. Edgar Ewing to Richard Steiner, March 7, 1966, Box 2, "BURHA—I," Folder "March 15, 1966," UBA.

21. "Anti-Poverty Aims Noted," *BMS*, June 29, 1965.

22. "City Council Backs Plan of Self-Help," *BMS*, February 7, 1967; "The Council Says Yes," *BMS*, February 7, 1967.

23. John E. Woodruff, "'Self-Help' Hiring Shift Is Proposed," *BMS*, February 2, 1967

24. John E. Woodruff, "Poverty Unit Calls Hiring Shift 'Insult,'" *BMS*, February 4, 1967, Box 145, "CGEE VI," Folder "February 1967," UBA.

25. Daniel Drosdoff, "Anti-Poverty Staff Runs Rally," *BMS*, February 7, 1967; Daniel Drosdoff, "Aid Cut-Off Is Claimed," *BMS*, February 5, 1967; "City Council Backs Plan"; "Council Says Yes."

26. "Self-Help Given Green Light," *BMS*, September 1, 1967.

27. J. Linn Allen, "Poverty War Critic May Soon Get Chance to Work with CAA Project," *Baltimore Afro-American* (hereafter *BAA*), May 21, 1966.

28. "Self-Help Given Green Light"; "Chase Dropped from Self-Help," *BAA*, May 20, 1969; Parren J. Mitchell, interview by author, February 26, 1997.

29. Parren J. Mitchell, interview by Nick Kotz, Series III: Equality Series, Kotz Papers.

30. Lynton, "Anti-Poverty 'Self-Help.'"

31. "Position Paper: The Community Action Commission," July 3, 1968, RG 9, Series 26, Box 530, Folder 598, "CAA Resignations," BCA.

32. Thomas D'Alesandro III Statement, July 5, 1968, Community Action Commission Statement, July 18, 1968, both in ibid.

33. Walter P. Carter Obituary, August 4, 1971, Maryland Vertical Files, Folder "Carter, Walter P., 1923–71," Enoch Pratt Free Library, Baltimore; "Activist Leaders Hit D'Alesandro," *BAA*, June 3, 1967; Peter J. Koper, "Carter: 'The Residents Have Been Cheated,'" *BAA*, May 6, 1969.

34. Lynton, "Anti-Poverty 'Self-Help.'"

35. Ibid.; Letter to Thomas D'Alesandro III, October 9, 1968, RG 9, Series 26, Box 530, Folder 598, "CAA Resignations," BCA; "Statement of the Staff of the CAA on the City Council Decision against Mr. Walter P. Carter as Executive Director," Series III, "BURHA," Box 2, Folder 29, "CAA," UBA; "A Slap at the Mayor," *BES*, October 1, 1968.

36. Peter Koper, "City Council 'Conservatives' Want Poverty Program Control," *BAA*, March 18, 1969.

37. Stephen J. Lynton, "The New Policy at the Anti-Poverty Agency Is to Keep Afloat, but Don't Rock the boat," *Sun*, June 8, 1969.

38. CAC Meeting, Minutes, November 13, 1968, RG 9, Series 26, Folder 356, "CAA Minutes," BCA; Lynton, "New Policy."

39. Lynton, "New Policy."

40. Community Action Agency of Baltimore City Summary Program Report, 11, January 1968, RG 9, Series 26, Box 497, Folder 355, "Community Action Agency (2)," BCA.

41. CAC Meeting, Minutes, February 26, 1969, RG 9, Series 26, Box 529, Folder 594, "CAA Minutes," BCA; "Self-Help Staff Protests, Faces CAA Showdown Soon," *BAA*, February 22, 1969.

42. CAC Meeting, Minutes, February 26, 1969.

43. "Self-Help Staff Pickets after Loss of Autonomy," *BAA*, March 1, 1969; "Self-Help Director Put 'on Leave,' Advisor Quits," *BAA*, March 8, 1969.

44. "Self-Help Staff Pickets"; "Chase Dropped"; "Self-Help Director Put 'on Leave.'"

45. Stephen J. Lynton, "Poor Funds Cutback Is Threatened," *Sun*, January 1969, RG 9, Series 26, Box 529, Folder 596, "CAA, General (2)," BCA.

46. David E. Sloan, "Ellis Describes Attempts to Show Concern for Poor," *BAA*, December 2, 1969.

47. Ibid.; "Schaefer Backs Ivey for CAA Director," *Baltimore News American*, August 16, 1970, RG 9, Series 26, Box 496, Folder 355, "CAA (1)," BCA; Josephine Smith to Buzzy Hettleman, January 15, 1971, Agenda for Open Meeting, January 21, 1971, both in RG 9, Series 26, Box 530, Folder 599, "Community Action Agency, Self-Help Housing," BCA.

48. Mitchell, interview by Kotz.

49. Ibid.

50. Lenwood Ivey, interview (1973) by Nick Kotz, Series III: Equality Series, Kotz Papers.

WESLEY G. PHELPS

Ideological Diversity and the Implementation of the War on Poverty in Houston

In Houston, the largest city in the American South, as in other cities and in some rural communities, the War on Poverty was profoundly shaped by a multifarious group of local actors that included public officials, financial elites, grassroots antipoverty activists, program administrators, federal volunteers, civil rights activists, and poor people themselves. In particular, the Community Action Program ignited fierce local political battles when implementers took seriously the federal mandate to empower the poor, organizing them to confront pillars of the local power structure. Yet few historians have analyzed the grassroots intellectual environment that created the battleground on which the War on Poverty was fought. An important part of the explanation for why and how Houston activists sought to use the War on Poverty to empower the city's poor lies in the antipoverty philosophy that fueled their actions.

In Houston, grassroots activists created a local context that was more diverse in its intellectual and political influences than the rather moderate liberalism of New Deal–Great Society liberalism. This moderate vision that motivated the architects of the federal War on Poverty helped galvanize local antipoverty activists, but even more prominent in their philosophy were Prophetic Christianity, confrontational civil rights activism, and the vision of participatory democracy and community organizing espoused by members of the New Left and iconoclastic figures such as Saul Alinsky. An eclectic intellectual fusion, this mix created a favorable environment in which to advance an agenda of social change that included empowering the city's poor and helping them engage in confrontations with local elites. By the same token, the diversity of ideas that fueled the implementation of the War on Poverty in Houston—especially grass-

roots activists' small victories in their quest to empower the city's poor—provoked a strong backlash from local public officials and conservative defenders
of the status quo. These interactions between the federal antipoverty program
and a broad range of local ideas gave the War on Poverty a distinctive flavor in
Houston that simultaneously created opportunities for grassroots activists to
bring about social change and set limits on what those activists could achieve.

Perhaps no one did more to create the local context for implementing the
War on Poverty in Houston than the Reverend Wallace B. Poteat, a minister of
the Ecumenical Fellowship United Church of Christ. His grassroots antipoverty
organization officially sponsored the Volunteers in Service to America (VISTA)
program in the city in 1966, and he trained participants in his model for community organizing. But his influence on the manner in which local activists implemented the War on Poverty would extend far beyond the VISTA program: By
1967, nearly all of the community organizers affiliated with the War on Poverty
in Houston had begun implementing Poteat's model of community organization and empowerment of the poor.

The conditions under which the Ecumenical Fellowship was born shaped the
way its members would interpret their role in the fight against poverty. The Fellowship emerged out of a bitter summer 1964 split between two factions within
the Garden Villas United Church of Christ, an all-white congregation in Southeast Houston. Garden Villas was located in an area that was gradually transition-
ing from all-white to majority African American and Latino. Many Garden Villas members as well as the congregation's young pastor, Poteat, wanted to reach
out to welcome the new neighbors. To begin this outreach program, Poteat and
several church members teamed up with a nearby African American congregation to sponsor a racially integrated vacation church school for children. A
significant majority of Garden Villas's members, however, steadfastly opposed
any challenge to entrenched patterns of segregation. After several months of
factional battles, the congregation voted to dismiss Poteat as pastor in October.
Several dozen members of the church responded by withdrawing their membership from Garden Villas and committing themselves to establishing a new
church under Poteat's leadership.[1]

The desire for active community involvement beyond the church walls propelled Poteat and his supporters to create the Ecumenical Fellowship United
Church of Christ. Houston desperately needed a new congregation whose members engaged with the outside world, Poteat argued, because most of the city's
churches had become "spiritual retreats from the rapidly changing patterns of

urbanization." Rather than cutting itself off from social problems, as he felt Garden Villas had done, this new congregation would seek solutions for societal ills and attempt to be a transformative force.[2]

Poteat and his followers had been profoundly influenced by early 1960s trends in Protestant theology, most notably (1) the renewed emphasis on original sin and on the Old Testament prophets spearheaded by Reinhold Niebuhr, (2) Harvey Cox's call for people of faith to engage more directly with the world, and (3) the ecumenical push coming from the National Council of Churches. In creating the Ecumenical Fellowship United Church of Christ, Poteat and his supporters hoped to combine these elements into a theology that called church members out into the slums as prophetic voices exposing the evil of poverty in an ecumenical way. These trends had significant implications for the way Poteat and his congregation viewed the opportunities created by the federal War on Poverty.

In January 1965, Poteat urged members of his new congregation to read carefully *Moral Man and Immoral Society*, Niebuhr's most widely known book, which called for a renewed emphasis on humanity's original sin and depravity. He criticized liberal theology (and postwar liberalism in general) for purporting that humans could ultimately be perfected. American liberals going back to John Dewey and other political theorists during the first few decades of the twentieth century had an unshakable faith in the inevitable progress of human civilization as a result of education and democracy. As society improved, conflict between groups and individuals would accordingly decline. Niebuhr disagreed with this faith in progress. Highlighting Old Testament prophets' role in exposing evil in society, Niebuhr argued that social conflict was inevitable because of humanity's depraved and fallen nature. Liberals, Niebuhr wrote, "completely disregard the political necessities in the struggle for justice in human society by failing to recognize those elements in man's collective behavior which belong to the order of nature and can never be brought completely under the dominion of reason or conscience. They do not recognize that when collective power, whether in the form of imperialism or class domination, exploits weakness, it can never be dislodged unless power is raised against it." Niebuhr argued that the only way to achieve justice on earth was through conflict and coercion. "Conflict is inevitable," Niebuhr stated, "and in this conflict power must be challenged by power." Niebuhr's revival of Prophetic Christianity provided Poteat with a powerful theological justification for his goal of exposing poverty and racism in Houston.[3]

In addition to being greatly influenced by Niebuhr, Poteat and his followers saw themselves as part of a religious movement whose participants were dedicated to establishing Christian missions in the country's urban centers. Foremost among the influential theologians in this movement was Cox, whose 1965 publication, *The Secular City*, synthesized an increasing number of calls to reengage with the outside world. In January 1966, Poteat asked his congregation to read this book, in which Cox lambasted Christians who feared secularization. Instead, Cox argued, the process of secularization was "the liberation of man from religious and metaphysical tutelage, the turning of his attention away from other worlds and toward this one. . . . The task of Christians should be to support [secularization] and nourish it." In the secular city, which Cox argued was quickly becoming ubiquitous, traditional religion, with its preoccupation with otherworldliness, had no place. Modern Christians should reject that kind of traditional religion and participate fully in the secular world. Most attractive to Poteat and his congregation was Cox's attempt to develop a theology of social change. "We are trying to live in a period of revolution without a theology of revolution," exclaimed Cox. "Our task is that of developing a theology of politics, and in particular a theology of revolutionary social change. . . . The secular city provides the starting point for such a theology." For grassroots antipoverty activists such as Poteat and his congregation, Cox provided a theological justification for political activism by advocating a democratization of the economy as a whole to produce a world without the evil of poverty.[4]

Poteat looked to Cox and other theologians for guidance in the attempt to establish an urban church. The minister rejected contemporary church congregations' tendency to leave the inner city and retreat to the suburbs. The city of Houston needed a new church, he told his congregation, that would actively and ambitiously reach out to the urban poor. "It is our conviction," proclaimed Poteat, "that those who stand outside the doors of the churches in an exploding metropolis with its problems and promise deserve to be served by faithfully witnessing churches rather than pious professions of concern."[5] In a brochure advertising the founding of the Ecumenical Fellowship, Poteat asked, "Will Sunday morning begin your eager week of involvement or will it hear your prayer of relief that toil is done? Will you attend a sanctuary where an inordinate claim on your time drags you out of the world and makes life one big retreat . . . where the emphasis is on ceremony, ritual, narrow-minded minutiae, pious platitudes . . . where exalted ideals are proclaimed but no attempt is made to implement them or live up to them . . . where charity is only a food basket from Lady Bountiful?" Or, Poteat asked, would congregants attend a church "where the whole church means the whole world . . . where the emphasis is on our common needs, racial and social justice, the brotherhood of man . . . where concern is courageous and the church will take a stand on issues . . . where charity recognizes human dignity and helps others raise themselves?" The Ecumenical Fellowship, according to Poteat, would exemplify this new brand of urban church, "committed to seeking a faith adequate to the challenge of today and the promise of tomorrow."[6]

The ecumenical movement that began slowly at the turn of the twentieth century also strongly affected Poteat and his supporters as well as the entire United Church of Christ body. In 1950, the National Council of Churches was formed, capping off a half century of efforts to create an interdenominational organization capable of encouraging dialogue between believers of different faiths. Council members wanted to shift the focus away from the relatively small doctrinal differences that divided people of faith and toward the many commonalities among the denominations. As founders stated in a message "To the People of the Nation," "we have forged an implement for cooperation such as America has never seen before. . . . The Council itself is a demonstration of [Jesus'] power to unite his followers in joyous cooperation. Let nation and nation, race and race, class and class unite their aims in his broad purposes for man, and out of that unitedness there will arise new strength like that of which we ourselves already feel the first sure intimations."[7]

As Poteat explained to his congregation in March 1966, "Denominational parochialism, static concepts, and competition" were and are "the worst enem[ies]" of the modern urban church, "a curse on the seamless robe of Christ." Suburban church congregations could cling to their denominational differences and remain financially viable, Poteat argued, but "competition and isolation spells doom to the inner city church. . . . In the cruel heart of the city, traditional middle class neighborhood churches are closing their doors and are objects of indifference and hostility." However, the growth of the National Council of Churches and the increasing strength of the ecumenical movement demonstrated to Poteat that "the walls of hostility between diverse religious groups, ethnic groups, economic groups, between suburb and inner city are being broken," thereby enabling churches to better serve "the poor, the blind, the deaf, the oppressed, the captives."[8]

Poteat and his supporters envisioned the Ecumenical Fellowship carrying out this prophetic Christian mission in Houston's inner-city neighborhoods, in part to expose and confront a racial caste system that kept many residents mired in poverty. In the fall of 1964, Poteat backers founded an antipoverty project in the predominantly Mexican American neighborhoods near the ship channel in Southeast Houston. The project's goals included "the development of indigenous 'grassroots' community organizations through which they can together prevent further deterioration of the area . . . and attack the root causes of economic, political, social, cultural, and spiritual deprivation, alienation, and discrimination." The Fellowship also sought to "provide a means whereby the barriers which prevent the exercise and enjoyment of the rights and responsibilities [of] full and equal citizenship by all the residents of the area may be overcome."[9] Such language dovetailed perfectly with that of the new Economic Opportunity Act.

This antipoverty program was the first of its kind in Houston. Poteat and Fellowship members recruited volunteers not only to provide services to the poor but also to empower the city's poor residents by organizing them. As Poteat explained to a potential volunteer, Houston could escape the fate of the northern ghettos "not by lady bountiful with a charity basket at Christmas, not by professional 'do-gooders,' not by expecting the government to do it all—but by voluntary, person-to-person involvement in projects in which the people, the churches, the businessmen, the clubs, and the schools are motivated and given an instrument and the necessary outside support by which they can unite in a concerted common effort to break the bonds of poverty—themselves!"[10]

Poteat hoped that newly organized neighborhood residents would effect widespread social change by pressuring local businesses and institutions to comply with federal desegregation laws and registering voters and educating them politically to prevent them from voting "against their own interests." He and his supporters hoped to organize residents to demand more public housing options from the city and from the federal government. Poteat planned to fight for rapid desegregation of local schools, adequate funding for schools in poor neighborhoods, more job opportunities, upgraded medical and welfare services, and an end to police harassment of poor and minority residents. As a recruitment brochure stated, "We believe in grassroots democracy. . . . We believe in Racial Justice now. . . . We believe in community organization and action. . . . We work with religious and secular organizations for justice now, for a new day in Houston." The time had come, Poteat believed, to force churches "to practice what [they] preach—i.e., Peace instead of killing. Brotherhood instead of Segregation."[11]

Searching for volunteers to carry out the new antipoverty project, Poteat discovered Houston's chapter of Students for a Democratic Society (SDS), whose idealistic young members were eager to assume an active role in the city's poor communities. SDS was a radical New Left organization formed in 1962 that set out to invigorate participatory democracy throughout the country. By the fall of 1965, Houston SDS activists were working closely with the Ecumenical Fellowship volunteers on "programs ranging from literacy work to recreation to tenants' organization work." They planned to "get to know the community, and then perhaps branch out into more specifically political programs—whatever issue, be it garbage, schools, housing or jobs, that the community feels is of importance." SDS sought primarily "to involve the people in political action." Poteat organized a training session to teach Houston SDS members his theories of community organizing and named the group's Gil Campos the project's youth director. Poteat hoped to influence SDS activists, while they hoped to transform their community-based antipoverty work into a vehicle for radical political action: "Do come!," they urged other students. "The possibilities for a dedicated, militant and sensitive organization are fantastic." Poteat was heavily criticized for welcoming student radicals into his organization but remained steadfast in his support for Houston SDS, proud that his was the city's only antipoverty organization that welcomed the organization's involvement.[12]

Poteat and his congregants were also looking for ways to tap into the new federal War on Poverty to advance and expand their efforts to organize and empower the city's poor. In so doing, they clashed with a city bureaucracy vying to control the implementation of the federal antipoverty program. Soon after the Ecumenical Fellowship created its antipoverty project, Houston mayor Louie Welch, Harris County judge Bill Elliott, and members of the city's welfare bureaucracy officially declared war on poverty in Houston. Welch wanted to use federal War on Poverty funding to build new infrastructure, such as sewers and water lines, in remote areas where the city had been rapidly annexing land. Elliott and members of the city's welfare establishment wanted to use federal funds to increase the level of social services provided by welfare agencies. After months of delay caused by these power struggles, the competing factions reached a compromise: Each would appoint individuals to a new antipoverty board, giving members of the two camps equal influence over the city's use of federal War on Poverty monies.[13]

Although Houston officials named a few representatives from the city's existing antipoverty agencies to the new board, many appointees were wealthy

businessmen. George H. W. Bush, an oil industry executive, Republican politician, and recent critic of the War on Poverty, was appointed, as were *Houston
Post* vice president William P. Hobby Jr. and Texas National Bank vice president Charles W. Hamilton. The mayor and county judge also appointed a few
middle-class African American business leaders, including Sid Hillard, a real
estate agent, and Francis Williams, a prominent African American attorney.
The committee would be chaired by attorney Leon Jaworski, a friend of President Lyndon Baines Johnson's who had been considered for the position of U.S.
attorney general after Johnson's 1964 reelection.[14]

A federal inspector dispatched to Houston in May 1965 expressed concern
about the makeup of the city's poverty board. He was most troubled by the complete absence of poor people and believed that the Houston antipoverty board
would fail to meet the minimum community action specifications for impoverished residents' participation. "If Houston is an example of what is being done
in other towns," he wrote in his report, "then I suppose the self-help ideal will
once again be defeated. . . . There is an obvious fear of including minorities or
poor people in any kind of function, administrative or operative." He concluded
that even the middle-class African American representatives on the executive
committee would not be allowed to have any voice, "except as it may have been
pre-determined." The inspector urged federal officials to take note of the "predominance of millionaires" on the board and argued that there was "every reason to believe that the board as it is constituted now has no intention of allowing communities to formulate their own programs much less decide policy."[15]

The report also warned that if Houston's antipoverty board continued on its
present course of action, the residents of the city's poor areas would likely continue to insist on true representation, possibly using mass demonstrations to
get their point across. The previous week, two thousand African American students and supporters had marched through Houston's streets to demand rapid
desegregation of the public schools. If a mass demonstration was mounted in
support of poor and minority representation on the antipoverty board, federal
War on Poverty officials would be forced to side with the poor against Houston's
political elites, a situation most War on Poverty officials wanted to avoid.[16]

Rev. Poteat had little hope that the recently created War on Poverty board
would make much of an impact in Houston. He saw his program as a more vital
alternative, more in keeping with the spirit of the federal program. While it was
unlikely that Office of Economic Opportunity (OEO) officials would fund more
than one community action agency for the city, Poteat approached VISTA offi-

cials and proposed using the young volunteers to advance his project's efforts to organize and empower the poor. By placing young and idealistic volunteers in poor communities under the supervision of local activist organizations, VISTA was contributing to a rise in community organizing and the use of confrontational tactics by the poor in many parts of the country. In Houston, the VISTA program would soon alter the official community action agency's approach.

Committed to social harmony and preserving the status quo, most national and local government officials saw the VISTA program as a benign idea. Attorney general Robert Kennedy and his task force on juvenile delinquency first came up with the idea for a domestic Peace Corps in 1962 as a way to give young people the opportunity to serve their country at home. Though a bill to establish the National Service Corps stalled in Congress, architects of the War on Poverty picked up the idea and included the volunteer program, now called VISTA, in the Economic Opportunity Act of 1964. The federal government proposed training and funding volunteers to serve one-year tours of duty in impoverished areas of the United States, most often working in conjunction with and under the supervision of local antipoverty organizations. What Peace Corps volunteers had done in remote villages in distant lands, VISTA volunteers were to do domestically—that is, helping poor families navigate some of the challenges associated with poverty.[17]

Most historians of the War on Poverty agree with this contemporary assessment of the VISTA program as thoroughly nonthreatening, which may be one reason why the program remains one of the most understudied parts of the poverty war. However, some individuals, including a few early architects of the federal War on Poverty, recognized VISTA's potential to become a transformative political force. According to War on Poverty planner Stephen J. Pollak, some of the most progressive members of the group that planned the Economic Opportunity Act—Kennedy, Richard Boone, and David Hackett—were the strongest proponents of including VISTA in the federal effort.[18]

Edgar May, a member of Sargent Shriver's early team, explained years later why so many VISTA volunteers became what he called "agents of change":

> It didn't take the VISTA volunteer a hell of a long time, whether he was in Harlem or in the South Side of Chicago or in Appalachia or in a Navajo reservation . . . to figure [out] who the bad guys are. . . . It didn't take him long to figure out that if the white people have got a municipal water system, and the Indians have got to travel in the same county five miles to get enough water in

a bunch of five-gallon cans, then there's something the matter with the public system, and if you're down there to do something about poverty, you begin showing up at the water authority meetings, and you say things that they really don't want to hear. . . . Yes, they're agents of change. We didn't need social workers. We didn't need a lot of people to teach little kids how to read.[19]

May's analysis of the profound impact of local material realities on VISTA volunteers applied to those who came to Houston. Although the national legislation contained the seeds of a VISTA program that would become a vehicle for social change, these seeds were fertilized and grew in the grassroots implementation of the program. Volunteers came face to face with the privation and living conditions of Houston's poor and realized that many of their problems were tied to their relative powerlessness, simultaneously exposing the volunteers to a wide range of ideas about how to bring about social change.

Poteat laid out his vision in the application to VISTA administrators in Washington, D.C. He proposed sending volunteers into neighborhoods to both organize the poor and allow them to play an active role in creating, planning, and developing antipoverty programs and projects. "The VISTA program as we have outlined it will be the most popular of all O.E.O. programs in Houston as the people to be served will have a real voice in its development. Most . . . are eager to participate because it will be their program, not something handed down to them from a central office."[20]

Poteat also proposed using VISTA volunteers to register voters in poor communities. "Political indifference of Latin Americans and Ghetto Negros has enabled [Houston's] political establishments to persuade the few who vote to often vote against their interests," Poteat wrote. Project volunteers would help establish people's organizations to "enable the poor to organize themselves to prevent further deterioration of their neighborhoods, to redevelop their communities and to attack the root causes of deprivation, alienation and discrimination." The ultimate goal, according to Poteat, was to make "a serious attempt to effect real change for the better." These types of activities would continue to grow with OEO funding, he asserted. Poteat and other project activists established a few service-delivery programs in their neighborhoods, but from the outset, they focused on empowering the poor through community organization.[21]

That emphasis had begun to change the direction of the city's community action agency. Around the time Poteat received the first VISTA volunteers in 1966, attorney William V. Ballew was appointed chair of the Houston–Harris

County Economic Opportunity Organization (H-HCEOO). Ballew's vision for the War on Poverty in Houston offered a striking contrast to the conservative views of the founding board members. He espoused a radical interpretation of community action based on his beliefs in participatory democracy and Alinsky's method for organizing and empowering the poor.

Ballew had long been a well-known figure in Houston's social welfare establishment. He had chaired a task force to study possibilities for implementing the Economic Opportunity Act, and Mayor Welch had appointed Ballew the first vice chair of the city's antipoverty committee in 1965. When Jaworski resigned as president of the antipoverty board in January 1966, Ballew was the logical choice to succeed him. Ballew had ample experience with Houston welfare and antipoverty efforts, had been an early advocate of the federal poverty program, and had remained a strong proponent.

Ballew's selection as the new head of H-HCEOO marked a dramatic shift in the focus and direction of the War on Poverty. While most of the early H-HCEOO staff had a conservative interpretation of community action, Ballew firmly believed that the most important part of the federal poverty program was mobilizing the poor to challenge elected officials and institutions. Ballew's views were well known, and when he took over, some board members argued that he was too radical for conservative Houston.[22]

Some wealthier and more conservative board members subsequently resigned, and Ballew replaced them with poor residents from target neighborhoods. Bush resigned to campaign for the Republican Party nomination to represent the west side of Houston in Congress. One federal official noted approvingly that "the course and pace of Houston's War on Poverty may have changed for the better."[23]

The history of the H-HCEOO makes clear that terms such as *community action* and *maximum feasible participation of the poor* had no real meaning outside of the local political context. Congress and OEO officials had defined these terms ambiguously, leaving grassroots implementers of the poverty program responsible for interpreting these concepts within the local context. When Welch and Elliott created Houston's first incarnation of the city's community action agency in 1965, the two men construed its mission very narrowly. They intended to keep the War on Poverty small and focused on improving the city's infrastructure and delivering social services. Jaworski, H-HCEOO's first chair, agreed with that assessment, and for the first few months, the agency simply gathered data.

Ballew, however, believed in the tactics espoused by Alinsky, a pioneering community organizer who in 1939 had helped create Chicago's Back of the Yards Neighborhood Council. Alinsky had subsequently garnered national attention by traveling the country to train organizers in his methods. He argued that individuals trapped in poverty had little hope of winning concessions from city government agencies or welfare organizations because of the overwhelming amount of power an urban bureaucracy possessed over poor citizens. According to Alinsky, only through organizing, as labor had done with the creation of industrial unions, could poor people attempt to match the power of a city's government and bring about needed changes. Alinsky's method of organizing and mobilizing poor communities attracted many antipoverty workers because he seemed to understand that the problems of poverty boiled down to one core issue—power relations. His followers, Ballew among them, believed that only through upending the traditional balance of power between a city's elites and its poor could the evils of poverty be eradicated.[24]

To remove any doubt about his antipoverty philosophy and commitment to community organizing, Ballew required that all H-HCEOO board members read *Reveille for Radicals* (1946), in which Alinsky laid out his blueprint for organizing poor communities. The first half of the book differentiated radicals from American liberals. "The Radical refuses to be diverted by superficial problems," Alinsky wrote. "He is . . . concerned with fundamental causes rather than current manifestations. He concentrates his attack on the heart of the issue. . . . The Radical recognizes that constant dissension and conflict has been the fire under the boiler of democracy." By contrast, Alinsky wrote, liberals "are hesitant to act." Their "opinions are studded with 'but on the other hand.'. . . Caught on the horns of this dilemma, [liberals] are paralyzed into immobility. . . . They discuss and discuss and end in disgust." The true American radical "does not sit frozen by cold objectivity. He sees injustice and strikes at it with hot passion." According to Alinsky, "society has good reason to fear the Radical. Every shaking advance of mankind toward equality and justice has come from the Radical. He hits, he hurts, he is dangerous. Conservative interests know that while Liberals are most adept at breaking their own necks with their tongues, Radicals are most adept at breaking the necks of Conservatives."[25]

The most important difference between liberals and radicals, according to Alinsky, lay in their disparate understandings of power. "Liberals fear power or its application," failing "to recognize that only through the achievement and constructive use of power can people better themselves. They talk glibly of a people lifting themselves by their own bootstraps but fail to realize that nothing can be lifted or moved except through power." Alinsky concluded that common people could attain power only by organizing: "If we strip away all the chromium trimmings of high-sounding metaphor and idealism which conceal the motor and gears of a democratic society, one basic element is revealed. The people are the motor, the organizations of the people are the gears. The power of the people is transmitted through the gears of their own organizations, and democracy moves forward."[26]

In the second half of *Reveille for Radicals*, Alinsky explained how to establish "People's Organizations" capable of empowering the poor to challenge oppressive structures and institutions. A People's Organization, according to Alinsky, was not like the community councils designed by liberals to remedy the symptoms of a community's problems; instead, it would attack the root causes of society's ills. "You . . . dare not, come to a people who are unemployed, who don't know where their next meal is coming from, whose children and themselves are in the gutter of despair—and offer them not food, not jobs, not security, but supervised recreation, handicraft classes and character building!" Alinsky wrote. "Yet *that is what is done!*" He continued, "To train men for a job when there is no job is like dressing up a cadaver in a full-dress suit; in the end you still have a cadaver." Alinsky acknowledged that most charity and social workers would disagree with his assessment, primarily because they "pride themselves upon their techniques and talents for adjusting people to difficult situations. They come to the people of the slums under the aegis of benevolence and goodness, not to organize the people, not to help them rebel and fight their way out of the muck—NO! They come to get these people 'adjusted' . . . so they will live in hell and like it too."[27]

After a community was organized, Alinsky contended, it needed to engage in conflicts that would upset the status quo: "A People's Organization is dedicated to an eternal war . . . against poverty, misery, delinquency, disease, injustice, hopelessness, despair, and unhappiness." This was a very different kind of War on Poverty than Houston officials or President Johnson had envisioned. However, Alinsky and many of his followers argued, the continuation of democracy itself depended on waging this kind of war. "The only hope for democracy," Alinsky wrote, "is that more people and more groups will become articulate and exert pressure upon their government." The alternatives would be "hellish." If "orderly revolution" was suppressed, the result would be "disorderly, sudden, stormy, bloody revolution, or a further deterioration of the mass foundation of democracy to the point of inevitable dictatorship. The building of

People's Organizations is orderly revolution, it is the process of the people gradually but irrevocably taking their places as citizens of a democracy."[28]

In February 1966, one month into Ballew's tenure as head of H-HCEOO, Alinsky brought his radical message directly to Houston's poverty workers, speaking on the campus of the University of Houston. The speech drew on his past experiences organizing poor communities and explained how the organizational tactics he had pioneered could be used in the federal War on Poverty. Alinsky diagnosed the antipoverty effort's main shortcoming as the fact that it saw "deprivation only in terms of money and not of power. . . . To expect to funnel federal funds through local administrations is like giving an employer money to funnel into the organization of labor unions that someday might strike against him." Alinsky argued that the only way that the War on Poverty could eradicate Houston's poverty was by organizing poor people into powerful blocs that could confront the power structure and force it to address the needs of impoverished neighborhoods. Alinsky's concept of orderly revolution did not go over well with some in the audience. After just a few minutes of Alinsky's speech, one woman in the front row jumped out of her seat and shouted, "Well, that's enough for me!" and walked out. About twenty-five other audience members followed her, including about a dozen Ku Klux Klan members in full regalia. When asked about Alinsky's visit a few days later, Mayor Welch stated, "I don't think extreme philosophies of either side are needed in this community. Any philosophy which sets class against class is, in my opinion, un-American." Ballew faced an uphill battle if he planned to apply the Alinsky model of community organizing in Houston.[29]

In the spring and summer of 1966, Ballew launched a public relations campaign to explain how he planned to use the Alinsky method among Houston's poor. During a speech to a group of Houston businessmen, Ballew argued that the grassroots antipoverty activists then at work in so many American cities were "fast replacing the Civil Rights movement as the number one domestic effort of our people." He admitted that the "basic concept is radical, yes, even revolutionary; but so was the beginning and the development of our American democracy and economy. . . . Recall the labor movement in America. Most manufacturers did not improve wages and working conditions until workers in America organized and became a political and economic force in our country." "The war on poverty," Ballew argued, "cannot be a mere extension of existing social and welfare programs. Existing agencies, for all their decent efforts and good intentions, were not getting through to the poor." He pledged that H-HCEOO would represent a "new departure" in fighting poverty, though he understood that his plan would "not necessarily [be] welcomed by existing power structures." Still, he committed H-HCEOO to encouraging "grass roots involvement of the poor in their own programs and . . . meeting their needs in the community. . . . When these people meet in their civic organizations and clubs, get to know each other and articulate their needs, requests are bound to be made upon the county courthouse, the city hall for services, etc. As labor organizers in the 20s and 30s were labeled agitators, or worse, community organizers today in the war on poverty may be likewise reviled. If we are wise, we will exercise extreme patience and understanding while these people go about their work."[30]

As Ballew moved toward implementing his vision, Rev. Poteat and his anti-poverty project activists were using VISTA volunteers to organize the poor. The effects were explosive. They also came as a bit of a surprise to many community organizers, who found themselves being educated by the people they had come to serve.

In May 1966 Winifred Pollack, a VISTA volunteer working in an impoverished African American neighborhood in Houston's Fifth Ward, helped organize a group of forty area residents to protest recent actions by the Houston school board. When Pollack had arrived in the neighborhood a few months earlier, one resident had approached her for help. School board members had asked to buy his home to clear land for a new elementary school. The school board had offered him just seven thousand dollars, though his home was valued at more than twenty thousand dollars. The offer was accompanied by a threat: if the man failed to sign the paperwork to sell the house within seven days, the board would petition the city to condemn the property. Pollack recognized the unfairness of the situation and promised to arrange a meeting of all neighborhood residents who had received similar threats from the school board.[31]

Forty neighborhood residents met a few days later. Pollack came into the meeting convinced of the need to address the unfair prices being offered by the school board and the threatening tone of their communications with residents. She quickly discovered that area residents had a larger critique of the school board's actions. Despite pressure from the federal government and civil rights activists, many Houston school board members continued to resist public school desegregation through subtle and devious tactics aimed at preventing African American and Mexican American students from attending "white" schools. One approach was to build new schools in African American neighborhoods that bordered white areas of the city instead of sending black students to existing white schools. Fifth Ward residents explained to Pollack that the school board's decision to build a new school in their neighborhood was part of their plan to transform the crumbling system of de jure segregation into a more permanent system of de facto segregation. Pollack told an interviewer that she "was very impressed that these elderly and not particularly literate people were so aware of the situation."[32]

After a series of neighborhood meetings, Pollack mobilized the residents to appear at school board meetings to voice their disapproval. Caught off guard, the school board members agreed to back off from their coercive actions. This victory emboldened Pollack and the residents to continue their efforts to organize the Fifth Ward and thus empower the poor to make demands on the institutions that affected their lives. According to Pollack, the only way for VISTA volunteers to leave a lasting impact on the area was to help residents learn how to organize to gain power. Power, in turn, "can help them acquire many of their smaller, mutual needs such as streetlights and better facilities. . . . If the fight against the School Board works, [community] organization may lead in the long run to the possibility of a quality education."[33]

Near the end of September 1966, Ballew arranged an informal meeting with Poteat and some VISTA volunteers. Ballew was struck by the effectiveness of the city's VISTA participants: Although they had been in the city for only seven months, they were organizing residents around important issues and empowering them to make demands on local officials and institutions. While most of H-HCEOO's community organizers were social workers who traveled daily into the neighborhoods they were trying to organize and were under strict supervision from the H-HCEOO board, the VISTA volunteers lived in the neighborhoods where they worked and enjoyed the freedom to pursue whatever courses of action they deemed necessary. Whereas poor Houston residents often distrusted H-HCEOO community organizers, the VISTA volunteers seemed to have earned trust. Ballew concluded that "we are doing it precisely wrong" and that H-HCEOO administrators must reevaluate the purpose of the organization and the role of their community organizers.[34]

Ballew decided to commit the majority of H-HCEOO's resources to organizing and empowering Houston's poor. In early November 1966, he wrote in a confidential memorandum to H-HCEOO executive director Charles Kelly, "Since money . . . is not only in short supply but is also restricted in many cases, our effective area of operation is in community organization, development and action. Our primary effort, I repeat, is in the neighborhoods and our primary responsibility is placing good people there as community organizers and neighborhood developers. This is essential." Just like the VISTA volunteers, Ballew argued, H-HCEOO community organizers should live in Houston's poor neighborhoods with the residents they were attempting to empower. Community organizers should be chosen based on whether they could commit to this new focus.[35]

"This requires a special commitment," Ballew continued, "not normally found in some social worker types who want a good paying job and spend too much time protecting that job. In the war on poverty, we are all expendable." Ballew advised giving individual community organizers as much freedom as possible to carry out their efforts: "Once we have good people working in the neighborhoods, we should give them as much independence and responsibility as possible." Ballew's sought to get community organizing activities initiated quickly and to that end hired a community organizing specialist from Chicago to administer a four-week training program for H-HCEOO organizers.[36]

In November 1966, Ballew chose Earl Allen to give H-HCEOO's community organizing effort clear direction as well as to build some credibility in the poor neighborhoods. Allen was a Methodist minister and director of the Wesley Foundation at all-black Texas Southern University, located in one of H-HCEOO's target neighborhoods in the Third Ward. Allen had been a regional representative of the Congress of Racial Equality in Dallas while attending seminary at Southern Methodist University and had organized a monthlong 1964 protest to desegregate downtown restaurants and cafeterias.

Like Ballew, Allen advocated organizing poor Houston residents to empower them to challenge public officials and city institutions that affected their lives, and his radical civil rights activism had convinced him that this tactic could bring about small victories for the poor. In hiring Allen to focus solely on community organizing and in assigning him a 140-member staff, Ballew sent a clear message that neighborhood organization, community empowerment, and even protest activity would be a major thrust of H-HCEOO's effort to implement the War on Poverty.[37]

On January 6, 1967, a deputy constable appeared at the doorstep of Houston resident Betty Gentry, who was eight months pregnant, to carry out an eviction order. Gentry lived in Settegast, a few miles from the Fifth Ward and one of the city's most isolated and impoverished areas. The deputy constable ordered Gentry out of her home and began removing her belongings. When Gentry's plea that she was being wrongly evicted went unheeded, she telephoned her landlord. The confrontation then turned physical. "When I was on the phone,"

Gentry recalled, "one of the men pushed me. . . . I hit him with the phone to defend myself; he threw me by the hair into the bedroom and handcuffed me and threw me across the bed." After removing all of Gentry's belongings, the deputy constable arrested her and charged her with aggravated assault. A few hours later, as news of the altercation spread, hundreds of angry Settegast residents showed up at Gentry's home and staged a spontaneous protest that lasted until the early morning of the next day.[38]

Allen quickly decided to concentrate his efforts in Settegast, sending eighty H-HCEOO community organizers to assess the needs of neighborhood residents and begin organizing collective action to demand remedies for their problems. Gentry's treatment illustrated two of the most glaring inequalities that Allen and his staff encountered: police brutality and a devious lending practice known as "contract for deed." Mortgage lenders in Settegast took advantage of an arrangement, common in black neighborhoods in many U.S. cities, whereby a prospective home buyer was allowed to make payments each month toward a down payment, after which the buyer could receive a mortgage loan. Although this practice seemed to enable poor people to buy homes, H-HCEOO staff found that many of these contracts contained exorbitant hidden fees and finance charges that trapped poor buyers in a deepening cycle of debt and that most ultimately lost their homes and all of the money they had paid.[39]

The evening following the incident at Gentry's home, more than two thousand Settegast residents, including Allen and his staff, met at a local Baptist church. They signed a petition calling for immediate dismissal of the deputy constable who had mistreated Gentry and vowed to protest at City Hall until their demand was answered. Allen immediately recognized the issue's potential to mobilize Settegast residents to confront the city's public officials about the problems of unfair housing contracts and police brutality. Allen later explained that "eviction wasn't the real issue. The real issues are lack of adequate housing which permits profiteers to insist on unfair terms, and the intimidation of the poor by police. But the people are concerned because a pregnant woman was roughed up. We had to help them to do something right then. Once mobilized they can get at other issues." Allen and his community organizing staff helped residents stage demonstrations outside city and county offices in downtown Houston until public officials responded to their concerns.[40]

A few days later, approximately eighty Settegast residents boarded buses and headed downtown. The protest did not result in the dismissal of the deputy constable but forced a response from city and county officials. Precinct 1 constable

W. H. Rankin, the deputy constable's immediate supervisor, told the protesters that Gentry was "agitated during the eviction proceedings" and at some point during the scuffle struck his deputy. "We can't allow our men to be beaten and abused," argued Rankin. "We only serve the papers after the court has decided on the eviction." Allen himself could not have portrayed the situation more succinctly and accurately: Gentry had not simply been roughed up by one county constable but was the victim of a web of oppression that included unscrupulous profiteers, local city ordinances, the courts, and law enforcement officials. Protesting Gentry's treatment was simply an avenue through which to confront the structural and institutional problems facing Settegast residents. As Allen had hoped, the protest at City Hall and city and county officials' response provided excellent illustrations of how a gut issue could alert poor residents to such major problems as inadequate housing, unfair business practices, and police brutality.[41]

Local activists thus transformed the federal antipoverty program into a vehicle for social change and engaged in widespread community organizing activities. The grassroots intellectual environment in which local activists implemented the federal antipoverty program and the confrontational tactics those ideas provoked complicate and deepen our understanding of the War on Poverty and its consequences for twentieth-century American politics. While national studies have been integral for detailing the broad context and illuminating the moderate New Deal–Great Society liberalism out of which the federal antipoverty program emerged, they have also obscured many important details about the War on Poverty. Because many of these national studies have assessed the success or failure of federal programs, they have overlooked the local context. Recent grassroots studies show that the War on Poverty was not simply imposed by Washington, and its implementation in Houston confirms these findings. Events in Houston also illustrate that the War on Poverty did not simply represent the culmination of New Deal–Great Society liberalism. Houston's War on Poverty included a fascinating patchwork of ideas and principles that do not fit neatly into the main currents of mid-twentieth-century American liberalism.

If the Houston context opened up significant opportunities for grassroots activists to transform the War on Poverty into a vehicle for social change, it also set the constraints that limited how much activists could achieve in the city. Poteat, Ballew, and Allen's implementation of their vision provoked a predictably swift and powerful backlash from local public officials and other conservative defenders of the status quo. Activists' ideological diversity and small victories emboldened opponents of community action and brought on an attack from members of the city's power structure that ultimately destroyed the War on Poverty. By the summer of 1967, Houston's mayor, police chief, and other public officials had effectively tamed the city's community action agency and the VISTA program by discrediting their leaders and linking them in the public mind with the threat of urban riots. By attacking the idea of organizing and empowering poor residents, public officials galvanized moderate and conservative Houstonians in a quest to weaken and destroy the poverty program. Because the conservative counterattack was quick and effective, it remains difficult to assess the legacies of Houston's federal antipoverty program. Small victories must not be confused with overall success. The implementation of the federal poverty program in Houston remains very much a tragedy despite the important lessons it offers about how the War on Poverty operated at the local level and its implications for the course of American politics in the twentieth century.

Notes

1. "Splinter Group Has Its Own Church Now," *Houston Chronicle*, March 9, 1965; Ecumenical Fellowship United Church of Christ, "Contract with Wallace B. Poteat," September 23, 1964, Vince Maggio to Council Members, September 25, 1964, Garden Villas United Church of Christ Board of Trustees to Garden Villas Members, October 28, 1964, Garden Villas United Church of Christ, "The Community Courier," October 31, 1964, Garden Villas United Church of Christ, "Annual Report," November 1964, all in Box 1, Volunteers in Service to America Collection, Houston Metropolitan Research Center, Houston Public Library, Houston (hereafter VISTA Collection).

2. Ecumenical Fellowship, "Questions Asked of the Ecumenical Fellowship by William Luthe and Henry Damm," January 15, 1965, Box 1, Scrapbook, VISTA Collection.

3. Ibid.; Reinhold Niebuhr, *Moral Man and Immoral Society: A Study in Ethics and Politics* (New York: Scribner, 1932), xxvi–xxvii.

4. Wallace B. Poteat, "Minister's Report," January 1966, Box 1, VISTA Collection; Harvey Cox, *The Secular City: Secularization and Urbanization in Theological Perspective* (New York: Macmillan, 1965), 17, 105–8.

5. Wallace B. Poteat, "Theology and Structure, Ecumenical Fellowship-LAC Project," March 1, 1966, Box 1, Scrapbook, VISTA Collection.

6. Ecumenical Fellowship, "Out of Adversity," n.d., in ibid.

7. National Council of Churches, "To the People of the Nation," 1950, in *A Documentary History of Religion in America*, ed. Edwin S. Gaustad and Mark A. Noll (Grand Rapids, Mich.: Eerdmans, 2003), 3:509–12.

8. Poteat, "Theology and Structure."

9. Jan Morgan, "Churchmen to Work in Harrisburg Area," *Houston Chronicle* (hereafter *HC*), September 11, 1965; Melvin Steakley, "Ship Channel Area to Get Outside Aid in Self-Help," *HC*, April 24, 1965; Don Britton to Charles Cross, November 3, 1964, Ecumenical Fellowship, "Voice," February 14, 28, March 28, 1965, all in Box 1, VISTA Collection; Ecumenical Fellowship, "Projected Program for LAC Project, Houston, Texas, 1965–1966," April 1965, Box 2, VISTA Collection; Wallace B. Poteat, "The Objectives of the LAC Project," August 1965, Box 1, Scrapbook, VISTA Collection.

10. Wallace B. Poteat to Lawrence H. Noonan, September 30, 1966, Box 1, VISTA Collection.

11. Ibid.; Jan Morgan, "Churchmen to Work in Harrisburg Area," *HC*, September 11, 1965; Wallace B. Poteat, "The LAC (LACK) Project," May 16, 1966, Ecumenical Fellowship, "Why Does the Ecumenical Fellowship UCC-LAC Project Ask You to Support Our Cause?" n.d., both in Box 1, Scrapbook, VISTA Collection.

12. Houston SDS Newsletter, November 12, 1965, Box 1, Scrapbook, VISTA Collection; Ecumenical Fellowship, "Why Does the Ecumenical Fellowship UCC-LAC Project Ask You to Support Our Cause?"; Bud Poteat to Ecumenical Fellowship Church Council Members, August 1, 1965, Box 1, VISTA Collection.

13. Mel Young, "$8 Million Poverty War in Harris," *HC*, October 13, 1964; Howard Spergel, "Youth Unwanted," *Houston Post*, December 13, 1964; Minutes of Houston–Harris County Community Council Membership Committee, November 19, 1964, Minutes of Houston–Harris County Community Council Committee on Appraisal of Needs, December 10, 1964, Minutes of Houston–Harris County Community Council Board of Directors, October 7, 1964, all in Box 2, Box 2, Records of the Community Welfare Planning Association of Greater Houston, Houston Metropolitan Research Center, Houston Public Library, Houston, Texas; "Poverty Funds Bid by City Is Rejected," *HC*, September 26, 1965; Fred Baldwin to Theodore Berry, Fred Hayes, and Bill Bozman, May 10, 1965, Box 9, Records of the Community Services Administration, OEO, Community Action Program, Records of the Director, State Files, 1965–68, RG 381, National Archives II, College Park, Maryland); Vince Ximenes to Bill Haddad, May 11, 1965, Box 77, OEO, Community Action Program, Records of the Director, State Files, 1965–68.

14. Vince Ximenes to Bill Haddad, May 11, 1965, Box 77, OEO, Community Action Program, Records of the Director, State Files, 1965–68; H-HCEOO, "Articles of Incorporation," May 1965, H-HCEOO, "By-Laws," May 1965, both in Box 265, Leon Jaworski Papers, Texas Collection, Baylor University Library, Waco, Texas.

15. Vince Ximenes to Bill Haddad, May 13, 1965, Box 77, OEO, Community Action Program, Records of the Director, State Files, 1965–68.

16. Ibid.; Vince Ximenes to Bill Haddad, May 11, 1965, Box 77, OEO, Community Action Program, Records of the Director, State Files, 1965–68.

17. Michael L. Gillette, *Launching the War on Poverty: An Oral History* (New York:

Twayne, 1996), 237–41. See also William H. Crook and Ross Thomas, *Warriors for the Poor: The Story of VISTA, Volunteers in Service to America* (New York: Morrow, 1969); T. Zane Reeves, *The Politics of the Peace Corps and VISTA* (Tuscaloosa: University of Alabama Press, 1988); Marvin Schwartz, *In Service to America: A History of VISTA in Arkansas, 1965–1985* (Fayetteville: University of Arkansas Press, 1988); Michael Balzano, "The Political and Social Ramifications of the VISTA Program: A Question of Ends and Means" (Ph.D. diss., Georgetown University, 1971); David Jacob Pass, "The Politics of VISTA in the War on Poverty: A Study of Ideological Conflict" (Ph.D. diss., Columbia University, 1975).

18. Gillette, *Launching the War on Poverty*, 237–41. In the section of his book devoted to the War on Poverty, historian Allen J. Matusow refers to early architects of community action such as Boone and Hackett as "closet radicals" (*The Unraveling of America: A History of Liberalism in the 1960s* [New York: Harper and Row, 1984], 243).

19. May quoted in Gillette, *Launching the War on Poverty*, 249–50.

20. Ecumenical Fellowship, "Revised VISTA Proposal—LAC Project: Description and Needs," Ecumenical Fellowship "Projected Program for LAC Project, Houston, Texas, 1965–1966," LAC, "History, Structure and Purposes of the LACK Project," all in Box 2, VISTA Collection.

21. Ecumenical Fellowship, "The LAC (LACK) Project," May 16, 1966, Box 1, Scrapbook, VISTA Collection; Ecumenical Fellowship, "Projected Program for LAC Project, Houston, Texas, 1965–1966," April 1965, Ecumenical Fellowship, "History, Structure and Purposes of the LACK Project," Ecumenical Fellowship, "Revised VISTA Proposal—LAC Project Description and Needs," n.d., all in Box 2, VISTA Collection.

22. W. V. Ballew Jr., "The Way We Were," Address Delivered at the Twentieth Anniversary Symposium of the Gulf Coast Community Services Association, November 19, 1986, Box 1, W. A. V. Ballew Collection, Houston Metropolitan Research Center, Houston Public Library, Houston; Minutes of H-HCEOO Board of Directors, January 10, 1966, Box 266, Jaworski Papers.

23. Minutes of H-HCEOO Board of Directors, January 10, 1966, Box 266, Jaworski Papers; George H. W. Bush to Bill Ballew, January 15, 1966, Box 265, Jaworski Papers; Leon Abramson, "Summary Report on the Investigative Task Force of the Ad Hoc Subcommittee on the War on Poverty Program," Box 6, OEO, Community Action Program, Records of the Director, State Files, 1965–68; Noe Perez, "Jaworski Quits Local Antipoverty Group," *HC*, January 11, 1966; "Bush Is 7th District Congress Candidate," *HC*, January 16, 1966.

24. Ballew, "Way We Were." On Alinsky, see Sanford D. Horwitt, *Let Them Call Me Rebel: Saul Alinsky—His Life and Legacy* (New York: Knopf, 1989).

25. Saul Alinsky, *Reveille for Radicals* (Chicago: University of Chicago Press, 1946), 23–29.

26. Ibid., 29–30, 70.

27. Ibid., 82–83.

28. Ibid., 154, 208, 213, 215.

29. Austin Scott, "Saul Alinsky, Professional Radical, Aids 'Have-Nots,'" *HC*, February 20, 1966; Noe Perez, "Slum-Dweller Organizer Hits Poverty War," *HC*, February 25, 1966.

30. W. V. Ballew Jr., "The Anti-Poverty Program in Houston," Address Delivered to the Young Presidents' Club of Houston, Texas, August 17, 1966, in author's possession.

31. Ibid.

32. Ibid.

33. Cate Ewing and Joy Hodge, "Winifred Pollack: Census Tract 18, Houston, Texas," Box 1, Houston Council on Human Relations VISTA Collection, Houston Metropolitan Research Center, Houston Public Library, Houston; "VISTA," Houston Council on Human Relations Newsletter, Box 2, Folder 3, Houston Council on Human Relations Collection, Houston Metropolitan Research Center, Houston Public Library, Houston.

34. William V. Ballew, "Anti-Poverty Program," October 3, 1966, Box 1, William V. Ballew Jr. Papers, 1965–1968, MS 254, Woodson Research Center, Fondren Library, Rice University, Houston.

35. William V. Ballew to Charles Kelly, November 2, 1966, Box 1, Ballew Papers.

36. Ibid.

37. Charles Kelly to Don Hess, July 26, 1966, Box 13, OEO, Community Action Program, Records of the Director, State Files, 1965–68; "E. E. Allen Named to EOO Post," *HP*, November 20, 1966; H-HCEOO, "The Settegast Report: A Program for Community Development," August 31, 1966, Box 59, OEO, Community Action Program, Records of the Director, State Files, 1965–68; Earl E. Allen, interview by author, December 11, 2008.

38. "Beating Pregnant Woman Arouses Resentment," *Houston Informer*, January 14, 1967; Ed Terrones to Edgar May, March 15, 1967, Box 73, Folder CAP, Houston, Harris County, Texas, January–March 1967, OEO Inspection Division, Inspection Reports, 1964–67, RG 381, National Archives and Records Administration, College Park, Maryland; Saralee Tiede, "Settegast—A Powderkeg or a Community on the Move?," *Houston Chronicle*, January 22, 1967.

39. See H-HCEOO, "Settegast Report."

40. Ed Terrones to Edgar May, March 15, 1967, Charles Kelly to Ed Terrones, March 17, 1967, both in Box 73, Folder CAP, Houston, Harris County, Texas, January–March 1967, OEO Inspection Division, Inspection Reports, 1964–67; Tiede, "Settegast."

41. Tiede, "Settegast."

MARC S. RODRIGUEZ

Defining the Space of Participation in a Northern City

Tejanos and the War on Poverty in Milwaukee

Many of the important social movements of the 1960s played out dramatically in Milwaukee, Wisconsin, a midwestern industrial city known for the brewing of beer. One of the largest metropolitan areas in the United States, Milwaukee is divided along a north-south axis by the Menomonee River. The river also divides the city's two largest minority communities, African Americans and Tejano migrants. In the 1960s, Milwaukee gave birth to a racially and ethnically diverse urban civil rights movement that is most often associated with a charismatic Italian American priest, James Groppi, who led some of the city's most dramatic protests and trained many young African American activists. Still, the emphasis on one person's heroic activism tells only part of Milwaukee's activist history. Led by farm labor organizer Jesus Salas and other Tejanos, a civil rights movement developed on the city's Latino South Side. These leaders maintained close relationships with local African American activists, with Father Groppi, and with the national Chicano civil rights movement emanating from Texas, California, and other western states. The story of the Milwaukee movement complicates both the history of civil rights activism in the city and narratives of the War on Poverty that explore the impact of African American migration on poverty politics but overlook that of Mexican Americans.

In urban areas of the North, the War on Poverty created tensions between the primarily white governing class and low-income minority communities that were politically galvanized by the Community Action Program (CAP) operated by the Office of Economic Opportunity (OEO). In Milwaukee, the Social

Development Commission (SDC), established in 1963 at the behest of the city's mayor, sought to respond to the problems faced by the region's poor. After passage of the Economic Opportunity Act (EOA), the SDC became the community action agency (CAA) for all of Milwaukee County. In 1964, a group of religious leaders who had long worked to assist migrant farmworkers began planning a CAA of their own. Their work led to the creation in 1965 of United Migrant Opportunity Services (UMOS). Headquartered in the suburb of Waukesha and set up as a statewide CAA, UMOS sought and won federal funding under the new federal poverty program's provisions for migrant workers.

Tejanos and other Latino migrants fought to define themselves as central to the "community" that UMOS had been created to help. They also increasingly sought political and administrative control of an agency that was supposed to incorporate maximum feasible participation of the community members it served. Late in the 1960s, UMOS experienced an organizational revolution as a direct consequence of the era's varied activist influences, including the establishment of a farm labor union in Wisconsin, support for the California grape boycott led by the United Farm Workers Union, and the growth of pan-Latino and interracial civil rights activism. The UMOS case provides insights into the ways poor people defined themselves into the space of an interstate and translocal community as well as a vantage point from which to consider the development of Mexican American activism and pan-Latino politics outside the American Southwest. It also reminds us that part of the original intent of the EOA and a focus of much organizing that grew out of it was to ameliorate the poverty of the nation's farmworkers.[1]

Although usually considered an urban program, the War on Poverty also sought to remedy the problems of the several hundred thousand migratory farmworkers who harvested the nation's crops. Nearly ignored by historians of the War on Poverty, Title IIIB of the EOA created separate program funding streams to address the special needs of America's migrant farmworkers. Following a well-established narrative, research into the War on Poverty has tended to focus on urban programs serving African American neighborhoods, with some more recent examination of rural programs assisting Appalachian whites, a population that had lived in the same place for generations. Unlike programs that sought to remedy the problems faced by fixed populations in poverty, the migrant program operated at statewide and interstate levels. As a result, this sort of CAA was free (at least in the Wisconsin case) from the control of city and county political machines.

The founders of UMOS in many ways provided a model for other Title IIIB programs. The EOA stimulated the creation of a different kind of antipoverty agency. By creating a new type of CAA, UMOS sought to centralize and expand the reach of a variety of statewide migrant service programs. Some had been operated by the Migrant Ministry of the Wisconsin Council of Churches, while others had been run by the Catholic and Episcopal Churches. UMOS brought together all of these programs.

Because Tejanos made up the majority of the migratory farmworker population in Wisconsin and the Midwest, UMOS became a Tejano-centered antipoverty organization (though it assisted others), and Tejanos were notable among its founders and earliest employees. Operating in both rural and urban areas, UMOS sought to ease the burden of migratory work and to convince farm laborers to abandon interstate employment in favor of fixed occupations. Toward that end, UMOS offered job training programs, basic education, health, and child care services.

TEJANOS AND LATINO MILWAUKEE

Several economic factors drew Latinos to Milwaukee After World War II. The eleventh-largest city in the United States in 1960, Milwaukee was home to abundant entry-level manufacturing jobs at wages higher than those available to agricultural workers, a primary factor in attracting the mainly working-class Tejanos and other Latinos who settled there. Employers targeted Latino workers by advertising in the city's bilingual newspapers and by recruiting through social service and religious agencies. With a population of 741,324 in the city and a metropolitan-area population of more than 1,000,000, Milwaukee was a vast metropolis compared to the farming communities elsewhere in Wisconsin and in South Texas. UMOS played an increasingly important role in recruiting migrant settlers to Milwaukee and assisting their adjustment to city life. Agency officials sought out community resources that could serve new arrivals and worked with urban employers to secure steady employment for families that had previously moved from location to location as farmworkers.[2]

In Milwaukee, Tejano migrants joined a diverse urban community that included residents of Mexican ancestry and Latinos. Just ninety miles north of Chicago, Milwaukee attracted chain migrants from the larger metropolis to the south as well as direct migrants from Texas and Mexico. A significant population of Mexican immigrants had settled in Milwaukee in the early 1920s, find-

ing employment mainly in the industrial section of the city near the Menomonee River in tannery, steel, and railroad work. Many of these workers came
directly from Mexico after working on the railroads and other industries. This
wave of immigrants established many of the city's first Mexican-origin institutions on the working-class South Side, where Mexicans lived alongside Polish
and European immigrants. Experiencing some decline in population during
the Great Depression, the Mexican-origin community rebounded during and
after World War II as opportunities attracted Mexicans and an ever-growing
population of Tejanos to Milwaukee. The census reported fewer than five thousand Spanish-speakers in the city in 1970, yet some observers estimated the actual number to be much higher, including a highly fluid Latino population of
between eight and twenty thousand.[3]

Unlike California and the Southwest, Milwaukee's Latino community included a significant Puerto Rican population. Puerto Ricans first settled in
Milwaukee in large numbers during and after World War II as labor migrants.
Local service agencies established programs that sought to ease the new arrivals' transition to life in Milwaukee. Some Puerto Ricans traveled directly from
their home island, while others migrated through the gateway cities of New
York or Chicago, which had large, established urban barrios. In the late 1960s,
several members of the Chicago-based Young Lords activist group settled in
Milwaukee and became key players in Latino politics. Puerto Ricans lived on
the South Side as well as in a barrio bordering the city's African American community. Adding to the milieu, a small group of Latin American students joined
social reform movements and community organizations after completing graduate work at Wisconsin universities. Puerto Ricans and this generation of Latin
Americans added to the diversity of the city's "Latin" influences.[4]

Milwaukee was also home to an active and organized African American protest movement with regional and national ties. The city's African American
population increased by nearly 200 percent after World War II.[5] Prior to the
war, African Americans lived just north of the downtown section of Milwaukee known as the "inner core." By the mid-1960s, a wave of southern migrants
changed the origin and nature of African American community life and tested
the limits of segregation in housing and education.

Home to an active branch of the Congress of Racial Equality and a militant
National Association for the Advancement of Colored People (NAACP) Youth
Council, Milwaukee became a key location in the northern civil rights move-
ment. Young African Americans, whites, and religious leaders increasingly joined

forces and played a prominent role in protest activism as Milwaukee earned the moniker Selma of the North. By the late 1960s, the city had witnessed a school boycott, open housing protests, sit-ins, mass arrests, an urban rebellion, and the filing of a high-profile desegregation case. The African American North Side and Latino South Side, including many moderates and elected officials, increasingly worked together to stage street demonstrations, support the California grape boycott, protest employment discrimination, demand welfare reform, and support other issues of mutual concern for minority and poor people. UMOS played an important role in bringing together the two communities.[6]

CREATING A CAA FOR MIGRATORY FARMWORKERS

Far removed from the militant activism of Milwaukee's urban neighborhoods, UMOS was from the outset committed to helping migrant farmworkers settle in urban Wisconsin. With origins in the service mission of Wisconsin-based religious organizations, the founders of UMOS had long assisted migrants under the auspices of the Wisconsin Welfare Council's Migrant Committee. These veteran migrant-aid workers greeted the 1964 passage of the EOA with optimism. As early as 1963, Wisconsin religious leaders, most prominently the Reverend Ralph Maschmeier, a Lutheran from Waukesha, and Father John R. Maurice, a Milwaukee Catholic, joined with the Wisconsin Council of Churches to identify funding sources for a statewide effort to provide aid and training to migrants and combine existing service programs.[7]

Incorporated as a not-for-profit agency in 1965 with assistance from Genevieve Medina, a former migrant from Crystal City, Texas, UMOS sought funding from the newly created OEO and received its first grant of thirty-one thousand dollars to operate day care centers for migrant farm families in southeastern and south-central Wisconsin agricultural areas.[8] These child care programs provided transitional learning experiences that enabled migrant children to prepare for elementary school, obtain English-language proficiency, and improve their health; in addition, according to planners, the programs would "extend the child's horizons and interests, stimulating interest in learning." Most important, perhaps, the UMOS schools allowed the children to leave the fields to learn and play. UMOS also hoped that the day care programs might encourage parents to take advantage of adult education and job training programs.[9]

Initially established in the nearby city of Waukesha with limited operations in Milwaukee, UMOS for a time escaped the management and participation problems that plagued the Milwaukee-based SDC. The SDC, a countywide antipoverty coordinating body made up of private and public institutions, began and continued in controversy. Like so many other urban CAAs, the SDC became an arena for budget and policy control wars between county and city governments and later for struggles between government and private interests, on the one hand, and advocates of greater participation by the poor, on the other. UMOS also sought to balance various agricultural interests, so its board included representatives of industry, the University of Wisconsin, labor unions, and religious leaders as well as a small group of Tejano migrants and former migrants representing the poor. The agency drew its board members from among those who worked at the statewide level on issues related to migrant reform. Both boards reflected Wisconsin's demographics—that is, they comprised mainly members of the European American community of long-term residents and included very few minorities or new migrants.[10]

The religious, academic, and labor leaders who created UMOS, did not envision the organization as an activist agency. UMOS officially sought to "avoid problems with employers" and other political difficulties by staying neutral in the area of civil rights and labor relations. Founders tried to limit its focus to migrant welfare and settlement from season to season. This neutrality initially paid off, as UMOS earned the backing of government, academic, and business leaders and became the statewide clearinghouse for all OEO-funded migrant antipoverty, job training, and child welfare programs. As a progressive social service agency, UMOS sought only to "make it possible for the migrant to break out of the cycle of poverty and enter a new and better life now enjoyed by the vast majority of Americans." To maintain the fragile relationships among the state, agriculture, and migrant workers, UMOS leaders avoided taking sides even in political issues affecting migrants.[11]

Notwithstanding their efforts to negotiate the middle ground between reform and radical advocacy, the world around UMOS underwent significant change after 1965. Most prominently, Mexican American labor and political activism emerged in the southwestern United States and spread to Wisconsin in the summer of 1966 following a farmworkers march to the capitol in Madison. Migrant activists in Wisconsin, inspired by the activism of California-based Cesar Chavez, established an independent farm labor organization with the assistance of the AFL-CIO. Moreover, Milwaukee-based activists joined the United Farm Workers effort by establishing a boycott committee and organizing boycotts of California grapes. In addition, University of Wisconsin research studies funded through the OEO-sponsored Institute for Research on Poverty brought migrant activists and young academics together to expose the low pay and poor working conditions of Tejano migrants.[12]

In Milwaukee, the African American civil rights movement expanded rapidly after 1964 school desegregation protests and related activities galvanized the community. Many of these activists pressed for poor people's participation on the OEO funded-SDC from 1965 to 1966 by staging sit-ins and street protests. These demonstrations, combined with outside pressure from the OEO offices in Chicago and Madison to implement maximum feasible participation, forced the SDC to allow fuller participation by poor people. The SDC opened more board and committee positions to African American and Latino community members. This mandate for community participation and community control would become a template for all of Milwaukee's OEO-funded organizations.[13]

UMOS established a "roving counselor" program as its main point of contact with the migrant community. The program relied on Tejanos who were former farmworkers to recruit these counselors. The counselor program created job opportunities for migrants; counselors came from the same South Texas sending communities as the farmworkers and often had family members still working in the migrant stream. The counselors brought citizenship training and community organizing to current field-workers, encouraged enrollment in UMOS educational programs, and provided referrals to government services. Many roving counselors also involved themselves in the effort to organize farmworkers in rural areas and in the civil rights movement in Latino Milwaukee. They were to become the foundation for a radicalized internal Tejano community at UMOS.[14]

Despite its higher level of grassroots mobilization, UMOS still resembled the SDC in some ways. The mainly white management sought to limit poor people's participation in program administration. Although it reached out through its counselor program directly to field-workers, UMOS allowed the all-white management team to maintain maximum control, a practice apparently not perceived as conflicting with the federal mandate for maximum feasible participation. Board management also limited the participation and leadership roles of migrants through a set of restrictive internal administrative rules.[15]

Migrant representatives were allotted only three board positions, two of which were to be chosen by existing board members, while the third was to be selected by a vaguely defined and largely powerless "migrant advisory committee," thereby limiting migrant access to the board. In various documents submitted to the OEO, "migrants" appeared last on the list of communities served by or participating in UMOS, trailing "interested citizens," "public agencies," and "growers and canners." The bylaws cited the "maximum feasible participation" requirement, but UMOS officials appear to have read this language as divisible into two parts. The first group included "residents of the areas," which meant mostly white Wisconsin nonmigrants, including canners, growers, religious leaders, and bureaucrats; the second included Tejano and other migrants. UMOS management saw itself as working for rather than with migrants.[16]

Still, because UMOS reserved grassroots positions as roving counselors for bilingual Tejano former farmworkers, they became the organization's public face and voice. These counselors tended to be from the same towns and regions in South Texas not only as the workers but also as farm labor organizers. The line between UMOS and the farm labor movement blurred as these counselors visited labor camps and neighborhoods radicalized by the heightened labor and political activism of the 1960s. In the 1966 and 1967 harvest seasons, the counselors entered migrant camps at the same time as union activists came in to try to organize the workers. Tejanos may not have had much input in UMOS management, but they were on the front lines of OEO-funded UMOS field efforts. And many migrants saw Tejanos as the face of an organization that seemed to have links to the broader struggle for Latino civil rights.[17]

That struggle began to create pressure for change from within UMOS. In 1967, a group of board members pressed for the promotion of current Tejano and Latino employees to management positions. The administration agreed but tried to maintain control over staff selected for promotion. For example, the UMOS executive committee resolved that "as soon as OEO approves the program change, the personnel committee is requested to promptly interview and promote such present Spanish-speaking staff members as *they* believe will satisfactorily fill the positions of Area Program Coordinators for the Milwaukee and Kenosha-Racine area." The board decided that Tejanos already working for UMOS would become eligible for promotion from front-line positions as roving counselors to "area program coordinators." Although these were promotions, they were not management positions but rather supervisory positions subordinate to the all-white management. The problem of Tejano and Latino participation in UMOS would remain unsolved until the agency became embroiled in the cauldron of social movement activism around poverty and community control that was sweeping the country, Milwaukee included.[18]

SOCIAL MOVEMENT ACTIVISM AND UMOS

Milwaukee had a central role in the unfolding civil rights protests in the northern United States after 1960. Like its much larger midwestern peers, Chicago and Detroit, the city's civil rights movement was multiracial and multiethnic, involving many different peoples in struggles to bring greater equality to minority populations. Growing civil and labor rights activity among Wisconsin's Mexican Americans began to affect UMOS more directly after it moved operations from Waukesha to the heart of Milwaukee's South Side in 1968.

The move from a suburban setting to the center of Wisconsin's largest barrio placed UMOS at the center of a Mexican American and Latino community poised for action. UMOS headquarters, located in a large former hospital, served as a gathering point for a variety of Latino constituencies. Community meetings regularly were held there. Close by, the local farm labor movement led by Obreros Unidos (United Workers) shared offices and leadership with the AFL-CIO activists employed to manage the Milwaukee piece of the national grape boycott. Several other community organizations, restaurants owned by people of Mexican ancestry, and a bilingual newspaper stood within walking distance of the new UMOS headquarters.[19]

African Americans and Latinos increasingly worked together in the civil rights arena, creating crosstown coalitions that linked the three main areas of minority settlement. Youth activists from the African American, Puerto Rican, and Mexican communities picketed grocery stores selling grapes and worked to raise funds for the Wisconsin and California-based farmworkers unions. In May, a contingent of UMOS employees joined African American, Puerto Rican, and other Milwaukee civil rights activists to charter buses for travel to the Poor People's March on Washington. Conceived by Martin Luther King Jr. shortly before his assassination, the campaign sought to bring poor people together across racial and ethnic lines to attack the structural roots of poverty. The Poor People's Campaign brought Father Groppi and the NAACP's Youth Council "Commandos" to UMOS offices to win Latino support and encourage interracial and interethnic participation. In Washington, Milwaukee activists of many races built temporary shelters as part of a multiethnic "Resurrection City."[20]

In the summer of 1968, members of the NAACP Youth Council and Latino activists came together to discuss employment discrimination at the South Side's landmark employer, the Allen-Bradley Company. The meeting included "recently returned Vietnam veterans, college students, Puerto Rican ex-gang leaders, and recently arrived Chicanos from southwest Texas." Held in the storefront offices of the Spanish Center, which was also home to El Centro Credit Union (another OEO-funded program with links to UMOS), the meeting began a series of collaborations regarding the issue of employment discrimination. Activists sponsored a march and protest in which Latinos joined with the NAACP's Youth Council and Father Groppi to demonstrate outside the Allen-Bradley factory. These protests gained media attention, linking the civil rights movements of African Americans, Puerto Ricans, and Mexican Americans in a larger struggle for employment opportunity as well as community control of local institutions.[21]

A core of activists from the Mexican American and Puerto Rican communities subsequently founded the Latin American Union for Civil Rights (LAUCR) to implement community control across the South Side. Drawing members from UMOS and the Spanish Center and former union organizers, LAUCR focused on protesting on behalf of involvement in and control of agencies offering social services to Latinos. The group also pushed for institutional change at community, city, and state agencies. Led by UMOS employee Ernesto Chacon, LAUCR attracted Mexican Americans and Puerto Ricans who were long-term Milwaukee residents along with Tejano former migrant workers and Puerto Ricans new to the city. Its ranks overlapped with those of the city's Brown Beret chapter. Because LAUCR's membership also included many current and former UMOS employees, that agency, with its large budget and federal funding independent of city control, became an obvious target for the group's protests.[22]

Riding a wave of community-control activism that was sweeping the city and the country, the group decided in the summer of 1968 that maximum feasible participation, as mandated by the EOA, needed to be implemented at UMOS. Jesus Salas, already well known for his leadership of the Wisconsin-based Obreros Unidos and as the Wisconsin coordinator for the United Farm Workers California grape boycott, Chacon, and a group of UMOS employees made a move to win control of UMOS. In 1967, Salas had criticized the agency for serving as merely "an educational program" and for failing to push for enforcement of state laws related to "workmen's compensation and housing code violations." Salas remembered this conflict when he decided to support Tejano employees' efforts to take over the organization.[23]

Salas and Chacon, both Tejanos, began to challenge UMOS's authority in the migrant community. According to Salas, the EOA's maximum feasible participation provision meant that advocacy should be "directed by participants, both migrants and ex-migrants."[24] The two men argued that the white managers did not allow for effective representation of and participation by migrants. Because of his established leadership position among migrant workers and his family and personal network at UMOS based on ties to South Texas, Salas became the leader of the push for Tejano and migrant control.

The takeover at UMOS grew from meetings held by several different Latino activist groups. In November 1968, after private discussions with influential Tejano employees, including Obreros Unidos cofounder Salvador Sanchez, now a UMOS field operations coordinator, and Chacon, the group formed an informal committee to pressure UMOS to hire more Tejanos and Latinos as managers and administrators. After submitting the call for affirmative action on behalf of "concerned south-side citizens," Salas and others demanded control of the agency and the ouster of the white management team.[25]

On November 25, 1968, South Side residents packed UMOS's offices to protest what they considered the mismanagement of this poverty program. The protesters had called for the agency to do a better job serving the needs of migrants and demanded that it hire more former migrant farmworkers and promote them to management positions. Many of those in the room were leaders of Obreros Unidos or the California grape boycott or were participants in the developing pan-Latino activism of Milwaukee's urban barrios.

Dolores Aguirre, a young former migrant, graduate of a UMOS basic education program, and UMOS board member, told the crowd how "those upstairs" were failing to manage the CAP in ways that helped employees who worked directly "with the people." Although she did not publicly request the ouster of the administrators based on their race, these serious charges implied that it was time for farmworkers, the majority of whom were from Texas, to control Wisconsin's largest migrant-serving agency.[26]

Protest and the call for community control shocked and dismayed UMOS's all-white management. Executive director William Kruse "was confused" by the requests since he had heard "no great outcry" for change before this meeting. Kruse's comments betrayed a lack of understanding of the growing pressure for community control and perhaps a lack of attention to the changing nature of migrant politics and the civil rights movement.

The protesters, in contrast, saw their demand for migrant management as falling in line with government policy and believed that the time had come for community control. In late 1968, OEO released a series of instructions to assist agencies in obtaining greater participation by poor people in CAA operations. According to the OEO, "CAP grantees have a responsibility to broaden the scope of opportunities within their own agencies . . . for participation of the poor, and to help the poor equip themselves to take advantage of these opportunities." Responding to these pressures from the federal government, the Tejano community, and the organization's board, UMOS felt confident that it was increasing the involvement of former migrants. UMOS founder and board chair Maurice remarked in 1968, "Probably the greatest headway was the increasing involvement on the part of migrants and ex-migrants [which] gave better direction and meaning to the whole project."[27]

Despite Father Maurice's intentions and commitment to making sure that organizations such as the Spanish Center and UMOS trained Latino activists, Tejano participation did not expand into management. Between 1966 and 1968, UMOS reported that in two primary employee groups, "Administrative and Field" and "Teaching" employees, "Latinization" had taken place and that Tejanos and a small number of Latinos comprised 73.3 percent of workers in the former category and 35.8 percent in the latter. "Administration" remained nearly lily-white, however, and Tejanos remained the lowest-paid employees.[28]

Following the protest, members of the UMOS board supported a rapid transition to migrant and Tejano management. In the winter of 1968, the board, chaired by William Koch, a professor at the University of Wisconsin at Madison, supported the appointment of several migrant representatives. After the expanded board took control, it voted to meet the protesters' demands. The migrant takeover with the assistance of supportive white board members prompted the immediate resignation of UMOS's white managerial staff, a move that may have been intended to cause confusion and disruption in the agency's programs. In April, the board supported Salas's appointment to direct UMOS and requested that the OEO provide a leadership transition consultant to assist in the change. Rather than polarization over the race issue, migrant control resulted in a high level of cooperation between supportive white and migrant board members and protest leaders.[29]

Some observers were not pleased by the news that Salas now directed a program with a budget that topped one million dollars. The placement of a labor union founder and activist at UMOS's head led to a backlash from Wisconsin's agricultural industry, some of whose leaders exerted pressure to cut the group's funding. Much of the opposition came from the same Waushara County vegetable growers and processors who had fought Obreros Unidos. They argued somewhat oddly that Salas's two years of leading and organizing a migrant farmworkers union should disqualify him from holding a leadership and organizational position assisting migrants. UMOS nevertheless received the support of Wisconsin's Senate delegation, several Milwaukee- and Madison-area members of Congress, and various heads of nonprofit agencies. Amid the clamor and complaints by growers, the OEO, now directed by Nixon appointee Donald Rumsfeld, approved UMOS's 1969 operating grant.[30]

By 1969, Tejano migrant control was a reality at UMOS, beginning a trend that saw Latinos expand their roles at other service organizations on Milwaukee's near South Side. The activists who led the movement for community control also did so at other CAAs, including the Spanish Center, various OEO-funded legal programs, and at the countywide SDC. Late that summer, Salas engaged in direct-action protests on behalf of another Latino-serving agency and marched alongside Groppi in a welfare mothers' rights march to the State Capitol in which participants took over the assembly chamber. Police arrested both Salas and Groppi under a statute banning "misconduct on public grounds and in public buildings." The new Nixon administration had begun issuing rules banning OEO employees from participating in political protests. Salas told the OEO that he had not been employed at the time of his arrest but had been "on leave" to participate in the march, a definitional turn that would keep him out of trouble with the state and the OEO. He returned to his job by the fall.[31]

In late October, Salas submitted his 1969 report to the UMOS board of directors. He lambasted the agency's preceding administrators for having "been too selfish and fearful" and for failing to allow "the indigenous . . . population" a place in the decision-making process. Salas called on the remaining white board members to "put the cards on the table." He proposed having board meetings conducted in "Spanish and translated into English" to make them more accessible for community members. He also thanked Koch and white UMOS employee Beverly Seekamp for their assistance and made it clear that he wanted to establish a policy of providing a "ladder within the program for the staff to climb, either economically or in responsibility," to retain good employees and to provide expanding opportunities for migrants and Tejanos. Salas concluded that it was "time for a change and for the development of more Mexican American indigenous leadership."[32]

Sanchez took over as UMOS's director in 1970, bringing a heightened commitment to direct action. In 1970, Sanchez, along with students, members of the LAUCR, and other Latino-serving CAA employees, participated in sit-ins at the University of Wisconsin at Milwaukee to protest the lack of educational opportunities for Latinos. These sit-ins combined with pickets of the chancellor's home and hunger strikes to lead the university to begin outreach efforts among the Spanish-speaking community. Sanchez helped to transform UMOS into an explicitly activist agency committed to "to do all [it] possibly could to find solutions to the problems, including making legal complaints." UMOS continued to operate programs with much success and relatively little scandal. The program settled 108 farmworker families in Milwaukee in 1970–71 and extended its educational programs into rural areas, offering training courses at satellite campuses near migrant work sites.[33]

Sanchez organized several marches on Madison between 1971 and 1974 to demonstrate the state's continued failure to enforce its laws related to migrants. On August 24, 1971, Sanchez and UMOS supporters completed a nine-day march to Madison, where they staged a massive sit-in at the Capitol. The marchers repeated many of the demands made by their predecessors in 1966: "Enforcement of equal employment opportunity (EEO) legislation; . . . Amendment of State Civil Service regulations to ensure equal opportunity for Latinos; an affirmative action program to remedy problems between police and the Latin communities; enforcement of [Wisconsin's] protective laws; action to correct problems within . . . Wisconsin's Spanish speaking communities; creat[ion of] an inspection and enforcement division . . . on the Housing Code."[34]

Much like the marchers of 1966, UMOS protested what it considered the administrative state's failure to execute laws related to migrants and minority groups. Sanchez asked many of the state's department heads to meet the marchers before the march began to discuss how to improve the current laws as well as their enforcement.[35]

In early 1972, UMOS was subject to a review of its funding by an independent outside agency. The review criticized the staff's strong commitment to "ethnic movements," a charge the agency rebuffed: "UMOS employees came to work for the program in support of their belief for change and betterment of conditions for migrant farmworkers and all poor people. We do not expect our employees to disengage themselves from commitments they have outside the agency; on the contrary, participation is encouraged and vital to the growth of the community as a whole."[36] UMOS had finally become an activist agency controlled by the Tejano migrant community.

Between 1965 and 1973, UMOS received steady funding from a number of sources in addition to the OEO and maintained a budget that fluctuated between $1 million and $1.3 million per year. Following nearly a decade of expansion, UMOS offered a widening array of programs serving the health, nutrition, housing, vocational, educational, day care, and job placement needs of Wisconsin's migrant workers. By 1973, UMOS's service area included thirty-two Wisconsin counties, and employees continued to engage in sustained direct action on behalf of migrant farmworkers. As OEO regulations evolved to constrain the political participation of staff paid with federal funds, UMOS broadened its funding sources. Sanchez resigned in 1974, leaving an organization known for its commitment to migrant advocacy and for producing dynamic Tejano leaders.

Lupe Martinez succeeded Sanchez, remaining UMOS's director for more than thirty years. Although the activist period of the late 1960s had ended and the OEO was in decline, UMOS continued to play a significant role in Milwaukee's migrant and Latino community. After 1973, it received funding from the Comprehensive Employment and Training Act, which provided federal funds for community organizations to create jobs in underemployed areas, as well as other post-OEO federal poverty programs. Under Martinez's stewardship, UMOS expanded its service mission and began to promote such important community events as a Cinco de Mayo festival, a Hispanic awards banquet, and other annual celebrations. Martinez guided UMOS through the changing terrain of public and nonprofit funding for poverty programs as the organization continued to serve Wisconsin Latinos and has increased its mission to Texas and other midwestern states. Expanding its vision of who migrants are, UMOS also assisted Cuban and Hmong refugees as well as others who came to the state following nonagricultural migration paths. As its mission diversified, so too did the UMOS staff. In the twenty-first century, UMOS employees include members of the African American, Hmong, and other migrant communities in addition to Wisconsin Latinos.

UMOS demonstrates the forty-year success of a single migrant-serving CAA in moving Tejanos and other migrants from temporary residents to community members and leaders. By calling for the participation of the poor in the management of OEO programs, the EOA enfranchised a group of workers long denied the rights, benefits, and protections of U.S. citizenship. For UMOS, the 1968–74 period laid the groundwork for decades of stability and program growth. Considering UMOS within the national context reveals how many CAAs experienced an era of protest followed by long periods of community control. Rather than collapse or failure, theirs is a story of success.

Notes

An earlier version of this essay was published as "Migrants and Citizens: Mexican American Migrant Workers and the War on Poverty in an American City," in *Reposi-*

tioning North American Migration History: New Directions in Modern Continental Migration, Citizenship, and Community, ed. Marc S. Rodriguez (Rochester, N.Y.: University of Rochester Press, 2004), 328–51.

1. The "Chicano movement" lacked the viable national institutions found in the African American civil rights movement of the period, such as the Congress of Racial Equality and the Southern Christian Leadership Conference. As others have pointed out, the Chicano movement can best be seen as several related like-minded local civil rights efforts. The broader Texas-Wisconsin civil rights activism that developed across this migrant network is discussed in Marc S. Rodriguez, "Cristaleño Consciousness: Mexican-American Activism between Crystal City, Texas, and Wisconsin, 1963–1980," in *Oppositional Consciousness: The Subjective Roots of Social Protest*, ed. Jane Mansbridge and Aldon Morris (Chicago: University of Chicago Press, 2001), 146–69. The term *Latin American* apparently was used in the late 1960s when an organization included and served the interests of people considered Latinos. In the early twenty-first century, in Milwaukee, the primary groups were Mexican Americans (including Tejanos) and Puerto Ricans. Several well-educated Central and South American natives were active in this pan–Latin American activism. Activists began to label such activism and activists *Latino* or *Latina* in local publications beginning in late 1968.

2. Anthony M. Orum, *City-Building in America* (Boulder, Colo.: Westview, 1995); Campbell Gibson, *Population of the 100 Largest Cities and Other Urban Places in the United States: 1790 to 1990* (Washington, D.C.: Population Division, U.S. Bureau of the Census, 1998); John Gurda, *The Latin Community on Milwaukee's Near South Side* (Milwaukee: Milwaukee Urban Observatory, University of Wisconsin-Milwaukee, 1976); Gary Pokorny, "The History of Hispanic Ministry in the Archdiocese of Milwaukee, 1920–1985" (1985) (unpublished research paper, University of Wisconsin-Milwaukee Library Archives); Joseph A. Rodriguez, Sara Filzen, Susan Hunter, Dana Nix, and Marc Rodriguez, *Nuestro Milwaukee: The History of the United Community Center* (Milwaukee: Wisconsin Humanities Council and United Community Center, 2000).

3. On Mexican and Mexican American Milwaukee, see Gurda, *Latin Community*; Agnes M. Fenton, *The Mexicans in the City of Milwaukee, Wisconsin* (Milwaukee: YWCA International Institute, 1930); *I Remember: Hispanic Heritage* (video), Episode 254 (Milwaukee: WMVS Public Television, 1999); Avelardo Valdez, "The Social and Occupational Integration of Mexican and Puerto Rican Ethnics in an Urban Industrial Society" (Ph.D. diss., University of California–Los Angeles, 1980).

4. On Puerto Rican Milwaukee, see Cristóbal S. Berry-Cabán, *A Survey of the Puerto Rican Community on Milwaukee's Northeast Side in 1976* (Milwaukee: Milwaukee Urban Observatory, University of Wisconsin-Milwaukee, 1976); Cristóbal S Berry-Cabán, "Puerto Rican Strategies for Survival: Work and Kinship among Esperanceños in Milwaukee" (Ph.D. diss., University of Wisconsin-Milwaukee, 1981); Avelardo Valdez, "Social and Occupational Integration."

5. Ronald Edari, *Black Milwaukee: A Social History and Statistical Profile* (Milwaukee: University of Wisconsin-Milwaukee, Department of Sociology, 1990), 5.

6. "Selma of the North" might have been an overstatement, but Milwaukee was a national center of civil rights protest for much of the period between 1964 and the mid-1970s. Far more diverse in its leadership than other cities, the city's Black Power movement included Groppi as a key activist force. See Patrick Jones, "'Not a Color, but an Attitude': Father James Groppi and Black Power Politics in Milwaukee," in *Groundwork: Local Black Freedom Movements in America*, ed. Jeanne Theoharis and Komozi Woodard (New York: New York University Press, 2005), 259–81; Jack Dougherty, *More Than One Struggle: The Evolution of Black School Reform in Milwaukee* (Chapel Hill: University of North Carolina Press, 2004); UMOS, *Helping People Help Themselves, United Migrant Opportunity Services, Inc.: Celebrating Twenty Years of Service* (Milwaukee: UMOS, 1985).

7. Minutes, Southwestern Wisconsin Migrant Health Committee, December 18, 1963, Box 6, Folder 7, Bureau of Community Health and Prevention, Migrant Health Program in Wisconsin, 1953–78, Wisconsin Historical Society, Madison (hereafter BCHP-MHPW). Attendees at this meeting considered applying for federal funds to operate a pilot program and to create a nonprofit organization.

8. "1965 Operation," Box 6, Folder 7, BCHP-MHPW. For information on UMOS's broad-based effort to assist migrants, see "Propose Migrant Aid Plan," *Hartford Times-Press*, May 13, 1965; "Secretary's Phone Call Notes, Mrs. Margaret Salick, State Economic Opportunity Office, to Dr. James L. Wardlaw, Jr., May 5, 1965," Box 6, Folder 7, BCHP-MHPW.

9. "Draft of Statement to Be Included with the UMOS Proposal to OEO and to Be Given the Summer Staff, the Purpose of UMOS Operated Pre School Day Care Centers," Box 7, Folder 9, BCHP-MHPW; Jesus Salas, interview by author, April 20, 2000; Robert Holzhauer to Carl N. Neupert, September 17, 1966, Box 6, Folder 7, BCHP-MHPW; John R. Maurice to Joseph C. Fagan, November 3, 1966, Box 121, Folder "Governor's Committee on Migratory Labor," Department of Industry Labor and Human Relations, Commissioner's Subject Files, Wisconsin Historical Society (hereafter DILHR-CSF). According to Salas, children did not play in the fields, as many growers told the public, but rather were important workers in their own right, bringing other workers sacks and baskets and, when old enough, working as laborers themselves regardless of mandatory-school-attendance or maximum-hours laws.

10. On the SDC, see Mark Edward Braun, *Social Change and the Empowerment of the Poor: Poverty Representation in Milwaukee's Community Action Programs, 1964–1972* (New York: Lexington, 2001).

11. UMOS, *Helping People*, 3, 59; "United Migrant Opportunity Services, Inc., Proposal Title III-B, Economic Opportunity Act, May 1966–May 1967," Box 7, Folder 10, BCHP-MHPW.

12. Bill Smith, interview by author, August 23, 2000; Elizabeth Brandeis Raushen-bush, *A Study of Migratory Workers in Cucumber Harvesting, Waushara County, Wisconsin 1964* (Madison: University of Wisconsin, 1966). Smith, a graduate student in history, became the Madison-based coordinator for the march on Madison.

13. On African American protest in Milwaukee, see Dougherty, *More Than One Struggle*; Patrick D. Jones, "'The Selma of the North': Race Relations and Civil Rights Insurgency in Milwaukee, 1958–1970" (Ph.D. diss., University of Wisconsin-Madison, 2002); Braun, *Social Change*, 66–75.

14. "A Report on Programs, October 25, 1967," Wisconsin Division of Economic Assistance, Economic Opportunity Section, Administrative Subject Files, 1964–1978, Unprocessed Collection, Box 24, Folder "s24 UMOS General, 1968/1969," Wisconsin Historical Society; "Milwaukee, Wisconsin (Migrant)," June 27, 1966, Box 516, Folder "United Migrant Opp. Services, Wisconsin," Entry 42, Records of the Community Services Administration, Office of Economic Opportunity, Office of Operations, Records of the Director, Migrant Workers Program, State Files, 1966–72, RG 381, National Archives II, College Park, Maryland (hereafter RG 381).

15. UMOS, "Proposal Title III-B."

16. UMOS, "Bylaws of United Migrant Opportunity Services, Inc.," (1966), 502(a)–(f), 509, Box 7, Folder 10, BCHP-MHPW; "Relationship of Local Communities to UMOS," Box 7, Folder 9, BCHP-MHPW. The "migrant advisory committee" apparently did not operate in 1966 or 1967. No minutes of meetings are available, and no mention of it occurs outside the OEO grant and UMOS bylaws.

17. Salas, interview; UMOS, "Proposal, Title III-B"; Pilar A. Parra, "United Migrant Opportunity Services, Inc.: An Historical and Organizational Analysis of Changing Goals" (master's thesis, University of Wisconsin-Madison, 1984), 56.

18. "Five Policy and Personnel Resolutions Recommended by the Executive Committee, 1967" (emphasis added), Box 151, Folder "United Migrant Opportunity Services, Inc.," DILHR-CSF; "Highlight Memorandum: Application for Grant under Title 11-A, May 24, 1967," Box 516, "United Migrant Opportunity Services, Wisconsin" Folder, RG 381.

19. Smith, interview. For more on the union, see Rene Perez Rosenbaum, *Success in Organizing, Failure in Collective Bargaining: The Case of Pickle Workers in Wisconsin, 1967–1968*(East Lansing: Julian Samora Research Institute, Michigan State University, 1991).

20. "Hundreds Join Caravan Here," *Chicago Defender*, May 9, 1968; "March on Capital Delayed at Start," *New York Times*, May 10, 1968; *Helping People*, 7–8.

21. Avelardo Valdez, "Selective Determinants in Maintaining Social Movement Organizations: Three Case Studies from the Chicano Community," in *Latinos and the Political System*, ed. F. Chris Garcia (Notre Dame, Ind.: University of Notre Dame Press, 1988), 236–54; Salas, interview; Bill Smith, interview by author, April 23, 2000. Accord-

ing to Valdez, the coalition did not hold for very long because the three communities focused mainly on local needs. The Spanish Center, created with support of the Catholic archdiocese and UMOS cofounder Father John Maurice, also operated as a CAA, training activists from Crystal City, Texas, as well as other Latinos (Lalo Valdez, "A Narrative History of the Latin Community since 1968, Part 1," *La Guardia*, November 1974).

22. Avelardo Valdez, "Selective Determinants"; Lalo Valdez, "Narrative History"; *The Chicano Civil Rights Struggle in Wisconsin: Interview with Ernesto Chacon, Irma Guerra, and Maria Flores* (video) (Chicano Studies Program, University of Wisconsin-Madison, May 1989).

23. William G. Kruse to Board Members, July 20, 1967, "Minutes, UMOS Board of Directors, July 26, 1967," both in Box 151, Folder "United Migrant Opportunity Services, Inc.," DILHR-CSF; Salas, interview.

24. Salas, interview.

25. Ibid.

26. "UMOS in Real Dialogue," *El Cosechador*, November 26, 1968, 1–2; "Staff Shortages: Debate Goes On," *El Cosechador*, Christmas 1968, 2–3.

27. OEO Instruction 6005-1, "Participation of the Poor in the Planning, Conduct, and Evaluation of Community Action Programs," December 1, 1968, OEO, *Participation of the Poor in the Community Decision-Making Process*, CAP Mission Guide, OEO Guidance 6005-1, August 1969, 2, both in Office of Economic Opportunity Collection, Wisconsin Historical Society; UMOS, *Annual Report* (Milwaukee: UMOS, 1968), 1–9; William R. Bechtel to Helen Bruner, May 28, 1969, Margaret Salick to Salvador Sanchez, May 21, 1969, in Box 24, Folder "S24 UMOS General, 69/69," Wisconsin Division of Economic Assistance, Economic Opportunity Section, Administrative Subject Files, Wisconsin Historical Society (hereafter WDEA-EOS); UMOS, *Annual Report* (Milwaukee, Wisconsin, 1968), 1.

28. UMOS, *Annual Report* (1968), 1; UMOS, *Helping People Help Themselves*, 3–4; Parra, "United Migrant Opportunity Services," 56.

29. Margaret Salick to Robert Neil Smith, "Telephone Conversation with Bill Koch about Migrant Grievances," December 5, 1968, Box 24, Folder "S24 UMOS General 1968/1969," WDEA-EOS. Some UMOS Advisory Committee members felt that the "en masse resignations" dealt "a serious blow to the UMOS organization" (Helen Bruner to C. L. Creiber, Arthur Kurtz, Bronson La Follette, Stephan Reilly, Frank Walsh, and Melvin Velhulst, January 17, 1969, Box 151, Folder "United Migrant Opportunity Service, UMOS," DILHR-CSF; "Five Administrators Quit Migrant Services Program," *Milwaukee Sentinel*, January 16, 1969; "Five Who Quit Migrant Unit Start Own Consulting Firm," *Milwaukee Sentinel*, February 17, 1969; "OEO to Run Migrant Unit 'Temporarily,'" *Milwaukee Sentinel*, February 8, 1969; "US Advises Changes in Migrant Program," *Milwaukee Journal*, February 21, 1969. Koch was new to the job, and his actions may have startled the UMOS management. See "Madison Man Heads Migrant Service Unit," *Waukesha Freeman*, Oc-

tober 2, 1968; "UMOS Board Will Accept Resignations of 5 Directors," *Madison Capital Times*, February 4, 1969.

30. Helen Bruner to C. L. Creiber, Arthur Kurtz, Bronson La Follette, Stephan Reilly, Frank Walsh, and Melvin Velhulst, January 17, 1969, Box 151, Folder "United Migrant Opportunity Services, UMOS," DILHR-CSF; Margaret Salick to Larry Powell, April 25, 1969, Gaylord Nelson to Donald Rumsfeld, June 12, 1969, Gaylord Nelson to Helen Bruner, all in Box 24, Folder "S24 UMOS 68/69," WDEA-EOS; "Wautoma Chamber to Seek Removal of Migrant Center," *Oshkosh Daily Northwestern*, December 4, 1968; Robert Neal Smith to Noel Klores, March 4, 1969, Margaret Salick to Larry Powell, April 25, 1969, Gaylord Nelson to Donald Rumsfeld, June 12, 1969, Robert W. Kastenmeier to Donald Rumsfeld, June 20, 1969, all in Box 24, Folder "S24 UMOS General, 69/69," WDEA-EOS; "Migrants React to Grant," *Appleton Post-Crescent*, July 3, 1969. See also "Flap #2, June 25, 1969," "Statement of CAP Grant, CG-8514, June 1, 1969," "Field Representative Assessment of CAA performance," all in Box 516, Folder "United Migrant Opp. Services, Wisconsin," RG 381. In "Salas Poorly Qualified," *Waushara Argus*, April 3, 1969, a rural newspaper reprinted a letter that attacked Salas written by Wautoma resident Donald M. Weyenberg and addressed to Wisconsin senator William Proxmire. One legislator pushed for an amendment to the state's antitrespassing statute to bar entry to migrant camps and keep groups such as UMOS from "stirring up trouble" ("Wilcox 'Anti-Trespass' Bill Can Slam Gates to Migrant Worker Aid," *Madison Capital Times*, July 29, 1969). Although informed of the controversy, the OEO considered that some Republicans were "mad" at Salas but that the board's choice of Salas was a "local thing and [the OEO] had no reason to object to it" (Box 516, Folder "UMOS," RG 381). The OEO field assessment of the organization commented that UMOS operated as "an effective voice for the farmworkers working and attempting to settle in Wisconsin" (Box 516, Folder "UMOS," RG 381).

31. Jesus Salas to Grace Lensmire, May 27, 1969, Beverly Seekamp to Grace Lensmire, July 10, 1969, Grace Lensmire to Jesus Salas, July 17, 1969, all in Box 24, Folder "S24 UMOS General, 69/69," WDEA-EOS; Margaret Salick to Chuck Hill, November 4, 1969, Box 24, Folder "S24 UMOS General 1968/1969," WDEA-EOS; "Migrant Project Fears Loss of Federal Funds," *Milwaukee Journal*, June 27, 1969; "Groppi Agrees to Pay $1,500 for Demonstration Damage," *New York Times*, December 23, 1972.

32. UMOS, Program Coordinator's Report, October 30, 1969, Box 24, Folder "S24 UMOS General 1968/1969," WDEA-EOS; Jesus Salas, "To All Board and Staff Members," June 1970, Box 24, Folder "S24 UMOS General 1970," WDEA-EOS; "Salas Quits UMOS," *La Guardia* 1:6 (June 1970).

33. Salvador Sanchez, interview by author, July 19, 2000; "Courses Brought to Migrants," *Elkhorn Independent*, September 23, 1971.

34. Margaret Salick to Salvador Sanchez, November 3, 1970, Box 24, Folder "UMOS General 1970," WDEA-EOS; UMOS, *Helping People Help Themselves*, 18.

35. Salvador Sanchez to Thomas Dale, August 20, 1971, Box 155, Folder 16, Gubernatorial Records of Governor Patrick J. Lucey, Series 2419, 1971–77, Wisconsin Historical Society; "Governor Tells Migrants: 'State Has Failed to Help Migrants,'" *Madison Capital Times*, August 25, 1971.

36. *An Evaluation of United Migrant Opportunity Services, Inc. (UMOS), Milwaukee, Wisconsin, Submitted to the Office of Economic Opportunity, Migrant Division, under Contract Number BIC-5275; sba0958.8 (a) 71* (Washington, D.C.: Development Associates, 1971), Box 24, Folder "UMOS 1972," WDEA-EOS; "Minutes, United Migrant Opportunity Services, Inc., Special Committee Meeting, January 20, 1972," Box 24, Folder "UMOS 1972," WDEA-EOS.

PART TWO

Poor Mothers and the War on Poverty

LAURIE B. GREEN

Saving Babies in Memphis

The Politics of Race, Health, and Hunger during the War on Poverty

Barbara McKinney, who has worked for the same African American community action organization in South Memphis, Tennessee, for more than forty years, first encountered severe symptoms of malnutrition among infants and children in her neighborhood in 1967, when she began visiting homes as a newly employed neighborhood aide in one of the most poverty-stricken sections of the city—and, indeed, the country. McKinney remembers her shock at entering rundown houses and witnessing children with the swollen bellies, visible rib cages, smaller-than-normal head sizes, and low activity levels that are telltale signs of malnutrition. "In talking with people," she recalled, "we learned that children were going to school without breakfast. And they were having problems with clothing and shoes for school." In the block clubs she helped organize, however, the aides and neighborhood women "had conversations with each other about what we could do. Sharing with one another helped."[1]

A resident of South Memphis, McKinney was in only slightly less dire straits than those she assisted. As a young black parent without a high school diploma, McKinney attended night school and learned from her teacher about the Memphis Area Project–South (MAP-South) and its recent federal funding for antipoverty work. She and the other seventy-five neighborhood aides, most of them poor South Memphis residents, helped make MAP-South—an organization that viewed the antipoverty struggle as a continuation of the black freedom movement—the city's most vibrant community organization from the mid-1960s to the mid-1970s. Conversely, MAP-South strived to help the community workers become "self-actualizing" by developing confidence and a sense of responsibility in their community.[2]

Their endeavors took an unusual turn when McKinney and other neighborhood aides literally carried the most critically malnourished babies to the recently founded St. Jude Children's Research Hospital, just north of the MAP-South area. The hospital's director, Dr. Donald Pinkel, was forming his own conclusions about the dire need to address hunger and malnutrition right in his "own backyard." The remarkable collaboration that emerged between MAP-South and St. Jude saved the lives of otherwise failing infants and young children and ultimately changed federal policy. Project directors convinced the Office of Economic Opportunity (OEO), the principal agency of the War on Poverty, to fund a nutrition program in Memphis that became a prototype for the Special Supplemental Nutrition Program for Women, Infants, and Children (WIC), approved by Congress in 1972. Pinkel recalled, "My perception when leaving St. Jude in 1974 was that the MAP-South/St. Jude program was our most important achievement, rather than our much heralded cure of childhood leukemia."[3]

This sort of activism by poor black women and their medical collaborators in the 1960s and 1970s challenged decades of cultural thought that blamed black infant mortality in the South on their mothers' presumed immorality. The MAP-South/St. Jude experience influenced medical approaches to malnutrition, including St. Jude doctors' decision to recast malnutrition as a catastrophic childhood illness, paralleling leukemia. And it prompted shifts in public health practice, with neighborhood aides such as McKinney, who served as a health coordinator for MAP-South and liaison for the St. Jude project, playing key roles in the health care process. Together, these changes temporarily reversed the top-down, usually racist production of medical knowledge by southern public health officials.

These conflicts over health and hunger have until recently remained in the shadows of civil rights scholarship, which has traditionally focused on desegregation and voting rights battles. Even the 1968 Memphis sanitation strike, hailed as a coalescence of labor and civil rights activism and the site of Dr. Martin Luther King Jr.'s assassination, looks different in light of MAP-South's work to obtain food donations for strikers' families. This effort anticipated MAP-South's later antihunger program. Strikers' families lived on the same streets and in the same housing projects as did MAP-South participants. Some were members of MAP-South. Welfare recipients and public housing tenants involved with MAP-South supported the strike, stressing the commonalities between their families and those of the sanitation workers.[4]

The story of MAP-South enables us to view the period following the land-mark Civil Rights Act of 1964 and Voting Rights Act of 1965 from a fresh per-spective. The activism of McKinney and other women in MAP-South strongly suggests that the black freedom movement was deepening and broadening at this historical juncture. Not only veterans but newcomers to the movement—including poor women, many of them struggling mothers forced to rely on public assistance as a consequence of their serious health issues—turned their eyes to aspects of racial and economic justice that were even more challeng-ing than segregation and political disfranchisement and in so doing ques-tioned and complicated the meaning of freedom. Activists in the welfare rights, public health, and public housing movements did not see themselves as sepa-rate from the black freedom movement. The crusade against hunger and mal-nutrition became central to this multilayered activism and provoked extensive controversy about historical and contemporary meanings of race and health in America.

This chapter explores the history of MAP-South and the Memphis antipov-erty movement in the context of national and international antihunger cru-sades. It exposes the egregious levels of malnutrition among African Ameri-cans that existed at the end of de jure segregation and traces the struggle to save babies and eliminate hunger. It also explores the turbulent politics of race and class that shaped the struggle to end hunger in this era, and vice versa. McKin-ney and other neighborhood aides' encounters with hunger and malnutrition in South Memphis homes paralleled other, more official "discoveries" of hunger that provoked an astounding level of national publicity. However, MAP-South's philosophical and political goal of self-actualization for poor black community workers, block club members, and program participants was distinct and often conflicted with entrenched political, economic, and medical frameworks for fighting hunger and malnutrition.

Hunger-induced malnutrition is a serious physiological condition that can result in permanent physical stunting, neurological impairment, and death if untreated, and it strikes infants and young children especially hard. Yet during this period, malnutrition was never understood as an exclusively physiological problem. Saving babies, as the MAP-South/St. Jude collaboration did, placed the U.S. economy, ethics, and political willpower on trial and challenged core understandings of race, gender, poverty, and liberation that shaped perceptions of the hunger crisis.

THE OFFICIAL "DISCOVERY" OF HUNGER IN AMERICA

The significance of the Memphis crusade against malnutrition can only be fathomed when considered in relation to the outcry over hunger that resounded across the United States—in urban and rural locales, in the mass media, in political debates. The War on Poverty officially began when President Lyndon Baines Johnson signed the Economic Opportunity Act in August 1964, just a month after he signed the 1964 Civil Rights Act. However, hunger and malnutrition did not become burning national issues until 1967, when members of Congress crossed paths with civil rights activists, human rights physicians, and journalists determined to expose the extent of hunger in America.

Systematic state-level efforts to address hunger and malnutrition among the poor began during the Progressive Era; however, national policymakers did not become directly involved until the Great Depression. In addition to its better-known relief and jobs programs, the 1935 Agricultural Adjustment Act contained a section authorizing the U.S. Department of Agriculture (USDA) to support agricultural prices by buying "surplus commodities" from farmers—whatever they might be in a particular season—and then channeling them to needy families and youth through school lunch and other programs. Nevertheless, as critics would point out, three decades later, the USDA remained focused largely on relief for farmers and less on nutritious food for the poor and hungry.[5]

After World War II, most U.S. attention to the problem of hunger went outside the country's borders—initially to war-torn Europe through the Marshall Plan and subsequently to the rest of the world through the creation of the United Nations Food and Agricultural Organization (FAO) in 1945, the United Nations International Children's Emergency Fund (UNICEF) in 1946, and the World Health Organization (WHO) in 1948. The United States also launched nonmilitary foreign aid agencies, most notably the Alliance for Progress, culminating with the 1963 establishment of the U.S. Agency for International Development.[6]

President John F. Kennedy, influenced by Michael Harrington's *The Other America* (1962), sought to address poverty in Appalachia by launching a pilot food stamp program.[7] But public discourse and action regarding hunger in the United States really surged in the spring of 1967, when news headlines drew attention to two trips to the Mississippi Delta. At the behest of civil rights activists including physicians, members of the U.S. Senate Subcommittee on Employment, Manpower, and Poverty held hearings in Jackson in April. A team of six prominent physicians commissioned by the Field Foundation followed in May. Delegates expressed shock at the levels of hunger and malnutrition they observed, identifying such extreme conditions with poor nations.

The dire conditions reflected, in part, economic and social changes in the Delta. Mechanization and other changes in cotton production, a process begun during the New Deal and completed during the 1960s, had left thousands of ex-sharecroppers and tenant farmers landless, impoverished, and unemployed or reliant on seasonal day labor. Many families picked up and moved to Memphis, while others, out of choice or necessity, stayed in the Delta. Hunger and malnutrition activism would emerge at both origin and terminus of this migration.[8]

In a letter to President Johnson the nine Senate subcommittee members who visited Mississippi in spring 1967 reported on hearings they held in Jackson and a tour through the Delta conducted by New York senators Jacob Javits and Robert Kennedy. "They told us that they had had grits and molasses for breakfast, no lunch, and would have beans for supper," Javits and Kennedy recounted from a visit with a family with thirteen children. "Some of the children could not go to school because they had no shoes, and had distended stomachs, chronic sores of the upper lip, and were extremely lethargic—all of which are the tragic evidence of serious malnutrition." This story reappeared in national news coverage of the senators' letter. The members of the Senate subcommittee charged that the current system of distributing food stamps was grossly inadequate, partly because few people could afford to pay the fees required for the stamps. This narrative framework—the coupling of devastating stories of malnutrition, particularly among children, with indictments of the USDA's surplus commodities and food stamp program—would structure official responses to hunger for the next several years.[9]

These forays prompted a flurry of investigations, hearings, and proposals by Congress, government agencies, and private nonprofits, some formed for this express purpose. In the fall of 1967, Congress charged the secretary of the Department of Health, Education, and Welfare (HEW) with undertaking a "comprehensive" six-month survey of the extent of malnutrition in the United States and making recommendations. The resulting *Ten-State Nutrition Survey* took from 1968 to 1970 to complete and included rural and urban areas in California, Kentucky, Louisiana, Massachusetts, Michigan, New York, South Carolina, Texas, Washington, and West Virginia. Hundreds of investigators (many fresh out of college) conducted interviews and medical examinations. The Citizens' Board of Inquiry into Hunger and Malnutrition in the United States, created in July 1967 and cochaired by Benjamin Mays, president emeritus of Morehouse College, and Leslie Dunbar, executive director of the Field Foundation, launched its own investigation and in April 1968 released a stinging report, *Hunger, U.S.A.*, that triggered a new wave of public outrage.[10]

Shortly thereafter, the airing of *Hunger in America*, a CBS documentary narrated by Charles Kuralt, sparked the widest outcry to date over severe malnutrition in the wealthiest nation in the world. First aired on May 21, 1968, and based on a ten-month investigation, the program, too, combined personal stories of hardship with an indictment of the limitations of USDA food programs. *Hunger in America* brought poignant interviews with poor Latinos, Appalachian residents, Navajos, and African Americans from Texas, Virginia, Arizona, and Alabama directly into living rooms and college dormitories. It powerfully challenged the image many young people had of American society and inspired some to plunge into social activism. Strong public response to *Hunger in America* made the documentary itself into news, especially after secretary of agriculture Orville Freeman condemned the film as "distorted, misleading, and oversimplified," and Mississippi congressman Jamie Whitten, as chair of the House Appropriations Subcommittee on Agriculture, arranged for an FBI investigation to determine the veracity of the film.[11]

Despite the appearance that hunger and malnutrition had been "discovered" by Congressmen, physicians, journalists, and social scientists, these revelations reflected deepening struggle regarding poverty, welfare, hunger, and health care in the mid-1960s. In the winter of 1965–66, for example, unemployed black workers had occupied a shut-down Air Force base in Greenville, Mississippi, to draw federal attention to the severity of their problems. "We are here," their leaflets stated, "because we are hungry and cold and we have no jobs or land."[12] Such actions reflected not only economic restructuring but also a shift in the freedom movement's focus.

In this context, the Tufts-Delta Health Center, one of the first two OEO-funded comprehensive community health centers, opened its doors in the fall of 1967 in Mound Bayou, a historically black town in Bolivar County, Mississippi. Center staff and community board members recognized the impossibility of achieving health while patients went hungry, working with area residents to establish a cooperative farm. Dr. Jack Geiger, founder of the center and its counterpart in Boston, began issuing prescriptions for food to combat malnutrition and related health ailments.[13]

In 1968, shortly after Martin Luther King Jr.'s assassination, activists from poor communities across the United States traveled to the U.S. Capitol for the Poor People's Campaign, initiated by King and the Southern Christian Leadership Conference. Participants from Mississippi, Texas, California, and elsewhere testified before the Senate Subcommittee on Employment, Manpower, and Poverty, offering stories about their families' dire hunger that evidenced the need for the federal government, especially the USDA, to alter its policies. The hearings and the airing of *Hunger in America* just a couple of weeks later fueled support for Senate Resolution 281, which created the Senate Select Committee on Nutrition and Human Needs. George McGovern became the new committee's first chair.[14]

In 1969, newly elected president Richard Nixon declared that the United States had the resources, willpower, and democratic system to eradicate malnutrition and hunger. In May, just months into his presidency, he announced the White House Conference on Food, Nutrition, and Health, to be organized by Harvard nutrition expert Dr. Jean Mayer. The December gathering brought together fifteen hundred public officials, health professionals, scientists, educators, food industry executives, and community activists. Representatives of the National Welfare Rights Organization, Southwest Council of la Raza, Appalachian Volunteers, and other groups denounced what they saw as organizers' focus on the food industry and food quality rather than on getting food to hungry people. The battle against hunger had become a crucible in which activists and poor people, public officials and medical professionals struggled over the meaning of American democracy and the future of U.S. society.[15]

HEALTH CARE AS RACIAL JUSTICE IN MEMPHIS

In the historical literature on Memphis, however, the struggle over race, poverty, and health has revolved largely around the sanitation strike, in which grave issues of health, safety, and overall well-being were bound up with strike demands to end the exclusion of black sanitation workers from the right to organize as municipal employees. Strikers described working in inclement weather and hoisting fifty-five-gallon tubs of garbage onto their shoulders. Because tubs leaked, the workers returned home filthy and covered in maggots. Men suffered from back injuries and other job-related problems, but without worker's compensation, they returned to work before fully healing. Workers ultimately voted to strike after two men were crushed when an electrical malfunction suddenly triggered the mashing mechanism as they waited out a storm in the back of their truck.[16]

The sanitation strike represented but the most visible marker of the deep poverty and poor health care that existed in majority-black neighborhoods. Low-income people encountered severe obstacles, including long bus rides and the lack of evening hours, when attempting to obtain medical care from public health clinics. At the Thomas Gailor Outpatient Clinic, McKinney recalled, "there were long lines and long hours of waiting to see student doctors at the University of Tennessee." Many poor black Memphians simply passed on medical care. McKinney believed that Gailor, for years the only public health clinic available to African Americans, saved lives, but it was staffed by the University of Tennessee Medical School, which had historically excluded black medical students. White student doctors therefore "practiced on poor, indigent, predominantly black people."[17] Years of frustration with the racism embedded in the public health system added to the discontent that festered in neighborhoods such as South Memphis.

In June 1962, well before either the sanitation strike or the advent of the MAP-South/St. Jude program, U.S. Civil Rights Commission hearings held in Memphis (part of a series of inquiries nationwide) established the city's significance to national debate about inequality in medical facilities. Chair John A. Hannah commented that the choice of Memphis partly reflected local complaints. Testimony by high-level administrators about Memphis hospitals exposed a web of racist practices that shaped nearly every aspect of health care for black Memphians. The commission zeroed in on an issue capturing national attention among black attorneys and physicians with the National Association for the Advancement of Colored People's Legal Defense Fund and the National Medical Association, the black medical society paralleling the American Medical Association. These activists were shifting focus from establishing black hospitals to pressuring the federal government to desegregate all-white facilities.[18]

The hearings revealed that every major private hospital in Memphis, all with church affiliations, excluded blacks. Moreover, in the 1950s, the federal government had granted funds for the building of two all-black hospitals—E. H. Crump Memorial, a public hospital that offered private care on a paying basis, and Collins Chapel, a tiny unaccredited facility—through the 1946 Hill-Burton Act (Hospital Survey and Construction Act). A 1949 amendment had prioritized projects for populations underserved as a consequence of "race, color or creed" but permitted southern states to fulfill the requirement with "separate but equal" facilities. An influential 1963 report on exclusionary policies in Hill-Burton hospitals issued by the Civil Rights Commission used evidence from these Memphis hearings to persuade HEW to issue new rules banning the use of federal funds to further rather than relieve racial equality. This report and a 1964 Supreme Court ruling, *Simkins v. Moses H. Cone Memorial Hospital*, which reversed the exclusion of a black doctor from practicing in a private hospital built with Hill-Burton funds, formed the basis for Title VI of the Civil Rights Act, which barred federally funded programs from excluding individuals on the basis of "race, color, or national origin."[19]

The commission also explored the sharp differential between white and black infant mortality rates. In 1961, Memphis's black infant mortality rate had reached 36.6 deaths per thousand babies, far higher than the rate of 24.4 per thousand among whites. Dr. Nobel Guthrie, assistant director of the city's health department, blamed the gap on out-of-wedlock births: "The illegitimately born children have a higher infant death rate than those born legitimately." Guthrie submitted tables and graphs charting rates of illegitimacy and infant mortality but never considered that, although both numbers might be higher among blacks, the rates might not be causally linked.[20]

The report submitted by Guthrie and the health department's director, Dr. L. M. Graves, did not discuss malnutrition resulting from deprivation as an explanation for infant mortality. Instead, Guthrie and Graves claimed that only quelling immoral behavior would prevent infant deaths. "Though this is a primarily social or moral problem it has strong health effects," the report concluded. "Some of the Negro's most severe health problems, such as venereal disease and infant mortality, are directly related to behavior patterns which lead to illegitimacy of more than one-third of all babies born in recent years."[21] These officials publicly articulated an otherwise tacit racial logic of health care. That their assumptions were greeted with sharp public questioning by a federal commission indicates the impact of the black freedom struggle. More than desegregation was at stake for poor black southerners.

MAP-SOUTH AND THE ANTIPOVERTY MOVEMENT

MAP-South epitomizes the broadening of the freedom struggle with the goal of addressing black poverty through self-determination. The project's target area included some of the poorest census tracts in the nation. From the mid-1960s forward, MAP-South stood as the city's most important community action organization, with hundreds of members and numerous programs. With the beginning of operations in January 1967, block clubs and staff identified and addressed a phenomenal array of problems. Health and the urgent need for emergency food provisions surfaced as two of the most pressing issues, along with substandard housing, incomes below the poverty line, environmental problems such as open drainage ditches, nearly insurmountable obstacles to welfare eligibility, and the lack of recreational facilities for youth.[22]

Although the women and men who founded MAP-South had previous experience in civic clubs, community groups, churches, and schools, they envisioned the new organization in expansive terms. MAP-South's constitution, adopted in December 1965, declared the group's dedication "to the improvement of the community working with the framework of the anti-poverty program seeking to develop the economic, environmental, and social conditions of the citizens of the area." This stated intention tacitly acknowledged the complex realities of this well-established black community. While well-heeled African American families had long resided alongside stable as well as poor working-class households, the area was now rapidly changing under the impact of significant urban migration by impoverished families from West Tennessee, Mississippi, and Arkansas. LeMoyne Gardens, a public housing project from which much neighborhood activism emanated, sat across from LeMoyne-Owen College and the prestigious Metropolitan Baptist Church, and owners of the black businesses on and near Beale Street shared neighborhoods with families living in dire poverty.[23]

When President Johnson announced the federal War on Poverty in 1964, MAP-South applied to operate as a delegate agency of the Memphis Office of Economic Opportunity, funded by the national OEO. Political controversy within Memphis and between the city and the OEO stalled funding until January 1967. Undeterred, a committee headed by J. D. Springer, principal of Booker T. Washington High School, held monthly meetings to hammer out a framework for developing grassroots community leadership and addressing urgent poverty-related problems. The group also accrued political power and public recognition through community efforts including voter registration and boycotts of local businesses. Its prominence—or notoriety, depending on one's perspective—increased with participation of such well-known leaders as the Reverend James Lawson, a visionary of the civil rights movement who had led Nashville's first sit-ins and had helped to found the Student Nonviolent Coordinating Committee prior to moving to Memphis to pastor at Centenary Methodist Church in 1962.[24]

MAP-South's political profile and early prominence in the antipoverty movement entangled the organization in power struggles with Mayor William Ingram that resulted in the funding delay. Congress's passage of the 1964 Economic Opportunity Act, with its provision for the Community Action Program
administered by the OEO, sparked heated conflict. Ingram moved to establish
the Community Action Committee, whose members would assure his control
and thwart an alliance between a federal agency and a black community organization. As in other cities, the most heated confrontations emanated from the
legislative requirement that Community Action Programs include "maximum
feasible participation" by poor people.[25]

As the founders of MAP-South proceeded with their planning and activism,
the National Association for the Advancement of Colored People, Tennessee
Commission on Human Relations, and Congressman George Grider pressured
the federal OEO to freeze funding until a plan with community involvement
rather than city control was hammered out. Even when the OEO finally approved an independent War on Poverty Committee (WOPC) and citizens' board
to oversee citywide funding and programming, conflict surrounded the hiring of Washington Butler Jr., an African American analyst with the Tennessee
OEO, as WOPC director. The OEO ultimately chartered MAP-South as a delegate
agency and beginning in January 1967 channeled funds directly to the organization, making it possible to employ Autry Parker as executive director, secure
office space, and launch its action plan.[26]

MAP-South truly ignited the neighborhood in the early months of 1967. The
much-anticipated first meeting of the MAP-South Citizens' Association drew
several hundred to the auditorium of Booker T. Washington High School on
April 20, 1967. Mary Collier reported for the membership committee that more
than eight hundred people had joined the organization, a number that would
double within months. By March, in addition to the staff of social workers and
clerks hired by Parker, MAP-South had hired and begun to train fifty neighborhood aides, including McKinney, who would organize others while expanding
their own horizons and skills. Aides, working with social workers, knocked on
doors on every street in the nine-census-tract area to initiate block clubs and
identify indigenous leaders (mostly women). The organization's 1967 annual report indicated that aides and social workers had established 73 clubs representing 1,621 members, had held 685 club meetings, and now had a contact list of
more than 5,000 people. Block club activists became members of the Citizens'
Association, the highest body of MAP-South, which in turn selected members

of the Policy Committee that oversaw the organization's ongoing work between Citizens' Association meetings. MAP-South also hired students as neighborhood aides and appointed college graduates, veterans of the civil rights movement, to its staff.[27]

Neither block clubs nor MAP-South programming underscored poverty on a single-issue basis. Clubs strategized about how to eliminate substandard housing, inadequate income, welfare ineligibility, and environmental problems (which in contemporary parlance referred not to forests and rivers outside the city but to open sewers, toxic waste, and the lack of streetlights and recreational facilities). For youth, MAP-South sponsored employment counseling, clubs, and summer workshops in writing, drama, art, and music. Aides initiated voter registration drives and established emergency centers, while social workers helped families, including migrants, identify public resources for addressing eviction, decrepit houses, unemployment, illiteracy, medical problems, and hunger. In 1968, a VISTA worker assisted women at LeMoyne Gardens in organizing a Welfare Rights Organization. MAP-South also helped activists initiate seven community action projects in other black neighborhoods, among them Southwest Shelby, North Memphis, and Orange Mound.[28]

In addition to material needs, staff members encouraged poor, working-class African Americans to think differently about poverty, race, and their lives. "Our people are burdened with a legacy of being ostracized politically, socially, economically and educationally from the mainstream of American life," declared MAP-South's 1968 annual report. Organization newsletters encouraged members to consider poverty as part of this legacy rather than as a result of personal failings or a racial attribute. One article spotlighted the summer youth program's rejection of menial jobs such as those assigned by the Neighborhood Job Corps. Instead, it aimed at "working with one's mind, a necessary condition-response to break the pattern of Negroes traditionally holding menial jobs, and to prepare children for our electronic age by teaching them to think and express themselves in modes not as dramatic as rioting but more sustaining."[29]

This language diverged from prevailing white liberalism, as articulated by Daniel Patrick Moynihan's 1965 report, *The Negro Family: The Case for National Action*. That report also evoked a burdensome historical legacy but added a new twist. "Three centuries of injustice," Moynihan argued, had "brought about deep-seated structural distortions in the life of the Negro American." The "structural distortions" to which he referred involved a "culture of poverty" that enveloped the black family—in particular, a matriarchal structure in which

Figure 3. Alice Williams and MAP-South arts and crafts program, June 16, 1976. One of the children is five-year-old Deborah James, who had been admitted into the supplemental food program at age six weeks, severely malnourished. *Memphis Press-Scimitar* staff photo, courtesy of the Mississippi Valley Collection, Special Collections, University of Memphis Libraries.

black men were weak or absent. This "tangle of pathology," he claimed, was "capable of perpetuating itself without assistance from the white world. The cycle can be broken only if these distortions are set right." Moynihan laid poverty at the feet of this distorted black family; resolution to poverty thus required outside intervention to strengthen "the Negro family so as to enable it to raise and support its members as do other families."[30]

Moynihan's call for "assistance from the white world" conflicted with MAP-South's emphasis on "working with one's mind." The organization's leaders both engaged and defied Moynihan's treatise on the cycle of poverty. The 1967 annual report, for example, seemed to echo Moynihan by asserting that the organization "was designed to mobilize every available resource to beat the cycle of poverty" in what it described as a self-help goal. The 1968 report, however, declared that despite the historical ostracizing of blacks, "we have demonstrated the imagination, initiative and thrift that many in the established order accuse us of not having." Rather than appealing for white intervention, the report emphasized that "we as a people can recognize the uniqueness of our situation even with the great problems we have which have caused many cities to explode with flames." The experience of that first year had prompted a direct challenge to the cycle-of-poverty thesis by embracing black imagination and "people involvement."[31]

MAP-South's intense support for the 1968 sanitation strike reflected this emphasis on self-determination. The headquarters for community support was in South Memphis, as were many of the workers' homes. Lawson headed the Committee on the Move for Equality (COME), founded by black ministers after some protesters were sprayed with mace during a march, and Lawson reached out for King's support. Strike families' dire circumstances spurred the MAP-South Policy Committee to solicit food donations from wealthy whites and Memphis-based food industries such as Quaker Oats and Ralston. This effort would provide the basis for a MAP-South's work on hunger and malnutrition.[32]

SELF-DETERMINATION, MEDICAL RESEARCH, AND THE STRUGGLE TO SAVE BABIES

MAP-South organizers confronted health crises caused by stress and malnutrition associated with persistent poverty, hard labor, and exposure to health and safety hazards. Statistics for the decade ending in 1970 showed far higher death rates from stroke, arteriosclerosis, degenerative heart disease, hypertension, and cancer for black forty-year-olds in the MAP-South area than for forty-year-olds in the city at large. MAP-South's first annual report described formidable barriers that led many area residents to skip basic medical care. In 1966, the U.S. Public Health Service's new Office of Equal Health Opportunity had picked up the Civil Rights Commission's trail by charging Memphis hospitals with continuing de facto segregation, in violation of the 1964 Civil Rights Act. Baptist, Methodist, and St. Joseph's had admitted a total of five, three, and two black patients, respectively. MAP-South attempted to offset these problems with such programs as a pilot tuberculosis skin test project cosponsored with the health department.[33]

MAP-South integrated its health care work with creative staff development. The 1968 annual report featured McKinney as the new director of health and nutrition programs, pointing out that she had benefited from a tutoring program for neighborhood aides. The report quoted McKinney as saying, "The manner of teaching makes a difference and the instructors have humane interest. Being in a class with those your same age makes a difference." It described her as "a perfect example of a talent that was overlooked by the outmoded ways of thinking and seeing in our culture. Through hard work and intelligence, she has helped MAP-South and has been rewarded on that basis rather than some artificial standard." In this view, she embodied the self-determination that MAP-South sought and that American society devalued.[34]

McKinney and other aides responded vigorously after meeting malnourished children and mothers unable to reverse these tragedies. They encountered babies and young children with distended bellies, visible rib cages, and spindly legs, with subdued activity levels and small head circumferences and bone measurements—indicators of potentially permanent mental and physical retardation. Their efforts to address this crisis resulted in a July 1968 agreement between MAP-South activists and research physicians at St. Jude Children's Research Center. Aides and social workers would refer malnourished infants and preschoolers to a pediatric nutrition clinic at St. Jude, where they would receive intensive care. MAP-South reported that 150 children were treated in the second half of 1968 alone. With Pinkel, a pediatric cancer expert, as director, St. Jude had opened its doors on a nonsegregated basis (including live-in accommodations) in 1962. The brainchild of Lebanese American entertainer Danny Thomas, St. Jude's mission was to research and cure catastrophic childhood illnesses. In 1967, the same year that MAP-South sent neighborhood aides out for block-by-block canvassing, Pinkel had confronted hunger and malnutrition among African American children in the area around St. Jude. His focus on this issue had been nudged by his daughter's participation in an OEO-sponsored summer youth program. However, he had already hired Dr. Paulus Zee, a pediatric nutrition specialist, to initiate a nutrition program among poor, predominantly black pediatric cancer patients at the clinic after observing how malnutrition obstructed their treatment.[35]

Individuals involved in the MAP-South/St. Jude collaboration emphasized the uniqueness of this relationship. Zee consistently commented on the crucial roles played by MAP-South, while Lawson noted the innovativeness and openness on the part of the St. Jude doctors. "Our block workers took malnourished babies over to St. Jude's," he recalled. "They proceeded to examine them. That wasn't supposed to be their work. Their specialty was supposed to be cancer research. But they didn't throw them out."[36]

This collaboration led St. Jude's doctors to break new ground in medical history. Pinkel reclassified malnutrition as a catastrophic childhood illness, with

kwashiorkor linked to liver failure and marasmus to physical and mental un-
derdevelopment. He worked with MAP-South to establish a health care program and initiated an investigation of malnutrition in infants and young children under Dr. Zee's supervision. MAP-South neighborhood aides and nurse
assistants received training on childhood illnesses. They visited homes in their
assigned areas; evaluated the health of infants, preschool children, and pregnant mothers; and sent babies with signs of malnutrition to the hospital clinic.
There, nurses and doctors examined them, administered health care, and sent
them home with Similac, a baby formula enriched with vitamins and minerals,
including iron. In extreme cases, they admitted infants to the hospital.[37]

These developments provided the scaffolding for an ambitious Surplus Commodities Food Prescription Program begun in 1969. Through an agreement
with the state agriculture department and the city/county health department,
MAP-South neighborhood aides identified women, children, and babies in urgent need of nutritional support. St. Jude medical staff wrote prescriptions for
food, as Geiger had been doing at the Tufts-Delta health center. Based on the
idea that food was the medicine of choice for poor people, MAP-South workers then distributed food commodities from a warehouse. St. Jude added iron-
and vitamin-enriched baby formula to its warehouse stock in 1970. By 1973, an
average of 140 individuals visited the warehouse each day.[38]

According to Pinkel, this combination of community involvement and medical research distinguished the MAP-South/St. Jude project from other community health programs and allowed those involved to project their experiences
far beyond Memphis. St. Jude's staff maintained records of head circumfer-
ence, weight, bone age, and levels of vitamins A and C and serum iron in children they encountered through MAP-South as well as those enrolled in Head
Start. This investigation tracked the impact of nutrients on babies' health and
development, including brain and bone growth, responsiveness, and anemia.
Zee extended his conclusions in a *Journal of the American Medical Association*
article by comparing Memphis findings to information from the rural Mississippi Delta.[39]

Lennie Lott, an African American nurse practitioner and researcher at St.
Jude, underscores the social impact of the nutrition project by relating a stunning story about the fate of a particular infant. Lott recalls a call she received in
the early 1970s from a woman who was worried that her four-week-old grand-
daughter might be malnourished. That the woman made this call reflected the
educational work MAP-South aides had been doing in her neighborhood. Lott

found the baby in grave condition, her head dangerously small and her anterior and posterior fontanels (the soft spots on babies' craniums that demarcate gaps between the immature, growing bones protecting the brain) closed, an indicator that the baby's brain had halted its development. Lott arranged for the baby to be admitted to St. Jude, where pediatric nurses fed and cared for her. Within weeks, the baby's condition had improved. "An X-ray revealed that her fontanels had reopened," Lott remembered. "Her brain had started growing again." Lott saw this story not as a narrative of helplessness and salvation or of immorality and morality but rather as reflecting activism by MAP-South, St. Jude, and the grandmother. Because childhood malnutrition could cause permanent developmental damage, combating it literally meant seizing the future.[40]

St. Jude and MAP-South rejected stereotypes of black women as dependent, lazy, or licentious, instead emphasizing their labor to combat hunger and malnutrition. St. Jude reports claimed that their staff would have been stymied without door-to-door visits by MAP-South aides, because a racial gulf would have prevented residents from trusting the medical professionals. Zee lauded MAP-South as a "black self-help organization" that "let the most significant problem of a block be defined by the people who live there" and that was "worked out by the combined efforts of the families, block captains, aides, and social workers." A *Redbook* journalist who authored a story on the program seemed awed at the extensive work accomplished by neighborhood aides. She noted that Johnnie Mae Jones, whom the writer accompanied on visits in December 1972, "seems to know almost every person, street and house in the area." McKinney declared that as a grassroots organization comprised of "mostly poor, uneducated people," MAP-South was doing something that "had never been done before. . . . We were like the little engine that could, that kept being told it couldn't be done."[41]

Zee declared in his article that poverty, not race, caused the stunted growth and anemia he had observed among poor black children and disparaged medical studies reminiscent of Moynihan's sociological conclusions: "A deprived emotional environment has been suggested as a cause of growth failure. However, [studies] have demonstrated that growth failure associated with maternal deprivation is from under-eating secondary to not being offered food, or not accepting it, and not because of some psychologically induced metabolic defect." Zee's study, in other words, drew conclusions that contradicted those of the city health officials who had attributed black infant mortality and low birth weight to illegitimacy and immorality. Elsewhere, Zee also refuted assertions that low birth weight among black newborns was caused by a genetic racial

Figure 4. Summer youth program at MAP-South, July 1968. *Memphis Press-Scimitar* staff photo, courtesy of the Mississippi Valley Collection, Special Collections, University of Memphis Libraries.

defect, reporting that black newborns treated in a well-baby clinic displayed no signs of the malnutrition and anemia commonly seen among other infants in the MAP-South poverty area.[42]

Zee's emphasis on economic explanations for malnutrition and his accolades for MAP-South as a black self-help organization must be considered in light of other political and ideological developments in the mid- to late 1960s. Although social scientists in this period rejected biological racial explanations in favor of cultural ones, the latter took on racial meanings when paired with characterizations of poor communities as dysfunctional or pathological. In embracing this perspective, the War on Poverty sought to jump-start poor people's mainstream economic participation by creating vehicles for "maximum feasible participation" and individual achievement. In this sense, the MAP-South/ St. Jude's collaboration paralleled at least the stated (if often controversial) goals of the OEO, which funded the project.

However, in this case, the reverse of the experts' expectations had also transpired: Poor black women had motivated medical professionals from outside their communities to become involved in their lives and publicly to articulate a different perspective on hunger. Zee's statements in the *Journal of the American Medical Association* and elsewhere reversed the flow of medical knowledge.

MAP-South also won support and assistance from white women philanthropists. After a tour of South Memphis, several women formed a group, the Women of Memphis, to address poverty, particularly its impact on children. Myra Dreifus, Selma Lewis, and Jocelyn Wurzburg further developed their ongoing work, with Dreifus's Fund for Needy Schoolchildren becoming the key advocate for free school lunches. Other projects proliferated under the aegis of the YWCA, Junior League, and Church Women United.[43]

Nonetheless, St. Jude and MAP-South faced formidable pressures, internally and externally. "Many people in Memphis didn't like it *at all*," recalled Pinkel. Many condemned the program as a civil rights rather than child health crusade and accused the effort of marring the city's image by exposing malnutrition. This conflict jeopardized the program's support: according to Pinkel, "Some of our St. Jude donors said they wouldn't contribute to the hospital anymore, which got our fundraisers pretty upset with me."[44]

Paradoxically, the nutrition program's success, including support from the USDA and the OEO, spurred tension within MAP-South. Leaders not centrally involved with the program worried that extensive concentration on mothers, infants, and young children, supported by state funding, siphoned energies from other goals. "We became the agency to prescribe food," Lawson observed. "We were feeding eleven hundred families a month when I left the city in 1974." He saw this focus on malnutrition as just a "drop in the bucket" of the problems that faced Memphis's poor.[45]

MAP-South's work with unemployed youth drew more political heat than any other program. In 1967, MAP-South came under fire for employing Coby Smith and Charles Cabbage, young activists widely identified with Memphis's Black Power movement. Their views sometimes clashed with those of Lawson, who hired them, yet he saw in them a means of connecting with unemployed youth. The WOPC recommended that MAP-South fire the men for associating with organizations whose goals contradicted those of the War on Poverty, a reference to the Student Nonviolent Coordinating Committee, which now espoused Black Power. Moreover, the U.S. Senate's Judiciary Committee, headed by Mississippi's James Eastland, investigated whether Smith and Cabbage (and others nationwide) were fomenting race riots. White attorneys Lucius Burch and Mike Cody defended Smith and Cabbage at a WOPC hearing requested by MAP-South's Policy Committee. Yet the larger questions remained: Who would control the War on Poverty in Memphis? And who would get to define black self-determination and self-help?[46]

HUNGER AS A CRUCIBLE

This local struggle in the urban South intersected with national and worldwide efforts to combat hunger. The dissension at Nixon's White House Conference on Food, Nutrition, and Health, which convened one year after the start of the Memphis food program, was reported in Memphis newspapers. "Not since the faltering attempts to forge a melding of the three predominant poverty groups in the country by the Poor People's Campaign," declared an "observer" quoted in the *Tri-State Defender*, "has there been a concentrated attempt to bring the disadvantaged together." Another commentator wondered whether these showdowns might spark another civil rights movement.[47]

The Nixon administration's steps to redirect and ultimately dismantle the War on Poverty also provoked anger in Memphis. The decision to remand authority for the Community Action Program to state and municipal officials resulted in the shuttering of the WOPC offices in October 1970, but not before a sit-in by some of the three hundred fired employees, the arrest of several participants, and a protest rally by their supporters. Butler, the fired WOPC direc-

tor and a participant in the sit-in, rebutted charges that wearing a dashiki and
a beard made him unfit to lead the committee, arguing that his dress made it
easier to approach poor African Americans.[48]

MAP-South reestablished itself as an autonomous organization, ending its
reliance on local, state, and federal agencies apart from the USDA. This independence, however, cost political power and narrowed MAP-South's program
to a focus largely on food distribution. The organization's conflicts with the city
came to a head after MAP-South (particularly Parker) and black physicians designed and won OEO approval to create the Memphis Health Center to serve
South Memphis. The center opened in 1975, but four years of fighting over control undermined the original vision and sapped community energies. By then,
city health officials, physicians, and the federal government had wrested control of the center from the neighborhood activists. MAP-South lost further clout
through gerrymandering of the Ninth Congressional District and the razing of
MAP-South territory around Beale Street as a consequence of urban renewal.[49]

Even as these conflicts heated up, the prescription food program gained a
national profile. Although the Nixon administration would soon replace the
OEO with the more decentralized Community Services Administration, Congress in 1972 approved and the president signed legislation sponsored by Senator Hubert Humphrey to create WIC under HEW's jurisdiction. WIC would distribute USDA surplus commodities to pregnant and lactating women, infants,
and preschool children. According to Pinkel, Humphrey had been inspired in
part by *Prescription: Food*, a documentary about the MAP-South/St. Jude program made by Memphis's WMC-TV.[50]

When McGovern's Senate Select Committee on Nutrition and Human Needs
convened hearings in June 1973 to address the USDA's and HEW's failure to implement WIC on more than a limited trial basis, committee members called on
Zee, who testified about his team's findings about the reversal of malnutrition
through prescription food. Zee also introduced into the record the *Redbook* article, "How to Save Babies for Two Dimes a Day," which displayed disturbing
photographs of malnourished babies alongside text detailing the MAP-South/St.
Jude collaboration. Committee members also viewed *Prescription: Food*, aired
by WMAL-TV on the opening night of the hearings, June 5, 1973, which similarly
revealed his team's research on the severity of child malnutrition.

Dr. Zee's testimony did not stand alone. Back-to-back statements by medical
researchers from prestigious universities and international agencies conveyed
findings from studies in Guatemala, Tunisia, Taiwan, Chile, Mexico, and the

United States. Most involved poor women and children; some used laboratory animals. The hearings thus shifted attention away from local results and toward the larger physiological and neurological effects of malnutrition. A Johns Hopkins biochemist had found that the offspring of malnourished pregnant rats suffered "behavioral damages. . . . [T]hey learn very slowly, and they make mistakes while learning." He compared his study to others involving pregnant women and babies in Taiwan. Comparing rats to humans and Guatemalans to Detroiters proved that poverty, not race, caused malnutrition and the associated physical, mental, and behavioral deformities. Researchers took pains to argue that white babies would respond to nutritional deprivation in the same ways that black babies did.

And yet in the fraught racial milieu of U.S. politics in the early 1970s, linking "inner cities" to indigenous populations in poor countries could translate malnutrition and its effects into problems of race in terms of ingrained dependency, high birth rates, and social volatility. Liberal senators such as McGovern and Humphrey underscored WIC's potential for preventing developmental deficiencies and insisted that the United States live up to its role as the leader of world democracy by eradicating hunger and poverty at home. Cognizant of the need to articulate these goals in pragmatic terms to win support from conservatives, however, they argued that federal expenditures for WIC were justified by the alternative: greater economic and societal costs if Congress waited for the babies to become teenagers and adults.[51] As *Redbook* put it, babies could be saved "for two dimes a day." In this view, unlike that espoused by MAP-South, mere nickels and dimes would allow the federal government to avoid riots and the potential costs of supporting adults incapable of functioning to their full capacity.

From today's perspective, WIC appears to be just one more social policy from the War on Poverty era that funnels public resources to presumably dependent women and children. Its continuing existence appears to support rather than contradict prevailing views that the cultural dependency and immorality of the poor results, as Moynihan put it years ago, in a self-perpetuating cycle of poverty. Viewed from a different historical vantage point, however, WIC emerged out of years of struggle by poor African American women, MAP-South organizers, and St. Jude professionals who undermined scholarly claims about "dysfunctional" and "pathological" black families that could be salvaged only by government intervention. This intervention and professional expertise mattered greatly in South Memphis. Engaging in this project of black self-determination allowed poor women simultaneously to save babies and to develop talents and skills. It profoundly impacted medical knowledge and practice. Interpretations of race as culture fueled new versions of racism in the post-civil-rights era. In the hands of organizations such as MAP-South, the idea of race as self-actualization opened possibilities for different kinds of relationships between poor African Americans, "experts," and the state, even in the face of repression.

Notes

1. Barbara McKinney, interview by author, June 14, 2007.

2. Ibid.; MAP-South 1967 Annual Report, 1–2, 4, Autry Parker, "Politics of Community Organization: MAP-South, Inc.," 12–13, unpublished paper, Memphis State University, 1975, both in MAP-South Papers, MAP-South Office, Memphis.

3. Donald Pinkel, e-mail to author, November 2, 2009; Donald Pinkel, interview by author, January 6, 2010.

4. McKinney, interview; Juanita Miller Thornton, interview by author, June 6, 2001.

5. Susan Levine, *School Lunch Politics: The Surprising History of America's Favorite Welfare Program* (Princeton: Princeton University Press, 2008), 45–49; U.S. Department of Agriculture, Food and Nutrition Service, "Legislative History: History of the Food Distribution Programs," http://www.fns.usda.gov/fdd/aboutfd/fd_history.pdf. President John F. Kennedy expanded the surplus commodities distribution program by executive order in January 1961.

6. Amy L. S. Staples, *The Birth of Development: How the World Bank, Food and Agriculture Organization, and World Health Organization Changed the World, 1945–1965* (Kent, Ohio: Kent State University Press, 2006), 76–81 (on FAO), 132–36 (on WHO), 101, 153–54 (on UNICEF), 105–21 (on FAO Freedom from Hunger Campaign).

7. Michael Harrington, *The Other America : Poverty in the United States* (New York: Macmillan, 1962)

8. Greta de Jong, "Staying in Place: Black Migration, the Civil Rights Movement, and the War on Poverty in the Rural South," *Journal of African American History* 90:4 (Fall 2005): 387–409.

9. U.S. Senate, Subcommittee on Employment, Manpower, and Poverty, to Lyndon Baines Johnson, April 27, 1967, Box 59, Folder: Hunger: Subcommittee on Employment, Manpower & Poverty 4/1967–5/1967, Robert F. Kennedy Papers, John F. Kennedy Presidential Library and Museum, Boston; Joseph A. Loftus, "Poverty Hearing Set in Mississippi," April 9, 1967, "Clark and Kennedy Visit the Poor of Mississippi," *New York Times*, April 12, 1967; "Johnson Is Asked to Rush Food Aid," *New York Times*, April 30, 1967; "Senators Ask Emergency 'Delta' Food," *Washington Post*, April 30, 1967.

10. U.S. Department of Health, Education, and Welfare, *Ten-State Nutrition Survey, 1968–1970* ((Atlanta: Centers for Disease Control, 1973), 1-1-1-5; Citizens' Board of In-

quiry into Hunger and Malnutrition in the United States, *Hunger, U.S.A.* (Boston: Beacon, 1968); Joseph A. Loftus, "Hunger of Millions Laid to Farm Policy," *New York Times*, April 23, 1968.

11. *CBS Reports: Hunger in America*, reported by Charles Kuralt, written by Peter Davis and Martin Carr, produced by Martin Carr; Orville Freeman to Frank Stanton, June 12, 1968, Box 1016 (1968, 1969 Hunger and Nutrition Committee), Hunger Research Folder, Papers of George S. McGovern, Seeley G. Mudd Manuscript Library, Princeton University, Princeton, New Jersey; Ben A. Franklin, "Freeman Asks Equal Time to Rebut C.B.S. Film," *New York Times*, May 28, 1968.

12. Citizens' Board of Inquiry, *Hunger, U.S.A.*, 15; John Dittmer, *Local People: The Struggle for Civil Rights in Mississippi* (Champaign: University of Illinois Press, 1995), 366–68.

13. John Dittmer, *The Good Doctors: The Medical Committee for Human Rights and the Struggle for Social Justice in Health Care* (New York: Bloomsbury, 2009), 231–36.

14. U.S. Senate, *Hunger and Malnutrition in the United States: Hearings before the Subcommittee on Employment, Manpower, and Poverty of the Committee on Labor and Public Welfare*, 90th Cong., 2nd sess., (Washington, D.C.: U.S. Government Printing Office, 1968); S. Res. 281, Report No. 1416, Calendar No. 1394, April 26, 1968, Box 1016, 1968, 1969 Hunger and Nutrition Committee, Folder: Senate Select Committee on Human and Nutrition Needs, S. Res. 281, McGovern Papers.

15. *White House Conference on Food, Nutrition, and Health: Final Report* (Washington, D.C.: U.S. Government Printing Office, 1970), 12; Jack Rosenthal, "Emergency Hunger Aid Given First Priority by Food Parley," *New York Times*, December 4, 1969; "Nixon's Conference on Hunger Called Sham by Lance 'Wine' Watson," *Tri-State Defender*, December 20, 1969.

16. Laurie Green, *Battling the Plantation Mentality: Memphis and the Black Freedom Struggle* (Chapel Hill: University of North Carolina Press, 2007), 224, 276–79.

17. McKinney, interview; MAP-South 1967 Annual Report, 9.

18. *Hearings before the U.S. Commission on Civil Rights: Hearings Held in Memphis, Tennessee, June 25–26, 1962* (Washington, D.C.: U.S. Government Printing Office, 1962), 4–5, III–V; Vanessa Northington Gamble, *Making a Place for Ourselves: The Black Hospital Movement, 1920–1945* (New York: Oxford University Press, 1995), 182–90.

19. *Hearings before the U.S. Commission on Civil Rights*, 7–82; *Report of the U.S. Commission on Civil Rights, 1963* (Washington, D.C.: U.S. Government Printing Office, 1963); Mitchell F. Rice and Woodrow Jones Jr., *Public Policy and the Black Hospital: From Slavery to Segregation to Integration* (Westport, Conn.: Greenwood, 1994), 93–95; P. Preston Reynolds, "Hospitals and Civil Rights, 1945–1963: The Case of *Simkins v. Moses H. Cone Memorial Hospital*," *Annals of Internal Medicine* 126:11 (June 1, 1997): 898–906.

20. *Hearings before the U.S. Commission on Civil Rights*, 16–17.

21. Ibid., 23.

22. MAP-South 1967 Annual Report.

23. "Constitution and Bylaws of Memphis Area Project-South, Inc., Adopted December 1, 1965," MAP-South Papers.

24. Minutes of the MAP-South Citizens' Association Meeting, April 20, 1967, MAP-South Papers; Parker, "Politics of Community Organization."

25. Parker, "Politics of Community Organization."

26. Washington Butler Jr., e-mail to author, December 2, 2009; "Poverty Committee Split over Top Job Issue," *Memphis Press-Scimitar*, March 31, 1966, "Nashvillian Gets 'Poverty' Job here," *Memphis Press-Scimitar*, August 19, 1966; William J. Miles, "Anti-Poverty Unit Tangled on Question Of Director," *Memphis Commercial Appeal*, March 31, 1966; William J. Miles, "Tempers Flare in Floor Fight of Poverty Group," *Memphis Commercial Appeal*, May 19, 1966; William J. Miles, "Negro to Head Poverty Panel," *Memphis Commercial Appeal*, July 23, 1966; Minutes of the MAP-South Citizens' Association Meeting, April 20, 1967.

27. Catherine Howell, telephone interview by author, July 28, 2010; McKinney, interview; Minutes of the MAP-South Citizens' Association Meeting, April 20, 1967; "Program Shutdown Deprives Families of Deedy [sic] Food," *Tri-State Defender*, July 7, 1969.

28. MAP-South 1967 Annual Report; Joseph Mullins, interview by author, July 17, 2009; Eloise Silmon Brown, interview by author, July 17, 2009; "North Memphis Action Project Sets High Goals," *Tri-State Defender*, November 29, 1969.

29. MAP-South 1967 Annual Report; "Report by WOPC Is Attacked," *Memphis Press-Scimitar*, June 11, 1968.

30. Daniel Patrick Moynihan, *The Negro Family: The Case for National Action* (Washington, D.C.: U.S. Department of Labor, Office of Policy Planning and Research, 1965), available online at http://www.blackpast.org/?q=primary/moynihan-report-1965.

31. MAP-South 1967 Annual Report; MAP-South 1968 Annual Report, MAP-South Papers.

32. McKinney, interview.

33. Parker, "Politics of Community Organization"; Powell Lindsay, "U.S. Wants Doctors Told Where to Send Patients," *Memphis Press-Scimitar*, May 5, 1966; MAP-South 1968 Annual Report.

34. MAP-South 1968 Annual Report, 16.

35. Pinkel, interview; S. A. Unger, "A Little Fire in the Belly," *Buffalo Physician* 36:1 (Summer 2001): 6–7.

36. McKinney, interview; MAP-South 1968 Annual Report, 15; St. Jude/MAP-South Nutrition and Health Program, Request for Renewal of Contract B3B-5429, submitted to U.S. Office of Economic Opportunity, June 22, 1973, MAP-South Profile, MAP-South Office, 1:3; James Lawson, telephone interview by author, July 10, 2007.

37. Virginia M. Hardman, "How to Save Babies for Two Dimes a Day," *Redbook*, April 1973, 68ff; Pinkel, interview.

38. MAP-South 1968 Annual Report, 15; Memorandum of Understanding between St. Jude Children's Research Hospital, MAP-South, Memphis/Shelby County Health Department, and the Tennessee Department of Agriculture, November 21, 1968–December 2, 1968, in MAP-South Profile, vol. 1; Hardman, "How to Save Babies"; Request for Renewal of Contract B3B-5429, 6.

39. Paul Zee, Thomas Walters, and Charles Mitchell, "Nutrition and Poverty in Preschool Children: A Nutritional Survey of Preschool Children from Impoverished Black Families, Memphis," *Journal of the American Medical Association* 213:5 (August 3, 1970): 739–41; Paulus Zee, "St. Jude/MAP-South Nutrition and Health Program, Summary and Evaluation," [ca. 1971] MAP-South Profile; Request for Renewal of Contract B3B-5429.

40. Lennie Lott, interview by author, June 15, 2007, July 15, 2009.

41. Zee, "St. Jude/MAP-South Nutrition and Health Program Summary and Evaluation," iii; Hardman, "How to Save Babies," 68; McKinney, interview.

42. Zee, Walters, and Mitchell, "Nutrition and Poverty," 741–42; St. Jude 1971 Annual Report, 18, in possession of the author.

43. "After Tour of Poverty Areas, Women Try to Solve Problems," *Tri-State Defender*, June 21, 1969; Lawson, interview by author; Kimberly K. Little, *You Must Be from the North: Southern White Women in the Memphis Civil Rights Movement* (Jackson: University Press of Mississippi, 2009), 106–7.

44. Unger, "Little Fire," 7.

45. Lawson, interview by author; James Lawson, interview by Joan Beifuss and David Yellen, September 23, 1969, Sanitation Strike Archival Project, Special Collections, McWherter Library, University of Memphis.

46. Charles A. Brown, "Anti-Poverty Group Demands Hearing for Two Controversial Workers," *Memphis Press-Scimitar*, August 11, 1967; Lawson, interview by Beifuss and Yellen; Lawson, interview by author.

47. Rosenthal, "Emergency Hunger Aid"; "Nixon's Conference on Hunger Called Sham."

48. "WOPC Is Dead," *Memphis Citizen*, June 24, 1970; Richard Lentz, "Sit-In at Defunct WOPC Ends in Arrest of 6," *Memphis Commercial Appeal*, October 31, 1970.

49. Mullins, interview.

50. My analysis of the WIC hearings is based on U.S. Senate, *Maternal, Fetal, and Infant Nutrition: Hearings before the Select Committee on Nutrition and Human Needs of the U.S. Senate* (Washington, D.C.: U.S. Government Printing Office, 1973), 2, 21, 58–58; *Prescription: Food*, directed by Craig Leake, WMC-TV News, ca. 1970.

51. Charles Percy in U.S. Senate, *Maternal, Fetal, and Infant Nutrition*, 63.

CHRISTINA GREENE

"Someday . . . the Colored and White Will Stand Together"

The War on Poverty, Black Power Politics, and Southern Women's Interracial Alliances

Few federal programs in the past four decades have been the target of as much vitriol and distortion as President Lyndon Baines Johnson's War on Poverty. Critics on the right deride it as a glaring example of federal waste, fraud, and misguided handouts to the undeserving poor. Some on the left complain about the failure to eradicate poverty, while feminists castigate its focus on angry young men. Convinced that taxpayer money was fomenting social unrest, both Republicans and Democrats realized that the antipoverty program's mobilization of the poor threatened powerful political machines and entrenched economic interests. In such southern locales as Atlanta, Memphis, and Sumter County, Alabama, white officials co-opted War on Poverty programs and refused to allow meaningful black participation, while in Las Vegas, Republican political operatives destroyed one of the most successful and remarkable antipoverty programs created and run by poor black women.

Scholarly attention similarly has been both overly broad and excessively harsh in its assessment of Great Society programs. Utilizing a national perspective or focusing largely on northern cities, scholars generally and to some extent correctly dismiss the federal antipoverty initiative as a mere skirmish rather than all-out war. Some scholars castigate southern officials for their usual obstructionist hostility to federal intervention. Others dismiss as naive or arrogant what they see as top-down social engineering.[1]

Forty-five years later, however, the program deserves another look. While most of these critiques contain some kernel of truth, an examination of local efforts, especially those of southern neighborhood women in Durham, North Carolina, and elsewhere, yields some surprising discoveries. Although historians have examined interracial alliances among southerners, few have thought to look for such efforts in low-income southern neighborhoods where racial segregation as well as racial antagonism seemingly prevailed.

The War on Poverty certainly eliminated neither poverty nor racism. But far from simply a failure or cynical ploy, the federal initiative—most notably the community action agencies (CAAs)—and its mandate for "maximum feasible participation" of the poor fostered a climate for creative community projects and interracial alliances among women in low-income neighborhoods. That the women failed to create the kind of multiracial poor people's movement that some organizers had envisioned makes their efforts no less remarkable. Moreover, their achievements, limited though they were, challenge interpretations of community organizing and racial politics in the 1960s and 1970s in at least three important ways. First, two groups seemingly among the least likely to reach across the racial divide—low-income southern whites and blacks—did so at a time when Black Power politics and a virulent white backlash supposedly had eroded the possibility for such a coalition. Second, women's interracial cooperation occurred in low-income neighborhoods, long considered sites of racial separation or racial hostility, especially after blacks who were displaced by urban renewal (or "Negro removal," as skeptics termed it) "intruded" into formerly all-white areas. Finally, the women's efforts complicate the gendered debate about service provision and antipoverty programs that presumably diverted mostly female recipients from engaging in more overtly political activities. This debate characterized not only Durham's antipoverty programs but also national groups, including the National Welfare Rights Organization and Students for a Democratic Society's Economic Recovery and Action Project.

Male radicals in particular tended either to ignore women's activities, especially those of poor women, or to view them as outside the realm of political activism. But as political theorist Martha Ackelsberg has observed, "Unless we begin to change our conceptual framework to incorporate a broader conception of politics, and of who can and does participate in it, much of the radical potential of actions that are already taking place will be lost—even to those who participate in them." Indeed, official efforts to thwart women's antipoverty activism not only in the South but across the country suggest that women's subsistence politics, which frequently displaced street demonstrations as the dominant form of black protest, constituted "political" activity, whether activists then or scholars since have recognized it as such.[2]

Women's local antipoverty activism also pushes us to rethink the links among civil rights protest, the War on Poverty, and Black Power.[3] The late 1960s have frequently been characterized by a shift from the nonviolent integrationist politics of the civil rights movement to a nationalist and even separatist focus on black institution building fueled by militant Black Power politics. Black Power was an elusive and vague slogan that spanned the ideological spectrum from black capitalism to armed revolution. Although most whites equated Black Power with racial separatism and antiwhite violence, groups such as the Black Panther Party saw no contradiction in working with supportive white allies. However, few such relationships have been presumed to exist among poor blacks and whites in the South. Nor have most scholarly interpretations of Black Power moved beyond the more visible hypermasculinized "gun-barrel" politics of radical men to include women's efforts, particularly those outside self-defined Black Power organizations.[4] But in a particularly striking collaboration, one of Durham's most respected black community activists who publicly supported the city's Malcolm X Liberation University and even boasted about her expertise in making Molotov cocktails joined forces with a local Ku Klux Klan leader. Even more surprising, this unlikely friendship between an impoverished black woman and a low-income white man developed over the volatile issue of school desegregation, suggesting the power of subsistence politics to transcend not only race but gender.

During the 1960s, low-income black and white women in Durham reached across the racial divide to forge a precarious yet impressive biracial neighborhood coalition. The alliance was the outgrowth of several years of organizing among poor blacks and whites by the city's antipoverty agency, Operation Breakthrough (OBT) which was part of a statewide but privately funded antipoverty initiative started in 1963.[5] Within a few years, OBT had spurred the formation of two low-income neighborhood federations, the all-black United Organizations for Community Improvement, created in 1966, and ACT, a federation of poor whites started in 1968 and modeled on United Organizations. Although neither was envisioned as a women's organization, low-income women quickly emerged as the backbone of both groups, especially United Organizations, which was about 80 percent female.

Some of the women had honed their racial and class politics in the labor and civil rights movements. Joyce Thorpe participated briefly in the civil rights movement before her 1965 armed standoff with a sheriff in McDougald Terrace, Durham's black public housing project, sparked the formation of United Organizations, and Bascie Hicks, a white former textile worker and union member, was a key figure in both ACT and Durham's low-income interracial alliance. However, most women responded to the War on Poverty because of its focus on daily survival issues with which they had long struggled.[6]

No ideological commitment to building "an interracial movement of the poor" propelled this unlikely sisterhood. Rather, class-based "motherist" politics led some women to cooperate on a range of fronts, from opening an integrated community-based health clinic to challenging the Durham school board's decision to close a racially integrated school. Despite their mutual suspicions, black and white women found common ground rooted in similar class-inflected conceptions of motherhood, neighborhood, citizenship rights, and a new relationship to the state. Especially for white women, the initial experience of working jointly with black women sometimes opened the door to other cooperative ventures. The ability of poor women to sustain even some degree of collaboration across the color line suggests that the basis for a transformed "beloved community," based not simply on shared moral or religious values but on similar experiences of economic exploitation, was more than a faded dream of naive activists. The interracial poor people's movement for which many activists, including Martin Luther King Jr., had hoped might not have succeeded, yet numerous instances of interracial cooperation, mostly among low-income neighborhood women, emerged.[7]

Indeed, women in United Organizations, many of whom leaned toward Black Power politics, and white low-income neighborhood women in ACT, many of whom still harbored vestiges of white supremacist ideology, breached the racial chasm to establish a limited partnership. Of course, the divisions among low-income black and white women, both real and imagined, often were stronger than the mutual interests that united them, and white women's embrace of racialized notions of protest and motherhood also fostered racial discord. In effect, racial cooperation operated alongside racial antagonism, each counteracting the other in a dialectical tension in which the outcome was often unpredictable.

From its inception, OBT deliberately targeted poor white areas as well as black neighborhoods and hired both white and black staff.[8] Many low-income whites, however, shunned the antipoverty program, seeing it as "just for the colored." They often were "resentful and bitter" toward blacks, who were perceived as better able to demand attention from white authorities.[9] The formation in 1966 of the all-black United Organizations, with its militant confrontations and Black Power rhetoric, did little to quell poor white people's trepidations. Sensitive to white prejudices but hoping to overcome such attitudes, organizers did not attempt to bring blacks and whites together, and white organizers tended to work in white communities. Thus, the program was biracial but not racially integrated.

White racial antipathy toward OBT contained a certain irony, however. Low-income blacks also harbored suspicions regarding the organization, especially its control by local officials. This wariness prompted the push to create the independent United Organizations, and by 1968, it dominated the freedom movement in Durham, with twenty-three councils and one thousand members, most of them female.

African American women were included in both OBT and United Organizations from their inception in part because of Howard Fuller, an astute young black community organizer. Fuller recruited low-income black women such as Ann Atwater, soon heralded as a veritable expert on public housing and welfare regulations, and Pat Rogers, who became a nationally recognized tenants' rights organizer. Fuller refused to run one of OBT's first community action workshops unless low-income black women were included. As Thorpe recalled, "They were encouraging everybody to get involved, not just the affluent, but the nobodies like me." By hiring local women as organizers, both OBT and United Organizations attracted other "strong" neighborhood women, "all of them with a militant bent." Even male organizers inadvertently used informal female spaces to their advantage, stitching together networks of women by organizing in black beauty parlors and even illegal neighborhood drink houses run by African American women. As one male organizer noted, "The women who ran the liquor houses had a great deal of influence on the neighbors and could act as informal leaders."[10]

By the end of the 1960s, poor black women were shaping both the agenda and direction of Durham's protest movement. One of the most impressive examples of black women's newfound collective strength was a seven-month boycott of white downtown merchants in 1968–69. The Black Power–initiated boycott represented the culmination of several years of local antipoverty campaigns among low-income blacks. Between 1965 and 1968, African American women stood at the center of a series of seemingly spontaneous protests throughout the city: a strike by cafeteria workers that shut down schools across the city; a labor union drive among housekeepers and janitors at Duke University; a sit-down demonstration and rent strike by public housing tenants; and an armed show-down between the county sheriff and Thorpe when sheriff's officers attempted to evict her from public housing that led to a landmark tenants'-rights ruling by the U.S. Supreme Court.[11]

Contentious city council meetings became almost the norm as crowds of angry blacks, mostly low-income and overwhelmingly female, demanded attention to a range of problems from substandard housing and police brutality to segregated schools and discriminatory employment and welfare policies. One July 1967 city council meeting was so heated that Viola Holman, a twenty-one-year-old for-mer school cafeteria worker and organizer for United Organizations, warned, "Durham will be another Vietnam." The following day, the *Durham Morning Herald* added to the mounting tension by proclaiming in an eight-column, front-page headline, "Another Newark Threatened Here," referring to the racial violence that had wracked that New Jersey city just days earlier.[12]

These events accentuated white failure to contain black demands, which of-ficials had hoped to do primarily through OBT. But such efforts backfired, and many of the racial conflicts in the mid- to late 1960s resulted directly from OBT and United Organizations community organizing projects, which harnessed both government resources and private foundation funds to challenge the eco-nomic and political status quo.

Around the same time, white organizers, some of whom worked with OBT, decided to focus more specifically on organizing poor whites into neighbor-hood councils. In 1968, Harry Boyte and Dick Landeman, two young, radical white men who had been involved in the southern civil rights movement, re-ceived an OEO grant through OBT for a white community organizing project, Experiment in Parallel Organization, out of which emerged an umbrella group, ACT. Some organizers even envisioned the ultimate emergence of a biracial poor people's movement.[13]

Building interracial alliances, however, was not an easy task. Affluent as well as low-income whites harbored deep-seated racial prejudices, and white su-premacist organizations had often found fertile ground in low-income white neighborhoods, such as the Edgemont section of Durham, a former mill hill. By the mid-1960s, the KKK was resurgent across North Carolina. Nearly eight thousand whites flocked to a 1965 Klan rally at a Durham stadium, where im-perial wizard Robert S. Shelton of Tuscaloosa, Alabama, lambasted President

Johnson for announcing the arrest of three men in connection with the recent Alabama murder of Viola Liuzzo, a white Detroit housewife and civil rights activist.[14]

White racial animosity, however, does not tell the entire story, and the racism of poor whites was not as impermeable as it seemed. Acutely aware of their grinding poverty and paralyzed by political powerlessness and economic insecurity, low-income whites looked across the racial divide at the events of the 1960s with both fear and admiration. "One thing about the blacks, they'll stick together and get what they want," a white Durham mill worker observed. "Whites will never do that. . . . [W]hite kids can be starving, [but] it don't make no difference to the big shots." Despite their resentment, Durham whites modeled their community organizing campaigns after those of blacks. As Hicks explained, "The colored people already had something to stand up for them. . . . But whether our people want to admit it or not, we're taking a lesson from [Operation] Breakthrough."[15]

The formation of Experiment in Parallel Organization and ACT reflected broader shifts in the civil rights movement, including the emergence of Black Power politics. By the mid-1960s, civil rights leaders both nationally and locally began to think more seriously about the need for whites to organize in white areas rather than continuing to work in black communities. In Durham, organizers felt that to ally with blacks, poor whites needed to develop a stronger sense of community. Between 1967 and 1971, ACT organized twenty-one neighborhood councils of low-income whites as well as a new welfare rights group. Just as United Organizations had attracted overwhelming numbers of poor black women, ACT, too, relied on the informal networks of local white women. The largely male and middle-class ACT leadership, which initially targeted unemployed, marginal men, would inadvertently come into contact with and use these female networks. Local women simply came to meetings and did the work.[16]

Hicks was one of the first neighborhood women to respond to ACT's organizing efforts in Edgemont, a historically poor white section that began to integrate in the early 1960s.[17] Hicks had grown up in a southern textile mill family and began working at the mill at age nineteen, during World War II. There she met her future husband, Doug Hicks, and both of them joined the Textile Workers Union of America, a CIO union. Like many low-income southern whites, Bascie Hicks lived in a neighborhood adjacent to a black area and included blacks among her friends. Although she did not consider herself a racist, Hicks was not unaffected by white supremacy. When a black man came into the mill looking for a job, the "boss man told the man he could not hire him because he was black," even though the war had caused a labor shortage. Hicks later wondered "why I didn't speak out for the black man." Yet speaking out against racial segregation, especially a white woman defending a black man's right to integrate white work space, might well have cost Hicks her job—or worse.[18]

Hicks provided a crucial link between ACT organizers and neighborhood residents because she was widely respected among both groups. One ACT founder described Hicks as "a very special person. . . . just personally very generous. . . . She was a woman in the neighborhood that helped out all the other neighborhood kids; [she] was just there." Another ACT organizer described her as "both leader and strategist, someone who contradicted the whole notion that people who understood organizing were cut off from the community."[19]

Working-class and low-income whites initially were suspicious of the mostly middle-class, male organizers from ACT, and some residents thought the organizers were spies from the welfare department. The local KKK even shadowed Boyte when he first started canvassing, but Hicks reassured the neighbors that he could be trusted. Hicks soon joined the ACT staff and began writing for the ACT newspaper, *The Action*. Her column, "People Power vs. Money Power," addressed a wide range of issues from brown lung disease and racial discrimination to the Vietnam War, which she opposed because "working people are the hardest hit." Despite her radical politics, Hicks refused to relinquish the cultural symbols that increasingly came to be associated with conservative whites—God, country, and law and order: "All my life I have been a 'God-fearing, law abiding' tax paying citizen of the United States," she declared proudly.[20]

Like Hicks, Inez Gooch, an African American woman living in Edgemont, commanded respect within her neighborhood. The mother of twelve, Gooch was a full-time health aide. In 1967, she assumed the presidency of the Edgemont Council, one of the most vocal and militant groups in United Organizations. The previous year, Edgemont Council members had pushed the boundaries of southern civility by picketing the home of slumlord Abe Greenberg. "Your Neighbor Is a Slumlord," read one sign, while another directed a pointed message to the landlord's wife: "Mrs. Greenberg, My Children Sleep with Rats."[21] Poor black women from Edgemont and other areas of the city soon were engaging in repeated and continuous public confrontations with city officials. Despite the Edgemont Council's militant embrace of Black Power politics, Gooch also believed that working cooperatively with poor whites could benefit neighborhood blacks. In this way, black separatism and the possibility for interracial alliances operated side by side.

Lacking formal authority but commanding great respect within their neighborhoods, Hicks and Gooch were what anthropologist Karen Sacks would call "centerwomen" or what sociologist Belinda Robnett would describe as "indigenous bridge leaders."[22] Such women were instrumental in mobilizing women's friendship and kinship networks, which formed the foundation for both United Organizations and ACT. Even leisure settings such as beauty shops, bridge clubs, and front stoops offered possibilities for organizing local women. Thorpe, who had graduated from Durham's DeShazor Beauty School in 1959, recalled that African American "women would go in the beauty parlor and talk about" local protest activities.[23]

There was nothing particularly magical or mysterious about women's predominance in community organizing efforts. As veteran civil rights organizer Ella Baker understood, personal relationships were the building blocks of successful organizing campaigns, and women's social roles, deeply embedded in family and neighborhood networks, made it easier for women to persuade other residents to join collective actions. Among low-income women, these networks were especially important since they facilitated daily survival. Remarked North Carolina native and Duke student Tami Hultman, who canvassed Edgemont with Hicks, "Bascie knew a lot of people, so we had that advantage." Thus, women's personal relationships and neighborhood bonds became pivotal assets in cementing community support for struggles against exploitative political and economic arrangements.[24]

Women quickly emerged as the backbone of both ACT and United Organizations neighborhood councils. The councils, in turn, facilitated more active public roles for low-income women, many of whom assumed leadership positions. Top decision-making positions, especially in ACT, remained in male hands, however. ACT and United Organizations nevertheless gave poor women a sense of self-confidence that, according to ACT member Deborah Cook, "we thought we'd never have." Both black and white women noted the humiliation they had endured as a result of their poverty. Atwater, one of United Organization's most effective black community organizers, recalled attending parent-teacher association meetings, but "me being low-income . . . they wouldn't pay me no nevermind. They counted me as a nobody." Black and white women who had previously thought of themselves as "nobodies" soon began speaking out at public meetings and confronting city officials. Others mastered the bureaucratic maze of welfare and public housing regulations and then used their newfound expertise to organize rent strikes and establish a welfare rights group.[25] Low-income women, black as well as white, thus claimed public spaces that had previously been marked as white, male, and affluent.

Although blacks and whites were organized separately in United Organizations and ACT, respectively, a number of community organizers hoped that these efforts would culminate in a biracial poor people's movement that would address issues of economic exploitation. As Hicks predicted, "Someday—I don't know when—when everybody sees there's something in it for him, I think the colored and white will stand together." But Durham's campaign was hindered by numerous obstacles, including the racial fears of poor whites and deliberate attempts by white officials to sow distrust among low-income residents of both races. For example, when authorities responded to demands from white public housing tenants for lighting but ignored similar complaints from black tenants a year later, African Americans were furious at the unequal treatment. Although the issue was a small one, such disparate responses from white officials fanned flames of distrust between the races. According to one white woman organizer, "They just didn't want us to get together."[26]

Despite these difficulties, some of ACT's most impressive accomplishments were interracial efforts established and/or sustained by low-income women in Edgemont. Edgemont had been on a downward spiral since the Great Depression and by World War II had become "one of the most blighted white areas in Durham." Thirty-five years later, a local journalist offered a more colorful description, perhaps alluding to its shifting racial composition: "The mean part of town: fatback and hominy grits. A bootlegger province. It was a neighborhood one avoided on the Sunday drive." By then, Edgemont was known as a "transition neighborhood," meaning that black newcomers displaced by urban renewal had prompted white flight. By 1968, 60 percent of the community's five thousand residents were African American. One-third were welfare recipients; another third claimed incomes of less than three thousand dollars per year. Eighty percent lacked high school diplomas, and 60 percent had never finished grade school. Almost 45 percent of the houses in Edgemont were "deteriorated" or "dilapidated."[27]

But racism—most notably, white fears of declining social status through association with or proximity to blacks—was not the only factor pushing whites out. Economic considerations, only partly shaped by white racial anxieties, also accounted for Edgemont's shifting racial composition. As black families moved in, unscrupulous landlords often raised rents, inducing poor whites to find less expensive housing elsewhere. Poor blacks had fewer options and were forced to pay the exorbitant prices. In fact, the first black newcomers reported little or no trouble from white residents, who were far more concerned with housing-code violations than with the color of their new neighbors' skin.

Several neighborhood characteristics may have helped to diminish racial tensions, at least to some extent. Despite the arrival of blacks in Edgemont, most blocks remained racially segregated. The fact that many Edgemont residents were renters rather than homeowners might have made them slightly more amendable to cross-racial alliances because they had less to lose. Cook recalled that whites in this section of Durham were far more receptive to interracial organizing than were the slightly more affluent former mill workers in West Durham, where people "were more secure than what our East End bunch was, so, see, that made a lot of difference. [They] were homeowners, mostly retired folk." People in the East End, by contrast, had "more poor housing, less jobs, more welfare." Renters also were more transient, however, providing a less stable community base.[28]

As Cook's comments suggest, low-income whites had complex and fluid racial attitudes. For example, whites refused to participate in the Edgemont Community Center after blacks started attending, even requesting white-only programs. However, closer proximity to blacks could also generate greater tolerance and a lessening of racial animosity. According to one contemporary observer, "Whites continue their verbal abuse of the blacks, but on an individual level their prejudices fall away to some degree." Hence, the seeds of both racial division and racial tolerance were present in these transition neighborhoods.[29]

One of the most successful interracial efforts in Durham, as in many other poor communities during that era, was the Edgemont Community Health Clinic, which offered free medical services to residents on a walk-in basis. The clinic was a black-initiated project that grew out of a fall 1968 series of community health workshops organized by Gooch. Gooch became president of the clinic board and remained influential in its operation for many years. The clinic was run by volunteers, medical students as well as neighborhood residents who cleaned and worked as receptionists and health aides. Most important, it was a community-controlled project. According to Gooch, "People feel a part of the clinic—it's ours, not something doctors plopped down on us." In a reversal of the patron-client relationship that characterized most conventional service providers and that male community organizers feared would diminish poor people's potential to organize politically, Gooch declared proudly, "The doctors are working for us." When asked who ran the clinic, she glanced around the crowded waiting room and responded with a smile and a wave of her hand, "We all!" Thus, service provision, particularly if it was community-based and community-controlled, as in the case of the clinic, did not create dependency, as ACT leaders had feared. It also did not thwart political protest. For many poor mothers, organizing on behalf of health care was an expressly political act.[30]

When ACT was formed, Gooch asked several doctors to approach the new organization about the idea of white participation in the clinic. Hicks agreed to join the clinic board and soon became treasurer. According to Gooch, Hicks's participation "eased people's suspicions and whites got confidence that they would get good care." Eileen Newcomb, a white woman who worked with ACT, offered similar sentiments: "It's wonderful. Everything is nice and friendly. . . . About everybody in the community uses it."[31]

Despite the facility's popularity among both blacks and whites, two fires hours apart destroyed the clinic in June 1969, shortly after it opened. Many suspected that the fires were arson, perhaps the work of those who opposed the interracial effort. But residents were determined to reopen the clinic, suggesting that at least among some residents, the desire and need for health care may have trumped both white supremacy and black separatism. As Gooch explained, "We didn't want the neighborhood to think we let them down." By the following year, the clinic had relocated to an abandoned beauty parlor in East Durham, expanded its hours to two nights a week, and was serving between fifty and one hundred people each week.[32]

Most of ACT's male leaders, although not overtly critical of the clinic, failed fully to appreciate the political potential of service-based projects. ACT leaders organized residents to push for neighborhood improvements such as traffic lights or paved streets, seeing these small victories primarily as vehicles toward greater community cohesion. However, male leaders dismissed service provision as apolitical, ignoring the fact that women's biracial service projects cemented community bonds that could be and were used for other more overtly political campaigns. Instead, ACT leaders favored mass confrontations with white officials "to clarify relations of power." According to this line of argument, only then would the rich "emerge as the real 'enemy' and blacks would be seen more and more as allies."[33]

Even a sympathetic local journalist-activist who acknowledged that essential services such as neighborhood-run day centers and health clinics helped residents form collective identities, underestimated the political possibilities offered by service provision, claiming that "unless their sense of identity is reinforced through political education they cannot move on to press for political and social change." Echoing ACT's call for mass protest, she insisted that "the most essential education comes only through political conflict. Poor and working class whites must now begin to confront the power of the city."[34]

On one level, ACT had good reasons to oppose projects that provided services to the poor, which had become a widespread means through which local officials across the country co-opted the War on Poverty. Yet women did not make these kinds of distinctions between protest politics and securing needed services. Organizing to get and sustain quality services for their families taught women about structures of government and of power. And the clinic did more than provide much-needed health care for impoverished blacks and whites. It also created a bridge between two communities that often viewed each other with fear and suspicion. In Hicks's words, "Both races use the clinic about equally. And I think working together on the clinic has meant a difference in other areas as well; it's taught people to get along better." Another resident claimed, "I don't know what the community did without it, and it's brought us together as a community on other issues too."[35]

Cook suggested that the community-controlled clinic politicized local residents, especially poor whites, by introducing the notion of health care as a right. It also taught Edgemont's inhabitants that when poor people worked in concert, they could make a difference. One white clinic supporter, Daphne Lassiter, a mother of five and wife of a mill worker, insisted, "He's got to back down sometime, the big man up there, if we stick together long enough. One individual isn't gonna change anything [but] with a group, you can change it." The male leaders of ACT who claimed that providing services diverted energy from collective action and political mobilization missed the point.[36] The success of the clinic offered tangible evidence of poor blacks' and whites' ability to find common ground, even at the height of Black Power politics and the white backlash.

Indeed, the success of the Edgemont Clinic opened the door for other interracial efforts among the poor. A group of black and white neighborhood women who had played key roles in the Edgemont Clinic spearheaded a biracial campaign to rid their neighborhood of drugs. In 1970, a racially integrated coalition made up of ACT, United Organizations, and members of the Health and Hospital Workers Union at Duke University Hospital protested the hospital's rejection of a plan that would have provided health benefits to thirty-eight thousand employees. Edgemont whites at times engaged in biracial protests despite some whites' concerns that public demonstrations constituted "civil rights" (that is, black) activities. After a teenager was shot outside the Edgemont Community Center in the spring of 1970, both black and white residents were outraged by media coverage that depicted their community as violence-ridden. Bascie's daughter, Theresa Hicks, who was active with an ACT teen group that had participated in biracial projects, expressed the community's outrage: "The stories in the paper were used to make Edgemont look bad. This often happens to low-income and working class communities and we don't like it." Black and white women from the Edgemont Clinic helped organize two neighborhood meetings, called a press conference, and finally, to guarantee that the white newspapers covered their protests, accompanied a larger group of black and white residents to a city council meeting.[37]

One of the most stunning interracial campaigns emerged in response to the Durham school board's decision to close the recently integrated Edgemont Elementary School. The board's announcement came in June 1970, as the city awaited a federal court decision on a lawsuit filed by the National Association for the Advancement of Colored People. As most of Durham's white residents mounted a last-ditch effort to resist school desegregation and middle-class whites fled to the suburbs, low-income white and black parents in Edgemont fought to save a racially integrated school that was 60 percent African American. According to both black and white parents, racial tensions were minimal in the school. Defying the stereotypes of white working-class opposition to school integration that would soon dominate national headlines, white mothers collaborated with black women, collecting more than 350 signatures opposing the school's closure in just a single afternoon.[38]

A biracial delegation made plans to go to the school board "and raise cain," but the school superintendent convinced them to wait for the desegregation decision. Weeks later, a federal judge upheld the board's decision to close the school. "We turned the petition in to the district judge, but he didn't say heck to us," complained Christine Richardson, a white mother with two boys at the Edgemont school. Although official explanations for the school closing varied, many local residents believed it resulted from Edgemont parents' demands for a voice in school decisions.[39] More striking than their defeat, however, was the fact that low-income southern whites had found common cause with their black counterparts in connection with the explosive and racially divisive issue of school desegregation. Such struggles, even those that failed, do not fit the standard narrative of white working-class racism and opposition to school desegregation. Despite their inability to keep Edgemont School open, the women's activism suggests that neighborhoods not only were sites of bitter racial conflict but also could become arenas for interracial cooperation.

By the late 1970s, pernicious city policies together with tensions between providers and patients led to the demise of the Edgemont Clinic. Durham officials had allowed Edgemont to deteriorate, predicting that the area would eventually be condemned and razed. New zoning laws allowed industry to intrude into the community, forcing out both black and white residents. Most clinic patients soon came from the East End, a black working-class section of the city that was well organized. With community involvement dwindling, the clinic staff voted to close the facility, and it reopened in 1979 in the predominantly black neighborhood as the East End Health Clinic. In the end, decisions made by city authorities with little regard for neighborhood needs undermined one of the most successful interracial experiments Durham had witnessed.[40]

It is difficult not to see the school and clinic closings, along with the abandonment of Edgemont, as part of an escalating move by white power brokers to thwart local community organizing campaigns. In Durham, as elsewhere, War on Poverty programs, particularly CAAS, had become convenient targets. Although attempts to undermine antipoverty programs often were bipartisan, after Republican president Richard Nixon's election in 1968, conservative Republicans, including Nixon-appointed OEO head Donald Rumsfeld and his assistant, Richard Cheney, led an all-out assault on the antipoverty programs, especially those they associated with black grassroots insurgency.[41] And in North Carolina, Nixon's "southern strategy" breathed new life into Tar Heel Republicans, who sensed a political opportunity in attacking War on Poverty programs and black community organizing. North Carolina Republican Party chair James Holhouser asked the Nixon administration to withhold an OEO grant for a United Organizations cooperative, demanding an investigation of "militants" and "troublemakers." As one observer wryly noted, "One million dollars in the hands of poor blacks! This is not the traditional mode of economic development in Durham." Nor were white officials reassured by Pat Rogers's Black Power–inflected instructions to Durham blacks to bypass white stores and patronize black-owned cooperatives—including the one Nixon appointees were attempting to destroy. According to Rogers, rather than "teaching hatred," her actions were "teaching unity."[42]

Cutting program funds and launching often-baseless investigations into the finances of local antipoverty programs was a favored and effective tactic of War on Poverty opponents, who mounted attacks under both the Johnson and Nixon administrations. Durham's white officials publicly castigated key black leaders, especially the more radical ones. Even if the allegations were eventually proven false, they prompted widespread coverage in local white media and helped to erode public confidence in the poverty program, particularly among whites, who rarely distinguished between the biracial OBT and the all-black United Organizations. The conservative *Durham Sun* captured the feelings of many local whites when it editorialized, "Regardless of whether or not any Federal law, civil service regulation or . . . rules has or has not been broken, . . . enough smoke has curled up . . . to lead many to the suspicion that there is a spark or a smoldering ember somewhere in the woodpile."[43] Local press coverage became so incendiary that South Carolina segregationist Strom Thurmond and Louisiana Republican John Rarick quoted the *Durham Morning Herald* on the House and Senate floors as evidence of federal programs gone awry. The legislators denounced the OEO for supporting "Marxism," "campus riots," and "insurrection" in North Carolina. Even the Ford Foundation, which Durham activists approached for help, found its hands tied by restrictive new federal guidelines. ACT also bore the brunt of interference from OBT and was the target of charges of financial mismanagement. These attacks, along with internal class and gender tensions, led to the organization's demise by the 1970s.[44]

As the Edgemont School closing and clinic experience suggest, most interracial collaboration among low-income Durham residents centered on issues that have traditionally involved women, especially mothers. Such concerns could generate racial conflict as easily as racial cooperation. Whites did not easily or readily abandon their allegiance to the "southern way of life." But under the right circumstances, women's shared experiences of poverty and the common concerns of motherhood—the convergence of gender and class—enabled women to transcend racial divisions, at least to some extent.

At the same time, racialized conceptions of motherhood, particularly among white women, also hindered the maintenance of interracial alliances. For example, both black and white women participated in the Christmas House, which enabled poor parents to shop without cash for gifts for their children. But the effort succeeded precisely because the women participated through racially separate organizations. ACT member Shirley Sherron made explicit the limits of interracialism: "This is for the people of Edgemont, whites and blacks, but separated by the community organization groups. ACT is working with whites and United Organizations . . . is working with blacks."[45] White mothers remained unwilling to share their vulnerability and destitution—from which whiteness could not protect them—in racially mixed company.

ACT's success, however limited, raises important questions about the complexities of racism among low-income whites and demonstrates the importance of examining local antipoverty movements. ACT generated biracial cooperation on specific, well-defined, short-term issues; however, despite its decision in the spring of 1970 to deal more directly with white supremacy, the organization was unable to bring to fruition its broader goal of establishing a biracial poor people's movement.[46] Still, that groups typically perceived as most likely to engage in racial conflict—poor blacks and whites—could find any area of unity was indeed noteworthy, particularly in the late 1960s. Low-income whites were both racist and at times willing to find common cause with blacks and frequently were more likely to do so than were middle-class whites, in part because of their closer proximity.[47]

Unlike African Americans, whose history of residential segregation had aided black community mobilization in Durham and throughout the nation, ACT's difficulty in organizing low-income whites citywide stemmed in part from poor whites' geographic dispersal. However, racially integrated transitional neighborhoods such as Edgemont offered new possibilities for interracial organizing because black and white women residents shared a sense of ownership. Women's efforts to create stability in their neighborhoods and their demands for control over their racially integrated institutions, including the Edgemont school and clinic, were indeed political. Thus, just as local studies of the civil rights movement have forced a reevaluation of the black freedom struggle, so too place-centered analyses of women's subsistence politics offer new insights concerning the War on Poverty.

By the early 1970s, the climate of interracial cooperation on subsistence issues had created space for an almost unimaginable interracial alliance that transcended racial as well as gender barriers. The unlikely partnership involved a Durham Klansman, C. P. Ellis, and United Organizations' Atwater. Atwater was a single mother who quickly emerged as one of Durham's most effective black community organizers. Willing to work with nearly anyone who could address the problems of poor blacks, including middle-class women's organizations and white officials, Atwater also embraced Black Power politics and was not averse to using retributive violence. Following Martin Luther King Jr.'s assassination, Atwater hinted that she had diverted police so that militants could wreak their damage in the city. She bragged that she "could make a Molotov cocktail better than the man who invented it." In 1969, she publicly endorsed the opening of Durham's black nationalist Malcolm X Liberation University.[48]

Ellis was a white maintenance worker and the son of a Durham mill worker who had died at age forty-eight from brown lung disease. Ellis's father had been a Klansman, and his son discovered a similar appeal in the white supremacist group: "Here's a guy who's worked hard . . . and struggled all his life . . . and here's the moment to be something. I will never forget it," Ellis said of his initiation into the Durham Klan. He soon rose to become Exalted Cyclops (president) of the local KKK and began attending public forums during the 1960s to represent his organization's views. With his .32 pistol tucked in his belt in full view, Ellis frequently launched into racist diatribes. At one stormy city council meeting shortly after King's assassination, Ellis announced to a packed room, "We're just tired of niggers taking over Durham." The comment drove several middle-class black leaders from the room, but Atwater had a more visceral response. Focusing on a small spot on Ellis's neck, she lunged at him, knife in hand, though her friends restrained her. Several years later, Atwater and Ellis would confront one another again in roles no one could have predicted.[49]

In the early 1970s, former Edgemont tobacco worker and white AFL-CIO state president Wilbur Hobby secured a federal grant to help ease the process of school desegregation that had been mandated by a federal court order. Ellis and Atwater cochaired the citywide school committee (known as a *charrette*) funded under the grant. Ellis initially was overtly hostile to Atwater. He insisted on showing her a gun in his car trunk and refused to sit with her at a cafeteria. But the Klansman somehow gradually came to see the similarities between the problems of poor whites and blacks. Ellis's transformation was neither smooth nor easy, as he wrestled with his conscience and his southern traditions. Years later, he sobbed openly as he recalled his conversion: "From that moment, I tell ya, that gal and I worked together good. I begin to love the girl, really." The two remained friends, and Ellis's family asked Atwater to speak at his funeral in 2005.[50]

The cooperation and eventual friendship between a Klansman and a militant United Organizations activist was indeed impressive. However, few KKK,

ACT, or United Organizations members attended the citywide school desegregation forums. Because both ACT and United Organizations had declined by that time, there was no mass base on which the experiences of the former Klansman and black activist might have been expanded. Moreover, Ellis was ostracized by many whites, and Atwater was similarly rebuffed by local blacks. Durham residents on both sides of the color line simply dismissed the "odd couple" as opportunists and publicity seekers.[51]

Much of the failure to build an interracial movement of the poor was a matter of timing. Perhaps had it not been the late 1960s, with all the cross-currents and conflicts concerning the direction and meaning of social protest, coupled with divisive pressures from powerful whites opposed to the empowerment of poor people, an interracial coalition might have had better success. Conversely, these upheavals, particularly the community organizing campaigns of the black freedom movement and War on Poverty, enabled low-income blacks and whites to reach across the chasm of distrust and forge fragile alliances.

White activists created ACT in July 1968, the same month that United Organizations solidified relations with middle-class blacks and launched its boycott of white merchants. But ACT was in reality a hollow organization with shallow roots in white neighborhoods. Had ACT been created earlier and become a stronger, mass-based organization by 1968, it might have supported the black boycott, creating a stronger foundation for a biracial poor people's movement in Durham.

For its part, United Organizations did not oppose interracial efforts but had more pressing matters to pursue, including the need to mount a defense against increased attacks by white officials locally and nationally. The move toward racial solidarity prompted by Black Power politics and black middle-class support for both United Organizations and the black boycott therefore precluded a stronger alliance between ACT and United Organizations. The two groups were on parallel but distinct historical paths that diverged rather than connected.

In the end, the combined forces of white racism, deliberate attacks by white officials on antipoverty projects, historical timing, and male organizers' failure fully to appreciate neighborhood women as vital political assets undermined any chance of sustaining a genuine interracial movement of the poor. Still, that groups typically perceived as unlikely to work together—poor southern whites and blacks—could find any area of solidarity is indeed noteworthy, particularly in the late 1960s when, scholars and activists have contended, Black Power, racial violence, and a white backlash made such alliances seemingly impossible.

The ideological predisposition to see Black Power politics and interracial activism as mutually exclusive, an emphasis on formal male leadership, the focus on workplace rather than neighborhood settings, and the tendency to see poor women's activities (especially those involving social service provision) as outside the realm of politics have obscured women's political activism. Similarly, the failure to establish an interracial movement of the poor—a goal of many movement activists at the time—has kept scholars from seeing how the work of neighborhood women built and sustained creative community organizing projects. Finally, the scholarly inclination to separate the War on Poverty from the Black Power movement, especially in the South, has obscured the interracial alliances among low-income neighborhood women. The War on Poverty broke down barriers during a period of hardening divisions by focusing on impoverished communities. And by addressing the concerns of the poor, women—especially mothers—were politicized in new ways, forging connections across racial lines and sometimes between women and men. That vision, which transcended race, lingering progressive trade union aspirations, and the nationalist impulse of Black Power activists, challenged local race, gender, and class hierarchies in profound ways. And poor mothers were at the center of this effort.

Notes

1. Melvin Small, *The Presidency of Richard Nixon* (Lawrence: University Press of Kansas, 1999), 191; Michael B. Katz, *The Undeserving Poor: From the War on Poverty to the War on Welfare* (New York: Pantheon, 1989), 95–98; Allen J. Matusow, *The Unraveling of America: A History of Liberalism in the 1960s* (New York: Harper and Row, 1984), 237–40, 267, 255–56, 269–70; Alice O'Connor, *Poverty Knowledge: Social Science, Social Policy, and the Poor in Twentieth-Century U.S. History* (Princeton: Princeton University Press, 2001), 202; Michael Brown, *Race, Money, and the American Welfare State* (Ithaca: Cornell University Press, 1999), 210, 215, 223–25; Irwin Unger, *The Best of Intentions: The Triumphs and Failures of the Great Society under Kennedy, Johnson, and Nixon* (New York: Doubleday, 1996), 152–53; Annelise Orleck, *Storming Caesars Palace: How Black Mothers Fought Their Own War on Poverty* (Boston: Beacon, 2005); Jennifer Frost, *An Interracial Movement of the Poor: Community Organizing and the New Left in the 1960s* (New York: New York University Press, 2001); Lee J. Alson and Joseph P. Ferrie, *Southern Paternalism and the American Welfare State: Economics, Politics, and Institutions in the South, 1865–1965* (New York: Cambridge University Press, 1999), 119–42; Charles Murray, *Losing Ground: American Social Policy, 1950–1980* (New York: Basic Books, 1984).

2. Martha A. Ackelsberg, "Communities, Resistance, and Women's Activism: Some Implications for a Democratic Polity," in *Women and the Politics of Empowerment*, ed. Ann Bookman and Sandra Morgen (Philadelphia: Temple University Press, 1988), 297–313; Frances Fox Piven and Richard Cloward, *Regulating the Poor: The Functions of Public Welfare* (1971; New York: Pantheon, 1993); Frances Fox Piven and Richard Cloward, *Poor People's Movements: Why They Succeed and How They Fail* (New York: Pantheon, 1979); Richard Cloward and Frances Fox Piven, *The Politics of Turmoil: Essays on Poverty, Race, and the Urban Crisis* (New York: Pantheon, 1974).

3. On these links in North Carolina, see Robert Korstad and James Leloudis, *Impoverished Democracy: The North Carolina Fund and America's War on Poverty* (Chapel Hill: University of North Carolina Press, 2010).

4. For a recent corrective, see Dayo F. Gore, Jeanne Theoharis, and Komozi Woodard, eds., *Want to Start a Revolution?: Radical Women in the Black Freedom Struggle* (New York: New York University Press, 2009).

5. The campaign was administered by the North Carolina Fund (NCF), a private consortium established by North Carolina governor Terry Sanford in 1963 to bypass the conservative state legislature. Eleven target sites, including Durham, were selected for the antipoverty initiative, and in 1964 OBT reorganized as a CAA to qualify for federal funds (Robert Korstad and James Leloudis, "Citizen-Soldiers: The North Carolina Volunteers and the South's War on Poverty," in *The New Deal and Beyond: Social Welfare in the South since 1930*, ed. Elna C. Green [Athens: University of Georgia Press, 2003], 142, 158–59); George Esser Jr., "The Role of a State-Wide Foundation in the War on Poverty," in *Anti-Poverty Programs*, ed. R. O. Everett (Dobbs Ferry, N.Y.: Oceana, 1966), 77–113.

6. ACT was not an acronym. For a fuller discussion of OBT, United Organizations, and ACT, see Christina Greene, *Our Separate Ways: Women and the Black Freedom Movement in Durham, North Carolina* (Chapel Hill: University of North Carolina Press, 2005).

7. Jennifer Frost, "Community and Consciousness: Women's Welfare Rights Organizing in Cleveland, 1964–1966," paper presented at the Berkshire Conference on Women's History, Rutgers University, June 1990.

8. "NCF Survey of Low-Income Families in North Carolina: Characteristics of Individuals in Areas Surveyed by the Community Action Program in Durham," Report 3F (NCF, August 1967), 36–37, North Carolina Collection, University of North Carolina–Chapel Hill; *U.S. Census Population: General Characteristics of the Population, 1960*, vol. 1, pt. 35, North Carolina, tables 33, 77; *A Profile of Community Problems: Durham County*, OBT Report, tables I, II, NCF Papers, Southern Historical Collection, University of North Carolina–Chapel Hill. The NCF papers were unprocessed when I first consulted them.

9. Korstad and Leloudis, "Citizen Soldiers," 148; Wayne Flynt, *Dixie's Forgotten People: The South's Poor Whites* (Bloomington: Indiana University Press, 1979), 118, 109;

Brown, *Race*, 279–80; "A Review and Assessment of Operation Breakthrough" (NCF, August 1967), in *NCF Process Analysis Report*, pt. 3 (NCF, 1969), 70, 140, North Carolina Collection; Anne Braden, "Durham's ACT: A Voice of the Southern Poor," *Southern Patriot*, March 1969, 3.

10. Greene, *Our Separate Ways*, 123, 119–21, 124.

11. Thorpe insisted for years that she was unarmed when the sheriff tried to evict her and her children, but she more recently admitted publicly that she had a gun, suggesting the existence of armed self-defense within the nonviolent protest movements of the 1960s (Joyce Nichols Thorpe, interview, December 9, 1993, Durham, North Carolina; "The Sisters behind the Brothers: Women in the Durham Civil Rights Movement," panel discussion, Hayti Heritage Center, July 24, 2005; "Social Transformation in Durham: Women and the Black Freedom Movement," panel discussion, Duke University, April 2, 2007).

12. Bertie Howard and Steve Redburn, "United Organizations for Community Improvement: Black Political Power in Durham," NCF Papers; Francis Steven Redburn, "Protest and Policy in Durham, North Carolina" (Ph.D. diss., University of North Carolina–Chapel Hill, 1971), 95.

13. Dick Landerman and Harry Boyte, "Supplement to Position Paper on White Organization" (1968), 5, Box 1, Harry Boyte Papers, Special Collections, Duke University, Durham, North Carolina.

14. *Durham Morning Herald*, April 25, September 18, 1965, Report of Formation of White Citizens Council Group in Durham, North Carolina, n.d., Early History of Local 208, all in Box 33, Wilbur Hobby Papers, Special Collections, Duke University, Durham, North Carolina; David Cecelski, *Along Freedom Road: Hyde County, North Carolina, and the Fate of Black Schools in the South* (Chapel Hill: University of North Carolina Press, 1994), 39.

15. Harry Boyte and Dick Landerman, "Poor Whites on the Move!," Box 1, Boyte Papers; Hicks quoted in Braden, "Durham's ACT," 3; Sara Evans, interview by author, March 22, 1994.

16. Boyte, Landerman, and Chuck Schunior were the key leaders and decision makers in ACT; all had prior experience in the civil rights and/or labor movements (Harry Boyte and Dick Landerman, "Position Paper on White Organization," April 1968, Harry Boyte, "The History of ACT," n.d., appendix 3, both in Box 1, Boyte Papers; Elizabeth Tornquist, "Standing Up to America: Poor Whites in Durham," *New South*, Fall 1969, 45–46.

17. Boyte, "History of ACT," 5.

18. *The Action*, [ca. 1969], April 13–27, May 27–June 15, 1970; Dick Landerman, interview by author, July 14, 1995; Harry C. Boyte, telephone interview by author, July 27, 1995.

19. Landerman, interview; Tornquist, "Standing Up," 46; Evans, interview.

20. *The Action*, July 14–27, 1970.

21. Patricia Wallace, "How to Get Out of Hell by Raising It: The Case of Durham," May 24, 1967, Series 4.8, no. 4562, NCF Papers.

22. Karen Sacks, "Gender and Grassroots Leadership," in *Women and the Politics of Empowerment*, ed. Bookman and Morgen, 77–94; Belinda Robnett, *How Long! How Long!: African-American Women in the Struggle for Civil Rights* (New York: Oxford University Press, 1997), l.

23. Thorpe, interview.

24. Tami Hultman, interview by author, July 21, 1999; Barbara Ransby, *Ella Baker and the Black Freedom Movement: A Radical Democratic Vision* (Chapel Hill: University of North Carolina Press, 2003), 369, 135–36.

25. Boyte, interview; Landerman, interview; Sara Evans Boyte, unpublished typescript, February 1969, 4, Box 1, Boyte Papers; Phyllis Freeman, "White Community Organization in Durham from 1966 to the Present," July 1968, 4, NCF Papers; *The Action*, February, April 25–May 9, 1970; Deborah Cook-Milan, interview by author, June 18, 1999; Studs Terkel, "Occurrence in Durham," in *Race: How Blacks and Whites Think and Feel about the American Obsession* (New York: Norton, 1992), 181–82.

26. Braden, "Durham's ACT," 3; Evans, interview; Ed Sylvester et al., "Evaluation of the Foundation for Community Development," October 1969, Mitchell Sviridoff to McGeorge Bundy, both in NCF Papers; *Carolina Times*, May 17, 24, June 7, 21, 28, July 26, 1969; City Council Meeting, June 16, 1969, Nathan B. White Sr. Tape Collection, Tape 11, Side 2, Hayti Heritage Center, Durham, North Carolina.

27. Leon Rooke, "Through the Streets of Edgemont: A Neighborhood in Transition," *North Carolina Anvil*, April 15, 1967, 2.

28. Cook-Milan, interview. In Atlanta, affluent rather than low-income whites were especially resistant to residential integration (Kevin Kruse, *White Flight: Atlanta and the Making of Modern Conservatism* [Princeton: Princeton University Press, 2005]).

29. Sidney M. Gospe Jr. et al., "The Edgemont Community Clinic: Durham's Student-Operated Free Clinic Begins Its Second Decade," n.d., Edgemont Clinic Papers, Southern Historical Collection; Tami Hultman, "The Edgemont Community Center," NCF Report, August 1968, NCF Papers; Cook-Milan, interview; Rooke, "Through the Streets," 2.

30. *The Action*, June 30–July 13, 1970; "We All" [magazine clipping], n.d., Edgemont Community Center Papers, Box A–C, Special Collections, Duke University, Durham, North Carolina.

31. *The Action*, June 30–July 13, 1970.

32. Quoted in *Durham Morning Herald*, November 22, 1969; "This Clinic Is Free," *Breakthrough* 7 (July 1970): 2, Edgemont Clinic Papers.

33. Evans, interview; Boyte, "History of ACT," appendix 1, 3.

34. Tornquist, "Standing Up," 45.

35. *The Action*, March 9–30, June 30–July 13, 1970; *Daily Tar Heel*, February 14, 1973, Edgemont Clinic Papers; John Hughes et al., "Patterns of Patient Utilization in a Volunteer Medical Clinic," *North Carolina Medical Journal*, May 1972, Edgemont Clinic Papers. Of the more than one thousand CAA boards established between 1964 and 1968, most merely distributed government funds and services to the poor (Matusow, *Unraveling of America*, 255, 267–70; Unger, *Best of Intentions*, 164). Many white officials, among them FBI director J. Edgar Hoover, also did not distinguish between protest politics and efforts to obtain needed services. Hoover claimed that the Black Panther Party's free breakfast program was the organization's "best and most influential activity . . . and as such, is potentially the greatest threat to efforts by authorities . . . to neutralize the [party] and destroy what it stands for" (quoted in Tracey Matthews, "'No One Ever Asks, What a Man's Place in the Revolution Is': Gender and the Politics of the Black Panther Party, 1966–1971," in *The Black Panther Party (Reconsidered)*, ed. Charles E. Jones (Baltimore: Black Classic, 1998), 292.

36. *The Action*, June 30–July 12, 1970; Cook-Milan, interview; Elizabeth Tornquist, "An Analysis of Durham Politics," *Durham Voters Alliance Newsletter*, May 1973. In response to neighborhood women's demands, ACT later opened a day care center, but it was short-lived (Hultman Interview; Boyte, "History of ACT," appendix 1, 6; *The Action*, June 15–28, 1970).

37. *The Action*, May 12–25, July 28–August 11, 1970, January 26–February 23, June–July, 1971; *Anvil*, July 17, 1971.

38. In the 1970s, Boston became the national symbol of white working-class women's opposition to court-ordered school desegregation (Julia Wrigley, "From Housewives to Activists: Women and the Division of Political Labor in the Boston Antibusing Movement," in *No Middle Ground: Women and Radical Protest*, ed. Kathleen M. Blee [New York: New York University Press, 1998], 251–87).

39. *The Action*, August 19–September 1, 1970. For similar interracial alliances among low-income parents, see *The Action*, February 24–28, March 2–April 10, July 28–August 8, 1970, February 28–March 24, 1971; Boyte, "History of ACT," 8–12, 13.

40. David Ross Garr, "An Examination of the Edgemont Community Clinic: A Study of Growth and Frustration," May 19, 1971, 5, Frances Strychaz, "Community Health Projects: A Closer Look at Problems," *New Physician*, April 1970, Staff-Community Meeting Minutes, November 12, 1975, all in Edgemont Clinic Papers; *Durham Morning Herald*, December 2, 1973, October 27, 1979.

41. Matusow, *Unraveling of America*, 270; Small, *Presidency*, 190–91, 194, 213–14; Joan Hoff, *Nixon Re-Considered* (New York: Basic Books, 1994), 33, 60–65, 136, 144; H. R. Haldeman, *The Haldeman Diaries: Inside the Nixon White House* (New York: Putnam's, 1994), 80, 114, 186–87, 208.

42. Pat Rogers, interview by author, April 23, 1993; Durham, North Carolina, Foundation for Community Development Report to NCF, October 9–August 1, 1969, Nathan Garret to "Dear Friend of FCD," May 8, 1970, all in Series 1.8, nos. 882, 874, NCF Papers; *Durham Sun*, April 24, 1970; *Durham Morning Herald*, April 25, 1970; "Crisis and Conflict: The Story of Operation Breakthrough," "A Case Study of the War on Poverty in Durham, North Carolina," both in *NCF Process Analysis Final Report*, pt. 3, 1, 5–13; Jill Quadagno, *The Color of Welfare: How Racism Undermined the War on Poverty* (New York: Oxford University Press, 1994), 47–59.

43. "Crisis and Conflict," 40. The phrasing was a blatant reference to the expression *a nigger in the woodpile*.

44. Boyte interview; Ed Sylvester, "Evaluation of FCD," Hugh Price, "Foundation for Community Development: A Unique Experiment in Community Development," March 1972, George Esser to Howard Dressner, July 23, 1969, all in series 1.8, NCF Papers. ACT never received the same level of official harassment as United Organizations.

45. *Durham Morning Herald*, [ca. December 1969], Box 1, Boyte Papers; Boyte, "History of ACT," 13; *The Action*, February 1970.

46. Boyte, "ACT: Survey of Changing Strategies," 5.

47. William H. Chafe, *Civilities and Civil Rights: Greensboro, North Carolina, and the Black Struggle for Freedom* (New York: Oxford University Press, 1981), 37–38; Bob Blauner, *Black Lives, White Lives: Three Decades of Race Relations in America* (Berkeley: University of California Press, 1989), 122–23.

48. Christina Greene, "Ann Atwater," in *African American National Biography*, ed. Henry Louis Gates Jr. and Evelyn Higginbotham (New York: Oxford University Press, 2007); Osha Gray Davidson, *The Best of Enemies: Race and Redemption in the New South* (New York: Scribner, 1996), 232–33.

49. C. P. Ellis, "Why I Quit the Klan," *Southern Exposure*, Summer 1982, 47–53.

50. Although this example involves an interracial alliance between a man and a woman, it revolved around school concerns, traditionally the responsibility of women (Ann Atwater, interview by author, January 12, 1993; Terkel, "Occurrence," 271–88; *North Carolina Anvil*, July 17, August 14, 1971; Mosi Secret, "Racial Reconciliation Leader Is in Need," *Durham Independent Weekly*, December 28, 2005.

51. Cook-Milan, interview. Only two ACT councils were still in existence by 1971.

ADINA BACK

"Parent Power"

Evelina López Antonetty, the United Bronx Parents, and the War on Poverty

Anyone in New York's City's South Bronx in the late 1960s would have found it hard to miss the "United Bronx Parents" sign at 791 Prospect Avenue. Stretching across the building's facade, the large sign hinted at a complex and until now mostly hidden history of life, politics, and economics in one of America's poorest urban communities. This history turns on the desires and aspirations of South Bronx families and the political activities they undertook to try to bring their children closer to achieving the dream of equal access to quality education. This history also illuminates the reach of the War on Poverty and the ways that populations very much out of the sight and the thoughts of Lyndon Baines Johnson and his planners were touched and transformed by community action.

A close examination would show that the sign pointed to the role of the federal and local governments in helping these families organize. The third line of the sign read, "For Good Education in Our Community." That wording is noteworthy. The sign's creators were not using the language of integration, desegregation, decentralization, or community control. This struggle for educational equality was driven not by a particular strategy but by a general imperative—*good education in our community*. The sign explained clearly who funded the United Bronx Parents (UBP). Its primary sponsor was the federal Office of Economic Opportunity (OEO), the clearinghouse for President Johnson's War on Poverty programs. The organization also noted support from New York's corporate and philanthropic sectors through the Urban Coalition, which was a public-private partnership of the kind that animated much community organizing even during the official War on Poverty years. This sort of mix of funds sustained community organizing in New York and scores of other American cities long after the OEO and its successor, the Community Services Administration, had passed into history.

In its heyday, UBP operated six satellite centers, trained thousands of parents to advocate for their children in their local schools, organized summer lunch programs that served more than 150,000 children a day throughout New York City, offered direct services, and provided technical services to parent advocacy groups across the country. In all of these efforts, UBP used War on Poverty funds to wage a battle against a school system that shortchanged the city's poor children. The group's organizers were Puerto Rican mothers who embodied the ideal of community action, convincing thousands of poor parents that they had the right and the ability to take control of and improve their children's education.

UBP challenged not only inferior schools in one underserved community but also the mind-set of New York City Board of Education officials, who labeled that community's children as victims of an impoverished culture that did not value education. The angry, articulate Puerto Rican mothers of UBP still challenge us, breaking down a panoply of myths and misconceptions about both the War on Poverty and the movement in northern cities for equal educational opportunities for children of all backgrounds.

The Spanish organization name at the top of the sign, *Padres Unidos del Bronx*, provided a visible reminder that the movement for educational equality in many urban areas around the country was not exclusively an African American struggle. UBP was a grassroots organization staffed and driven by Puerto Rican parents, but its members were not exclusively Puerto Rican or exclusively of any one race. And a sign over the front door bore the image of two clasped hands, one light, one dark, announcing to visitors that this movement was multiracial.

Leaning out the window above the organization's sign, visitors often saw a woman with a big hat. Described by some in her community both as brilliant and gorgeous, Evelina López Antonetty had founded the UBP in 1965, leading a group of parents in the takeover of a city-owned South Bronx building intended for demolition. That building, located at 791 Prospect Avenue, became the UBP headquarters.[1]

Contrary to the popular political critique of the War on Poverty as essentially a failure, the story of the UBP offers powerful evidence that grassroots communities effectively used antipoverty funding to empower parents. The UBP battled not only to improve education in the South Bronx but also to shatter a pervasive "culture of poverty" ideology that explained poverty as a consequence of individual pathology rather than systemic inequality. The UBP's existence offered a direct retort to the widely accepted belief that Puerto Rican parents—as well as African Americans and Afro-Caribbean immigrants—were passive and uncaring about their children's education. Antonetty's life story also demonstrates the continuities between the movements for economic and racial justice of the New Deal and postwar decades, in which she cut her teeth as an activist, and grassroots organizing in the 1960s.

COMING OF AGE IN EL BARRIO

"I was the Puerto Rican who could speak a little English so I became the president of the PTA," explained Antonetty in a 1976 interview. "They thought we were supposed to drink tea. When I began asking the wrong questions, the principal realized he had made a mistake." Antonetty "was organizing parents and asking why our children could not read. I asked that the assistant superintendent be dismissed. Then I was called down to the Board of Education. I had to remind them that I didn't work for them. So I went to the politicians. They laughed at me. . . . So I began to organize all different people in our community to get rid of the assistant superintendent."[2]

Already in her forties when she decided to take on the New York City school system, Antonetty brought to her activism a political mind that had been sharpened by a childhood of poverty in Puerto Rico and by emigration to New York City, where she was exposed to the radical politics of the Depression era, to an internationalist and anticolonial consciousness, and to the trade union movement. Evelina López was born in the small fishing village of Salinas, Puerto Rico, on September 19, 1922. "My family, like the rest of the villagers, was very poor. The men went fishing every day, so we ate lots of fish, crabs and cornmeal. Pineapples and bananas were plentiful. Imagine—no one ate the lobster. We used to feed it to the pigs."[3]

Eva Cruz López sent the eldest of her three daughters, Evelina, to live with her aunt and uncle in New York in the fall of 1933. Elba Cabrera, Evelina's youngest sister, later recalled that their mother, recently widowed, "was having difficulty. There were no jobs in Puerto Rico. People were suffering [in the United States] in the depression, so you can imagine how it was in Puerto Rico.

It was worse." Eva joined Evelina in "El Barrio" (Spanish Harlem) three years later, bringing along her two younger daughters, Lillian and Elba.[4]

Evelina went to Public School 103 in East Harlem, where her initial experience of rejection shaped her responses to later immigrants to New York. As she explained, "The Hispanics from Central America, the Haitians, the blacks from the south and the Puerto Ricans all have problems with language and social customs. They experience rejection like I did. They feel like outsiders! That's why I began to fight for bilingual education and tolerance. My own memories are still quite vivid."[5]

An academically talented student, López went to Harlem's Wadleigh High School, one of the best schools in the city. One of only a few Puerto Rican students there, López experienced discrimination, as administrators did not encourage black and Latino students to participate in cocurricular activities other than singing and dancing, viewing them as "just good for that."[6] Though many of Wadleigh's graduates went on to college, López's family lacked the resources to enable her to continue her education.

Much of López's education thus took place in her community, influenced by the hardships of the Great Depression and the atmosphere of progressive politics and Puerto Rican culture swirling around her. Many landlords offered free rent for the first three months, and the Lópezes, like many other Depression-era families, took advantage of the practice, moving every time that grace period expired. The family always stayed within the Latino community—between 110th and 116th Streets on the north and south and Park and Lenox Avenues on the east and west. Eva López worked in the Hotel New Yorker's laundry six and a half days a week; her starting salary was seven dollars a week, an amount that ultimately rose to twelve dollars.[7]

As part of the working poor, López's family was relatively fortunate. Many of her neighbors were unemployed and received public assistance in the form of food allotments. López often helped her neighbors claim their free food packages, since many were ashamed to need "home relief" and refused to go to the YWCA on West 137th Street to pick up their food. The self-described "businesslike" López would gather her neighbors' vouchers, collect their food (riding the trolley for free courtesy of her cousin, Santos, a transportation worker). When she delivered the food, neighbors would pay her with some of the food, which she would bring home to her mother and sisters.[8]

The young López melded this entrepreneurial spirit with a strong sense of justice and entitlement. Her grandfather was the longtime mayor of Salinas, and her mother had been active in island politics. Vincenta Godreau, the aunt with whom López lived when she first came to New York, was a vibrant community and political activist who introduced the girl to some of the community's radical leaders, including Puerto Rican labor activist and politician Jesús Colón. López's mother and aunt helped organize a hotel workers' union and served as union representatives.[9]

During the Great Depression, López protested alongside neighbors evicted from their homes, helping them to move furniture that had been tossed out onto the sidewalk back into their apartments. While she was in high school, she and three classmates staged a school boycott to draw attention to what they perceived as inadequate medical care provided when a fellow student fell ill at school. "Two Jewish, one black girl and myself decided to stay away from the school until changes were made. Well we won. A nurse was hired for the medical room." Her multiracial Bronx neighborhood thus shaped López's political vision.[10]

López was also informed and influenced by the radical internationalist and nationalist politics fermenting around her. Colón "paid my insurance so I could be a member of the International Workers' Order," Antonetty recalled. "I knew what was going on in Russia, and the struggle to organize in the United States." Some of López's friends went to fight against the fascists in the Spanish Civil War. Moreover, after police shot into a crowd of proindependence marchers in Ponce, Puerto Rico, on Palm Sunday 1937, López was among tens of thousands who congregated in Central Park to protest and mourn.[11]

Antonetty's childhood was also infused with Puerto Rican culture and Latin music. Her uncle, Godreau, was a dance promoter who worked with many prominent and emerging Latin-Jazz and Afro-Cuban musicians. Antonetty's sister, Elba Cabrera, recalled that noted musicians including Machito, Mario Bauzá, Alberto Iznaga, and Bobby Capó frequented the Lópezes home, even playing for the sisters' birthdays.[12] El Barrio was alive with musical activity and Antonetty's home was a center. Sometimes the political and cultural intersected as in the case of Cuban musician, Iznaga, who joined the International Workers Order Symphony Orchestra in the mid-1930s, which brought together the political and cultural by using revolutionary songs to stir the audience to rise up against injustice.

By the late 1930s, López was organizing young people for Vito Marcantonio, the only Communist member of the U.S. Congress. First elected to office in 1932 in a largely Italian district of Harlem, Marcantonio later won fierce support among many Puerto Ricans for his support of the island's independence. Like many El Barrio Puerto Ricans, López felt that Marcantonio "belonged to" the community. Residents had enormous "love and trust" for the congressman, believing "that he could fix anything, even rotten chicken sold by the grocer."[13]

After graduating from high school, López eloped in 1941 with draftsman Binaldo Montenegro. The young couple moved to Jackson Avenue in the South Bronx, and Evelina convinced her mother and sisters to rent an apartment around the corner. With Eva López working during the day, Evelina generally went to meet with Elba's teachers, "and she would fight when things weren't right," Cabrera recalled.[14] The Montenegros soon had a new baby, Lorraine, and Evelina spent the war years caring for her daughter, attending Brooklyn College part time, and continuing to organize on behalf of the community.

When her marriage fell apart, Evelina began working full time at the District 65 United Auto Workers Union, one of the first Latina women hired by the union. Over the next ten years, she served as an organizer and job developer, helped create the union's medical programs and security procedures, and opened the doors for other Latinos looking for union jobs.[15] In 1955, Evelina married Donato Antonetty, a cousin of her mother who left Puerto Rico to court her. After the birth of Anita, her second daughter, in 1957, she resigned from the union to stay home and raise her children.

The Antonettys added a son, Donald, to the family, and when the two youngest children entered Public School 5 in the early 1960s, Evelina Antonetty got a firsthand view of the educational system in her South Bronx neighborhood. Parents were frustrated and confused that their Spanish-speaking children were not learning to read and that after doing poorly on English-language tests, these children were placed in classes for mentally retarded students. "I began to see the schools as an island. After 3 o'clock, the school officials closed the doors and left the community. They made no input into the community. There were no teachers in the school from the community."[16]

THE UBP CONFRONTS THE CULTURE OF POVERTY

Antonetty first tried to work within the traditional venues available to parents. She was elected president of the PTA, a position that enabled her to learn more about parents and teachers in her district and thus accumulate valuable insights into the community's needs and strengths. When a teacher was accused of sexually abusing some students, Antonetty fought not only to have the teacher discharged but also to dismiss the district superintendent who had initially refused to pursue the parents' complaints or investigate the teacher.

Antonetty solicited support and assistance from various community groups and business leaders in her effort to force a reluctant board of education to address the community's concerns. Building on this coalition of parents, local groups, and neighborhood businesses all concerned about the education of their community's children, Antonetty founded the UBP in 1965. "Our children can become the educators, doctors and leaders of tomorrow," Antonetty asserted. "Don't let anyone tell us differently . . . that our children [are] uneducable or mentally retarded." In that simple, forceful assertion of all parents' faith in their children's potential, Antonetty was offering a response to prevailing theories that suggested otherwise about Puerto Rican parents.[17]

At that time, arguments that Puerto Rican children were impossible to educate strongly influenced the perspective and policies of the city's educators. While theories about African American and Puerto Rican "inherent inferiority" had been common for decades, in the mid-1960s these arguments about behavioral pathology were formalized into a theory of culture. Anthropologist Oscar Lewis coined the phrase "culture of poverty" in his 1959 study, *Five Families: Mexican Case Studies in the Culture of Poverty*, to describe the social and familial pathology of his subjects.[18] The phrase caught on and became widely used, particularly by liberal policymakers, shaping the War on Poverty as well as the educational vision of the self-described liberals who ran the New York City school system.

While histories of culture-of-poverty theories have tended to focus on how they shaped perceptions of African Americans, Lewis's work focused first on Mexicans and then on Puerto Ricans. In his 1966 book, *La Vida: A Puerto Rican Family in the Culture of Poverty—San Juan and New York*, Lewis tried to legitimize the study of poor people, to put a human face on poverty by focusing in depth on a single urban slum family. Lewis was passionate about giving "a voice to people who are rarely heard" and hoped that the study would serve as a bridge between the poor and the middle-class professionals who serviced them—"teachers, social workers, doctors, priests and others—who bear the major responsibility for carrying out the anti-poverty programs."[19]

As Lewis admitted, good intentions too often backfire. Professionals had drawn negative conclusions about the poor people about whom Lewis had written in his earlier works, and he feared they would do so again about the Puerto Ricans in *La Vida*. He tried to prevent his work from being used to stigmatize his subjects. Yet Lewis's descriptions were fraught with judgments that implied that one set of values was preferable to another. He described Puerto Rican families living in San Juan slums and New York City ghettos as prone to "acting out more than thinking out, self-expression more than self-constraint, pleasure more than productivity, spending more than saving, personal loyalty more than impersonal justice." Poor Puerto Ricans, he wrote in *La Vida*, seemed "less reserved, less depressive, less controlled and less stable" than the poor Mexicans he had observed. Lewis described his Puerto Rican subjects as showing a "great zest for life, especially for sex, and a need for excitement, new experiences and adventures."[20]

Though Lewis's characterizations may well have fed his readers' prejudices, his culture-of-poverty framework was intended to shift the paradigm for social workers and education professionals from a genetically based theory of racial and cultural inferiority to one of environmental determinism. Lewis argued that the "brutalizing environment" in which poor Puerto Ricans lived had generated the culture of poverty he found in generation after generation. Though frank in his admiration for his subjects' resilience and "ability to cope with problems that would paralyze many middle-class individuals," he concluded that those caught in a culture of poverty tended to be impulsive and irresponsibly self-indulgent and had low self-esteem and "very little sense of history." While it may have been innovative to suggest that the poor had any culture, it was at best a "thin culture" that Lewis described, and it was certainly not the culture in which Evelina Antonetty and the Bronx parents she helped to organize saw themselves living.[21]

The culture-of-poverty theory gained tremendous political currency. As Lewis predicted, it was used and misused by policymakers and education and social service professionals throughout the country. Senator Daniel Patrick Moynihan's 1965 policy report, *The Negro Family: The Case for National Action*, was the most famous offshoot of Lewis's work, arguing that the black family was pathological and was controlled by overbearing "matriarchs." But Moynihan's work was part of a long strain of influential theorizing on the Negro problem, including the work of sociologists E. Franklin Frazier in the 1930s and Gunnar Myrdal in the 1940s. As historian Regina Kunzel has argued, while postwar social policymakers and politicians were strongly influenced by Frazier and

Myrdal's work, "They were less inclined . . . to focus on aspects of [Frazier's] analysis that indicted racism and more likely to name the black family itself as the dilemma that demanded national attention."[22]

The culture-of-poverty theory also took hold among education policy strategists. As education historian Jerald Podair has described, *Equality of Educational Opportunity*, James Coleman's 1966 report to the U.S. Commissioner of Education, was also premised on this idea. Coleman explained the low educational achievement of the nation's students of color as the consequence of culturally inferior family and community environment. In other words, poor reading and math scores among black and Puerto Rican students resulted not from poor schools, inadequate funding, or inexperienced teachers but from the students' homes and parents.

For the UBP and other old and newly emerging Puerto Rican civil rights organizations, the issue was not that generation after generation perpetuated the culture of poverty. Quite the contrary. They asked why generation after generation of educators persisted in believing and behaving as if Puerto Rican children were simply not educable. Since a 1935 report by the U.S. Chamber of Commerce's Special Committee on Immigration and Naturalization had "proved" that Puerto Ricans had significantly lower IQs than did other children, Puerto Ricans had been suspicious of "official" findings. More than twenty years later, the New York City Board of Education's much-touted *Puerto Rican Study* offered anecdotal evidence of teachers and schools operating under the assumption that Puerto Rican students' homes were to blame for children's failings at school. And in 1968, ASPIRA, an organization founded in the early 1960s to train and develop leaders among Puerto Rican youth on the U.S. mainland, published *The Losers: A Report on Puerto Ricans and the Public Schools*, which affirmed that the culture-of-poverty theory remained strong in the culture of educators.[23]

Puerto Rican children did not need to read Lewis's work or any of the other many reports generated by researchers and policymakers that characterized them as culturally deficient and used this theory to explain their educational failures. They experienced this perspective firsthand in the classroom. *The Losers* compiled example after example of Puerto Rican schoolchildren being told directly that they had no intellectual abilities. One Puerto Rican honor student requested college catalogs from her guidance counselor and was told, "Now this is just my opinion, but I think you'd be happier as a secretary." More often than not, according to the report, Puerto Rican students were simply ignored.

One ethnographer recorded that a teacher in a Spanish Harlem school during the mid-1960s had said, "The Puerto Ricans seem to learn absolutely nothing, either here or at home." Another teacher agreed: "All they seem to care about is sleeping, eating, playing and having parties." Educator Hernan LaFontaine, who taught at a large junior high school in New York City during this period, described sitting in the teachers' lounge and hearing his colleagues call the students "spics" and "animals" while assuring him that he was "different."[24] As Lewis hoped, the culture-of-poverty theory had trickled down to the classroom, and as he feared, his theory was used to disparage his research subjects.

The UBP was part of a national movement of grassroots organizations that subscribed to a fundamentally different theory on the causes of poverty and the culture of poor people. Leaders such as Antonetty brought to their War on Poverty strategy an understanding of economic inequities that had been shaped by the harsh experience of the Great Depression and the animated discussions of class struggle in which she and other Harlem activists had engaged during that era. She also brought to her analysis of poverty insights from the culture in which she was raised, a Caribbean Latino worldview strong on family and neighborhood ties and mutual aid. Finally, by the mid-1960s, Antonetty had been exposed to the "opportunity theory" that drove War on Poverty's Community Action Program. Before creating UBP, she had worked for the Puerto Rican Community Development Project and the Head Start program at Public School 25. Antonetty's experience and outlook meshed with the guiding principles of the OEO-funded Community Action Program.

Antonetty was excited by the possibility of drawing OEO funding to empower Bronx parents with knowledge about their rights and responsibilities. The UBP's central political intention was to enable an articulate and informed group of parents to demand improvements in their children's schools. The types of improvements for which Bronx parents asked would change over time, but the idea of giving parents the tools to fight for those improvements meshed well with the principle of maximum feasible participation, enabling Antonetty to win federal funds for UBP and then to leverage OEO funds to raise money from local government as well as New York City–based corporations.

As a first step, UBP began offering workshops to train parents to evaluate the schools in their communities. Antonetty and her staff developed a hands-on interactive training approach complete with role-playing materials. UBP gave parents copies of official documents so that they could educate themselves about board of education regulations regarding such matters as suspensions and the accepted procedures for handling disruptive children. Trainers focused directly and explicitly on shifting the locus of blame and power. After being told repeatedly by teachers and administrators that bad Puerto Rican parenting produced bad Puerto Rican children, these parents now learned about lack of accountability in the board of education bureaucracy, racial and ethnic discrimination by teachers, and an inequitable distribution of resources that left certain city schools with crumbling buildings and incompetent teachers.[25]

UBP sent workshop participants on a "treasure hunt" that took them into a middle-class Bronx neighborhood and then back to their local community. In what was billed as a "treasure hunt for parents who blame themselves," participants carried checklists asking them to note public libraries, dime stores, banks, restaurants, and furniture stores and to compare the two neighborhoods. With checklist in hand, they were asked to compare and contrast: Did the library schedules in the middle class neighborhood compare to the one in their poor neighborhood? Did libraries in both neighborhoods offer evening and weekend hours? How did the quantity and quality of children's books at the two libraries compare? Which dime store sold educational materials, toys, flashcards? What kinds of paperback books and magazines did the local newspaper store carry? In which community could parents find the *New York Times*? Parents asked bank managers whether their institutions offered school savings accounts and whether the banks lost money on those accounts. Did the banks offer loans to families with school-age children? Did bank branches even exist in the poor neighborhood?[26]

Parents hunted for family restaurants without bars that offered affordable, "decent and clean" meals. At the furniture stores, parents noted the availability and prices of a child's desk, lamp, and bookcase. Parents searched for local entertainment such as bowling alleys or movie theaters. What was playing? What was the price? Finally, parents surveyed real estate: Were there four- or five-room apartments for rent, and at what price? Did the apartment building come with services—doormen, maintenance workers, elevator operators?[27]

Parents found that such middle-class neighborhoods as Fordham Road and the Grand Concourse offered resources that were completely unavailable in the poor neighborhoods, even though just a few blocks often separated the two communities. The treasure hunt essentially represented an attempt to quantify and name key dimensions in children's daily experience of poverty and to analyze how that daily experience had a damaging impact on learning.

The UBP parent-training programs drew from the language and ideology of freedom movements at home and around the world. Taking a page from Brazilian educator Paulo Freire's *Pedagogy of the Oppressed*, a philosophy of democratic education very popular among 1960s civil rights activists, authors of the UBP treasure hunt created a series of exercises designed to "re-educat[e] parents who have been turned around against their own."[28] Antonetty brought to the UBP's training program the critique of imperialism and its effects on the young that she had developed over years in the Puerto Rican independence movement. UBP training director Ellen Lurie brought to the parent-training activities the philosophical and strategic insights she had gained during her many years as a community and civil rights activist.

Involved in the movement for school integration since the mid-1950s, Lurie was a white mother of five children who attended the city's public schools in Upper Manhattan. Deeply passionate about racial equality and social justice, she cofounded and led a grassroots parents' organization, EQUAL, that sought to build support for school integration in white communities and to counter opposition to integration from such white parent organizations as Parents and Taxpayers, a group that by the early 1960s numbered half a million members. Lurie worked with Annie Stein and the Reverend Milton Galamison on the citywide school boycotts of 1964. She agitated within the system as well, serving as a member of Local School Board 6 for five years until she resigned to protest parents' lack of power to effect substantive change. In 1966, she joined with new and old allies, including Antonetty, and formed the New York City People's Board of Education.[29]

The training materials that Lurie developed advocated "Parent Power."[30] The materials precisely and concisely explained to parents their rights in both English and Spanish. Years of doing battle with the board of education clearly informed the militant tone that permeated the materials that Lurie produced. But she was not only registering her frustration; more important, she was capturing the daily experiences of Puerto Rican parents trying to gain entry into their children's schools so that they could better understand why these schools were failing their children.

From nationally commissioned reports to local studies, the conclusions were the same: Puerto Rican children were not succeeding in school. The Coleman Report documented that test scores of sixth-grade students placed the average Puerto Rican child about three years behind the average white child in verbal ability, reading comprehension, and mathematics and about one year behind the average African American child. Antonetty recalled these dismal statistics in starker terms: "69% of our children could not read. By 1967, 89% could not read. Things were getting worse and worse." The UBP charted every fifth grade in the Bronx and ranked reading scores from highest to lowest based on the results of a 1967 standardized reading test. The results surprised no one. In schools with predominantly Puerto Rican and black students, fewer than 25 percent of children read at grade level. In some schools, the figure was just 8 percent. But the UBP insisted that ethnic and racial demographics were not sufficient to understand why children were doing so poorly. UBP studies correlated the schools with the lowest percentage of children reading on grade level to school population size and teacher experience. (They drew these numbers from board of education figures). The fifth-graders with the lowest reading scores attended the most overcrowded schools and were taught by the most inexperienced teachers.[31]

The UBP gave Puerto Rican parents the language of rights and power but also statistics to back up their analysis, urging parents to "let the numbers speak for themselves" and to reject the paradigm that they were to blame for their children's failures in schools. Like many of the era's other civil rights organizations, UBP taught parents their legal rights and urged them to use those rights to demand improvements. Bronx parents found, for example, that they had the legal right to see and obtain copies of everything that was in their children's school records. Citing Education Law 310, Decision 6849 of the state education commissioner, the UBP pointed out that parents were allowed to see their child's complete records at any time and to get a copy of these materials. They also had the right to challenge any information they considered incorrect and could "sue the teacher and the school system for slander and libel." "We at the United Bronx Parents will help you obtain a free lawyer." One UBP pamphlet described how a mother found this unsigned, undated note in her child's record folder: "A real sickie—abs[ent], truant, stubborn & very dull. Is verbal only about outside irrelevant facts. Can barely read (which was a huge accomplishment to get this far). Have fun."[32]

In addition to their rights, UBP argued, parents had a responsibility to evaluate schools, and to that end, Lurie's training department developed a variety of forms to assist parents in measuring school efficacy. In response to statistics on low reading scores among Puerto Rican schoolchildren, UBP directed parents to interview principals about reading programs and then to evaluate the school's strategies for teaching children to read. The UBP taught parents to begin by collecting data, demanding precise information in writing and refusing to accept guesses or excuses: "If your principal tells you that it is normal for half the children to read below grade level, tell him he is being ridiculous. Private and suburban schools would be ashamed if they only had half the children reading at level. In most middle class schools outside New York City *all* of the children are reading on or above grade norm. *Your children will have to compete with those children for jobs!"*[33]

Puerto Rican and African American parents' experiences of being insulted and ignored by school principals contributed to the unequivocal quality of the UBP's directives. Principals at times addressed parents as if they were first-graders. Even after New York City school superintendent Bernard Donovan directed that reading score data be made available to the public, parents had difficulties obtaining the information. According to one East Harlem school board member, "It was always like pulling teeth. Our local school board did some good by informing parents when Donovan's orders came that they could demand the scores. When this was done parent associations could get them, although grudgingly. Even then the principals could give them a hard time and the district superintendent gave an equally hard time in enforcing Donovan's order."[34]

Public school administrators' willingness to cooperate with parents' demands for greater transparency became important parts of the UBP's list of criteria for judging principals and other administrators. One document explained that the principal "should want to change the school—not your home." The UBP continued by advising that the principal "should not tell you the children are not 'ready to learn'—he should be getting them ready and making them learn! He should like the children and not be afraid of them."[35] Such exhortations reflected poor Spanish-speaking parents' too-often negative experiences with public school administrators. At issue was not only the educational quality of a school but also the school's attitude toward its students and their families. If the parents decided that a principal was sincere about wanting to improve the school's reading program, then the UBP would recommend that the parents make public their findings, design "performance standards" for the school, work with the principal to get needed financial support, and hold the school accountable for its promises. But the UBP also had no qualms about directing parents to "immediately organize to have [principals] removed for incompetence" if they refused to respond to parents' concerns.[36]

The language of "removing" resonated for New York's Puerto Rican and black parents because their children seemingly were being removed en masse. New York parents perceived a campaign of rampant suspensions with racial and ethnic underpinnings. A coalition of fourteen civic organizations led by the Citizen's Committee for Children released a spring 1967 report charging that the public schools often wrongly accused students of unruly behavior and suspended pupils without fair hearings. The report showed that more than twelve thousand children had been suspended during the previous school year on charges that included absenteeism, failure to do homework, making noise in class, talking back to teachers, and fighting with other children. Representing a range of organizations from the New York Civil Liberties Union, ASPIRA, CORE, the Public Education Association, and the United Parents Association, the report's authors voiced concerns about students' civil liberties and due process and the lack of educational services to help suspended students "become willing and able to learn in the regular school setting."[37]

Several days after the report was released, as the board of education was digesting the findings, federal judge Constance Baker Motley ruled that a student suspended from public school had the right to be represented by a lawyer at a board of education hearing because "proceedings which involve the loss of liberty and the loss of education are of critical importance to the person involved and to our system of justice." Motley's ruling involved a fourteen-year-old junior high school student who had been suspended by the school's principal for allegedly hitting a teacher. A hearing was to be held before the district superintendent, but the student's parents were informed that no lawyer could be present. Motley's ruling reasserted the due process rights of suspended students and their families. While civic organizations hailed Motley's ruling, educators across the city, including the Council of Supervisory Associations and the High School Principals' Association, inveighed against it, claiming that the hearings were intended not to be punitive but to serve as guidance conferences for the student's benefit.[38]

The U.S. Court of Appeals subsequently reversed Motley's ruling. The board of education's new special committee on disruptive pupils met to assess the situation and to make recommendations. And the United Federation of Teachers passed a resolution insisting that a "disruptive child" clause, giving teachers the right to expel a "seriously misbehaving" student, be included in the collective bargaining agreement to be negotiated with the board of education in the fall of 1967.[39]

Puerto Rican and black parents sought to evaluate the situation. Were some children truly out of control? Did they qualify as juvenile delinquents? The UBP suggested that parents invert the question: "How do you know if you have a bad kid or if your kid has a bad teacher?" Here, too, the UBP offered parents a checklist for analyzing cause and effect: "Does the teacher have a pattern of *rules and procedures* which are *consistent*, fairly applied to all? Have these rules been developed *with* the children, and are they *understood* and *expected* by the children? Do the children have *times* when they may talk, and times when they should be silent? Are the lessons dull and repetitive? Or are they planned inadequately without any goal, setting no standard of achievement for the children? Does she treat all the children with respect?" The UBP concluded with some parenting advice. "Before you start yelling at your child when you get a note from school saying that he has been 'bad,' try to find out the answers to these questions." The UBP also reassured parents with the information that these questions had been almost completely copied from a memo that the board of education was circulating to new teachers.[40]

The UBP's "report card" for schools framed the group's philosophy about a school's role in the community: "A Good School Involves Its Students in the Life of Their Community." The report card scored schools on evidence of vibrant interactions between the community and the school. For example, did local shops hang posters advertising school activities? Was artwork by the community's seniors displayed in the school? Was the building open beyond normal school hours for recreational and educational activities for neighborhood residents of all ages? Did the school hire a mixed staff of idealistic and energetic professional and lay educators who lived primarily in the community? Did the school allow local lawyers to teach classes on tenants' rights on its premises? Were doctors from nearby hospitals invited to teach students how to test for lead poisoning? The report card urged parents to consider whether "the staff believes that the school's main job is to teach its students how to cope with a changing world . . . and how to improve it."[41]

UBP parents looked for school curricula that stressed independent, critical thinking skills and that recognized different learning styles. They considered whether schools created links between students and their communities through work-study programs and off-site learning. The UBP encouraged parents to assess whether the curriculum was relevant. Did it offer students ways to study about themselves and their pasts as well as subjects that focused on current events and contemporary politics? Did the schools "prepare students for the real world"? Finally, Lurie urged parents to score whether schools had a democratic governance structure that included student participation.[42]

The UBP's worldview was based on a philosophy of education that had its roots in the nineteenth-century thinking of Horace Mann, who argued that all citizens, no matter their race or economic status, should have equal access to a tuition-free, tax-supported public school system. In addition, UBP leaders incorporated an emphasis on participatory democracy drawn from the radical politics swirling around the community in the 1960s.

Like antipoverty organizations around the country, the UBP firmly believed that community members—in this case, poor and working-class migrants—were entitled to a voice in shaping the decisions that affected their lives. In Antonetty, the community had a leader who had what her sister described as "a sense of history." Antonetty "read and read and read. And, you know, she was just brilliant." Kathy Goldman, UBP's Summer Meals Program coordinator, said that Antonetty "had a presence, and she knew it. And so when she walked into a hearing, you were so glad if you were on her side. . . . She was a real force, a political force."[43]

Antonetty derived that gravity and that presence from her years of political experience as a child of the Depression who helped neighbors to get the federal assistance they were owed, as a teenage volunteer developing insights into the machinations of electoral politics through her work for Congressman Marcantonio, and as a young adult working for the United Auto Workers. By the early 1960s, that experience had helped her to earn the trust of OEO officials, who channeled funds to her Bronx parents' group. By the mid-1960s, New York City's elected officials had begun to recognize Antonetty as a player. She received calls from Mayor John Lindsay and met with local members of Congress and national leaders including Martin Luther King Jr. In 1968, she was appointed cochair of Lindsay's Council against Poverty; the same year, the Urban Coalition, a consortium of antipoverty groups, named her cochair of its Education Task Force.[44]

By that time, the UBP's Parent Leadership Training Program was tied to a larger campaign building in the city's black neighborhoods that called on the city to grant parents ultimate control of the schools their children attended. Antonetty was widely acknowledged as one of the key figures in the community-control movement. While other Puerto Rican leaders had feared and opposed aligning their community with the black civil rights movement, Antonetty's history of cross-race organizing enabled her comfortably to link her community's education struggles to those of black parents.[45] She understood the deep disillusionment among New York's school integration activists. After more than ten years of parent organizing to desegregate the city's public schools, integration proponents had begun to adopt a different strategy. If central authorities refused to act on parent demands that their children be allowed to attend higher-quality schools in white neighborhoods, nor would they allocate greater resources to improve schools in poor and black communities, parents would demand that they be allowed to control the schools. At demonstrations throughout New York's poor neighborhoods in the late 1960s, a new cry was heard: "Parent Power."

The next phase of Antonetty's struggle would take her into the heart of this struggle for parental control of public schools that spread from Harlem and the Bronx throughout the city and would culminate in a divisive 1968 confrontation involving parents and teachers in the Ocean Hill–Brownsville school district. Area parents boycotted subpar schools and organized separate institutions, including the People's Board of Education. The Reverend Milton Galamison, a well-known Brooklyn desegregation activist, was chosen as the new body's president, while Antonetty was appointed vice president.[46]

The People's Board used UBP research to give failing report cards to the city school system and called for the creation of local boards that would be run by parents and would have ultimate control over local education. Antonetty addressed crowds around the city, urging the school board "to cede its authority to the people." Parent activism and unrest ultimately led the city to decide in 1968 to experiment with "decentralization" of city schools to increase parent control. The Ocean Hill–Brownsville struggle emerged out of community action during the War on Poverty. For Antonetty, the idea of Parent Power represented the continuation of that politics as well as the politics of community self-help that she had learned during the Great Depression. But for the majority of unionized teachers, this shift from demands for school integration to an insistence on local control threatened an intolerable loss of teacher autonomy. A fissure soon opened up between the city's poor black and Puerto Rican parents and the predominantly white teachers' union. The city's 1968 experiment in school decentralization turned this fissure into a great divide that split the city.[47]

In the aftermath of the Ocean Hill–Brownsville struggle, parents continued the campaign for local control through the Citywide Coalition for Community Control, for which Antonetty served as spokeswoman. Drawing on training materials that the UBP had produced, the coalition conducted "Trainings for Local Control" for parents and community activists in poor neighborhoods around the city. The sessions focused on all aspects of operating a school—creating a local school board, selecting school personnel and textbooks, maintaining the physical plant. In contrast to her first impressions of her children's neighborhood school as an "island" where none of the teachers or other personnel came from the community, Antonetty and the UBP envisioned local schools steeped in the community. In asking who should control the lunch program, these activists were arguing that the meals not only should be healthy and tasty but also should represent the cultural cuisine of the student body. The UBP gathered employment statistics to make the case for challenging "racism in the building trades" and advocated hiring black and Puerto Rican workers to construct and maintain local schools. The UBP had shifted from teaching parents how to evaluate the schools that their children attended to showing them how to run schools.[48]

While positing a modern-day utopian vision of self-sufficient and self-determined urban community, the UBP and Citywide Coalition for Community Control demanded that any education policy changes proposed by the city and state be translated into Spanish and fully aired in local communities. When hearings were scheduled over Christmas break, Antonetty reacted angrily: "We will not go through a process just so the Board of Education can pretend it consulted with the community."[49] Feeling disrespected by the board, the South Bronx leaders organized an alternative neighborhood gathering, open to everyone, to discuss the new plan. All the while, the United Bronx Parents continued to run training sessions aimed at promoting local control.

In the spring of 1969, New York governor Nelson Rockefeller signed a decentralization bill into law. The new law disbanded experimental districts such as Ocean Hill–Brownsville that were to be fully controlled by parents but established thirty-three school districts that would be governed by their own local school boards. Community-control leaders and activists were enraged that the law gave parents little autonomy. Antonetty built on her history in Puerto Rican independence politics and accused the city of making colonies of its poor communities: "The Masters have given the local colonies three clear powers. We are given the power to be in charge of the cafeterias, the recreational centers and student discipline. That is all they think we can do. We are to feed the children, teach them to play and sing and dance, and then spank them when they don't behave. How much longer will we do what they tell us to do?"[50]

Antonetty and the parent activists she had helped to organize held onto their anger. In response to the board of education's 1971 fiscal crisis, a large coalition of black and Puerto Rican community leaders asserted, "Don't give more money to preserve a corrupt school system; let the communities run the schools and close down central headquarters." Led by Antonetty, the leaders argued against the city and state giving more money to the board of education. "We are tired of fighting for increased budgets," they said, "only to find more and more of our children cannot read every year."[51]

Determined to continue organizing until schools improved, the UBP remained an important presence in New York school debates into the late 1970s. Like other organizations with roots in the War on Poverty, the UBP faced funding cuts and budget crises and did not achieve all its goals. Nevertheless, the War on Poverty had provided money and legitimacy that allowed parents to attack the structural foundations of economic and social inequality in their communities and the city at large. "It was," said Antonetty, "up to parents and community activists to exploit that potential." What began as a small group of parents in one Bronx neighborhood grew into a movement that galvanized parents throughout the city of New York, home to the nation's largest public school system. Those challenges had lasting effects on the city's schools.[52]

For Antonetty and the parents she organized, challenging the culture of poverty—precisely the ideology used to justify educational inequality in their community—constituted the first point of attack, in a struggle that upended traditional power relations in the city's schools. Despite dwindling funds, the UBP subsequently continued to empower parents by training them to change the schools, disseminating its *Parent Evaluation Handbook* not only throughout the city but across the country.[53]

In the late 1960s, in coalition with other Puerto Rican groups, the UBP shifted its focus, spearheading programs and schools devoted to bilingual education. In the fall of 1968, the South Bronx became home to one of the nation's first bilingual public schools. That victory was a tribute to the UBP's tenacity, And that victory gave parents the emotional energy needed to continue their struggle for "Good Education in Our Community."[54]

Notes

1. "For Latinos, the Loss of a Guiding Light," *New York Daily News* (hereafter *NYDN*), November 22, 1984; "Roomful of Wisdom to Remember Evelina By," *NYDN*, February 5, 1987.

2. Evelina López Antonetty, interview by Lillian Lopez, February 19, 1976, Library and Archives, Centro de Estudios Puertorriqueños, Hunter College, City University of New York (hereafter Centro Library).

3. "Dr. Evelina Antonetty," in Essie E. Lee, *Women of Distinction*, Box 2, Folder 6, Records of United Bronx Parents, Library and Archives, Centro de Estudios Puertorriqueños, Hunter College, City University of New York (hereafter UBP Records).

4. Elba Cabrera, interview by Lillian Jimenez and Adina Back, August 6, 2007; interview conducted with Evelina Antonetty and Juan Flores for the video program *Island Images*, October 24, 1986, Centro Library, Vertical Files BP-18F—Bios on Evelina; Aurora Flores, "A Celebration of the Life of Evelina Antonetty," March 16, 1985, Box 3, Folder 19, Centro Library; Antonetty, interview by Lillian Lopez; "Dr. Evelina Antonetty."

5. "Dr. Evelina Antonetty."

6. Ibid., 5; Lopez, interview.

7. "Dr. Evelina Antonetty"; "Island Images" interview, op. cit.

8. "Dr. Evelina Antonetty," 7; Nicholasa Mohr, *All for the Better: A Story of El Barrio* (Austin, Tex.: Raintree Steck-Vaughn, 1993); Cabrera, interview.

9. "Gov. Hails Puerto Rican Heroine," *NYDN*, November 14, 1985.

10. "Dr. Evelina Antonetty," 6. For more on 1930s antieviction protests, see Annelise Orleck, *Common Sense and a Little Fire: Women and Working-Class Politics in the United States, 1900–1965* (Chapel Hill: University of North Carolina Press, 1995), 215–49; Mark Naison, *Communists in Harlem during the Depression* (Urbana: University of Illinois Press, 2005).

11. Lopez, interview.

12. Cabrera, interview.

13. Lopez, interview; "Sketches of Winners for Congress in City Races; Vito Marcantonio," *New York Times* (hereafter *NYT*), November 6, 1946. On radical leaders in the community, particularly Jesús Colón, see Winston James, *Holding Aloft the Banner of Ethiopia: Caribbean Radicalism in Early Twentieth-Century America* (London: Verso, 1999).

14. Cabrera, interview.

15. Ibid.

16. Flores, "A Celebration of the Life of Evelina Antonetty"; "Dr. Evelina Antonetty," 9.

17. "Gov. Hails Puerto Rican Heroine"; "Open Letter to the Puerto Rican Parents and Children of the City of New York," . . . *Toward the Dream*, October 1969, 4, Box 2, Folder 7, UBP Records.

18. Oscar Lewis, *Five Families: Mexican Case Studies in the Culture of Poverty* (New York: Basic Boos, 1959).

19. Oscar Lewis, *La Vida: A Puerto Rican Family in the Culture of Poverty—San Juan and New York* (New York: Random House, 1966), xii.

20. Ibid., xxvi. See also Oscar Lewis, *The Children of Sánchez: Autobiography of a Mexican Family* (New York: Random House, 1961).

21. Lewis, *Vida*, xxix, xlviii, lii.

22. Daniel P. Moynihan, *The Negro Family: The Case for National Action* (Washington, D.C.: U.S. Department of Labor, 1965); E. Franklin Frazier, *The Negro Family in the United States* (Chicago: University of Chicago Press, 1939); Gunnar Myrdal, *An American Dilemma: The Negro Problem and Modern Democracy* (New York: Harper, 1944); Regina Kunzel, "White Neurosis, Black Pathology: Constructing Out-of-Wedlock Pregnancy in Wartime and Postwar United States," in *Not June Cleaver: Women and Gender in Postwar America, 1945–1960,* ed. Joanne Meyerowitz (Philadelphia: Temple University Press, 1994), 320; Michael B. Katz, "The Urban 'Underclass' as a Metaphor of Social Transformation," in *The Underclass Debate: Views from History* (Princeton: Princeton University Press, 1993); see p. 12 for Katz's discussion of conservative interpretations of the culture of poverty.

23. Virginia Sanchez-Korrol, *From Colonia to Community: The History of Puerto Ricans in New York City, 1917–1948* (Westport, Conn.: Greenwood, 1983), 155–56; Sonia Nieto, "Fact and Fiction: Stories of Puerto Ricans in U.S. Schools," *Harvard Educational Review* 68:2 (Summer 1998): 148; Richard J. Margolis, *The Losers: A Report on Puerto Ricans and the Public Schools* (New York: ASPIRA, 1968). Marcantonio protested the Chamber of Commerce study on behalf of his Puerto Rican constituency in East Harlem; see Adina Back, "Up South in Nueva York" (Ph.D. diss., New York University, 1997), chap. 4.

24. Margolis, *Losers*, 3, quoted in Nieto, "Fact and Fiction," 150; E. Bucchioni, "The Daily Round of Life in the School," in *The Puerto Rican Community and Its Children on the Mainland,* ed. F. Cordasco and E. Bucchioni (Metuchen, N.J.: Scarecrow, 1982), quoted in Nieto, "Fact and Fiction," 150; Hernan LaFontaine, telephone interview by author, May 29, 1996. Nieto notes that *The Losers* included a bibliography of 450 articles and studies related to Puerto Rican children in U.S. schools ("Fact and Fiction," 156).

25. Parent Leadership Training Program, Materials Kit 4, 1967, Box 4, Folder 4, UBP Records.

26. Ibid.; "The New Redlining," *U.S. News and World Report,* April 17, 1995; Mario Luis Small and Monica McDermott, "The Presence of Organizational Resources in Poor Urban Neighborhoods: An Analysis of Average and Contextual Effects," *Social Forces* 84:3 (March 2006): 1697–1724.

27. Parent Leadership Training Program, Materials Kit 4, 1967, Box 4, Folder 4, UBP Records.

28. Ibid. See Paulo Freire, *Pedagogy of the Oppressed* (Harmondsworth: Penguin, 1972).

29. Jerald E. Podair, *The Strike That Changed New York* (New Haven: Yale University Press, 2002), 30–33, 71–73; Clarence Taylor, *Knocking at Our Door* (New York: Columbia University Press, 1997), 163; Ellen Lurie, *How to Change the Schools: A Parents' Action Handbook on How to Fight the System* (New York: Random House, 1970), back

cover; Ellen Lurie Biographical Information, Box 1, Folder 4, UBP Records. Lurie's book was dedicated to Antonetty and the UBP.

30. Various UBP materials and leaflets from this period use the term *parent power*. See Centro Library, Vertical Files b—Organizations f—UBP.

31. Figures from the Coleman report quoted in Frank Bonilla, "Opening Statement," in "'Hemos Trabajado Bien': A Report on the First National Conference of Puerto Ricans, Mexican-Americans and Educators on 'The Special Needs of Urban Puerto Rican Youth,'" May 14–15, 1968, New York City, available at http://www.eric.ed.gov/PDFS/ED023780.pdf; and Richard J. Margolis, "The Losers: A Report on Puerto Ricans and the Public Schools," in *Puerto Ricans and Educational Opportunity*, ed. Eugene Bucchioni, Maximilliano Soriano, and Diego Castellanos (New York: Arno, 1975); "Three Sisters," a segment of *Visiones* including Evelina Antonetty, interview by David Diaz, October 14, 1983, Series VIII, Oral Histories, Lillian Lopez Collection, New York State Archives, Albany; *Would You Like to Know How Your Schools Compare with the Rest of the Schools in the Bronx????*, n.d., UBP Files, United Federation of Teachers Records, Tamiment Library and Robert F. Wagner Labor Archives, New York University, New York.

32. *Would You Like to Know*; *Parents Have the Right to See Their Child's Record*, n.d., Centro Library, Vertical Files b—Organizations f—UBP; *What's in Your Child's Folder?*, n.d., Box 4, Folder 3, UBP Records.

33. *All the Children Should Read*, n.d., Centro Library, Vertical Files b Organization f-UBP.

34. David Rogers, *110 Livingston Street: Politics and Bureaucracy in the New York City Schools* (New York: Random House, 1968), 501.

35. Ibid.

36. Ibid.

37. "14 Civic Groups Charge Pupils Are Often Unfairly Suspended," *NYT*, April 6, 1967.

38. "Student's Access to Lawyer Backed," *NYT*, April 11, 1967; "Educators Score Discipline Ruling," *NYT*, April 12, 1967; "'I Want a Lawyer!,'" *NYT*, April 16, 1967.

39. "Decision Reserved on Pupil's Rights," *NYT*, June 9, 1967; "Suspension from School," *NYT*, April 14, 1967. Podair describes the issue of the "disruptive child" as one of the central points of conflict between the UFT and the African American Teachers Association. As he notes, the latter group put the term in quotation marks as a way of underscoring that the problem of the "so-called disruptive child" was the fault of the education system (*Strike*, 160–64).

40. "Parent Leadership Training Program Materials Kit #4, Discipline & Suspensions," 1967, Box 4, Folder 4, UBP Records.

41. "UBP Report Card, a Health, Education and Welfare School Evaluation Project," n.d., Centro Library, Vertical Files b—Organization f—UBP.

42. Ibid.; *How Good Is Your Child's School: A School Evaluation Handbook*, March 17, 1972, Box 4, Folder 3, UBP Records.

43. Cabrera, interview; Kathy Goldman, interview by author, April 20, 2006.

44. Cabrera, interview; Rogers, *110 Livingston Street*, 130.

45. Many Puerto Rican community leaders and parents supported school integration at the height of the movement and were active in the Citywide Coordinating Committee for Integrated Schools. During the citywide school boycott for integration in February 1964, the areas where Puerto Ricans predominated had the highest rate of absentees. However, divisions within the movement deepened over disagreements about a second boycott and the lack of support from African Americans that some Puerto Rican leaders felt when they organized a silent march across the Brooklyn Bridge.

46. "Brooklyn Sit-In Bars 2d Hearing by School Board," *NYT*, December 21, 1966; "Galamison and 11 Seized in Sit-In at School Board," *NYT*, December 22, 1966.

47. "Insurgents Propose a Plan for Schools," *NYT*, March 1, 1967. The history of the conflict in the Ocean Hill–Brownsville school district has been recounted by activists and educators involved as well as several historians. See, for example, "Ocean Hill–Brownsville, 1967–1968: 'Everything Became More Political,'" in *Voices of Freedom: An Oral History of the Civil Rights Movement from the 1950s through the 1980s*, ed. Henry Hampton and Steve Fayer (New York: Bantam, 1991), 486–509; Maurice R. Berube and Marilyn Gittell, eds., *Confrontation at Ocean Hill–Brownsville* (New York: Praeger, 1969); Jerald Podair, "Like Strangers," in *The Strike That Changed New York* (New Haven: Yale University Press, 2002), 123–52; Marjorie Murphy, *Blackboard Unions: The AFT and the NEA, 1900–1980* (Ithaca: Cornell University Press, 1990), chap. 12.

48. "Training for Local Control" documents included *The Issue of Due Process, Procedures for Evaluating and Dismissing Personnel, Selection of Personnel, How Shall the Local School Boards Be Selected?, Local Districts—How Many Should There Be?, School Construction, Repair, and Maintenance, The Physical Plant and Local Control, How Does a New School Get Constructed?, Who Should Control the School Lunch Program?, School Construction: Scandals, Delays, and Frustration, Racism in the Building Trades, Who Should Control the Repair and Maintenance Program?, How Much Do Custodians and Their Staff Earn?*, all in Folder "Decentralization—UBP, 1968–1972," United Federation of Teachers Records.

49. Press Release, January 3, 1969, Bilingual Flyer about Special Community Hearing, January 25, 1969, both in Folder "Decentralization-UBP 1968–1972," United Federation of Teachers Records.

50. "Summary and Analysis of School Decentralization Bill," Folder "Decentralization—UBP 1968–1972," United Federation of Teachers Records.

51. Press Release, March 10, 1971, Folder "Decentralization-UBP 1968–1972," United Federation of Teachers Records.

52. "45 Antipoverty Projects Here to Lose Federal Aid," *NYT*, March 21, 1968; "An Urgent Appeal to All Friends of the United Bronx Parents," January 1970, Folder "Decentralization-UBP 1968–1972," United Federation of Teachers Records. Kenneth Clark and Jeanette Hopkins, *A Relevant War against Poverty: A Study of Community Action Programs and Observable Social Change* (New York: Harper and Row, 1969), offered strong criticism of the antipoverty programs, arguing that they "were doomed to failure because they reflected a total lack of commitment to eliminate poverty, to share power with the powerless."

53. The *Parent Evaluation Handbook* and related training materials were funded by the U.S. Department of Health, Education, and Welfare (correspondence with the Department of Health, Education, and Welfare, June 28, 1971, Box 4, Folder 3, UBP Records; request for twenty thousand copies of handbook by California Legislature Joint Committee on Educational Goals and Evaluation, June 9, 1972, Box 4, Folder 3, UBP Records).

54. "A 3rd City School to Offer Spanish-English Instruction," *NYT*, July 7, 1969.

ROBERT BAUMAN

Gender, Civil Rights Activism, and the War on Poverty in Los Angeles

Three women of color, Opal Jones, Francisca Flores, and Graciela Olivarez, made signal contributions to the War on Poverty in Los Angeles. In the process, these women challenged the racial and gender status quo in that city's African American and Mexican American activist communities, in Los Angeles city government, and in the administration of the federal War on Poverty. Jones, Olivarez, and Flores had long and consistent connections to civil rights and social service organizations, giving them experience that informed their leadership of community organizations during the War on Poverty. Tracing these women's involvement with the federally funded Community Action Program illustrates the ways in which the War on Poverty was linked to and became an extension of important social movements of the era, particularly the black freedom struggle, the Chicano movement, and working-class feminism. Such an examination also provides a clearer understanding of how activists such as Flores and Jones, with deep roots both in their communities and in civil rights movements, used the structure of the War on Poverty, particularly its mantra of "maximum feasible participation" of the poor, to provide more opportunity for and advance the causes of African American women and Chicanas.

This exploration of the intersection between civil rights and antipoverty work expands and challenges our understanding of both histories in three distinct ways. First, it emphasizes the significant role women played in civil rights/ empowerment movements and in the War on Poverty in Los Angeles as well as the ways in which women's activism forced male colleagues to rethink their assumptions both about women's capacity as leaders and about the gendered nature of the poverty program. Second, Jones's, Flores's, and Olivarez's stories highlight challenges, tensions, cooperation, and conflict between Chicanos and African Americans as they attempted to create interracial coalitions through the War on Poverty. The War on Poverty in Los Angeles, like the city itself, was a multiracial enterprise. This view offers an important corrective to the popular imagery and historiography of the poverty program that has created a misconception that community action occurred only in racially homogeneous communities. Finally, these determined, motivated women fashioned careers that challenge the traditional chronology of the War on Poverty as ending with Richard Nixon's election as president. As these women's careers illustrate, a "long war on poverty" continued to evolve and grow after the demise of the Office of Economic Opportunity (OEO).

Flores, Jones, and Olivarez challenged the racial and gendered status quo by changing the definition of women's roles in the War on Poverty. Its architects originally focused almost exclusively on men, omitting from the programs professional employment opportunities and antipoverty programs geared for women. In 1967, when the OEO announced a conference on women in the War on Poverty, the idea likely was generated by women directly involved in state and local OEO programs who were dissatisfied with the male-centered focus of OEO's job training programs and with women's general share in the antipoverty effort.

Olivarez, who in the late 1960s headed Arizona's OEO, had badgered agency officials in Washington for some time to do something to increase opportunities for women in the War on Poverty. And when the conference was announced, she encouraged her longtime friend, Flores, to attend. But most OEO officials saw women involved only as an interest group lobbying for funding or as volunteers aiding the operation of programs. OEO director Sargent Shriver wrote to President Lyndon Baines Johnson that one purpose of the conference was "mobilizing the various women's organizations for legislative backing." Perhaps as a result of this view, most of the delegates came from mainstream, white-dominated women's groups. Shriver and other OEO officials who spoke at the conference emphasized the large numbers of women who had volunteered in War on Poverty programs and encouraged women to continue to do so. Flores asked why she was one of the few conference attendees who represented organizations of women of color, even though they suffered disproportionately from poverty. She, Olivarez, and Jones challenged OEO's limited vision by arguing that the agency should broaden its focus to include pathways for women to well-paid employment and programs geared specifically to serve women's needs.[1]

Race consciousness played a significant part in all three women's participation in the War on Poverty and in the response to their work. The African American Jones and the Mexican American Flores particularly challenged the racial status quo in fundamental and unique ways. When the War on Poverty was declared in 1964, many observers saw it essentially as a program for African Americans and for whites in Appalachia, and scholars subsequently have reinforced that idea. The War on Poverty in multiracial Los Angeles was much more complicated, however. Relationships between blacks and Chicanos in Los Angeles both frayed and strengthened as the boundaries of race shifted. The War on Poverty helped shape new racial and cultural identities, and these shifts changed the direction and meaning of the city's antipoverty programs.

Jones and Flores had different experiences with race as a factor in the War on Poverty, however. Jones headed an interracial and sex-integrated organization and found that interracialism was difficult to practice, particularly as the ideologies of Black Power and Chicano Power became more prevalent. Race-related controversies would cloud her tenure as a poverty program administrator, a situation further complicated by her status as a woman in a male-dominated field. Flores, inspired by the Chicano movement, became director of an explicitly Chicana organization in the early 1970s, when racially distinct organizations had become typical. Flores's agency, built on racial pride and unity, was less riven by divisions, probably at least in part because her agency was run for and by women.

These women's stories also illustrate the double-edged sword of government involvement in poverty programs. Jones headed a government-controlled agency (at least in its early years) and continually battled male government officials. Flores operated a grassroots Chicana community agency. While she at times struggled with male government officials over contracts and funding, those officials did not have control over the daily operations of her organization.

Scholarly discussions of women's roles in the War on Poverty have been a relatively recent development. Nancy A. Naples, Annelise Orleck, Christina Greene, and Rhonda Y. Williams have begun to examine gender, women's leadership, and women's activism in the War on Poverty.[2] This essay contributes to that discussion by examining the interaction of racial, ethnic, and gender-based rights movements, providing a new lens through which to view issues of gender and race in the War on Poverty. Finally, this essay roots the War on Poverty in pre-1964 movements for civil rights and social justice and examines some ways that antipoverty efforts have continued well beyond the 1970s. The antipoverty work of Flores and Olivarez in particular continued well beyond the 1970s. Indeed, the antipoverty organization founded by Flores continues combating poverty in East Los Angeles in the twenty-first century. For these women, fighting a long war on poverty was a lifelong commitment. For activists like them the War on Poverty never ended.

THE MULTIRACIAL WAR ON POVERTY

Little is known about Opal Jones's early years. She was born in Texas in the 1920s and moved to Los Angeles, along with tens of thousands of other African Americans, after World War II. Jones found herself in a Los Angeles that was highly segregated. Racially restrictive covenants established in the 1910s and 1920s limited blacks to the Central Avenue District and to Watts, a residential area seven miles south of downtown Los Angeles. Combined with the growth of the black population by seventy thousand during the war years, these restrictions meant that the black community faced limited, overcrowded housing, inadequate public transportation, and a lack of access to jobs.

The city's deteriorating social and economic conditions led Jones to seek a profession through which she could help to ameliorate the suffering she saw around her. By the mid-1950s, she had become a social worker at South-Central Los Angeles's Avalon Community Center. Jones quickly became active in citywide professional organizations, among them the Los Angeles Federation of Settlements and Neighborhood Centers, and political causes, including Tom Bradley's 1963 campaign for the Los Angeles City Council. By the early 1960s, Jones was well known both among social workers and within the African American community and had become the community center's executive director.[3]

Francisca Flores became politicized during the early 1930s, when she was a tuberculosis patient at a sanatorium in San Diego. There, she met and interacted with veterans of the Mexican Revolution who sparked what would become a lifelong interest in public activism. By the early 1960s, Flores already had an impressive activist résumé. She was a member of the Democratic Minority Conference, founder of the League of Mexican-American Women, and one of the founders of the Mexican-American Political Association (MAPA). She, too, was a well-known figure among Mexican American civil rights activists well before her encounter with the War on Poverty.[4]

Los Angeles's Mexican American population doubled to three hundred thousand during the 1950s, and Flores became an active champion of civil rights causes. The postwar period also brought increased segregation to East Los Angeles, and by 1965, more than 75 percent of the area's residents were Latino. East Los Angeles had become the major entry point for immigrants, with more than half of the area's residents born in Mexico or Latin America. When President Johnson declared the War on Poverty, unemployment and poverty rates in East Los Angeles sat at double the county average. Latino immigrants in East Los Angeles, like the African American migrants of Watts and South-Central Los Angeles, faced racially segregated housing and schools as well as high unemployment and poverty rates. The War on Poverty provided Flores and Jones with the opportunity further to expand their activism.[5]

When Johnson signed the Economic Opportunity Act in August 1964, creating the OEO to administer grants to local antipoverty organizations, communities and organizations across the nation began planning to apply for funding. Los Angeles officials announced plans to create a citywide organization, the Economic and Youth Opportunities Agency (EYOA), that would manage grants and distribute funds.

Jones was one of the chief critics of the EYOA plan, believing, as did many of the city's African Americans, that it did not adequately represent the poor. Jones hosted a meeting of African American social workers, public officials (including Bradley), and community activists to discuss strategies for channeling some federal antipoverty money to organizations in their community. Jones and her colleagues believed that Mayor Sam Yorty intended to control EYOA and limit any participation by legitimate representatives of the poor, so they created the Economic Opportunity Federation as a direct challenge to Yorty.

Like city and state officials in many other parts of the country, Yorty and other Los Angeles administrators sought to control War on Poverty funds and to resist challenges by community-based organizations. The infusion of federal antipoverty funds led to power grabs by urban mayors at the same time that the language of maximum feasible participation was galvanizing protest in impoverished communities. Such efforts forced some mayors to negotiate (although Yorty resisted) and ultimately expanded the political class in many poor communities, creating new power and jump-starting political careers. Bradley, for example, emerged as a clear leader of Los Angeles's African American community, earning a reputation for being unafraid to challenge the mayor. Bradley ran unsuccessfully against Yorty in 1963 but defeated the incumbent four years later, serving as the city's highest elected official for the next twenty years.

Jones also emerged as one of those new political leaders. Because of her long history of community work and perhaps to temper her opposition to the city's antipoverty efforts, Jones was appointed to head the Neighborhood Adult Participation Project (NAPP). The city initially proposed NAPP to OEO in November 1964 as an employment and job training program. The following month, Jones met with a representative from the President's Task Force on the War on Poverty, agreeing that NAPP would become one of the program's community service centers, outposts that focused more on community organization than employment. Supervised by the EYOA and by the Los Angeles Area Federation of Settlements, NAPP established headquarters in an office at the old Wrigley Field, a derelict forty-year-old minor league stadium in the heart of South-Central.

NAPP opened its doors on April 1, 1965, one of the few War on Poverty programs in Los Angeles to begin before the Watts revolt four months later. NAPP differed from the era's other OEO programs because it was directed by a woman and consisted of mostly female employees, presaging the community antipoverty organizations of the late 1960s and 1970s. Jones's position of leadership as a woman of color would put her at the center of two significant controversies during her tenure as NAPP's executive director, one regarding participation of the poor, the other regarding racial strife between blacks and Mexican Americans.[6]

NAPP had offices or outposts in each of thirteen poverty areas identified by the Los Angeles Welfare Planning Council. Each outpost employed thirty workers, or aides, all of whom were poor and previously unemployed residents of the communities in which they worked and most of whom were women. Jones had insisted that the aides be paid and referred to them as "change agents," first because social welfare agencies usually did not hire poor women of color and second because Jones believed that hiring neighborhood women would change the methods employed by those agencies. Jones understood that the notion of change agents was "frightening to the agencies," but, as she explained, NAPP was "only trying to bring them in closer touch with the grass roots." Some of these women served in schools as teacher aides, registering children for Head Start early childhood education centers, another War on Poverty program. Some served as liaisons between community residents and government agencies. And three employees at each outpost worked as information aides, answering residents' questions. These aides went door to door, asking families about their needs, those of the neighborhood, and how community members could work together to accomplish change. In other words, they essentially served as community organizers.

NAPP initially organized neighborhoods for better street lighting, weekly garbage collection, child care centers, and food banks. NAPP also provided adult education classes, conducted voter registration drives, and provided employment services as well as job training programs. NAPP's 1966 annual report featured a cartoon with a baby (NAPP) struggling under a "heavy load"—the agency's programs and responsibilities. In the middle of the sack, as at the center of NAPP, was "citizen participation."[7]

In April 1966, Jones was fired. The *Los Angeles Sentinel*, the city's largest black newspaper, editorialized that Jones had been dismissed because of the "philosophy behind the operation of her NAPP program." The paper also argued that NAPP would continue to succeed only if it was "taken completely from under the political thumb of the EYOA and . . . Mayor Yorty." Jones attributed her firing to the fact that she had made grassroots citizen participation a reality and that she was a woman. She told the *Sentinel*, "I will fight for my own right and reputation as a social worker and for NAPP to become an independent, vital community action program." She also asked city leaders to deal with her as a staff member, not as a woman. Jones's firing touched off a storm of protest. More than three hundred people, most of them African American and Latino and many NAPP employees, congregated in the parking lot outside NAPP headquarters. Led by Congressman Augustus Hawkins, the crowd protested Jones's firing and blamed Yorty. Another group led a march to picket the EYOA offices.[8]

Jones's firing and the public response created a crisis for federal OEO officials. Following negotiations that included Shriver, Yorty agreed to rehire Jones and divest NAPP from EYOA control, thereby enabling city officials to disclaim responsibility for Jones's activities. What municipal leaders had initially found appalling now seemed reasonable. NAPP received greater independence under the eye of the Federated Settlements and Neighborhood Centers. Jones had effectively wrenched control of NAPP from Yorty and the EYOA.[9]

Though the issue of representation and control had been resolved, NAPP experienced further controversy as a result of interracial tensions. Many of Los Angeles's African Americans, like Jones, were recent migrants who had lived in primarily black communities in the South before migrating to predominantly black South-Central Los Angeles. Many of these people were unused to interacting with Mexican Americans. But Latinos comprised the city's largest minority group and understandably believed that they should have an equal share of War on Poverty services and resources. Because the outlay for War on Poverty programs never approached levels that would adequately have addressed the problems associated with poverty, groups competed for the scarce resources. Los Angeles's Latino groups began to demand greater funding and more services from and greater control over War on Poverty programs. From the beginning, Mexican Americans had questioned why only three of the thirteen NAPP outposts (in East Los Angeles, Boyle Heights, and Pacoima) were located in majority Mexican American neighborhoods and employed Mexican American directors, while the rest of the offices were in African American areas. NAPP and Jones became targets for those who felt that Mexican Americans were not being adequately served or represented.[10]

These tensions peaked in September 1966, when Jones fired Gabriel Yánez, director of the Boyle Heights field office. Jones claimed that Yánez had told his aides not to attend meetings she called and had discouraged residents in his area from involvement in NAPP because it favored African Americans. Jones also argued that Yánez was contributing to the split between Mexican Americans and African Americans both within NAPP and in Los Angeles as a whole. Yánez's dismissal infuriated many Latinos, and forty people picketed NAPP offices, criticizing NAPP and EYOA for showing favoritism toward blacks. Bob Ramirez, a NAPP aide from the Boyle Heights outpost, told a reporter, "Until now it was the Negroes who used these tactics. Now we're picketing. And we're going to keep picketing until our problems are recognized."[11]

Jones initially defended the placement of NAPP offices, arguing that the locations were based on a Welfare Planning Council study of pockets of poverty. A few days later, under extreme pressure and at the insistence of the Federation of Settlement Board of Directors, Jones rehired Yánez, but the damage had been done. Irene Tovar, Latina director of the NAPP outpost in Pacoima, resigned to protest Yánez's firing, saying that the incident made "it very clear . . . that I can no longer work within the framework of NAPP." Tovar succinctly summed up the racial tensions and trouble that lay ahead for the War on Poverty in Los Angeles: "What's good for Watts and the civil rights movement is not necessarily good for the Mexican-American community."[12]

Edward Roybal, who represented East Los Angeles in the U.S. Congress, tried to use the NAPP controversy to deepen Mexican Americans' involvement in the War on Poverty. He wrote to a Mexican American NAPP employee that Yánez's dismissal was "unfortunate. It did, however, bring to the forefront a troublesome problem of long-standing, as well as highlight the many inequities which should have been resolved long ago." Roybal was troubled by the ongoing and escalating tensions between blacks and Mexican Americans as well as by the small number of NAPP outposts in Mexican American neighborhoods. The congressman hoped to encourage Latino organizations "to sponsor additional Teen Post programs." Moreover, Roybal hoped that with "the cooperation of all concerned, the Mexican-American community will eventually receive the attention due them in the anti-poverty war."[13]

In 1967, Roybal, Hawkins, and Congressman George Brown Jr., along with Bert Corona, MAPA's president, met with Jones to develop strategies to increase Mexican American representation in NAPP. Jones later expressed her appreciation for Roybal's help, writing, "It was like our old association back at the Avalon Center. . . . I am glad that we were able to be together again after our years of absence." She also thanked Corona, calling him a "life-saver" who "recognizes, as I do, the importance of our teamwork and cooperation together, for that will be the only way that we will make it." Jones, Roybal, Corona, and other leaders in both the African American and Mexican American communities understood that their mutual interests required them to work together rather than in conflict with each other. Their cooperation reflected the opportunities for interracial, interethnic collaboration opened up by the War on Poverty. But these efforts grew out of deep rifts that the myopia of federal poverty administrators had made more painful and that took extraordinary efforts to heal.[14]

Jones came to understand that interracial cooperation was essential to community activism and success in the War on Poverty, but she continued to battle racial tensions throughout the remainder of her time at NAPP. In 1971, the members of the Los Angeles Federation of Settlements and Neighborhood Centers elected her the group's president. She continued in that role through the 1970s before retiring and moving back to Texas.[15]

Jones rarely spoke openly or directly about women's roles in the War on Poverty and apparently had no direct links to feminist organizations. Yet her example as a paid director of a War on Poverty program that openly encouraged participation by poor women challenged OEO's notions of women's appointed roles in the War on Poverty. In addition, by hiring women as most of the directors and staff of the thirteen NAPP outposts, she modeled an alternative vision of the War on Poverty that acknowledged poor neighborhood women's expertise in determining their communities' needs and that made clear the importance of programs that offered poor women paid, meaningful work. Although she did not explicitly say so, the fact that she hired mostly women as NAPP aides suggests that she believed that poor mothers were the true experts on poverty and the people who knew best what their neighborhoods needed.

Jones's vision meshed with a strategy for fighting poverty espoused by other black women community activists in the West. Like Ruby Duncan, founder of a Las Vegas community organization, Operation Life, that was led by black mothers, Jones subscribed to the vision that poverty programs should hire poor mothers to help provide services to poor communities. That vision was also shared by Johnnie Tillmon, who formed one of the first grassroots welfare mothers' organizations, Aid to Needy Children Mothers Anonymous, in 1963. Tillmon served as director of NAPP's Watts outpost before becoming one of the key figures of the welfare rights movement. This essentially radical idea of empowering poor women certainly encouraged some the opposition against Jones and NAPP.[16]

As an African American woman with connections to black male political leaders and civil rights activists, Jones provided an important link between the black freedom struggle and the War on Poverty. But her roots in and ideological affinity with racial solidarity movements also became a point of conflict for her as Mexican Americans challenged her leadership of NAPP. These rifts worsened as the African American and Chicano civil rights movements shifted from an integrationist ideal to one more rooted in racial and ethnic identity. NAPP became the chief battleground of the War on Poverty in Los Angeles between African Americans informed by Black Power and Mexican Americans influenced by the emerging Chicano movement.

Gender and race also played significant roles in Flores's War on Poverty career but did so somewhat differently than they did for Jones. Flores was directly involved in feminist causes and headed an explicitly ethnically based and gender-distinct organization. She helped to establish the Chicana Service Action Center (CSAC) as a community action agency in June 1972. CSAC was directly affiliated with a larger Chicana feminist federation, the Comisión Femenil Mexicana Nacional (CFMN), founded in 1970. The CSAC combined the framework of the War on Poverty and the ideology of a burgeoning Chicana feminism to provide services and leadership training for Mexican American women in East Los Angeles. Most of the women who founded CSAC had come out of the Chicano civil rights movement, but they wanted to establish organizations free from the sexism they had encountered there. They considered themselves feminist but wanted to create an organization independent of a women's movement they believed did not adequately address issues of concern to women of color, most notably underemployment and poverty. Building on the growing demand for more programs for women in the War on Poverty and on women's attempts to obtain a greater voice within the Chicano movement, these activists created an agency that would organize and train East Los Angeles women for leadership positions. Using the War on Poverty's community action model and the ideologies of the Chicano and feminist movements, these women built an antipoverty agency focused on the cultural, economic, and political empowerment of Chicanas in East Los Angeles.

CSAC was a child of crosscurrents and conflicts within the Chicano movement. In 1970, Sacramento, California, was the site of the National Issues Conference, sponsored by a coalition of Chicano organizations: the GI Forum (a Hispanic veterans' organization), the League of United Latin American Citizens, MAPA, and the Association of Mexican-American Educators. About thirty Chicanas at the conference, including Flores, met in a women's issues workshop to discuss topics of importance to them, such as abortion, birth control, child care, poverty, Chicano stereotypes, machismo, and Chicana leadership. Angered by their exclusion from leadership roles in Mexican American organizations, the women created the CFMN to organize and train women leaders and to address issues of importance to Chicanas. Members of the new group immediately passed resolutions advocating bilingual, bicultural sixteen-hour child care centers; legalized abortion and birth control; and the creation of a woman-run antipoverty organization.[17]

Flores always envisioned the CFMN as separate from Anglo feminist organizations. The thirty original members noted the organization's dual inspiration from the Chicano and feminist movements but explained that the "effort and work of Chicana/Mexicana women in the Chicano movement is generally obscured because women are not accepted as community leaders, either by the Chicano movement or by the Anglo establishment." Group members pledged to develop Chicana awareness, advocate for Chicana rights, provide leadership training, ensure the welfare of the Chicana community, and remain a female-dominated organization.[18]

Flores argued that the CFMN was organized "to provide a platform for women to use for thinking out their problems, to deal with issues not customarily taken up in regular organizations, and to develop programs around home and family needs." The "regular organizations" to which Flores referred included such Mexican American civil rights and antipoverty organizations as the GI Forum and the League of United Latin American Citizens that were led by and focused on men. Flores later said that the male-dominated organizations "used us; the men had us doing the work and they couldn't have operated without the women. Yet women were never nominated for president, vice president, or any other executive office." Flores and the other founders of CFMN were motivated by "the realization that it didn't matter how long we worked together with the men in MAPA and other organizations. We were not part of the leadership, and they weren't going to allow us to be part of it." Thus, Flores saw the creation of CFMN in part as "a subconscious attack against women's' auxiliaries" of traditional Mexican American civil rights organizations, groups with which Flores was quite familiar and had substantial connections.[19]

Flores maintained a close friendship and correspondence with Graciela Olivarez, a Chicana activist who had helped found the National Organization for Women in 1966. President Johnson appointed Olivarez as head of the Arizona OEO, and President Jimmy Carter later made her director of the Community Services Administration (the successor agency to OEO).

Olivarez was born in 1928 in the mining town of Sonora, Arizona, to a Spanish American father who worked as a machinist in the copper mines and a Mexican American mother. She dropped out of high school and moved to Phoenix, where she worked at a Spanish-language radio station for fourteen years, eventually becoming the station's program director. In 1962, Olivarez made the first of several appearances before the U.S. Civil Rights Commission, testifying about the living and working conditions faced by impoverished Mexican Americans in the Southwest. From 1962 to 1966, Olivarez also worked for the Choate Foundation, where she served as an advocate for Mexican American civil rights.

Flores and Olivarez corresponded regularly during the early 1960s about what they saw as languishing Mexican American struggles for social justice. In November 1963, Olivarez complained to Flores about Mexican Americans' lack of progress toward full civil rights: "In spite of all the noise we have been making in the southwest, none of it has reached Washington and so we can spend the rest of the year and next making speeches, noises, holding conventions and everything else but . . . we are just spinning our wheels. . . . We need to do a lot of work in the field of orienting and training. We are way behind the Negro." Olivarez believed that what was needed was a "democratic coalition of the southwest" including blacks, Mexican Americans, and Jews.[20]

Olivarez's dismay over the lack of progress by Mexican Americans and what she saw as a lack of leadership by some Mexican American politicians steadily deepened. She wrote to Flores that "Our people are very green when it comes to politics, and it hurts me to see some of us deceive the rest." In 1964, Olivarez complained that the U.S. Civil Rights Commission had been in Los Angeles "and got absolutely nowhere with their investigation. After my plea and my 'ruegos' [requests] to the Commission two years ago . . . they send out investigators who can't get any information because everyone keeps saying that all is fine with the Mexicanos." Olivarez's frustration with the bureaucracy, her passion for social and economic justice, and her intelligence impressed Notre Dame president Theodore Hesburgh, who encouraged her to go to law school. Olivarez followed his advice and in 1970 became Notre Dame law school's first female graduate.[21]

The War on Poverty offered Olivarez a chance to attack the problems of Mexican Americans from a different angle. In October 1964, two months after President Johnson signed the Economic Opportunity Act, Olivarez became a consultant to the program. She immediately told leaders of the Volunteers in Service to America (VISTA) program about Flores. Over the next few years, Olivarez became consumed with War on Poverty activities and duties. In addition to her position with the Arizona OEO, she served on the agency's national advisory council and as executive secretary of the National Conference on Poverty in the Southwest. She also continued to encourage Flores's involvement.[22]

Flores nevertheless resisted becoming enmeshed in the federal poverty bureaucracy, instead becoming an unofficial liaison between War on Poverty officials and Mexican Americans. War on Poverty officials often attempted to entice Flores to become more actively involved with antipoverty programs. She rejected an offer from the director of the Job Corps Center for Women to join the center's advisory committee, though she accepted a request to serve on the advisory committee for the Upward Bound program at the University of California at Los Angeles. VISTA director William Crook consulted her, as did other OEO officials, and she participated in various conferences and agency programs.[23]

By 1970, Flores was intimately familiar with the programs and policies of the OEO and the War on Poverty and saw the antipoverty program as a way to extend her involvement in civil rights efforts. Following her graduation from law school, Olivarez worked as the director of Food for All, an OEO-funded program created to improve federal food programs in Arizona.[24]

Flores began to move the CFMN to create an antipoverty organization run by and for Chicanas. In the early 1970s, the CFMN applied for and received a fifty-thousand-dollar grant to create a community action agency to assist low-income Chicanas. Initially funded as a one-year demonstration project, the CFMN opened the CSAC on Boyle Street in East Los Angeles in August 1972.

Flores's CSAC proposal noted that there were numerous government programs and social service agencies designed to aid the unemployed and underemployed but argued that "little, if any, emphasis has been placed on the needs of women. . . . Childcare, women's health needs in family planning, general health, education, and employment are the needs of women within the disadvantaged community." Because poor Chicanas lacked not only the time and resources to travel to other communities for social and health services but also "English language skills," CFMN "proposed to establish a women's center in the Mexican-American community" run by and for Chicanas. The CSAC would help women who needed services, develop new employment opportunities for Chicana women, negotiate with politicians and social service professionals to see that these women's needs were met, and publish a Spanish-language newsletter to disseminate information to the broader community. Finally, the center's employees would be "trained to understand the problems of all women, and in particular Chicanas." The CSAC clearly reflected the confluence of feminism, Chicana activism, and the community action aspect of the War on Poverty.[25]

Flores and the CSAC focused much of their efforts on job training. In 1970, 15 percent of Los Angeles Chicanas were unemployed, and their median income was less than one-third of Chicanos. In addition, 25 percent of the city's Chicanas worked in service positions, while 27 percent held clerical jobs and only 5 percent received paychecks for professional employment. The fact that 42 percent of Mexican American families in Los Angeles County headed by women were living at or below the poverty level highlighted the importance of well-paid employment for Chicanas. Early indications at CSAC reinforced Flores's and other CSAC leaders' beliefs about the importance of job training. More than 50 percent of Chicanas who came to CSAC were unskilled or untrained women under the age of thirty. Most were high school dropouts and single mothers.[26]

In 1974, CSAC applied for a nine-hundred-thousand-dollar Comprehensive Employment and Training Act (CETA) grant from the Los Angeles County CETA Appeals Committee. Initially proposed in 1969 and signed into law by President Nixon in 1973, CETA essentially replaced the Manpower Development and Training Act (MDTA) as the most significant federal jobs program. CETA differed from MDTA in that it centered more job and job training programs at the local level rather than with the state or federal governments. Many of these programs were housed in what became called community-based organizations—mostly community action agencies, like CSAC, created under OEO auspices. President Carter signed legislation doubling the number of public service jobs funded through CETA, greatly expanding funding for job training programs and increasing participants' earned income. For CSAC and other community organizations that focused on job training, CETA was vital. The Reagan administration killed CETA in 1982 as part of its anti-big-government campaign, but until that time, CETA funds helped provide job training and placement for thousands of women through CSAC and millions of women nationally.[27]

The Los Angeles CETA committee rejected most of CSAC's 1974 proposal, funding only the 10 percent of the request that was slated for counseling and supportive staffing services. Los Angeles county staff argued that Mexican American women did not need job training services because they did not need jobs. Administrators also reasoned that CSAC's program would discriminate by serving only Chicanas. One male member of the CETA Appeals Committee derisively referred to the CSAC board members present as "those feminists."[28]

Flores and CSAC were not deterred by such antifeminist hostility. The CSAC newsletter's first issue bore a front-page article, "The Emancipation of the Mujer," that asserted that the agency was committed to Chicanas' cultural, political, and economic freedom. Articles in other CSAC newsletters informed readers on issues of concern to Chicanas and highlighted the accomplishments of women of Mexican descent. Flores believed in print culture's power to promote the ideals and ideology of the Chicana feminist movement. In 1970, she had founded a journal, *Regeneración*, and she had been part of a core group of California Chicanas involved in the creation of other publications intended to promote Chicana artistic expression, scholarly analysis, and political and cultural ideology. The CSAC newsletters, focused on issues of "collective self-knowledge" and "collective self-determination," served as "organizing tools" for the Chicana movement that "helped to constitute and document new forms of Chicana insurgency during this period."[29]

Flores and the CSAC board fought for their CETA proposal. Throughout the fall of 1974, Flores badgered local, state, and federal CETA officials. She refuted the claims that Mexican American women did not need the services and that CSAC's program would not provide any new services. In early December, she penned a letter to all CFMN members asking for their support in CSAC's battle for CETA funds. Late in the month, Flores received word that CSAC would receive the CETA funding.[30]

CSAC became one of the longest-lasting of Los Angeles's War on Poverty agencies. At the end of the 1990s, it provided job training, counseling, and health services to more than twenty-five thousand Chicanas in East Los Angeles annually. Flores remained active in the agency until her death in 1996. Her funeral, held at CSAC headquarters, drew many younger Chicana women whom she had served or mentored. Her activist experience was far less conflicted than that of Jones or even that of Olivarez because Flores remained outside of government agencies but still tapped into the resources made possible by the War on Poverty.[31] Olivarez had died in 1987. Jones, too, had already passed away, and her NAPP had predeceased her.

Though Flores's experiences differed significantly from those of Jones and Olivarez, the three women are united by their lifelong pursuit of economic, social, and cultural empowerment for people of color and particularly for women. All three challenged gender norms both in government and in their communities, and all faced backlashes on that score.

Many federal programs started during the War on Poverty remained active at the end of the twentieth century, and some, such as Head Start and Legal Services, even flourished, in part because of the commitment of activists who made defending those programs their life's work. Community organizations such as NAPP and CSAC, formed as a result of the War on Poverty and energized by the civil rights and cultural empowerment movements as well as by feminism, reshaped the landscape of urban social services and political organizing. CSAC, the Watts Labor Community Action Committee in Los Angeles, Communities Organized for Public Service in San Antonio, Texas, and other organizations continue to serve many tens of thousands of people.

Flores's, Olivarez's, and Jones's stories demonstrate the centrality of gender and women activists to the struggle against poverty. Women grassroots activists, women's neighborhood organizations, and women leaders and administrators became a vibrant part of the War on Poverty in the late 1960s and early 1970s. As in Las Vegas, Durham, Baltimore, and other cities across the United States, these Los Angeles activists believed that women of color had specific economic needs that could be met only through a organizations run by and for women. Jones's experiences with NAPP further demonstrated the difficulties that women of color faced working in male-dominated interracial organizations.[32]

The leadership styles and positions of Jones, Flores, and Olivarez raise questions about the roles of women in social movements. These women clearly served as more than "bridge leaders," although their organizations did at times serve as bridges between their clients and Chicano or black political leaders. More often, however, these women provided political and economic leadership. Indeed, their collective style also challenges Karen Sacks's description of "center women," who sustain women's networks but allow male leaders to be the public spokespersons for organizations, causes, or movements. Through their writings, public testimony, press conferences, and political activism, Flores and Jones worked as more than sustainers of networks, serving as the public faces and voices for the cause of Los Angeles's poor Chicanas and African Americans. Olivarez filled much the same role for the Mexican American poor nationwide. In some ways, these women most closely resemble Naples's description of activist mothering—using social activism to address the needs of the community rather than for individual advancement.[33]

Jones, Olivarez, and Flores, the movements they helped to galvanize, and the organizations they shaped and drove clearly exemplify the coming together of movements for social, political, economic, and cultural empowerment with the War on Poverty. These grassroots movements and organizations, centered on race and/or gender, attempted to use the framework of the War on Poverty to gain economic, social, and cultural power for poor women and people of color. The careers of these women also demonstrate that the War on Poverty and those social movements were not static. As those movements interacted with community antipoverty programs, both evolved and changed, shifting tactics and strategies and redefining poverty politics and gender and racial politics in America. Some of the programs that these women helped to shape collapsed from budget cuts and political opposition in the 1980s and 1990s. But others, like CSAC, continue to thrive. Often unknown outside of their own communities, these vibrant coalitions continue to wage war on poverty into the second decade of the twenty-first century.

Notes

1. OEO, *Conference Proceedings: Women in the War on Poverty* (Washington, D.C.: U.S. Government Printing Office, 1967), 57; Sargent Shriver to Lyndon Baines Johnson, April 20, 1967, Lyndon Baines Johnson Library, Austin, Texas; OEO, *Women in the War on Poverty* (Washington, D.C.: U.S. Government Printing Office, 1969), 1–3; Kazuyo Tsuchiya, "Race, Class, and Gender in America's 'War on Poverty': The Case of Opal C. Jones in Los Angeles, 1964–1968," *Japanese Journal of American Studies* 15 (2004): 218–20.

2. Nancy A. Naples, *Grassroots Warriors: Activist Mothering, Community Work, and the War on Poverty* (New York: Routledge, 1998); Annelise Orleck, *Storming Caesars Palace: How Black Mothers Fought Their Own War on Poverty* (Boston: Beacon, 2005); Christina Greene, *Our Separate Ways: Women and the Black Freedom Movement in Durham, North Carolina* (Chapel Hill: University of North Carolina Press, 2005); Rhonda Y. Williams, *The Politics of Public Housing* (New York: Oxford University Press, 2004).

3. Tsuchiya, "Race," 213–36.

4. "Francisca Flores Vitae," Box 40, Folder 1, Comisión Femenil Mexicana Nacional Papers, California Ethnic and Multicultural Archives, University of California Santa Barbara Special Collections Library (hereafter CFMN Papers).

5. California Department of Industrial Relations, *Negroes and Mexican-Americans in South and East Los Angeles* (San Francisco: State of California, 1966), 23–24.

6. NAPP Progress Report, August 1, 1965, Box 3, NAPP Records, California Social Welfare Archives, University of Southern California, Los Angeles.

7. NAPP Progress Report, August 1, 1965, Box 3, NAPP Records; NAPP Annual Report, 1966, Box 2, Los Angeles Area Federation of Settlements and Neighborhood Centers, University of Southern California, Los Angeles; Jack Jones, "Opal Jones Mellows as Poverty Project Grows," *Los Angeles Times*, March 30, 1967; "NAPP Fights Poverty with Total Grass-Roots Approach," *Los Angeles Sentinel*, June 10, 1965.

8. Betty Pleasant, "Opal Jones Views Fight: Hearing on Dismissal Set Wednesday," *Los Angeles Sentinel*, April 7, 1966; Roy Rogers, "Crowd Holds Rally to Protest Firing of Poverty Aide," *Los Angeles Times*, April 6, 1966.

9. "EYOA Reinstates Mrs. Opal Jones," *Los Angeles Sentinel*, April 28, 1966.

10. Opal Jones, "The Mexican-Americans in NAPP," n.d., Box 3, NAPP Records.

11. Opal Jones to Gabriel Yánez, September 8, 1966, Box 3, NAPP Records; Art Berman, "Latin-American Quits Antipoverty Job in a Row," *Los Angeles Times*, September 16, 1966.

12. Jack Jones, "Irate Mexican-American Units Demand Poverty War Equality," *Los Angeles Times*, September 25, 1966.

13. Edward Roybal to Paul Ramirez, October 5, 1966, Box 193, Folder 25, Edward R. Roybal Papers, Special Collections Library, California State University–Los Angeles.

14. Opal Jones to Edward Roybal, August 28, 1968, Box 190, Roybal Papers.

15. Tsuchiya, "Race," 230.

16. On Duncan and black mothers in Las Vegas, see Orleck, *Storming Caesars Palace*, 208–78. On Tillmon, see Guida West, *The National Welfare Rights Movement* (New York: Praeger, 1981).

17. "History of Comisión Femenil de Los Angeles, Feb. 1983," pt. 1, Collection 30, Box 1, Folder 6, Comisión Femenil de Los Angeles Papers, Chicano Studies Research Center, University of California–Los Angeles.

18. Ibid.

19. Francisca Flores, "Comisión Femenil Mexicana," *Regeneración* 1:2 (1971): 6–7; Francisca Flores, interview by Gloria Moreno-Wycoff, October 19, 1982, Box 46, CFMN Papers.

20. Graciela Olivarez to Francisca Flores, November 26, 1963, Box 38, Folder 1, CFMN Papers; Jimmy Gurulé, "Amazing Grace: A Tribute to Graciela Olivarez," *Notre Dame Lawyer*, Fall 2006, 18–19.

21. Graciela Olivarez to Francisca Flores, December 17, 1963, July 28, 1964, both in Box 38, Folder 1, CFMN Papers; Gurulé, "Amazing Grace," 18–19.

22. Graciela Olivarez to Francisca Flores, October 6, 1964, January 6, 1965, both in Box 41, Folder 4, CFMN Papers.

23. "Francisca Flores Vitae," Box 40, Folder 1, CFMN Papers; William Crook to Flores, May 19, 1967, Box 41, Folder 6, CFMN Papers.

24. Gurulé, "Amazing Grace," 19.

25. CSAC Original Proposal, Box 38, Folder 6, CFMN Papers.

26. Anna Nieto Gomez, "Chicanas in the Labor Force," *Encuentro Femenil* 1:2 (1974): 28–33.

27. Grace A. Franklin and Randall B. Ripley, *CETA: Politics and Policy, 1973–1982* (Knoxville: University of Tennessee Press, 1984), xi–xiii, 3–22.

28. CSAC Executive Board Meeting Minutes, November 14, 1974, Box 39, Folder 2, CFMN Papers.

29. CSAC Newsletters, 1973–77, Collection 30, Box 2, Folder—"Chicana Service Action Center," Comisión Femenil de Los Angeles Papers; Maylei Blackwell, "Contested Histories: *Las Hijas de Cuauhtémoc*, Chicana Feminisms, and Print Culture in the Chicano Movement, 1968–1973," in *Chicana Feminisms: A Critical Reader*, ed. Gabriela F. Arrendondo (Durham, N.C.: Duke University Press, 2003), 62, 78.

30. Steven M. Porter to Francisca Flores, December 23, 1974, Box 39, Folder 4, CFMN Papers; Francisca Flores to CFMN Members, December 2, 1974, Box 70, Folder 5, CFMN Papers.

31. Francisca Flores Funeral Program, Box 24, Folder 19, CFMN Papers.

32. Orleck, *Storming Caesars Palace*; Greene, *Our Separate Ways*; Williams, *Politics of Public Housing*.

33. Karen Sacks, *Caring by the Hour* (Champaign: University of Illinois Press, 1988); Belinda Robnett, *How Long? How Long?: African-American Women in the Struggle for Civil Rights* (New York: Oxford University Press, 1997); Naples, *Grassroots Warriors*.

PART THREE

The War on Poverty, the Civil Rights Movement, and Southern Politics

KENT B. GERMANY

Poverty Wars in the Louisiana Delta

White Resistance, Black Power, and the Poorest Place in America

A quarter century after President Lyndon Baines Johnson declared an unconditional War on Poverty, the U.S. Census revealed Lake Providence,
Louisiana, to be the poorest place in America. In 1990, an almost four-square-
mile census block covering the town's southern half earned the troubling distinction of having the nation's lowest median annual income, beating out other
low-income areas in the Southwest borderlands, the Appalachian Mountains,
the Alabama agricultural Black Belt, and American Indian reservations. The
small town's average annual income of $6,500 for a family of four was not even
half of the national poverty line of $14,700; 72 percent of the people in the cen-
sus block lived below that line.[1]

Set along the Mississippi River in the far northeastern corner of Louisiana,
eight miles north of a place called Transylvania, Lake Providence lies in the
heart of a vast agricultural area known simply as the Delta. In 1990, Lake Providence was the poorest town in the poorest parish in the poorest region of one
of the poorest states in the Union. Twenty-six years after the passage of the Civil
Rights Act and the launching of the War on Poverty, Lake Providence remained
largely segregated by race, operated a weak and poorly funded public education system, and was most famous for being among the least attractive places to
live in the United States. During that time, the town had lost half its population
and had become essentially insignificant in a national economy booming as a
consequence of innovations in technology and information. For an astute *Time*

magazine journalist, the town had become a symbol of what had gone wrong in America.[2]

Why did the War on Poverty not prevent Lake Providence from becoming so poor? An easy answer is to agree with President Ronald Reagan's cynical declaration in his 1988 State of the Union Address that poverty had won that war. Accepting that answer, however, requires ignoring the actual history of the War on Poverty. One of the major reasons that it never reached the lofty goals espoused in Johnson's rhetoric was the intense and often violent opposition the antipoverty effort generated. In the late 1960s, the War on Poverty was little match for the Delta's poverty and traditions, which engendered extreme white resistance to black advancement and racial inclusion, an economy too dependent on the land and on low wages, and an education system designed to perpetuate white privilege. Judging from the struggle to implement the War on Poverty in the area, President Johnson's beloved initiative was not equipped to alter the social, cultural, and economic conditions of a region whose leadership tended to prefer preserving white supremacy over economic innovation, quality public education, and investment in human capital. For some of the region's most powerful leaders, the War on Poverty and its supporters were the enemies, and if they could not be denied, they needed to be curtailed and controlled. In the Delta, perhaps the better question is not "What won the War on Poverty?" but "What won the war on the War on Poverty?"

On satellite maps, the Delta looks like an ancient accident that spilled out of Illinois and came to rest midway into Louisiana. The largest and most written about part of it lies in Mississippi, the dusty plain between Memphis and Vicksburg that historian James Cobb has declared "the most southern place on earth."[3] On the Louisiana side, the Delta takes up approximately ten thousand square miles and accounts for about one-fifth of the state's land mass.

In the early 1960s, the Louisiana Delta, similar to its counterparts in Mississippi and Arkansas, was home to a plantation culture that had produced intense devotion to white supremacy and high concentrations of both wealth and poverty. White citizens controlled virtually every aspect of public life at least to some degree. This situation was intensified in the parishes (Louisiana's term for *county*) bordering the Mississippi River, which typically had majority black populations and poverty rates nearly five times the national average. At least two of those parishes, Madison and East Carroll (the home of Lake Providence), had no black voters as late as 1962. In the 1950s and 1960s, cotton remained king there, springing forth every summer from the rich alluvial soil, but fortunes were also built from lumber and petroleum. The Delta, however, was changing in those years, as developments in technology, mechanization, and race relations forced the region's residents to adjust to the South's social and economic modernization.

Beginning in 1964, the War on Poverty was poised to become a significant part of that process, offering programs to help improve education, to cope with the loss of farm jobs, and to facilitate racial integration. In the early years, however, the federal effort to address long-standing poverty became part of the battle over ending the approximately eighty-year-old system of racial segregation known as Jim Crow. This battle turned the War on Poverty into a target for white supremacists, including the Ku Klux Klan, and substantially limited the effort's potential to transcend its chaotic beginnings.

Across the region, War on Poverty organizers and workers faced violence, intimidation, economic reprisals, and politically motivated investigations from white supremacists intent on weakening the Community Action Program and its Head Start programs. Beginning in 1966, Head Start, a seemingly innocuous initiative to teach letters, colors, etiquette, and hygiene to five-year-olds, sparked yet another outbreak of white supremacist terrorism and showed that black leaders wanting any significant voice in public life had to be courageous, cunning, and creative. These struggles to create antipoverty agencies and Head Start centers illustrated that any efforts at economic development, workforce rehabilitation, or social welfare investment would be defined by entrenched notions of black and white.

The War on Poverty was foremost about creating economic opportunity. Most white leaders and their constituents in the Delta, however, saw the antipoverty effort in that light only if it was under their power. Accustomed from the time of the New Deal to controlling federal programs in the area, particularly when they involved agriculture, rural life, or social welfare, white Delta leaders rushed to establish their authority over programs emerging from the Great Society. Refusing to concede even the slightest ground to African American leaders, committed white segregationists fought against black participation in the War on Poverty (and ultimately against the War on Poverty itself) with a mix of violence, subterfuge, and bureaucratic manipulation. Intimidation helped curb participation in antipoverty programs and helped affirm white residents' perception that the War on Poverty was for black residents and should be avoided by whites. Equally important was determining who would control the funds flowing in from Washington. White segregationists continued to dominate the local economy and much of its politics, but after the Civil Rights Act of 1964 and the Voting Rights Act of 1965, a new generation of black leaders used the War on Poverty to confront Jim Crow and to carve out a foothold of bureaucratic and political power.

In three Delta parishes in the mid- to late 1960s, black antipoverty leaders withstood segregationist resistance long enough to build small but relatively long-term antipoverty agencies. In all three instances, the leaders benefited from previous civil rights organizing work by the Congress of Racial Equality (CORE), the national civil rights organization that had led the Freedom Rides in 1961 and had become a major force throughout the Deep South.[4] Zelma G. Wyche, Father August Thompson, and the Reverend Philip Rayfield Brown took on powerful segregationists and won. Wyche and Brown received national attention, Wyche for his bravado and eventual electoral success, and Brown for tangling with the Ku Klux Klan and other whites who wanted to refocus local War on Poverty efforts more exclusively on poor whites. Wyche became one of the first black chiefs of police in the modern South and the president of the local War on Poverty agency, while Brown survived a brutal showdown with the Klan and the area's elite white leadership, including Otto Passman, a nine-term congressman renowned as one of the staunchest segregationists on Capitol Hill.

The greatest bureaucratic ally of these black leaders was the new Office of Economic Opportunity (OEO), created by the Economic Opportunity Act of 1964 to administer the War on Poverty initiatives. Because the OEO required the racial integration of Head Start programs at a time when almost all Louisiana school boards were still defying federal desegregation rulings, white segregationists came to see preschool classes as a despised symbol of federal power and black advancement. The OEO's "extremely conservative" estimate found that, in 1966 alone, terror tactics by the Ku Klux Klan in the area directly affected 375 students and 45 teachers and aides. Approximately two-thirds of those students and three-quarters of those teachers and aides were white.[5]

Two easy tools of intimidation were the phone and the flyer, bringing threats of bombs, fires, and bad luck. The number of anonymous warnings is impossible to count and their impact hard to assess. In several documented cases, however, clandestine calls were enough to cause white teachers to quit, white politicians to avoid publicly supporting the programs, and white parents to keep their children out of Head Start classes. In East Carroll Parish, where Lake Providence was the seat of government, four female college students resigned their positions as teacher's aides after several "days and nights" of threats against them, their parents, and in one instance a younger brother. Another white teacher quit on the first day because her room had gotten "too hot." Further south, in Avoyelles Parish, the birthplace of future four-term Democratic governor Edwin W. Edwards, the sheriff received several messages promising to "blow up a Head Start class."[6]

In Grant Parish, a pine-hills parish on the western edge of the Delta known for populism, a local Klan group burned crosses in opposition to the Head Start program and forced people to leave antipoverty programs. Klan members attached dire warnings to Head Start buses, whose drivers received notices reading, "Do not carry any kids to Head Start any more[.] You loose [*sic*] your home and even your life." Another flyer read:

NOTICE

BIG BIG BLACK NIGGER
   SAY YOUR PRAYERS BEFORE YOU OPEN THIS DOOR SO YOU[R] SOUL
WILL REST IN PEACE IF ANY HEAD START GO ON DOWN HERE THIS PLACE
WILL BE BLOWN INTO BITS.
   UNDERSTAND BIG BIG NIGGER
   P S DON'T OPEN THIS DOOR

KKK NO 40.

Robert Shelton, the national leader of the United Klans of America, Knights of the Ku Klux Klan, characterized his group's opposition to the War on Poverty as an "educational campaign" designed to let people know how the federal government was using Head Start to "completely demoralize and degenerate the American society." In contrast, an OEO regional administrator pleaded with white parents in Louisiana not to be intimidated and to join Head Start classes because the United States could not break the "poverty cycle" without confronting the "terror cycle."[7]

One incident in Tensas Parish, one of the plantation parishes abutting the Mississippi River, showed that terror did not have to come in the form of an early morning telephone call or a midnight Molotov. Terror could also come if a person's name was accidentally leaked to the Louisiana office of the OEO, which was under the governor's control. A white Methodist minister, Wallace P. Blackwood, complained to the national OEO about a local planter's attempt secretly to form a local OEO to forestall any participation by civil rights activists. The national OEO let the minister's name slip in communications with the state

OEO office, and one day later, a Louisiana OEO official arrived at the minister's home wanting to know who was "making trouble." Rev. Blackwood soon came to fear for his family's safety because of "implied threats" by others in his hometown. A few weeks later, he officially withdrew his complaint. Announcing that he had cleared up the matter with the local planter, he asked the national OEO to help him change the impression that he had "slandered" the other man because "we live in a small community here, and it could become quite unpleasant if this untruth is not corrected."[8]

While terrorism and intimidation were powerful parts of white resistance to the War on Poverty, a more legitimate tactic involved controlling the bureaucracies that administered local community action agencies (CAAs). Most such agencies were created as new nonprofit corporations, with varying levels of participation by local governing bodies. To ensure "maximum feasible participation" of impoverished area residents, the OEO required the inclusion of the poor in the planning process and as representatives on the CAA boards of directors. This arrangement helped antipoverty activists bypass traditional sources of local and state power and appeal directly to the federal government for assistance. Therefore, these CAA boards became the most powerful link to the money and power flowing out of Washington. Holding an appointment to a CAA board was more than a symbolic good deed; it could make the difference in bringing thousands of dollars in programs and contracts to an impoverished community. Louisiana governor John McKeithen, a lawyer from the Delta region who had won office in 1964 as the more racially conservative candidate, understood the potential of these CAAs and tried to stack the state-level OEO office with political cronies and diehard white supremacists. Only an intense campaign by civil rights groups and an OEO refusal to fund the state-level agency prevented McKeithen from appointing an archsegregationist as deputy director of the state office.[9]

McKeithen was not alone in his tactics. Throughout the South, CAA boards of directors became battlegrounds to determine who best represented the poor and in many cases to identify which black officials should lead agencies in black communities. Several historians have outlined this process in Alabama, Mississippi, Texas, North Carolina, and South Louisiana. The most widely chronicled episode concerned the campaign against the activist-driven Child Development Group of Mississippi (CDGM). In a few places in Louisiana—most notably, Alexandria, Bossier City, and Shreveport—severe divisions emerged among black antipoverty leaders. One OEO inspector claimed that the state's white conservative "power elite" had "deliberately and systematically" worked to "split the Negro community into rival factions and played them against each other."[10]

In the Delta, OEO investigators found "secretively and poorly formed" boards of directors to be the norm.[11] To counteract these tactics, grassroots activists relied on bureaucratic guile and the national OEO to secure outright control of War on Poverty grants. In Madison Parish, along the Mississippi River, Wyche, a barber and longtime civil rights activist in the small town of Tallulah, led a campaign against the segregationist control of the Delta Community Action Agency and became its president. In mostly rural Concordia Parish, situated across the river from Natchez, Mississippi, Thompson engineered a quiet coup that wrested control of the South Delta CAA from prominent segregationists. In the more urban Ouachita Parish, Brown, an African American minister and president of the National Association for the Advancement of Colored People in the twin cities of Monroe and West Monroe, faced some of the most intense resistance in Louisiana. Opponents shot up his home, bombed his car, and had police monitor his daily activities, but Brown did not quit.

THE TALLULAH MOVEMENT

Sixty miles east of Monroe, Louisiana, and a mile or so across a wide spot in the Mississippi River from Vicksburg, Mississippi, Madison Parish was in the heart of the Delta. One of the most politically segregated places in the South, it had no black voters in its modern history until two years before the passage of War on Poverty legislation. The prospect of any black political participation caused one prominent white resident to tell Wyche that he "would wade up to my knees in blood 'fore these goddam darkies go to the polls" and would not "stand by and see niggers put their feet on white people's necks." In 1965, approximately two-thirds of Madison's residents were African American, but only three hundred of the parish's approximately five thousand eligible black residents were registered to vote. Around two-thirds of the black population lived below the poverty level.[12]

The largest town and parish seat was Tallulah. Founded in the 1850s, it had emerged in the twentieth century as a relatively prosperous place where timber, cotton, and other agricultural products were processed. By the mid-1960s, it was home to approximately twelve thousand citizens, but it was in the early stages of a historic decline. Black residents had been fleeing for years, many of them for work in booming Las Vegas.[13] Tallulah and the rural areas surrounding it had been the focus of civil rights organizing work by CORE activists, whose presence had emboldened the grassroots leadership of the local civil rights group, the Madison Parish Voters League.

Leading that organization was Wyche, a tall, rotund, cigar-smoking barber and World War II veteran in his late forties. A legendary figure in the local civil rights movement, he had been arrested multiple times for his activism and was renowned for having stood down the Ku Klux Klan on numerous occasions, each time threatening violent retaliation. Wyche told *Ebony* magazine that "five white men" had "put guns in my face and I called each one of 'em a damn coward and dared him to pull the trigger." In one of the incidents, he told the gunslinger to "get out of my face. . . . We're not working on this nonviolence no more."[14]

Wyche's intransigence bolstered boycott campaigns, at least one of which involved a national grocery chain and lasted for four months. Wyche claimed that the strategy forced seventeen businesses to close and others to give in to demands to desegregate their public accommodations and hire black workers as clerks. By 1967, enough black residents had registered in Tallulah to give Wyche a legitimate shot at public office. Citing a longtime love of detective stories and the *Perry Mason* television show, he decided to run for police chief. After coming up short by 196 votes in a race against two white opponents, he accused local whites of tampering with voting machines and sued (using outside counsel because of difficulties finding any local lawyers willing to risk ostracism). Federal judge Benjamin Dawkins eventually decreed that a new election be held, and Wyche squeaked out a win. He began his new job in May 1969.[15]

Wyche's historic victory resulted in part from the War on Poverty. Four years before taking office as Tallulah's first black police chief, Wyche had led a group of activists in taking control of the local CAA, giving him valuable experience and time to develop political networks. In 1965, Wyche and others identified several problems with the formation the Delta Community Action Association (DCAA). Working out of Mose's Tire Service on U.S. Highway 80 in Tallulah, Wyche fought to restructure the DCAA with the help of local black businessman and activist Moses Williams and white CORE activist Harold M. Ickes, the son of prominent New Dealer Harold Ickes and future deputy chief of staff to President Bill Clinton. In July, the three men demanded that the OEO change DCAA's twenty-nine-member board of directors. Occupying nine of the slots on the board were members of the all-white Madison Parish Police Jury, and according to Wyche, the board's five black members were "under the thumb of the whites"—an electrician with many white customers, a veterinarian who depended almost entirely on white clients, a junior high school principal employed by the white superintendent, a mother and homemaker, and a day laborer for a local oil company owned by one of the most affluent white families in the area.[16]

Resistance to Wyche, Williams, and Ickes on this and other civil rights matters was intense. This same year, Ickes was beaten so severely by three white attackers that he lost a kidney. In October, Williams's tire shop was burned down. Instead of giving in to the intimidation, these men used these episodes to demonstrate the new strength of the black community. "We let them know where we stood," Wyche explained to *Ebony*, "and they knew that these black folks in Tallulah were getting ready to let loose on 'em." The arson at the tire shop sparked what Wyche described as a "street meeting" where the leaders used a bullhorn to tell the crowd, "White folks, you've burned us out for the last time. You burn us one more time and we're gonna burn you right back. You hurt one of us and we're going to hurt the first white person we run across." In this majority-black Delta community, according to Wyche, white residents "got the message and they didn't do much messing with us after that."[17]

This spirit not only helped get Wyche elected when black voters became a majority of registrants but also helped Wyche secure authority over the local War on Poverty. In his words, local white residents learned that he was "one black man who don't take no stuff." After the early conflicts, he established a new look for the DCAA and its board, eventually serving as its leader. Wyche continued to oversee the DCAA throughout the late 1960s, and in 1969 and 1970, he led the effort to consolidate several Delta parishes under the DCAA in the wake of the Green Amendment's requirement that each CAA serve at least fifty thousand residents. This organization continues to operate Head Start, drug rehabilitation programs, migrant worker programs, and other community programs in the area.[18]

FATHER AUGUST THOMPSON AND CONCORDIA PARISH

In Concordia Parish, a group of black activists used a combination of subterfuge and quiet maneuvering to get control of the local CAA. Directly south of Madison and Tensas Parishes, Concordia was another typical river parish, although only 46 percent of its 20,500 residents were black. Forty-one percent of parish residents lived in poverty. Concordia had produced several celebrities. A wild piano player named Jerry Lee Lewis and a sober ABC news anchor named Howard K. Smith were already household names across the United States, with Lewis's cousins, Jimmy Swaggart and Mickey Gilley, soon to make it big as a charismatic televangelist and a country music star and Houston honky-tonk owner, respectively. The parish's most prominent politician was the virulent segregationist Shelby Jackson, the man whom Governor McKeithen tried to make deputy director of the state's OEO office in 1965.

Concordia Parish, named for the Roman goddess of harmony, was ironically known as one of the most violent spots along the Mississippi River. Situated across from Natchez, Mississippi, the cities of Ferriday and Vidalia had seen their share of bloody river-town quarrels, and the area had been the site of a number of civil-rights-related bombings and violence. On December 23, 1964, Frank Morris, a black shoe-store owner reportedly affiliated with the National Association for the Advancement of Colored People, caught two white men pouring gasoline inside his business. They used guns to force him to remain in the building as they set it aflame. The severely burned Morris survived for a few days but did not finger his assailants. Concordia Parish assistant district attorney Roy Halcomb told the *New York Times* that Morris had been a kind man who handed out balloons to customers and that his "ten-year-old daughter prayed for that nigger every night." No one was ever charged with the crime.[19] Adding to the tension at the time was an ongoing black boycott of white businesses, to which white officials retaliated by halting surplus food distribution. According to an OEO investigator in January 1967, the "KKK was waiting in the wings" for any opportunities to lash out.[20]

In this environment, Father August Thompson, a black priest at the St. Charles Catholic Church, pulled off what the OEO called "a major breakthrough in Louisiana" in early 1967.[21] Head Start classes in Concordia had initially been run by the Southern Consumers' Education Foundation (SCEF). Led by two black men, Father Albert McKnight of the Catholic Diocese in Lafayette, Louisiana, and John Zippert of CORE, the SCEF administered the controversial Acadiana Neuf CAA in several South Louisiana parishes, with Thompson serving on its board of directors. Unhappy with the arrangement, key white leaders in Concordia formed the South Delta Community Action Program to put those classes in the hands of the local government and to keep them from the SCEF, a group being targeted by Louisiana's Joint Legislative Committee on Un-American Activities.

In response, the SCEF accused the South Delta leaders of creating a board that did not adequately represent the black community. Others complained that South Delta's programs were "run paternally by the whites for the Negroes." In a compromise, Father Thompson was added to the South Delta board, changing the board's composition to ten black and eleven white members. Thompson had aspirations of leading the board, and he quietly negotiated the support of all of the black members and waited for the opportunity to implement a takeover plan. One evening, when only seven white members showed up for a meeting to replace an outgoing president, Thompson defeated the white director of the parish's school lunch program by a vote of nine to seven. Thompson's election infuriated the white members of the board, and the board had difficulty selecting a vice president because none of the whites wanted "to serve under a Negro."[22]

Despite continuing friction between Concordia's white and black leaders, South Delta successfully operated an adult-education-centered Seasonal Farm Workers program for approximately one hundred participants, a Neighborhood Youth Corps program for ninety students (seventy African Americans, twenty whites), and a well-reviewed Head Start program. Head Start was particularly helpful in arranging medical care for the many children who needed attention. In one semester, seven students were diagnosed with heart disease, eight with lung problems, thirty-eight with blood disorders, fifty-six with nutritional problems, seventy-four with dental issues, twenty-one with eye disorders, and twenty-six with hearing problems. Five of the students were found to need significant mental health treatment.[23]

RAYFIELD BROWN, THE KKK, AND CONGRESSMAN OTTO PASSMAN

The Reverend Rayfield Brown was not from the Delta. Born in New Orleans and educated at the city's Xavier University and Union Theological Seminary, he had come to the Delta in 1959 to lead the Calvary Baptist Church. He soon became active in the local civil rights movement, pressing for school desegregation and political reapportionment.[24] His organizing efforts would lead him to seek War on Poverty funding in 1965 and eventually to establish a CAA.

Dr. Brown and his wife, Bertha, lived in West Monroe in a home not far from the Ouachita River, a stream that drained out of southern Arkansas and formed one of the western boundaries of the Delta and separated the town from Monroe, the Delta's hub city. Monroe lay on the Ouachita's eastern bank on Interstate 20. The city of approximately fifty thousand residents was an extension of the region's plantation culture whose leading white citizens prized their debutante rituals and family lineages and tended to look askance at West Monroe, a smaller sawmill city. Monroe's entrepreneurs had helped turn a crop-dusting business into Delta Airlines and a drugstore bottling system into a cornerstone of the Coca-Cola Company. While the consciously genteel Monroe thrived on cotton and Coke, West Monroe looked more to lumber and low wages. Like other Louisiana mill towns, it was known for having an active Ku Klux Klan and a white police force hostile to blacks.[25] For African Americans, these twin cities were notoriously harsh and were perhaps best known for those who had fled it as children, including Huey Newton of the Black Panthers and Bill Russell of the Boston Celtics.

West Monroe's key employer was the Olin Mathieson Chemical Company, one of the few significant industrial complexes in a predominantly rural region. Olin's sprawling factory on the south side of town crushed young pine trees from nearby forests into pulp, reshaped the fibers into material for sacks and boxes, and then shipped them out to the rest of the world. The startling aroma from the nearly nonstop process left the city smelling like a cross between a sewage treatment plant and a recently lit match. Despite the odor, the community prized the mill, since it and its suppliers provided much-needed jobs. They did not provide enough well-paying employment, however; the poverty rate for the metropolitan area was 33 percent, more than double the national average of 14 percent. The rate for black citizens approached 50 percent, typical for the region but better than most of the other Delta parishes and similar southern counties economically dependent on the land.[26]

Hoping to improve the opportunities for locals to escape that poverty, the heavyset Reverend Brown helped to found the Ouachita Multi-Purpose Community Action Program (OMCAP) and the local Head Start program. OMCAP became the OEO's designated CAA in May 1966, ten months after the agency's founding.[27] During that time, a group of black community leaders, white moderates, and white Catholic priests cultivated the support of the Ouachita Parish Police Jury and the city governments of Monroe and West Monroe and appeared to have won their backing. When members of the local Ku Klux Klan discovered the arrangement, they demonstrated at a Police Jury meeting, prompting the governing bodies to withdraw. The city of Monroe and its mayor, Jack Howard, continued to assist on an unofficial basis, but most white civic and political leaders shied away from any association.

This development left OMCAP to Brown, several of his black colleagues, and two white priests, whom Brown described as "the only people" willing to associate with him. The Klan responded by distributing a circular among members of one of the priest's churches. As a result of the reluctance of elected white officials to participate, OMCAP became an anomaly in the Delta. Instead of having a board with a few black representatives and a majority of white members, OMCAP's board included eighteen blacks and only eight whites. Unlike boards in most other parishes, it met approval from CORE activists working in Monroe.[28]

In the year after OMCAP became the OEO's official agency in Ouachita Parish, Rev. Brown received numerous threats from white supremacists, including the West Monroe police chief, who reportedly promised a group of white men that "this nigger Brown" would "either go to Angola [State Prison] or . . . turn up missing one night. My men will se[e] to that." Over the next three years, white extremists linked to the Ku Klux Klan burned a cross in Brown's yard, placed a bomb in Brown's car, and fired bullets into Brown's home. For good measure, they also shot up a vehicle owned by the preschool program. Reports of these attacks went to the OEO and then to the Federal Bureau of Investigation. In one instance, a member of the Klan was arrested for firing into the Browns' home, but the charges were later dropped.[29]

Between 1966 and 1969, despite the paucity of local governmental support and the repeated threats against its leadership, OMCAP received a total of $925,000 in federal grants, mostly to support its summer Head Start program but also to fund neighborhood service centers, health services, and summer recreation programs.[30] The summer Head Start program operated in more than a dozen sites, employing more than fifty teachers and teacher's aides and offering education and occasional health exams to well over one thousand children. Like most Louisiana CAAs, the vast majority of OMCAP's participants were black, and only one center, located in a Catholic church, had any significant numbers of white students. That center had sixty-two white children and three black children.[31] The OMCAP functioned in this form until a national scandal erupted in 1969.

After 1967, reports of incidents of intimidation declined in the Delta, and the poverty wars seemed to settle down. The growth of black electoral power due to post–Voting Rights Act registration undoubtedly contributed, as did the passage of the 1967 Green Amendment to the Economic Opportunity Act. From 1965 to 1967, the CAP had produced intense controversies by encouraging assertive local groups to challenge existing leadership. Pressure built in Congress to kill the program. To salvage it and OEO's funding for 1968, Oregon Democrat Edith Green proposed restructuring CAA boards to give local government the chance to take control of the agencies. Many locales chose not to add these often unwieldy agencies to their workload but rather to exercise authority in informal ways.[32] In Louisiana, however, some segregationists seized the opportunity to try again to assert control over the War on Poverty.

On some occasions, government officials or other prominent whites accused black War on Poverty leaders of corruption, calling for intensive investigations of their programs. One of these scenarios played out in the twin cities of Shreveport and Bossier City, along the Red River in Northwest Louisiana. In 1967, Governor McKeithen vetoed a six-hundred-thousand-dollar Head Start grant because of conflicts in the local War on Poverty agency. Congressman Joe D. Waggonner was irate about the political actions of black board members he labeled a "militant clique" and pushed for a series of federal audits. The four-term representative worried about reports "of thefts, of lavish trips to New Orleans where steaks and champagne flowed like a Roman orgy, of supplies paid for that never existed, of political threats and black mail, of illicit relationships between Negroes and whites, of check forgeries, nepotism, padded payrolls, of malfeasance and nonfeasance." The investigations found little to substantiate such hyperbole, but struggles in Shreveport-Bossier continued until at least 1971, when members of a local Ku Klux Klan group attacked a rural Head Start center, throwing Molotov cocktails, burning crosses, and nailing threatening messages to the door. Soon thereafter, the local CAA underwent another reorganization, with the predominantly white Police Jury becoming the sponsoring agency.[33]

The most attention went to Ouachita Parish, however. Segregationists who had been rebuffed in 1966 saw the Green Amendment as their chance to get rid of Rayfield Brown and to use OMCAP to help more white residents. This time, the story moved beyond the Delta and became a national news event.

According to the House Un-American Activities Committee (HUAC), Ouachita Parish was home to two founders of the extremely violent splinter group known as the White Knights of the Ku Klux Klan and had fourteen functioning KKK cells. In early 1969, the New York Times revealed that the Ouachita Parish Police Jury was infested with Klansmen, three of whom had been part of a group of white police jurors who had engineered a takeover of the OMCAP board in September 1968. The OEO report on the situation noted that the FBI had identified those men as having "definite links" to the Klan. Leading the white effort was powerful state senator William D. Brown, although he was not publicly linked to the KKK and vehemently denied that he or any member of the Police Jury had any association with the Klan.[34]

Adhering to the new rules for CAA boards, the Police Jury created a governing body split equally among elected officials, the poor, and community leaders. Almost overnight, the board had shifted from being two-thirds black to two-thirds white. This shake-up made Bernie J. Van, the Police Jury's vice president and a deeply committed segregationist, the board's new president. One of his first actions was to replace the associate director of OMCAP, a white woman who had criticized him, with an aide to Senator Brown. The senator defended these actions, explaining to the *New York Times* that he wanted a more efficient program that spent more money "on poor white people."[35]

The white leadership on the new board flexed its considerable political power and sought financial audits and criminal prosecutions of Rev. Brown and his supporters. In addition to Senator Brown, the key political figure in the dispute was Otto E. Passman, a restaurant supplier and notorious segregationist from Monroe who had represented an ultraconservative Delta district in the U.S. Congress since 1947. His conservatism was such a problem for the White House that President Johnson referred to him as a "caveman." Known for his bluntness, Passman blamed the Klan story on a conspiracy of "the liberal left-wingers and do-gooders from the New York Times and elsewhere."[36] Rayfield Brown and his supporters fought back by appealing to the OEO and by turning the incident into a public relations fiasco for the area's business boosters.

As Passman told anyone who would listen, he knew poverty. A tall, thin man born on the pinelands north of New Orleans, he had grown up in deprivation of mythic proportions. He had constructed his life story to celebrate his transformation from a humble barefoot boy who survived on cornbread and milk to a successful entrepreneur and then one of the most powerful representatives on Capitol Hill. Passman's dirt-farmer memories caused him to react strongly to CBS News's 1968 exposé, *Hunger in America*, decrying its claims of starvation as one of the greatest exaggerations "in the history of America." Anyone in Louisiana could get plenty of food in less than an hour, he contended. Any "deprivation" came from "bad moral parents" who preferred "to spend their money on strong drink and gambling rather than their families." In his view, people who were poor were just "too trifling to work."[37]

His views on race were equally blunt. Like most of his white constituents, he believed that God had intended whites to be superior to blacks and that any challenge to that notion endangered family and society. In an April 1965 form letter responding to constituent complaints about a HUAC investigation into the Klan, Passman suggested that the federal government instead focus on "this thick-lipped Negro preacher, Martin Luther King." He was shocked that someone "with such limited ability as this King negro could so arouse the minorities." A "sexual pervert" with communist speechwriters, King needed to be stopped. In the aftermath of King's April 1968 assassination, Passman wanted to be "abundantly clear" that he believed the "murdered preacher brought about more heartaches, injuries, murders, violence, looting and destruction of property than any other man in America." Only a few days after the shooting, Passman told his Delta voters that he opposed murder in principle but was equally upset by the fact that "so many Americans in high places" made "such fools of themselves" in their mourning of King.[38]

The intensity of Passman's opposition to desegregation was equaled only by his commitment to fiscal austerity. He penned countless letters and made numerous public statements extolling the virtues of limited government, minimal taxation, and administrative efficiency. The War on Poverty combined his worst fears—racial integration and liberal social spending. To one local white politician, Passman described President Johnson's pet initiative as "without a doubt the most wasteful, inefficient, ineffective program ever conceived by the Congress." To the local district attorney, he went a step farther, labeling the War on Poverty "the most corrupt, unnecessary and ill-administered program ever conceived by the mind of man." Passman openly derided the intentions of "extreme liberals and do-gooders" and the "vindictive" LBJ. He saw the issue as simple. The OEO was created merely "to appease" the "colored belligerents, militants, agitators and troublemakers."[39]

It is not clear whether members of the Ouachita Parish Police Jury were members of the Klan, although such charges are plausible. OEO administrators were so troubled by the restructured OMCAP board that they withheld its funding. Congressman Passman called the charges against his Ouachita Parish friends an ugly episode of "name-calling" by people who were "just waiting to pounce on me."[40]

Passman soon turned his animosity into an assault on Rev. Brown's handling of the organization. Four days after the New York Times story appeared, Passman asked the Government Accounting Office (GAO), the federal government's nonpartisan accounting arm, to audit OMCAP to "protect the American taxpayer and establish the facts." Four months later, the GAO reported that OMCAP had some financial accounting problems but that investigators had found no evidence of malfeasance. When a Monroe accountant produced another clean audit in January 1970, Passman went on the offensive, charging that thousands of dollars were missing. Rev. Brown shot back that Passman's continued allegations were "malicious" and "irresponsible political propaganda." Two weeks after the January 1970 local audit, a grand jury investigation ordered by the local district attorney announced that it, too, could find no evidence of criminal activity, though it criticized the OEO for its confusing regulations and lack of oversight. A month later, the Southwest Office of the OEO released yet another audit of OMCAP that cleared Brown and others of any wrongdoing, although this one found that Van, who had resigned as president of the OMCAP Board after the *New York Times* article, had been intrusive and had violated OEO policy.[41]

Van told Passman, "This negro is trying to make you look like a fool" and asked for another GAO audit to look into abuse of the food stamp program. Congressman Passman demurred but promised his constituents that he would continue to fight against programs such as OMCAP because he was not a "political coward" or a "political prostitute." The restored OMCAP board passed a vote of confidence in Brown by a two-to-one margin.[42]

Brown and OMCAP survived these attacks, and the minister went on to a long career at Calvary Baptist and as executive director of OMCAP, retiring from the War on Poverty agency in 1984 and his church in 1993. The local government eventually named a park after him in a majority black neighborhood in the southern section of Monroe. Passman's career ended in disgrace in 1976 after allegations surfaced that he received $190,000 in bribes from South Korean rice dealer Tongsun Park. Jerry Huckaby, an upstart farmer with considerable backing from black voters, ended Passman's bid for a fifteenth term in Congress. Three years later, Passman escaped a criminal conviction when a friendly Ouachita Parish jury found him not guilty. A legendary enemy of foreign aid, Passman was done in because he allegedly could not resist taking aid from a foreigner.[43]

CONCLUSION

For Rayfield Brown, Zelma Wyche, August Thompson, and others, victories in the War on Poverty established precedents for developing political and bureaucratic power, but their long-term impact was gradual and incremental. Through cautious management and political perseverance, they secured power connected to Washington, D.C., and used that influence to address severe deficiencies in early childhood education and a few other areas. Antipoverty programs, however, did not change the fact that most of the region's land and wealth were controlled by white citizens who liked racial segregation, and nothing short of an actual war was likely to change that attitude. Activists' efforts usually resulted at best in white toleration, not cooperation. In addition, the Nixon administration's restructuring of the OEO and other antipoverty efforts in the early 1970s and the Reagan administration's cuts to jobs programs and other antipoverty initiatives significantly weakened an already feeble antipoverty structure. In 2007, only five CAAS remained in the region, mostly administering Head Start and struggling to respond to Hurricanes Rita and Katrina through the newly formed Louisiana Community Action Partnership Consortia.

Perhaps the War on Poverty's greatest legacy was not the programs it left behind in some small Louisiana towns but the long-term impact of initial resistance to those programs. For too many white residents and leaders, black education and black political power represented threats to rather than opportunities for economic development. For the next few decades, in addition to being hobbled by the region's reputation for harboring unrepentant white supremacists, the Delta's economic leaders could muster few incentives beyond cheap land and cheap wages. Divided by race and class, isolated by geography, and constrained by the presence of too many workers with too few skills, the Delta has had little to offer nonagricultural investors. The persistence of poverty among the Delta's black and white populations and white residents' resistance to black civic participation and to black progress were long-term problems.

After the 1970s, the Delta's economic story was one of rural isolation and stagnation, magnifying the historic problems of racial inequality. A poorly diversified economy was too much at the mercy of world agricultural markets, petroleum prices, and federal spending. A few million dollars from the War on Poverty in the late 1960s could do little to fix the region's larger economic and infrastructural troubles. By 1990, the economic situation in Lake Providence resembled what too much of the Delta had become and what the War on Poverty could likely never have overcome.

The story is familiar. In the second half of the twentieth century, the expanded use of the tractor and the cotton-picking machine forced families off the land, priced out small farmers, and required enormous capital investment. In a dangerous game, growers often had to take catastrophic risks. Racial inequality persisted, as did inadequate investment in public institutions, particu-

larly in education. Most white children attended private segregationist acade-
mies, often with strong evangelical curricula. These intractable divisions left the
region holding hazily onto history, barely able to survive in the world economy.
The collapse of petroleum prices in the 1980s proved especially devastating and
exposed the region's weak civic and economic foundations. Jobs disappeared.
People left. What remained was the ancient soil (and the bits of oil and natural
gas left under it), the few who could make use of it, and the others who clung
to family and survived on agricultural subsidies, Social Security, and/or other
social welfare programs. One 2006 study found that the federal government
was the most significant contributor to the economy of East Carroll Parish, the
home of Lake Providence.[44]

In 1989, Congress created the Lower Delta Development Commission. Eighteen months later, the commission, chaired by Arkansas governor Bill Clinton,
produced a report that was supposed to identify both problems and opportunities. Ten years later, the federal government helped establish the Delta Regional Authority. Between 2000 and 2006, Washington disbursed fifty-six million dollars for a wide variety of health and economic development programs,
a remarkably small sum considering that the authority stretches over 252 counties in eight states.[45]

In Louisiana, the Delta region, once a major contributor to the world's cot-
ton/textile market, is now mostly irrelevant to the rest of the world. In a state
heavily dependent on tourists, few come to the Delta on purpose. Local and
state governments beg businesses not to leave and offer massive sums to entice
new enterprises to come. The great economic hopes of the 1990s were the day-
dreams of the desperate: private prisons and casino gambling. But Mississippi
got the gambling boats, and a private juvenile prison in Louisiana shut down
amid scandal. In 2004, the region lost one of its few white-collar industries when
State Farm Insurance moved one of its major hubs. A hurried package of thirty-
three million dollars in incentives from the state could not keep the good neighbor from taking its one thousand jobs and heading to Tulsa, Oklahoma.[46]

Since then, Louisiana leaders have bet the region's future on chickens, sweet
potatoes, and, in a curious move, green-economy automobile manufacturing.
In 2008–9, the state's Republican governor, Bobby Jindal, a strong proponent
of free markets, supported giving approximately $150 million in public money
to help three different corporations while calling for hundreds of millions of
dollars in cuts to elementary, secondary, and higher education. Governmental
subsidies kept a bankrupt chicken-processing plant from shutting down, bank-

rolled a new factory manufacturing potato products, and encouraged a wildly speculative and ultimately unsuccessful venture by California computer moguls to build a small, fuel-efficient vehicle known as the V-Car.

Lake Providence, however, revived an old solution to a bad economy, a convict-lease system echoing the system in use in the state a century earlier. The sheriff put the parish's prison population to work in local businesses and in the community doing cooking, cleaning, landscaping, and making hot sauce. In 2006, prisoners accounted for 10 percent of the local labor force.[47] Almost a half century after the so-called War on Poverty limped into existence in the Delta, the winner seems to be the culture that produced the resistance to it. The war on the War on Poverty helped to affirm the worst tendencies in the local economy and society and helped to preserve the Delta as one of the poorest places in America.

Notes

1. Lyndon Baines Johnson, "Annual Message to the Congress on the State of the Union," January 8, 1964, in *Public Papers of the Presidents of the United States, 1963–1964* (Washington, D.C.: U.S. Government Printing Office, 1965), 1:113–14; "Population, Land Area, and Poverty Data for 1990 Census Tracts," http://www.census.gov/geo/www/ezstate/LA.pdf.

2. Jack E. White, "The Poorest Place in America," *Time*, August 27, 1994, http://www.time.com/time/magazine/article/0,9171,981266,00.html.

3. James C. Cobb, *The Most Southern Place on Earth: The Mississippi Delta and the Roots of Regional Identity* (New York: Oxford University Press, 1992). See also Nan Woodruff, *American Congo: The African American Freedom Struggle in the Delta* (Cambridge: Harvard University Press, 2003).

4. Adam Fairclough, *Race and Democracy: The Civil Rights Struggle in Louisiana, 1915–1972* (Athens: University of Georgia Press, 1995), 313–14, 393–402; Joe E. Leonard Jr., "'We Are Catchin' Hell Down Here': The Struggle for Public Accommodations and Voter Franchisement by the Congress of Racial Equality in Louisiana, 1960–1965" (Ph.D. diss., Howard University, 2004), 180–88; Greta de Jong, *A Different Day: African American Struggles for Justice in Rural Louisiana, 1900–1970* (Chapel Hill: University of North Carolina Press, 2002), 175–206.

5. William Crook to Sargent Shriver, July 14, 1966, Box 31, Folder "Klan Activity—Louisiana," Records of the Community Services Administration, Office of Economic Opportunity, RG 381, National Archives II, College Park, Maryland (hereafter RG 381).

6. Daniel W. McBride to Shirley Powell, July 7, 1966, William Crook to Sargent

Shriver, July 13, 1966, Earl Rhine to William Crook, July 13, 1966, all in Series 74, Box 31, Folder "Klan Activity—Louisiana," RG 381.

7. Mike Coleman, "Office of Inspection Sign-Off Check List," February 17, 1966, Series 74, Box 30, Folder "Louisiana 1966 2–3," RG 381; Edgar May to Sam Yette, August 9, 1966, Series 74, Box 31, Folder "Klan Activity—Louisiana," RG 381; Robert Heard, "Klan Threats Cited by Crook," *New Orleans Times-Picayune*, July 14, 1966.

8. Wallace P. Blackwood to Sargent Shriver, January 18, 1966, Drawer 53, Folder 31, "War on Poverty," Otto E. Passman Collection, 1947–1978, Special Collections, University of Louisiana-Monroe; Wallace P. Blackwood to OEO Southwest, March 30, 1966, Mike Coleman to Peter Spruance, April 19, March 29, 1966, Wallace P. Blackwood to Sargent Shriver, February 26, 1966. all in Series 74, Box 30, Folder "Louisiana April–June 1966," RG 381.

9. Kent Germany, *New Orleans after the Promises: Poverty, Citizenship, and the Search for the Great Society* (Athens: University of Georgia Press, 2008), 49–53.

10. John Dittmer, *Local People: The Struggle for Civil Rights in Mississippi* (Urbana: University of Illinois Press, 1994), 363–88; Joseph Crespino, "Strategic Accommodation: Civil Rights Opponents in Mississippi and Their Impact on American Racial Politics, 1953–1972" (Ph.D. diss., Stanford University, 2002), 207–35; David C. Carter, "'Two Nations': Social Insurgency and National Civil Rights Policymaking in the Johnson Administration, 1965–1968" (Ph.D. diss., Duke University, 2001), 61–115; David C. Carter, "Romper Lobbies and Coloring Lessons: Grassroots Visions and Political Realities in the Battle for Head Start in Mississippi, 1965–1967," in *Making a New South: Race, Leadership, and Community after the Civil War*, ed. Paul A. Cimbala and Barton C. Shaw (Gainesville: University Press of Florida, 2007); Nicholas Lemann, *The Promised Land: The Great Black Migration and How It Changed America* (New York: Knopf, 1991), 324–27; Polly Greenberg, *The Devil Has Slippery Shoes: A Biased Biography of the Child Development Group of Mississippi* (London: Macmillan, 1969); Robert J. Gentry, "Consulting Assignment to Alexandria, Louisiana (June 17th and 18th)," June 19, 1966, Series 75, Box 102, Folder "Rapides," RG 381. On a split between white labor leaders and local activist black leaders, see material in Series 1030, Box 4, Series 74, Boxes 28, 30, RG 381; ; Boxes 1, 2, Joe D. Waggonner Jr. Papers, Collection A58, Prescott Memorial Library, Special Collections, Louisiana Tech University, Ruston. For studies of the war on poverty in various locales, see Susan Youngblood Ashmore, "Carry It On: The War on Poverty and the Civil Rights Movement in Alabama, 1964–1970" (Ph.D. diss., Auburn University, 1998), 153–55; Carolyn Thompson, "A Story of Hope: Southern Consumers' Cooperative and the Origins of the War on Poverty in Southwest Louisiana" (master's thesis, Tulane University, 2000); Fairclough, *Race and Democracy*, 393–94; de Jong, *Different Day*, 200–206; Lisa Hazirjian, "Negotiating Poverty: Economic Insecurity and the Politics of Working-Class Life in Rocky Mount, North Carolina, 1929–1969" (Ph.D. diss.,

Duke University, 2003), 480–555; William Stephen Clayson, "Texas Poverty and Liberal Politics: The Office of Economic Opportunity and the War on Poverty in the Lone Star State" (Ph.D. diss., Texas Tech University, 2001).

11. Mike Coleman to Peter Spruance/Ed Terrones, March 29, 1966, Series 74, Box 30, Folder "Louisiana 1966 2–3," RG 381.

12. Charles Sanders, "Black Lawman in KKK Territory," *Ebony*, January 1970, 64; Zelma Wyche and Harold M. Ickes to Fred Baldwin, July 13, 1965, Series 74, Box 31, Folder "October–December 1965," RG 381.

13. Annelise Orleck, *Storming Caesars Palace: How Black Mothers Fought Their Own War on Poverty* (Boston: Beacon, 2005), 7–36.

14. Sanders, "Black Lawman," 64; Fairclough, *Race and Democracy*, 397.

15. Sanders, "Black Lawman," 59–60, 64, 66; Martin Waldron, "Black Police Chief in Louisiana Concedes He's Not Winning White Support," *New York Times* (hereafter *NYT*, October 3, 1969; Jack Nelson, "Rights Leader Testifies about Lawyer's Fears," *Los Angeles Times*, January 30, 1968; Thomas A. Johnson, "Louisiana Negroes Seek Power," *NYT*, September 29, 1971; Fairclough, *Race and Democracy*, 395–98.

16. Wyche and Harold M. Ickes to Baldwin, July 13, 1965, Series 74, Box 31, Folder October–December 1965, RG 381.

17. Todd S. Purdum, "A Political Whodunit," *NYT*, February 14, 1993; Fairclough, *Race and Democracy*, 396; Sanders, "Black Lawman," 64, 59.

18. Sanders, "Black Lawman," 59; Zelma Wyche to Hale Boggs, April 8, 1969, Drawer 85, Folder 27, "OEO-OMCAP 1969," Passman Collection; Fred Baldwin to Earl Oswalt, August 8, 1969, Walter Richter to Earl Oswalt, September 17, 1969, both in Drawer 98, Folder 37, "OEO 1970," Passman Collection.

19. John Herbers, "Burning of a Negro Arouses Louisiana," *NYT*, December 24, 1964; Stanley Nelson, "Retired FBI Agents Unsure Who Killed Morris, Edwards," *Concordia Sentinel*, November 5, 2009, http://www.concordiasentinel.com/news.php?id=4334. Investigators are continuing to attempt to solve the Morris case.

20. Tom McRae to Edgar May, January 27, 1967, Series 74, Box 30, Folder "Louisiana January 1966," RG 381.

21. Edgar May to Sargent Shriver, January 27, 1967, Series 74, Box 30, Folder "Louisiana January 1967—Jan–Feb," RG 381.

22. Tom McRae to Edgar May, January 27, 1967, Edgar May to Sargent Shriver, January 27, 1967, both in Series 74, Box 30, Folder "Louisiana 1967 January," RG 381; Tom McRae and Ele Chassy to Edgar May, January 30, 1967, Series 74, Box 30, Folder "Louisiana 1967 January–February," RG 381.

23. Tom McRae and Ele Chassy to Edgar May, January 30, 1967, Series 74, Box 30, Folder "Louisiana January–February 1967," RG 381.

24. "P. Rayfield Brown, III Dies at Age 79," *Monroe Free Press*, July 26, 1997.

25. Lance Hill, *Deacons for Defense: Armed Resistance and the Civil Rights Movement* (Chapel Hill: University of North Carolina Press, 2006); Fairclough, *Race and Democracy*, 313–14, 342–45, 357–85.

26. Mike Coleman, "Report on CAP application, LA CAP 66-5175," Series E74, Box 30, Folder "Louisiana OEO Programs (Compilation) April–June 1966," RG 381; OEO Information Center, Community Profile, 1966, "Ouachita Parish, Louisiana," 8, Series 23, Box 202, RG 381.

27. Comptroller of the United States to Otto Passman, Drawer 85, Folder 27, "OEO-OMCAP 1969," Passman Collection.

28. Ibid.; Mike Coleman to Peter Spruance/Ed Terrones, May 5, 1966, Gordon Wilcox, Inspector's Field Report for OMCAP, Inc. Head Start, June 28, 1966, both in Series 74, Box 30, Folder "Louisiana OEO Programs (Compilation) April–June 1966," RG 381; Gordon Wilcox to Frank Moffitt and Hamah King, March 27, 1967, Series 75, Box 102, Folder "Ouachita," RG 381.

29. Philip Rayfield Brown, "A Statement" [OMCAP letterhead], late September 1966, Series 75, Box 102, Folder "Ouachita," RG 381; OEO, "Situation Report—Region V, Monroe, Louisiana," December 30, 1967, Series 74, Box 30, Folder "Louisiana November–December 1967," RG 381; "Whites in Louisiana Town Take Control of Poverty Board from Negroes," *NYT*, March 16, 1969.

30. Comptroller of the United States to Otto Passman, Drawer 85, Folder 27, "OEO-OMCAP 1969," Passman Collection.

31. Wilcox, Inspector's Field Report; Gordon Wilcox to Frank Moffitt and Hamah King, March 27, 1967, Ed Steinman, Administratively Confidential Inspector's Field Report, OMCAP Head Start, July 24, 1967, both in Series 75, Box 102, Folder "Ouachita," RG 381; Norma L. Sherman to author, August 15, 2007.

32. Allen J. Matusow, *The Unraveling of America: A History of Liberalism in the 1960s* (New York: Harper and Row, 1984), 270.

33. Tom McRae to Edgar May, August 8, 1967, Series 74, Box 28, Folder "Caddo-Bossier," RG 381; Joe Waggonner, "Government Audit of Caddo-Bossier–CAP-CAB," Statement to the U.S. House of Representatives, July 25, 1968, Box 2, Folder 33, "Poverty Program Audit," Waggonner Papers; "CAP-CAB's Rodessa Center Is Target of Harassment by KKK," *Shreveport Sun*, April 29, 1971; Phil Cate, "Protection Asked in Rhodessa Area: Board Conditionally Okays CAP-CAP [*sic*] Reorganization," *Shreveport Times*, July 23, 1971.

34. "Whites in Louisiana Town"; Bernie J. Van to Otto Passman, January 6, 1969, Drawer 85, Folder 27, "OEO-OMCAP 1969," Passman Collection; "Senator Billy Brown Sets the Record Straight," *East Carroll Delta News*, March 27, 1969.

35. Comptroller of the United States to Otto Passman, Drawer 85, Folder 27, "OEO-OMCAP 1969," Passman Collection; "Whites in Louisiana Town"; "Senator Billy Brown."

36. Lyndon Baines Johnson and John McCormack, December 20, 1963, in *The Presidential Recordings, Lyndon B. Johnson: The Kennedy Assassination and the Transfer of Power*, vol. 2, *December 1963*, ed. Robert David Johnson and David Shreve (New York: Norton, 2005), 567; Otto Passman to Mrs. E. A. Coons, April 3, 1969, Drawer 85, Folder 27, "OEO-OMCAP 1969," Passman Collection.

37. Jack Anderson and Les Whitten, "U.S. Loath to Indict Ailing Passman," *Washington Post*, October 27, 1977. Otto Passman to Mr. and Mrs. Michael Yerger, May 27, 1968, Drawer 68, Folder 22, "Hunger," Passman Collection). Passman did not know if the Yergers were black or white but wrote to them "as though they were white."

38. Otto Passman to Fred C. Rogers, April 5, 1965, Drawer 42, Folder 20, "Ku Klux Klan," Passman Collection; Otto Passman, form letter, Drawer 33, Folder "King, Martin Luther," Passman Collection.

39. Bernie J. Van to Otto Passman, March 18, 1969, Otto Passman to Bernie J. Van, March 19, 1969, Otto Passman to Albin P. Lassiter, August 18, 1969, Otto Passman to Rayfield Brown, January 21, 1969, all in Drawer 85, Folder 27, "OEO-OMCAP 1969," Passman Collection.

40. Otto Passman to Paul Galloway, January 21, 1969, Otto Passman to Mrs. E. A. Coons, April 3, 1969, both in Drawer 85, Folder 27, "OEO-OMCAP 1969," Passman Collection.

41. Otto Passman to Lawrence J. Powers, March 20, 1969, Albin P. Lassiter to Otto Passman, January 26, 1970, both in Drawer 85, Folder 27, "OEO-OMCAP 1969," Passman Collection; "CAP Director Denies Charges," *Monroe Morning World* (hereafter *MMW*), January 23, 1970; "Grand Jury Lashes Poverty Program," *MMW*, January 23, 1970; "OEO Gives Action Agency Here Clean Slate in Report," *MMW*, February 18, 1970.

42. Bernie J. Van to Otto Passman, [January 1970], Drawer 98, Folder 38, "OEO Ouachita Parish Community Action Agency," Passman Collection; "Police Juror Calls for Another Audit," *MMW*, January 29, 1970; Otto Passman to Paul Grimes, April 28, 1970, Drawer 98, Folder 37 "OEO, April–June 1970," Passman Collection; "CAP Board Gives Confidence Vote," *MMW*, February 3, 1970.

43. "P. Rayfield Brown, III Dies at Age 79," *Monroe Free Press*, July 26, 1997; Nicholas Gage, "Tongsun Park Said to Have Given $190,000 to Former Rep. Passman," *NYT*, November 2, 1977; "Park Says in Court Passman Took Cash," *NYT*, March 15, 1979; A. O. Sulzberger, "Investigation into Influence-Buying by Korean Figure Comes to an End," *NYT*, August 17, 1979. Passman was eventually accused of taking $273,000.

44. Dominique Duval-Diop, "Rediscovering the Delta: A Reassessment of the Linkages between Poverty, Economic Growth, and Public Policy Using Geographically Weighted Regression Analysis" (Ph.D. diss., Louisiana State University, 2006), 51.

45. Clyde Adrian Woods, "Development Arrested: The Delta Blues, the Delta Council, and the Lower Mississippi Delta Commission" (Ph.D. diss., University of California–Los Angeles, 1993), ix–x, 1–6; "All-White Panel Leads to Boycott," *NYT*, December 25,

1988; Ronald Smothers, "Hope Is Seen for Poor in 7-State Area," *NYT*, November 22, 1989; Duval-Diop, "Rediscovering the Delta," 1–4; Delta Regional Authority homepage, http://www.dra.gov/.

46. James Matthew Reonas, "Once-Proud Princes: Planters and Plantation Culture in Louisiana's Northeast Delta, from the First World War through the Great Depression" (Ph.D. diss., Louisiana State University, 2006); "State Farm's Monroe Center to Close After All," *Insurance Journal*, February 5, 2004, http://www.insurancejournal.com/news/southcentral/2004/02/05/36441.htm.

47. Kim Quillen, "Foster Farms to Bring Jobs Back," *New Orleans Times-Picayune*, July 10, 2009, http://blog.nola.com/tpmoney/2009/07/foster_farms_to_bring_jobs_bac .html; News Release, Louisiana Office of the Governor, "Governor Bobby Jindal and Ron Foster Mark Opening of New Foster Farms Facility in Farmerville," July 11, 2009, http://gov .louisiana.gov/index.cfm?md=newsroom&tmp=detail&articleID=1422; News Release, Louisiana Economic Development, "ConAgra Foods Lamb Weston's New Processing Facility Will Become One Of Northeast Louisiana's Top 10 Private-Sector Employers," August 8, 2009, http://www.louisianaeconomicdevelopment.com/news—multimedia/news-releases/conagra-foods-lamb-weston-announces-new-processing-facility.aspx; Greg Hilburn, "V-Vehicle: Real Car under Wraps," *Monroe News Star*, October 14, 2009; Adam Nossiter, "With Jobs to Do, Louisiana Parish Turns to Inmates," *NYT*, July 5, 2006.

GRETA DE JONG

Plantation Politics

The Tufts-Delta Health Center and Intraracial Class Conflict in Mississippi, 1965–1972

I n 1965, the federal Office of Economic Opportunity (OEO) approved a proposal to establish a community health center in the all-black town of Mound Bayou, Mississippi. The center promised to serve impoverished residents of northern Bolivar County, who had almost no access to medical care. Initiated and staffed by civil rights activists, the project sought to move beyond providing medical services to address the underlying causes of poor people's health problems. The Tufts-Delta Health Center (TDHC) began operating in November 1967 and launched a full-scale assault on the oppressive structures associated with the region's plantation economy. Dilapidated housing, poor sanitation, malnutrition, inadequate social welfare services, and political powerlessness became targets of TDHC staff and the local activists involved in the project. Organizers encouraged poor people to participate in decision making and recruited them for training and jobs at the center, disrupting long-standing class and race hierarchies in the Delta. Some of the poor people most closely associated with the program would go on to long and satisfying careers in health care delivery.

The TDHC's connections to the civil rights movement and the challenges it posed to the social order generated the usual protests from racist white officials. Less predictably, the project exposed class divisions within the African American community that hindered efforts to empower poor black people. White elites in Mound Bayou, as in other southern communities, were threatened, but just as important, the economic and political interests of Mound Bayou's black middle class were threatened by antipoverty projects and the political mobilization they generated. The situation was further complicated by the rise of the Black Power movement in the late 1960s and demands that African Americans be allowed to control their own affairs. Pressure from local black elites making arguments about the importance of black-controlled institutions ultimately would persuade the federal government to order a reorganization of the TDHC, which had a white founding director. Ironically, this reorganization shifted most decision-making authority away from rural poor people and restored the power of local white elites and middle-class black community leaders to determine the distribution of resources. The history of the TDHC highlights the complex forces that hindered antipoverty work in the Delta and demonstrates that struggles for social justice in the South cannot be understood without reference to class oppression as well as to the racism that characterized the region.

HEALTH CARE AS A BATTLEFRONT IN THE WAR ON POVERTY

The health needs of low-income Americans emerged as an area of concern for the OEO soon after the agency was established in 1964. Proposals received from groups seeking to set up agencies under the Community Action Program (CAP) often included requests for money to provide medical services to poor people, and in its first four years, the OEO allocated 11 percent of CAP funds for this purpose. At the same time, suggestions for a more comprehensive approach came from H. Jack Geiger and Count D. Gibson, two white professors of preventive medicine at Boston's Tufts University. Geiger's approach to health care was shaped by his experiences working at a community health center in South Africa that served a black housing project just outside of Durban. The South African clinic was part of a network of centers created by Sidney Kark, whose holistic philosophy of medicine emphasized the connections between health and the social environment. In these clinics, Geiger explained, "One never saw an individual patient; one saw patient, family, and community, with the community as the ultimate focus of concern."[1]

After returning to the United States, Geiger helped to found the Medical Committee for Human Rights, an organization of health professionals that provided medical services to civil rights workers in the South. Through his participation in 1964's Freedom Summer, Geiger realized that conditions resembling those he had encountered in developing nations existed in his homeland. He shared his experiences in South Africa with other volunteers and suggested set-

ting up a similar health clinic in Mississippi. Gibson arranged for his department at Tufts Medical School to sponsor the project, and the two men drafted
a proposal to apply for federal funding. After convincing the OEO that community health centers could instigate social change and address the underlying
causes of disease, they received a grant to test this model at two sites, one serving an urban poor population in the North and the other located in a rural poor
community in the South. Columbia Point housing project in Boston was chosen for the urban demonstration, and the search for a Mississippi town willing
to host an OEO experiment followed.[2]

Meetings in 1965 and 1966 between the Tufts doctors and white officials in
Mississippi drew a mostly negative response. Governor Paul Johnson opposed
the project and reported that the state board of health, the Mississippi Medical Association, and the Mississippi Association of Hospital Administrators
were also against it. He wrote to OEO director Sargent Shriver in March 1966
requesting that the clinic be located elsewhere. When Tufts began to focus on
Mound Bayou as the most amenable site, Bolivar County's white doctors and
political leaders called on Mississippi senator John C. Stennis to block the university's plans. R. T. Hollingsworth of Shelby Community Hospital argued that
TDHC was a "blueprint for socialized medicine." Cleveland lawyer William Alexander expressed similar concerns. Moreover, he thought the project unnecessary, since the county already had "one of the finest Health Departments in
the State," along with community clinics at Rosedale and Shelby and two black
hospitals in Mound Bayou.[3]

White Mississippians' claims that the state provided adequate health services to its people were inaccurate. Wealthy residents who could afford to pay
for treatment might have been well cared for under the existing system, but
Tufts's target population of rural poor black people had little or no access to
health care. In 1960, Mississippi had 77 doctors per 100,000 residents, just over
half the national average of 142. Most of the state's general practitioners were
located in urban communities and charged fees for their services; according
to the OEO, almost no publicly funded health care was available in the state.
Many black Mississippians never sought treatment for their ailments because
they could not afford to pay or because they lacked transportation to doctors'
offices. As Tufts staff noted, numerous social and environmental factors also
compounded poor people's health problems, including lack of income and
substandard housing and sanitation facilities. In addition, outright racism and

complicated bureaucratic procedures discouraged needy families from applying for public aid.[4]

These conditions resulted from the systematic discrimination that restricted
black people's opportunities in all aspects of life during the Jim Crow era. Yet
in Mound Bayou, where local officials, business leaders, and civic organizations
were entirely African American, poor black people fared little better than in
other parts of Mississippi. Founded in 1887 by a group of former slaves, Mound
Bayou was promoted as a community where black people were free to develop
according to their abilities, unhindered by the obstacles to economic and political progress that slowly strangled black aspirations in the decades after the
end of Reconstruction. Town leaders adhered to Booker T. Washington's philosophy of racial uplift, emphasizing the possibilities for African Americans to
succeed within the capitalist system through hard work, thrift, and adopting the
proper moral values.

Even as they rejected the white supremacist racial order being constructed
to keep black people subordinate, Mound Bayou's inhabitants embraced the
dominant economic values of the time. Class stratification, exploitation, and
the monopolization of political power by the town's wealthiest citizens characterized Mound Bayou, just as they did other communities in Mississippi. Like
their white counterparts, Mound Bayou's black leaders appealed to residents'
racial pride to minimize challenges to dominance. Residents who complained
about the high prices charged in the stores, economic hardship, or the lack of
public services were called "race traitors" and told that their problems resulted
from their own deficiencies, not the actions of town elites.[5]

Despite the founders' goal of fostering black autonomy, Mound Bayou could
not insulate itself from the wider economic trends that affected rural southern communities in the twentieth century. A chronic shortage of capital and
credit kept local farmers constantly on the edge of debt, and when the cotton
economy collapsed after World War I, many were forced to sell their properties to white landowners. The Great Depression in the 1930s had similar consequences, driving several of the town's black-owned businesses into bankruptcy.
Over the next few decades, agricultural mechanization displaced thousands of
black workers from the plantations, leading unemployment and poverty rates
to skyrocket in Mississippi's rural counties.

The influx of former sharecroppers into urban areas strained the resources
of local governments and generated hostile reactions from existing residents.

Like the state's white leaders, Mound Bayou's black rulers failed to respond adequately to the crisis. In February 1967, an analyst for the Economic Development Administration reported that the needs of the community were "all inclusive—housing, water, sewage, streets, sidewalks, utilities, modern government, police and fire protection, town hall, community facilities, schools, vocational programs, park and recreation area, industrial park, industry, and jobs and jobs." He urged federal and local officials to support the Tufts project for its economic impact as well as its health benefits.[6]

Increasing poor people's access to health care in Bolivar County was a pressing need despite Mound Bayou's two black hospitals. Both facilities were operated by black fraternal organizations that charged members an annual fee in return for hospitalization and burial benefits. Nonmembers could receive care by paying for treatment as needed. Much like the town itself, the fraternal orders functioned as both public services for the larger community and as money-making ventures. The International Order of Twelve Knights and Daughters of Tabor founded the Taborian Hospital in Mound Bayou as a way to attract new members and funds for the organization. The hospital opened in 1942 with Dr. Theodore Howard as its chief surgeon.

Most patients were sharecroppers and laborers from the plantation counties surrounding Mound Bayou, but the top officials in the fraternal order were ministers, teachers, and other members of the black middle class. Fraternal leaders at times seemed more interested in members' money than in ensuring their health or well-being. State director Perry Smith urged recruiters carefully to screen potential members and avoid those who could become too costly for the organization. "Don't enlist them when they are too old," he advised, "or when they are in bad health and when they are of bad morals."[7]

In 1946, Howard's practice of forcing patients to be seen at his private clinic for a one-dollar fee before being admitted to the hospital precipitated a split within the fraternal order and the eventual defection of the surgeon and his supporters. They formed the United Order of Friendship and opened the Friendship Clinic in 1948, offering essentially the same services as the Taborian Hospital. Unable to recruit a surgeon to replace Howard, the Taborians worked out an arrangement with Meharry Medical College in Tennessee under which medical residents completed the last few months of their training at the hospital.[8]

Although the fraternal orders helped to fill the void left by white health care providers who refused to treat black patients, neither hospital offered the same quality of care that white Mississippians received or that the Tufts-Delta clinic promised to make available. Overcrowding, inadequate equipment, and inexperienced staff plagued both facilities. Taborian's practice of encouraging indigent patients to seek treatment at other hospitals, where they could qualify for state assistance, caused some observers to conclude that its administrators were not interested in providing health care to those who could not afford to pay.

One woman who grew up in Mound Bayou accused the fraternal orders of selling "so-called hospital insurance to the Black poor people in the same way they sold expensive funeral insurance, taking the money from the poor and giving them almost nothing for it. Like a lot of other things in Mound Bayou . . . it was just a business run by some Black people to rob other Black people." Others were less harsh, citing lack of money rather than mercenary motives as the main cause of the problem. Doctors and administrators at the fraternal hospitals adamantly defended the quality of the services they provided. Their facilities might not measure up to the modern, high-tech hospitals to which white northern doctors such as Geiger were accustomed, they said, but staff were competent and did the best they could with their limited resources.[9]

The fraternal hospitals' financial straits grew worse in the 1950s, when state regulators began to pay more attention. The state demanded that facilities be brought up to standard, forcing the fraternal hospitals to spend thousands of dollars on renovations and new equipment. During the following decade, the federal government began to offer incentives to induce white practitioners who had previously refused to treat African Americans to compete with black health providers for patients. Both of Mound Bayou's fraternal hospitals raised their membership fees and increased charges for some services; nevertheless, they remained near bankruptcy when Tufts began its forays into the Delta. With help from Tufts staff, hospital administrators applied for an OEO grant to merge the two facilities, and in 1967 they consolidated into the Mound Bayou Community Hospital (MBCH). Despite white Mississippians' opposition, the OEO also went ahead with its plans to fund the Tufts-Delta clinic. Under the terms of the grants, Mound Bayou offered free hospital treatment to poor people in Bolivar and neighboring counties, and the new clinic would provide preventive health services, outreach, and outpatient care for a population of fourteen thousand people in an area covering five hundred square miles.[10]

The Tufts-Delta Health Center began seeing patients in November 1967. For the first year, the clinic was housed in an old movie theater and a church parsonage renovated it for the clinic's use while more permanent facilities were under construction. According to Mary Stella Simpson, a Catholic nun and nurse-midwife who moved to Mound Bayou to help with the center, it was clear from the outset that the health needs of the community were acute: "Many people in the area had never visited a doctor in their lives, and virtually every family we cared for needed much more than obstetrical and newborn care." Between 1967 and 1969, Simpson wrote numerous letters to her friends and supporters in the North describing dilapidated homes, filthy conditions, and hungry people.[11]

Agricultural mechanization had pushed the region's unemployment rate up to 75 percent, and the state's restrictive welfare practices meant that many families were ineligible for public assistance. Some plantation owners allowed former sharecroppers to continue to inhabit their crumbling shacks rent-free, but without work or income, displaced farmworkers faced a constant struggle to obtain adequate food, clothing, and other necessities. After visiting one family, Simpson reported, "The children in this home have heads that are masses of matted hair from ringworm and sores. They wear rags for clothes. When the rags fall off them, they look for more rags." In April 1968, Simpson helped to treat a baby who was "almost dead from starvation." "The mother had taken him to two other doctors and they did nothing for him," she wrote. "She lives quite a distance from us but heard about our good doctors."[12]

Rural poor people's enthusiastic responses to the new clinic contradicted opponents' claims that local sentiment was unanimously against the project. Clinic doctors and nursing staff often worked overtime, attending to the long-neglected needs of the dozens of patients who came to the clinic every day. By the time permanent clinic facilities were completed in December 1968, staff were treating between 150 and 175 people a day at the clinic and visiting another 30 to 40 people in their homes. "The cases just appear—some patients walking for miles, sleeping under the stars the night before they are seen," Simpson wrote.[13]

Local resident Irene Williams explained that the rural poor were willing to go to such lengths to get to the Tufts-Delta clinic because it offered thorough examinations, accurate diagnoses, and effective treatment that contrasted greatly with the indifference shown toward poor people by doctors at the fraternal hospitals and in private practice. Similarly, John Brown believed that his wife would not have survived a serious illness and operation had it not been for the free medical care she received at the center. Clinic nurses offered advice and guidance to pregnant women and new mothers, a service that local women very much appreciated. Clinic reports show that these local women diligently followed the proffered advice about prenatal nutrition and breast-feeding. Mothers of young children were also grateful for information about what sanitation measures they could take to minimize the incidence of childhood diseases. Evening parenting classes were another popular service. "We seem never to get away from the sessions," Simpson wrote. "Well, hardly ever. They ask questions for *hours!*"[14] Viewing health in a holistic sense, the clinic offered adult-education classes, which were also well attended by local residents eager to earn high school diplomas and to learn new skills.

Clinic staff took people that local elites—black and white alike—had long deemed "unemployable" and trained them for careers in the medical profession. Irene Williams was one of the first people from Bolivar County to be hired by the center. Like most other poor residents of the clinic's target area, Williams had acquired only a rudimentary education and no skills other than picking cotton. As a clinic trainee, however, she received fifty dollars per week, and she subsequently went on to a rewarding career as a nurse's aide. "It was wonderful," she stated. "I was able to raise my children half decent, give them some of the things I never would have been able to give them. . . . I couldn't have done that without [the TDHC], and I'm thankful."[15]

L. C. Dorsey's life was similarly transformed by the project. Dorsey was a former sharecropper, a high school dropout, and a civil rights activist struggling to support a family of seven on thirty-six dollars per week when the Tufts-Delta clinic hired her as an outreach worker. She attended the center's evening courses to get her high school diploma and to acquire the foundations for a medical education. She went on to graduate studies at the State University of New York at Stony Brook, eventually earning a doctorate. She returned to Bolivar County in the 1980s to take over as director of the health center after Tufts' involvement with the project had ended. Approximately sixty other local residents from the TDHC service area completed college or trade school courses or were trained in-house, leading to careers as nurses, doctors, social workers, nutritionists, environmental health experts, office managers, and administrators. Some health center employees went on to found similar projects in other rural poor communities in Mississippi. According to Dorsey, the clinic acted as an "incubator center for the development of leadership for the community health center movement."[16]

Both the Tufts-Delta clinic and the Columbia Point project served as models for a new, comprehensive approach to health care. In 1966, the OEO approved grants for similar initiatives for poor neighborhoods in Chicago, Denver, Los Angeles, and New York. After visiting Columbia Point, Senator Edward M. Kennedy became a powerful congressional advocate for the community-based model of health care delivery. Kennedy was the driving force behind 1967 legislation that created a national network of neighborhood health centers and mandated active participation by low-income community residents in the administration and governance of the clinics. By 1974, the federal government had funded eight hundred health centers serving four million people across the United States. President Jimmy Carter expanded the network yet again. This strategy increased life expectancy in impoverished communities, and the system has thrived, becoming the nation's largest provider of health care in the twenty-first century.[17]

But what was most dramatic about the Tufts-Delta model was its insistence on empowering its low-income client base. Enabling poor people to take control of the project was one of TDHC's goals from the start, and it made significant progress in this area within a few years. In 1969, 21 of the 26 members of the center's nursing staff were local people, and a total of 75 area residents held paid jobs in the clinic. A year later, the center employed roughly 200 people, including 180 from Bolivar County.[18]

These people did not come from the educated middle class but were some of the poorest of the Mississippi poor. According to a report by the clinic governing board, "Community Development staff who were past recipients of food stamps and commodity food programs are now *managing* the Health Center Supplemental Food Program." African Americans comprised roughly 70 percent of the center's staff, and most nonlocal employees were black southerners who had trained as health professionals at northern colleges or at predominantly black institutions in southern cities. Assistant project director John Hatch, for example, spent his childhood in rural Arkansas and knew what it was like to work in the cotton fields. He trained as a social worker at Atlanta University and joined the Tufts-Delta clinic after taking a position as an assistant professor at Tufts. Obstetrician-gynecologist Helen Barnes was a native Mississippian who earned a degree at Howard University in Washington, D.C., and returned home to work as a general practitioner in Greenwood before being hired by the TDHC to set up a prenatal care program in 1968. As the center's training programs prepared more people for employment, local residents filled more of the jobs at the health center.[19]

Center staff also worked to involve rural poor people in the governance and direction of the project. Hatch emphasized the need to avoid patterns that had characterized white Americans' relationships with black people in the past, where small groups of educated, middle-class African Americans were anointed as "leaders" who represented the entire black community. Hatch spent several months living with poor black families in Bolivar County during the organizing phase of the project. During that time, his hosts repeatedly expressed the mistrust they felt toward "white folks and gate keeper blacks." These conversations convinced him that building a successful health care project required meaningful participation and decision making by the people to be served. Geiger agreed that selecting only those African Americans with college degrees to serve on citizens' committees did "not involve the great majority of the community's population in any way." He urged TDHC staff to make sure that poor people had real power to shape the project according to their needs.[20]

Among their responsibilities, local people served as outreach workers who scoured the countryside to tell residents about the center and to gauge community sentiment about what sorts of programs the center should offer. According to Geiger, local activists "literally knocked on the door of every house in northern Bolivar County inhabited by a black family" as well as met with residents in churches, schools, and workplaces. Hundreds of people attended public meetings to learn more about the project, and organizers held special forums at which Mound Bayou's health professionals and political leaders discussed concerns about potential competition from the TDHC and threats to the town's traditions of black autonomy. As a result of these efforts, Hatch reported, the project gained "broad based community support."[21]

That support was ongoing and was shaped and worked out through democratic engagement. Residents in the towns and hamlets that the clinic served chose representatives to serve on local health associations, which met regularly to decide how best to address their constituents' needs. By February 1970, ten local health associations had been organized and membership totaled 2,835 people. Attendees at health association meetings, a clinic staffer wrote, were "the rural poor—the overwhelming majority of our target population—rather than the black townspeople and middle-class elite." Those among the rural poor who became most active in the work of the clinic became delegates to a larger regional group, the North Bolivar County Health Council (NBCHC), formed in July 1968 as a clinic steering committee. Service on this council was intended to prepare local people to assume control over the project. NBCHC members attended twice-monthly meetings where they discussed community concerns, heard reports from clinic staff about the status of various initiatives, and made the decisions needed to keep the clinic programs running. Hoping to enhance local initiative and autonomy, Tufts staff refrained from closely directing council activities.[22]

Members in each community set priorities and developed programs. Many members of local health associations were keenly aware that they had to meet basic survival needs in their communities before they could begin to address specific health issues and consequently worked to feed the hungry, rehabilitate housing, construct sewage systems, and ensure safe water supplies—the top priorities for rural poor people. Residents of some communities held picnics and barbecues to raise money when particular families or communities were experiencing unusual hardship. Health associations established community centers, recreational facilities, youth programs, rural transportation systems, and services to care for the disabled and elderly, among many other activities.[23]

All of these activities were in keeping with the holistic approach that the Tufts-Delta clinic and other neighborhood health centers established as an effective model for addressing the health needs of the nation's poorest citizens. As Geiger explained, preventive medicine sought "not merely to treat illness but to help provide a road out of the conditions—poverty, unemployment, lack of educational opportunity, dangerous physical and biological environments— that greatly increase risk. In short, medicine must bring about change in the social order." This broad agenda meant that TDHC staff often engaged in activities that went far beyond just treating sick people. Obstetrics nurses visited all new patients in their homes to determine the overall health needs of the entire household, not just the individuals who had sought medical care. Workers from the environmental health unit helped prevent the spread of disease by digging drainage ditches and wells, building sanitary toilets, fitting windows and doors with fly screens, removing garbage, and poisoning rodents at hundreds of homes.[24]

In February 1968, TDHC nurses visited a home in which they found a mother and daughter with barely any food. "We pulled a few strings and a few legs and got food stamps for them," Simpson wrote. "Usually . . . it takes awhile to wade through all the red tape. Today, we talked faster than the welfare agent, and he gave them to us at once." TDHC clinical director Leon Kruger believed that monitoring welfare agencies and pushing for policy changes to address the unmet needs of poor people were legitimate functions of the center, which he believed "in addition to providing direct services must help achieve physical, mental, and social well-being by participating in social action." By 1970, Tufts-Delta staff were confident that they were working not only to address malnutrition and illness but to help achieve the wider goals of the War on Poverty. "The idea of intervention in the poverty cycle is no longer a dream but a reality, and health services have become a point of entry for broad social intervention within the community."[25]

Although the conditions of OEO grants prevented the health center staff from becoming directly involved in voter registration or civil rights work, the center clearly encouraged and fostered political activity among its rural poor clientele, in part because staffers and their clients had come to see access to health care as a right. Local health associations offered many residents their first experiences in democratic participation, their first chance to elect representatives and to influence decisions affecting their communities. To address poverty and unemployment in their communities, these residents at times had to resort to protest politics.

Members of a Rosedale, Mississippi, group who had gotten their first taste of politics as activists in the local health association organized a 1970 boycott of white-owned stores to push for an end to employment discrimination. The activists also demanded better water and sewage systems, housing code enforcement, streetlights, paved roads in black neighborhoods, and more hiring of African Americans by the municipal government and private businesses. The NBCHC endorsed the boycott and urged members of each local health association to donate funds to help sustain it. In response to white complaints about TDHC involvement in the protest, center director Andrew James acknowledged that some of the participants were probably employed at the center but stated that they did not engage in civil rights activity during working hours. However, the distinctions between health center work and political activism were not always obvious, and that fact lay at the heart of the center's approach. As staff member Theodore Parrish observed, the health associations were made up of citizen volunteers who understood the roles that elected officials played in the provision (or nonprovision) of health care and other services. For that reason, "the Health Association members are greatly involved in voter registration activities."[26]

BACKLASH POLITICS

Opponents of the TDHC had from the start feared the increasing politicization of poor black people. During the negotiations over the location of the project, Tufts staff repeatedly found themselves trying to reassure nervous officials that the center would not promote civil rights activity. These efforts failed to allay the suspicions of many white Mississippians, however, and their allegations that federal funds were being spent in a wasteful manner elicited a promise from Senator Stennis to look into the matter. Stennis had already undermined other antipoverty efforts in Mississippi by demanding audits of programs he said were using taxpayers' money to fund political revolutions. Stennis vowed to Hollingsworth, "I will use all of my influence on the Appropriations Committee to see that [the TDHC] gets a thorough going over." In 1971, the OEO investigated accusations that center staff and vehicles had been used to support the campaigns of black political candidates. The following year, the agency conducted an audit of TDHC financial records dating back to 1969.[27]

White Mississippians were not alone in fearing that Tufts-Delta's organizing activities would have disruptive consequences. Mound Bayou's black leaders recognized the threats to their dominance posed by the economic and political empowerment of poor people and joined their white counterparts in efforts to undermine the project. Cleveland lawyer Alfred Levengston wrote to the Mississippi congressional delegation in August 1968 at the request of a "prominent citizen" whose views represented those of "the more substantial people" in the town. He claimed that the TDHC had created "untold dissension among the citizenry of and around Mound Bayou" by paying people salaries that were far above prevailing labor rates—double what some local people had made in their previous jobs.[28]

The following year, a representative of a consulting firm based in Washington, D.C., wrote to Congressman Thomas Abernethy on behalf of MBCH to make sure the congressman fully grasped the distinction between the "good local people" who operated the hospital and the "Tufts crowd" at the health center. "It is common knowledge that the Tufts people are trying to undermine the local Mound Bayou Community Hospital program and to eventually take over the complete health services program in the Delta," the letter asserted. "Much of the racial unrest has been fomented by Tufts' staff of civil rights activists."[29]

Just as many white Mississippians believed that black southerners would not think to participate in civil rights activity without encouragement from northern agitators, Mound Bayou's black elite also assumed that the rural poor—former plantation workers, sharecroppers, and maids—were incapable of acting without white direction. Rather than accepting the health associations as legitimate vehicles through which poor people could express their concerns and carry out plans for improving conditions in the community, the town's black leaders attacked them as agents of white colonialism.

The *Mound Bayou Voice* echoed this view in its coverage of decisions made in the early 1970s by the NBCHC. When Geiger moved from Tufts to the State University of New York at Stony Brook, health council members voted to affiliate their clinic with that university. A January 1971 article in the *Voice* ridiculed that decision as an example of council members simply following their white "boss": Geiger "decided to change his affiliation, and decided to let the local group 'decide' to come with him." A few months later, the *Voice* carried a lengthy piece about the TDHC in which it quoted comments made by a Black Power advocate who had worked there for one summer: "The people of the community do not yet realize that the center belongs to them, and not 'Mr. Tufts.' The overwhelming majority of the consumers are still revolving in the plantational cycle of life where you accept what is given and dare not ask for any more and are not encouraged to do so."[30]

The *Voice* accused the TDHC of denying local people any say in planning or decision making and suggested that the real power lay with Geiger and the white universities that funded the project. Such an arrangement was simply a new plantation system, the newspaper editorialized, and should not be tolerated by Mound Bayou's independent black leaders. "Blacks do not need whites to think for blacks," an unsigned article asserted. "*NO* white can be allowed to choose the black leader any more." Using the same arguments, Mound Bayou mayor Earl Lucas and other leading townspeople urged the OEO to merge the health center with MBCH to bring the project under the control of local African American health professionals instead of white outsiders.[31]

TDHC staff and patients were outraged by these attacks. Local people were actively involved in directing the project—just not the people that Mound Bayou's elites thought should be in charge. One health council report noted that initiatives such as improved sanitation, nutrition education programs, hot lunch programs, and transportation services were "the accomplishments not of the health center, but of the rural black community (which is still regarded, in some official quarters, as 'plantation slaves incapable of social change')." Local health associations had played major roles in setting the center's priorities, and the NBCHC was an autonomous entity that made decisions on its own rather than meekly following white advice.[32]

In February 1970, for example, the TDHC board voted to accept two new communities into the council, believing it was wrong to deny health services to people who needed them just because they were not included in the original grant. The NBCHC also requested and received more control over hiring at the TDHC after some rural residents complained that only people from Mound

Bayou were getting jobs. By 1971, NBCHC functions had expanded to include screening and approving applicants for positions at the center, monitoring the administration of health services, hiring staff for support services such as transportation and day care, and maintaining outreach facilities for the local health associations. Its employees answered only to the board, and council decisions were accepted both by university administrators "and Center staff as the final voice on local issues and Center policies impacting the community." The idea that the TDHC operated like a plantation, Geiger believed, was baseless. He saw the charges as part of "a political, ideological and social-class campaign (by one segment of the Black local community) for take-over, through the mechanism of merger with the Mound Bayou Community Hospital, which that segment controlled."[33]

In contrast to the TDHC's achievements in health care and black empowerment, MBCH's record of service to and inclusion of rural poor people since it received its first OEO grant was unimpressive. In 1967, civil rights activist Jake Ayers had complained that the newly reorganized "community hospital" had shut most residents out of elections for its board members by giving responsibility for outreach activities to "teachers and ministers who have little or no contact with poor people." As a result, the board came to be composed of black businesspeople and professionals. "The whole election was run by a middle-class group which made no effort to really involve the poor, and . . . it was so irregular that it should be nullified," Ayers reported. A year later, OEO officials found multiple violations of agency guidelines and procedures in MBCH operations. According to investigator George Dines, the program had no clear goals, democratic procedures were lacking, and most decisions were made by a small group of people on the executive committee who ran the hospital "as they see fit and most of all for their own personal aggrandizement." Many people in the Mound Bayou service area were unaware that the hospital had received federal funds to provide free care to poor people regardless of whether they belonged to the fraternal orders. Indeed, MBCH continued to charge nonmembers for treatment. "Double fees are being paid and there is every evidence that [the doctors] are receiving kick-backs from private insurance companies as well as many of the poverty patients they serve," wrote Dines. Local people also complained that MBCH doctors and staff at often mistreated patients who had been referred there by clinicians at TDHC, labeling them "Tufts patients" and asking them to pay for services that were supposed to be free.[34]

Conditions at the hospital were not much better than they had been when

Simpson first saw "Mound Bayou Hospital, such as it is" and commented, "Oh, it would take me all night to describe *that* situation!" Outside investigators revealed that, among other things, the hospital was often short of beds, provided substandard care to many patients, and would not allow mothers to breast-feed their babies because it was "too much trouble." One MBCH critic observed, "If the Hospital were a white Mississippi institution giving its present quality of medical care, there would be picket lines, explosions of protest, and lawsuits."[35]

Poor black people's experiences at MBCH convinced many that those who were demanding a merger of the health center and hospital were more concerned with consolidating their own power than with providing higher-quality medical care to local residents. A local black woman who had worked as a nurse at both facilities before moving out of the area provided a scathing analysis of the real motives she believed lay behind Mound Bayou elites' pressure on the OEO: Lucas wanted to gain control over federally funded jobs for political patronage purposes. His efforts were supported by civil rights activist Owen Brooks, a black northerner who had come to Mississippi in 1965, as part of an attempt to build an independent black political base in the Delta. Fraternal order leaders also resented TDHC, preferring a system that would allow them to keep charging poor people for services and lining their own pockets in the process. "Lucas and Brooks and those people hate the rural Black poor people and are full of prejudice against them," the nurse wrote. "I myself heard them call them 'niggers' and 'slaves' over and over. The way they kept trying to take the health center over was to yell that *they* were the Black leaders (only none of the poor people ever chose them) and to pretend that the health center was 'white outsiders' and to go to OEO every month and demand a 'merger' of the health center and hospital." In the view of Shelby resident Lucinda Young, Lucas's charge that the TDHC was a white-run "plantation" ignored its achievements and discounted poor black people's deep appreciation for the project. "I don't care what he say, we was doing mighty good with [the] plantation," she asserted.[36]

Aware of the problems at MBCH, the OEO resisted the idea of a merger until 1971. By that time, a major reorganization of the agency and new priorities set by President Richard Nixon had caused the departure of many OEO staff who supported the TDHC. The OEO's original mission of empowering poor people to solve their own problems was abandoned in favor of more traditional approaches that emphasized the efficient delivery of services by professionals. This shift in federal priorities and philosophy affected the administration of community-run antipoverty programs across the country. In one locale after another, con-

trol was taken from the hands of poor people and given to traditionally creden-
tialed professionals.

New administrators at OEO's Office of Health Affairs worried that MBCH
and TDHC were offering redundant services. Arguments for cost and service
efficiency thus reinforced complaints made by proponents of local black elite
control of health care delivery in northern Bolivar County. Transferring power
over the project to the Mound Bayou faction also fit with Nixon's "new federalism," which focused on restoring local oversight of antipoverty projects instead
of centralizing supervision in the federal OEO. Restoring control to Mound Bayou's administrators was politically appealing because it allowed the president
to make points with advocates of greater black autonomy even as he appeased
conservative southern supporters who expected action on election promises to
roll back federal interference in their states.[37]

In April 1971, the OEO ordered the health center and hospital to merge by the
following September as a condition of renewing the TDHC funding. Protests by
TDHC staff and the State University of New York at Stony Brook persuaded the
agency to renew the grant for six months under the original terms and allow
more time to plan the merger. Negotiations between the two hospital boards
began in November. Attempts to provide for the continuation of the NBCHC as
a delegate agency that could receive OEO funds failed, and in January 1972 OEO
officials demanded that the two boards form a new corporation and submit a
new grant proposal. An agreement to merge programs and facilities was finally
reached in February, and in May the OEO granted $5.5 million to the newly cre-
ated Delta Community Hospital and Health Center (DCHHC) to continue services to poor people in Mississippi's Bolivar, Coahoma, Sunflower, and Washington Counties.[38]

Rather than ensuring black independence, the merger increased the new
health center's vulnerability to attacks from white Mississippians seeking to destroy programs that served the poor. Under the terms of the original grant, with
federal funds channeled through northern universities such as Tufts and Stony
Brook, the TDHC was immune to the governor's veto. This element was crucial
in maintaining the program's independence, since Deep South governors had
frequently used the veto power granted under the Economic Opportunity Act
to try to keep federal funding from community projects seeking to empower
the poor. As might be expected, civil-rights-oriented organizations trying to
empower the black poor generated special hostility. As an independent clinic,
the health center also had not been subject to regulation by the state hospital

commission. The merger created a state-chartered corporation, giving Mississippi officials much more power to meddle with the project.

Geiger explained the postmerger situation: "To stop the whole project—including the Health Center—at any time under the new grant, the state has only
to lift the hospital's license, something for which it can find 50 valid reasons."
Governor William Waller exercised his new authority over the project immediately by vetoing the federal grant to the DCHHC. In a letter to the OEO, Waller
cited concerns over safety code violations, duplication of services, and the proposed program's inability to meet the needs of poor people.[39]

Supporters of the newly merged hospital and clinic refuted Waller's claims,
and the OEO eventually overrode the governor's veto. In November 1972, an
evaluation by the American Public Health Association praised the Delta health
program's achievements over the previous five years and attributed many of its
failures to government policies that hindered long-term planning and staff recruitment. "The project has boldly, creatively, and with some measure of success demonstrated a way to improve health for rural people," the study group
noted. "It could very easily become an important forward step along the path to
improving health services for all Americans." The report urged state and federal
officials to lend their full support to the DCHHC and find a way to ensure adequate and reliable funding for the project.[40]

These recommendations came at a time when the Nixon administration was
interested in reducing rather than expanding the federal commitment to antipoverty programs. In 1973, Nixon transferred most OEO functions to other government agencies, and the Department of Health, Education, and Welfare took
over responsibility for the nation's community health centers. In an effort to
cut costs, department officials restricted DCHHC activities to services directly
related to medical care, undermining the original mission of using holistic approaches to spark changes in the social order. Annual funding of the project declined from $5.5 to $3.3 million, and services such as home nursing care, education and outreach, youth programs, supplemental food distribution, delivery of
meals for the elderly, and the environmental health unit were cut. As Geiger observed, the changes meant a return to "the usual deal of just providing services
for people [instead of] developing people's capacity to do it themselves."[41]

Within the DCHHC, power passed from the rural poor clientele to middle-
class administrators. In April 1972, the NBCHC reluctantly agreed to sign over
its responsibilities to the new board of the DCHHC. Earlier plans to provide
management training to health council members and enhance their ability to

administer programs were abandoned, and council members' role in planning and implementing services was curtailed. Whereas the NBCHC had been made up of elected representatives from local communities, the DCHHC board of directors included politicians and business leaders appointed to represent specific interests. No mechanism was created to ensure democratic participation by program recipients.

With little involvement by the community in decision making at the new hospital and health center, a small group of board members distributed key positions and resources to their families and friends. Board member Olivia Johnson reported that Mayor Lucas's wife was appointed head of the nursing program and that staff were now punished if they criticized the new administrators. Shelby alderman Robert Gray accused board members Lucas, Brooks, and Richard Polk of being more interested in building a political empire using federal funds than in providing services for poor people. "Lucas and Brooks and that bunch are not concerned about health care," Gray claimed. "All they want is control."[42]

In the years following the merger, the quality of services provided by the DCHHC steadily declined. Many staff members left the project because of the funding problems, substandard conditions at the hospital, and a sense that administrators were no longer committed to the community health center ideal. The same conditions that drove the DCHHC's existing employees away made it hard to replace them. Within a year, the DCHHC had only three doctors on its staff. According to Dorsey, one of the doctors was a drunkard who often abused patients; the second was trying to recover from a mental illness; and the third was "old, senile, and alcoholic." Many poor people no longer used the hospital or the health center, preferring to go without care or spend what little income they had to see private doctors. To Geiger it seemed like a "return to the days before the health center arrived—a combination of unrepresentative local control and Meharry, with those two groups profiting while the people get screwed—except now it is happening to the tune of 4 million dollars a year."[43]

Although the TDHC's original goal of initiating broad social change was undermined in the 1970s, its activities left a positive legacy. Improvements to housing, sanitation, and infrastructure as well as to direct medical services raised living standards for many Delta residents. Local people who completed their education and trained for careers at the center earned higher incomes than would otherwise have been the case. In interviews conducted in 1992, residents of Bolivar County noted that the presence of the DCHHC continued to exert a constructive influence even though the programs had become less comprehensive. According to William Crockett Jr., a majority of young people in the area went on to college after completing high school, helping to break the cycle of poverty in the region. Many of them chose to work in health professions. Irene Williams told John Hatch, "I . . . will always have a special part in my heart for you all, because [you] thought enough of peoples like myself to come down to the Mississippi Delta and try to start a comprehensive health center, and give peoples like myself a chance."[44]

At the same time, the deeper social problems that TDHC tried to address in the 1960s continued to plague the region into the twenty-first century. Responsibility for persistent poverty, racism, and poor people's limited ability to influence the decisions that affect their lives falls heavily on national and regional political leaders who undercut the transformative potential of antipoverty programs. Yet the fate of the TDHC demonstrates that these forces were not the only obstacles to social justice in the Mississippi Delta. In a town where African Americans held a monopoly on political power, opposition from local elites obstructed activists' efforts just as much as did the actions of the white racists who governed other southern communities. Although complaints that outsiders initiated and financially sustained the TDHC were technically accurate, the project encouraged participation and leadership by the rural poor black people it served. By offering participants a genuine voice in shaping policy and dramatically improving the economic prospects of thousands of people in Bolivar County, the TDHC fulfilled the goals of the Black Power movement more completely than the black-controlled health program that Mound Bayou political leaders proposed. Yet the OEO was persuaded that blackness alone qualified people to run programs for African Americans and turned the project over to a group that did not adequately represent or serve the poor. In forcing the TDHC to merge with the MBCH, the OEO ignored the class dimensions of the Delta's social problems and facilitated the continuation of precisely the conditions the agency had been created to eradicate.

Notes

1. H. Jack Geiger, "A Life in Social Medicine," in *The Doctor Activist: Physicians Fighting for Social Change*, ed. Ellen L. Bassuk (New York: Plenum, 1996), 15.

2. Sar A. Levitan, "Healing the Poor in Their Back Yard," in *Neighborhood Health Centers*, ed. Robert M. Hollister, Bernard M. Kramer, and Seymour S. Bellin (Lexington, Mass.: Lexington, 1974), 51–52; Geiger, "Life in Social Medicine," 12–16.

3. Paul B. Johnson to Sargent Shriver, March 25, 1966, Box 16, Folder "Administrative—Mississippi—1967," Records of the Community Services Administration, Office of Economic Opportunity, Community Action Program, Records of the Director, State Files, 1965–68, RG 381, National Archives II, College Park, Maryland (hereafter RG 381); R. T. Hollingsworth to John Stennis, April 8, 1966, William B. Alexander to John C. Stennis, April 25, 1967, both in Series 25, Box 7, Folder "Tufts Medical College Mound Bayou, 1966–68," John C. Stennis Collection, Special Collections, Mitchell Library, Mississippi State University, Starkville.

4. "Health Problem in Mississippi," 1–2, Box 16, Folder "Administrative—Mississippi—1967," , RG 381; H. Jack Geiger, "Community Control—or Community Conflict?," in *Neighborhood Health Centers*, ed. Hollister, Kramer, and Bellin, 139; Mary Stella Simpson, *Sister Stella's Babies: Days in the Practice of a Nurse Midwife* (New York: American Journal of Nursing, 1978), 57.

5. Norman L. Crockett, *The Black Towns* (Lawrence: Regents Press of Kansas, 1979), 9–15, 42–43, 50–51, 67, 182–83.

6. Ibid., 156, 158–62, 177–78; Geiger, "Community Control," 139; Jacob R. Henderson to Ross D. Davis, February 28, 1967, Box 9, Folder "Tuffs [*sic*] Mississippi Medical Project," Subject Files, 1965–69, Executive Secretariat, Office of Administration, Economic Development Administration, RG 378, National Archives, Washington, D.C.

7. David T. Beito, "Black Fraternal Hospitals in the Mississippi Delta, 1942–1967," *Journal of Southern History* 65:1 (February 1999): 119.

8. Ibid., 113–19, 120–28.

9. Ibid., 125–26, 129–32; "Sad Nurse" to A. B. Albritton, July 31, 1972, Box 25, Folder "March–December 1972," Delta Health Center Records, Southern Historical Collection, University of North Carolina–Chapel Hill (hereafter DHCR).

10. Beito, "Black Fraternal Hospitals," 135–38; Russell E. Miller, *Light on the Hill: A History of Tufts University since 1952* (Cambridge, Mass.: MassMarket, 1986), 2:355, 358.

11. Simpson, *Sister Stella's Babies*, 19–20, 65.

12. Cynthia Kelly, "Health Care in the Mississippi Delta," *American Journal of Nursing* 69:4 (April 1969): 760; Simpson, *Sister Stella's Babies*, 5, 19–20, 65.

13. Simpson, *Sister Stella's Babies*, 11, 82.

14. Sandra Blakeslee, "To Rural Negroes, Health Center Is Hope," *New York Times*, August 28, 1970; Irene Williams, interview by John Hatch, July 18, 1992, tape recording, T-4316/19, DHCR; John Brown, interview by John Hatch, [1992], tape recording, T-4316/2, DHCR.

15. Williams, interview.

16. Ibid.; L. C. Dorsey, "Dirt Dauber Nests, Socks Nailed over Doorways, Salts, Prayer and OTC's: Space Age Medicine in the Poor Community," [1990], 10–12, 14, Box 12, Folder 252, John W. Hatch Papers, Southern Historical Collection; Jennifer Nel-

son, "'Hold Your Head Up and Stick Out Your Chin': Community Health and Women's Health in Mound Bayou, Mississippi," *NWSA Journal* 17:1 (Spring 2005): 104–5.

17. Joseph A. Loftus, "Cohesion Sought in Medical Aids," *New York Times*, May 22, 1966; Geiger, "Life in Social Medicine," 18; Nelson, "Hold Your Head Up," 100.

18. Kelly, "Health Care," 760.

19. Ibid., 760; Leon Kruger, "Role of the Comprehensive Health Center in Social Change," [1969], 5, Box 1, Folder 10, Lee Bankhead Papers, Wisconsin Historical Society, Madison; Blakeslee, "To Rural Negroes," 30; "Progress Report," February 1970, [14], Box 39, Folder "Health Assoc. Council Progress Reports etc. 1969–70," DHCR; Miller, *Light on the Hill*, 2:359; Nelson, "Hold Your Head Up," 106–7, 109; Joseph J. Huttie Jr., "New Federalism and the Death of a Dream in Mound Bayou, Mississippi," *New South* 28:4 (Fall 1973): 22; Geiger, "Life in Social Medicine," 17.

20. [John Hatch], "Citizen Participation in the Tufts-Delta Health Center," December 1, 1967, 2, Box 39, Folder "J. Hatch—Health Council—Comm. Org. Prog. Rep.," DHCR; John W. Hatch, "Community Development in a Rural Comprehensive Community Health Program," paper presented at the New York Academy of Medicine Annual Health Conference, April 24, 1970, 2–3, Box 1, Folder 16, Hatch Papers; Geiger, "Community Control," 135; "Wednesday Meeting," July 18, 1968, 2–3, Box 1, Folder 11, Bankhead Papers.

21. Geiger, "Community Control," 139; [Hatch], "Citizen Participation," 1; Hatch, "Community Development," 4–5.

22. "Progress Report," February 1970, [4]; North Bolivar County Health Council, General Description, n.d., 2, Box 13, Folder "North Bolivar County Health and Improvement Council" (1 of 2), DHCR; North Bolivar County Health and Civic Improvement Association, "Progress Report," February 1970, 1, Box 39, Folder "Health Assoc. Council Progress Reports, etc. 1969–70," DHCR.

23. John Hatch, "Community Shares in Policy Decisions for Rural Health Center," *Hospitals*, July 1, 1969, 110, 112; "Progress Report," February 1970, [4]; Hatch, "Community Development," 7; K. Biggs, "Gunnison-Perthshire-Waxhaw Health Association Report," [1970], 1–2, Box 9, Folder "Health Council 1970," DHCR; North Bolivar County, "Progress Report," 1.

24. Geiger, "Life in Social Medicine," 25; Simpson, *Sister Stella's Babies*, 20, 87; H. Jack Geiger, Statement Presented to the Subcommittee on Employment Manpower and Poverty, U.S. Senate, May 21, 1969, 17–18, Box 1, Folder 15, Bankhead Papers.

25. Simpson, *Sister Stella's Babies*, 57; Kruger, "Role," 8; "Tufts-Delta Health Center Annual Report, 1970," [draft], [2], Box 1, Folder "Annual Report, 1970," DHCR.

26. Rosedale Black Community to Merchants of Rosedale, August 25, 1970, Box 22, Folder "Rosedale, Town of," DHCR; Minutes, North Bolivar County Health Council Meeting, September 27, October 11, 1970, 2, Box 13, Folder "North Bolivar County Health

and Improvement Council" (1 of 2), DHCR; Andrew B. James to M. J. Dattel, November 2, 1970, Box 22, Folder "Delta White Community," DHCR; Theodore Parrish to Andrew B. James, March 16, 1971, 1, Box 25, Folder "January–June 1971," DHCR.

27. John Stennis to R. T. Hollingsworth, October 16, 1968, Series 25, Box 7, Folder "Tufts Medical College Mound Bayou, 1966–68," Stennis Collection. See also Jordan, this volume; John Dittmer, *Local People: The Struggle for Civil Rights in Mississippi* (Urbana: University of Illinois Press, 1994), 371–72; H. Jack Geiger to Edmund D. Pellegrino, April 13, 1972, 3, Box 25, Folder "March–December 1972," DHCR.

28. Alfred A. Levingston to James Eastland, John Stennis, and Thomas Abernethy, August 2, 1968, Box 182, Folder "Tufts College—Mound Bayou," Thomas G. Abernethy Papers, Archives and Special Collections, University of Mississippi, Oxford.

29. Charles R. Holm Jr. to Thomas Abernethy, May 14, 1969, Box 182, Folder "Tufts College—Mound Bayou," Abernethy Papers.

30. "N.B.C. Health Council," *Mound Bayou Voice*, January 17–30, 1971; "Who's Fighting Who?," *Mound Bayou Voice*, February 11–March 1, 1971.

31. "N.B.C. Health Council"; "Who's Fighting Who?"; H. Jack Geiger to Edmund D. Pellegrino, April 13, 1972, 3, Box 25, Folder "March–December 1972," DHCR; [John Hatch], "Thoughts on University Relationship with Delta Health Center," July 2, 1971, 1, Box 25, Folder "January–June 1971," DHCR.

32. North Bolivar County Health and Civic Improvement Association, "Progress Report," February 1970, Box 9, Folder "Health Council 1970," DHCR; H. Jack Geiger to Edmund D. Pellegrino, April 13, 1972, 3, Box 25, Folder "March–December 1972," DHCR.

33. "Progress Report," February 1970, [6]; North Bolivar County, "Progress Report," 2; "Role of Consumers," [1972], 1–2, Box 25, Folder "March–December 1972," DHCR; H. Jack Geiger to Edmund D. Pellegrino, April 13, 1972, 3, Box 25, Folder "March–December 1972," DHCR.

34. Jake Ayers to Sargent Shriver, August 19, 1967, Sidney W. Maurer to William Lafayette, April 3, 1968, both in Box 23, Folder "Mound Bayou (Mississippi) Correspondence," Box 23, DHCR; George B. Dines to Sidney Maurer, October 16, 1968, Box 22, Folder "Mound Bayou (Mississippi) Reports," DHCR.

35. [John Hatch], "Summary of Comments to the Health Council Board of Directors," [December 1971], 5, Box 25, Folder "July–December 1971," DHCR; Simpson, *Sister Stella's Babies*, 14, 40, 47, 76, 90, 135; "Reflections on a Merger of the Mound Bayou Community Hospital and the Delta Health Center, and a Staged Plan for Functional Merger," [1971], 3, Box 25, Folder "July–December 1971," DHCR.

36. "Sad Nurse," 2–3; Mark Newman, *Divine Agitators: The Delta Ministry and Civil Rights in Mississippi* (Athens: University of Georgia Press, 2004), 42, 126; Lucinda Young, interview by John Hatch, n.d., tape recording, T-4316/22, DHCR.

37. H. Jack Geiger to Andrew James, January 26, 1971, Box 43, Folder "OEO Grant

Correspondence 1971–72," DHCR; H. Jack Geiger to Mike Holloman, September 1972, Box 25, Folder "March–December 1972," DHCR; Robert F. Clark, *The War on Poverty: History, Selected Programs, and Ongoing Impact* (Lanham, Md.: University Press of America, 2002), 60–68, 133–35; Kenneth O'Reilly, *Nixon's Piano: Presidents and Racial Politics from Washington to Clinton* (New York: Free Press, 1995), 282–86.

38. Huttie, "New Federalism," 22; "Brief History of the Delta Health Center 1970–1972, and of the Events Leading to Merger with the Mound Bayou Community Hospital in a New Corporation Beginning March 1, 1972," [February 1972], 1–3, Box 25, Folder "March–December 1972," DHCR; "OEO Continues Mississippi Delta Health Program," 1, OEO News Release, July 29, 1972, Box 181, Folder "Mound Bayou Community Hospital," Abernethy Papers.

39. H. Jack Geiger to Edmund D. Pellegrino, April 13, 1972, 3, Box 25, Folder "March–December 1972," DHCR; Bill Waller to E. Leon Cooper, June 1, 1972, Box 3, Folder "Cooper, Leon, Director, Office of Health Affairs, OEO," DHCR.

40. Congressional Task Force Report, [1972], 14–16, 44, Box 5, Folder "Mound Bayou Community Hospital," Tombigbee Council on Human Relations Collection, Special Collections, Mitchell Library, Mississippi State University, Starkville; Nancy Hicks, "Health Projects Get Funding Plan," *New York Times*, November 14, 1972.

41. H. Jack Geiger to Andrew James, January 26, 1971, Box 43, Folder "OEO Grant Correspondence 1971–72," DHCR; Huttie, "New Federalism," 21, 23–24.

42. "Role of Consumers," 1, 3; H. Jack Geiger, Notes on Impact of Merger, 1972, encl. in Geiger to Mike Hollomon September 1972, Box 25, Folder "March–December 1972," DHCR; James Rundles to Bill Waller, August 14, 1972, Folder 262, Hatch Papers.

43. Thomas Gualtieri et al. to Thomas Georges, September 14, 1972, Box 25, Folder "March–December 1972," DHCR; Jack Geiger to Mike Holloman, July 19, 1973, 1–2, Box 25, Folder "1973," DHCR.

44. William Crockett Jr., interview by Martha Mounett, July 31, 1992, tape recording, T-4316/6, dhcr; Williams, interview.

AMY JORDAN

Fighting for the Child Development Group of Mississippi

Poor People, Local Politics, and the

Complicated Legacy of Head Start

The Child Development Group of Mississippi (CDGM), a network of child care and educational centers and one of the most controversial programs to emerge from the Community Action Program (CAP) of the War on Poverty, began as a hopeful outgrowth of the movement schools established during the 1964 Freedom Summer campaign. Civil rights activists organized Freedom Schools to sustain local young people through the difficult, slow, and violent organizing campaigns of the early 1960s. More generally, the CDGM grew out of a determined struggle to overturn Mississippi's repressive power structure, which subjected blacks to rampant discrimination. In their day-to-day operation, the CDGM local centers empowered poor black families in ways that contrasted starkly with the state's tradition of top-down segregated education. And segregationist whites recognized the challenge that CDGM posed: The program's federal funding was intermittent, constantly under threat, and ultimately cut off entirely. But its legacy survived, and it stands as an example of grassroots activists using organizing strategies of the civil rights movement along with funding and expertise from the federal antipoverty program to record tangible gains in the fight against poverty.

THE BIRTH OF THE CDGM

McComb, Mississippi, the site of one of the early Mississippi Freedom Schools, was also where Tom Levin, key organizer of the Medical Committee for Human Rights and a Freedom Schools volunteer, was exposed to the student-centered pedagogical approach that defined these schools. As the summer of 1965 approached, Levin, inspired by his experiences the previous summer, reached out to other veteran organizers to develop a proposal for creating "freedom preschools" in Mississippi. Art Thomas, the director of the Delta Ministry, an organization deeply committed to carrying on the civil rights traditions of the first half of the decade, was looking for a federal program in which poor people could play meaningful roles in structuring institutions that could change their lives. Similarly, Marian Wright, a brilliant strategist and a Jackson-based attorney for the National Association for the Advancement of Colored People, envisioned tapping into the emerging federal War on Poverty. She was particularly concerned about providing a means of empowerment for preschool-aged children who would soon face the daunting task of desegregating the state's white public schools.[1]

In the months before civil rights veterans began to lay plans for "freedom preschools," debates were raging in Washington about President Lyndon Baines Johnson's CAP, the initiative authorized by the Economic Opportunity Act of 1964 that emphasized channeling federal funds directly to local communities rather than to established government agencies. Out of these debates in Congress and among War on Poverty officials came a growing concern about how to address the needs of young children living in poverty. Sargent Shriver, director of the Office of Economic Opportunity (OEO), convened a committee of early childhood experts early in 1965. By February, they had begun to lay plans for a nationwide network of early childhood education centers. The planning for Operation Head Start, conceived on the federal level as a preschool medical/nutritional community action program, coincided with Levin's efforts to apply Freedom School principles to poor children in Mississippi. Levin's proposal, a modest plan to open ten early childhood education centers for about 150 children, was accepted in April 1965, a month before Johnson gathered reporters in the White House Rose Garden to announce the creation of Head Start as an experimental summer program. That summer, more than half a million children attended 13,400 preschools across the United States. In August, Johnson made the program permanent.[2]

Even as they wrote and submitted their proposal, Levin and Thomas were wary of working with a federal agency. After years of economic and violent reprisals with little federal intervention, veteran organizers in Mississippi rejected the idea that the federal government could be trusted to support the building of experimental and alternative institutions among poor African Americans. However, Levin and Thomas quickly became convinced that this was an opportunity for black Mississippians to exercise some real control over the kind of antipoverty programs brought into the state. The CAP's transformative potential lay in the idea of "maximum feasible participation" by low-income residents affected by programs, a progressive goal written into the Equal Opportunity Act legislation of 1964. OEO officials were eager to bypass entrenched local and state power structures that worked to maintain the status quo.[3] Although OEO policy guidelines betrayed a professional bias that dismissed poor people's ability to exercise critical leadership in early childhood education programs, CDGM organizers saw a potential to use the program to achieve War on Poverty goals with grassroots means.

The CDGM began with a short-term $1.5 million OEO grant to fund early childhood education centers through the summer of 1965, making the CDGM one of the first Head Start centers funded. Organizers recruited a network of professionals from the fields of education, psychology, and social work; hired a central staff; and created an administrative structure while mobilizing local communities to locate and renovate buildings for the centers and hire resource teachers, teacher trainees, and aides—all in a period of just three months.[4]

Activists from the Student Nonviolent Coordinating Committee (SNCC) and the Delta Ministry spread the word about CDGM throughout the state. Working-class African Americans were skeptical of both the federal government and formal educational programs. As Adam Fairclough has pointed out in his recent study, *A Class of Their Own: Black Teachers in the Segregated South*, working-class African Americans in the South held ambivalent attitudes regarding formal education. Doubtful about CDGM's potential effectiveness, one mother stated, "Books is stuffed with white man lies. Those books ain't never gonna put down stories the 'ol people tell about black people."[5]

Nevertheless, by early April, local activists had persuaded their neighbors that CDGM could represent their communities' traditions, history, and aspirations for the future. One canvasser exhorted, "Get in there and help teach. It's the parents' program. That's how we overcome fear in our community. We say, you don't have to give up your kids to nobody. Come, too."[6]

For fifteen years, Hattie Saffold, a resident of Holmes County, had weighed and recorded cotton for five dollars a day and transported agricultural workers to the fields for fifty cents a person. During the winter, she did domestic work for three dollars a day. In the early stages of the civil rights movement, she and her husband, Eugene, had organized meetings at her church. Hattie Saffold was deeply committed to voter registration as an activist with the Mississippi Freedom Democratic Party (MFDP) and helped to organize black farmers to run for positions on federal farm policy boards. She and her neighbors drew from these experiences to help create CDGM centers. They met as area committees, quickly located sites for centers, hired staff, and mobilized locals to build or renovate buildings for six centers in Holmes County.[7]

When the CDGM's central staff and local organizers gathered in mid-April, sixty-four communities had signed up 4,200 children. One elderly African American man proudly announced that he personally had signed up 107 children. Mount Beulah, a former black college in the countryside outside of Jackson, became the site of the hastily constructed central staff headquarters. CDGM rented several campus buildings from the Delta Ministry. In one of the buildings, a local black printer printed picture books. The campus also contained a large auditorium, places for staff to live, and a sweeping rural landscape where children and adults could play the games and activities that would animate CDGM classrooms.[8]

Rather than provide a precise template for how CDGM centers were to operate, the central staff, headed by Levin and Polly Greenberg, provided broader ideas as well as some firm principles regarding leadership. Very little time was available between the program's approval and the opening of the centers. The CDGM orientation sessions, which occurred at Mount Beulah in early July, proved critical for many CDGM organizers. A participant from Rolling Fork described an atmosphere permeated with "a feeling of real respect . . . [b]reathing fresh air and feeling free." She was surprised at the degree of openness and genuine feeling. Interactions involved not only laughter and singing but debates about teaching methods.[9]

SNCC organizer Frank Smith led sessions in the large auditorium at which local people expressed themselves through testimonials, freedom songs, and spirituals. Contrary to OEO expectations, local teacher trainees rather than outside experts led the small workshop sessions. Local people played children's games, tried different art projects, and shared ideas. CDGM staff encouraged the resource teachers, most of whom had been recruited from outside of the state, to remain available but in the background. These recruits struggled to meet what many saw as at best open-ended and at worst outrageously vague expectations. Since resource teachers did not receive specific assignments, these experts in the field had to cultivate some humility and work out patiently with local staff on the community level how they could be useful.

Greenberg described orientation as a "backwards slave market" where communities "looked over the imported goods" and selected which resource teachers best suited them. Levin expected resource teachers, once chosen by a community committee, to adapt themselves to the local context without imposing specific curricula on individual centers. Instead, the centers would reflect the communities that created them. A local person compared resource teachers to water that needed to be hauled from a well: "Haul out the resources without blasting the people's ways."[10]

Many community residents relished the open-ended quality of CDGM guidelines, the lack of required lesson plans, and the lack of ironclad prescriptions for running the centers. Without preset activities and lesson plans, participants felt free to imagine educational centers that contrasted sharply with their experiences in Mississippi's schools. The process of defining CDGM helped many residents begin to find their voices. One Mississippian facilitated an engaging discussion on the "limits of freedom" by asking her small group what freedom would mean for a young child. The participants stressed the importance of providing children with opportunities to choose activities, use their imaginations, and exercise some independence.

When a trained kindergarten teacher warned the group against promoting chaos, the participants at first hesitated to contradict her; however, they subsequently argued persuasively that order and the ability to sit quietly and follow directions should not be prioritized. One participant envisioned freedom occurring in the context of hearing a story being read: "If I'm readin' him a story, say, and he breaks in an' talks, say, I'd let him tell. . . . [M]aybe the story has reminded him of something. I mean we ain't reading to him to keep him still."[11] These discussions reflected participants' experiences with a segregated educational system in which discipline and shaming techniques ruled. In these orientation sessions, poor African Americans articulated their dreams for a more liberating educational experience marked not by fear, discipline, and humiliating punishments but rather by empowering children to develop their creativity. Participants wanted an educational environment that valued the children and the communities from which they came.

In those first hectic months, CDGM opened eighty-four centers for six thousand children, creating a program that reflected the ideals and ambitions of the surrounding communities. CDGM drew teacher trainees as well as teacher guides, aides, drivers, cooks, designers and builders, and equipment operators from local community committees. Poor, unemployed, underemployed, and displaced workers thronged the flurry of community-level meetings, workshops, and social gatherings with an eagerness to pursue a concrete expression of the campaigns for racial and economic justice. CDGM teacher Lavaree Jones, a resident of Hollandale, Mississippi, recalled that the "people became the curriculum." Activities, books, art supplies, and playground equipment reflected the language, images, and lived experiences of local people. CDGM embraced the creative energy and vision of the dispossessed.[12]

INSIDE THE CDGM CENTERS

During the first year, the teachers experimented with many imaginative approaches to nursery education. The flexibility of the CDGM model allowed local adults to infuse centers with personal experiences. Some adults shared their relationship to the surrounding rural landscape, while others showed children how to build equipment and toys; still others taught children to use discarded materials to make beautiful objects. Centers shared these creative ideas through frequent visits and social gatherings as well as through the CDGM newsletter. One former McComb teacher recalled that the public school system told teachers "everything to do," whereas with CDGM, "you can't feel anyone taking your right to plan away from you." In her view, CDGM and the newsletter in particular offered "flavorings" that teachers could add to their own recipes.[13]

A June 1966 visitor to one of the centers would have seen a lot of outdoor activity, such as children painting on handmade easels, playing dress-up with dolls and mirrors, or listening to an adult reading stories aloud. Another extension of the emphasis on self-made equipment involved carpentry and crafts made outside. Men in the community made child-size work benches and provided scraps for children to use to build their own toys. Children also used big needles to sew hems, a skill they might put to use at home, even if their efforts were crooked.[14]

The rural Hollandale center was in many ways typical in that it not only exemplified many of the CDGM centers' greatest strengths but also experienced persistent challenges. Excitement about the creation of the Hollandale center had led to overenrollment and thus overcrowding. Still, an outside evaluator reported, the staff gave the impression that they "knew what they were doing and that they enjoyed doing it. . . . The place looks like a nursery school." The center had four "clean and bright looking" rooms, each housing thirty children. All of the rooms featured colorful materials designed to stimulate the children to play and create.

> In one room chains made of colored construction paper hung from the ceiling—about 15–20 strips of them. They gave it a real carnival air. . . . It seemed that every bit of available space was being used to good advantage—shelves line almost every wall and all supplies seemed to be neatly stored and easily accessible [to the children]. Every room had an easel arrangement. One had a large piece of heavy cardboard that nearly covered one wall. . . . Work was displayed attractively on the walls—string painting, pasting of colored shapes.

Outside was a "good-sized wooden box filled with dirt ready to do some planting."[15]

Hollandale staff were excited about taking five- and six-year-olds on a field trip to see a house under construction, and their enthusiasm was contagious: the children returned to the center and began collecting bits of wood to build toy houses. The center thus gave young African American children the opportunity to be inspired by their parents' and neighbors' ingenuity and creativity. In contrast, parents and the CDGM staff associated county-run nursery schools with alienation and fear. In orientation meetings, parents had made it clear that they did not want their children to be cowed into silence by school and that they hoped that the CDGM centers would encourage children to confidently express their ideas, engage in imaginative play, and begin an educational adventure. In short, they wanted their children's school experiences to be the opposite of what they had found in Mississippi's segregated public schools.[16]

Most important, CDGM nurtured children's capacity to create, imagine, play, and discover their surroundings. Resource teacher Nancy Babcock noted that one "child's ideas have taken noticeable shape, as seen in his artistic expression as well as his 'academic' work, such as counting, writing his name, etc." CDGM staff felt that providing primers that used the children's language was critical to enhancing their identification with the printed word. An African American printer active in the movement printed a book, *The Pond*, that taught

CDGM children to read by using their own descriptions of experiences at local ponds.[17]

> I been swimming up in the pond.
> Lee found a big tree snake he killed it with an axe.
> Ole preacher caught two snakes on a hook when he was fishing. Frances and me found tree toad around the tree.
> I didn't get scared.
> If toad frog hop up on you and wet on you.
> He make a big blister on your feet.
> Fish live in a green pond.
> I caught a fish this big.
> A cat fish has a mouth like a big smile.
> We eat 'em up he tastes good.

Some licensed black teachers objected that *The Pond* did not use standard English, but local adults were gratified to see their children's words in print and believed that the children also would be proud.[18] In many ways, *The Pond* represented the flowering of children's creative intellect that the CDGM staff had hoped would occur.

This free-flowing exchange of ideas was exhilarating and empowering, but it also complicated and slowed decision making at the centers. Committees whose members were elected by residents constituted arenas in which conflicting perspectives of leadership and decision making were worked out, a process that did not always go smoothly. The central staff noted parents' concerns about specific teachers or committee chairs but refused to present solutions to such problems, instead encouraging local committees to work out these issues themselves. At times, long-simmering personality conflicts and jealousies threatened the functions of local centers.

Jones became frustrated with the leadership style of the chair of the Hollandale center, whom Jones described as having a "throttle neck hold over the staff." She became "afraid something is going to happen that not good for us. I can't say all I want to say now but I did get up and the people know how I felt towards the way [the chair] has been treating me lately. . . . I am going to have to try to find time to get some other people out in the community to help me."[19]

CDGM leaders advised Jones to discuss these differences with the chair, but follow-up reports and letters suggest that tensions lingered, as did conflicting ideas about how to exercise authority. Jones nevertheless was promoted to the position of area teacher guide because she "respects and draws out the ideas" of others. Still, she struggled, finding "it very, very hard for me to get an idea over when people are use to being told what to do." The Hollandale staff ultimately thrived under Jones's guidance. In the spring of 1966, a woman who trained teachers for the University of Maryland was impressed by what she saw at Hollandale, concluding that parents there could "do just as good a job" as conventionally trained teachers.[20]

Other observers disagreed. CDGM's dedication to providing Mississippi's poor adults with training in early childhood education led to some notable struggles over authority. CDGM's detractors exploited the program's use of unlicensed teachers as a way of challenging the program's legitimacy; in what became a standard line of attack against the CAP, critics argued that CDGM employees were not qualified and that the program therefore should not be receiving public funds.

However, poor adults in the community responded with enthusiasm to CDGM's commitment to providing them with training, in part because they felt the sting of negative assumptions about their capacity to be teachers. "They don't think we are qualified," one participant in the program wrote. Eager to prove otherwise and hungry for education, local resource teachers and area teacher guides flocked to take eight-week courses in early childhood education at area colleges. A faculty member for the Tuskegee Head Start training course, for example, noted that CDGM teachers often led discussions and were "adequate in all respects . . . bringing a superior attitude and quest for information."[21]

Because the CDGM centers attracted participation from a wide range of adults in the community, not just those who became teachers or aides, the program expanded the possibilities for local adult participation in children's education. Parents contributed clothes, food, and labor of various kinds to the centers, leading to a sense of communal pride and accomplishment. That sense of pride was nurtured by CDGM's philosophy, which acknowledged poor parents' important role in their children's education by encouraging meetings, insisting on local hiring committees, and building curricula that drew from parental experiences. In these ways, the CDGM centers echoed and built on the empowerment-centered pedagogical strategies pioneered and spread widely through the civil rights movement by the citizenship schools of "freedom's teacher" Septima Clark. By 1964, Clark had founded two hundred schools throughout the South that incorporated into the curriculum the knowledge and participation of poor African American adults, particularly women.[22]

By drawing African American mothers into CDGM as trainees, the program empowered them in two ways. First, it transformed the possibilities they envisioned for their educational development. Second, and just as critical, it provided them with an immediate source of income, a huge benefit for people who had previously worked in seasonal agriculture, domestic service, or subsistence farming. Flora Howard, a Mileston farmer with nine children, wrote that her work at the Mileston Center "put food in there mouth and clothes on there backs." At the same time, she noted, I "really have learn a great deal since I been here with the children." According to Hollandale's Lorese McAllister, CDGM "put food in [her] house" and gave her "money to pay bills," but it also made her feel good that she helped "some Body Child to learn." McAllister was proud of her ability to work with shy and withdrawn children and gradually to encourage them to take the lead in play activities. Many letters written in support of the program commented on how previously withdrawn children slowly blossomed. Teacher trainees enjoyed walking, talking, and playing with children as they learned to express themselves.[23]

Other letters commented on CDGM's less tangible effects. A participant from Glenn Allen had previously worked for three dollars a day and valued not only the regular employment but also the focusing of communal energy on building and sustaining CDGM. She suggested that "the program has changed many people minds. It has made people feel there are someone. It has encouraged them to want more and feel it need for Education."[24] Thus, CDGM quickly had a major impact on the lives of poor families in Mississippi, giving them the confidence they needed to fight for their rights in many arenas.

CDGM emerged at a time when agricultural workers were facing steep declines in the demand for their labor and consequently becoming even more vulnerable to evictions and punitive welfare policies. Between 1959 and 1965, the number of sharecroppers in the Delta dropped by half. In the fall of 1965, when CDGM's first session ended, the Mississippi Employment Security Commission predicted that the region's cotton planters would hire about half as many seasonal laborers as the previous year. Some of this decline resulted from mechanization and other changes in the economic landscape, but countless plantation laborers also had been evicted as a consequence of their civil rights activity.

In many ways, federal involvement in the Delta prior to the War on Poverty had deepened the problems of African Americans who made their living from the land. Programs enabled farmers to use federal funds to invest in mechanization and to dominate local agricultural committees, which made sure that acreage allotment and loan practices would benefit large planters. For example, the Agricultural Stabilization and Conservation Service provided loans to local farmers to diversify crops, plant trees, and implement other conservation practices. Elections to conservation service committees became a hotly contested arena, as African American farmers, mostly affiliated with the MFDP, sought to change their place in the rural economy. Such organizing brought a backlash from Mississippi's political elites that dovetailed with and intensified the resistance to the CDGM. As Mississippi's rural African Americans organized their neighbors to build an autonomous preschool program, they faced reprisals from farm committees, welfare departments, and the local educational bureaucracy.[25]

INEVITABLE CONFLICT

The CDGM got caught up in a broader backlash against black students, their parents, and the desegregation process that began in the fall of 1965. The organization had emerged from the Mississippi civil rights movement, and even had its developers wanted to stay aloof from the struggle against racial segregation, they could not have done so. Keenly aware of the lack of decision-making power among African American parents and teachers, they saw the CDGM as a tool to increase local power and autonomy. In her memoir, *Barefootin': Life Lessons from the Road to Freedom*, Mayersville activist Unita Blackwell exclaimed, "CDGM centers truly were about our black Mississippi Delta people for the first time being totally in charge of running and staffing an educational program that was not controlled by the white establishment." For that reason, the CDGM movement "drove the white establishment in Mississippi wild." In Mayersville, a small rural enclave in Issaquena County, Blackwell and Pauline Sias, Minnie Ripley, and Dorothy Carter organized a CDGM center in an old church, provoking strong reprisals from the white community. Church leaders subsequently voted against continuing to allow their church to be a CDGM site, forcing the organizers to find another location. White pressure did not succeed, however, and nearby communities of Rolling Fork and Hopedale also organized CDGM centers.[26]

The need for autonomous black educational institutions was further dramatized by an extended battle between black families and Mississippi public school authorities that began in the months before CDGM received its first federal funding and continued through the summer of 1965. The battle swept up many of the black high school students in Issaquena and Sharkey Counties at the same time that the CDGM centers were getting started.

In late January 1965, students at Henry Weathers High School decided to wear SNCC pins that depicted black and white hands clasped in a handshake. Principal O. E. Jordan asked the students not to wear the pins, but 179 students did so anyway. The principal repeatedly demanded that the students stop wearing the pins, and fearful teachers refused to allow the students back into their classrooms. At one point, students asked Jordan why the school board had no African American members and whether he would want his daughter subjected to the same corporal punishment they had endured. After four days of open student defiance and mounting pressure from the school board, Jordan suspended the students. In response, more than eleven hundred students boycotted the Issaquena-Sharkey public schools.[27]

When students were offered an opportunity to return to school if they signed a document pledging not to participate in civil rights activities, three hundred students refused. SNCC organizers opened Freedom Schools in small churches in Hopedale, Mayersville, and Valewood. There, the boycotting students were exposed to curricula drawn, as at the CDGM centers, from student and parent experiences and rich with historical examples of African American resistance to slavery and racial inequality. K. D. Steward and other Freedom School participants founded and ran a newspaper, the *Freedom Fighter*, that ran many articles underscoring the connection between the lack of African American power to shape educational goals and the gaps in local people's understanding of the broader political economy that shaped their plight. In one piece, Steward highlighted the irony of an annual Weathers tradition in which classes competed to raise money by picking bales of cotton. While seasonal labor was an integral part of the school tradition, Steward argued, the Weathers curriculum did not allow for an honest exploration of the labor exploitation so deeply embedded in their lives.[28]

Confronted with the intractable power of white-dominated county school boards and the conflicted loyalties of African American educators, black parents signed a petition demanding that the district desegregate its schools. When the school board refused to budge, Blackwell became the lead plaintiff in an April 1965 suit against the school system. Under increasing pressure from the U.S. Department of Health, Education, and Welfare, Issaquena and Sharkey Counties finally submitted a plan to desegregate the first, second, third, and twelfth grades in the fall of 1965. Similarly, after years of fierce resistance to the integration of public schools, several other Mississippi counties grudgingly submitted gradual desegregation plans between 1964 and 1969. As fall approached, boycotting students faced the dilemma of returning to school to repeat a grade with an eye toward eventually attending a desegregated school or continuing the boycott while attending Freedom Schools.[29]

As students and their parents marshaled their resources to sustain the boycotting students, the CDGM centers continued to develop their pedagogical approaches to early childhood education, working to explore various ways of drawing from the knowledge of resource teachers and coming up with creative ways of circumventing the lack of funding, equipment, and adequate facilities. CDGM supporters hoped that their efforts would enable their children to walk into public elementary schools prepared to deal with the pressures of the desegregation process.

In August 1965, white citizens described in MFDP reports as hoods and Klan members stepped up their harassment of tenant and farmworker families whose children enrolled in newly desegregated schools. Willie Baltimore of Rolling Fork enrolled her four children in formerly white schools and was evicted from Bernard Lovin's plantation on the same day. Throughout August and into the fall, planters pressured sharecropper and farm families to remove their children from the integrated schools or leave their plantation homes. Some of these plantation owners held critical posts in local government and law enforcement, increasing the sense of threat and vulnerability felt by black families. After enrolling his children at a Rolling Fork school, Johnnie Hurns was evicted from the plantation of J. A. Darnell, who was also the Issaquena County sheriff. Over the next few months, a spate of cross burnings occurred, including seven in Sharkey County on the night of August 18.[30]

As in Delta counties across the Mississippi river in Louisiana, Head Start centers became popular targets of vandals and Klan threats. Head Start participation reflected working-class African Americans' aspirations for a more effective path into the formerly white public school system. Many white Mississippians saw that idea alone as provocation enough. CDGM centers stood as visible symbols of change in the Delta's planter-dominated racial and economic order. While CDGM employees and volunteers persuaded a few white parents to enroll their children, the movement still inflamed deep-seated white fears about desegregation.

Support from and participation by white allies from outside the state intensified local white resistance. After being seen in the company of a white Head Start teacher, Carl Davis was "haunted by a threat that some white folks would pay ten dollars to have him killed." In late August, a "white hood in Rolling Fork shot at the Head Start Center." In response, local people sustained a twenty-four-hour watch over the Head Start Center, a café frequented by Head Start workers, and several homes of MFDP members who had reason to fear arson attempts. Around the same time, the St. John Church in Valewood, which housed the CDGM center and MFDP precinct meetings, "burned to the ground."[31]

Parents faced less violent forms of harassment as well. Public school teachers, threatened by CDGM's location outside of the existing educational bureaucracy, discouraged parents from participating in CDGM centers. Teachers pressured parents to enroll their children in public preschool programs where they were available. Shortly before the start of CDGM's first eight-week session in the summer of 1965, Frances Alexander called to alert CDGM staff that teachers from the Henry Wells Grammar School

> have been campaigning . . . to the parents of pre-school children to enroll them in the Henry Wells Grammar School pre-school program. If they do not enroll them in this program the parents have been told that their children will not receive any credit when they come to the school. . . . The parents have been told that the teachers at Henry Wells will be making out report cards for the children and insinuating that those children without a report card from Henry Wells Grammar School will have a "bad mark" against them.[32]

CDGM organizers urged parents to document such intimidating treatment, but the dynamic recurred.

Parents remained committed to CDGM despite these threats because they fervently hoped that their children would enter the first grade with some degree of confidence and pride, and the CDGM schools gave the children experiences that built precisely those feelings. As the chair of the CDGM center in Rolling Fork pointed out, in the fall of 1965, parents enrolled numerous children who attended the summer CDGM preschool in previously all-white schools, but none of the children who attended local public school preschool programs enrolled in desegregated schools. Public school officials were correct in their fears that CDGM would spearhead desegregation.[33]

CDGM provided important leverage to poor and working-class families that had been left out of the public school system's decision-making processes. According to one small farmer in Sharkey County, local public schools "leaves me out; so I stays out, all the way out. They got no use fer me cause they says I ain't got sense. I got no use fer them, neither, cause they ain't got sense enough to treat peoples human." CDGM offered a powerful alternative.[34]

CDGM organizers developed a remarkably autonomous leadership structure that contrasted sharply with the Mississippi officials' general disregard for the federal government's emphasis on "maximum feasible participation" by the poor in fighting poverty. The flurry of activity in CDGM communities engaged the energy and commitment of a wide range of community residents, including displaced agricultural laborers, recent high school graduates, disaffected teachers, returning migrants, and small farmers. In keeping with both the goals of the civil rights movement and the holistic vision of early Head Start planners, CDGM became the focal point for a range of concerns that began with preschool children but also encompassed issues of welfare, surplus commodities, food stamps, medical care, federal loans for small farmers, and farm cooperatives.

CAP analysts Marvin Hoffman and John Mudd argued that CDGM provided poor people the opportunity to learn to administer a large federal program. The development of these skills would dramatically shift the relationship between poor communities and governance. This orchestrated assault on the multiple dimensions of poverty was most effectively carried out not through the elite-dominated CAP agencies that would emerge the following year in Mississippi but through the local people who built the CDGM centers.[35] Local committees met on a weekly basis in centers that they had helped to build or renovate. They made decisions that enabled staff to pursue progressive early childhood education methods and became a nexus for community efforts in school desegregation, welfare rights, health care access, and farm programs.

Mileston in Holmes County was a prime example of how CDGM both built on and expanded existing foundations for community activism. This Delta farm community had a high percentage of African American landowners who had collectively run the Mileston Farm Cooperative Association since its founding during the New Deal. Following Freedom Summer, volunteers from California joined with local people to build the Holmes County Community Center, which began operating in October 1964. Mileston's small farmers were less vulnerable to economic reprisals than were sharecroppers and tenant farmers; their community center served as a polling place for MFDP elections and hosted meetings, voter education programs, and a health clinic. The community showed an interest in early childhood education even before the CDGM was created, opening a kindergarten with an enrollment of fifty students at the center in December 1964.

Young people educated in community meetings and Freedom Schools later worked at the Mileston CDGM center, which was strengthened by this infusion of the dynamism and pedagogy of the civil rights movement. Zelma Williams, a graduate of both a Freedom School and the local high school as well as an MFDP activist and a kindergarten teacher at the pre-CDGM Mileston kindergarten, helped shape Mileston's CDGM. Elease Gallion, a young cook at the segregated public school, quit her job to canvass for CDGM, voter registration, and school desegregation. She found the center a wonderful site of learning, a place to "work out things on my own." And Rosie Head, a young mother of five and an early community center staff member, eventually became the head teacher at the Mileston Head Start Center. Even before federal funding became available, Mileston residents thus understood the transformative possibilities of locally run schools.[36]

The civil-rights-oriented community center became the site of a federally funded Head Start program only after the Holmes County School Board refused a community request to run a 1965 summer preschool program at the local public school. The superintendent rejected the request on the grounds that "the Holmes County Board of Education and I feel that it would be improper and unwise to authorize the use of the Mileston public school . . . to any organization that has no official connection with the public school system in the county."[37]

The CDGM center continued operating at the Mileston Community Center even during periods when harassment was severe and when federal funds were cut off because of the center's ties to civil rights activity. In the autumn of 1966, 125 students were enrolled, and the center became what one community member described as the site where "most of our strategy and all our information dispersed from." Mileston resident Griffin McLaurin later remembered the white community's reprisals, which included police ticketing of people walking or biking along the road to the center and merchants' refusal to provide butane to light the center. However, most white hostility was directed toward the building itself: "They wasn't targeting homes as much as they were targeting the center," McLaurin recalled. "They'd come in late at night and try to get to the center, but we had our guards. We stood our ground, and whenever we heard something that we thought wasn't right, we had our firepower."[38]

Farmers' commitment to early childhood education was based in part on their recognition that these programs offered a path to work other than seasonal agriculture and domestic labor. Recent high school graduates seemed particularly excited by the prospect of meaningful employment. Other War on Poverty programs that offered job training in Mississippi included the Migrant Farmers Educational Project (an initiative of Title IIIB of the Economic Opportunity Act, which provided assistance to the nation's migrant farmworkers) and Systematic Training and Redevelopment (STAR). STAR was administered by the Catholic Church and emphasized literacy training for adults, while the Migrant Farmers Educational Project was sponsored by Saints Junior College in Lexington and focused on teaching skilled trades such as carpentry and masonry.[39] The CDGM thus offered a unique mix of employment and educational opportunities that creatively addressed the question of community autonomy over local programs.

Maude Hemphill, a 1965 graduate of Mound Bayou High School and a seasonal agricultural worker, was acutely aware of her marginal position in the labor market: "We would go a half a day from school and we would go to the fields. The mothers would be out there all the time." When someone came into the fields to inform workers about CDGM meetings, she "just dropped my hoe and . . . came."[40] For her as for many other Mississippians, CDGM meetings began a process of learning that would last a lifetime.

THE NATIONAL FUNDING BATTLE

The CDGM was vulnerable to challenges from powerful white Mississippi politicians. From the outset, Mississippi's political elite balked at the influx of federal funding in support of a poverty program whose participants were so clearly allied with the civil rights movement. In May 1965, a *Jackson Daily News* reporter assured readers that the seemingly innocuous program appealed "to the most tender senses assisting infant youngsters" but in actuality bore "an ugliness which keeps making itself felt, well over the sound of crisp dollars being rustled as a conscience-appeaser."[41]

Before the first summer session was over, Mississippi's John Stennis, a veteran member of the Senate Appropriations Committee, urged investigators to examine the CDGM's hastily assembled financial structure. Congress not only focused its investigations on protest activities in which CDGM employees had been involved but also subjected the CDGM's petty cash and administrative practices to very close scrutiny, a strategy that was used against War on Poverty programs in many other locales. Results of these audits put CDGM funding in jeopardy.

Mount Beulah's center housed staff from the CDGM as well as the Delta Ministry and the MFDP, so the lines between civil rights and CDGM overlapped on a daily basis. When demonstrators were arrested at the State Fairgrounds in Jackson, a CDGM administrator advanced a paycheck to be used as bail. In addition, local center staff had difficulty keeping track of purchases of food and other supplies when grocery stores and banks refused to cash checks. There were few experts in finance among either the local employees or the network of professionals recruited by Levin. As the political pressure mounted, the OEO agreed to conduct an audit, finding problems with less than $5,000 of the $1.5 million grant. They found no evidence to substantiate charges of fraud. In mid-October, investigators submitted a report to the Senate Appropriations Committee detailing the use of funds to bail out CDGM staff, arrests of CDGM employees at an antiwar protest, and a significant number of former SNCC and Delta Ministry organizers on CDGM's payroll.

The most unsettling aspect of this attack was the OEO's willingness to appease Mississippi's segregationist leaders. Before the end of the summer, the agency had called an emergency meeting at which members of the CDGM board of directors and central staff were told that they had to relocate from the Mount Beulah campus, which Stennis viewed as a civil rights stronghold, to Mary Holmes Junior College in West Point, Mississippi, more than two hundred miles from many of the centers. Turmoil ensued as central staff members and the board disagreed over whether to comply. Levin was incensed that OEO would force a move three weeks before the first session ended, while Smith argued that such betrayals were to be expected from a federal agency.[42]

Many staff members felt demoralized and voted to resign from CDGM and run the program without federal input. The OEO ultimately backed off of the forced relocation but ousted Levin as director and replaced him with John Mudd, a Harvard graduate student in political science who had worked with black farmers to develop a farm cooperative in Batesville. Mudd was charged with the difficult task of addressing CDGM's administrative inefficiencies while preserving its autonomous grassroots character.

In the autumn of 1965, local communities continued to draw from the central staff's resources to develop and apply the "people's ways." During this period, fifty centers operated on a volunteer basis. Because many local employers refused to hire people who had worked for CDGM during the summer, volunteers endured great financial hardship.[43]

VOLUNTEERS: BUILDING FROM THE GROUND UP

In November 1965, CDGM remained unfunded by OEO but received an interim grant of $17,975 from the Field Foundation to support ambitious plans for preparing and opening centers. Greenberg recruited area teacher guides (ATGS) from among the locals who had worked at CDGM centers the previous summer, selecting people who had a passionate commitment to their communities and a hunger to learn and develop new ideas. With the uncertainty of OEO's future support, the ATGS provided the critical grassroots link that conveyed the mix of Freedom School and progressive early childhood education methods to resource teachers in the local centers. At a two-week orientation session in Jackson, ATGS created a sample classroom and explored and practiced reading-readiness activities: grouping and matching games, word cards, and ways to promote concentration. Among these trainees was Hattie Saffold, whose home had been shot up the day before the session began.[44]

Despite the ongoing harassment, Greenberg urged the ATGS to examine their conceptions of freedom and think about how to teach children to embody this cherished ideal. They observed children, considering "how the activity . . . relates in the way you want . . . to the social action." Finally, Greenberg exhorted, participants should "have faith in nothing. Find out." Ideas from these sessions were typed up and included in an ATG notebook, a resource from which they could draw to conduct orientation sessions for resource teachers at the centers. For the first orientation session at Mount Beulah, one attendee decided to stage a "demonstration" with picket signs that read "ENCOURAGE ME TO EXPLORE NEW THINGS" and "DEVELOP MY OPINION OF MYSELF."[45]

Fueled by the excitement of the Mount Beulah workshops, ATGS and resource teachers traveled to centers to encourage and inspire teachers and parents. Lavaree Jones's ongoing education enabled her to see more clearly what was wrong in the public school system: "I found out that many public school teachers were trained in home economics. Well home economics had a lot of influence on growth and development, but it didn't have the well-rounded way of how you talk to a child, how do you allow a child to use his own creativity. And how in that child's own expressions you supply him with what he needs to further build on those God-given potentials."[46]

Communities struggled to keep their CDGM centers going as investigations dragged and OEO funding was withheld. But these hardships also brought opportunity. For example, the need to build playground equipment inspired broad communal involvement, and the resulting homemade playgrounds provided artistic visual markers that brightened and transformed the surrounding rural landscape. Such efforts also seemed to bring men more centrally into the daily work of creating the centers and infused them with energy needed for the uphill battle of running the centers. CDGM newsletters offered ideas and instructions that staff could read aloud, not only providing local people the chance to contribute ideas but also engaging local residents who could not read.[47]

As in many other War on Poverty efforts, CDGM activists understood that students needed more than books and art supplies to learn. CDGM staffers checked on students who lacked food or clothing, essential prerequisites for good school attendance and performance. Such efforts required a significant degree of self-sacrifice by CDGM staff. For example, when the OEO restored limited funding to CDGM centers in March 1966, Cary Center employees contributed money from their first paychecks to purchase new clothing for the center's children.[48]

The volunteer period compelled CDGM staff to draw on informal social welfare strategies. Community members adapted discarded clothing to make outfits for the center children. They grew vegetables and shared the contents of their families' deep freezers. Hemphill recalled that in Winstonville, near Mound Bayou, local people brought surplus agricultural commodities such as pork and gravy and peanut butter to feed to the children at the centers. CDGM made a concerted effort to provide an entry point for local residents into the fiercely guarded social welfare system. In response to local protests, Mississippi authorized food stamp and emergency commodities distribution, but availability varied throughout the state, and many Mississippians without incomes could not afford even the minimal outlay required to buy food stamps. CDGM staff gathered information about what services were available in their regions and shared it with their local communities.

Hemphill recalled meetings with staff from Coahoma, Sunflower, Bolivar, and Washington Counties at which people exchanged information about what programs were available in the individual counties. One staff member at the Mileston CDGM program was "learning how to type and how to solve welfare problems, and about things I never heard of before."[49] Community-level workshops about local health departments, Social Security Administration offices, and county welfare departments not only demystified how these local agencies operated but also pointed to the need for sustained activism in the areas of health and social welfare. Greenberg heard a welfare case worker from Leflore County complain that African Americans did not need more information since they were determined to get "more than they deserved" from welfare departments.[50]

Despite the struggle for daily subsistence, local communities drew a collective strength from their volunteerism and their shared resources and resisted attempts to coerce them away from the centers. One mother of six children had worked for a tailor but was essentially unemployed when the CDGM centers opened. She received six weeks of training there and was able to prepare her children for school with supplies and clothes. But volunteering at CDGM was frowned on by the Mississippi Employment Services, which channeled African American women to domestic work, and when the woman "went to welfare [the] welfare lady told me to go to the employment service. I did, about a factory job, but they said I needed ninth grade education, and I only had seventh, and they didn't offer any education and training. The employment man said he had some maid jobs . . . paying fifteen dollars a week and I told him I couldn't work full time, because we were trying to work full-time to keep the center open." The caseworker then told her that welfare recipients "can't afford to do no volunteer work." As her debts mounted and she struggled to provide required reading materials for her children's schoolwork, she ultimately gave up volunteering and began receiving a meager welfare stipend. Fellow volunteers looked askance at her, but she felt she had no choice.[51] Though she remained a believer in CDGM, the county welfare agent had underscored the relationships between enforced work norms, social welfare, and the ways that volunteerism represented a challenge to these mechanisms of control.

In January 1966, displaced workers staged a dramatic sit-in at the vacant Greenville Air Force Base to dramatize the lack of adequate food, land, and housing for poor people. The Delta Ministry negotiated with the OEO for an emergency food program, which eventually materialized, but local authorities fought to control the distribution of the food.[52]

Parents and staff from the Sunny Mount Center in Lexington, which had been operating on a volunteer basis since October 1965, wrote to Washington in mid-February 1966 that "the poor Negro people of Mississippi need your support more than ever. We need jobs to help give our children better education." The Sunny Mount Center relied on parents, staff, and other supporters to contribute fifty cents or a dollar once a week and had volunteers build play materials. Sunny Mount eventually sent forty-eight five-year-olds, accompanied by their teachers, to Washington to hold a "play-in" in the hearing room of the House Education and Labor Committee, where they sang and colored. Later in the month, the OEO approved a $5.6 million grant that would fund CDGM centers for nine thousand children for six months. The following summer, Mississippi parents enrolled twelve thousand children in the program.[53]

THE LEGACY

In September 1966, however, CDGM supporters were devastated when the OEO turned down their request for a full year of funding. Despite the broad community involvement in early childhood education, the OEO caved into political pressure to redirect the money to "qualified" established educational institutions. In the fall of 1966, Rust College received a $1.2 million grant for a full twelve-month program. Mississippi Action for Progress, composed mostly of middle-class African Americans and moderate white Mississippians with deep ties to old patterns of authority, received $3 million for a yearlong program. CDGM won a final grant in January 1967 but eventually lost the fight to lead the early childhood education movement in Mississippi.[54]

As in many parts of the country, tensions over black leadership came to dominate Mississippi's Head Start programs. OEO officials tightened conditions for grants and left little room for the kind of grassroots character that CDGM encouraged. According to Lavaree Jones, middle-class residents, both black and white, simply stepped into CDGM offices and said, "You no longer work here. . . . They were just that harsh and rough." The Friends of Children of Mississippi (FCM), a group of CDGM stalwarts, emerged during the final stages of the fight over funding and maintained an active presence in the state. Jones worked for FCM for a few years as an associate director, but she found the struggle over local control disheartening. For Jones, the beauty of CDGM was that "people became the curriculum." Not only did local people contribute to curriculum development, but children also were encouraged to make choices and to contribute their ideas. Under tightened federal guidelines, Jones was expected to produce a detailed curriculum that precluded the kind of openness and flexibility for which CDGM strove. Jones left FCM in the early 1970s.[55]

After 1967, amendments to the CAP created community action agencies that oversaw local Head Start centers. Grassroots organizations in different parts of Mississippi responded to tightened regulations in varied ways, with different degrees of success in maintaining autonomy and creativity. But once a community action agency was approved by Washington, a single-purpose agency such as CDGM could not exist independently; rather, it automatically came under the authority of the local community action agency.

Some local movements in Mississippi tried to create community action programs. Holmes County had nine strong Head Start centers and a vigilant grassroots leadership that effectively challenged attempts to pack Central Mississippi Inc., a six-county community action agency, with middle-class professionals. Ralthus Hayes, the chair of the Holmes County MFDP, tried in vain to get information about the process for creating an agency board. In March 1966, a newspaper notice announced a meeting at the county courthouse with a temporary committee that would eventually set up community elections for representatives to the agency's advisory board. Local MFDP activists organized multiple meetings to discuss strategies for getting a one-person, one-vote principle incorporated into the process for electing the community action agency's advisory board. These meetings also served as workshops in which community residents could learn about OEO and agency elections. The county sheriff kept movement representatives out of the courthouse meeting, allowing in only people appointed by the country supervisor. The president of nearby Saints Junior College was the only African American allowed into this meeting. Nevertheless, plantation workers prevailed in their battle to vote in these elections, and "reasonably strong Negroes" from fifteen communities were elected to the community action agency.[56]

Bernice Montgomery Johnson, a civil rights movement veteran, became the director of Holmes County's Head Start in 1967, shortly after its last OEO grant. She believed she "could have done a much better job directing the program that I was directing without that CAP agency." Yet she added that "sometimes community people would have to get the black CAP Board members in line." Like Jones, Johnson lamented the entrance of teachers who lacked meaningful experience in community action but felt qualified to take leading roles in Central Mississippi Inc. "So you had a lot of teachers that came out of the classroom saying, 'I want to work with this CAP agency,' but they knew nothing about community involvement, what the needs of the people are, because they always thought they were so high-minded; they didn't want to come down there to these people in the movement." Johnson credited grassroots people for the successes of CDGM and the CAP in Holmes County.[57]

CONCLUSION

The conception of freedom nurtured in CDGM playgrounds posed a critical challenge to a very different kind of learning environment in Mississippi public schools. As one CDGM teacher with thirteen years of experience in the public schools explained, CDGM represented a communal effort to "prepare the children for a new life we never could give them in Mississippi before." Her public school principal asked her to join his nursery school staff and emphasized his intention to stress discipline, a necessary corrective to "wild" children. Yet this teacher left the relative security of the local school district because she believed that CDGM would nurture "free-thinkers." Greenberg described a school-board-run nursery in Holly Springs as a sterile and paralyzing environment for children. "I saw staring immobile children, sitting at desks with their hands folded." Black mothers were "sitting in classroom corners ready to jump up when chores and errands were requested by the teachers. . . . Golden Books [were] arranged attractively on window sills high above the children's reach."[58]

CDGM parents hoped to bring education within the reach of their children. The chance to play a role in the shaping of such a future constituted a dramatic shift for black education in Mississippi, where the economic prerogatives of planters and the plantation economy limited most African Americans' access to education. For some, like Maude Hemphill and Hattie Saffold, CDGM began a longer educational process that led to careers in early childhood education. Lavaree Jones, too, continued to work on behalf of the state's children by monitoring compliance with federal school lunch regulations. Despite CDGM's demise, its spirited insistence on quality preschool education for poor children left a definitive mark on Mississippi's educational landscape. Though CDGM is no more, its imprint can be felt on Head Start centers across the state. In 2003, more than twenty-five thousand Mississippi children enrolled in Head Start. It remains the subject of contentious debate at both the state and national levels, yet when Unita Blackwell spoke at the Head Start Center in Rolling Fork early in the twenty-first century, she said that she "felt a spirit of community that uplifted me and reminded me of the original spirit of CDGM and the movement—open, communal, and full of faith that progress is possible."[59]

Notes

1. Andrew Kopkind, "Bureaucracy's Long Arm: Too Heady a Start in Mississippi?," Reel 15, Child Development Group Papers, Community Services Division, Wisconsin Historical Society, Madison (hereafter CDGM Papers); U.S. Senate, Committee on Labor and Public Welfare, *Hearings before the Subcommittee on Employment, Manpower, and Poverty: Preschool Education and the Communities of the Poor—A Report on the Child Development Group of Mississippi*, 90th Cong., 1st sess., Jackson, Mississippi, April 10, 1967, 863–80; Nancy A. Naples, *Grassroots Warriors: Activist Mothering, Community Work, and the War on Poverty* (New York: Routledge, 1998); Jill Quadagno, *The Color*

of Welfare: How Racism Undermined the War on Poverty (New York: Oxford University Press, 1994); Polly Greenberg, *The Devil Has Slippery Shoes: A Biased Biography of the Child Development Group of Mississippi* (Toronto: Macmillan, 1969), 4–5, 30.

2. On the origins of Head Start, see Maris Vinovskis, *The Birth of Head Start: Preschool Education Policies in the Kennedy and Johnson Administrations* (Chicago: University of Chicago Press, 2005). See also Lyndon Baines Johnson, "Remarks on Announcing Plans to Extend Project Head Start," August 31, 1965, http://www.presidency.ucsb.edu/ws/index.php?pid=27204.

3. Quadagno, *Color of Welfare*, 28–31.

4. Greenberg, *Devil Has Slippery Shoes*, 6, 18–57.

5. Adam Fairclough, *A Class of Their Own: Black Teachers in the Segregated South* (Cambridge: Harvard University Press, 2007); U.S. Senate, Committee on Labor and Public Welfare, *Hearings*, 866.

6. Greenberg, *Devil Has Slippery Shoes*, 21.

7. Child Development Group of Mississippi, Records, 1962–1969, "Histories of: Children, Employees, Centers, Community Support," Marvin Hoffman Papers, Reel 15, Wisconsin Historical Society.

8. Greenberg, *Devil Has Slippery Shoes*, 19–22, 50–51.

9. Ibid., 59.

10. Ibid., 58–59, 60–61, 69–70, 70–71.

11. Ibid., 74–77.

12. Kay Mills, *Something Better for My Children: How Head Start Has Changed the Lives of Millions of Children* (New York: Plume, 1999), 63; Lavaree Jones, interview by author, June 10, 1996; *Issaquena MSU: Freedom Fighter*, December 1965, Box 9, Folder 3, Mississippi Freedom Democratic Party Papers, Martin Luther King Jr. Library and Archives, Atlanta (hereafter MFDP Papers); Unita Blackwell and Jo Anne Prichard Morris, *Barefootin': Life Lessons from the Road to Freedom* (New York: Crown, 2006), 147–48.

13. Greenberg, *Devil Has Slippery Shoes*, 79, 114.

14. Polly Greenberg to Teachers and Committee, June 13, 1966, Reel 2, CDGM-Papers.

15. Report on Hollandale, January 23, 1966, Community Visit, Hollandale, June 23, 1966, both in Reel 2, CDGM Papers.

16. Lillie Ayers, Hollandale Center Report, January 5, 1966, Reel 2, CDGM Papers; Greenberg, *Devil Has Slippery Shoes*, 114.

17. Nancy Babcock, Rolling Fork Center Evaluation, n.d., Reel 2, CDGM Papers.

18. Wats Report, September 1, 1965, "A Report on School Integration in Issaquena and Sharkey Counties, Mississippi," both in Box 9, Folder 4, MFDP Papers; U.S. Senate, Committee on Labor and Public Welfare, *Hearings* 866–67.

19. Lavaree Jones to Chuck, December 9, 1965, Reel 2, CDGM Papers.

20. Mary Emmons to Annie Mae Jones, March 27, 1966, Reel 2, CDGM Papers.

21. Greenberg, *Devil Has Slippery Shoes*, 417–18.

22. See Katherine Mellen Charron, *Freedom's Teacher: The Life of Septima Clark* (Chapel Hill: University of North Carolina Press, 2009).

23. Flora Howard, August 23, 1966, Reel 1, CDGM Papers; Tecella McCurry, August 30, 1966, Lorese McAllister, August 29, 1966, both in Reel 2, CDGM Papers.

24. Tecella McCurry, August 30, 1966, Reel 2, CDGM Papers.

25. James C. Cobb, *The Most Southern Place on Earth: The Mississippi Delta and the Roots of Regional Identity* (New York: Oxford University Press, 1992), 255–56; Bruce Hilton, *Delta Ministry* (New York: Macmillan, 1969), 70–76; Mark Newman, *Divine Agitators: The Delta Ministry and Civil Rights in Mississippi* (Athens: University of Georgia Press, 2004), 95–97; John Dittmer, *Local People: The Struggle for Civil Rights in Mississippi* (Urbana: University of Illinois Press, 1994), 363–64; Charles Bolton, *The Hardest Deal of All: The Battle over School Integration in Mississippi, 1870–1980* (Jackson: University Press of Mississippi, 2005); "SNCC Program: ASCS Elections, 1965," Box 51, Folder 3, Student Nonviolent Coordinating Committee Papers, Martin Luther King Jr. Library and Archives, Atlanta.

26. *Freedom Fighter*, December 1965, Box 9, Folder 3, MFDP Papers; Blackwell and Morris, *Barefootin'*, 147–48.

27. Hattie Mae McFarland and Lizzie Lee Sias, "History of School Boycott," *Freedom Fighter*, August 1965, Box 9, Folder 3, MFDP Papers; Bolton, *Hardest Deal*, 142–45.

28. K. D. Steward, "Henry Weathers School: An Uneducation School," *Freedom Fighter*, December 1965, Box 9, Folder 3, MFDP Papers; McFarland and Sias, "History."

29. Bolton, *Hardest Deal*, 157; Unita Blackwell, interview by Mike Garvey, University of Southern Mississippi, 1977; Lizzie Sias, "Why Parents Should Send Children to Desegregated School This September"; Steward, "Why We Should Go Back to School."

30. Wats Report, September 1, 1965, "A Report on School Integration in Issaquena and Sharkey Counties, Mississippi," both in Box 9, Folder 4, MFDP Papers.

31. Wats Report, September 1, 1965, "A Report on School Integration in Issaquena and Sharkey Counties, Mississippi," both in Box 9, Folder 4, MFDP Papers.

32. Memo regarding telephone call from Frances Alexander to Tom Levin, June 18, 1965, Reel 2, CDGM Papers.

33. Sidney Alexander to Sargent Shriver, August 3, 1965, Reel 2, CDGM Papers.

34. Greenberg, *Devil Has Slippery Shoes*, 100.

35. Marvin Hoffman and John Mudd, "The Grand Illusion: The Community Action Program in Mississippi," Reel 15, CDGM Papers.

36. Holmes County Community Center, Messages from Staff, Box 8, Folder 19, MFDP Papers; Youth of the Rural Organizing and Cultural Center, *Minds Stayed on Freedom: The Civil Rights Struggle in the Rural South* (Boulder, Colo.: Westview), 1991), 129.

37. L. R. Thompson letter quoted in U.S. Senate, Committee on Labor and Public Welfare, *Hearings*, 863.

38. Youth, *Minds*, 10–11, 31, 125; *Holmes County Community Center*, Harriet Tanzman Papers, Wisconsin Historical Society; *Mileston Minute*, July 27, 1964, Wisconsin Historical Society; Griffin McLaurin, interview by Harriet Tanzman, 2000, Tougaloo College Archives, Tougaloo, Mississippi.

39. Jill Quadagno, *Color of Welfare*, 41–44; Roy Elmore, "A Socio-Economic Profile of Holmes County, Mississippi" (master's thesis, Louisiana State University, 1969).

40. Maude Coleman Hemphill, interview by author, May 20, 1997.

41. Jack Ward, editorial, *Jackson Daily News*, cited in Greenberg, *Devil Has Slippery Shoes*, 55.

42. Kopkind, "Bureaucracy's Long Arm," 21–22; Greenberg, *Devil Has Slippery Shoes*, 259–88; Dittmer, *Local People*, 371–72.

43. Dittmer, *Local People*, 370–77; Greenberg, *Devil Has Slippery Shoes*, 329–437.

44. Greenberg, *Devil Has Slippery Shoes*, 383–424.

45. Ibid.

46. Jones, interview by author.

47. Ibid.

48. Sidney Alexander to Sargent Shriver, August 3, 1965; *Area Four in Action*, Reel 2, CDGM Papers.

49. Hemphill, interview; *Holmes County Community Center*, Tanzman Papers; Dittmer, *Local People*, 385–86.

50. Mills, *Something Better*, 67; Greenberg, *Devil Has Slippery Shoes*, 201–3; Hemphill, interview.

51. Greenberg, *Devil Has Slippery Shoes*, 354; Quadagno, *Color of Welfare*, 44–46. Quadagno points out that Mississippi Employment Services has institutional links to the Labor Department that date back to the New Deal, so Labor Department programs were locked into traditional mechanisms for channeling African Americans into low-wage service jobs.

52. Gene Roberts, "Job Losses Facing Mississippi Negro," *New York Times*, November 18, 1965; Greenberg, *Devil Has Slippery Shoes*, 437–40; "Greenville Air Base: What Happened, and Why," *Delta Ministry Reports*, Box 142, Folder 7, Paul B. Johnson Papers, University of Southern Mississippi, Hattiesburg; Erle Johnston Jr. to P. D. Armstrong, February 4, 1966, State of Mississippi Sovereignty Commission Files, Mississippi Department of Archives and History, Jackson.

53. Sunny Mount and Poplar Springs Center to Powell, February 14, 1966, Reel 1, CDGM Papers; Mills, *Something Better*, 68; Joseph A. Loftus, "Youthful Lobby Asks School Fund," *New York Times*, February 12, 1966, cited in Mills, *Something Better*, 68.

54. Mills, *Something Better*, 70–71.

55. Jones, interview by author; Dittmer, *Local People*, 377–82; Mills, *Something Better*, 73.

56. Susan Lorenzi, "Calendar of CAP Events," September 24, 1966, Reel 15, CDGM Papers.

57. Ibid.; Bernice Montgomery Johnson, interview by Kenneth Sallis and Tamara Wright, in Youth, *Minds*, 67–80; Greenberg, *Devil Has Slippery Shoes*, 668–70.

58. Greenberg, *Devil Has Slippery Shoes*, 72, 111.

59. Hemphill, interview; Jones, interview; "Head Start: Barbour Right, It's Good for Miss," *Jackson Clarion-Ledger*, subject file, Head Start Project, Mississippi Department of Archives and History; Blackwell and Morris, *Barefootin'*, 156.

SUSAN YOUNGBLOOD ASHMORE

Going Back to Selma

Organizing for Change in Dallas County after the March to Montgomery

> Political action is an inevitable consequence of anti-poverty programs, for any effort to better the condition of the poor raises fundamental issues of citizenship and political influence. . . . In short, how much political revolution can a publicly funded program afford to sponsor? Localized control of programs—to the extent that this has been possible in the anti-poverty programs—only exacerbates this political dimension. No giver of money can long remain neutral: it must decide how much to give, and to whom, and for what purposes.
> Roger H. Davidson, "The War on Poverty," 1969

The national history of the civil rights movement is often remembered by using specific locations to explain how racial segregation met its end. In popular memory, the dramatic events that unfolded in Montgomery, Little Rock, Birmingham, the Mississippi Delta, Selma, and Memphis are commemorated most. Museums have been built to explain what happened, monuments have been erected to honor courageous leaders, and in some cases, annual celebrations have taken place to ritualize important victories. Every spring, a Bridge Crossing Jubilee is held in Selma, Alabama, to observe the passage of the Voting Rights Act by acknowledging the March 7, 1965, attack on civil rights marchers at the Edmund Pettus Bridge. As important as it is to recognize achievements and claim public space, celebrations like the one in Selma convey a false sense of accomplishment. While it is true that the Voting Rights Act changed America in fundamental ways, people who think this law removed the last obstacle to southern racial justice will be confused when they cross the Edmund Pettus

Bridge going into Selma and see a languishing city of once-beautiful houses in need of repair, vacant downtown streets, and boarded-up businesses.

The history of the War on Poverty in and around Selma provides an opportunity to explain what happened in this Black Belt town after 1965, during the third phase of the civil rights movement. In this phase, African Americans tried to use the new laws to change their circumstances in fundamental ways. Understanding how President Lyndon Baines Johnson's Great Society program worked in the Deep South enables us to see why racial and economic justice remained so elusive. The struggles over who controlled the programs supported by the Office of Economic Opportunity (OEO) make visible the difficulty of dislodging Jim Crow customs that contributed to the poverty of so many of the region's residents. Selma's longtime mayor, Joseph Smitherman, exploited the divisions within the black community for political gain. The structure of the OEO, functioning through a national headquarters, regional offices, state divisions, and local programs, made it hard for its officials to know exactly what was happening on the ground. What looked like progress from the perspective of the nation's capital turned out to be the same old story from the viewpoint of rural folk in Dallas County, Alabama. By going back to Selma, many activists in the region learned firsthand that despite the passage of federal legislation, the civil rights movement faced continued challenges in the enforcement of the new laws. Implementing an antipoverty program in a divided city such as Selma brought many forces into play that explain why the War on Poverty could not bring about economic and racial justice in some of the nation's poorest places.[1]

Selma is the seat of Dallas County, located along a bend in the Alabama River in the heart of the Black Belt. Although the city served as an important regional trade center, the county had all the characteristics of a region in transition during the 1960s. The voting rights protests revealed an engaged and active fight against Jim Crow, yet the power of white supremacy persisted. In the spring of 1965, schools, restaurants, and hotels remained segregated despite the passage of the Civil Rights Act the preceding year. Even the names of the city's public housing projects reflected the racial divide: the George Washington Carver public housing project housed African American families in town, and the Nathan Bedford Forrest public housing project served white families who lived near Craig Air Force Base. White residents of the Alabama Black Belt found it perfectly acceptable to honor Tuskegee's famous scientist in similar fashion as the Confederate general who created the Ku Klux Klan.[2]

Signs of white commitment to Jim Crow were everywhere. In January 1965, Selma's city council and county revenue board approved a resolution to seek OEO funds. When Mayor Smitherman applied for an OEO community action grant, the agency's governing board was all-white, and there were only tentative plans for a biracial policy committee. His actions shut out precisely the people who needed the most assistance from the War on Poverty. Turmoil also arose within Dallas County's black community, contributing to a weak response to the mayor's antipoverty plans. When Randolph Blackwell visited the city in early May as part of his work for the Southern Christian Leadership Conference (SCLC), he reported back to Atlanta that local black people were "confused, divided, and often hostile" toward Martin Luther King Jr.'s organization. Many missed King's presence after the march to Montgomery. By July, more disorder arose after a grand jury indicted Frederick D. Reese, the president of the Dallas County Voters League (DCVL), on three counts of embezzling $1,650 from the organization. The DCVL had played a central role in the voting rights protests.[3]

In response to these problems, Dr. King sent the Reverend Harold Middlebrook to Dallas County to try to reassemble the Selma movement. Shirley Mesher joined him, working as a paid SCLC field staff member. She had come from San Francisco to participate in the march from Selma to Montgomery that started on March 21, 1965. As the march got under way, the SCLC tapped Mesher to handle the press. After the march, she stayed to continue working for racial and economic justice. When the cameras left, she recalled, "it wasn't glamorous anymore; there was no romance to it. It was just grinding head-on work. . . . You were dealing now with the real guts issues. You couldn't keep looking at a man who earned his dollar a day in the field or couldn't get a job at all." She wanted to help create lasting change. "I think what needs to be realized and perhaps is realized now," she clarified in 1968, is "that once you tear open an area you leave it to a worse fate if you don't have an intention to build an indigenous community organization that's going to be able to fight the battle on from there."[4]

Middlebrook and Mesher were not the only civil rights organizers who stayed in Selma. They set up their office one floor below the Alabama headquarters of the Student Nonviolent Coordination Committee (SNCC) at 31½ Franklin Street. The SNCC members concluded that the DCVL had not done a good job of representing the needs of the local people and made plans to operate in the rural parts of the county. Working near these young people influenced Mesher's approach. These activists believed that with effective political participation, the black citizens of Dallas County might be able to change some of their harsh living conditions. The SNCC members believed that antipoverty efforts needed to address the structural issues associated with poverty—racial discrimination, educational deficiencies, unemployment, declining agricultural opportunities, substandard housing, neglected infrastructure, lack of health facilities—rather than the personal characteristics of rural folk many observers labeled as mired in a culture of poverty. These were not pressing issues for the middle-class African Americans who led the DCVL and lived in Selma.[5]

For the next year, the SCLC office in Selma buzzed with activity resembling what was taking place at the city's SNCC headquarters. In September, the SCLC staff, especially Mesher, began to organize an antipoverty committee to counter the mayor's all-white program. The SCLC activists worked through rural churches, distributing handbills, visiting farms, and attempting to contact every poor person in Dallas County. Earning twenty-five dollars a week from SCLC, Mesher initially lived with families in the community and tried to organize around issues they wanted addressed. She "appreciated how smart those people were out in the rurals," she later explained, "how much it took to get by when they had nothing."[6]

Mesher's hard work began to make headway. Her year-end report to the SCLC noted that eleven thousand black people had registered to vote in Dallas County; that every rural community in the county had been organized to meet once a week to discuss problems; that she had counseled people on matters of welfare, federal housing, and federal farm programs; that the Lawyers Constitutional Defense Committee had decided to set up an office in Selma; and that a free lunch program had been established in the county schools. This organizing work was particularly significant because many of these local people had not participated in earlier civil rights campaigns. As Mesher recalled, "These people had not registered, they hadn't voted. They hid in the bushes when the march went by. They didn't participate in anything. And that was true largely of the rurals. The rurals were largely untouched." But the civil rights movement continued to inspire and change people—in this case, both Mesher and the local residents. When the people living out in the county came forward, Mesher found them to be "much stronger than the people in the city" because "they knew adversity." After Mesher had spent a year working in the rural areas, one woman told the activist how much she had learned. Mesher responded, "'No, Mrs. Harris, I learned it from you.' And she said, 'Oh, but we didn't know we could tell it.'" These relationships sustained Mesher, and her organizing work began to bear fruit, especially as Dallas County organizers began an effort to create a community action agency (CAA).[7]

Middlebrook first sought information on the Community Action Program (CAP) from the Department of Agriculture in late July 1965. As other SCLC volunteers talked up the idea of an antipoverty program among local people, the DCVL's Reese spoke out against these actions. Chuck Fager, an SCLC volunteer, reported to the group's Atlanta headquarters that the DCVL "announced that no projects are to be initiated or even meetings scheduled, without prior consultation with them." Fager wanted to make his position clear in case conflicts later arose with the DCVL. Reese had taken similar stands in other matters in an attempt to maintain his position as the political power broker for Selma's black community. When SNCC conducted the East Selma People's Convention, he told the citizens of Ward 5 that they had "no right to go off on their own without consulting him." Brushing off the desires of Reese and the DCVL, Middlebrook created the Dallas County Economic Employment Opportunity Committee in hopes of capturing OEO funds for the county by the fall. "You see," Middlebrook told a reporter, "what we're going to do is take over the white folks' program — which we think is very good — add our own proposals to it, and submit the whole thing to the OEO." The next challenge involved bringing in white people from Selma to join the SCLC effort.[8]

At the second organizational meeting, held in October, William Zierden, a field representative from the OEO's Southeast Regional Office in Atlanta, came down to oversee the process and answer any questions. Because the mayor's proposal excluded black people, OEO officials decided to give technical support to the SCLC plan with the idea of funding single-purpose programs that would not need the support of the city or county government. Zierden urged those at the meeting "not [to] let the race problem stand in the way of the anti-poverty program." The SCLC antipoverty committee reached out to the white community, inviting thirty people to take part in the plan. Seven accepted, including Arthur Capell, managing editor of the *Selma Times-Journal*; two city council members; and the superintendent of Selma's schools. At the end of the meeting, the Reverend Ernest Bradford, who chaired the SCLC-sponsored committee, put several white attendees on the spot by asking them to tell the group how they would help in the antipoverty effort. Most agreed to join a committee and gave statements of support to the program. By November, the mayor challenged this biracial committee, which had begun to encroach on his plans for the city.[9]

On November 4, Smitherman sponsored a public meeting at the Selma Armory at which he discussed the War on Poverty program and revealed a complicated plan for creating a biracial committee. He wanted eleven men from the black community to select fifty African Americans to serve on a one-hundred-person county antipoverty committee. Smitherman and probate judge Bernard Reynolds would have final approval of the fifty black representatives. Smitherman and Reynolds would then choose a thirty-five-member board of directors from among the committee members. The board of directors would control the money for the program. The many African Americans in attendance saw the mayor's plan as designed to maintain white elites' hold over the black majority. When black leaders balked, Smitherman told them, "You've got to start somewhere with good faith. This is the key to it. Until proven otherwise, I think this is the route we should take." That black community had good reason to be suspicious of the mayor. In August, the *Southern Courier* reported that he had told members of the Alabama League of Municipalities that the way to avoid civil rights conflict was by "building up leadership among local Negroes to keep the civil rights people from taking over." Before the unrest that occurred in Selma in the spring of 1965, Smitherman had tried his hand at this strategy, calling in three local black men and telling them that "we would build them up as leaders." All three left his office and never returned. By mid-November, however, things had changed so much in the city that Smitherman found a willing participant in Reese.[10]

After the mayor disclosed his plans, the SCLC-led antipoverty committee regrouped for a third organizational meeting at the Greene Street Baptist Church on November 9. Reese told attendees that he favored the mayor's plan, while Rev. Bradford, whose church was out in the county, not surprisingly disagreed. The meeting broke up before any final decision was made. The Reverend Francis Walter, a white Episcopal priest who grew up in Mobile and served as the director of the Selma Inter-Religious Project, was in attendance and recorded his thoughts: "Many more prosperous Negroes (I guessed) wanted to accept. From the acknowledged accurate report of the meeting between Mayor and committee of this group I don't see how anybody could accept his proposal." The SCLC-led group, now going by the name Self-Help against Poverty for Everyone (SHAPE), tried to convince Smitherman to change his plan by using tactics learned from the earlier voting rights campaign. About one hundred SHAPE supporters held a protest march that began at the First Baptist Church and proceeded to the probate judge's office and the mayor's office. Neither man met with the protesters, but those gathered read a statement of their grievances outside the courthouse and carried placards declaring their positions. A mass meeting followed that night. On December 4, about two dozen SHAPE members met with the mayor and suggested that he allow the people who had been elected at mass meetings to manage the antipoverty program. They wanted "*NO* formal education requirements" for board members and stated that it was "*not* necessary that a person be able to read or write" to serve. The only requirement was that "people in the area feel that the persons they select will faithfully and fairly represent their interests and do a good job." Here was the clear expression of what the black freedom struggle meant. OEO's mandate of including the "maximum feasible participation of the residents served" provided the opportunity to confront Selma's elite and demand a seat at the table. Smitherman dismissed the group and told the delegation that he would study the plan, but the mayor could no longer ignore the challenge to the old order.[11]

Four days later, SHAPE met and hammered out a complete strategy for selecting a board of directors for a future CAA. This process taught SHAPE members valuable lessons on the mechanics of representative democracy. In addition to having board members from the traditional government/public welfare/nonprofit organizations, SHAPE also wanted to include a percentage of the poor based on the total population, an equal number of city and rural residents, and numbers of white and black people that reflected their percentages of the population. Once the areas and numbers of people to serve from each community had been set, SHAPE held neighborhood meetings at which participants elected representatives to the board. SHAPE's plan took to heart the OEO's maximum feasible participation mandate. An OEO official in Washington, D.C., later commented that SHAPE's method "led to the most effective elections by the poor that have been held in the South, and perhaps in the nation." SHAPE members thought they had executed a solid program. The board would have middle-class and low-income members as well as representation from government and social welfare groups. SHAPE's proposal called for a board composed of 155 people (90 black and 65 white), which reflected the county's population (58 percent black, 42 percent white). Impoverished people would have had a larger voice than ever before. From the perspective of the grass roots, the plan was truly revolutionary—the black poor had the potential to influence a federally funded program in the heart of the Alabama Black Belt. In this case, the War on Poverty gave meaning to federal civil rights laws that had not yet been fully implemented.[12]

SHAPE members did not give up trying to convince Smitherman to go along with their plans. On December 15, Bradford asked the mayor to reconsider the structure of the antipoverty committee and to attend a December 20 meeting with other members of the white community. However, Smitherman told Bradford that "a meeting would not be granted to me but only to people of good faith." Smitherman further explained his position in a letter to SHAPE that also uncovered the mayor's plan for controlling the program. In his opinion, SHAPE represented only "a segment of the community," and he did not "recognize the organization as . . . being 'broad base' in the overall concept of the Office of Economic Opportunity." The mayor thought that a broad-based organization had to be assembled before anyone could discuss the structure of how the CAA would operate: "I think that the only guidelines necessary at this point is [sic] an understanding by both the Negro and white communities that each will have equal representation from top to bottom in whatever structure evolves." The mayor concluded with the information that he planned to form an antipoverty committee after January 1 "without further reliance upon your organization, as such to provide recommendations for the Negro representation on it." SHAPE's attempt to create a biracial CAA that included both the African American poor and city and county elected officials had come apart. Smitherman recognized SHAPE's revolutionary potential and worked to define the reach of the War on Poverty more to his liking.[13]

The SHAPE members moved on with their plans, unaware that they lacked support from OEO officials in Atlanta and Washington. "We won't try to make contact with [Smitherman] any more," Bradford said. "There might be meetings with other representatives of city and county government, but I'm not saying yes." The mayor and OEO also moved on. An official of the OEO Inspection Division later reported that "when it became apparent that no meeting could be held, Atlanta began working more closely with the Mayor, who had agreed to go to any reasonable length to get a program." Administrators from the OEO's Southeast Regional Office planned to hold an open meeting to elect sixty community representatives who could sit down with sixty representatives of the mayor's office and work out a solution. SHAPE complained emphatically to OEO officials in Washington about this meeting and in response were told that SHAPE members could elect people to this committee, just as anyone else could. But the OEO had been told that "SCLC, SNCC, and the other way out groups just don't have the support of the majority of the Negro population." The regional office clearly was satisfied with integration on the most superficial level, focusing only on race and not class. This approach enabled Atlanta OEO officials to disregard the large numbers of people from across the county who made up SHAPE's board. Demonstrating the attitude other Black Belt counties had encountered with OEO's Atlanta office, one of the regional administrators remarked that he doubted "SCLC could get even one bus-load of Selma Negroes to ride to Washington in their behalf."[14]

Why would SHAPE receive such treatment from the OEO? The problem resided in its bureaucratic structure and in the people who filled its positions. Fred O'R. Hayes, the official in charge of CAP at the OEO's Washington headquarters, pushed for quick funding and for leaving the details of implementing maximum feasible participation of the poor for another day. He did not want perceived foot-dragging over civil rights compliance to dampen enthusiasm for the CAP across the country. He focused on getting CAAs functioning without too much friction. In March 1965, Hayes's contacts in Alabama reassured him that "if the federal government insists on what it wants in Community Action organizations, the vast majority of the communities will comply and will, themselves, be able to take care of any problem that creates in the State House." Hayes concluded that the OEO "should begin funding eligible programs in Alabama without further delay." In the Alabama Black Belt, where city and county officials dominated community action, bureaucrats at the OEO's Atlanta office took this directive as permission to look the other way when elected officials controlled CAA boards and supported programs that maintained the racial status quo. Only the appearance of community action was required for programs to receive funding. Bad publicity hurt the OEO's ability to do its job across the country. Thus, as long as national OEO officials remained unaware of blatant racial discrimination and as long as the Alabama governor did not draw further attention to a CAA, funding was assured. With Smitherman in control, Governor George Wallace would not step in.[15]

The Alabama field representative from the OEO's Southeast Regional Office had a history of discriminatory behavior, underscoring the fact that white supremacist beliefs died hard. While evaluating the Huntsville Community Action Agency, Lawrence Duncan Sturm made derogatory comments about African Americans to Janet Nussmann, a CAP official from Washington, D.C. She reported that he "lamented the paperwork involved in being a Field Representative, but was quick to add that he would never object to processing Head Start applications because nothing pleased him more than to see those 'cute little brown-eyed niggers learning to brush their teeth.'" Sturm also told Nussmann that he resented "people who feel they have to come down from the North to meddle in the South's affairs." He said, "The Northern cities are the ones that burn; have you ever heard of riots in the South? The South knows how to handle its problems." Sturm even commented that Viola Liuzzo, a Detroit woman who had been murdered while driving marchers home after the 1965 Selma-to-Montgomery march, had been killed because she "lay down with the colored boys." Nussmann told her bosses that Sturm's "attitude alone (especially since it was expressed so freely) is inappropriate and unsuitable for a Federal employee, and particularly a representative of OEO." With an official with such views responsible for oversight in Alabama, CAAs such as Smitherman's could continue to operate in violation of the spirit of OEO's mandates.[16]

At a January 18, 1966, SHAPE meeting, the divisions within Dallas County's black community came out into the open. Father J. P. Crowley of Selma's Catholic Society of Saint Edmund Mission announced that Smitherman's plan must have meant that the mayor was ready to form a biracial group with "no strings attached." "Once they get together," the priest argued, "the mayor will have no control over it." Crowley thought this new approach would give white liberals "a chance to raise their heads." Bradford interpreted Smitherman's détente differently, telling the group, "The mayor hasn't done anything so far without being pushed." One middle-class African American said, "We don't think people who make under $4,000 a year can go downtown and talk to the mayor. We don't want them to represent us."[17]

The Reverend P. H. Lewis of Brown's Chapel African Methodist Episcopal Church chaired the nominating committee that chose the delegates for the compromise sixty-person group. Twelve people on his list had no previous connection to SHAPE. Others complained that Lewis's committee chose delegates even when local meetings could not be organized. Flabbergasted by these events and remarks, Mesher pointed out their ramifications: "It is ironic that the poor black people are now hearing from the black middle class the same thing they heard from the white power structure." The class conflict split SHAPE between those who agreed with the mayor's plan and those who wanted to apply to the OEO without city and county officials' support. Mesher and others in her camp continued to put her faith in the OEO's commitment to the maximum feasible participation of the poor, while an ally of Lewis's, the Reverend J. D. Hunter, and those who agreed with him continued to put their trust in the leadership of middle-class African Americans. "The purpose of the whole program is really that people do things for themselves," Mesher told the group. Hunter replied, "Nobody is trying to shove the poor people out. But when I go to court I want a lawyer, and when I go to church I want a preacher." Hunter's statement implied that someone with more standing was needed to speak for the black community in meetings with the mayor.[18]

Walter believed that the conflict resulted from differences in leadership style that revealed how much had really changed as a result of the black freedom movement. According to Walter, the leaders of the black community before the voting rights campaign sought to maintain their positions after the Selma march ended. While Walter did not "want to take away anything from a man like Reese who's suffered personally, who could be killed any time or hit over the head or put in jail," he believed that "when the tide went out, [existing black leaders] felt they had to consolidate. And what were they going to do now? Well, economic things, register to vote, try to get political structure set up," thus "assuring . . . that [they] are going to be the leaders in this community." Men such as Reese and Lewis had in mind leadership qualities established before 1964, which Walter thought "was an error because the movement had brought to the common Negro the idea . . . of a mass meeting, where the group makes the policy. And the idea of the open meeting in the Negro church . . . was just unheard of."[19]

Walter also pointed out that loyalty to the leader was another important part of the old form of leadership: "You show loyalty to the organization by showing loyalty to the leader. And . . . one of the ways you show loyalty to the leader is by unquestioning loyalty, unquestioning obedience. If he's the one who keeps the books, and he says the money's all accounted for in a meeting, you just don't stand up and say, 'Well I'd like to examine the books,' or 'I'd like to question that.'" Under this structure, a slippery slope of blame easily developed. In Walter's words, "The leader can stand up and say, 'You do not back the xyz improvement association because you question me, and therefore you don't back the civil rights movement, and therefore you don't back Martin Luther King and God. . . . So sit down.'" Walter remembered hearing that many months after the march to Montgomery a man "from the country" stood up in a meeting and disagreed with a prominent black Selma minister. The minister's response included an insult about the man's choice of words: "He stood up and said, 'You don't even know how to talk good English.' In other words, 'How can you have an opinion about that?'" The audience then booed the minister. "That's what the movement did. . . . The decisions are made by the whole group, no closed meetings, and then the idea [that] the fellow of the rural could stand up, and he could say for the first time in his life—he could stand up just like any preacher and voice his opinions, and his opinion carried just as much weight because he had discovered that he was a man. Well, if you're an old-time leader, how do you make the adjustments to this new kind of stuff? And I think that's what happened . . . and why people got put off in Selma." Walter defined the group-centered leadership style "personally by the personality of Shirley Mesher," and her role created a clash with the city's traditional black leaders: "You've just got automatic conflict, fireworks and everything else."[20]

Dallas County's War on Poverty–related organizing activities clearly re-ignited the smoldering coals from the previous spring. The *Selma Times-Journal* made sure that if Smitherman made any çompromises with SHAPE's demands, residents would see his actions as capitulation—a step in the wrong direction. The editors threatened to withdraw their tentative support for the program if it did not stay in the hands of elected officials. The paper's willingness to back the antipoverty effort hinged on city and county officials working with the OEO to organize a program to benefit the entire area. "From the start, unfortunately, there have been brazen efforts by individual SCLC and SNCC professionals to torpedo any structure that failed to place their man—a Negro preacher named Bradford—in a position at the elbow of those who dispense the goodies," the *Times-Journal* complained. "This, of course, under the ever watchful eyes and outstretched palms of SCLC and SNCC." The editors thought civil rights orga-nizations were illegitimate and therefore warned of dire consequences if ac-tivists sat on the CAA board. "The question is whether [OEO director] Sargent Shriver has any business helping to shake up anybody else's city hall," the edi-tors announced. "The question is also whether, in the name of local flexibil-ity, Mr. Shriver should help impose federally financed revolutionary move-ments that could become, given enough money, local quasi-governments." In this charged atmosphere, the mayor created a biracial CAA with the help of the OEO's Southeast Regional Office. Smitherman's actions had effectively divided the black community between those people willing to work with him and those who continued to distrust his motives and wanted more say in the process. Lewis and Reese withdrew their support for SHAPE and started holding meet-ings with the mayor.[21]

By the end of March 1966, a CAA had been formed with a forty-eight-member board. It had an equal number of black and white members, with one-third coming from public and private agencies, one-third from private leadership, and one-third from the poor, thereby complying with OEO guidelines. Lewis and Reese served as the arbiters of the black community, choosing the sixteen people who represented the poor community from the ninety-eight representatives previously elected by SHAPE. They told an OEO inspector that they picked "those with whom they felt they could deal most effectively." Although four of the sixteen had supported Bradford and SHAPE, they were now completely outnumbered on the CAA. Smitherman did not sit on this board, but Reynolds did. The mayor kept control of the new organization by appointing a friend, thirty-four-year-old Joseph S. Knight, as executive director of the new Dallas County–City of Selma CAA. Knight admitted to OEO officials that he would be loyal to the mayor.[22]

To no one's surprise, SHAPE protested the creation of the new antipoverty agency. The grassroots organization complained that its initial work had been taken over by the "white power structure with their chosen minute faction of the Negro community" and with the official sanction of the OEO's Southeast Regional Office. SHAPE leaders angrily "protest[ed] all of this and more on the grounds of DISCRIMINATION against the Negro and against the poor." The protest fell on deaf ears at the OEO's national headquarters. A biracial group with local government support outranked a truly autonomous, integrated, multiclass organization. After investigating, OEO inspectors concluded that Smitherman's committee "includes political leadership, charitable and service organizations, civil rights leaders, and representatives of the poor elected from all areas of the county." For OEO's purposes, the effort appeared to be a breakthrough—an integrated antipoverty program in a city that stood out as one of the nation's icons of racial hatred and polarization. "This CAP is probably the only one in the South in which the militant civil rights leaders will sit on the Board of Directors with the power structure," inspector Robert L. Martin reported to his boss in Washington.[23]

It is not clear how much Martin knew about the internal leadership struggle within Selma's black community. It is true that Lewis and Reese could be called militant leaders in the context of the Selma voting rights campaign—Brown's Chapel had served as the movement's headquarters during the spring protests, and Reese led the local civil rights organization and lost his job as a science teacher for his activism. Yet much had transpired since March 1965. When the OEO examined the issues brought up by Bradford and Mesher, officials in Selma blamed the two activists for their unwillingness to negotiate. "Miss Mesher is aware that OEO funded the Child Development Group of Mississippi—a non-power structure, civil rights oriented group, and cannot be persuaded that conditions which dictated formation of CDGM do not exist in Selma," Martin relayed back to Washington. "Her reasoning is that SHAPE unquestionably represents the Negro poor, and that OEO will not fund a program which is positively opposed by the poor." Smitherman had mastered the art of what historian Joseph Crespino has labeled "strategic accommodation." As a "practical segregationist," the mayor avoided taking a hard line, hoping to reduce federal interference so that he could control the pace of change. Working with Reese signaled to Washington that the mayor was willing to join with African Americans, but Smitherman also knew the DCVL president was engaged in a struggle for authority within the black community. This approach enabled the mayor's continued dominance of Selma's antipoverty program. By ignoring the sharp differences within the black community, however, the OEO's actions helped spark a movement for a third political party in Dallas County. In this case, OEO's capitulation to Smitherman encouraged greater militancy among many African Americans who lived in the rural areas of Dallas County and who had been left out of the new CAA. The developments in Dallas County frustrated many people who had dreams of using OEO programs to confront the region's real problems of racial and economic injustice. In this sense, despite SHAPE's failure, the War on Poverty helped to destabilize traditional race and class relationships and thus marked the third phase of the civil rights movement.[24]

As the first election since the passage of the Voting Rights Act approached, DCVL members' actions against SHAPE reinforced the sense that economic justice could not come about without political power. SNCC activists in the Black Belt wanted to create a "freedom organization" in Dallas County in the mold of the Lowndes County Freedom Organization. Not surprisingly, Mesher and the SCLC's Selma office also supported the idea: "We figured we'd be at this two thousand years," she remembered. "You couldn't go through them, you'd have to go around them, and that's when we started doing our own thing."[25]

In mid-March, about one hundred people gathered to elect temporary officers and form the Dallas County Independent Free Voters Organization (DCIFVO). The new party's name spoke clearly about its supporters' intentions. Most of the third-party supporters came from the rural areas where black people more significantly outnumbered white people than was the case in the city of Selma. These numbers meant there was a real possibility of electing their candidates. According to Walter, "SHAPE workers as a committee of DCVL really got out there in the bushes and worked and found all these rural people and got them to create something—I think they used political precincts and got these people to elect their delegates to the CAP board from their precinct. And they got all these people who had never gotten involved in a Negro organization before. . . .

At this point, SHAPE was deep into politics, as I saw. It happened to give birth to a political arm, a natural thing." Experience gained from organizing SHAPE paid off in the creation of DCIFVO. As party chair, organizers chose Clarence Williams, a shop steward at the Curtis, King, and McKensey Products Company, the first unionized plant in Selma with a black voting majority. Williams had set up a base of "soul folk" that SNCC contacted in its effort to organize the county. A. D. Bush, Mary Jane Sims, and Nathan Payne rounded out the new party's board; all but Sims had been elected to the original SHAPE board before the mayor commandeered it. Attendees at the initial DCIFVO meeting also chose the party's slogan and symbol: a black-and-white diamond inside a chain circle with the words *Strength through Unity*. This message of black political independence clearly bothered many members of the white community. Because of her political activism, Sims's landlord evicted her and her brother from their home.[26]

The founders of the new party saw many reasons to follow the lead of their Lowndes County neighbors by forming a third party. This was Black Power Alabama style. Many voiced their disappointment that the DCVL had not backed African American candidates for all of the county offices in the upcoming May 1966 Democratic Party primaries. Shortly after Reese agreed to work with Mayor Smitherman on the antipoverty program, circuit judge L. S. Moore dropped the charges against Reese for misusing DCVL funds. Historian J. Mills Thornton has written that Earnest Doyle of the DCVL "testified that the Voters League's steering committee had authorized Reese to cover his personal expenses from league funds." Many members of the black community wondered if Reese's legal problems contributed to the DCVL's decision to support Selma's chief of public safety, Wilson Baker, in his bid to oust notorious incumbent Jim Clark as Dallas County sheriff. Finally, the motivations for a new political party stemmed from the middle-class nature of the DCVL. "We find that people out in the rurals have never heard of the Dallas County Voters League," Williams told a reporter; SHAPE, however, had contacted many of these people, and they could be recruited to support the third party.[27]

To mark the first anniversary of the Selma-to-Montgomery march, the DCIFVO sponsored a Freedom Rally on April 11 at the National Guard Armory. People came from far and wide. Comedian Dick Gregory spoke to the crowd in favor of the third-party movement. SNCC's Julian Bond participated, and Stokely Carmichael and John Hulett came from Lowndes County to lend their moral support. In defense of their bold move, Williams asked, "People say this is black democracy and that that's bad. But how could black democracy be any worse for us than the white democracy we've been living under for the last 100 years?" Speakers from various Dallas County grassroots organizations also addressed the crowd to reinforce the third-party effort. Rev. Bradford reminded listeners of his experiences with white municipal officials. SHAPE, he said, had been formed by "the Negro people themselves," but the mayor's biracial committee had handpicked only those African Americans who would be "responsive to the whites." Others took the opportunity to highlight other black independence issues. Pearl Moorer spoke about the Dallas County Farmer Movement, which was trying to address the needs of evicted tenants who refused to sign their allotment checks over to their landlords. All the speakers at the rally voiced their commitment to defining their freedom on their own terms.[28]

After the rally, DCIFVO supporters printed fliers to explain the details regarding the third party and the reasoning behind the political movement. "The white people will not help us win control of our government. They will not give us candidates to vote for who will work for our welfare," one handbill proclaimed. "The Democrats will not represent us. They will give us Jim Clark and Wallace over and over again if we let them, or they will give us Toms who will work for them, not us. We have to choose our own people, if we want to win." The announcements also encouraged people to "talk to everybody we meet," so they would understand what was being planned for Dallas County.[29]

The divisions created by the formation of the Dallas County–City of Selma Community Action Agency continued to play a role in the spring political campaign. The DCVL supported black Democrats for various county offices except sheriff. In that case, the DCVL backed Baker as a racial moderate. Louis Anderson, pastor of Tabernacle Baptist Church and board member of the mayor's CAA, ran for mayor against Smitherman, earning Reese's public criticism "for running against a progressive mayor who had shown himself willing to negotiate with blacks." Following the Alabama Code for forming a third party, thirty members of the DCIFVO met on primary day to put together a slate of candidates to appear on the November 3 ballot. Samson Crum, a postal worker who lived in Selmont but worked in Birmingham, agreed to run for sheriff. Nine other people came forward to seek county positions; two of them had been elected to the original SHAPE board of directors. The DCIFVO also nominated Jimmy L. Stanley and Pearl Moorer to run for the Alabama House of Representatives from the Twenty-eighth District.[30]

In spite of the unprecedented numbers of newly registered black voters, the results of the May 3 primaries disappointed many African Americans in the Black Belt. Voting irregularities surfaced in some precincts. In Selma, officials placed black stickers on ballots cast by African Americans. Sheriff Clark locked up six boxes that contained more than sixteen hundred ballots from black neighborhoods, charging that he had found them unattended and thus should throw them out as tainted goods.[31]

The outcome of the primary served as a hard lesson in politics. Even a black majority in a county did not guarantee the election of an African American candidate. In several races, black Democrats received enough votes to advance to the May 31 runoff. Others lost close elections. Nevertheless, it had become more difficult for authorities to permit blatant disregard for the law. In Dallas County, the U.S. Justice Department filed a complaint against Clark for locking up the six boxes of ballots, and federal district judge Daniel Thomas ruled that the ballots must be counted, clearing the way for Baker's victory. Despite such victories, the African Americans who remained on the November 8 ballot faced voter apathy since few chances remained to elect African Americans to office. Only Lowndes and Dallas Counties, with their third-party movements, retained significant numbers of black candidates in the fall election.[32]

DCIFVO faced a serious setback in early October when Crum withdrew from the race for sheriff. According to Williams, Crum's job with the postal service kept him from actively campaigning. DCIFVO decided that it would not endorse a candidate for sheriff. Third-party supporters in the Selma area distributed leaflets encouraging people to vote for the party that favored "strength through unity." The DCVL, in contrast, supported the Democratic ticket from top to bottom, including Lurleen Wallace, George Wallace's wife, for governor and Smitherman for mayor. Reese wanted to make sure that Baker won the sheriff's office in spite of Clark's write-in campaign, but this stance turned many people away from supporting viable black candidates from the DCIFVO.[33]

The hopes that accompanied the presence of third-party candidates on the ballot faded by the time the polls closed. None of the DCIFVO's candidates won; in fact, all lost by wide margins, failing to receive enough votes even to win the DCIFVO consideration as a bona fide political party. Williams took the long view: "We're not concerned with being listed as a party. We're trying to establish a democratic system in the county. The next four years will determine what the Negro does with himself, where he'll be placed." The DCIFVO chair was concerned with the process: "We intend to stand up politically, any way we can. We're going to keep fighting."[34]

In the first two years after the passage of the Civil Rights Act, residents of the Alabama Black Belt experienced numerous setbacks. After the 1966 elections, the strong presence of national civil rights organizations in the region came to an end. After the May primaries, King shifted his focus to Chicago, and by June only a skeleton SCLC staff remained in Alabama, with most of the activists in Selma under the direction of Stoney Cook. Mesher resigned from SCLC but remained in Selma, working independently but sharing office space with the Lawyers Constitutional Defense Committee, which came to Selma at her urging in June.[35]

SNCC also began reorienting its overall goals as a result of discussions held during a conference at Kingston Springs, near Nashville. Inspired by Carmichael's successes in Lowndes County, SNCC's executive staff elected him chair on May 8. Thirteen people continued working in Alabama for SNCC, but by the November election, there would be some doubt as to whether anyone from the organization would remain in the state.[36]

Without the grassroots support of SHAPE, the Selma–Dallas County CAA lacked the desire and determination to address the issues that mired so many people in poverty. Under Smitherman's heavy hand, the programs operated by the CAA were uninspiring and full of corruption. In 1967, board member Louis Anderson admitted to Shriver that "the only thing our CAP Board has done is to provide minimal, temporary relief-type programs whose small benefit . . . ends when the project terminates." He confessed, "We have not been a success." A 1968 OEO review of all CAAs uncovered the results of the mayor's dominance over Selma's antipoverty program. Inspector Dwain Alexander of the OEO's Midwest Regional Office, in Kansas City, noted Selma's structural problems that contributed to the impoverishment of so many people in the county: racial discrimination, educational deficiencies, unemployment and underemployment, lack of industrial growth, declining agricultural prosperity, and lack of health facilities. He found that none of these issues had "been addressed by the CAA, and the evaluation indicated that external influences upon the CAA have caused it in many instances to support the causes of poverty."[37]

The Selma CAA developed two programs for Dallas County's targeted population. One, Operation Mainstream, sought to train unskilled people for jobs that would benefit both them and the county. Low-income residents would be hired to repair streets, pick up garbage, and maintain city property. In reality, Alexander found that target-area employees were restoring "the curbing in front of homes in the middle class and well to do white neighborhoods" while being supervised by prison guards, a violation of the Economic Opportunity Act. Prior to Operation Mainstream, convicts had performed this work, which meant that the CAA broke an important maintenance-of-effort clause contained in all OEO contracts. CAA work crews also planted and cared for shrubs, bought from Smitherman's nursery, at a private park and pool. The CAA's purchase of these plants had not followed an established bidding process, a blatant conflict of interest that financially benefited the mayor. Finally, Operation Mainstream workers used lime to sanitize outside toilets throughout the city. A Selma housing ordinance prohibited the renting of houses without indoor plumbing: The CAA work program thus facilitated the violation of local laws and supported the persistence of substandard housing. As its name indicated, Operation Mainstream simply kept the antipoverty program from challenging the mainstream of a Jim Crow world.[38]

The lack of vision was also apparent in the second program, which established eight Neighborhood Service Centers to serve as resources for job placement and counseling, community organization, rural recreation, and health education. Training courses were planned for domestic work and gardening, and each center would then serve as an employment agency for maids, yard workers, babysitters, and day laborers. But many of those whom the centers were supposed to serve wanted year-round Head Start programs rather than employment agencies. Since the city refused to comply with civil rights laws as required by the early childhood development program, Head Start was out of the question. To accommodate Jim Crow and get around the mandate, the CAA planned to run kindergartens in the centers, but in practice, they became day care programs. The Neighborhood Service Centers failed to accomplish any of their original goals. Staff members did not do community outreach because they were busy taking care of young children. Area residents had not been involved in choosing the locations for the centers, none of the centers were well marked, many served as recreation centers for young people, and there was little evidence of programming for adults. Not surprisingly, investigators found that many poor people living near the eight community centers thought that the "Selma–Dallas County Economic Opportunity Board is carrying out the wishes of the 'establishment' in maintaining the *status quo*." None of the programs sponsored by the Neighborhood Service Centers had the chance to transform the lives of Dallas County's impoverished. The use of federal funds to train people to continue working in subservient jobs neither fostered economic independence nor offered hope for a productive future.[39]

Crossing the Edmund Pettus Bridge out of Selma resonates in our national memory. It is as if walking over the muddy waters of the Alabama River lets us leave behind the reality of what it meant to live in a segregated society. As nice as that is, it does a disservice to our deeper understanding of the breadth and depth of Jim Crow and what the civil rights movement meant. We need to be reminded that the goal of racial segregation was the maintenance of white supremacy in all its manifestations. Jim Crow forced black people to struggle to gain decent housing, adequate health care, meaningful educations, and worthwhile jobs that offered a living wage. Civil rights advocates understood the structural nature of segregation and consequently used the War on Poverty to open up another avenue for the black freedom movement. Selma became notorious because officials there remained firmly committed to maintaining Jim Crow; it should not be surprising that white supremacy carried on in spite of federal civil rights laws.

The work to put together a CAA in Selma provided previously excluded African Americans with a chance to participate. In many ways, the idea of maximum feasible participation of the poor worked, although it did not do so as the OEO had envisioned. Maximum feasible participation took place not within Selma's antipoverty program but outside of it as a result of the OEO's initial acceptance of Smitherman's "strategic accommodation" and the complicity of Reese and other DCVL members. The Selma–Dallas County CAA was a failure. If the story ended there, our assessment of the War on Poverty would be very different. But black people in the poorest parts of Alabama did not let the OEO's failures stop them from defining their freedom for themselves. The formation of SHAPE offered Dallas County's poor a chance to learn the mechanics of democracy, electing delegates, choosing representatives, negotiating with officials, and exerting some political power. They used these new skills to create a third party that voiced their desired independence from the old ways of the past.

The confrontations with elites both black and white eventually assisted in undermining the old order, a fact that should be part of any assessment of the overall impact of the War on Poverty. The OEO's structure was a weakness. The Southeast Regional Office reflected the racist customs of its region in funding the Selma–Dallas County CAA's ineffective and corrupt programs. Yet the political struggle that nurtured the third-party movement eventually pushed the Alabama Democratic Party to integrate its ranks. Although most of the third-party incarnations did not reach all of their stated goals, their presence permitted many black people to gain political office in the Black Belt by the early 1970s, an accomplishment that should not be minimized.

The history of the War on Poverty in Selma after 1965 prevents us from romanticizing and simplifying the civil rights struggle. Dismantling hundreds of years of white supremacy takes perseverance, organization, vigilance, and a lot of time. SHAPE's experiences reveal how much had indeed changed and how much still needed to be addressed. While it was not easy for the mayor to keep control, it was even more difficult for the full goals of the civil rights movement to be met. Dallas County remains one of the nation's poorest places. Selma remains a polarized city because elites figured out ways to maintain control and power in spite of the federal civil rights laws and the grassroots activism of energized and committed citizens. Smitherman remained Selma's mayor until 2000 by using his contacts with the city's traditional black leaders to his advantage. An examination of the local level enables us to see more fully what civil rights activists hoped to accomplish in the third phase of the movement. This was a dynamic struggle among those in power, those who traditionally brokered power, and those who fought to include representatives of people from the grass roots in the power structure. Thornton has noted that after everyone could vote, black people sought "to influence the political process through electoral competition rather than, as previously, through boycotts and marches in the streets. . . . The national movement was focused upon the transformation of laws and the vindication of rights; the local movements were bound up with the continuing process of compelling authority to hear one's voice." Selma's failed poverty program reminds us of the reality of white supremacy and demands that we pay attention to the voices that continued to work for racial and economic justice.[40]

Notes

1. Cleveland Sellers, "The Curricular Legacy of Southern Student Activism," paper presented at the conference Student Activism Southern Style: Organizing and Protest in the 1960s and 1970s, University of South Carolina, Columbia, March 21, 2010. Sellers's talk explained his idea of the third phase of the civil rights movement.

2. Gay Talese, "Where's the Spirit of Selma Now?," *New York Times Magazine*, May 30, 1965, 9, 41, 44.

3. Frederick O'R. Hayes to Theodore M. Berry, March 31, 1965, Box 1, Records of the Community Services Administration, Office of Economic Opportunity, Commu-

nity Action Program, Records of the Director, State Files, 1965–68, RG 381, National Archives II, College Park, Maryland (hereafter RG 381); Adam Fairclough, *To Redeem the Soul of America: The Southern Christian Leadership Conference and Martin Luther King Jr.* (Athens: University of Georgia Press, 1987), 261; "Selma Wonders after Reese Arrest," *Southern Courier* (hereafter *SC*), July 16, 1965; David M. Gordon, "Selma: Quiet after the Battle," *SC*, July 23, 1965.

4. Shirley Mesher, interview by author, July 21, 2005; Shirley Mesher, interview by Stanley Smith, 1968, RJB 388, 1–4, 8, 10–11, 16, 18, Ralph Bunche Oral History Collection, Moorland Spingarn Research Center, Howard University, Washington, D.C.

5. Fairclough, *To Redeem the Soul*, 261; Shirley Mesher, "Selma—One Year Later—What?," April 12–13, 1966, Series II, Box 144, Southern Christian Leadership Conference Papers, Martin Luther King Center for Nonviolent Social Change, Atlanta. "Alabama Staff Workshop," April 21–23, 1965, Doc 1213, A-AX-10, Reel 36, Student Nonviolent Coordinating Committee Papers; "Special Report No. 4: Selma and Dallas County, Alabama: A Statistical Roundup," March 1965, Doc 0061, C-I-1, Reel 53, SNCC Papers; J. Mills Thornton III, *Dividing Lines: Municipal Politics and the Struggle for Civil Rights in Montgomery, Birmingham, and Selma* (Tuscaloosa: University of Alabama Press, 2002), 419–20.

6. Mesher, interview by author.

7. Shirley Mesher, "Special Report: Dallas County, Alabama," April 12–13, 1966, Series II, Box 144, SCLC Papers; Mesher, interview by author.

8. John A. Baker to Harold A. Middlebrook, July 18, 1965, Chuck Fager to Randolph Blackwell, July 31, 1965, both in Series II, Box 146, SCLC Papers; Doug and Tina Harris, Janet Jermott, and Jim to Silas Norman, August 3, 1965, Doc 1061, A-VIII-70, Reel 18, SNCC Papers; Edward M. Rudd, "Race Complicates Black Belt Anti-Poverty Plans," *SC*, October 16–17, 1965; Frank Prial to Robert Clampitt and Jack Gonzales, "Alabama Contact," November 7, 1965, Box 1, "Inspection Reports Evaluating CAP," RG 381.

9. Edward M. Rudd and Mary Ellen Gale, "Two Fronts in the War on Poverty . . . ," *SC*, October 23–24, 1965; Robert L. Martin to Edgar May through C. B. Patrick, "Dallas County–City of Selma Economic Opportunity Board," June 20, 1966, Frank Prial to Robert Clampitt and Jack Gonzales, "Alabama Contact," November 7, 1965, both in Box 1, "Inspection Reports Evaluating CAP," RG 381.

10. Robert L. Martin to Edgar May through C. B. Patrick, "Dallas County–City of Selma Economic Opportunity Board," June 20, 1966, Box 1, "Inspection Reports Evaluating CAP," RG 381; Edward M. Rudd, "Poverty Dispute in Selma," *SC*, November 13–14, 1965; David R. Underhill, "Governor Wallace Comes out Fighting, Hits Attacks on Local Government," *SC*, August 28–29, 1965.

11. Edward M. Rudd, "Mayor: I'll See Selma Negroes of 'Good Faith,'" *SC*, December 18–19, 1965; Francis X. Walter Diary, November 9, 16, 1965, Francis X. Walter Collection, Sewanee, Tennessee.

12. Robert L. Martin to Edgar May through C. B. Patrick, "Dallas County–City of Selma Economic Opportunity Board," June 20, 1966, "Method for Selecting Board of Directors—Adopted at SHAPE General Meeting," December 8, 1965, both in Box 1, "Inspection Reports Evaluating CAP," RG 381.

13. Rudd, "Mayor"; Ernest M. Bradford to Joe T. Smitherman, December 15, 1965, Box 1, "Inspection Reports Evaluating CAP," RG 381; Joe T. Smitherman to Ernest Bradford, December 21, 1965, Box 24, Records Relating to the Civil Rights Program in the Regions, 1965–66, RG 381.

14. Edward M. Rudd, "Poverty Dispute in Selma," SC, November 13–14, 1965; Robert L. Martin to Edgar May through C. B. Patrick, "Dallas County–City of Selma Economic Opportunity Board," June 20, 1966, NA to BLB, "Selma, Alabama," January 15, 1966, both in Box 1, "Inspection Reports Evaluating CAP," RG 381.

15. Frederick O'R. Hayes to Theodore M. Berry, March 31, 1965, Records of the Director, State Files, 1965–68, RG 381; W. Edward Harris to R. Sargent Shriver, March 13, 1965, Records Relating to the Administration of the Civil Rights Program in the Regions, 1965–66, Box 24, RG 381. Susan Youngblood Ashmore, *Carry It On: The War on Poverty and the Civil Rights Movement in Alabama, 1964–1972* (Athens: University of Georgia Press, 2008), 63–64.

16. Janet Nussmann, "Alleged Racist Attitudes of a Member of the CAP Staff," February 3, 1969, Box 3, Records of the Community Services Administration, Office of Economic Opportunity, Regional Offices, Organizations Planning Files, RG 381, National Archives, Southeast Region, Morrow, Ga. (hereafter RG381SE); Evaluation Team of City of Selma–Dallas County Economic Opportunity Board, Anti-Poverty Program Evaluation, Community Action/Anti-Poverty, Box 5, RG 381SE.

17. Bill Mahoney, "'SNICK' in Alabama," [ca. 1966], Doc 0970, A-VIII-66, Reel 18, SNCC Papers; John Klein, "Selma Negroes Wonder, What Did Mayor Mean?," SC, February 5–6, 1966; "Stu House Reports from Selma, Alabama," February 13, 1966, Doc 1049, A-VIII-70, Reel 18, SNCC Papers.

18. Mahoney, "'SNICK' in Alabama"; Klein, "Selma Negroes Wonder"; "Stu House Reports from Selma, Alabama," February 13, 1966, Doc 1049, A-VIII-70, Reel 18, SNCC Papers.

19. Francis X. Walter, interview by Stanley Smith, 24–25, Ralph Bunche Oral History Center.

20. Ibid., 26–28.

21. "Editorial: Antipoverty Probe?," *Selma Times-Journal*, March 10, 1966; Robert L. Martin to Edgar May through C. B. Patrick, "Dallas County–City of Selma Economic Opportunity Board," June 20, 1966, Box 1, "Inspection Reports Evaluating CAP," RG 381; Walter, interview, 32–33.

22. Joseph S. Knight Résumé, March 25, 1966, Box 1, "Inspection Reports Evaluating

CAP," RG 381.; Robert L. Martin to Edgar May through C. B. Patrick, "Dallas County–City of Selma Economic Opportunity Board," June 20, 1966, Box 1, "Inspection Reports Evaluating CAP," RG 381.

23. Ernest M. Bradford, "Protest from the People of Dallas County Regarding the Community Action Program by Dallas County SHAPE," March 29, 1966, Ernest M. Bradford to Samuel Yette, March 31, 1966, both in Box 24, Records of the Office of the Director, Records Relating to the Civil Rights Program in the Regions, 1965–66, RG 381; "Selma's Poor Object to Poverty Set-Up," *SC*, April 9–10, 1966; Robert L. Martin, to Edgar May through C. B. Patrick, "Dallas County–City of Selma Economic Opportunity Board," June 20, 1966, Box 1, "Inspection Reports Evaluating CAP," RG 381.

24. Robert L. Martin to Edgar May through C. B. Patrick, "Dallas County–City of Selma Economic Opportunity Board," June 20, 1966, Box 1, "Inspection Reports Evaluating CAP," RG 381; Thornton, *Dividing Lines*, 482, 491; Joseph H. Crespino, *In Search of Another Country: Mississippi and the Conservative Counterrevolution* (Princeton: Princeton University Press, 2007), 11–12, 19.

25. Unknown to Bill [and] Gwen, March 16, 1966, unknown to Bill, March 17, 1966, both in Doc 0066, A-VIII-28, Reel 18, SNCC Papers; Mesher, interview by author.

26. Larry Freudiger, "A Rally in Selma," *SC*, April 16–17, 1966; SNCC News Release, "Dallas County Independent Voters League," March 17, 1966, A-VIII-71, Reel 18, SNCC Papers; John Klein, "Dallas County Voters Start Third Party," *SC*, March 19–20, 1966; Walter, interview, 32–35.

27. "Rev. Reese Cleared of Charges in Selma," *SC*, April 9–10, 1966; "Selma Wonders"; Thornton, *Dividing Lines*, 491–92; Klein, "Dallas County Voters."

28. Tina Harris, "Freedom Organizations in Alabama," April 21, 1966, Doc 0543, A-VII-3, Reel 14, SNCC Papers; Larry Freudiger, "Dick Gregory: Selma," *SC*, April 16–17, 1966; "First They Listened, Then They Danced," *SC*, April 16–17, 1966; Freudiger, "Rally"; Terry Cowles, "Tenants Say Planter Won't Share Payments in U.S. Cotton Plan," *SC*, April 2–3, 1966.

29. Tina Harris, "Freedom Organizations in Alabama," April 21, 1966, Doc 0543, A-VII-3, Reel 14, SNCC Papers; "Dallas County Independent Free Voters Organization Information," n.d., Doc 1136, A-VIII-22, Reel 17, SNCC Papers.

30. "Big Political Day in Dallas County," *SC*, April 30–May 1, 1966; "Alabama Candidates Running for Public Office in the May Primaries," May 1966, Series IV, Box 165, SCLC Papers; SNCC Press Release, May 4, 1966, Doc 0552, A-VII-3, Reel 14, SNCC Papers; "News of the Field No. 3 from the New York Office of SNCC," May 6, 1966, Doc 0030, A-VII-16, Reel 17, SNCC Papers; Dallas County Report, [ca. 1966], Doc 0065, A-VIII-28, Reel 18, SNCC Papers; Dallas County Report, May 2, 1966, Doc 0067, A-VIII-28, Reel 18, SNCC Papers; Michael S. Lottman, "Slim Chance for Negroes to Win Legislative Races," *SC*, May 7–8, 1966; Thornton, *Dividing Lines*, 499.

31. SNCC Press Release, "Report on Alabama Elections," May 6, 1966, Doc 0553, A-VII-3, Reel 14, SNCC Papers; SNCC Press Release, n.d., A-VIII-71, REEL 18, SNCC Papers; Stephen E. Cotton, "Negro Voters All over State Say, 'I Waited,'...," SC, May 7–8, 1966.

32. Michael S. Lottman, "How Did Your County Vote?," SC, May 7–8, 1966; Lottman, "Slim Chance"; SNCC Press Release, "Report on Alabama Elections," May 6, 1966, Doc 0553, A-VII-3, Reel 14, SNCC Papers; "Baker Named Winner, but Clark Can Fight," SC, May 28–29, 1966; "By George—No Run-Off," SC, May 7–8, 1966.

33. Viola Bradford, "Samson Crum Withdraws from Dallas Sheriff Race," SC, October 8–9, 1966; DCIFVO Flier, [ca. 1966], Doc 0119, A-VIII-29, Reel 18, SNCC Papers; DCIFVO advertisement, SC, November 5–6, 1966; "November 8 Nears—Political Plots Thicken," SC, October 22–23, 1966; James Chisum, "Negro Voter May Cast Deciding Ballot Tuesday," Birmingham News, November 6, 1966.

34. SNCC Press Release, "Election Reports (Georgia, Alabama and Mississippi)," November 10, 1966, Doc 0584, A-VII-3, Reel 14, SNCC Papers; "Dallas: DCIFVO Head Not Discouraged," SC, November 12–13, 1966.

35. "Rights Staff Studies Vote 'By the Sea,'" SC, May 14–15, 1966; Terry Cowles, "SCLC Moves out of Alabama," SC, June 4–5, 1966; Mesher, "Special Report"; Robert E. Smith, "Rights Lawyers open Selma Office," SC, June 18–19, 1966.

36. Clayborne Carson, In Struggle: SNCC and the Black Awakening of the 1960s, (Cambridge: Harvard University Press, 1981), 200–203; "Black Panther Party to Import Observers," Alabama Journal, May 24, 1966, Box SG 6944, Public Information Subject File—General Files, Alabama Department of Archives and History, Montgomery; John Dittmer, Local People: The Struggle for Civil Rights in Mississippi (Urbana: University of Illinois Press, 1994), 392; unknown to Stokely Carmichael, August 10, 1966, Stokely Carmichael to Alice L. Moore, August 22, 1966, both in A-1-52, Reel 2, SNCC Papers; SNCC Staff and Assignments List, May 1966, Doc 1064, A-III-1, Reel 3, SNCC Papers; Central Committee Meeting Minutes, October 22–23, 1966, Doc 0604, A-II-11, Reel 3, SNCC Papers.

37. Louis Lloyd Anderson to Sargent Shriver, April 9, 1967, CAP Office Records of the Director, Subject Files 1965–69, Box 45, RG 381; Dwain Alexander, "Official Report of On-Site Findings," Dallas County–Selma Economic Opportunity Board, November 19–22, 1968, Anti-Poverty Program Evaluation, Community Action/Anti-Poverty, Box 5, RG 381SE.

38. Alexander, "Official Report"; "Comments by Dwain Alexander," November 25, 1968, Anti-Poverty Program Evaluation, Community Action/Anti-Poverty, Box 5, RG 381SE.

39. "Comments by Dwain Alexander," November 25, 1968, Anti-Poverty Program Evaluation, Community Action/Anti-Poverty, Box 5, RG 381SE; Thaddeus Olive Jr., "Assignment Report," November 19, 1968, Selma–Dallas County Economic Opportunity

Board, Andre W. Moore, "Assignment Report," Selma–Dallas County Economic Opportunity Board, November 19, 1968, Donald Thielke to Dwain Alexander, December 5, 1968, all in Anti-Poverty Program Evaluation, Community Action/Anti-Poverty, Box 5, RG 381SE.

40. Thornton, *Dividing Lines*, 501–2; Douglas Martin, "Joseph Smitherman, Mayor in Selma Strife, Dies at 75," *New York Times*, September 13, 2005.

WILLIAM CLAYSON

The War on Poverty and the Chicano Movement in Texas

Confronting "Tio Tomás" and the "Gringo Pseudoliberals"

In October 1967, U.S. president Lyndon Baines Johnson went to El Paso, Texas, to meet with Gustavo Diaz Ordaz, the president of Mexico, and Texas governor John Connally. The purpose of the visit was to return the Chamizal Territory, a six-hundred-acre strip of land along the Rio Grande, to Mexico. Mexico had disputed U.S. claims to the land since the late nineteenth century, when the Chamizal had shifted away from the Mexican side of the border with the river's current. Always on the lookout for an opportunity, Johnson wanted to make the most of the occasion.

No politician in American history had benefited as much from the support of Mexican Americans as did LBJ. One might also argue that no politician had provided as much benefit to Mexican Americans. Yet by 1967, a new generation of Mexican American civil rights activists, young militants who defiantly called themselves *Chicanos*, had become disillusioned with Johnson and the liberal agenda he represented. While liberals had introduced revolutionary civil rights legislation and ambitious antipoverty initiatives, many Chicanos felt that Johnson had all but ignored the chronic poverty of the nation's barrios. If anything, the escape from poverty promised by the liberal agenda seemed to oblige Chicanos to abandon the culture that made them unique. Embracing the Great Society seemed to require that Mexican Americans forgive and forget the history of exclusion and abuse that had created barrio poverty. At the same time, a disproportionate number of Mexican Americans were coming home in flag-draped coffins from the president's failing war in Vietnam.

As a politician from Texas, the president had many Mexican American friends. He sought out their advice on what to do about the Chicano militants. At the urging of his Mexican American allies, Johnson created the cabinet-level Interagency Committee on Mexican American Affairs. To head the committee, the president appointed Vicente Ximenes, who was already working with the White House as a member of the Equal Employment Opportunity Commission. Although Johnson was leery of protesters, Ximenes urged the president to use the Chamizal summit to shore up his relationship with the Mexican American community. Ximenes organized a series of cabinet committee hearings on Mexican American affairs to coincide with the Diaz Ordaz visit.[1]

Like Ximenes and LBJ, the young Chicano activists recognized an opportunity in the Chamizal summit. The emerging leadership of the *movimiento* organized a protest and a rump conference in El Paso the same weekend. Chicanos and Chicanas lined city streets to shout at the president's motorcade. They shook picket signs with angry slogans in English and Spanish: "Today We Protest, Tomorrow Revolution!," and "Don't Ask Rich Mexicans to Talk for the Poor."[2] It must have been difficult for LBJ to maintain his composure. The Mexican president probably sympathized with Johnson. After all, Diaz Ordaz, too, had radicals to deal with in Mexico. Governor Connally would have been accustomed to angry shouts in Spanish by late 1967, but Johnson had always considered himself a friend to Mexican Americans. Yet there he was, riding in a limousine with the president of Mexico to a conference on Mexican American affairs planned by his Mexican American friend while scores of angry Chicanos jeered.

Ximenes had invited many of the protesters to attend the conference, but most had refused. Rodolfo "Corky" Gonzales of Denver's Crusade for Justice believed that a boycott of the conference would send the clearest message to Johnson. But José Angel Gutiérrez, the leader of the Mexican American Youth Organization (MAYO) from San Antonio, convinced Chicano leaders to hold the rump conference. They enlisted local Roman Catholic clergy, who opened the doors of the Sacred Heart Church in El Segundo Barrio for the protesters. In the dim light of the old church, the leadership of the Chicano movement first agreed on the term *La Raza Unida* (The Race United) to describe the political and cultural objectives of their movement.[3]

Controlled by absentee Anglo slumlords who refused to provide basic sanitation and safety, El Segundo Barrio ranked among the country's poorest neighborhoods, with few well-paying jobs. The Chicanos saw the barrio as a living demonstration of the failures of the liberal agenda. Johnson had declared war on poverty three years earlier, yet the residents of El Segundo Barrio continued to live in Third World conditions. El Paso was home to a variety of programs financed by the Office of Economic Opportunity (OEO), which Johnson had created in 1964 to fight his War on Poverty, but they had done little to ease the city's chronic poverty. Anglos and middle-class Mexican Americans from outside the barrios had created and administered the antipoverty programs, with little input from residents. Gutiérrez recalled that activists at the Sacred Heart Church condemned "the virtual exclusion of Chicanos in the developing of War on Poverty programs" and set out to rectify that omission.[4]

The War on Poverty and the Chicano movement influenced each other. Many young Chicanas and Chicanos received political educations while working for OEO programs. Movement leaders depended on War on Poverty funding and infrastructure to build and strengthen their nascent organizations. And yet Chicanismo was in many ways a critique of the liberal values of the previous generation of Mexican American political leaders. Many Chicano activists rejected the fundamental premises of postwar American liberalism that had shaped the War on Poverty. As a result, tensions arose within Texas OEO programs between younger Chicano community activists and older liberal allies of the Johnson administration, among them many leading Mexican American politicians.

Through the postwar era, a cadre of Mexican American politicians, led by San Antonio congressman Henry B. Gonzalez, had become stalwarts of the liberal wing of Texas's Democratic Party. They championed the goals of postwar liberalism, especially racial integration, a view that would become a key point of contention. The Chicanos saw integration as a vision that would require them to assimilate into an Anglo culture that had abused and oppressed their people for generations. When they demanded control of OEO funding in the barrios, they planned to use the money to promote a starkly contrasting ideal of Chicano self-determination, cultural celebration, and political empowerment.

By the time LBJ left office in January 1969, both the liberals and the militants seemed to have lost sight of the ultimate goal: eliminating poverty. Both the Chicano movement and Johnson's War on Poverty had run their courses by the early 1970s, leaving lasting imprints on Texas politics and culture. Nevertheless, the problem of chronic Mexican American poverty remained. In the wake of the Chicano movement and the OEO, a quieter, longer-lasting, and more effective grassroots War on Poverty emerged in cities across Texas. It built on and came out of Johnson's vision and structure but enacted more fully the core ideal of local leadership and community control.

LIBERALS AND THE WAR ON POVERTY IN TEXAS

The Chicano movement had not quite gelled nationally when its young leaders gathered in El Paso in 1967. With the exception of Reies Lopez Tijerina, who had been in constant confrontation with authorities for more than a decade over land claims in New Mexico, Chicano militancy was primarily an urban phenomenon. Small groups, mostly college students, had begun to coalesce in cities with large Mexican American populations. Leaders emerged under the influence of the Black Power movement in the cities, the New Left at universities, and Marxist revolutionaries from Latin America. Some of the founders had been active in the leading student organizations of the decade—the Student Nonviolent Coordinating Committee and Students for a Democratic Society, among others. In Los Angeles, budding Chicano activists had formed United Mexican American Students. Denver Chicanos created Crusade for Justice. In Texas, Chicano activism had begun to spread beyond college campuses in San Antonio.

Chicano activists built on a long tradition of political activism among Mexican Americans in Texas. The cadre of leaders that preceded the Chicano movement have been described by historian Mario T. García as the "Mexican American generation." They had made significant strides in advancing the cause of civil rights through the GI Forum, a service organization for Mexican American veterans and their families, and the League of United Latin American Citizens (LULAC). Both groups had waged legal battles against the discrimination and segregation Mexican Americans faced in South Texas, Los Angeles, and elsewhere. Their movement produced political figures of national significance, including such key Johnson allies as Congressman Gonzalez and Dr. Hector García, the leader of the GI Forum. The GI Forum had proved instrumental in mobilizing Texas Democrats through Viva Kennedy and Viva Johnson voting drives during the 1960 and 1964 presidential campaigns.[5]

The Mexican American generation's ideological stance clearly fell in line with the values of postwar liberalism. Military service in World War II had imbued many of these Mexican Americans with a sense of patriotism and loyalty to the United States. Like Johnson's Democratic Party and like Martin Luther King Jr., the political leaders of the Mexican American generation viewed racism, segregation, and chronic poverty as obstacles that activism, legal action, and progressive government could overcome. Unlike black leaders, however, the Mexican American generation viewed its struggle as akin to those of earlier immigrant groups that sought to integrate into the American mainstream, as Irish Americans and Italian Americans had done by the mid–twentieth century.

The Chicano activists rejected this value system, however, arguing that the Mexican experience in the United States differed from those of both European immigrant groups and African Americans. Many Chicanos had not descended from immigrants but came from families with roots in Texas and the Southwest that predated the creation of the United States and even the arrival of Europeans. They had become Americans not by choice but through military conquest. They had been denied civil rights, swindled or squeezed out of property, and brutalized by armed militias such as the Texas Rangers. By the twentieth century, Mexican Americans in Texas lived in an apartheid society that was, in the words of David Montejano, "as complete—and as 'de jure'—as any in the Jim Crow South."[6] Anger and an unwillingness to forgive this history motivated the Chicanos in the 1960s more than any other factor.

Cultural pride was the most salient aspect of Chicanismo. While the members of the Mexican American generation had encouraged their children to learn English, Chicanos considered the Spanish language a fundamental symbol of identity. Pride in culture led the Chicanos to reject integration and assimilation. As the Chicano movement picked up steam, leaders combined anger over historic injustices and cultural pride to develop an agenda of political self-determination and economic justice. When the War on Poverty came along, the Chicanos viewed it as an opportunity to realize these goals. They did not recognize any paradox in rejecting the liberal values that had inspired the War on Poverty while using OEO programs to further their aims. The Chicanos viewed the War on Poverty as long overdue recompense for centuries of discrimination, neglect, and abuse.

Chicanismo came directly out of what Ignacio M. García has called a "slightly new breed" of Mexican American political activist that came to the movement's forefront in the early 1960s. Foremost among this new breed in Texas was Albert Peña, the Bexar County commissioner. Peña had served as a leader in the Viva Kennedy clubs that contributed decisively to the Democratic victory in the state in 1960. In Texas, these clubs organized into the Political Association of Spanish-Speaking Organizations (PASSO) in 1961, with Peña as president. He had a confrontational, clamorous style that diverged from that of most public figures of the Mexican American generation. Along with PASSO executive secretary Albert Fuentes and the support of the Teamsters Union, Peña orchestrated the 1963 electoral takeover of Crystal City, in South Texas. Like many towns and cities in the state's border region, impoverished Mexican Americans comprised the majority of the population in Crystal City, yet wealthy Anglos controlled the municipal government and economy. PASSO put five Mexican Americans on the election slate for city council, and when they won, a shock wave reverberated through the state.[7]

Peña was a transitional figure in Texas politics. He remained loyal to the national Democratic Party even as Chicano leaders abandoned LBJ and the liberals. But Peña accused Connally and the state Democratic Party of racism and obstructionism because the governor resisted the 1964 Civil Rights Act and other liberal initiatives. Peña was a leading figure in the insurgent liberal coalition of the state party, comprised of minority groups, organized labor, and white progressives. They considered U.S. Senator Ralph Yarborough the leader of the Texas party. The War on Poverty ranked among this liberal coalition's highest priorities through the 1960s.

The two factions of the Democratic Party fought hard for control of federal War on Poverty programs in their state. The liberals, led by Peña, Congressman Gonzalez, and Senator Yarborough, worked to make local and state War on Poverty efforts a success. LULAC and the GI Forum, which remained steadfast supporters of LBJ, promoted the Great Society as the "Big Chance" to raise Texas's largest minority from deprivation. The conservatives, conversely, often obstructed individual OEO programs on state and local levels, especially if those programs seemed connected to LBJ's civil rights legislation. Conservatives viewed these programs as a waste of taxpayer money. Connally described to Marvin Watson, Johnson's chief of staff, the prevailing sentiment in Texas about the War on Poverty: "Most of the people down here don't like the program. . . . [R]eporters, every one of them thinks [the War on Poverty] is a big boondog."[8]

As governor, Connally had little power to influence OEO programs; however, to reduce political hostility to the program, the Economic Opportunity Act gave governors veto power over programs within their states. In late 1965, Connally became the first state chief executive to use his veto power when he shut down a Neighborhood Youth Corps program for Mexican Americans in the Rio Grande Valley. The veto surprised OEO officials in Washington, who had expected obstructionism from Alabama's George Wallace but not from LBJ's protégé.

Connally objected to the plan because it required a $1.25 minimum wage, which, he argued, would have placed the teenaged enrollees at a higher wage than most of their parents. Peña lambasted the governor for his view of poor Mexicans:

> Connally argued that the Mexicans in Texas shouldn't rely so much on the national government to solve their socio-economic problems; they should pull themselves up by their own boot straps. This is all well and good, but we do not wear boots. And they stole our huaraches. But we got some good shoes made with strong American leather in American factories and we are going to pound the pavement in the barrios until the soles of our shoes are worn thin.... Our feet may blister, our toes may break out the side of our shoes, but Mr. Governor we are going to do everything we can to make the War on Poverty a reality in Texas.[9]

The fight that began with "Connally's disparaging remarks" escalated into a major confrontation between the governor and the liberals. The United Farm Workers (UFW) became involved in early 1966. The UFW was led by Mexican Americans but remained in the liberal Democratic camp in Texas. To confront the governor, the UFW moved beyond the War on Poverty to demand a raise in the minimum wage for all Texas workers, organizing the most dramatic civil rights protest in Texas history, a 490-mile march from the Rio Grande Valley to Austin on Labor Day 1966. The march illustrates further the great hope that Texas liberals attached to OEO programs as tools of economic advancement, particularly for minorities. As Yarborough, who accompanied the marchers to Austin, stated, "Amigos, compadres—fellow marchers . . . as our senior U.S. Senator, I *hold* the highest elective office and with all the power and good will which the people of Texas can give . . . I welcome you with open arms. . . . A hundred years ago we ended physical slavery. We are here to end economic slavery."[10]

The passion of activists such as Peña and the power of the Labor Day march and other political demonstrations inspired the young people who would form the leadership of the Chicano movement. Unlike Peña and the UFW, however, the Chicanos would come to doubt the value of maintaining loyalty to the Democratic Party on any level. Many came to such doubts while working in War on Poverty programs.

THE OEO AS CHICANO MOVEMENT TRAINING GROUND

Civic-minded young people across the country took advantage of employment offered by various OEO programs, especially local community action programs.

In Texas, the OEO agencies that employed Mexican American young people showed a preference for college students as the most capable, most motivated, and most idealistic people available. While these qualities were a natural fit for the War on Poverty, the same group of young people was also drawn to some of the more militant strands of 1960s racial politics. In his book on the Chicano movement, Carlos Muñoz explains that War on Poverty programs provided a "training ground" for future Chicano activists across the nation. Many prominent figures of the Chicano movement worked for OEO programs. Best known was Gonzales, who directed Community Action in Denver and sat on a national committee appointed by LBJ to develop War on Poverty programs for the special needs of the Southwest. Gonzales, who authored *Yo Soy Joaquin*, a poem considered a manifesto of the Chicano movement, left the OEO in protest to create the independent Chicano group Crusade for Justice in 1966.[11]

In Texas, the most prominent future militants to work with a War on Poverty program were the founders of MAYO. Gutiérrez became the most vocal member of the group and among the most influential figures of the Chicano movement. Mario Compean, another MAYO founder, worked in Volunteers in Service to America (VISTA), a domestic version of the Peace Corps. Ramsey Muñiz worked for the Model Cities Program in Waco. Muñiz became the first Mexican American to appear on the ballot for Texas governor when he ran on the Raza Unida Party ticket in 1972. The party grew out of MAYO and became the most influential political product of the Chicano movement in Texas. Muñiz took only 6 percent of the vote, but that showing made conservative Democrat Dolph Briscoe the first governor in state history to take office without winning a majority of the electorate.[12]

Gutiérrez worked as a counselor in the San Antonio Neighborhood Youth Organization (SANYO) in 1967 and 1968 while a graduate student in political science at St. Mary's University. During this time, Gutiérrez and Compean created MAYO with fellow students Willie C. Velásquez, Ignacio Pérez, and Juan Patlán. SANYO was a local affiliate of the Neighborhood Youth Corps, one of several "national emphasis" programs developed by OEO for local agencies to administer. Gutiérrez later recalled that his day-to-day duties mostly involved counseling SANYO enrollees on "punctuality, work ethic, appearance, hygiene, skills, the whole gamut."[13]

The tasks performed for programs such as SANYO may have been mundane, but working for War on Poverty agencies provided budding activists with a political apprenticeship. Irma Mireles, who would became the director of San Antonio's

Mexican American cultural center, recalled that her experience as a SANYO employee "opened my eyes to how the politics worked . . . and gave me a sense of how people working together as a community can do something." "It was the first time," Mireles remembered, "that I saw the Mexican-Americans speaking out." SANYO helped politically to mobilize the community through neighborhood centers housed in Catholic parishes. These centers evolved into the Greater San Antonio Federation of Neighborhood Councils, which one local journalist called "a vibrant, if unwieldy, political force." The federation established councils in neighborhoods where Mexican Americans formed a majority and ultimately represented nearly 250,000 people, about one-third of San Antonio's population. The federation became so politically influential that some Anglo elites feared a repeat of the Crystal City takeover.[14]

In El Paso, activist José Aguilar used OEO funding to create the Mexican American Committee on Honor Opportunity and Service (MACHOS). Aguilar used the agency and funding to mobilize the city's Mexican American majority to stage demonstrations and boycotts to demand the enforcement of safe building codes as well as improved services and infrastructure. MACHOS organized economic boycotts to pressure absentee slumlords to improve living conditions in the dilapidated tenement buildings in El Segundo Barrio. Members developed a cooperative in South El Paso to help poor families purchase food and utilities. OEO officials praised Aguilar and MACHOS: According to one assessment, "The only successful organizing in El Paso is done by MACHOS. They are efficient, they do their homework, and pick their fights carefully."[15]

Along with employment and lessons in political confrontation, OEO programs also provided access to people. Gutiérrez recalled that many young people he counseled "wanted to get involved [and] expressed frustration about political issues in school or the neighborhood, and MAYO offered an outlet for that." In his autobiography, Gutiérrez explained that the Chicano movement followed the example of other militant groups that had "infiltrated" War on Poverty programs and "used those structures and resources to expand their organizing." Gutiérrez recalled that "many future organizers for MAYO came from these . . . programs."[16]

The early Chicano movement also used VISTA to expand its organizing. According to historian Ignacio M. García, VISTA, provided MAYO with "a larger financial base" that assisted the organization's growth "from one chapter in San Antonio to more than thirty" by the end of the 1960s. Thanks to VISTA, Compean explained, "MAYO had 200 people loose. . . . We had a budget. We had salaries for people. We had transportation. We had telephones. We had travel monies. So consequently that really allowed MAYO to expand."[17]

War on Poverty programs facilitated the growth of Chicano organizations as the movement took shape later in the decade. However, central to the movement ethos in relation to government antipoverty programs were suspicions of white welfare paternalism. In *Chicano Manifesto*, native Texan Armando Rendon singled out the OEO to explain this sentiment: The OEO's "gringo pseudoliberals and guilt ridden do-gooders" attempted to solve the problems of the barrios with a complete disregard for local culture. As an example, Rendon described an encounter between OEO consultants and a Mexican American community group in an unnamed South Texas town. OEO staffers insulted the local people by failing to translate an evaluation into Spanish. According to Rendon, "Only a handful of the audience understood the gringos [who were] so presumptive as to belittle their program but not even being able to do so in their own language." Rendon viewed Anglo antipoverty workers' efforts as ultimately self-serving and hoped that "Chicanos will no longer permit their barrios to be used as laboratories, at least not by Anglo cientificos [and] at least not for free."[18]

Rendon wrote *Chicano Manifesto* as the movement reached its crescendo in the early 1970s, but such suspicions of white welfare paternalism in the OEO bureaucracy had existed since the agency's inception. In 1966, OEO director Sargent Shriver created the Office of Civil Rights to ensure that all War on Poverty programs complied with the Civil Rights Act of 1964. Shriver appointed Samuel Yette, a former editor at *Ebony* magazine, to run the office, and Yette in turn appointed seven civil rights coordinators, with one operating out of each OEO regional office. For the Southwest Region, the civil rights coordinator was Gregorio Coronado, a GI Forum representative from Lubbock, Texas. Regional director Bill Crook immediately clashed with Coronado.

Crook eventually accused Coronado of deliberately creating a "backlog" of community action program applications because of his suspicions that regional staff were excluding Mexican Americans. Crook informed Yette that Coronado acted "with suspicion towards the office and everyone in it [as if] he is the only one standing between the minorities and a raw deal by OEO." "Frankly," Crook complained further to Shriver, "I resent the hell out of the suspicion that seems to be the basic premise for the operation of civil rights here."[19]

Other OEO officials reinforced Crook's assessment of Coronado. Deputy regional director Astor Kirk reported that when he attempted to talk about civil rights issues, Coronado refused to discuss such matters with Anglo officials who "just don't understand the civil rights problems in Texas." Kirk believed that Coronado had "reservations regarding the commitment of the Southwest Region Staff . . . to the centrality of civil rights in our work [and] seems inclined to 'find' civil rights issues in policy." Fred Baldwin of the OEO's Office of Inspection was sent to Austin to investigate the matter and reported that Coronado assumed that the regional staff lacked concern for civil rights issues "when, in fact, the backgrounds of our people show the opposite."[20]

Although Gregorio Coronado created friction at the regional office, no individual in Texas protested the underrepresentation of Mexican Americans in War on Poverty programs more than Coronado's wife, Dominga. She insisted that white paternalism could be solved only by placing Mexican Americans in positions of responsibility. When the Lubbock County Community Action Board applied for a grant in late 1965, Dominga Coronado politely asked Crook to encourage the city to include members of minority groups on the program's board of directors. In 1966, she became chair of the Lubbock GI Forum's War on Poverty Committee. By April of that year, her patience exhausted, Dominga Coronado threatened to stage a major protest over the "undemocratic" manner in which the program had developed its board of directors. She warned that a public demonstration remained the only weapon available to minority groups "as long as local groups are controlled by RACIST power structures, as is the regional office" of the OEO. She declared that "the politicians and power structures" bore responsibility for explaining "to the Mexican-American boys fighting in Viet Nam why we are still discriminated against."[21]

Dominga Coronado also requested that the Texas state OEO hire a Mexican American person to run a regional office rumored to be opening in Lubbock. She complained to Governor Connally that "if a Mexican-American is not placed in this office, then only the Power Structures will be advised again and again, and the poor Mexican-American people will not be advised and consequently will not benefit." Walter Richter, director of the state OEO, informed her that the governor had no plans to open a regional office in Lubbock but had named Joe Meador to act as a consultant for the Panhandle-Plains region. While nine of the state office's twenty-one staffers were Mexican American, the Texas OEO had "not selected any staff people on the basis of race, but on qualifications, which must include a deep concern and compassion for the poor, whatever their race. I cannot believe that you subscribe, as your letter clearly suggests, that members of only one race are capable of carrying out the spirit and the letter of the Economic Opportunity Act."[22]

According to a report from the Lubbock community action agency, the situation became "sticky" when both Coronados became involved. Just after Dominga Coronado stood up to speak at a meeting of the Lubbock Community Action Board, "who should appear on the floor but Mr. Coronado from the Office of Economic Opportunity." As a consequence of his position as an OEO administrator, local officials felt that he "was attempting to destroy the confidence of the people . . . the implication being that we were misleading the people when we said that we were attempting to follow the instructions of the OEO." Dominga Coronado ended the rebuke with a comment that would have threatened local officials even in remote Lubbock: "You remember Watts, don't you?"[23]

OEO headquarters stepped in and silenced the Coronados. Crook pleaded with Yette, "It seems that Mrs. Coronado WANTS a demonstration in Lubbock. . . . I see no way for this office to escape involvement and embarrassment. Perhaps you are better at handling wives than I am. What do you suggest?" Shriver ordered Yette to quiet the Coronados, especially Dominga: "Your man, Coronado, has got to keep his wife out of activities which impede our whole program state-wide. If he wants to continue this work, maybe he should leave us and do something else." Yette had Gregorio Coronado transferred to become the civil rights coordinator at the San Francisco regional office. Dominga Coronado later became the national chair of the GI Forum Ladies Auxiliary and served as an adviser for the Job Corps women's program.[24]

Chicano and Chicana activists also accused the OEO of tokenism or cronyism in employing Mexican Americans. Gutiérrez described the Mexican Americans employed by the Johnson administration as "token Mexicans" who were for the most part close allies of the Johnson administration. Ximenes's ties to LBJ, Gutiérrez argued, seemed to make him the "Chicano destined for all appointments."[25] The Chicanos defined any Mexican American who bought into the liberal agenda as a lackey of the Anglo power structure—a "Tio Tomás" (Uncle Tom).

To the Chicano militants, the Mexican American leader who best exemplified the Tio Tomás image was Gonzalez. His friendship with LBJ was at least partly responsible for San Antonio's large War on Poverty allocation, but Chicanos criticized his view of himself as "a congressman for all Americans, not solely Mexican-Americans." Gutiérrez described Gonzalez as a man who ran the Democratic Party in San Antonio like a machine politician, with little use for "the indigenous leadership" of the barrios. Gonzalez's reluctance to support any legislative agenda targeted specifically at Mexican Americans made him, in Gutiérrez's words, "the couch for the racist gringos to sit on." In response, Gonzalez referred to MAYO leaders as "brown thugs" or "professional Mexicans" who styled Chicanos as "the embodiment of good" and Anglo Americans as "the incarnation of evil. That is not merely racist, it is drawing from the deepest wellsprings of hate."[26]

Wresting the War on Poverty from Anglo and Mexican American liberals became a primary focus for the *movimiento Chicano* as it gained momentum in the late 1960s. Political scientist Rodolfo Rosales has explained that as the Chicano militants assumed center stage in Mexican American politics in San Antonio, leaders dealt "almost exclusively with Chicano issues that were related to civil rights, the War on Poverty, and the inclusion of Chicanos in national politics." Arnoldo De Leon has reiterated the same idea for Houston, where Mexican American civil rights organizations led drives to improve employment and education opportunities but also strove "to secure a share of the poverty program for the Mexican-American neighborhoods."[27] By 1968, the Chicanos clearly wanted more than just "token Mexicans" in positions of responsibility in OEO programs: activists wanted control of War on Poverty funds in the barrios and the freedom to use those funds to advance the movement's values.

The OEO proved willing to accommodate the Chicanos' demands to a limited extent. In 1968, VISTA opened an experimental Texas program, the Minority Mobilization Program (MMP). Activists José Urriegas and Gonzalo Barrientos introduced the idea to the OEO regional office. Historian Julie Pycior explains that the two men "had watched well intentioned volunteers from outside Texas spend their whole VISTA stint trying to learn the barrio culture while, at the same time, people in those neighborhoods searched desperately for employment." To avoid this paradox, Urriegas and Barrientos proposed recruiting local residents into VISTA, giving them a short course in VISTA procedures, and then putting them to work doing community organizing in the barrios. With support from Texas state senator Joe Bernal, Urriegas and Barrientos launched the MMP, enrolling more than seventy volunteers in 1968. Jeff Stromer, a VISTA volunteer from New York, explained that MMP participants "have a great awareness of poverty and can work more easily with the people" than Anglos could. VISTA soon switched to hiring local people instead of bringing in outsiders in many other minority communities.[28]

San Antonio MMP volunteers abandoned the VISTA playbook to turn to militant tactics that quickly got them in trouble. In fall of 1968, they organized a student walkout at the Edcouch-Elsa Independent School District in Hidalgo

County, reminiscent of Sal Castro's Los Angeles "Blowouts" earlier that year. Urged by the MMPs and MAYO organizers, student protesters demanded that the district add Spanish-language instruction and Chicano culture and history to the curriculum. Students also sued the district for fifty thousand dollars in miscellaneous damages. Administrators expelled the walkout's organizers, while federal judge Reynaldo Garza, a Kennedy appointee and another Johnson ally, rejected the students' suit. Garza called the walkout concept "ridiculous" but ordered the district to readmit the expelled students. Students reported that VISTA volunteers had offered to finance the school strike and to provide attorneys through OEO's Legal Services program.[29]

In San Antonio, the SANYO Federation of Neighborhood Councils sponsored a thirty-person project using MMP and regular VISTA volunteers. The MMP volunteers placed greater emphasis on teaching barrio children about Mexican art and culture and spent more time in the neighborhoods, informing residents about the availability of resources or trying to get them involved in community activities. The MMP generated controversy in San Antonio when the volunteers became "deeply involved in organizing neighborhood residents to win decision-making power in agencies that directly affected them." MMP volunteers, for example, mobilized residents to oppose a proposed amendment to the Texas Constitution that would have capped individual welfare assistance.[30]

The MMP drew vociferous opposition when Congressman Gonzalez accused the volunteers of distributing "hate gringo" literature in the barrios. One Gonzalez aide recalled the MMP as "a special headache because lots of kids who later became Hispanic radicals in the late 60s were involved in those programs." The congressman sought to close the program because these "radicals" were using VISTA to expand MAYO's influence. Gonzalez argued that MAYO leaders were "really advocating violence" because of occasional statements by leaders calling on Chicanos to "eliminate the gringo." The congressman also voiced a Cold War concern that "Cuban-trained revolutionaries" had infiltrated the Chicano movement, leading to a "fierce hassle" that ended in the dismissal of two MMP volunteers.[31]

In 1969, newly elected governor Preston Smith, a conservative Democrat who had served as Connally's lieutenant governor since 1962, closed down the MMP in Val Verde County at the request of county commissioners, who blamed the volunteers for instigating a rally protesting police brutality and for "fomenting racial tension." The governor went further, ordering the VISTA volunteers to leave Val Verde County and mobilizing state troopers with machine guns to silence the protests. The Del Rio community action agency and the OEO regional office objected to Smith's actions, calling the use of force heavy-handed. Despite these objections, the governor closed the VISTA program, opining, "The abdication of respect for law and order, disruption of democratic processes, and provocation of disunity among our citizens will not be tolerated."[32]

Smith's actions emboldened Chicano activists. More than two thousand young militants from all over the Southwest descended on Del Rio in hopes of instigating a "Chicano Selma" to reveal Anglo racism to the rest of the country. The protest inspired the Del Rio Manifesto, a statement of principles that expressed the values of the Chicano movement and defended VISTA in specific terms. The manifesto accused county commissioners and the governor of shutting down the program because "nervous power-wielders [saw] the growing assertiveness of the poor served by VISTA Mexican-Americans as a threat to their traditional supremacy." The manifesto argued that "arbitrary termination by local and state officials" offended the "VISTA principle of self-determination." The manifesto called for legislation to protect the MMP because "unless the ideal of self-determination is upheld with our poor at home, the entire world will judge us as hypocritical in our attempt to assist the poor abroad." And, as leaders of poor people's movements in many American cities were doing that year, the Texas activists warned the governor and the county commissioners that they invited "serious social unrest if they do not immediately rescind their VISTA cancellation."[33]

The Del Rio Manifesto went on to express the "magnificence of La Raza [as a] spiritual and biological miracle" and to confirm the centrality of the Spanish language to the survival of Chicano culture. The document also condemned the entire "Anglo-controlled establishment" for waging a war of cultural genocide on the Chicano people: "There must be something invincible in our people that has kept alive our humanity in spite of a system bent on suppressing our difference and rewarding our conformity. . . . In a color mad society, the sin of our coloration can be expiated only by exceptional achievement and successful imitation of the white man who controls every institution of society. La Raza condemns such a system as racist, pagan, and ultimately self destructive. We can neither tolerate it nor be part of it." After reading the manifesto aloud, Gutiérrez imitated Martin Luther and nailed the document to the courthouse door. Despite the protests, no Chicano Selma occurred, and the OEO never reestablished the Val Verde County MMP.[34]

The alarmism with which Gonzalez and Smith responded to Chicano rhetoric helps illustrate why the War on Poverty became so controversial. In reality, the Chicano militants were educated, articulate, and understandably angry about the conditions in which their people lived. It was common in 1968 for young people to predict violence or talk about revolution. The endemic urban violence of the late 1960s led people in authority, including Gonzalez and Smith, to conclude that the radicals intended to make the rhetoric a reality. The involvement of militants, even in minor programs such as the MMP, fueled opposition to the OEO even among liberals who supported the War on Poverty as politicians overreacted to perceived threats to law and order. Militants, radicals, and other "troublemakers" who worked in OEO programs also provided easy targets for those who would dismantle the War on Poverty after LBJ left office. Yet the War on Poverty continued in Texas, demonstrating with measurable successes key flaws in the approaches of both the OEO and the Chicano militants.

A POLITICS THAT BEGINS WITH COMMUNITIES: FIGHTING POVERTY IN SAN ANTONIO SINCE 1970

The federal government's long retreat from the War on Poverty did not stop the fight in Texas. Several local programs continued for decades after the OEO departed the scene. SANYO, for example, continued operations in San Antonio until 1994, funded mostly by the U.S. Department of Labor. Julian Rodriguez, who assumed control of the organization in 1970, kept the program alive by deemphasizing its political role and focusing on education and recreation programs for children. The Federation of Neighborhood Councils faded away in the mid-1970s, but SANYO secured nearly one hundred million dollars in federal funds from various public and private sources in the two decades after the OEO ceased to exist. Project BRAVO, a similar community-based agency funded during the War on Poverty era, continues to operate in El Paso today. Like SANYO, BRAVO avoided political confrontations to focus on providing services to the poor: repairing housing, delivering health care, employment assistance, and adult education. BRAVO eliminated funding for the more confrontational MACHOS when the Nixon administration slashed the OEO budget in 1973.[35]

New, independent, grassroots organizations also emerged in the 1970s to continue the poverty fight. Most significantly, the Industrial Areas Foundation (IAF), a nationwide network of antipoverty groups founded in 1940 by Saul

Alinsky, picked up where the Community Action Program left off. The IAF's "iron rule" that organizers must "never do anything for anybody that they can do for themselves" indicates that the agency had pioneered the idea of maximum feasible participation long before the OEO. IAF affiliates remain active in Mexican American communities across Texas, including San Antonio's Communities Organized for Public Service (COPS), the El Paso Interreligious Sponsoring Organization, Valley Interfaith, and Border Interfaith.

The IAF exposes major flaws in the model of federally administered antipoverty programs but also exemplifies programs that had real staying power. The IAF made abundant use of federal funds. In its first ten years of operation, COPS received some eighty-six million dollars in Community Development Block Grants from the U.S. Department of Housing and Urban Development. But the IAF remained independent of the federal bureaucracy and the local political pressures it faced. Using churches as organizational foundations strengthened antipoverty efforts and credibility in the Mexican American community. Churches were, in the words of COPS founder Ernesto Cortés, "the only institutions in society that are fundamentally concerned with the nature and well-being of families and communities."[36] Furthermore, tax-eating governmental bureaucracies proved soft targets for opponents, but attacking church groups for helping the poor requires conservative (and ostensibly Christian) opponents to devise more complex rationalizations.

COPS also focused on specific goals, in contrast to the OEO's promise of quickly resolving a problem as complex as American poverty. Cortés's organizers urged low-income people to identify and organize around their problems. One of COPS's big early victories, for example, was drainage improvement in San Antonio's West Side barrios, a serious and long-standing problem that brought flooding and unsafe conditions for West Side residents after every rainstorm. Focusing efforts on specific issues one at a time rather than advancing a broad agenda helps to maintain agreement. Just as important, IAF organizers built alliances across class lines. Cortés's tactics emphasized building personal relationships among individuals—what Alinsky called "social capital." For example, the IAF opened several job training programs in the Rio Grande Valley in the late 1970s. Rather than beginning with the workers in the mode of OEO programs such as the Job Corps, the IAF established relationships with potential employers. Organizers asked what skills employers needed, then secured an agreement from those employers to hire people who learned those skills in IAF jobs programs.[37]

Soliciting input from companies on job training and city officials on infra-structure concerns humanized individuals who had been demonized as face-less, heartless, racist businessmen or bureaucrats. IAF groups turned to political confrontation only when local or state officials refused to listen or ignored re-quests. The IAF's voter registration efforts motivated politicians and city offi-cials to deal with the organization. The IAF model works. In 1981, thanks to COPS, the predominantly Mexican American wards of South and West San An-tonio voted in larger numbers than the Anglo north side of town for the first time. By 1993, COPS alone had secured an estimated $750 million in funds for San Antonio's low-income communities.[38]

The IAF's success also exposes key weaknesses in the Chicano movement's approach. Most of the IAF volunteers in Texas were Mexican American, but the organization avoided the use of race or culture as organizing principles. Al-though the IAF did not deny or reject Mexican heritage, affiliates focused on building an understanding of common interests beyond race to involve as many people as possible. Racial nationalism hindered the solidarity of the poor or the working class as a whole and blinded people from different backgrounds to their common interests, Cortés believed: "There is much misplaced anger, resentment and fear among working people," he argued. "Elected officials and candidates for public office exploit these misplaced sentiments."[39]

Racism and discrimination created the chronic poverty of the barrios, but defining poverty as primarily a racial problem turned the War on Poverty into a competition among racial nationalist groups. The IAF avoided race politics be-cause it obstructs coalition building and often alienates whites who might oth-erwise be sympathetic. "When somebody is willing to deal with you," Cortés advised, "for you to be confrontational, you're just being a bully. We're teaching people politics. Politics means negotiation and being reciprocal and thinking about the other person."[40]

The IAF also recognized the need to include women in leadership roles and women's issues on its agenda more readily than either the Chicano movement or the OEO. Former Chicano and Chicana activists disagree on the extent to which Chicanas were involved in shaping the movement. MAYO's Gutiérrez and Compean recalled Chicanas playing direct roles in organizing chapters and set-ting the agenda for the group. Compean remembered that "large numbers of women were involved, especially at the local level, in MAYO's activities. There was no formal definition of roles."[41]

Chicanas involved with MAYO agree with Compean but also note that women served primarily in support roles while men led and served as spokespersons for the organization. Women did clerical work and other supporting activities because, according to MAYO activist Choco Meza, "males generally see themselves as ones who can out-strategize and out-think females"; men believed that they could "gain respect for their ideas better than females." According to Luz Gutiérrez, the Chicanas in MAYO tolerated the patriarchy and machismo of the organization's male leaders because "we didn't want the feminist issue to divide us."[42]

Yet as the movement evolved, Chicanas challenged the patriarchal structure of organizations such as MAYO and refused to be constrained by traditional gender roles. Chicanas forced the inclusion of women in leadership roles and women's issues on the agenda and forged independent organizations. Unlike their male counterparts, Chicanas confronted oppression from three sources: as nonwhite females in a male-dominated political system, as part of an ethnic culture infused with the values of machismo, and as poor people. These circumstances led to the development of a Chicana feminism that altered the trajectory of the Latino civil rights movement in the 1970s.[43]

While Chicanas muscled their way into the movement, the OEO included almost no women in leadership roles and seemed unwilling to recognize lower-income women as a significant constituency for the agency's services. No women worked in management positions in the OEO's Southwest Regional Office in Austin or in any of the major Community Action Program agencies in Texas cities. The OEO seemed to assume that if it helped men escape poverty, they would take responsibility for women and pull them along, ignoring obvious issues such as single motherhood and the fact that women were often the primary breadwinners in lower-income families. When Shriver commissioned an ad campaign to recruit people into the Job Corps in 1966, he had to be reminded to recruit women to avoid violating the Civil Rights Act. Christopher Niebuhr of the OEO's Office of Inspection explained to the director, "maximum feasible participation should not be exclusive, I believe, of any significant group within a community. Women constitute a significant group in most communities."[44]

In contrast to both the Chicano movement and the OEO, the IAF included women in positions of responsibility from the beginning. After Cortés organized COPS in 1974, for example, all but one of the group's presidents have been women. Beatrice Cortéz, who held the office in the early 1980s, explained that "women have community ties. We knew that to make things happen in a community, you have to talk to people. It was a matter of tapping our networks." Rodolfo Rosales has traced the rising influence of Chicana activists in San Antonio in the late twentieth century, finding that women changed the nature of politics in that city because they remained focused on the needs of the community. Men seemed more focused on their personal ambitions for "position and power," creating a "political environment that has historically been able to co-opt those who successfully challenge the system's exclusionary politics." Women activists, Rosales suggests, forged "a politics that begins with community and remains connected to that community's issues, sometimes at the expense of electoral or otherwise personal achievements."[45]

Now in its fourth decade in Texas, the IAF also shows that the battle for economic justice requires patience. Within three years of launching the War on Poverty, the Johnson administration began scaling back the OEO. Within a decade, the agency was gone. The Chicano movement also faded by the mid-1970s as leaders aged and moved into political or academic careers.[46] In contrast, Cortés spent three years in Chicago learning how to organize before he started in his native San Antonio. Another three years passed before COPS made significant headway. A decade or more passed before Valley Interfaith or the El Paso Interreligious Sponsoring Organization made any impact.

Although the federal government dismantled the OEO and the Chicano movement faded away, both contributed to a transformation of the political culture of Texas that remains under way. The OEO left behind a reputation for failure and controversy that helped fuel the Republican ascendancy in the state. Only now have historians begun to uncover the success stories of LBJ's War on Poverty in Texas, but even the most liberal Democratic politicians in the state remain gun-shy about supporting antipoverty programs. Indeed, the idea that government has a responsibility to fight poverty faded as a focal point of liberalism in Texas after the Johnson era, as it did through the rest of the nation. The Chicano movement also transformed the liberal agenda in Texas. While only a minority of the state's Mexican Americans ever embraced Chicanismo, the cultural pride the movement introduced reshaped not only the barrios but also public school and college curricula across the state. Further, liberals accepted the basic premise of the Chicano critique of liberalism itself—the implicit cultural insult of the ideal of integration. In response to the militants, liberals changed their focus from equality and integration to inclusion and diversity. Mexican Americans and African Americans now form the core of Texas's Democratic Party, but the party has struggled to remain relevant in the face of Republican dominance of the state. The fight against poverty seems to have been removed from the agenda.

Notes

1. Juliet Pycior, *LBJ and Mexican Americans: The Paradox of Power* (Austin: University of Texas Press, 1997), 25–26; Gladys Gregory and Sheldon B. Liss, "Chamizal Dispute," *Handbook of Texas Online*, www.tsha.utexas.edu/handbook/online/articles/CC/nbc1.html.

2. Pycior, *LBJ and Mexican Americans*, 202–4, 206–14.

3. José Angel Gutiérrez, *The Making of a Chicano Militant: Lessons from Cristal* (Madison: University of Wisconsin Press, 1998), 110–11.

4. Gutiérrez, *Making*, 111.

5. Mario T. García, *Mexican Americans: Leadership, Ideology, and Identity* (New Haven: Yale University Press, 1989), 21.

6. David Montejano, *Anglos and Mexicans in the Making of Texas, 1836–1986* (Austin: University of Texas Press, 1987), 262.

7. Ignacio M. García, *Chicanismo: The Forming of a Militant Ethos among Mexican Americans* (Tucson: University of Arizona Press, 1997), 24, 26.

8. Ibid., 151; James Reston, *The Lone Star: The Life of John Connally* (New York: Harper and Row, 1989), 304.

9. "Laber Peña of PASSO Attacks Connally for Declaring War on the War on Poverty," *Houston Chronicle*, July 11, 1965.

10. Reston, *Lone Star*, 10; Pycior, *LBJ and Mexican Americans*, 176.

11. Carlos Muñoz, *Youth, Identity, Power: The Chicano Movement* (New York: Verso, 1989), 58; Ignacio García, *Chicanismo*.

12. Teresa Palma Acosta, "Raza Unida Party," *Handbook of Texas Online*, http: www.tsha.utexas.edu/online/articles/RR/war1.html.

13. José Angel Gutiérrez, telephone interview by author, September 5, 2000.

14. Irma Mireles, telephone interview by author, September 5, 2000; Rodolfo Rosales, *The Illusion of Inclusion: The Untold Political Story of San Antonio* (Austin: University of Texas Press, 2000), 94, 99.

15. William Stephen Clayson, "Texas Poverty and Liberal Politics: The Office of Economic Opportunity and the War on Poverty in the Lone Star State" (Ph.D. diss., Texas Tech University, 2001), 193; Benjamin Marquez, *Power and Politics in a Chicano Barrio* (Lanham, Md.: University Press of America, 1985), 98–99, 116, 136–39; Tom Sinclair to Frank Curtis, September 19, 1968, Frank Curtis to Hannah King, "Thoughts on El Paso," December 18, 1968, both in El Paso File, Records of the Community Services Adminis-

tration, Office of Economic Opportunity, City Economic Opportunity Boards Files, RG 381, National Archives, Southwest Region, Fort Worth, Texas.

16. Gutiérrez, interview; Gutiérrez, *Making*, 104.

17. Ignacio M. García, *United We Win: The Rise and Fall of La Raza Unida Party* (Tucson: University of Arizona Press, 1989), 22; Pycior, *LBJ and Mexican Americans*, 216.

18. Armando Rendon, *Chicano Manifesto* (New York: Macmillan, 1971), 87–88.

19. Bill Crook to Samuel Yette, April 6, 1966, Bill Crook to Sargent Shriver, April 15, 1966, both in Region V File, Records of the Community Services Administration, Office of Economic Opportunity, Records, Office of Civil Rights, Records Relating to Civil Rights in the Regions, RG 381, National Archives II, College Park, Maryland (hereafter RG 381).

20. W. Astor Kirk to Bill Crook, April 5, 1966, Fred Baldwin to Bill Crook, April 5, 1966, both in ibid.

21. Dominga Coronado to Bill Crook, December 20, 1965, Mike Garza to John Connally, April 7, 1966, Bill Crook to Sam Yette, April 19, 1966, all in "Special Greg File," RG 381

22. Dominga Coronado to John Connally, April 12, 1966, John Connally Papers, Series 38, Box 25, Lyndon Baines Johnson Presidential Library, Austin, Texas; Walter Richter to Dominga Coronado, April 15, 1965, "Special Greg File," RG 381.

23. "The Community Action Board in Lubbock," April 29, 1966, Box 30, "Special Greg File," RG 381.

24. Bill Crook to Sam Yette, April 19, 1966, Sam Yette to Sargent Shriver, May 6, 1966, both in "Special Greg File," RG 381; U.S. House of Representatives, Committee on Education and Labor, *Ad Hoc Hearing: Task Force on Poverty* (Washington, D.C.: U.S. Government Printing Office, 1969), 2042. Shriver wrote his message on Crook's memo and rerouted it to Yette.

25. Gutiérrez, *Making*, 112.

26. Ibid., 104, 84, 121; Gutiérrez, interview; Ignacio García, *United We Win*, 27; William S. Clayson, "The Barrios and Ghettos Have Organized: Community Action, Political Acrimony, and the War on Poverty in San Antonio," *Journal of Urban History* 28:2 (January 2002): 173.

27. Rosales, *Illusion of Inclusion*, 99; Arnoldo DeLeón, *Ethnicity in the Sunbelt: A History of Mexican Americans in Houston* (Houston: University of Houston Press, 1989), 181–82.

28. Pycior, *LBJ and Mexican Americans*, 216; Joe Bernal to Walter Richter, April 23, 1968, Joe Bernal Papers, Benson Latin American History Collection, Austin, Texas; Melodie Bowsher, "VISTA in Turmoil," *Wall Street Journal*, November 5, 1969.

29. "Judge Orders Students Readmitted," *Harlingen Valley Morning Star*, November 26, 1969.

30. Bowsher, "VISTA in Turmoil."

31. Ibid.; Pycior, *LBJ and Mexican Americans*, 217; Terry Anderson, *The Movement and the Sixties* (New York: Oxford University Press, 1995), 310.

32. Rodolfo Acuña, *Occupied America: A History of Chicanos*, 3rd ed. (New York: HarperCollins, 1988), 339; Pycior, *LBJ and Mexican Americans*, 238; Ignacio García, *United We Win*, 27; Rendon, *Chicano Manifesto*, 332.

33. Anderson, *Movement*, 308; Rendon, *Chicano Manifesto*, 332, 336.

34. Rendon, *Chicano Manifesto*, 334–35; Texas, Office of Economic Opportunity, *The Texas Front in the Nation's War on Poverty* (Austin: Texas Office of Economic Opportunity, 1969).

35. Veronica Flores, "Agency's Program Opened Doors for Many Members," *San Antonio Express-News*, October 9, 1994; www.projectbravo.org; Marquez, *Power and Politics*, 32.

36. Ernesto Cortés, *Justice at the Gates of the City: A Model for Shared Prosperity* (Dallas: Dallas Area Interfaith, n.d.), http://www.dallasareainterfaith.org/justice.htm.

37. Robert Putnam and Lewis Feldstein, *Better Together: Restoring the American Community* (New York: Simon and Schuster, 2003), 13, 14, 19; Benjamin Marquez, "Organizing the Mexican-American Community in Texas: The Legacy of Saul Alinsky," *Policy Studies Review* 9:2 (Winter 1990): 355–73.

38. William Clayson, *Freedom Is Not Enough: The War on Poverty and the Civil Rights Movement in Texas* (Austin: University of Texas Press, 2010), 153; Pearl Caesar, *Communities Organized for Public Service (COPS)*, http://www.grass-roots.org/usa/cops .shtml; William Greider, *Who Will Tell the People?: The Betrayal of American Democracy* (New York: Simon and Schuster, 1992), 229.

39. Cortés, *Justice*.

40. Clayson, *Freedom Is Not Enough*, 152; Greider, *Who Will Tell*, 229.

41. Armando Navarro, *Mexican-American Youth Organization: Avant-Garde of the Chicano Movement in Texas* (Austin: University of Texas Press, 1998), 110.

42. Ibid., 111.

43. Ignacio García, *Chicanismo*, 136; Robert Bauman, *Race and the War on Poverty: From Watts to East L.A.* (Norman: University of Oklahoma Press, 2008), 111; Rosales, *Illusion of Inclusion*, 161.

44. James H. Quillen to Sargent Shriver, April 5, 1966, Records of the Community Services Administration, Office of Economic Opportunity, Records of the Office of Civil Rights, Director's Records, Alphabetical Files, 1966–69, RG 381, National Archives II, College Park, Maryland.

45. Vicki Ruíz, "Communities Organized for Public Service," in *Latinas in the United States*, ed. Vicki Ruíz and Virginia Sánchez Korrol (Bloomington: Indiana University Press, 2006), 170; Rosales, *Illusion of Inclusion*, 160.

46. Gutiérrez, *Making*, 290; Ignacio García, *Chicanismo*, 143–44.

PART FOUR

What Do They Really Mean by Community Development?

THOMAS KIFFMEYER

Looking Back to the City in the Hills

The Council of the Southern Mountains and a Longer View of the War on Poverty in the Appalachian South, 1913–1970

Though usually associated with racial minorities in decaying urban centers, the War on Poverty rhetorically and symbolically began with Appalachia. Shortly after he declared "unconditional war on poverty" in his January 8, 1964, State of the Union address, President Lyndon Baines Johnson announced that he would "launch a special effort in the chronically distressed areas of Appalachia." On April 24, the president visited Martin County, Kentucky, located in the heart of the Appalachian coalfields, with the express intention of putting a "white face" on his nascent reform program. Coming on the heels of nearly a decade of varying degrees of racial unrest precipitated by the civil rights movement, this "white face" helped sell his agenda to the American public.[1]

Perhaps unintentionally, Johnson's visit linked his reform efforts with a much longer history of Appalachian reform that dated to the late nineteenth century. This essay takes that longer view, tracing the history of the Council of the Southern Mountains (CSM), an Appalachian aid society founded in 1913 that channeled much of the War on Poverty money that came into rural Kentucky. It also argues that looking at Appalachia creates a different interpretation of the War on Poverty from those that focus on cities. Poor mountain whites failed to harness—or, more properly, rejected—the possibilities presented by what they labeled "other people's programs, instead channeling public and private monies into programs of their own." This essay attempts to make sense of that history and to fit it into our understanding of the War on Poverty.

In 1964, focusing on those white southerners who left Appalachia for northern cities following World War II, Cleveland, Ohio, resident Adelbert Bodnar informed the CSM, headquartered at Kentucky's Berea College, that his city had "trouble . . . with 'Sam' [an acronym for *southern Appalachian migrant*] in the area of behavior." While the adults were responsible for drunken brawls, robbery, burglary, vandalism, and gang fights, "Sam's" children used the foulest language. No wonder, Bodnar wrote, that decent people called these migrants "poor white trash." They also threatened the economic security of established residents. Since the 1930s, industry had increasingly relocated to the Piedmont South, lured by right-to-work laws and tax breaks; in contrast, Appalachian residents, jobless in large part as a consequence of the mechanization of the coal industry, moved north in hopes of gaining industrial employment. This migration, which began during the Great Depression and rapidly increased during and immediately after World War II, brought thousands of mountaineers to America's industrial centers: Cleveland and other cities now faced "hordes of hillbillies [who came] up here to take away what jobs [were] left." Bodnar ordered the CSM to "keep them back in the hills where they belong" and teach them respect for order and property.[2]

That a Cleveland resident would know about, let alone contact, the CSM is not surprising. The CSM had long advocated reform in Appalachia. Comprised mostly of fairly conservative members of the Congregationalist and Presbyterian churches, the council was a loose confederation of individuals bent on remedying the region's problems through a cooperative approach that allowed virtually anyone—from outside industrialists to local church leaders—a seat at the table.

Perley Ayer, who became the CSM's executive director in 1951, reflected this consensual approach to social reform through his "call to partnership." While Ayer recognized the destructive capabilities of extractive industry, he sought ways to include "*all segments* of society; public *and* private, dominant *and* dependent; . . . affluent . . . as well as poor" in his consensus-building reform programs. By embracing everyone, Ayer believed that he could create a sense of ownership among all parties in the CSM's reform efforts and that beneficial change would then result. As Ayer took his message across the country in the 1950s and 1960s, the CSM became well known and more open to all Americans.[3]

In 1983, nearly twenty years after the council received Bodnar's letter, a CSM member explained why the organization finally rejected Ayer's cooperative ap-

Figure 5. By the early 1970s, the CSM leadership reflected the region's racial, gender, and generational diversity. Included in this photo are Mike Smathers (second from left); Ben Poage (third from left); Judy McKinney, who became the CSM's first woman president in 1977 (fourth from left); and Almetor King (far right), who became president in 1980. Council of the Southern Mountains Records, 1970–1989; Southern Appalachian Archives, Berea College.

proach in 1969 and underwent a profound transformation. During the 1960s, the CSM received millions in federal funds, much of it through the Office of Economic Opportunity (OEO). During that time, the CSM resembled a traditional "top-down" charitable association. Near the end of the official War on Poverty, however, many of the CSM's more politically motivated members (some of them middle-aged) rejected the War on Poverty and the cooperative council "because of its role in the sixties as facilitator of other people's programs . . . especially the government's antipoverty programs." Equally important, these militant CSM staff cast off the "outside young activists" who came along with those government programs and shifted control to "real mountain community leaders." From that point forward, the CSM relied on Appalachian residents rather than outside volunteers. The group reorganized into various semiautonomous "commissions," among them the Black Appalachian Commission, the Poor People's Self-Help Commission, and the Youth Commission. Operating out of Clintwood, Virginia, the CSM adopted a highly politicized agenda that severely restricted its base of support so that it never again enjoyed the status it had attained during the War on Poverty. Nevertheless, functioning as a loosely organized coalition of diverse interests, the CSM focused on environmental concerns such as strip mining and on occupational hazards faced by local people, including black lung disease. Ironically, CSM was more successful at mobilizing Appalachian activism after it lost federal money and widespread support. Finally, in 1989, after working for change in the Appalachian South for seventy-six years, the CSM officially disbanded.[4]

Bodnar's 1964 letter and the unofficial history of the CSM written two decades later highlight the complex, often confusing and hostile relationship between the United States and one of its most persistently impoverished regions, the central Appalachians. Bodnar's letter illustrates the popular conception that mountain people were violent, uncouth hillbillies. It also highlights the remedy to their condition accepted by the vast majority of mountain reformers, including many involved in the War on Poverty—the instillation of urban, middle-class values. The unofficial council history written by the militants who later drove the activism of CSM saw Bodnar and many antipoverty activists who invaded the region during the 1960s as the problem—just one more wave of outsiders attempting to transform Appalachian residents (and Appalachia) into something more akin to urban America. As early as 1921, John C. Campbell, the founder of the CSM (then known as the Southern Mountain Workers Conference) recognized that "the Southern Highlander . . . does not relish the idea of being uplifted or missionary-ized."[5] War on Poverty activists as well as their predecessors failed to heed Campbell's warning, a failure that illustrates the difficulties with transforming people from the top down.

Nevertheless, despite the negative reaction of many southern mountain residents to the volunteers who descended on their region in the 1960s, the War on Poverty reinvigorated grassroots Appalachian people associated with the CSM. "In the year in which OEO dies," exclaimed one member at the CSM's 1970 conference, "we try maximum feasible participation of [the] poor. In the year [of] alienation and separation, we attempt a broad-based coalition. The only thing we have in common—with all but the Department of Defense—no money. . . . *Point is that what we do here is move against that mainstream of American life into which OEO . . . tried for years to make Appalachia's poor move.*" But why did these different trajectories arise? This question is especially pertinent since

Figure 6. Appalachians gather to organize in the wake of a February 1972 Buffalo Creek slurry pond failure in Logan County, West Virginia. Owned by Pittston Coal, the burst pond sent approximately 132 million gallons of waste from Pittston's surface mining operation into the valley below. The resulting flood killed 125 people and rendered over 4,000 homeless. Because compliant federal mine inspectors recently had found the dam "satisfactory," Pittston declared the disaster an "act of God." Council of the Southern Mountains Records, 1970–1989; Southern Appalachian Archives, Berea College.

racial minorities and southern mountain whites were equally motivated by the War on Poverty and sought the same objective—control over their own lives.[6]

Perhaps mountaineers remained so hostile to efforts, both public and private, to improve their lives because so many of these attempts were rooted in the idea of a "culture of poverty." While this term was not used until the mid–twentieth century, the implications of this label were present in the literature and language of much earlier Appalachian reformers. Using labels such as "contemporary ancestors" and "a strange land and peculiar people," William Goodell Frost, president of Berea College at the turn of the twentieth century, identified a "unique" and intractable mountain culture. Long before the idea of a culture of poverty was used in the 1950s and 1960s to explain persistent poverty among

Puerto Ricans, Mexicans, and African Americans, reformers described Appalachian peoples as perpetuating their impoverishment by clinging to outmoded customs, values, and traditions.

Because the people of the mountains still lived in log cabins, spoke the language of Chaucer, dressed in "sorry clothing," and exhibited an "awkward demeanor," Frost wrote in 1899, Appalachia had become a land of primitive people, a place "in" but not "of" America. Appalachia inherited the label of Otherness, which for reformers meant poverty. The sense of Otherness about this region seemed especially true when Appalachia was viewed in light of the economic and technical achievements of the late nineteenth and early twentieth centuries. Mountaineer lifestyles, according to this explanation, more closely resembled those of generations past, typified by sparsely settled communities, subsistence farming, a Calvinistic sense of fatalism, and, most important, a value system that was incongruent with modern, urban standards. Such views precipitated a century of reform efforts in the southern mountains.[7]

While Frost spoke of "Elizabethan" mountaineers, women reformers, in the form of teachers, established settlement schools in the southern mountains. Programs designed to bring progressive education, community development, and better living to Appalachia attracted reformers "fascinated by the remnants of the past found in the highland culture." Still, outsiders who remained in the mountains for more than a few years were continually dismayed by residents' lack of modern knowledge and of community spirit. These traits, they believed, most significantly hindered their reform efforts in the mountains.[8]

That this attitude continued through the twentieth century is evidenced in New Deal programs including the Resettlement Administration and the Tennessee Valley Authority. Created with the goal of addressing the same issues that the Progressives had identified—that is, a dispersed and atomized population that lacked any "modern knowledge" and "community spirit"—these programs attempted to bring rational living and the machine age to the hills through the creation of planned communities and the introduction of flood control and hydroelectric power.[9]

The poverty warriors of the early 1960s continued the unquestioned assumption that the values and lifestyles of the dominant culture were inherently superior to those of the mountains. Jack Weller's *Yesterday's People*, published in 1963, served as a "training manual" for reformers who entered Appalachia during the first few years of the War on Poverty.[10]

These reformers did not know, however, that the region had already begun to modernize, albeit in ways that escaped outside notice, perhaps because the reformers themselves were part of that modernization process. As Ronald Eller illustrates, by the mid-1910s, Appalachia was "a new frontier for expanding industrial capitalism" that left few highlanders unaffected. The consequences of these "improvements" included the concentration of land in the hands of absentee owners (mostly coal and timber companies), a decline in farm production, and perhaps most significant, a shift in political power into the hands of an emerging "urban" (county seat or company town) elite that operated at the behest of those same corporations. In the end, Eller contends, mountaineers were more dependent and more isolated after industry came to Appalachia than before. For the most part, mountaineers did their best to resist these changes and the accompanying social and cultural alterations. While engaged in "public work" (work performed away from the family farm) during the off-season, they attempted to return to their homesteads for planting season. Because Appalachian residents fought attempts to impose on them the "habits of industry," corporate America saw them at best as old fogies who retarded progress and prosperity. At worst, because they would leave their wage-labor jobs whenever they wanted, mountaineers were seen as stereotypical lazy hillbillies. This image reinforced the culture-of-poverty model. Ironically, reformers offered to combat this "fogeyism" by industrializing Appalachia. As residents saw it, this proposed solution to the problems of industrialization was more industrialization.[11]

During the late 1940s and in particular the 1950s, the nation underwent an ideological shift in the culturally dominant views of both city dwellers and residents of the southern mountains. As practitioners of the normative lifestyle in the United States, urban dwellers—including many social theorists and other academics—saw in their home environment those basic interrelated elements essential to progress, order, and affluence. They described cities as settings conducive to cultural and economic growth and as providing a forum for identifying, analyzing, and overcoming obstacles to growth. With their immediate access to markets, educational and cultural facilities, and political institutions, cities provided the environment in which citizens organized, exercised democracy, and lobbied for those goods and services that they determined were necessary. Because they faced a coherent, cogent group, businessmen and politicians responded favorably to demands made by city dwellers. In short, cities made possible pluralism, the process by which interest groups expressed themselves, influenced the distribution of goods and services, and "achieve[d] their various rights." This vision of urban centers as the cradles for robust democracy contrasted sharply with reformers' views of "isolated mountaineers." This ideological shift in American beliefs about the relative health of urban and rural living would have dire consequences for rural antipoverty activists.[12]

In a second ideological change, Americans altered the concept of the culture of poverty articulated by noted anthropologist Oscar Lewis in the 1950s and 1960s. According to Lewis, the culture of poverty amounted to a rational response to the devastating social and economic conditions faced by those who ultimately adopted that culture. In this way, Lewis's model was as much an indictment of the circumstances that surrounded the culture of poverty as a critique of the culture itself. By the 1960s, however, the culture of poverty came to be seen as pathological, a disease in an otherwise healthy country. In this way, Americans could attack the behavior of the poor without calling into question the socioeconomic conditions that created it. This conceptualization of a pathological culture of poverty protected the status quo because it blamed the poor for their condition. Antipoverty warriors' notion of a pathological culture of poverty and belief that urban centers gave rise to democratic pluralism significantly hindered their efforts in the mountains.[13]

President Johnson's Great Society, of which the War on Poverty was a part, reaffirmed these changes. Contrary to the New Deal, which addressed quantitative issues such as jobs and income, Johnson hoped that the Great Society would improve Americans' quality of life by developing educational, cultural, and social opportunities. Speaking at the University of Michigan in May 1964, Johnson declared that "the city of man serves not only the needs of the body and the demands of commerce, but the desire for beauty and hunger for community." A few years later, he asserted that "in the midst of abundance modern man walks oppressed by forces which menace and confine the quality of his life, and which individual abundance alone will not overcome." To satisfy these concerns, Johnson shepherded through Congress an impressive array of programs—among them the Elementary and Secondary Education Act, Medicare and Medicaid, and the Civil Rights Act of 1964—designed to create a "flourishing community where our people can come to live the good life." This focus on quality, coupled with the move toward "participatory democracy" included in the Economic Opportunity Act, made the War on Poverty less useful in addressing the realities of the southern Appalachians than the New Deal had been. In this region, the issues were more quantitative than qualitative, at least in the eyes of many residents. As reformers entered the region in early 1964, they failed to recognize this critical distinction. In the end, this failure further complicated their chances for successful reform.[14]

Johnson's initial proclamation of a war on poverty nevertheless set off a flurry of activity in Appalachia. Because the Kennedy administration had begun addressing Appalachian poverty, Tom Gish, editor of the *Whitesburg (Kentucky) Mountain Eagle*, facetiously complained that most Americans figured that by the summer of 1964, the problems were already solved: The "great national emphasis and interest in eastern Kentucky, the Appalachians, depressed areas and pockets of poverty largely is a thing of the past. . . . The average citizen in the United States, if he thinks about Appalachia at all this summer, thinks that the problems are being handled—that there is no reason for him to be particularly concerned."[15]

Gish, however, knew that Americans needed to be very concerned. Despite the growth precipitated by World War II, the southern mountains remained full of "depressed areas and pockets of poverty" in the 1950s. A University of Kentucky sociologist, Thomas R. Ford, led a team of researchers into the region in an attempt to understand and explain its problems, publishing his results in *The Southern Appalachian Region: A Survey* (1962). Demographers James S. Brown and George A. Hillery Jr., for example, found that the Appalachian counties of Kentucky had lost 250,000 people in the 1940s, while the state of West Virginia experienced a population decline of 400,000. During the 1950s, these regions respectively lost another 35 percent and 25 percent of their populations. These migrants settled in places like Bodnar's Cleveland.[16]

Technological innovation, legal doctrine, and labor politics had led to this migration. Postwar labor-saving devices such as conveyor belts and automatic coal cutters and loaders spelled the end of the hand (shovel) loading method, while the introduction of oversized bulldozers a few years later enabled strip mining (now called "mountaintop removal"). Compounding the unemployment problem created by these new practices, state courts enforced "broad form deeds" that protected mine owners at the expense of local landowners. Coal speculators, most of whom were absentee owners, bought only mineral rights, not land. Stripping practices removed the coal, in the process destroying the land and leading to surface owner protests. But courts ruled that the original deeds, some of which were nearly a century old, gave mineral owners the right to extract the wealth in any way they saw fit. This legal doctrine at best threatened traditional land-use patterns and at worst destroyed them.[17]

Appalachian residents also suffered from labor politics. While the wartime demand for energy helped accelerate the pace of mine mechanization, it also resulted in the creation of a multitude of small, nonunion "truck mines." These operations, located along smaller seams that the major producers found unprofitable, offered men jobs, but the pay was poor and employees received no benefits. Such operations accounted for 38 percent of Kentucky's coal production. In 1950, however, the United Mine Workers of America ratified a new agreement with the nation's largest producers. Hoping to secure higher wages, better health and retirement benefits, and control over production that would allow coal to compete with more efficient fossil fuels such as oil, United Mine Workers president John L. Lewis agreed to accept mechanization. Though the agreement created well-paying jobs in the larger mines, it also meant that the truck mines, which predominated in the Appalachian coalfields, could not compete. As a result, thousands of smaller Appalachian mines closed, and machines "replaced an entire generation of miners."[18]

These ideological and economic changes placed Appalachian peoples, both those who had migrated to the North and those who remained in the highlands, at the center of the War on Poverty. As early as 1959, the CSM sponsored a series of "Urban Workshops." Designed to acquaint city officials, police, and social service agencies with the habits and culture of mountain people who had moved north, these workshops introduced urban professionals to a "dysfunctional" culture ill suited to city life. According to historian Bruce Tucker, workshop speakers "described a society weak in institutional structures, lacking in political and social cohesion, deprived of material resources, and burdened by archaic family and religious customs." Of the many criticisms of the southern mountain region offered by workshop speakers in the late 1950s and early 1960s, two of the more significant were Appalachian peoples' "environmental circumstances" (which city workers needed to understand to "help . . . the mountain migrant") and the notion that the highly individualistic, family-oriented mountain culture prevented people from realizing that "voluntary cooperation [was] required for urban living."[19] In addition to keeping alive the national dialogue about Appalachia, these workshops reinforced reformers' pathological version of the culture of poverty.

While the War on Poverty did not officially begin until the passage of the Economic Opportunity Act, the CSM anticipated the effort. Already in contact with federal officials involved in planning the antipoverty efforts, the council created an Appalachian Volunteers program that would position the group to take advantage of the federal effort should it come to fruition. On the third weekend in January 1964, the first AVs, college students from the region, traveled to Upper Jones Creek in Harlan County, Kentucky, to "winterize" the local school (that is, paint the building and repair broken windows and doors). This effort marked the beginning of the War on Poverty in Appalachia. The CSM's reason for the school renovation project reflected group leaders' overriding conception of poverty in the region, a conception that one of the first AVs later termed a "power company, chamber of commerce kind of vision." From this perspective, poverty was seen as beginning with the schools. If the school buildings themselves were attractive, the council reasoned, poor mountain children would be more likely to value and thus complete their education. An educated population, in turn, would draw industry to the region. This analysis placed the burden of poverty on the poor and ignored its real sources.[20]

The following June, the CSM decided to place a pair of AVs in the small community of Mill Creek, Clay County, Kentucky, for the entire summer. According to the council's information, not one of Mill Creek's seventy adults had finished high school, and most of those under the age of sixteen were two to five years behind in their educations. Further, the county could not place a qualified teacher in Mill Creek and issued "emergency certificates" that enabled unqualified "educators" to serve as instructors at the school. Mill Creek was also chosen because staff member Flem Messer, a Clay County native, had relatives there. The CSM devised a two-tiered school reform and "community development" effort for Mill Creek. This program, a "demonstration project" for the AVs, meshed with previous reform efforts in Appalachia and reflected preconceived notions regarding the culture of poverty.[21]

Funded by a combination of grants from the Ford Foundation, the Area Redevelopment Administration (a federal agency created to stimulate economic development in "depressed areas"), and the American Friends Service Committee (AFSC), the Mill Creek program's first tier began on June 8, 1964, when two AVs traveled to Mill Creek, where they would spend the next three months. According to Milton Ogle, the CSM staff member charged with administering the nascent AV program, the council hoped the project would "bring to the community through Audio Visual Aids and a wide selection of books and records a modern educational experience that goes far beyond anything that was ever attempted in a similar Eastern Kentucky community."[22]

Throughout the summer, the AVs engaged in activities they believed would end the mountaineers' cycle of poverty, operating a summer school and taking impoverished mountain children on field trips designed to broaden their experiences. By improving the school environment, the AVs hoped to alter the value system of the mountain people—to "stimulate desire" and "interest" in education. Appalachian residents were believed to place no value on learning. As much as anything else, the AVs hoped to change this attitude, and from their perspective, this aspect of the program realized immediate results with virtually every resident. "The parents were very cooperative," claimed the AVs. "They might not have understood the things I did, and sometimes they found them strange, but they were tolerant. . . . And we talked—*talking takes them out of their environment and gets them interested in the world.*" Children, for their part, openly embraced the volunteer effort. Nevertheless, the job remained challenging. The "healthy, intelligent, and enthusiastic children . . . responded extremely well" to the lessons offered in summer school. Yet there were "so many things they didn't know *because of their way of life.*" Still, the most significant results would come from the "young minds brought alive, stirr[ed] from the lethargy induced by an existence circumscribed by the hills that surround Kentucky's countless Mill Creeks." Simply by "kindl[ing] the imaginations" of poor mountaineers, the *Louisville Courier-Journal*'s Jim Hampton reported, these antipoverty workers pulled back the veil of "isolation and poverty" that kept an Appalachian "settlement" such as Mill Creek "locked . . . in the mold of yesterday."[23]

That autumn, following the departure of the two AVs, Carol Irons, an AFSC volunteer, arrived in Mill Creek and started the second part of the project. Under the CSM's direction, Irons reported doing only those "things" that the people could do even without her help. For example, she drove local residents to Manchester, the county seat, to see a physician, or just helped around their homes. She found her role less than satisfying, informing Robert Sigmon, the director of the AFSC's program, that she hoped to provide the community with services they could get only with her assistance. She argued that Mill Creek needed a community center where she could conduct what Irons considered to be the more important aspects of her program, a literacy project and instruction in healthy cooking. Because a community center would serve as a focal point, antipoverty workers stressed the importance of school-oriented projects that would improve residents' literacy rates and job skills.[24]

Since the building was a prerequisite for all other reforms, this effort all but monopolized Irons's attention through the fall and winter. Her attempts engendered confusion, animosity, and hostility among the CSM, the AFSC, the local community, and the local church. At various times during the ensuing ten months, all of these stakeholders had different ideas about the volunteer program and the location of the center. Irons's troubles forced Sigmon to question the AV program's leadership and supervision, and the local community and the local church eventually abandoned the project. According to Irons, after specific plans and resources failed to materialize, the people of Mill Creek "resigned" themselves to failure. Irons, too, gave up on the project and left Clay County about two months prior to her scheduled departure date.[25]

Evaluated by the council's own criteria, the CSM's Mill Creek project was a dismal failure. Mill Creek did not get its community center, and the volunteer left prior to completing her assignment. Worse, at least for the council and the direction of the War on Poverty in Appalachia, were the lessons learned—or not learned. On a surface level, the Mill Creek project represented a departure from the CSM's plan to employ local people to staff projects. Second, Irons's and the council's commitment to the community center revealed an approach to "community development" that was more concerned with qualitative developments than purely "facility development." By improving impoverished mountaineers' health, recreation, and most important educational facilities, the CSM believed that it would foster a local interest group that would precipitate economic opportunity through the creation of a better-educated, healthier workforce that would attract outside industry. Finally, both Sigmon's and Irons's concerns about her experiences revealed that they were more focused on her activities than on the community.

While a lack of evidence makes it difficult to assess the attitudes of the people of Mill Creek, their reactions are most important. Because the nature of the effort resembled that of previous Appalachian reforms—an attempt to bring to the mountains a proper education and better living through community development—it is reasonable to conclude that the mountaineers did not view it in the best of lights. For example, Irons's repeated references to the "indecisiveness of the community" as well as locals' "negative reactions," "resignation," and silence reflected residents' stances. These responses suggest that the people of Mill Creek were at best indifferent toward yet another reform effort that treated them as objects. Though the voices of the poor rarely appear, their silence is deafening. The Mill Creek project, an effort to improve a place where reformers believed that "the cycles of ignorance and poverty [had] become a way of life," conformed to the long-established pattern of reform in the region.[26]

In addition, however, potential problems of which the CSM was ignorant existed within the community itself. Much of the War on Poverty in Appalachia—

and of rural development in the twentieth century—focused on questions concerning the market and those who supposedly failed to reap any of its benefits. That market, moreover, was male-dominated, and the region's poverty largely resulted from job loss in the male-dominated industries of mining and timber combined with the lack of local control resulting from the sale of mineral rights. This response to industrialization had another important consequence in post–World War II Appalachia. As the coal industry increasingly mechanized, men migrated to northern industrial centers in search of employment. This process created a vacuum at precisely the place the Appalachian men had cherished so much—the head of the household. In response, the region began to undergo a gender shift. By the 1970s, as Susan Tallichet illustrates, women had moved into much more powerful social and economic positions, ultimately including working in the mines. Irons's position as a volunteer may have upset the emerging local gender balance.[27]

Further, as Robert Weise argues in *Grasping at Independence: Debt, Male Authority, and Mineral Rights in Appalachian Kentucky, 1850–1915*, men sold their mineral rights in an attempt to maintain independence and control over their households. While modern reformers found this effort to sustain local and household independence anachronistic, it also "favored the interests of the individual or kin-based household over a civic sense of the public good." As the market descended on Appalachia (as opposed to bypassing the region as many War on Poverty reformers believed), male heads of households competed with each other to ensure survival. Collective action might not have prevented economic dislocation, Weise concludes, but it might "have helped guide them to a better end."[28] This internal division became manifest during the debates over the Mill Creek community center; in short, Irons was not dealing simply with the interaction of competing groups that would, through the democratic process, reach a consensus. Instead, she had become enmeshed in a contest for local control in which the AV program probably represented an unwanted intrusion.

For the duration of the War on Poverty, the council attempted to avoid open conflict and continued with its inclusive, open-forum method of reform. According to Loyal Jones, the CSM's assistant executive director, the OEO's "three legged stool" approach to its Community Action Program was congruent with the CSM's cooperative strategy and attracted the federal organization to the council. Intended "to be a way in which all important segments of the community would mobilize all available resources to deal with local poverty," the OEO's stool incorporated a community's public and private sectors as well as the "maximum feasible participation" of the poor. Anticipating a certain degree of conflict, which was considered healthy in a participatory democracy, Sanford Kravitz, associate director of the Community Action Program, claimed that this inclusive approach would force the antipoverty effort to "'remain honest' to its purposes" by including every possible voice. Kravitz associate John Wofford described a "painful . . . process . . . toward a local consensus."[29]

From 1964 through 1966, the CSM expanded the AV program. Participants in the Volunteers in Service to America (VISTA) program arrived in the southern mountains in 1965, operating as the AVs. Because VISTA participants served for a year, the council labeled them "full-time AVs." College students, mostly from Kentucky, also joined the AV program but usually only worked on weekends or semester breaks. Members of both groups nevertheless performed many of the functions that the CSM had believed would end poverty. For example, in the weeks leading up to Christmas 1964, five AVs who also were students at the University of Kentucky traveled to Salt Rock, in Jackson County, and built bookshelves and made Christmas ornaments for the school's tree. Immediately after the new year began, this AV chapter constructed a basketball court and conducted science demonstrations—what the CSM called "curriculum enrichment" projects—at the Lick Branch School in Knott County. In the summer of 1965, the CSM deposited 150 volunteers in eastern Kentucky to renovate schools and enhance curriculum. Following the departure of the college AVs at the end of the summer, the full-time AVs were supposed to continue these programs.[30]

By early 1966, however, some council members, particularly those who worked on the AV project, began to question the validity of the cultural explanation. Spending time in the mountains exposed these reformers to the destructiveness of strip mining and to the coercive power of local officials, especially school superintendents. Reformers began to argue that the region should be seen as a colony of corporate energy interests.

One volunteer declared that the War on Poverty was an "obvious paradox" because it wanted to end poverty "without disturbing the present situation." To be effective, he argued, the AV program needed to reorganize or abolish "those institutions which initially led to the impoverishment . . . of the mountain people." At around this time, this realization struck community activists in many parts of the country, urban as well as rural. It was in many ways the core problem of the War on Poverty. With the goal of attacking and reorganizing the institutions that led to the impoverishment of mountain people, the AVs tried to organize mountaineers around some of the same issues that other poor communities were addressing, including welfare rights and inadequate schools. As the largest employers in their counties, superintendents used their ability to hire and fire as a means to maintain their powerful positions. Poor parents in urban as well as rural areas were addressing similar power imbalances, in part motivated by War on Poverty rhetoric of maximum feasible participation. But Appalachia had unique issues that affected the lives of the local poor—most important, strip mining. AVs began to organize against that practice, with its devastating environmental effects.

By May 1966, Ogle, backed by many participants, took the AVs from under the CSM's umbrella and created a separate organization, the Appalachian Volunteers, Inc. Mountaineers now had two agencies that sought to take the lead in Appalachian reform. One was traditional and conservative, seeing culture as the source of poverty; the other sought to lead mountain residents into a more radical camp.[31]

In a September 1966 attempt to understand the increasing tensions surrounding the War on Poverty, President Johnson created the National Advisory Commission on Rural Poverty (NACRP). Charged with making a "comprehensive study and appraisal of the current economic situations and trends in American rural life as they relate to . . . income and community problems of rural areas," this organization, like Bodnar, connected urban and rural issues. It also went a step further, blaming urban unrest on the rural folk now residing in cities. "Because we have been oblivious of the rural poor," declared the NACRP in a blatant reference to the War on Poverty, "we have abetted both rural and urban poverty, for the two are closely linked through migration. . . . The commission is unanimous in its conviction that effective programs for solving the problems of rural poverty will contribute to the solution of urban poverty as well." Reflecting common assumptions about Appalachians and blacks and the validity of the country's social, economic, and political structures, commission members argued that poverty was not simply the consequence of an inadequate income but resulted from a lack of access to respected positions in society, an "unstable" home, living "outside [the] market economy," and the disappearance of the "community . . . as an effective institution." Most important, in keeping with the conception of the culture of poverty, this "wretched existence . . . perpetuate[d] itself from one generation to the next," contributing significantly to the year's widespread urban riots. To remedy this situation, the country should work to improve life in rural America and thus remove the incentive to migrate. Furthermore, the NACRP hoped to find ways by which state and federal governments as well as private industries could provide ways "for the rural population to share in America's abundance." Among the first steps in this direction was to organize the poor so that they might better take advantage of the benefits of existing antipoverty programs.[32]

Though its focus was rural, the commission, led by Kentucky governor Edward Breathitt, held three 1967 hearings in Tucson, Arizona; Memphis, Tennessee; and Washington, D.C. In January 1967, perhaps in recognition of the irony of holding the hearings in major urban areas, Breathitt, along with two other Kentucky members of the commission, Berea College president Francis Hutchins and the University of Kentucky's Ford, met briefly in Berea. Designed to examine the weaknesses and shortcomings in the Great Society, the NACRP hearings provide some insights into how local people felt about and reacted to the War on Poverty.

Comprised mostly of antipoverty workers in and around Madison County, Kentucky, witnesses at the Berea hearing, like those at the three official meetings, represented the various ways Americans generally thought about poverty. Alvin Boggs from the Pine Mountain Settlement School vacillated between structural issues—those that took into account factors such as jobs and wages— and personal ones. In response to a question from Breathitt concerning income among rural nonfarm Appalachian residents, Boggs claimed that "even if a person does receive twenty-five dollars . . . or thirty dollars a day, he is not sure that this is going to continue for the next week. And if that mine should close, he wouldn't feel like investing much in something that would tie him for a period of years . . . and the taxes that go with it. So a very expensive car may win out in this contest of how he spends his money." Such testimony indicated that poor mountaineers made rational decisions with their economic resources but also implied that mountaineer culture did not necessarily adhere to or understand the urban values of thrift and saving. Boggs asserted that he could "think of plenty of people who have earned a great salary or income, but didn't know how to use it. And they were in much worse condition than those who might have received considerably less."[33]

Others spoke more directly about issues that had little to do with either mountaineers or their culture, focusing instead on corruption and mismanagement of funds, job-creation programs that did not really create jobs, and inadequate delivery of educational and welfare services. Berea College sophomore Bobby Wayne Burchette, a native of Charleston, West Virginia, contended that as a consequence of local political corruption and the manipulation of federal funds, "inside the Charleston city limits you have communities that are [so] isolated [that y]ou might as well be a hundred miles away." Ravenna, Kentucky, resident Robert Johnson claimed "that many of the resources of these counties, which are available, such as Head Start . . . backfires on the people it was intended for and is used as a weapon against them instead of an opportunity for them." Responding to Hutchins's query about employment prospects in Estill County, Kentucky, Margie Jones called into question the efficacy of the types of education offered in the public school system, the War on Poverty, and the Manpower Development and Training Act: "We don't have any job opportunities or anything. The schools offer all types of vocations and things like that, but it's nothing to employ the young people after they are out of school." In reference to another of the federal administration's favorite antipoverty efforts, the Elementary and Secondary Education Act, another witness informed Breathitt that the state Department of Education received funds based on the number of families below the poverty line (that is, earning three thousand dollars or less per year). Local school boards received the money from the state but spent "it pretty much as they see fit." Finally, one participant declared that "one of the major problems with the welfare program is that the more you have the easier it is to get more; the less you have, the harder it is to get anything . . . and that before a family can be helped, it has to fall apart entirely." Boggs was bothered by both the philosophical and geographic origins of the War on Poverty: "When this is aimed at a certain group of people [there] is an isolation that causes them to feel the stigma of this sense of poverty. I doubt that there are very many here who are in the same, or as poor a circumstance, as I was as a boy. But we never thought of it as poverty. I think it has a lot to do with the mental attitude. . . . But I believe that if somebody had stuck me in a little group and said 'You are here because you're poor' it would have hurt me perhaps beyond recovery."[34]

The Berea hearing demonstrates the problems with the War on Poverty in Appalachia and outlines the reasons for its immediate failure. Witnesses expressed resentment of reform efforts that labeled them as poor or that, as in the case of the Mill Creek experiment, attempted to "take them out of their environment." They also recognized that in many cases their poverty resulted not from their behavior but from larger structures—an unresponsive political system, a corporate world that cared little for the region's land and people, and an education/job-training program that essentially forced them to leave their homes because it did not create enough of the jobs for which they received training. Finally, many Appalachian residents saw the War on Poverty as just another in a century-long tradition of reform efforts that ultimately saw them as objects, as tools to fulfill someone else's agenda.

In many ways, these people remained objects in the contest between the various reform strategies in the mountains. As late as 1968, as support for the overall War on Poverty began to wane, conservative members of CSM continued to try to transform Appalachian people and thus reform Appalachia into something akin to urban America. "There is a basic difference . . . between poverty in the central cities and in rural areas," former NACRP staffer C. E. Bishop reiterated to the CSM. "In the central cities the poor are concentrated. They are organized. They have a clearly defined leadership structure. They are vocal. They are making their wants known and they are getting assistance. In contrast, the rural poor are widely separated. They are unorganized, they have no identifiable leadership, they are not vocal, and they receive little assistance." Moreover, the CSM's Ayer took an obvious swipe at his former Appalachian Volunteer colleagues, asking whether it was "desirable to help the poor adjust to contemporary society and make the most of it" or preferable to transform them from "their politically pristine state . . . into revolutionaries." Ayer's version of help, however, revealed his ambivalence toward and perhaps lack of understanding of one of the fundamental sources of poverty in the region and one of the reasons Appalachians resisted his reforms. His version of modernization and urbanization included "training centers and industrial establishments turning on the concept of *automation* . . . without the handicaps of *traditionalism* in either the minds of the people or the architecture and tooling of production facilities." In short, Ayer saw eastern Kentucky as an unspoiled, untapped, primitive reserve in which a modern "city on the hill," "designed, built and developed in accord with Space Age concepts," could be built.[35]

By early 1969, many Appalachian residents began to reject the council's conservative stance, and the CSM began to implode. Financial strains exacerbated internal divisions as War on Poverty funds began to dry up. In addition to the defection of the AVs in 1966, Ayer died in 1968. Many mountaineers saw the CSM's splintering as an opportunity to remake the organization, a development that puzzled Jones, who became the CSM executive director after Ayer's death. At the organization's 1969 annual conference, he stated that he "never saw an organization with so much wrong with it that people fought to be part of it." In 1970, after nearly a century of Appalachian reform programs dominated by people who saw mountaineers as "yesterday's people," "regular" Appalachian residents gained control of the CSM. One new leader exclaimed that "the sharpness of the anger, frustration, sorrow, joy obscured the fact that people, ordinary people, poor people, plain people, people began to take the CSM, not seriously, not ambitiously, maybe not even hopefully, but as their own. In a . . . world of repression and revolution, it just maybe [sic] that [the] CSM can be a help to a whole lot of human beings who need each other to make life worth celebrating."[36]

Despite its sanguine attitude, the new CSM understood that any work would be difficult, especially in the waning years of the War on Poverty. Nevertheless, it adopted President Richard Nixon's phrase from his November 3, 1969, Silent Majority speech, declaring that mountaineers were not reticent and fatalistic but rather "a do it yourself people." One of the first items on the agenda was to define the problems the new CSM faced. While the idea of poverty dominated the discussion, the conversation was quite nuanced. Some participants, for example, focused on economic poverty, setting a minimum income level; others talked about political and social poverty. They defined political poverty as "being part of a system which does not consider who you are, what you need, and whether you live or die," while social poverty was being of part of a system that fails to provide a "positive reflection of who you are in your cultural heritage" and isolates you from "participation in the institutions which affect your [life]." These two definitions moved the CSM in a new direction.[37]

Also critical to the new council was its organizational structure. Though it consisted of many different commissions that at times overlapped, the most important ones were the Welfare Rights Commission and the Black Appalachian Commission. In a statement that reflected the CSM's new direction and its critique of the War on Poverty, the Black Appalachian Commission asserted that when the council became more "people oriented," it offered more opportunities for blacks. Most important, African Americans in the region now had a "vehicle for action" with which to combat the popular perception that Appalachia was a "white poverty area."[38]

Led by Jack Guillebeaux from Asheville, North Carolina, the Black Appalachian Commission (BAC) originally expressed resentment toward white America and white Appalachians. Because the southern mountains were associated with "white poverty," the commission contended, blacks had even more to overcome to gain access to the "meager available poverty resources." In short, blacks in Appalachia were "bypassed by the war on poverty." This situation was all the more dire because the region's racial minorities not only lost jobs in the coal industry, as whites did, but were displaced by whites in the lower-paying

Figure 7. *Mountain Life and Work*, March 1973. Council of the Southern Mountains Records, 1970–1989; Southern Appalachian Archives, Berea College.

service-sector economy. The BAC sought to organize to "gain power to exercise meaningful influence and control of the resources that affect the black community." In addition to spreading word about the CSM in black neighborhoods to get more African Americans involved and thus make the council more responsive to blacks, the BAC promoted black culture and heritage in the region.[39]

At least one member of the commission, Leon Williams, understood that blacks needed to unite with Appalachian whites who opposed racism and "struggle for social justice for all people." The fluid nature of the new CSM commission structure allowed for this possibility. Many blacks served on the Committees for Social and Economic Justice (CSEJ).[40]

The CSEJ grew out of the Dickenson County, Virginia, Welfare Rights Orga-

Figure 8. As the shirt says, Appalachian residents just want to "be left alone." Council of the Southern Mountains Records, 1970–1989; Southern Appalachian Archives, Berea College.

nization, which in 1968 began working to help the poor receive fair hearings regarding their welfare cases and thus better benefits. Organization members soon discovered, however, that by focusing on individual cases, they failed to address larger, more significant issues. "The real question," they determined, "is 'Why are people poor' and 'What can we and the CSEJs do about that?' or more accurately 'What can *people* do about that and how can the CSM and the CSEJs help?'" CSEJ members already realized that people were the key to the struggle for social and economic justice.[41]

Building on this realization, the committees organized chapters in Letcher, Knott, and Perry Counties, Kentucky, and attacked a wide range of fundamental problems confronting poor Appalachian residents. Free breakfast and lunch programs, funneled through the county school system, for example, dominated many discussions. Equally important, the committees embraced environmental and health issues stemming from the devastation of the coal industry. The CSEJ worked with miners to help those suffering from black lung disease gain disability benefits and "publicized the problems of strip mining . . . talked, traveled, [took] pictures. . . . Strip mining is more important to fight every day." In Dickenson County, the CSEJ realized perhaps its greatest success in 1973, when "we have two black people elected to town councils" and another African American appeared on the ballot for the county board of supervisors. "This will be a process of change," the CSEJ proudly predicted.[42]

Important though these developments were, perhaps the greatest change precipitated by the evolution of the CSM was the genesis of an "Appalachian nationalism." Along with a "new period of self-criticism," the reorganized CSM hoped to establish a "deeper analysis" of Appalachian issues and to develop more "strategic alternatives" for dealing with those problems. The process would include compiling "data on the changing working class and ruling powers of Appalachia," conducting an intense analysis that would permit the council to advocate on behalf of "safer workplaces, more equitable systems of taxation, to improve human resources and education" and to fight "racism and derogatory stereotypes." The "struggle for social justice," the CSM concluded, "must come from Appalachians themselves." Ayer's philosophy had allowed "industrial establishment leaders" to run programs, while government money "meant we sponsored many programs but had few of our own." After the CSM came under the control of mountain people in the late 1960s, "sweeping changes" took place, and the new version took on positions that rejected that old consensual approach and challenged such practices as strip mining and the broad form deed, supported welfare rights, and advocated "community control of programs." At the new CSM, "The talk [was] about poverty as we live it."[43]

Notes

1. Lyndon Baines Johnson, *A Time for Action: A Selection from the Speeches and Writings of Lyndon B. Johnson, 1954–1963* (New York: Atheneum, 1964).

2. Adelbert Z. Bodnar to Council of the Southern Mountains, March 10, 1964, Box 102, Council of the Southern Mountains Papers, 1912–70, Southern Appalachian Archives, Hutchins Library, Berea College, Berea, Kentucky (hereafter CSM Papers, 1912–70). On the migration of Appalachians to the North, see Chad Berry, *Southern Migrants, Northern Exiles* (Urbana: University of Illinois Press, 2000); Pete Daniel, *Lost Revolutions: The South in the 1950s* (Chapel Hill: University of North Carolina Press, 2000), esp. chap. 1. For southern industrialization strategies, see James C. Cobb, *The Selling of the South: The Southern Crusade for Industrial Development* (Urbana: University of Illinois Press, 1982).

3. Perley Ayer to Jack Ciacio, May 28, 1966, Box 129, CSM Papers, 1912–70. On the

CSM's early years, see David Whisnant, *Modernizing the Mountaineer: People, Power, and Planning in Appalachia* (Boone, N.C.: Appalachian Consortium, 1980), esp. chap. 1; John M. Glen, "The War on Poverty in Appalachia—A Preliminary Report," *Register of the Kentucky Historical Society* 87:1 (Winter 1989): 53–57; Thomas Kiffmeyer, *Reformers to Radicals: Appalachian Volunteers and the War on Poverty in Kentucky* (Lexington: University Press of Kentucky, 2008), chap. 1. On Ayer's partnership philosophy, see Loyal Jones, interview by Tom Kiffmeyer, March 15, 1991, War on Poverty in Appalachian Kentucky Oral History Project, King Library, University of Kentucky, Lexington.

4. "Introduction: History and Description of CSM and Mountain Life and Work," ca. 1983, handwritten notes, ca. 1980, both in Box 1, Council of the Southern Mountains Papers, 1970–89, Southern Appalachian Archives, Hutchins Library, Berea College, Berea, Kentucky (hereafter CSM Papers, 1970–89). On the split from the old, traditional CSM, see "Council of the Southern Mountains Seek New Paths," *Berea College Pinnacle*, May 2, 1970; Glen, "War on Poverty"; Kiffmeyer, *Reformers to Radicals*, chap. 5.

5. John C. Campbell, *The Southern Highlander and His Homeland* (New York: Sage, 1921), xvii; Berry, *Southern Migrants*; Ronald D. Eller, *Uneven Ground: Appalachia since 1945* (Lexington: University Press of Kentucky, 2008).

6. Junaluska Speech, April 25, 1970, Box 2, CSM Papers, 1970–89. On the idea of a "longer view," see Jacquelyn Dowd Hall, "The Long Civil Rights Movement and the Political Uses of History," *Journal of American History* 91:4 (March 2005): 1233–63; Kent Germany, "The Politics of Poverty and History: Racial Inequality and the Long Prelude to Katrina," *Journal of American History* 94:3 (December 2007): 743–51.

7. William Goodell Frost, "Our Contemporary Ancestors in the Southern Mountains," *Atlantic Monthly* 83:492 (March 1899): 311. On the "culture of poverty," see Oscar Lewis, *Five Families* (New York: Basic Books, 1959). On the concept of Appalachian Otherness and how it affected America's responses to the region, see Henry Shapiro, *Appalachia on Our Mind: The Southern Mountains and Mountaineers in the American Consciousness, 1870–1920* (Chapel Hill: University of North Carolina Press, 1978). For the early reformers in the mountains, see esp. Whisnant, *Modernizing the Mountaineer*; David Whisnant, *All That Is Native and Fine: The Politics of Culture in an American Region* (Chapel Hill: University of North Carolina Press, 1983); Nancy Forderhase, "Eve Returns to the Garden," *Register of the Kentucky Historical Society* 85 (Summer 1987): 237–61; Campbell, *Southern Highlander*; Jack Weller, *Yesterday's People: Life in Contemporary Appalachia* (Lexington: University Press of Kentucky, 1963).

8. Whisnant, *All That Is Native*; Forderhase, "Eve Returns," 244, 249.

9. Allen Batteau, *The Invention of Appalachia* (Tucson: University of Arizona Press, 1990); Weller, *Yesterday's People*.

10. Weller, *Yesterday's People*; Tom Parrish, interview by Tom Kiffmeyer, April 1, 1991, War on Poverty in Appalachian Kentucky Oral History Project.

11. On the negative reaction of mountain folk to industrialization, see Ronald D. Eller, *Miners, Millhands, and Mountaineers: The Industrialization of the Appalachian South, 1880–1930* (Knoxville: University of Tennessee Press, 1982), xix. Eller carries his story into the twenty-first century in *Uneven Ground*. See also Ronald L. Lewis, *Transforming the Appalachian Countryside: Railroads, Deforestation, and Social Change in West Virginia, 1880–1920* (Chapel Hill: University of North Carolina Press, 1998), esp. chap. 9. On "old fogeyism" that retards progress, see Lewis, *Transforming the Appalachian Countryside*, 239. On "habits of industry," see John C. Hennen, *The Americanization of West Virginia: Creating A Modern Industrial State, 1916–1925* (Lexington: University Press of Kentucky, 1996).

12. Robert Dahl, *Dilemmas of Pluralist Democracy: Autonomy versus Control* (New Haven: Yale University Press, 1982), 11. See also Robert Dahl, *A Preface to Democratic Theory* (Chicago: University of Chicago Press, 1956); Robert Dahl, *Polyarchy: Participation and Opposition* (New Haven: Yale University Press, 1971).

13. Oscar Lewis, *Five Families*. As Alice O'Connor argues in *Poverty Knowledge: Social Science, Social Policy, and the Poor in Twentieth-Century U.S. History* (Princeton: Princeton University Press, 2001), this focus on the poor rather than on poverty allowed planners of antipoverty programs to ignore structural issues that resulted in poverty, essentially permitted them to blame the poor for their own condition, and ultimately rendered moot any discussion of fundamental political, social, or economic change.

14. Lyndon Baines Johnson, *The Public Papers of the Presidents of the United States: Lyndon Baines Johnson, 1963–1964* (Washington D.C.: U.S. Government Printing Office, 1965), 1:704; Lyndon Baines Johnson, *Public Papers of the Presidents of the United States: Lyndon Baines Johnson, 1966* (Washington D.C.: U.S. Government Printing Office, 1967), 1:3–7.

15. Tom Gish, speech before the CSM, Box 31, Appalachian Volunteers Papers, Southern Appalachian Archives, Hutchins Library, Berea College, Berea, Kentucky (hereafter AV Papers).

16. James S. Brown and George A. Hillery Jr., "The Great Migration, 1940–1960," in *The Southern Appalachian Region: A Survey*, ed. Thomas R. Ford (Lexington: University Press of Kentucky, 1962), 59.

17. Eller, *Miners, Millhands, and Mountaineers*; Eller, *Uneven Ground*.

18. Eller, *Uneven Ground*, 15–20.

19. Bruce Tucker, "Imagining Appalachians: The Berea Workshop on the Urban Adjustment of Southern Appalachian Migrants," in *Appalachian Odyssey: Historical Perspectives on the Great Migration*, ed. Phillip Obermiller, Thomas Wagner, and Bruce Tucker (Westport, Conn.: Praeger, 2000), 105; "Hands-across-the-Ohio" Program, Newsletter 4, September 10, 1962, Grant PA 61-62, Section 4, Reel R-0255, Ford Foundation Archives, Ford Foundation Headquarters, New York; Roscoe Giffin, pamphlet, [ca. 1958], Grant PA

58-42, Section 5, Reel R-0170, Ford Foundation Archives. See also Roscoe Giffin, "Some Aspects of the Migration from the Southern Appalachians," 1957, James Gladden, "How the Church May Increase the Resources of the Community," both in Grant PA 58-42, Reel R-0170, Ford Foundation Archives. See also Docket Excerpt—Board of Trustees Meeting, Public Affairs: Council of the Southern Mountains, September 26–27, 1963, Grant PA 61-62, Reel R-0255, Ford Foundation Archives. The records of the Urban Workshops are located in Boxes 280–84, CSM Papers, 1912–70.

20. On the Harlan County project, see Kiffmeyer, *Reformers to Radicals*, 42; George Brosi, interview by Tom Kiffmeyer, November 3, 1990, War on Poverty in Appalachian Kentucky Oral History Project.

21. Kiffmeyer, *Reformers to Radicals*; Summary of Special Projects Aided by the Council of the Southern Mountains Ford Foundation Grant, 1964, Box 20, AV Papers.

22. Kiffmeyer, *Reformers to Radicals*; Proposal to the Council of the Southern Mountains Education Committee, Project Area, Mill Creek, Clay County, Kentucky, [ca. June 1964], Box 28, AV Papers; CSM and ARA Contract for Grant Allocation, 1964, Box 3, AV Papers; Summary of Special Projects Aided by the Council of the Southern Mountains Ford Foundation Grant, 1964, Box 20, AV Papers. Ford gave the CSM thirty-three thousand dollars, while the ARA granted fifty thousand dollars.

23. Proposal to the Council of the Southern Mountains Education Committee, Project Area: Mill Creek, Clay County, Kentucky, [June 1964], Box 28, AV Papers; Jim Hampton, "Volunteers Pioneer Classes at Mill Creek," *Louisville Courier-Journal*, August 9, 1964 (emphasis added).

24. Robert Lee Sigmon to Milton Ogle, December 3, 1964, Box 25, AV Papers; Quarterly Report, U.S. VISA Volunteer, Carol Irons, Mill Creek, Kentucky, October 9, 1964–December 21, 1964, Box 25, AV Papers. See also Robert Lee Sigmon to Milton Ogle, December 3, 1964, Box 117, CSM Papers, 1912–70; Carol Irons VISA-US, Reports, October 19–29, 1964, January 1965, Youth Services Division, 1964, VISA Program, Projects: United States, Reports—Volunteers, American Friends Service Committee Papers, American Friends Service Committee Archives, Philadelphia.

25. Carol Irons to Milton Ogle, February 21, March 6, 1965, both in Box 25, AV Papers.

26. Proposal to the Council of the Southern Mountains Education Committee, Project Area: Mill Creek, Clay County, Kentucky, [June 1964], Box 28, AV Papers.

27. Susan Tallichet, *Daughters of the Mountain: Women Coal Miners in Central Appalachia* (State College: Pennsylvania State University Press, 2006).

28. Robert Weise, *Grasping at Independence: Debt, Male Authority, and Mineral Rights in Appalachian Kentucky, 1850–1915* (Knoxville: University of Tennessee Press, 2001), 292.

29. Jones, interview, November 19, 1990, March 15, 1991, War on Poverty in Appala-

chian Kentucky Oral History Project; John G. Wofford, "The Politics of Local Responsibility: Administration of the Community Action Program—1964–1966," in *On Fighting Poverty: Perspectives from Experience*, ed. James L. Sundquist (New York: Basic Books, 1969), 79; Sanford Kravitz, "The Community Action Program: Past, Present, and Its Future?," in *On Fighting Poverty*, ed. Sundquist, 60.

30. On the many AV programs between 1964 and the split between the AV and the CSM, see Kiffmeyer, *Reformers to Radicals*, chaps. 3–4; on the relationship between AVs and VISTA participants, see 111.

31. AV Background Information, [Chapter] VII Case Study—Report on Verda, Box 8, AV Papers. On the CSM-AV split, see Kiffmeyer, *Reformers to Radicals*, chap. 5.

32. Executive Order 11306, 31 FR 12769, 1966 WL 7724 (Pres.), in *The American Presidency Project*, ed. John T. Woolley and Gerhard Peters, http://www.presidency.ucsb.edu/ws/?pid=60544; "The People Left Behind: Summary," September 6, 1967, "The Fourteen Million," September 5, 1967, both in Box 6, National Advisory Commission on Rural Poverty Papers, Southern Appalachian Archives, Berea College, Berea, Kentucky. See also "Six Reasons for Action Now," September 4, 1967, "Poverty in Rural America: Summary," July 27, 1967, "The Current Situation: The Concept of Poverty," July 19, 1967, all in Box 6, National Advisory Commission on Rural Poverty Papers. In 1967, Tampa, Cincinnati, Atlanta, Newark, Detroit, and other cities experienced devastating urban racial violence. President Johnson created the National Advisory Commission on Civil Disorders to investigate the causes of these riots. See *U.S. Riot Commission Report: Report of the National Advisory Commission on Civil Disorders* (New York: New York Times Company, 1968).

33. Meeting in Connection with the National Advisory Commission on Rural Poverty, testimony of Alvin Boggs, January 21, 1967, 28–30, Box 2, National Advisory Commission on Rural Poverty Papers.

34. Testimonies of Bobby Wayne Burchette, Robert Johnson, Margie Jones, Leonard Gallimore, Richard Schneider, and Boggs, all in ibid., 59, 44, 32, 46, 2, 25.

35. Proposal for an Experimental Program in Model Community Development in Rural Appalachia, December 14, 1968, 12, Box 185, CSM Papers, 1912–70; P. F. Ayer to Paul Ylvisaker, February 23, 1966, Box 185, CSM Papers, 1912–70; Suggested Copy for Fund-Raising Brochure, [ca. 1965], Box 25, AV Papers.

36. Junaluska Speech, April 25, 1970, Box 2, CSM Papers, 1970–89.

37. Campaign for Human Development Application for Funding, Dickenson County Welfare Rights Organization, 1973, Box 97, CSM Papers, 1970–89.

38. Proposal to the Southern Education Foundation from the Black Appalachian Commission, March 24, 1972, Box 90, CSM Papers, 1970–89.

39. [Black Appalachian Commission], "The Problem," [ca. 1972], *Seeking a Fair Share: The Story of the Black Appalachian Commission*, [ca. 1972]; *Black Appalachian*

Commission, [ca. 1971], Black Appalachian Commission Proposal, n.d., all in Box 90, CSM Papers, 1970–89. See also Proposal for a Research Project in the Problems of Black People in Appalachia, February 1970, Box 90, CSM Papers, 1970–89.

40. *Seeking a Fair Share*.

41. "Citizens for Social and Economic Justice Proposal," [ca. 1973], "Problems with CSEJ's," August 18, 1977, both in Box 97, CSM Papers, 1970–89.

42. "Citizens for Social and Economic Justice Proposal."

43. *People's Appalachia*, [ca. 1973], Box 95, CSM Papers, 1970–89; "History" (handwritten), [n.d.], Box 1, CSM Papers, 1970–89; "Request for Funding from the Poor People's Self-Help Committee," [ca. 1970], Box 95, CSM Papers, 1970–89; "Council of the Southern Mountains," n.d., Box 1, CSM Papers, 1970–89.

DANIEL M. COBB

The War on Poverty in Mississippi and Oklahoma

Beyond Black and White

The War on Poverty is typically seen in black and white. Economists and political scientists marshal statistics to argue that it either succeeded or failed.
Sociologists debate whether the approach taken toward poverty was right or
wrong. These disputes are seldom painted in shades of gray. Historians have
looked through a similar lens. Historical assessments overwhelmingly focus either on local case studies of black or white communities or on a national narrative that situates the antipoverty campaign in the context of the civil rights movement. The experiences of other ethnic communities fall outside the field of view.
A case study of the War on Poverty among Indian communities in Mississippi
and Oklahoma sheds light on additional struggles for racial and economic justice, complicating the historiography of the Great Society's most controversial
undertaking.

CONTEXTS

On a most basic level, the antipoverty campaign intersected with and ultimately
enhanced an ongoing battle for what one Native scholar has called "civil rights
of a different order."[1] Through the 1960s and into the 1970s, Native and non-
Native rights advocates used the War on Poverty as leverage against their opponents in Congress and their supposed friends within the Bureau of Indian
Affairs (BIA). A vestige of colonialism, the BIA consisted of a central headquarters in Washington, D.C., and a host of regional and local offices that administered federal programs for Indians. Citing the bureau's penchant for paternalism, disempowerment, and overcontrol, reformers effectively translated the

War on Poverty's philosophy of "maximum feasible participation of the poor" into demands for more tribal self-government, self-determination, and sovereignty. They met with both success and failure.[2]

All told, more than sixty Indian-run community action agencies (CAAs) encompassed more than one hundred reservation communities. Some of them served only one nation, while others in California, Nevada, New Mexico, Wisconsin, and Washington were regional and multitribal in scope. In addition, several regional Indian community action projects located at major universities provided training and technical assistance, and War on Poverty initiatives including Legal Services, Head Start, Job Corps, and Volunteers in Service to America (VISTA) operated in many parts of Indian Country. The most visible and generously funded programs could be found in the northern Plains and Southwest. But across the Pacific Northwest, California, and in southern states from Maryland and North Carolina to Florida and Texas, American Indians residing both on and off reservations engaged in the assault on poverty.[3]

Indian community action became implicated in power struggles not unlike those found in urban areas. Newly formed CAAs upset institutionalized structures of power by channeling resources to tribal communities. BIA superintendents had long been criticized for being insensitive toward Indian people. Some administrators mismanaged individual and tribal finances or jealously guarded control over everything from economic development to education. Even when they operated efficiently, local BIA offices were not seen as indigenous institutions but instead as colonial impositions. The architects of the War on Poverty understood the situation and realized that Native people perceived the bureau the same way as residents of other impoverished communities across the United States perceived mayors, city council members, and social service providers. "It was very threatening to vested interests," observed Richard Boone, one of the lead designers of the attack on poverty.[4]

Tribal governments held a less certain place in this matrix. Throughout the nineteenth century, the United States set about undermining indigenous political institutions for a number of reasons, not the least of which was that policymakers were either unable or unwilling to see such institutions as "civilized" and therefore legitimate governing mechanisms. By the end of the nineteenth century, Native communities had been defined in federal law as "domestic dependent nations" and deemed incapable of self-governance. The BIA exerted tremendous control over reservations under the auspices of "trusteeship." In the infantilizing language of federal Indian law, the United States served as "guardian" and tribes as "wards." The reform movement known as the Indian New Deal, which led to the authoring of tribal constitutions during the 1930s and 1940s, attempted to resuscitate tribal self-government, with mixed results.[5]

The governing institutions that emerged during the first half of the twentieth century possessed limited power, with the secretary of the interior reserving the right to nullify any decision. The BIA also retained firm control over the money and programs that flowed from the U.S. Capitol. While some tribal governments fought for more power and aggressively advocated their communities' interests, others seemed to act as the BIA's pawns—as tools of subjection and assimilation. The idea of strengthening governing institutions through the War on Poverty, then, was problematic at best. Native people generally welcomed—and the BIA resisted—the idea of having federal money and programs channeled directly to tribes. Whether the tribal governments were seen as legitimate representatives of the whole community or merely certain segments of it was a different matter.[6]

The picture grew increasingly complex at the local level. On reservations, internal debates regarding representation often revolved around kinship, clan, and cultural orientation. In other areas, the boundaries between Indian and non-Indian political, legal, cultural, and social spaces were more ambiguous. Native Americans asserted the right to participate in the antipoverty campaign as Indians forced non-Natives to confront the discomfiting reality of the indigenous struggle for survival. In Mississippi and Oklahoma, the Community Action Program's mantra of "maximum feasible participation of the poor" disrupted the political, legal, and economic relationships between Indians and local, state, and federal institutions. In Mississippi, the results were enriching and empowering. In a far larger, more ethnically mixed swath of Oklahoma, the process and the results were more ambivalent. The different outcomes should not be surprising and offer insight into the War on Poverty not just in these specific places but also throughout Native America.[7]

MISSISSIPPI

The Mississippi of the 1960s is easily recognized as a focal point of the struggle for black equality. Its status as an indigenous homeland is less frequently observed. During the early to mid–nineteenth century, the federal government sanctioned a policy of ethnic cleansing intended to drive American Indians from territory east of the Mississippi River. Although the policy proved devastatingly

Figure 9. Even after the wreckage of forced removal during the nineteenth century, Choctaws continued to live in their ancestral homelands. Map by Joshua A. Sutterfield, © Joshua A. Sutterfield, 2007, used with permission.

effective, a Native presence endured. Fleeing into the backcountry, electing to take allotments, or returning from the Indian Territory after being forcibly removed there, American Indians set about reconstituting their communities. The Choctaws, a Muskogean-speaking people with deep roots in the Southeast, reestablished themselves across ancestral lands in Neshoba, Leake, Kemper and Newton Counties in east-central Mississippi, one of the most segregated and racist regions of the country.[8]

During the early twentieth century, ambiguity surrounded the legal status of the Mississippi Band of Choctaws. The federal government did little to acknowledge their persistence as a tribal community until 1918, when it established a BIA agency in the Neshoba County town of Philadelphia. As took place elsewhere in the South, white-dominated local and state governments defined Indians as "colored" and applied discriminatory laws to them. Landless and poor, Choctaws lived in a state of debt peonage, carving out meager existences through sharecropping, tenant farming, and seasonal labor in the cotton fields. They also experienced disfranchisement and were expected to observe the doctrine of "separate but equal" in public spaces. In short, Mississippi Choctaws found themselves, along with African Americans and people of mixed racial ancestry, on the wrong side of the color line.[9]

Despite this relegation to second-class citizenship, shared language, strong family ties, tightly woven extended kinship connections, social dances, church activities, and stickball games enabled the Indian community to survive. Ironically, extreme isolation contributed to the persistence of Choctaw as a widely spoken first language and the ongoing practice of traditional lifeways. Through the 1930s, an undeterred drive for political autonomy and economic stability bore at least some fruit when the federal government agreed to purchase and bring into trust more than fifteen thousand acres of reservation land. By 1945, the Choctaws had secured not only a checkerboard land base scattered across seven counties but also federal acknowledgment of the tribe's special legal relationship with the United States.[10]

The battle for sovereignty continued, however. Local whites controlled the BIA agency in Philadelphia and stifled the exercise of Choctaw self-government.[11] Though the potential for Native leadership existed, discriminatory hiring practices ensured that whites secured jobs at the agency and at federally administered schools in Pearl River, Tucker, Standing Pine, Bogue Homa, Red Water, Conehatta, and Bogue Chitto. To complete high school, Choctaw students attended federal boarding schools outside the state. When one Choctaw family attempted to integrate a local public school shortly after the *Brown* decision in 1954, resistance flared. To make matters worse, the appointment of a string of prejudiced agency superintendents culminated with the 1956 arrival of Paul Vance, husband to the niece of Mississippi's powerful Democratic senator, James Eastland. A native of Neshoba County, Vance showed himself to be indistinguishable from a segment of the local population that Choctaws characterized as "race fanatics and segregationists."[12]

Led by Emmett York and Phillip Martin, the Mississippi Choctaws took action. During the late 1950s and early 1960s, they allied with the Association on American Indian Affairs (AAIA), a prominent Indian-rights advocacy organization, to pressure the federal government either to remove Vance from office or discreetly to transfer him to a place "where he would not have to work for the racial equality of Indians." The AAIA surmised that Vance had allied with individuals within the sheriff's office, schools, and churches to forestall the tribe's efforts to deal with a host of issues, among them poverty, poor housing, discrimination, segregation, unfair business practices, predatory lending, and police abuse. The Choctaws did not secure a new superintendent until 1965, but the process of replacing Vance reinforced a valuable lesson. To effect change, they needed to circumvent the power of the local institutions that subordinated them to "the lowest rung of the economic ladder."[13]

ENTER COMMUNITY ACTION

The Economic Opportunity Act promised to give Indians precisely that ability. The Choctaw Tribal Council believed that the measure would inject into the community much-needed funds for education, job training, housing, health, and legal representation. No less important, the Community Action Program would channel federal money directly to the tribal government rather than to the BIA and other non-Native institutions, thereby giving Choctaws the leverage needed to realize at least a modicum of self-determination. For the Mississippi Choctaws to be taken seriously as a nation—that is, as a self-governing indigenous community with a legal status other than the state—they needed power. They believed that such power might come first from the antipoverty campaign. With such a foundation, the tribe could begin to build its own economy, provide opportunities to cultivate future leaders, take control of the education of its young people, and aggressively assert its distinct legal, social, and cultural identity.[14]

Mississippi Choctaws' desire to circumvent the South's white power structure dovetailed with the aims of the Office of Economic Opportunity (OEO). To the OEO's embarrassment, however, it had yet to establish a CAA in the state a year and a half into the War on Poverty. "Make no mistake," wrote an agency official in Washington, D.C., "we have a crisis in Mississippi." That crisis, driven by the state government's fear that federal money would be used to politically mobilize black communities, made the Choctaws an attractive grant recipient from the OEO's perspective. Administrators viewed indigenous people as a "safe" minority group, and Native Americans were widely perceived as being among the "deserving poor."[15]

The OEO awarded a program development grant to the Choctaw Tribal Council in the spring of 1966. The grant established a CAA to administer programs for seven reservation communities across five counties. Channeled through the OEO's Indian Desk, the Choctaw CAA would also be required to ensure representation of and extend services to non-Indian residents of the immediate surrounding areas. For a government that had been decimated in the nineteenth century, dominated by the BIA, and often ignored by other white institutions, such an acknowledgment of authority mattered. Community action served as the means through which the Mississippi Band could collaborate with BIA personnel and other non-Native power holders on an agenda set by Choctaws.

The tribal council appointed Martin to serve as director of the Choctaw CAA, a position he held into the 1970s. Born in 1926, Martin grew up in an area where Choctaw language was spoken and cultural practices were observed. After joining the military and attending local community colleges, Martin served two years on the Choctaw tribal council. In 1959, he was elected tribal chair, a position from which he led the campaign to remove Vance as agency superintendent. Martin stepped down as tribal chair in 1965 and began laying the foundation for the Choctaw community action program the following summer. By July, the tribe had established the Choctaw CAA headquarters in Pearl River, eight miles west of Philadelphia, and was cooperating with the BIA to conduct neighborhood surveys of the population, income, living conditions, and needs of both Indian and non-Indian families.[16]

The OEO's initial fifteen-thousand-dollar grant carried with it a meaning greater than its purchasing power. It represented the first time that the federal government had directly funded the tribe. Under Martin's leadership, the Choctaw community mobilized to make the most of the opportunity. Rather than disassociating themselves from the BIA, however, the Choctaws formed partnerships that encouraged the agency to support the tribe's agenda. Between 1966 and 1968, the Choctaws served as the administrative agency for an adult basic education program, senior citizens work training project, neighborhood center, and home builders' training program as well as such national-emphasis programs as the Neighborhood Youth Corps, Head Start, and Legal Services. Tribal members living within reservation boundaries welcomed the fact that Choctaw people now worked on beautification projects, built homes, served as community aides, provided support for accessing welfare assistance, and orchestrated voter registration drives.[17]

By the end of the decade, the War on Poverty added fuel to a Choctaw renaissance. Martin spoke in the summer of 1967 of a "tremendous surge upward of both personal and Tribal morale." A new tribal headquarters in Pearl

River, constructed in large measure by enrollees in the senior citizens work training program, was one visible expression of this positive turn toward self-determination. The same program supplied the muscle necessary to erect seven prefabricated schoolrooms that improved the Choctaw educational system. In light of the way that whites resisted integration, the tribal office and the schools signaled a future in which equality would be achieved not only by pressing for civil rights but also by exercising tribal sovereignty.[18]

The Legal Services program, which allied lawyers with a legal aide fluent in Choctaw, signaled similar possibilities. In addition to untangling difficult personal issues and confronting civil rights violations, Legal Services addressed complex jurisdictional disputes. When the War on Poverty began, the Choctaws had no law-and-order code, and civil and criminal jurisdiction rested in the state and federal courts, but which of these two had authority and under what circumstances was seldom clear. By 1968, a federal court ruling partially filled the vacuum that existed relative to crimes committed on the reservation when it found that the State of Mississippi did not have jurisdiction over the Choctaw Reservation. A decade later, the U.S. Supreme Court reaffirmed this basic component of tribal sovereignty, clearing the way for the development of a more robust tribal legal apparatus.[19]

In January 1968, Helen Scheirbeck, a Lumbee originally from North Carolina, traveled to Mississippi to evaluate the Choctaw CAA. "I was impressed by the tremendous movement forward being made by the Choctaws and the climate of change and opportunity sought by these people and stimulated by the Community Action Program," she reported. "The interest of the local Mississippian in the Choctaw area seems to be changing from direct prejudice to limited acceptance and a feeling that the Indians might even be somewhat of an asset to Mississippi after all." Over the next several years, the Choctaw CAA grew significantly. It employed eighty people in 1971, constructed thirty-five mutual help and thirty low-rent homes, and created a tribal housing authority to assist the Department of Housing and Urban Development in building more than two hundred units. In addition to an operating budget of $227,000 for the War on Poverty, the tribe administered a $415,000 Department of Health, Education, and Welfare–funded Follow Through program for children in kindergarten through third grade.[20]

Martin and York also consolidated the regional power of other resurgent indigenous communities by joining with the Miccosukees and Seminoles in Florida and Eastern Cherokees in North Carolina to found the United Southeastern

Tribes (USET) in 1968. As attacks on the antipoverty campaign intensified, USET lobbied for the effort's continuation. Acting in his capacity as the organization's president, Martin argued that the OEO should not be dismantled and transferred to another federal agency. "It was through OEO that the Indian people first received a chance to carry out their own programs to meet the broad scope of poverty-related needs on reservations that were not being met by established bureaucracies," he wrote to President Richard Nixon in February 1973. "While other agencies are attempting to expand their Indian programs in the directions first established by OEO, OEO remains the primary support for Indian governments attempting to achieve Self-Determination and self-development."[21]

Martin served as tribal chair from 1977 to 2007, proving so successful at promoting economic development that the tribe became the state's third-largest employer by the end of his tenure. With an enrollment of ninety-five hundred members, 85 percent of whom speak Choctaw as their first language, and a reservation of thirty-five thousand acres in ten counties in Mississippi and one in Tennessee, the Mississippi Choctaws have emerged as one of Native America's most dynamic communities. The War on Poverty served as a turning point, providing federal money that could be used to improve living conditions not only for tribe members but also for other Mississippians. In addition, the tribe gained leverage it needed to reassert an institutional presence as an indigenous nation in Mississippi. That empowerment did not lead to racial strife, as some had feared; instead, it laid the foundation for a symbiotic relationship among local, state, and tribal governments that anthropologist Jessica Cattelino has described as "sovereign interdependency."[22]

OKLAHOMA

The War on Poverty took a different turn for Indians living in Oklahoma, a state that took pride in its Native past while denying its Native present. In 1964, it contained within its boundaries more than sixty federally recognized tribes and more than two hundred thousand Native people but only one federally recognized reservation. This situation grew out of more than a century of dislocation and dispossession. Prior to statehood in 1907, Oklahoma had been divided into Oklahoma Territory to the west and Indian Territory to the east, with the latter, policymakers believed, serving as a permanent refuge for tribes. Between 1887 and 1898, the federal government passed legislation that led to the dismantling of the tribal land base throughout much of Indian Country. In all, some one hundred million acres were lost, with devastating results for Oklahoma Indians and other tribal communities.[23]

After the advent of statehood, Oklahoma, like Mississippi, gradually exerted civil and criminal jurisdiction over most of the land within its borders. Even though the allotment legislation did not explicitly abrogate tribes' federal trust status or dissolve reservation boundaries, succeeding generations of Oklahomans acted as though it had. Over time, a myth of Indian disappearance became real, at least in terms of practical consequences. By the 1960s, a majority of Oklahomans accepted the fiction that tribes had lost their sovereignty and that all tribal authority had been assumed by the state. But thousands of Native people from dozens of tribal communities had never accepted these ideas, and they, like the Mississippi Band of Choctaws, protested long before the coming of the War on Poverty. The antipoverty campaign would not, however, have as transformative an impact in Oklahoma as it did in Mississippi.[24]

In the spring of 1965, federal and state OEO field representatives convened meetings in eastern Oklahoma to promote Cherokee participation in the War on Poverty. In the towns of Hulbert, Tahlequah, and Jay, bilingual interpreters explained the Economic Opportunity Act at churches and public buildings. Hundreds of Cherokees attended and welcomed the OEO's promise to provide money to design and administer programs for their communities. In June, however, the OEO distributed a memo indicating that funding CAAs for any one racial or ethnic group would violate civil rights provisions. All War on Poverty programs would have to include an area's entire population.[25]

The formation of Cherokee County's CAA tested the efficacy of the OEO's approach. As a consequence of allotment and the infusion of non-Native people into northeastern Oklahoma, Cherokees represented approximately 20 percent of the population and a greater percentage of the poor in Cherokee County. Leading non-Indian residents mobilized to submit a community action proposal during the summer of 1965. Despite the OEO's efforts to involve Cherokee communities, the advisory board did not provide for equitable representation of low-income Cherokees. The OEO's Southwest Regional Office refused to fund the project.[26]

Cherokee County Community Development Foundation board members initially refused to accept an amendment to add more Cherokee-speaking, low-income representatives to its advisory board, arguing that "many people on the Board had Cherokee bloo[d]." OEO field representatives countered that to achieve "true Indian representation," the county must include a bilingual assistant director selected and trusted by the Cherokee population. A second mandate compelled the agency to ensure that Indians would participate in numbers commensurate with their population. The Cherokee County Community Development Foundation ultimately conceded, but many Cherokees withdrew, leaving unanswered the question of what it meant to achieve "true Indian representation."[27]

OKLAHOMANS FOR INDIAN OPPORTUNITY

What happened in Cherokee County was not an isolated event. Growing concerns that Native people would be left out led to the formation of Oklahomans for Indian Opportunity (OIO) in 1965. The organization grew out of a struggle for racial justice in the southwestern part of the state that predated the War on Poverty. During the early 1960s, a loosely knit multiracial organization known as "the Group" organized in Lawton, home of the Fort Sill army base, to address issues of segregation and discrimination. A second cohort came to OIO through the Indian Education Project, which was coordinated by the University of Oklahoma's Southwest Center for Human Relations Studies and which began as a BIA-funded pilot project in Lawton in November 1962. Over the next two years, Indian people in Ponca City, Carnegie, Watonga, Anadarko, and Hobart founded additional centers. By 1964, inspired in part by the rising tide of civil rights activism, the Indian Education Project addressed controversial issues such as police brutality, the misuse of the judicial system, discrimination, and voter registration.[28]

Members of the Group and the Indian Education Project found that the Community Action Program's principles of maximum feasible participation and local initiative reaffirmed the belief that ordinary people needed to be empowered to effect change in the communities in which they resided. The notion of bringing together all segments of a community in a common effort also complemented ongoing efforts in western Oklahoma. Community action called for the kind of interaction these activists believed would lead to mutual understanding while offering an alternative to the BIA's paternalism.

The unexpected rise to power of Oklahoma state senator Fred Harris and his wife, Comanche activist LaDonna Harris, made OIO possible. In 1964, Fred Harris was elected to fill the U.S. Senate seat made vacant by the death of Democrat Robert S. Kerr. The Harrises had previously been active in both the Group and the Indian Education Project. With their newfound prominence, they pressed for the active involvement of Oklahoma Indians in the antipoverty campaign.

Figure 10. LaDonna Harris (right) and Iola Hayden (left) provided the leadership necessary to make Oklahomans for Indian Opportunity a political force during the 1960s. Photograph courtesy of Oklahomans for Indian Opportunity.

Organizational meetings in June and August 1965 brought participants in the Group and Indian Education Project together with representatives from the state OEO, principal chiefs and governors of Oklahoma tribes, BIA officials, county CAA directors, church leaders, and university personnel.[29]

At these meetings, isolation, exclusion, and nonparticipation were identified as the primary impediments to Native economic self-sufficiency. As a means of rectifying these problems, OIO proposed Indian involvement in what the organization called the "total community." This integrationist approach proved to be anything but a panacea. The use of a shared language at the organizational meetings disguised profound disagreements over what that "total community" should look like. Members of both the state bureaucracy and the BIA, for example, considered integration synonymous with assimilation. The notion of "fuller participation in the culture and economy of the state and nation" meant something fundamentally different to the Harrises and the majority of their allies, none of whom expected Native people to lose their identities as Native people.[30]

Over the next several months, OIO initiated a broad array of programs. Field representatives encouraged Indians to participate in the county and city CAAs being established across the state. Community leaders who had the confidence of their neighbors were asked to enroll in leadership training seminars and drum up support for oio youth programs and urban centers. Work orientation programs prepared Indians to enter the labor force, while community development efforts fostered cooperation and mutual understanding across racial and cultural divides. Dozens of Indian youth councils were established in high schools, and a statewide Indian youth conference brought participants to the University of Oklahoma to receive scholarships and hear speakers such as Robert F. Kennedy and George McGovern. During annual Indian Achievement Week celebrations, oio donated books about Indians to school libraries, recognized towns that reached out to Indian communities, and sponsored keynote addresses by members of President Johnson's cabinet.[31]

During this flurry of activity, tensions among oio, county caas, and several tribal governments in eastern Oklahoma became evident. In the spring of 1967, a task force that included Fred and LaDonna Harris, oio executive director Iola Hayden (Comanche), members of Oklahoma's congressional delegation, and oeo personnel toured northeastern Oklahoma. Shortly thereafter, oio received a multicounty research and demonstration project grant to promote economic development in Haskell, LeFlore, Adair, Cherokee, and Sequoyah Counties. Hayden described the effort as "a poverty program and not just for Indian people" that would begin with start-up loans for cooperative buying clubs, feeder pig farms, agricultural industries, and brick manufacturing companies. However, non-Indian caa directors argued that they should control the funds and intimated that oio would discriminate against whites. The dispute climaxed in the summer of 1967 with a failed attempt to oust Hayden.[32]

The attempted coup reflected the caa directors' interests in self-preservation. But Maynard Ungerman, a Tulsa attorney and political ally of Fred and LaDonna Harris, detected additional motivations. "What now worries myself . . . and others . . . is that we may well have hit the level that we anticipated of somewhat of a conflict between oio and the tribal organizations," he confided to the Harrises. "I think you may recall . . . that we did discuss the possibility that oio sooner or later would through it's [sic] projects threaten the status quo relationship that the Tribal Chiefs have with the various tribes. Just as the Mayors of cities feel threatened by activities of vista and other governmental workers in the poverty area." In his view, tribal leaders in eastern Oklahoma were lashing out at oio because its projects were altering the balance of power within Indian communities.[33]

Amendments to the Economic Opportunity Act in November 1967 made matters worse. One of the changes mandated that all rural CAAs serve no fewer than fifty thousand people.[34] This alteration raised the stakes of Indian inclusion in Oklahoma because it meant that to retain their current funding levels, CAA directors needed to present themselves to OEO as vital, inclusive representatives of the poor. The directors, many of whom already felt threatened by OIO, argued that they should maintain their original role of merely facilitating Indian participation in their programs.

OIO was not the radical organization some observers made it out to be. It had, however, distinguished itself from CAAs, the BIA, and tribal governments in eastern Oklahoma. "The initial reason that we used to get money was to more fully draw Indian people into local community agencies," recalled Hayden. "They were not involving Indian people," she added. "It takes work to do that. . . . And they just weren't interested in doing it. It just takes too long, it just takes too much time and frankly they just probably didn't give a damn." Hayden's tenure with the Comanche County Community Action Foundation in southwestern Oklahoma had demonstrated this lack of caring, and her experience with OIO provided confirmation.[35]

Figure 11. Iola Hayden (standing) meets with Oklahomans for Indian Opportunity board members, 1967. Photograph courtesy of Oklahomans for Indian Opportunity.

Figure 12. LaDonna Harris (second from left), Senator Fred Harris (third from left), and Iola Hayden (fourth from left) meet with participants in Project Peace Pipe, an Oklahomans for Indian Opportunity–sponsored effort to pretrain native youths for service in the Peace Corps, August 1968. Photograph courtesy of Oklahomans for Indian Opportunity.

But the problem went beyond noninvolvement. Indians who participated in community action often did so under prejudicial circumstances. From OIO's perspective, too many CAA personnel believed that giving up cultural and social distinctiveness was the price of progress, and their caretaker mentalities stifled autonomy. At a 1968 Senate hearing, Hayden explained OIO's position: "We do not want you to come in and inflict charity upon people. . . . [W]e want you to come in and give people a chance to help themselves." Like the Mississippi Band of Choctaws, OIO concluded that to reclaim power, Indian people needed independent institutions rooted in the community.[36]

The War on Poverty had a less transformative impact in Oklahoma than it did in Mississippi, however. As OIO began its economic development program, the tenor of race and class politics changed. A backlash against the War on Poverty ultimately led to amendments that handicapped CAAs' ability to engage in local-level empowerment. And by 1970, the OEO, now under the direction of the Nixon administration, extended a research and development grant to the

State of Oklahoma that enabled it to serve as a regional office with full control over community action grants. Not coincidentally, this plan gained momentum after the 1968 elections produced a much stronger conservative presence in Oklahoma's congressional delegation.[37]

Now in the minority, Fred Harris led an effort to overturn what came to be called the Oklahoma Plan because it threatened to stifle local community involvement. When members of Congress, along with support from Native organizations such as the United Southeastern Tribes, derailed a similar plan in 1969, he contended that Congress had "decided specifically against giving control of OEO anti-poverty programs to the states." Harris questioned whether the OEO now sought to accomplish administratively what Congress had refused to legislate. Of particular concern was the fact that governors would gain veto power over grants such as the ones on which OIO depended for its existence. Despite Harris's repeated requests for hearings before its enactment, the Oklahoma Plan went into effect in July 1970.[38]

Without the OEO's support, OIO lost an important countervailing force against the governor's office. The state had already impinged on the efficacy of OIO's buying clubs by refusing to issue sales tax permits. The conservative resurgence in Congress only compounded matters, essentially leaving the organization with nowhere to turn. By 1970, as one of Republican congressman Page Belcher's assistants accurately noted, "No one in the entire Oklahoma Delegation, outside of Fred Harris really wants to be associated with O.I.O."[39]

The organization persevered through several more tumultuous years, surviving the final dismantling of the OEO between 1973 and 1974. Although OIO did not close its doors until 2005, the organization suffered the same fate as many other CAAs. Having lost the ability to use federal money in experimental, innovative, and potentially controversial ways, it survived by becoming adept at securing narrowly conceived grants authored by experts in faraway places.

The conflicts surrounding OIO do not fully explain the War on Poverty's shortcomings in Oklahoma. Indeed, its relative inefficacy extended from the OEO's critical decision regarding the funding of Indian community action. From the outset, the OEO removed appropriations for reservation programs from state budgetary allocations and created a separate Indian Desk within the Community Action Program to administer those programs. OEO director Sargent Shriver reasoned that since "these federal reservations have historical and legal ties to the federal government and not to the state governments," grants would be "awarded to the reservation *as a unit of geography* to serve all the poor people who live within the bounds of that community."[40] This geographical definition of community worked relatively well where large numbers of Indians lived on reservations, but it meant that nonreservation Indians would not fall under the aegis of the Indian Desk. For this reason, tribal governments in Oklahoma were not chosen to sponsor CAAs, and Indians were expected to participate in county-wide programs, in which Natives were invariably a minority population.

Poverty planners should have known better. In January 1965, a young Ponca activist, Clyde Warrior, submitted a paper for OEO's National Conference on Poverty in the Southwest in which he explained what it meant to be born and raised in north-central Oklahoma. He questioned whether the War on Poverty would be able to grapple with the depth of racism in and around his hometown of Ponca City. "I do not doubt that all of you are men of good will and that you do intend to work with the local community," Warrior wrote. "My only fear is what you think the local community is." The areas OEO considered communities geographically were hardly that in terms of relationships, he argued. "There is no Kay County, Oklahoma, community in a social sense," Warrior said of the region surrounding his people. "We are not a part of it except in the most tangential legal sense. We only live there."[41]

A paper written by Albert L. Wahrhaftig, a doctoral candidate in anthropology at the University of Chicago, bolstered Warrior's analysis. Wahrhaftig attempted to convince the OEO that a definition of community based on sociological and anthropological principles would be necessary to effect change. Drawing on his involvement in the Carnegie Cross-Cultural Education Project in the Cherokee Nation, Wahrhaftig contended that any other course of action would preclude tribal Cherokees from participating because they lived in nongeographical communities defined in terms of kinship, shared language, and common places of worship. "Tribal Indians are not going to move until they have been approached *as Indians* and offered a clearly defined place *as Indians* in the Great Society," Wahrhaftig concluded. "Since socially there are no local communities which embrace both Indians and whites, Indians are not going to join in planning mutual local programs with whites."[42]

CONCLUSIONS

Warrior and Wahrhaftig were right. Seen from a national perspective, the philosophy of community action—a commitment to local control over decision making that Native rights advocates effectively translated into the language of tribal self-determination—played a pivotal role in redefining federal-Indian relations in way that benefited all tribal communities in the decades that followed. But when the OEO's geographical definition of community led tribal governments, such as the Mississippi Band of Choctaws, to receive direct funding through the Indian Desk, Native nations gained momentum in their push for more local autonomy. Tribal communities in Oklahoma and in other non-reservation areas had to wait for the federal government's larger shift toward tribal self-determination beginning in the 1970s. Indeed, the limited vision of the War on Poverty's architects made OIO necessary. Bureaucrats' definition of Indians as members of distinct political communities did not extend beyond the most obvious of reservation boundaries; at least to those officials, Indians outside those boundaries assumed the status of a racial minority.

Scholarship on the War on Poverty is incomplete without the inclusion of Native people. American Indians actively participated in many of the same contests over the meaning of community, poverty, and identity that tore at the national fabric during the 1960s. Like so many alienated youths, disillusioned intellectuals, and people marginalized by poverty and discrimination, outspoken Native-rights advocates emerged from the decade with the conviction that the problem lay with the dominant society, not with them. In Mississippi, in Oklahoma, and across Indian Country, Native people engaged in their variant of the rights revolution, underscoring the reality of indigenous survival and the endurance of tribal sovereignty. Grasping this larger and more expansive legacy of the War on Poverty requires going beyond black and white, colorizing and complicating, and acknowledging that plenty of gray remains.

Notes

I thank Allan Winkler, Katherine M. B. Osburn, and Annelise Orleck for providing critical readings of earlier drafts of this chapter.

1. D'Arcy McNickle, *Native American Tribalism: Indian Survivals and Renewals* (1973; New York: Oxford University Press, 1993), 122.

2. See Daniel M. Cobb, *Native Activism in Cold War America: The Struggle for Sovereignty* (Lawrence: University Press of Kansas, 2008); George Pierre Castile, *To Show Heart: Native American Self-Determination and Federal Indian Policy, 1960–1975* (Tucson: University of Arizona Press, 1998); Thomas Clarkin, *Federal Indian Policy in the Kennedy and Johnson Administrations, 1961–1969* (Albuquerque: University of New Mexico Press, 2000).

3. Sar A. Levitan, *The Great Society's Poor Law: A New Approach to Poverty* (Baltimore: Johns Hopkins University Press, 1969), 263–70; Sar A. Levitan and Barbara Hetrick, *Big Brother's Indian Programs—With Reservations* (New York: McGraw-Hill, 1971).

4. Daniel M. Cobb, "Philosophy of an Indian War: Indian Community Action in the Johnson Administration's War on Indian Poverty, 1964–1968," *American Indian Culture and Research Journal* 22:2 (1998): 71–103; Richard W. Boone, interview by author, November 8, 2002. The Cobell case, settled in December 2009, revealed how badly the federal government had mismanaged its trust responsibilities. See http://www.cobellsettlement.com/.

5. Vine Deloria Jr. and Clifford Lytle, *The Nations Within: The Past and Future of American Indian Sovereignty* (New York: Pantheon, 1984).

6. Thomas Biolsi, "'Indian Self-Government' as a Technique of Domination," *American Indian Quarterly* 15:1 (Winter 1991): 23–28; Thomas Biolsi, "The Birth of the Reservation: Making the Modern Individual among the Lakota," *American Ethnologist* 22:1 (February 1995): 28–53.

7. For case studies, see Daniel M. Cobb, "'Us Indians Understand the Basics': Oklahoma Indians and the Politics of Community Action, 1964–1970," *Western Historical Quarterly* 33:1 (Spring 2002): 41–66; Paivi Hoikkala, "Mothers and Community Builders: Salt River Pima and Maricopa Women in Community Action," in *Negotiators of Change: Historical Perspective on Native American Women*, ed. Nancy Shoemaker (New York: Routledge, 1995), 213–34.

8. Ronald Satz, "The Mississippi Choctaw: From the Removal Treaty to the Federal Agency," in *After Removal: The Choctaw in Mississippi*, ed. Samuel J. Wells and Roseanna Tubby (Jackson: University Press of Mississippi, 1986), 3–32; Patricia Galloway and Clara Sue Kidwell, "Choctaw in the East," in *Handbook of North American Indians*, vol. 14, *Southeast* (Washington, D.C.: Smithsonian Institution, 2004), 499–519.

9. This treatment of Native Americans was customary rather than statutory until 1927, when the U.S. Supreme Court's *Gong Lum v. Rice* decision upheld separate but equal and determined that "colored" included other nonwhite races. See http://supreme.justia.com/us/275/78/case.html. I am indebted to Katherine M. B. Osburn for pointing out this information to me.

10. Clara Sue Kidwell, "The Choctaw Struggle for Land and Identity in Mississippi, 1830–1918," in *After Removal*, ed. Wells and Tubby, 64–93; Katherine M. B. Osburn, "'In a Name of Justice and Fairness': The Mississippi Choctaw Indian Federation versus the BIA, 1934," in *Beyond Red Power: American Indian Politics and Activism since 1900*, Daniel M. Cobb and Loretta Fowler (Santa Fe, N.M.: SAR, 2007), 109–25.

11. At times, Mississippi Choctaws forged alliances with non-Native local, state, and national political leaders. See Osburn, "'In a Name'"; Katherine M. B. Osburn, "Missis-

sippi Choctaws and Racial Politics," *Southern Cultures* 14:4 (Winter 2008): 32–54; Katherine M. B. Osburn, "The 'Identified Full-Bloods' in Mississippi: Race and Choctaw Identity, 1898–1918," *Ethnohistory* 56:3 (Summer 2009): 423–47.

12. Phillip Martin and Emmett York, report for American Indian Chicago Conference, http://www.choctaw.org/history/chronology.htm. Detailed correspondence on these issues can be found in Box 249, Folders 10–11, Association on American Indian Affairs Archives, Seeley G. Mudd Manuscript Library, Princeton University, Princeton, New Jersey.

13. Executive Director's Report, Mississippi Choctaws, June 8, 1962, La Verne Madigan to Phillip Martin, March 21, 1961, June 8, 1962, La Verne Madigan to Oliver La Farge and Dick Schifter, June 25, 1962, Richard Schifter to Oliver La Farge, July 13, 1962, Oliver La Farge to Betty Rosenthal, December 18, 1962, all in Box 249, Folder 11, Association on American Indian Affairs Archives; Martin and York, report.

14. Fergus M. Bordewich, *Killing the White Man's Indian: Reinventing Native Americans at the End of the Twentieth Century* (New York: Doubleday, 1996), 302–11.

15. Tersh Boasberg to Fred Hayes et al., March 8, 1966, Box 34A, Folder "RG 381 Restricted Records: FOIA (b)(c) Local Problem Areas File," Entry 5, Local Problem Areas File, 1966, Records of the Community Services Administration, Office of Economic Opportunity, Records of the Director, RG 381, National Archives II, College Park, Maryland (hereafter RG 381). On the notion of the "deserving poor," see Michael B. Katz, *The Undeserving Poor: From the War on Poverty to the War on Welfare* (New York: Pantheon, 1989).

16. Biographical Data, Mississippi Band of Choctaw Indians Application for Operation Mainstream Program under Nelson-Scheuer Amendment, December 4, 1967, Box 45, Folder "Application for Operation Mainstream Program under Nelson-Scheuer Amendment, Choctaw (Mississippi)," Entry 1023, Records of the Office of Operations—Indian Division, Grant Files, 1965–69, RG 381; Benton R. White and Christine Schultz White, "Phillip Martin: Mississippi Choctaw," in *The New Warriors: Native American Leaders since 1900*, ed. R. David Edmunds (Lincoln: University of Nebraska Press, 2001), 195–209.

17. Theodore Berry to Clay Gibson, October 17, 1966, Box 45, Folder "Mississippi Band of Choctaw MISS/CAP-8080 A/O Correspondence [2 of 2]," Entry 1023, Grant Files, 1965–69, RG 381. Information also derived from eleven CAP Narrative Progress Reports submitted between July 1966 and August 1967, Box 45, Folder "Mississippi Band of Choctaw MISS/CAP 8080 A/O Correspondence [1 of 2]," Entry 1023, Grant Files, 1965–69, RG 381.

18. Phillip Martin to Lloyd Moses, September 15, 1967, Box 45, Folder "Mississippi Band of Choctaw MISS/CAP A/O Correspondence [2 of 2]," Entry 1023, Grant Files, 1965–69, RG 381.

19. CAP Narrative Progress Report 11; Phillip Martin to Theodore R. Mitchell, September 17, 1966, Clay Gibson to "Gentlemen," April 18, 1967, both in Box 45, Folder "Mississippi Band of Choctaw MISS/CAP-8080 A/O Correspondence [2 of 2]," Entry 1023, Grant Files, 1965–69, RG 381; CAP.4 Eligibility of Applicant, Application for Community Action Program, n.d., Box 46, Folder "Choctaw Legal Service Program, Mississippi Band of Choctaw Indians (Miss) CG 8081," Grant Files, 1965–69, RG 381; Legal Service Report for April, Choctaw Legal Service Report for May, Choctaw Legal Service Report for June, Box 47, Folder "Quarterly Reports, Legal Service Reports, Observations on Technical Assistance and Training Needs, Correspondence," Grant Files, 1965–69, RG 381; Satz, "Mississippi Choctaw," 23–24; Galloway and Kidwell, "Choctaw in the East," 517.

20. Helen M. Scheirbeck, "Choctaw Report," January 18, 1968, 10, Box 47, Folder "Quarterly Reports, Legal Service Reports, Observations on Technical Assistance and Training Needs, Correspondence," Grant Files, 1965–69, RG 381; Operation Mainstream Grant, December 4, 1967, RG 381; *Self-Determination: A Program of Accomplishments* (n.p.: Arizona Affiliated Tribes, May 1971), 135, Box 77, Folder "Self-Determination," General Subject Files, Records of the National Council on Indian Opportunity, RG 220, National Archives II, College Park, Maryland.

21. Phillip Martin to Lloyd Moses, September 15, 1967, Box 45, Folder "Mississippi Band of Choctaw MISS/CAP A/O Correspondence [2 of 2]," Entry 1023, Grant Files, 1965–69, RG 381; Herbert Bechtold to Noel Klores, June 20, 1967, Box 45, Folder "Mississippi Band of Choctaw Indians—Philadelphia, Mississippi," Grant Files, 1965–69, RG 381; Phillip Martin, to Richard Nixon, February 25, 1973, Series 6, Box 38:49, Folder "OEO Shutdown," National Congress of American Indians Papers, National Anthropological Archives, Smithsonian Institution, Suitland, Maryland.

22. Bordewich, *Killing the White Man's Indian*, 302–11; White and White, "Phillip Martin," 199–208; Jessica Cattelino, "Florida Seminole Gaming and Local Sovereign Interdependency," in *Beyond Red Power*, ed. Cobb and Fowler, 262–79. A 2000 study found that tribal businesses employed more than sixty-seven hundred individuals at an annual payroll of $123.7 million. Tribal businesses generated more than twelve thousand jobs across the state and almost $100 million of spending with Mississippi businesses (http://www.choctaw.org/history/chronology.htm#part5).

23. I am referring here to the General Allotment (Dawes) Act of 1887 and the Curtis Act of 1898. On the former, see Janet McDonnell, *The Dispossession of the American Indian, 1887–1934* (Bloomington: Indiana University Press, 1991). On allotment in Oklahoma, see Angie Debo, *And Still the Waters Run: The Betrayal of the Five Civilized Tribes* (1940; Princeton: Princeton University Press, 1968). The official 1960 census reported 64,689 Indians in Oklahoma; as many as 140,000 were not counted.

24. John H. Moore, "The Enduring Reservations of Oklahoma," in *State and Reser-*

vation: New Perspectives on Federal Indian Policy, ed. Robert L. Bee and George Pierre Castile (Tucson: University of Arizona Press, 1992), 92–107.

25. Albert L. Wahrhaftig, "Making Do with the Dark Meat: A Report on the Cherokee Indians of Oklahoma," in *World Anthropology: American Indian Economic Development*, ed. Sol Tax and Sam Stanley (The Hague: Mouton, 1978), 481.

26. Ernest C. Woods to Donald B. Mathis, September 8, 1965, Bruce Babbitt to Chris Aldrete, December 14, 1965, Max Witzel to Bob Haught, March 2, 1966, all in Box 11, Folder "Cherokee County," Records of the Community Services Administration, Office of Economic Opportunity, Records of the Community Action Program, Records Relating to County Community Action Agencies, RG 381, National Archives, Southwest Region, Fort Worth, Texas; Cherokee (Oklahoma) County Development Foundation, Inc., Application for Program Development Grant, Box 7, Folder 51, Fred R. Harris Collection, Carl Albert Center for Congressional Research and Studies, University of Oklahoma, Norman.

27. Bruce Babbitt to Chris Aldrete, December 14, 1965, Bruce Babbitt to Chris Aldrete et al., January 13, 1966, Donald B. Mathis to Earl Squyres, n.d., Max Witzel to Bob Haught, March 2, 1966, all in RG 381, National Archives, Southwest Region; Sol Tax to Sidney Woolner, August 19, 1965, Series 4, Box 152, Folder 3, Sol Tax Papers, Joseph Regenstein Library, University of Chicago; Robert K. Thomas to Jack Conway, November 19, 1965, Earl Boyd Pierce Collection, Cherokee National Archives, Tahlequah, Oklahoma.

28. Maggie Gover, "We Called Ourselves the Group," unpublished manuscript in author's possession, 1–4, 6–7, 11–13; Sarah Epler Janda, "'Her Heritage Is Helpful': Race, Ethnicity, and Gender in the Politicization of LaDonna Harris," *Great Plains Quarterly* 25:4 (Fall 2005): 211–27; Fred R. Harris and LaDonna Harris, interview by author, May 14, 2001; LaDonna Harris and Iola Hayden, interview by author, May 27, 2002; *Southwest Center for Human Relations Studies, Annual Report, 1963*, 10, *Southwest Center for Human Relations Studies, Annual Report, 1964*, i, Box 2, Folder 51, Robert L. Miller Collection, Western History Collections, University of Oklahoma, Norman; Indian Education Faculty and Summary, Indian Education Meetings, August 6, 1964–June 7, 1965, Box 1, Folder 20, Miller Collection; *HRC Newsletter*, Spring 1963, 2, November 1963, Box 3, Folder 3, American Indian Institute Collection, Western History Collections, University of Oklahoma, Norman; Iola Hayden, interview by author, June 22, 2001; *Southwest Center for Human Relations Studies, Annual Report, 1964*, 5; *Indian Education Newsletter*, April 1964, 3–4, Box 3, Folder 3, American Indian Institute Collection.

29. *Indian Education Newsletter*, September 1965, 2, Box 3, Folder 3, American Indian Institute Collection; "Minutes of Initial Meeting," Oklahomans for Indian Opportunity Corporation Books, June 1965–November 1968, in author's possession. On Fred R. Harris's senatorial career, see Richard Lowitt, *Fred Harris: His Journey from Liberalism to Populism* (Lanham, Md.: Rowman and Littlefield, 2002).

30. Press Release, June 6, 1965, "Minutes of Initial Meeting," Oklahomans for Indian Opportunity Corporation Books; "OIO Ideas," July 13, 1966, Box 283, Folder 9, Harris Collection; "Oklahomans for Indian Opportunity, University of Oklahoma," June 14, 1965, Box 282, Folder 5, Harris Collection.

31. LaDonna Harris to Clayton Feaver, April 4, 1966, Box 283, Folder 11, Harris Collection; Kay M. Haws to LaDonna Harris, April 12, 1966, Box 282, Folder 12, Harris Collection; "New Training Center Is Set at OU," *Ada Evening News*, July 7, 1966, Box 12, Folder "Cleveland County News Clippings," RG 381, National Archives, Southwest Region; Minutes, Board of Directors Meeting, Oklahomans for Indian Opportunity, July 15, 1966, "Minutes," Oklahomans for Indian Opportunity Corporation Books; "Nominations Due for Award for Oklahoma Indians," *Tonkawa News*, September 22, 1966; "Wewoka to Get Special Award," *Tulsa World*, October 13, 1966; "No Kidding," *Anadarko Daily News*, October 13, 1966.

32. "Oklahomans for Indian Opportunity, Incorporated, Rural Development Program Proposal for Refunding Grant, November 20–December 1, 1970," 4, attached to CLW to Mr. A [Carl Albert], n.d., Box 89, Folder "OEO—Oklahomans for Indian Opportunity," Carl Albert Collection, Carl Albert Center for Congressional Research and Studies, University of Oklahoma, Norman; Harris and Harris, interview; Minutes of Executive Committee Meeting of Oklahomans for Indian Opportunity, May 6, 1967, "Reports of Executive Committee," Oklahomans for Indian Opportunity Corporation Books; "Memo to Executive Board Members of OIO from Iola Taylor," May 9, 1967, Box 68, Folder 5, Harris Collection; "Five Counties Tapped in Poverty Project," attached to Carl Albert to Fred R. Harris, May 13, 1967, Box 68, Folder 1, Harris Collection; Ed Edmondson to Clark McWhorter, April 14, 1967, C. E. Cummins to Dick Morrison, April 3, 1967, Ed Edmondson to Sargent Shriver, April 14, 1967, Sargent Shriver to Ed Edmondson, April 1967, all in Box 78, Folder 7, Ed Edmondson Papers, University Archives, John Vaughan Library, Northeastern State University, Tahlequah, Oklahoma; Lon F. Kirk to Fletcher Baker, April 25, 1968, OEO (1968) CAP—Program Data folder, Albert Collection. On the ouster attempt, see Cobb, "'Us Indians.'"

33. LaDonna Harris to Bob Miller, August 7, 1967, Box 2, Folder 17, Miller Collection; Maynard I. Ungerman to Fred and LaDonna Harris, July 18, 1967, Box 284, Folder 16, Harris Collection.

34. Susan Abrams Beck, "The Limits of Presidential Activism: Lyndon Johnson and the Implementation of the Community Action Program" (Ph.D. diss., Columbia University, 1985), 108–14.

35. Hayden, interview.

36. Iola Taylor Hayden in U.S. Senate, Committee on Government Operations, *Human Resources Development: Hearings before the Subcommittee on Government Research*, 90th Cong., 2nd sess., Pt. 1, April 8, 10, 18, 1968 (Washington, D.C.: U.S. Govern-

ment Printing Office, 1968), 16; William G. Hayden, "Oklahomans for Indian Opportunity, Inc., and Economic Development for Non-Reservation Indian People," in *Toward Economic Development for Native American Communities: A Compendium of Papers Submitted to the Subcommittee on Economy on Government of the Joint Economic Committee* (Washington, D.C.: U.S. Government Printing Office, 1969), 418–41.

37. "Statement of Senator Fred R. Harris before the Senate Subcommittee on Appropriations for the Departments of Labor and Health, Education, and Welfare," June 18, 1970, Box 215, Folder 22, Harris Collection.

38. Statement of Senator Fred R. Harris, March 12, 1970, Box 187, Folder 22a, Harris Collection. The position statement issued by United Southeastern Tribes can be found in Alvin Josephy, ed., *Red Power: The American Indians' Fight for Freedom* (Lincoln: University of Nebraska Press, 1971), 155–66.

39. NAN per J.C., September 8, 1971, Box 167, Folder 6, Page Belcher Collection, Carl Albert Center for Congressional Research and Studies, University of Oklahoma, Norman.

40. Sargent Shriver to Dewey F. Bartlett, May 1, 1967 (emphasis added), Box 121, Folder 1f, Belcher Collection.

41. Clyde Warrior, "Poverty, Community, and Power," *New University Thought* 4:2 [Summer 1965]: 5–10. Warrior claimed that organizers prevented him from giving his talk because they considered it too controversial.

42. Albert L. Wahrhaftig, *Indian Communities of Eastern Oklahoma and the War on Poverty* (Chicago: Carnegie Cross-Cultural Education Project, 1965), 4, 10, 26. On the Carnegie Project, see Daniel M. Cobb, "Devils in Disguise: The Carnegie Project, the Cherokee Nation, and the 1960s," *American Indian Quarterly* 31:3 (Summer 2007): 465–90.

KAREN M. TANI

The House That "Equality" Built

The Asian American Movement and the
Legacy of Community Action

President Lyndon Baines Johnson liked to quote the prophet Isaiah. "Come, let us reason together," Johnson sometimes said (assuming the voice of God) as he prepared to exercise his famous powers of persuasion.[1] But Johnson was no literalist. Jesus told his disciples that the poor would be "with you always." Johnson and the other architects of the Great Society disagreed. Convinced that privation had no place in modern America, they confidently launched the concatenation of federal initiatives known as the War on Poverty. That war is now over; the poor, as predicted, remain. Yet the battle mattered—not because it was effective or ineffective (a question that scholars, activists, and policymakers continue to debate) but because of what it did on the ground and apart from its creators' intentions. The War on Poverty fundamentally altered how government largesse reaches the poor as well as who enjoys the power that comes from channeling state beneficence. One of the locations in which that imprint is clearest is New York City's Chinatown.

As a consequence of a long history of restrictive immigration policies and an even longer history of discrimination, Asian Americans were relatively insignificant to the U.S. government in 1964, remaining far from the minds of the policymakers behind the War on Poverty. Yet that legislative program and its subsequent incarnations affected Asian American communities, especially as a social, political, and cultural Asian American movement gained momentum and as changes in immigration law sent thousands of Asian immigrants into already stressed and overcrowded ethnic enclaves.

Funds from the War on Poverty provided, however modestly, services that some Asian Americans needed (job training, housing assistance, youth programs) but had not often received from sources outside their communities. War on Poverty programs helped inspire Asian American activism. As they watched federal dollars flow into African American neighborhoods, young Asian Americans (and their older activist predecessors) rejected the idea that poverty was a normal and necessary part of the Asian immigrant experience. But most important, War on Poverty programs helped some Asian American political organizations survive and thrive in the midst of the 1970s urban crisis and in the face of opposition from those who had long purported to speak for impoverished Asian immigrant communities. By channeling War on Poverty funds (as well as antipoverty funds from the private sector that accompanied federal dollars) into densely populated ethnic enclaves, Asian American activist groups transitioned from bit players in urban politics to major actors. Poor Asian Americans were a far-flung and neglected front when the federal war against indigence was conceived and first executed; however, that campaign helped reorder the power structures in the spaces where many Asian Americans continue to live and work.

Building on the work of other scholars who have noted how War on Poverty initiatives reconfigured local political systems,[2] this essay uses the story of Asian Americans for Equality (AAFE), founded in New York's Chinatown in 1974, to explore how that phenomenon operated in a place that is not remembered as a War on Poverty target. A civil rights group with radical origins, AAFE began by critiquing local government for failing to deliver the opportunities, services, and civility it had promised. AAFE organized some of the largest demonstrations that Chinatown had ever seen, challenging the stereotype that Asian Americans were a passive minority, neither desiring nor deserving of "outside" help. Many groups with similar origins lost momentum and disbanded, but AAFE put down roots and grew. By the end of the 1980s, nourished by remnants of the War on Poverty's community action initiatives, AAFE was not only a well-known advocate for Asian American rights but a successful housing developer and a force in local electoral politics. By the end of the twentieth century, leftists in Chinatown would view AAFE as the establishment.

AAFE's story parallels that of other Asian American community-based organizations from the same era and thus can be used to demonstrate the significance of federal antipoverty policy for other Asian American enclaves. For example, activists founded the Philadelphia Chinatown Development Corporation in 1969 in response to an urban renewal project that threatened to destroy the area. Using government funds and foundation grants, the group eventually became a housing developer. Seattle's International District Improvement Association (InterIm) followed a similar path: it began in 1969 as a group dedicated to revitalizing Chinatown and assisting its residents; in the late 1970s, it started securing public and charitable funds; and today it channels millions of dollars into low-income housing, social services, and community programs. Similarly, San Francisco's Chinatown Community Development Center (formerly the Chinatown Resources Center) now uses funding from government and private foundations to develop housing, manage properties, and provide community services. In 1977, when it began, the group was essentially a collection of grassroots advocacy organizations.[3] These stories show that not all poor communities benefited from the War on Poverty in its early days but that the power and legitimacy that attached to War on Poverty funds eventually helped ostensibly radical groups become respectable enough to attract private patrons, win resources in an era of scarcity, and ultimately change the local political landscape. Whether poverty won or lost, this legacy remains.

"FORGOTTEN" TARGETS IN A LOCALIZED WAR

The War on Poverty, like many wars, was neither coherent nor well planned. As Alice O'Connor has explained, it emphasized not only "local organizing for direct, transformative action" but also and contradictorily "rational, 'top-down' planning toward readily achievable national goals."[4] It sought simultaneously to rehabilitate the poor, spur economic growth, appease vocal African Americans (as well as those who feared them), and demonstrate America's greatness. Whatever its goals, however, the War on Poverty was not designed with Asian Americans in mind.

Many Americans in the late 1950s and early 1960s developed a sense that they, as a society and a nation, were affluent; small, specific groups of Americans were far worse off. Those "other Americans" were poor, and not in the same way as earlier generations of Americans. They were isolated, downtrodden, and dangerously out of touch with "mainstream" American values and standards. They were no monolith, to be sure, but they fell into particular categories. Michael Harrington famously identified the dirt-poor "mountain folk" of the Appalachians; the friendless elderly; and most prominently "ghettoized" African Americans. "In, but not of, American society," these groups became the targets of the War on Poverty. President Johnson's assistants presented the Economic Opportunity Act (EOA) to Congress as a hand up specifically for children and the elderly, "those bypassed by industrial change," "rural families," and "minority members"—"Negroes," "Puerto Ricans," and "Spanish-speaking Americans."[5] Asian Americans were not on the list. At less than 1 percent of the U.S. population, Asian Americans remained invisible even to a nation attuned to the "invisible poor."

Yet the listed groups had much in common with Asian Americans, especially the many living in crowded ethnic enclaves. According to a 1966 Columbia University study, the median family income in New York's Chinatown was between $4,000 and $4,999, drastically lower than the median income for all families in the United States ($7,436) and lower even than that of nonwhite families in notoriously troubled cities such as Chicago and Detroit ($6,018). An Asian American Field Study commissioned by the Department of Health, Education, and Welfare reported several years later that nearly 70 percent of the Chinatown families it surveyed lived below the federal poverty level. Residents of Asian ethnic enclaves also encountered shortages in health care, housing, and government services; underrepresentation in the political process; difficulties accessing and qualifying for decent jobs; and strained relations with local law enforcement.[6]

Other minority groups with these concerns tapped into funding available through the Community Action Program (CAP), the heart of the War on Poverty. The CAP made available funding for local organizations "developing employment opportunities, improving human performance, motivation and productivity, or bettering the conditions under which people live, learn and work"—in other words, almost anything. CAP money could go to organizations administering "national emphasis" programs such as Head Start and Upward Bound, but the CAP was based on the belief that community needs differed widely and that only community members were capable of identifying those needs. Though great conflict arose in Washington and almost everywhere else in the nation about the CAP's goal of empowering the poor, the federal Office of Economic Opportunity tried to ensure, at least for a while, that grantee programs were "developed, conducted and administered with the maximum feasible participation of residents of the areas and members of the groups served."

Between 1964 and 1968, the Office of Economic Opportunity channeled funds into more than one thousand local community action agencies (CAAs), which administered services ranging from legal assistance to job training. A Puerto Rican community in East Harlem used CAP funds to fashion parks out of former garbage heaps; a Navajo reservation implemented a Head Start program; a group of black students in Washington, D.C., started the nation's first accredited student-run school.[7] Additional funds flowed into poor communities via the Juvenile Delinquency Act, the Manpower Development and Training Act, the Neighborhood Youth Corps program, and the Model Cities program.

Some Asian American groups also took advantage of War on Poverty funds in these early years. For example, in 1965 Asian American community activists in San Francisco formed a CAA, the Chinatown–North Beach Economic Opportunity Council (CNBEOC), which managed a million-dollar antipoverty fund. The previous year, a group of second-generation Asian American professionals in New York formed the Chinatown Planning Council (CPC) and obtained federal funds for a Head Start program. Other organizations tapped into War on Poverty funds a few years later. San Francisco's Chinese Newcomers Service Center and Chinese for Affirmative Action received funds in 1969, Northeast Mental Health Services did so in 1971, and Kai Ming Head Start followed in 1975.

But these organizations struggled. The CNBEOC faced opposition from Chinatown's de facto government, an "all-male hierarchy of fraternal, district, family, business, and charity organizations." From the late nineteenth century well into the late twentieth, Chinatowns functioned largely as self-governing islands: secret societies, family-name associations, and village associations administered civic, social, and protective services; district associations helped new immigrants find employment and housing. In San Francisco and New York, the most important of these associations created a conglomerate, the Chinese Consolidated Benevolent Association (CCBA), known as the Six Companies.

The CCBA served as the primary provider of education and health services, the arbiter of all local conflicts, and the intermediary between Chinatown and the white business community. It had concomitant privileges, including the power to exact membership dues, commercial and judicial fees, and community "property taxes." In the 1960s, members of this conservative elite continued to operate outside the American political system (many remained loyal to the Kuomintang [Chinese National Party]) and saw no need take part in the Great Society. They also had no interest in losing their monopoly on providing services to the Chinatown community, a role that helped guarantee these elites cheap labor. A related obstacle was the poor themselves, who might not have been content with CCBA leadership but had little experience with outsiders and no reason to trust them. Finally, the thorny issue of immigration status played a role. Some of the Asian American agencies that CNBEOC funded, including Self-Help for the Elderly (recognized by the White House as a model aging program), found that local residents would not accept help for fear of deportation.[8]

New York's CPC lacked relationships with the residents it purported to serve, but its bigger problem was that it had to battle for its small share of federal funds, succeeding only after it protested (and apparently sued) one of the umbrella organizations that distributed the city's antipoverty funds. In the contentious mid-1960s, when the city developed a confusing array of councils, committees, corporations, and agencies to take advantage of the CAP, Chinatown agencies were consistently overlooked. For a period in 1966, CPC and two other groups were delegates to a community corporation that was to distribute federal antipoverty funds throughout the Lower East Side, but rearrangements in 1967 left the Chinese groups powerless. Moreover, in 1966, Chinatown received none of New York's Model Cities funding, and the city skipped Chinatown when it created urban-action task forces to provide sanitation, fire, and police services to needy neighborhoods. By 1969, the city had fifty task forces, none of them in Chinatown.[9]

Into the 1970s, Chinatown groups accused the city of denying Chinatown its proportionate share of antipoverty funds. As the editor of the *Chinese American Times* put it, "They say, 'oh you do all right, you take care of your own problems' . . . and when the money is available, we don't get it." Government reports later conceded that "Asian Americans . . . suffer much of the social deprivation and economic discrimination experienced by other minority Americans" but that federal, state, and local agencies had ignored Asian Americans' plight. A 1977 report noted that no Asian group had ever received any of New York City's "so-called 'ethnic grants,'" that Asian Americans were underrepresented in state and city employment referral and job training programs, and that affirmative action programs often excluded Asian Americans because government regulations did not recognize them as a "separate minority group." They were, the report concluded, a "forgotten minority."[10]

"ASIANS BUILT THE RAILROAD; WHY NOT CONFUCIUS PLAZA?"

As the 1970s dawned, poor and working-class communities continued to grapple with the problems that the War on Poverty was supposed to remedy: joblessness, inadequate housing, poor health and education, and lack of meaningful power. In Asian American communities, even as popular media outlets proclaimed Asian Americans a "model" of quiescence and achievement,[11] socio-economic difficulties as well as political activism reached new heights as a consequence of both a sharp change in U.S. immigration policy and the development of an "Asian American movement."

The effects of the Immigration and Nationality Act Amendments of 1965, which removed restrictive quotas on Asian nationalities, were dramatic. An estimated 277,000 Asian immigrants, largely from China, Taiwan, India, and South Korea, arrived between 1965 and 1970. By 1970, the number of Asian Americans had climbed to 1,369,000, still less than 1 percent of the total population but a dramatic increase from the 878,000 counted in 1960. Some immigrants were highly skilled and headed straight to universities and other well-paying jobs, but many others packed into ethnic enclaves, where they sought low-wage work. By 1970, the population density in San Francisco's Chinatown was eleven times that of the rest of the city. The only location in the nation with a higher density was New York's Chinatown.[12]

Government data regarding other indicators of well-being among Asian Americans during the 1960s and 1970s are problematic as a result of the undercounting of the most vulnerable members of the population and the failure to record data that would allow disaggregation by ethnicity and place of birth. But it is reasonable to conclude that in the areas where new immigrants flocked, income levels were low and government services (for example, income support) were underused. Asian Americans had a relatively low national unemployment rate, but that figure masked a high rate of underemployment. Asian Americans often engaged in low-paid, part-time, or seasonal work—that is, dead-end work that was insecure and carried no benefits.[13]

The changes wrought by the Asian American movement in this time were also significant. Inspired by the antiwar movement, Black Power, women's liberation, and the Maoism of the Chinese Cultural Revolution, individuals of various ages, classes, and Asian ethnicities declared the existence of an "Asian American" identity, claiming this term as their invention. These activists demanded "self-determination and self-reliance" for Asian Americans and other Third World peoples and dedicated themselves to serving their communities.[14] Asian Americans had long organized around issues of labor, discrimination, and maltreatment, but these efforts now took on a scope, scale, and coherence that struck both participants and onlookers as unprecedented. Hot spots of Asian American activism emerged around the country, often in and around universities and ethnic enclaves.

In New York, the movement manifested itself in organizations such as I Wor

Kuen, a group of students, educators, and youth dedicated to implementing their broad revolutionary platform (much like the Black Panther Party and the Young Lords in other communities); I Wor Kuen operated out of a Chinatown storefront. Basement Workshop, a more moderate student organization, used the arts and education to explore Asian American identity and issues. AAFE also emerged during this time.[15]

Young activists Jerry Tung and Lydia Tom, along with various members of a Marxist-Leninist-Maoist collective, the Asian Study Group (ASG), came together to form what was then known as Asian Americans for Equal Employment. ASG viewed the Chinese in the United States as "an integral part of the leading force and the main force of the revolution" and called for participation in "the immediate day-to-day struggles of the people" in Chinatowns. According to some sources, AAFE "was meant to function as ASG's 'serve the people' mass-based arm," with an eye toward ultimately building a "true" (Maoist) communist party.[16] But AAFE's stated goal, like that of Asian American activists in San Francisco and Boston, was to join the many women and racial minorities seeking to break into the construction industry and its unions, using tactics pioneered by groups such as Harlem Fight Back.

Good jobs were on the line, as was symbolism: the construction industry was a well-known bastion of white, male privilege. Construction workers, notorious in New York City for their violent attacks on antiwar protesters, were "a rallying point for those nostalgic for a putative time when men were men, women knew their place, and social and familial authority remained unquestioned."[17] Construction was also a logical target because AAFE and similar groups had some leverage. In 1969, the Nixon administration instituted a policy requiring federal contractors to set goals for the hiring of minorities, and New York City had adopted a similar measure.

According to Tung, AAFE's first campaign, at a construction site at 2 Mott Street, ended in failure. But then the group hit on Confucius Plaza, a forty-million-dollar middle-income housing development in the heart of Chinatown. Confucius Plaza was itself an artifact of the War on Poverty. By at least one account, it was the brainchild of a humble Chinese shopkeeper, Kumshui Stephen Law, who lived in a Model Cities housing project in Upper Manhattan and wondered "why the same thing could not be built" in the "trash-filled lot" across the street from his store. Law organized a group of local businessmen, and the group secured federal urban renewal funds. By AAFE's account, however, the project was a joint venture of a greedy construction company, opportunistic local businessmen ("many of whom are local slum landlords"), and injudicious local government.[18]

AAFE leaders initially used established channels of influence. (The group's ASG founders, unlike other leftists at the time, did not oppose "working thru legitimate channels" or seeking "concessions under capitalism," according to one draft working paper. "As Chairman Mao Tse-tung has said, in principle we have to be firm as the oak, in tactics we should be as flexible as the willow.") AAFE joined a number of Chinatown social service agencies in approaching the equal opportunity office within the city's Housing and Development Administration. The groups reported that the contractor in charge of the Confucius Plaza project, the DeMatteis organization, was out of compliance with the city's affirmative action plan and urged the enforcement of the rules regarding minority hiring. According to AAFE sources, the office director was unsympathetic and threatened to call the police if protesters took action.[19]

AAFE had more success at the ground level. Members quickly located Asian American workers with construction experience and urged them to apply for jobs at the site, though as expected, DeMatteis rejected all of these applicants. AAFE also blanketed Chinatown with petitions and leaflets, informing residents about their exclusion from the economic opportunities in their "own backyard." By mid-May 1974, AAFE was leading daily demonstrations at Confucius Plaza, sometimes stopping work. The following month, the crowd had reportedly swelled to several hundred, representing a wide swath of the Chinatown community, "from schoolgirls carrying their books to wizened members of the Chinese Golden Age Club." Demonstrators carried provocative signs, accusing the construction company of racism and challenging anti-Asian stereotypes: "DeMatteis, you are a big racist"; "The Asians built the railroad; Why not Confucius Plaza?" Local restaurants donated food, and garment factories released their workers into the street. Drawing on their experience with antiwar protests, AAFE leaders came with bullhorns and staged protests at City Hall. AAFE also drew up a list of demands for the construction company, including that it raise the proportion of Asian American workers at the site to 25 percent.[20]

In mid-June, city and federal officials met with representatives of the contractor and the unions, AAFE spokespersons, and other Chinatown leaders, including Man Bun Lee, president-elect of the CCBA and therefore Chinatown's unofficial mayor. Lee was also a financial sponsor of the project. The parties reached an agreement that called for the hiring of twelve Asian American journeymen and twenty-seven Asian American trainees. The numbers did not match AAFE's earlier demands, and Lee's influence troubled AAFE leaders, who accused him of using liberal rhetoric to divert attention from Chinatown's truly progressive elements. AAFE members nevertheless viewed the agreement as a victory, proving that they could mobilize the Chinatown community and provoke an official response. AAFE subsequently acquired a storefront on East Broadway and began planning its next move.[21]

AAFE intended to pursue hiring breakthroughs for Asian Americans in other industries, but a spring 1975 incident prompted the group to focus on police brutality. On April 26, a white motorist and a Chinese American motorist got into a traffic argument. A crowd formed as the white man made his way to the nearby Fifth Precinct police station; in the ensuing confusion, a bystander, twenty-seven-year-old architectural engineer Peter Yew, was allegedly dragged into the precinct, stripped, and beaten. On May 12, AAFE led an eleven-hour demonstration including more than twenty-five hundred Chinatown residents who objected to Yew's treatment. AAFE again issued a list of demands, among them the dismissal of all charges against Yew and an end to "discrimination in employment, education, health, housing and all other social services to the minorities and working people."[22]

The incident reflected ongoing friction between Chinatown and the police as well as residents' willingness to engage in street-level protest tactics. It also dramatized the difference between groups such as AAFE and Chinatown's traditional leaders, whose business and fraternal associations comprised the CCBA. The CCBA was aware of the community's indignation and had planned to co-sponsor the protest but backed out at the last minute. One Chinese-language newspaper suggested that City Hall had "bought" the CCBA off. CCBA leaders insisted that they had simply been waiting for a permit from the city and organized a second demonstration a week later. By that time, a police captain's public statements implying that the community supported criminal activities seemed to have raised the stakes. An estimated ten thousand protesters, encouraged by a CCBA mandate closing all Chinatown shops, turned out on May 19. The three-and-a-half-hour demonstration ended after Lee emerged, supposedly victorious, from a meeting with police officials: "We are angry because we are opposed and discriminated against," Lee told a cheering crowd, to AAFE's consternation. "We will fight to the end until all our demands are satisfied."[23]

AAFE deemed the resulting agreement a sellout: the police conceded to the transfer of one captain, but the incident received no acknowledgment from the mayor's office. The AAFE's newsletter asked whether the community's sup-

Figure 13. Asian Americans for Equality leads a demonstration against police brutality, May 12, 1975. Chinatown's traditional leaders staged a competing protest one week later. © Corky Lee, all rights reserved.

posed representatives had not been "clear that the sentiments of the community were not just in support of Peter Yew's case, but an outcry of anger against our day to day oppression, e.g. bad housing, poor medical services, lousy schools, unemployment, etc." Later that day, AAFE gathered some two thousand protesters to throw eggs at the front of the CCBA headquarters, illustrating the growing divisions within the Chinatown community. By the mid-1970s, AAFE and other movement-oriented organizations (such as I Wor Kuen) existed side by side with traditional leaders (and with groups such as the CPC, which focused primarily on service). Like other community-based groups nationwide, AAFE wanted to pressure the government to respond to neighborhood-level demands, but the existence of so many competing voices meant that AAFE could not yet claim to speak for the community.[24]

THE GRASS ROOTS GROW DOWN, THE GRASS ROOTS GROW UP

After 1975, AAFE continued to call attention to discriminatory employment actions and police brutality, problems compounded by municipal budget cuts. Gouverneur, the local hospital, was targeted for closing or conversion to an outpatient clinic. Cuts in education and child care loomed on the horizon, and AAFE encouraged Chinatown residents to demand these services as their entitlement as well as objected to the city's efforts to "renew" and "redevelop" Chinatown. Noting that city planners across the nation were seeking to replace ethnic enclaves with luxury high-rises, commercial developments, and highways, AAFE urged Chinatown residents to claim their space. The AAFE newsletter told its young readers to fight for slots in the remaining local War on Poverty initiatives, such as the Neighborhood Youth Corps, because public programs were their right as much as anyone's.[25]

At the same time, AAFE was trying to sustain itself. Despite its fairly mainstream civil rights demands, the group relied on radical tactics and rhetoric. "We have a saying," AAFE member Lee Chong told the *New York Times* in 1975, "You can call me a Chink or a Chinaman. . . . But if you step on my toes I'll hit you back." An editorial in a 1976 edition of the AAFE newsletter declared that "the rotting, dog-eat-dog, money-centered system" was decaying and doomed to fail. The efficacy of that brand of radicalism seemed to be dwindling, however; the Vietnam War was winding down, the civil rights movement had apparently peaked, and the Chinese Cultural Revolution was over. These developments contributed to the feeling, Tung recalled, that "you can't simply picket, picket, picket." "You cannot just do things by agitation, you had to begin to stabilize yourself and you had to have institutions to make it last."[26]

In the summer of 1975, AAFE turned to stabilizing and institution building. It published a statement of purpose and enumerated "work objectives"— fighting for workers' rights, equal opportunities for minorities and women, and the rights of youths and elderly. The group exchanged ideas with like-minded Asian American organizations around the country and dedicated itself to cultivating a real base in the Chinatown. By the late 1970s, AAFE not only advocated on behalf of workers' rights but sponsored instruction sessions on construction, provided English classes and translation services, offered a recreation program, ran an unemployment legal clinic, and published a bimonthly newspaper.[27] In sum, AAFE was looking outward and encouraging Chinatown residents to claim their rights as members of a broader polity; at the same time, it cultivated the soil of Chinatown, hoping to grow where it was planted.

The fuller agenda gained grassroots support for AAFE but came with a price. As the decade closed, a rift developed between AAFE members who had come from ASG and those who had not. The former were self-identified revolutionaries interested in class-oriented political work and with vague plans to establish chapters across the country and unite the working class; the latter prioritized local service delivery. Many community-based groups of this era experienced similar rifts, but in AAFE's case, internal politics turned ugly, reportedly culminating in several violent altercations. In January 1979, twenty-six members of the service-oriented faction withdrew from the group, formed competing organizations, and began chipping away at the base AAFE intended to use to launch its national political movement. Organizer Wing Lam formed the Chinese Staff and Workers Association, which began winning significant victories for Chinatown laborers. This and several subsequent battles suggest that the intragroup split may also have involved disagreements over whether to confront the Chinese factory and restaurant owners who benefited from Chinatown's low-wage labor pool.[28]

On November 3, 1979, a terrible act of violence occurred, decisively pushing AAFE away from large-scale, revolutionary political work. ASG had first changed its name to Workers' Viewpoint Organization (WVO) and then, under Tung's leadership, renamed itself the Communist Workers Party (CWP) and allied with a Greensboro, North Carolina, group. The new organization's first major event was a rally on behalf of antiracism, unionism, and communist revolution and was advertised as a "Death to the Klan" protest. Fifteen members of a Nazi/Klan coalition appeared at the demonstration site, car trunks loaded with shotguns, pistols, knives, and brass knuckles. Despite the daylight hour, the presence of bystanders from the nearby public housing project, and at least one news camera, they opened fire, killing five CWP members and wounding nine. The incident was a political disaster for Tung's CWP, and it forced him to reevaluate the potential of radical politics. Tung encouraged AAFE to pursue its goals through more conventional channels, such as the Democratic Party and the union movement.[29] And while it is unclear whether AAFE took direction from Tung at this time, the group clearly toned down its rhetoric, refocused on serving the community, and began using its political capital to effect change in ways that other Chinatown groups could not.

Perhaps the best example of AAFE's new direction was its fight against gentrification in Chinatown. In 1981, the New York City Board of Estimate released a plan to create the Special Manhattan Bridge District. The plan rezoned a twelve-block stretch of Chinatown to permit high-density development. The timing was terrible for the Chinatown community: A steady stream of new immigrants meant that low-income housing was in high demand, while real estate prices had skyrocketed. Affluent New Yorkers seeking to live near Manhattan's Financial District had already taken over nearby SoHo and Greenwich Village, while uncertainty in Southeast Asia and Hong Kong had propelled Asian investors to move capital into Chinatown real estate. Indeed, the first developer granted permission to build in the new district was the Overseas Chinese Development Corporation, which planned two towers of luxury condominiums.[30]

The rezoning was opposed by many Chinatown-based groups, including the Asian American Legal Defense and Education Fund (AALDEF) and the Chinese Staff and Workers Association (CSWA), but AAFE used its grassroots base and its political connections outside Chinatown to garner maximum attention. AAFE not only sued the city (a tactic that AALDEF, CSWA, and the social service agency Mobilization for Youth also deployed) but captured mainstream media coverage of the issue. AAFE spokesman and former journalist Bill Chong coined the phrase "the Manhattanization of Chinatown," which became a *New York Times* headline. AAFE also accused other community groups of misrepresenting the interests of Chinatown's poor. When a collection of Lower East Side groups and government officials came together as the Manhattan Bridge Area Coalition to devise an alternative development proposal, AAFE led a "chaotic protest."[31]

At the coalition's September 1985 public meeting, AAFE labeled coalition members "running dogs" and "traitors." Some observers recall that AAFE objected to any negotiation with municipal officials, whom the group likened to colonial exploiters.[32] Others recall the disagreement as strategic: AAFE, perhaps anticipating its future as a developer, believed that more could be achieved by working directly with those who proposed to build in the area. Perhaps AAFE hoped that its ongoing lawsuit would resolve the zoning battle on more favorable terms.

In any case, a scaled-back version of the luxury development ultimately moved forward. But politics in Chinatown was shifting. After trying its hand at organizing beyond Chinatown, AAFE rededicated itself to its local base and emerged as the most visible of the new generation of community organizations. Through the antigentrification struggle, AAFE also acquired important knowledge about housing development, land use, and New York City politics. AAFE was one step closer to participation in a sanitized, corporatized, but still community-oriented War on Poverty.

THE HOUSE THAT "EQUALITY" BUILT: AAFE AS COMMUNITY DEVELOPER

After the court battle, AAFE decided to build housing. The choice was, in AAFE's view, a natural outgrowth of the struggle against gentrification. It also met a clear need. Existing government-subsidized housing did not serve most China-town residents, and the city had no plans to build low-income projects in the area. Although the federal government continued to give cities funds for housing development, Chinatown rarely saw them.[33] But going into housing development also served an important function for AAFE, giving stability and legitimacy to members who seemed to be growing out of their radicalism or who were never radical at all.

In 1984, AAFE sought grants for self-development and converted from a volunteer-run organization to one with a paid staff. The first grant came from the National Conference of Catholic Bishops' domestic antipoverty campaign. AAFE was not unique in making this change. In their synthetic study of the trajectory of the Asian American movement, Michael Liu, Kim Geron, and Tracy Lai have observed that between 1976 and 1982, "the 'social service activist' became 'the social service professional.'" During this period, the Chinatown Health Clinic started getting federal grants for a project on Asian health education and development and became a federally qualified health center; by the mid-1980s, it was a multi-million-dollar service agency.[34] In AAFE's case, professionalization meant that the cheap newsletters with hand-drawn cartoons and dramatic headlines were replaced by glossy mailings with photos of grateful Chinatown residents, members began paying dues, and Doris Koo, a volunteer since 1979, took the title of executive director.

In 1985, the well-funded and newly professionalized AAFE prepared to build. In some aspects, AAFE's position looked bleak: the group had spent its existence denouncing city officials and agencies, while wealthy real estate developers were eager to claim any available space in the area. Yet three years later, AAFE had completed a fifty-nine-unit rental project for low-income and elderly tenants, dubbing the structure Equality House and thus suggesting both AAFE's origins and its direction over the next two decades. "We drifted into housing," Koo told the *New York Times* in 1989, "but we are here to stay."[35]

The building of Equality House illustrates the War on Poverty's contribution to AAFE's sustenance and growth. Many accounts portray that war as short-lived, but community-based antipoverty initiatives demonstrate that the federal government, along with states and cities, continued to sponsor War on Poverty programs for decades, and foundations picked up where government funds left off. The EOA's community action programs received years of government support despite provoking immediate controversy. More than a thousand CAAS still operated at the turn of the twenty-first century. Community development

Figure 14. Mayor David Dinkins, councilwoman Miriam Friedlander, AAFE executive director Doris Koo, and New York State assemblyman Sheldon Silver lay the first brick at Equality House, September 28, 1988. © Corky Lee, all rights reserved.

corporations (CDCs) focused on partnering with the private sector to bring jobs and investment to poor urban neighborhoods are even more numerous than CAAs and still receive abundant government funding. AAFE became one of those CDCs.[36]

Perhaps anticipating the neoliberal turn, Senator Robert F. Kennedy brought the CDC model to Congress in 1966. Legislators quickly signed on, eager to redirect the War on Poverty and impressed by Kennedy's experimental CDC in Brooklyn, the Bedford-Stuyvesant Restoration Corporation. Funding went through a new subsection of the EOA, Special Impact Programs; six years later, such programs had become just one part of an entire Community Economic Development title. Subsequent Congresses supported CDCs through Community Development Block Grants, regulatory waivers, and tax benefits, and CDC programming shifted accordingly,[37] but the underlying philosophy of locally initiated community development with resident participation continued largely unchanged.

As the consequence of a combination of discrimination, disinterest, and lack of community recognition, AAFE did not join the earliest generation of CDCs, but in the 1980s, as the group attempted to solidify its gains and adjust to a more conservative political climate, it benefited from the government's embrace of the CDC model. As a legislative package, the War on Poverty was then moribund, but CDCs (sometimes also called community-based organizations) were thriving. By the mid-1980s, these groups had figured out how to attract the support of foundations and take advantage of incentives for low-income housing development. Indeed, the number of CDCs more than doubled during the Reagan years.[38]

AAFE's story illustrates just how favorable the climate was. When AAFE sought funding for Equality House, it found an ally in the New York Department of Social Services, which eagerly encouraged neighborhood efforts to address the state's severe low-income housing shortage. Similarly, when AAFE sought land, the New York Low-Income Housing Trust Fund, created in 1985 for the express purpose of channeling loans and grants toward nonprofit housing developers, came forward with two vacant city-owned buildings, which it sold to AAFE for one dollar each. And when a fire caused a $1.5 million increase in construction costs, Jim Rouse's Enterprise Foundation, a champion of decentralized housing development, stepped forward to fill the gap. AAFE's project also benefited from the newly instituted federal Low-Income Housing Tax Credit.[39]

New York's fiscal crisis, combined with a retrenchment in the welfare state and a broad consensus around localized economic development, made AAFE and other former "thorns in the sides of city officials" welcome partners in the city's struggle to provide for its citizens. Other groups with origins in the Asian American movement, including Boston's Chinatown Housing and Land Development Task Force, Los Angeles's Little Tokyo People's Rights Organization, and Seattle's InterIm, pursued similar projects and strategies.[40]

AAFE's turn to low-income housing development went hand in hand with the group's participation in the Democratic Party's Rainbow Coalition. In 1984, the year before AAFE pitched its plan for Equality House, AAFE spokesperson Bill Chong served as the national vice chair for Asian Pacific Americans in Jesse Jackson's presidential campaign. The following year, Chong ran for Democratic district leader. And in 1986, Margaret Chin, AAFE's president, was elected a state committeewoman for New York's Democratic Party. Other AAFE members sought seats on community planning boards and school boards.[41] Chin recently became the first Asian American to represent Chinatown on the city council, succeeding where other participants in the Asian American movement (including I Wor Kuen affiliate Rocky Chin and CPC cofounder Virginia Kee) had failed.

Not all of AAFE's political bids met with such success—indeed, Chin was defeated in earlier elections—but AAFE showed it could play the game, thereby strengthening its position as a developer. Some observers linked AAFE's one-million-dollar grant from the New York Department of Social Services for construction of a homeless shelter to the organization's support of Mario Cuomo's 1988 gubernatorial campaign. At the same time, Chinatown's traditional leadership grew weaker. Divided over politics in China and Taiwan, unable to command the respect of the new immigrants, and powerless over the new money coming in from overseas, the CCBA could only look on as AAFE usurped more and more of the older group's functions.[42]

AAFE is now an award-winning nonprofit. It has developed and preserved nearly seven hundred units of affordable and senior housing, again and again packaging community development funds from public and private sources. Not coincidentally, at least several former AAFE leaders now work in local government or at major foundations. AAFE has expanded into small business assistance and homeownership services, channeling hundreds of millions of dollars toward home buyers and entrepreneurs. It also continues to provide social services, both on the Lower East Side and at a branch in Flushing, Queens. And every step of the way, AAFE leaders argue, the group has empowered the community.[43]

This aspect of AAFE's work ironically has proven the most contentious. The same group that fought to give Chinatown a voice in the 1970s has been criticized for cutting residents out of its decision-making processes and abandoning their interests. In 2001, Tung remembered walking through Chinatown and encountering old AAFE members who broke down and cried: "One guy told me he went to an AAFE meeting and then . . . he couldn't get into the meeting because the security fellow in the front wouldn't let him. But he was one of the earliest AAFE members, on the board for many decades. They don't even know who you are, some of the people and the staff members." "They're poverty pimps," charged labor organizer and former AAFE member Wing Lam. "They're like Donald Trump in Chinatown." Criticism has also come from activists with no AAFE history: "I think AAFE has aligned itself with business interests and political interests at the expense of Chinatown's residential and low-wage workers," a Chinatown-based legal advocate told the New York Times in 2003. Chinatown's preeminent historian, Peter Kwong, has expressed similar views, opining that AAFE sacrificed its original beliefs "for real estate develop-ment and political power."[44]

AAFE staffers and board members have rejected these charges, arguing that the group maintains a strong connection to the community. In so doing, they echo the retorts of many community development groups born in an era of protest. Confronted with allegations that they have sold out and abandoned their radical roots, these groups argue that serving the community is empower-ing the community; that accomplished, professional Asian Americans are au-thentic and responsive representatives of poor and working-class residents; and that participation for participation's sake is not meaningful. As Bill Chong re-marked, "Ideas don't shelter people. Ideas don't clothe them. Ideas don't feed them. . . . How do you empower people and at the same time bring resources into the community?" In this question, which bedeviled the earliest community action programs, the War on Poverty lives on.[45]

The War on Poverty's most important legacy for Chinatown, however, is po-litical. Because of a steady stream of government and nonprofit support, groups such as AAFE competed with and in many ways supplanted the institutions that traditionally governed Chinatown. Ethnic voluntary associations, such as those that comprise the CCBA, will remain influential as long as Chinatown receives new immigrants, but those associations can no longer credibly claim to repre-sent the community to outsiders. AAFE can and does make that claim. AAFE's government-sponsored achievements in housing development and concomi-tant political clout have also allowed it to surpass other community-based or-ganizations of its generation. As the dominant voice among Chinatown's com-munity groups, AAFE now faces criticism from the grass roots. And AAFE now responds as power does in a democratic system, by urging "consensus build-ing" and "open dialogue."[46] "Come," AAFE is finally in the position to say, "let us reason together."

Notes

The author thanks Merlin Chowkwanyun, Michael Katz, Annelise Orleck, and Tom Sugrue for their close readings and generous comments. Peter Kwong offered invaluable corrections and insights.

1. Monroe Billington, "Lyndon B. Johnson: The Religion of a Politician," *Presidential Studies Quarterly* 17:3 (Summer 1987): 522. The quotation is from Isaiah 1:18.

2. See, e.g., Robert O. Self, *American Babylon: Race and the Struggle for Postwar Oakland* (Princeton: Princeton University Press, 2003); Nicole P. Marwell, *Bargaining for Brooklyn: Community Organizations in the Entrepreneurial City* (Chicago: University of Chicago Press, 2007).

3. Other Asian American community-based organizations followed different arcs. See generally Michael Liu, Kim Geron, and Tracy Lai, *The Snake Dance of Asian American Activism: Community, Vision, and Power* (Lanham, Md.: Lexington, 2008): 97–146.

4. Alice O'Connor, *Poverty Knowledge: Social Science, Social Policy, and the Poor in Twentieth-Century U.S. History* (Princeton: Princeton University Press, 2001), 166–67.

5. Michael Harrington, *The Other America: Poverty in the United States* (New York: Macmillan, 1962), 6; *The War on Poverty: The Economic Act of 1964, a Compilation of Materials Relevant to S. 2642*, prepared for the U.S. Senate, Select Subcommittee on Poverty of the Committee on Labor and Public Welfare, 88th Cong., 2nd sess. (Washington, D.C.: U.S. Government Printing Office, 1964), 36.

6. Chin-Yu Chen, "Social Impact of the Immigration Law of 1965 on Chinatown, New York City" (Ph.D. diss., Indiana University of Pennsylvania, 1988), 27; Chi-Wing Ho cited in New York State Advisory Committee to the U.S. Commission on Civil Rights, "The Forgotten Minority: Asian Americans in New York City," November 1977, 8; Stuart H. Cattell, *Health, Welfare, and Social Organization in Chinatown, New York City* (New York: Community Service Society, 1962).

7. Edgar Cahn and Jean Camper Cahn, "Maximum Feasible Participation: A General Overview," in *Citizen Participation: Effecting Community Change* (New York: Praeger, 1971), 18–23. For detailed studies of community action efforts in particular cities, see Kent Germany, *New Orleans after the Promises: Poverty, Citizenship, and the Search for the Great Society* (Athens: University of Georgia Press, 2008); Leila Meier Rice, "In the Trenches of the War on Poverty: The Local Implementation of the Community Action Program, 1964–1969" (Ph.D. diss., Vanderbilt University, 1997).

8. William Wei, *The Asian American Movement* (Philadelphia: Temple University Press, 1993), 172, 178; Ronald Takaki, *Strangers From a Different Shore* (Boston: Little, Brown, 1989), 117–18; Jan Lin, *Reconstructing Chinatown: Ethnic Enclave, Global Change* (Minneapolis: University of Minnesota Press, 1998), 124; Peter Kwong, *The New Chinatown* (New York: Noonday, 1987), 81–106.

9. Lin, *Reconstructing Chinatown*, 129; David Chen, interview by Teri Chan, July 13, 2004, http://911digitalarchive.org/chinatown/full_page.php?display=657; Chai-ling Kuo, *Social and Political Change in New York's Chinatown: The Role of Voluntary Associations* (New York: Praeger, 1977), 120–21.

10. "Chinatown Panel Asks Poverty Aid," *New York Times* (hereafter *NYT*, October 15, 1969; David Tong, "Asians Protest Poverty, Immigration Bias," *East/West*, July 24, 1974; "Youths Organize to Fight Back!," *Asian Americans for Equal Employment*, August

1977, New York Public Library, Chatham Square Branch, New York (hereafter NYPL); "City Chinese Also Have Problems," *New York Post*, May 21, 1978; New York State Advisory Committee, "Forgotten Minority," 1, 3, 27–28. See also California Advisory Committee to the U.S. Commission on Civil Rights, "Asian Americans and Pacific People: A Case of Mistaken Identity," February 1975, 58; U.S. Commission on Civil Rights, "The Federal Civil Rights Enforcement Effort—1974," June 1977, 11, 43. Similar complaints occurred in other cities: see, e.g., "Here, There, and Everywhere; Asians Tell SBA: 'We're Minorities,'" *San Francisco Journal*, July 18, 1979. Some evidence indicates that Chinatown's traditional elite concealed and denied residents' needs "in order to avoid losing face and political power." And at least one group, the San Francisco youth organization Leway, refused to apply for federal antipoverty funds to avoid the possibility of cooptation (Wei, *Asian American Movement*, 13–14, 173–74).

11. See, e.g., "Success Story of One Minority Group in the United States," *U.S. News and World Report*, December 26, 1966.

12. Urban Associates, *A Study of Selected Socio-Economic Characteristics of Ethnic Minorities based on the 1970 Census*, vol. 2, *Asian Americans* (Washington, D.C.: Department of Health, Education and Welfare, 1974), 11; Wei, *Asian American Movement*, 3; Ginger Chih and Diane Mei Lin Mark, *A Place Called Chinese America* (Washington, D.C.: Organization of Chinese Americans, 1993), 112. The actual figure in 1970 was probably even higher; see Fortunata M. Azores, "Census Methodology and the Development of Social Indicators for Asian and Pacific Americans," in U.S. Commission on Civil Rights, *Civil Rights Issues of Asian and Pacific Americans: Myths and Realities* (Washington, D.C.: U.S. Government Printing Office, 1979), which estimates that the official count of 1.4 million failed to acknowledge approximately 70,000 Koreans, 9,000 Pakistanis, and 76,000 Indians and points out that many immigrants probably avoided census takers. Figures on overcrowding tell a similar story: according to the 1970 census, one-fifth of the housing stock occupied by Chinese Americans nationwide was overcrowded; in New York City, the figure was one-third (Urban Associates, *Study*, 131).

13. Urban Associates, *Study*, 127, 122–26; Charles Sullivan and Kathlyn Hatch, *The Chinese in Boston, 1970* (Boston: Action for Boston Community Development, 1970); Irene Hirano, "Poverty and Social Service Perspectives," in U.S. Commission, *Civil Rights Issues*, 125–32; Bok-Lim C. Kim, "Problems and Service Needs of Asian Americans in Chicago: An Empirical Study," *Amerasia* 5:2 (1978): 23–44; Sucheng Chan, *Asian Americans: An Interpretive History* (Boston: Twayne, 1991), 168–69; Amado Cabezas and Harold T. Yee, *Discriminatory Employment of Asian Americans: Private Industry in the San Francisco-Oakland SMSA* (San Francisco: ASIAN, 1977).

14. See generally Liu, Geron, and Lai, *Snake Dance*; Steve Louie and Glenn Omatsu, *Asian Americans: The Movement and the Moment* (Los Angeles: UCLA Asian American Studies Center Press, 2001); Fred Ho, ed., *Legacy to Liberation: Politics and Culture of*

Revolutionary Asian Pacific America (San Francisco: Big Red Media/AK, 2000); Wei, *Asian American Movement*; Daryl J. Maeda, "Forging Asian American Identity: Race, Culture, and the Asian American Movement, 1968–1975" (Ph.D. diss., University of Michigan, 2001). For a useful historiography of the Asian American movement, see Diane C. Fujino, "Who Studies the Asian American Movement?: A Historiographical Analysis," *Journal of Asian American Studies* 11:2 (June 2008): 127–69.

15. Liu, Geron, and Lai, *Snake Dance*, 53, 81–84; Kuo, *Social and Political Change*, 65–73; Wei, *Asian American Movement*, 184–89, 212–25; Rocky Chin, "New York Chinatown Today: Community in Crisis," *Amerasia* 1:1 (March 1971): 282–95.

16. Wei, *Asian American Movement*, 217–25; Jerry Tung, interview by author, May 11, 2002; Asian Study Group, *Preliminary Draft on the Asian National Question in America*, pt. 1, *The Chinese National Question* (1973); Peter Kwong and Dusanka Miščević, *Chinese America: The Untold Story of America's Oldest New Community* (New York: New Press, 2005): 293–94. See also Asian Study Group, *Preliminary Draft*, 44–45 (describing "legal and broad struggles for democratic rights" conducted by "mass organizations" as the mechanism best suited to the "struggle in Chinatown"; opposing "open communist organizational forms and open communist participation in broad democratic struggles"; and noting that "legal struggles" for "bourgeois democratic rights" were a way "to mobilize the maximum number of people, to propagate our government, to force concessions from the American monopolies and government in the day-to-day interests of our people," and to take advantage of the contradictions between "liberal politicians" and Chinatown's conservative leadership).

17. Joshua B. Freeman, *Working-Class New York: Life and Labor since World War II* (New York: New Press, 2000): 238–39.

18. Tung, interview; Phil Tajitsu Nash, "Kumshui, Tsiwen, and Confucius Plaza," *Asian Week* 4:7 (October 5–11, 2007): 6; R. Takashi Yanagida, "The AAFEE Story: Asian Americans for Equal Employment," *Bridge* 3:4 (February 1975): 47–48.

19. Asian Study Group, *Preliminary Draft*, 45, 58; Yanagida, "AAFEE Story," 47–51.

20. Yanagida, "The AAFEE Story"; Willem Lee, "Confucius Plaza," http://www.aafe .org/index.html; Paul L. Montgomery, "Asians Picket Building Site, Charging Bias," *NYT*, June 16, 1974; "Asian-Americans Demand Construction Jobs," *The Militant*, June 14, 1974, 15.

21. Yanagida, "AAFEE Story"; New York State Advisory Committee, "Forgotten Minority," 29; Selwyn Raab, "New Militancy Emerges in Chinatown," *NYT*, June 8, 1975; "Ground Is Broken for Huge Project Serving Chinatown," *NYT*, September 12, 1973; Henry Chung, interview by Florence Ng, February 26, 2004, http://911digitalarchive.org/chinatown/ full_page.php?display=268.

22. Yawsoon Sim, "A Chinaman's Chance in Civil Rights Demonstration: A Case Study" (paper presented at the Annual Conference on Ethnic and Minority Studies, La

Crosse, Wisconsin, April 23–26, 1980); "2,500 Chinese Protest Alleged Police Beating Here," *NYT*, May 13, 1975; "Our Statement on the Reply," *Asian Americans for Equal Employment*, June 1975, NYPL; Carmody, "Thousands." Chinatown, like many other minority neighborhoods, suffered from a potent mix of underpolicing, overpolicing, and police brutality. See Deirdre Carmody, "Thousands in Chinatown March in Police Protest," *NYT*, May 20, 1975; Raab, "New Militancy"; Dena Kleiman, "Closing of Police Station Is Protested in Chinatown," *NYT*, October 29, 1975. The *NYT* later suggested that powerful tongs, which had profited from the city's long tolerance of illegal gambling in Chinatown, played a significant role in encouraging the protest (Raab, "New Militancy").

23. Sim, "Chinaman's Chance," 9–11; Carmody, "Thousands"; Selwyn Raab, "Chinatown Head of Police Shifted," *NYT*, May 24, 1975.

24. "Our Statement"; Raab, "New Militancy"; Carmody, "Thousands"; Kuo, *Social and Political Change*, 111 (describing AAFE as one of "five major conflict groups in New York's Chinatown" in 1977).

25. "Unite to Fight All Budget Cuts!!!" *Asian Americans for Equal Employment*, June 1975, NYPL; "Boycott Tuesday's Rally," *Asian Americans for Equal Employment*, November 1975, NYPL; "Cash Your Bonds!" *Asian Americans for Equal Employment*, November 1975, NYPL; "Urban Renewal/Redevelopment: No Answer for Working Class Housing," *Asian Americans for Equal Employment*, December 1976, NYPL; "Youths Organize to Fight Back!" The title of this section borrows from a retrospective on the nonprofit Banana Kelly Community Improvement Association. Like AAFE, Banana Kelly was "born in protest" but grew up to become a sophisticated nonprofit, a major player in neighborhood development, and, ironically, a landlord (David Gonzales, "In the South Bronx, the Grass Roots Grow Up," *NYT*, January 7, 1993).

26. Raab, "New Militancy"; *Asian Americans for Equal Employment*, January 1976, NYPL; Tung, interview.

27. "What Is AAFEE?," *Asian Americans for Equal Employment*, June 1975, NYPL; "Good News!," *Asian Americans for Equal Employment*, August 1977, NYPL; "Asian Americans for Equality" (Profile Sheet), 1979, NYPL. In 1977, in keeping with this broader program, AAFE dropped "employment" from its name to become Asian Americans for Equality.

28. "New York Groups Attack Each Other," *San Francisco Journal*, June 6, 1979, 1; Wei, *Asian American Movement*, 223. As a result of a heightened focus on toeing the correct political line, splits had occurred within almost all the major leftist groups in the nation's Chinatowns by the late 1970s. See Kwong, *New Chinatown*, 165; Scott Kurashige, "Pan-Ethnicity and Community Organizing: Asian American United's Campaign against Anti-Asian Violence," *Journal of Asian American Studies* 3:2 (2000): 172; Liu, Geron, and Lai, *Snake Dance*, 99–100; Max Elbaum, *Revolution in the Air: Sixties Radicals Turn to Lenin, Mao, and Che* (New York: Verso, 2002), 227–66; Xiaolan Bao, *Holding Up More Than*

Half the Sky: Chinese Women Garment Workers in New York City, 1948–1992 (Champaign: University of Illinois Press, 2001), 202 (noting AAFE's ambivalence about a 1982 garment worker strike); Tung, interview (explaining his reluctance to interfere with Chinatown's "self-contained economy"). AAFE at least briefly had offshoots in other cities, but the paper trail is sparse. See, e.g., Alton Chin, "Growing Pains in Chinatown," *Los Angeles Times*, September 9, 1979 (mentioning an AAFE chapter in San Francisco); Ray Hebert, "Chinatown Renewal Plan OKd," *Los Angeles Times*, January 17, 1980 (noting that AAFE led opponents of an urban renewal project in Los Angeles's Chinatown).

29. Elizabeth Wheaton, *Codename GREENKIL: The 1979 Greensboro Killings* (Athens: University of Georgia Press, 1987), 3, 112; Wei, *Asian American Movement*, 224; Tung, interview; Tockman, interview. See also Sally Avery Bermanzohn, *Through Survivors' Eyes: From the Sixties to the Greensboro Massacre* (Nashville: Vanderbilt University Press, 2003); Signe Waller, *Love and Revolution: A Political Memoir* (Lanham, Md.: Rowman and Littlefield, 2002); Greensboro Truth and Reconciliation Commission, *Greensboro Truth and Reconciliation Commission Final Report*, May 25, 2006, http://www.greensborotrc.org; *Greensboro: Closer to the Truth* (DVD, directed by Adam Zucker, 2007). For more on Tung's unusual political trajectory, see Elbaum, *Revolution in the Air*, 281–83. AAFE now prefers not to discuss its connection with radical groups or individuals, but the overlap with ASG, WVO, and the Communist Workers Party is well documented; see Wei, *Asian American Movement*, 222–24; Kwong, *New Chinatown*, 164; Elbaum, *Revolution in the Air*, 200; Fred Ho, "'Make It Snappy!': What Rhymes with 'Soviet Social-Imperialism'? The Line, the Music, and the Movement," in *Legacy to Liberation*, ed. Ho, 249; Tung, interview; Earle Tockman, interview by author, September 22, 2009.

30. Chin-Yu Chen, "Social," 34; Kwong, *New Chinatown*, 54–56; Laurie Cohen, "Bar to Chinatown Luxury Units," *NYT*, November 14, 1982.

31. Steve Dobkin, Geoffrey Smith, and Earle Tockman, "Zoning for the General Welfare: A Constitutional Weapon for Lower-Income Tenants," *New York University Review of Law and Social Change* 13 (1984–85): 911–29; Marvin Howe, "Chinatown's Have-Nots Fear 'Manhattanization,'" *NYT*, September 21, 1984; Jane Anderson, "Influx of Investors," *Los Angeles Times*, April 21, 1985; Lin, *Reconstructing Chinatown*, 154.

32. Lin, *Reconstructing Chinatown*, 151–55.

33. Chin-Yu Chen, "Social Impact," 35; Liu, Geron, and Lai, *Snake Dance*, 572; U.S. Commission, *Civil Rights Issues*, 585.

34. Liu, Geron, and Lai, *Snake Dance*, 97–98.

35. "We Did It! Equality House Breaks Ground," *Asian Americans for Equality*, Winter 1988–89, NYPL; Thomas J. Lueck, "The Tenant-as-Landlord Movement," *NYT*, July 2, 1989.

36. On the close relationship between CAPs and CDCs, see William H. Simon, *The*

Community Economic Development Movement (Durham: Duke University Press, 2001), 7; Nicole P. Marwell, "Privatizing the Welfare State: Nonprofit Community-Based Organizations as Political Actors," *American Sociological Review* 69:2 (April 2004): 269.

37. For cogent accounts of how government support changed over time, see Simon, *Community Economic Development Movement*, 7–19; Alice O'Connor, "Swimming against the Tide: A Brief History of Federal Policy in Poor Communities," in *Urban Problems and Community Development*, ed. Ronald F. Ferguson and William T. Dickens (Washington, D.C.: Brookings Institution Press, 1999), 108–17.

38. On developments during and after the Reagan administration, see Simon, *Community Economic Development Movement*, 16–26.

39. "State to Give Housing Aid," *NYT*, September 2, 1985; Dennis Helvesi, "Chinatown Journey: From Protesters to Developers," *NYT*, January 12, 2003.

40. Lueck, "Tenant-as-Landlord Movement"; Liu, Geron, and Lai, *Snake Dance*, 127.

41. "Chong Runs for N.Y. Demo Post," *Asian Week*, June 14, 1985; Lin, *Reconstructing Chinatown*, 130.

42. Kwong and Miščević, *Chinese America*, 299; Kwong, *New Chinatown*, 107–8. Nicole Marwell has discerned such trades of support for grants in other modern community-based organizations and labeled it a variant of "machine politics." I hesitate to speculate about AAFE without conducting the sort of rich sociological research that supported Marwell's findings. Marwell concluded that some community-based organizations function as replacements for "defunct political party organizations in poor neighborhoods": They "create and turn out a reliable voting constituency" in return for government financial support for service provision ("Privatizing the Welfare State," 269–70).

43. Testimony of Christopher Kui before U.S. House of Representatives, Committee on Government Reform, Subcommittee on Federalism and the Census, 109th Cong., 1st sess., July 25, 2005, http://aafe.org/pgs/Hilite_090605.html; Asian Americans for Equality, *Advocacy and Community Education*, http://aafe.org/pgs/services_advocacy.html.

44. "New Yorkers & Co.; What a Difference Two Decades Make," *NYT*, January 21, 1997; Tung, interview; Lincoln Anderson, Albert Amateu, and Laurie Mittelmann, "Rhetoric on Rezoning Ramps Up as Public Review Continues," *The Villager* 78:11 (August 13–19, 2008); Helvesi, "Chinatown Journey." This criticism stems in part from AAFE's role in a 1991 redistricting battle. That year, the city council agreed to redraw districts in an effort to bring in more minorities, and some politicians and activists proposed joining Chinatown to the heavily Latino and working-class Lower East Side. AAFE lobbied successfully for allying with the whiter, wealthier West Side. See Andrew Hsiao, "Chinatown in Limbo: Will Asian Americans Ever Elect a Councilmember of Their Own?" *Village Voice*, May 29, 2001; Andrew Hsiao, "Crashing the Party," *Village Voice*, January 18, 2000.

45. Bill Chong, interview by author, August 8, 2001. The conflict between commu-

nity participation and economic development is familiar to students of the CAP and CDCs. Because of that conflict, which seems inherent to the CAP and CDC models, some participants and observers have concluded that policymakers used community-based antipoverty initiatives to co-opt the poor people's movement. See, e.g., Harry Edward Berndt, *New Rulers in the Ghetto: The Community Development Corporation and Urban Poverty* (Westport, Conn.: Greenwood, 1977); Frances Fox Piven and Richard Cloward, *Poor People's Movements: Why They Succeed and How They Fail* (New York: Pantheon, 1979).

46. Chris Kui, "AAFE: Why It's Wrong to Call Rezoning Plan Racist," *The Villager* 78:10 (August 6–12, 2008). On similar political reconfigurations in other Chinatowns, see Yvonne Abraham, "New Voices, Voters Empowering Chinatown," *Boston Globe*, June 25, 2007; Min Zhou and Rebecca Y. Kim, "Formation, Consolidation, and Diversification of the Ethnic Elite: The Case of the Chinese Immigrant Community in the United States," *Journal of International Migration and Integration* 2:2 (June 2001): 227–47. AAFE was recently accused of supporting precisely the sort of rezoning that it once opposed; see Albert Amateu, "Planning O.K.'s Rezoning and Antis Cry 'Dump Mike!,'" *The Villager* 78:19 (October 8–14, 2008); Anderson, Amateu, and Mittelmann, "Rhetoric."

ANNELISE ORLECK

Conclusion

The War on the War on Poverty and
American Politics since the 1960s

We were told four years ago that 17 million people went to bed hungry each night. Well that was probably true. They were all on a diet.
  Ronald Reagan, *A Time for Choosing*, October 1964

My friends, some years ago, the Federal Government declared war on poverty, and poverty won.
  Ronald Reagan, 1988 State of the Union Address

If there is a prize for the political scam of the 20th century, it should go to the conservatives for propagating as conventional wisdom that the Great Society programs of the 1960s were a misguided and failed social experiment that wasted taxpayers' money.
  Joseph A. Califano, aide to President Lyndon Johnson and secretary of health, education, and welfare under Jimmy Carter, 1999

THE WAR ON POVERTY FROM LBJ TO JIMMY CARTER

The War on Poverty and the programs it spawned have had a complicated and ambivalent history since the 1960s. They have been attacked rhetorically on all fronts. Politicians across the political spectrum have consistently portrayed Lyndon Baines Johnson and his Great Society as symbols of all that is wrong with big government and as arguments against future expansions of federal poverty programs, especially those built on the idea of mobilizing the poor on their own behalf. That widely accepted narrative of the War on Poverty as both an exercise in naïveté and a destructive failure played a crucial role in the ascendancy of conservative thought in U.S. national politics from the 1960s to the 1980s. This idea has continued both to drive conservative politics and to constrain the liberal policy imagination into the twenty-first century. For almost half a century, conservative politicians have deployed negative imagery of the War on Poverty to drain public support from liberal policy initiatives. At the same time, Democratic leaders from Jimmy Carter to Bill Clinton to Barack Obama have carefully distanced their policies from those of Johnson and his poverty planners. Yet behind this public politics lies a very different, largely hidden, policy reality.

Antipoverty programs initiated under LBJ and built on, adapted by, and extended by several of his successors make up some of the most enduring and unassailable strands of the national social safety net. It is not hyperbole to say that the War on Poverty programs have had a vast impact on U.S. government policy from the municipal to the federal level. The transformations in the federal government and the American social welfare state that began as part of the Great Society have, despite their bad name and decades of criticism from both the Left and Right, proven as durable as those of the New Deal.

Almost all of the most important and visible poverty programs created during the Johnson years have survived—even if in altered form—into the twenty-first century. Their long-term existence has created a sense of permanence and inevitability that has not been easily dismantled, even by presidents with deep ideological commitments to doing so. The most conservative presidents since the 1960s, Ronald Reagan and George W. Bush, publicly made war on federal poverty programs and their beneficiaries. These presidents enacted deep program cuts and empowered investigatory agencies to crack down on "waste" and "corruption" in poverty programs. These crackdowns deepened the suffering of millions already mired in poverty. But at the same time, each of these presidents quietly increased allocations for a variety of poverty programs. And after Johnson, the president who oversaw the greatest expansion of War on Poverty programs was a Republican, the complicated and paradoxical Richard Nixon.

Nixon's presidency in many ways exemplifies how public rhetoric around the War on Poverty often diverged from the hidden mechanics of policymaking. Nixon publicly condemned the centralization of federal power that the War on Poverty had promoted. He campaigned for president insisting that Johnson's poverty program had been a wasteful failure: accepting the 1968 Republican presidential nomination, Nixon said,

For the past five years, we have been deluged by government programs for the unemployed; programs for the cities; programs for the poor. And we have reaped from these programs an ugly harvest of frustration, violence and failure across the land.

And now our opponents will be offering more of the same—more billions for government jobs, government housing, government welfare.

I say it is time to quit pouring billions of dollars into programs that have failed in the United States of America.[1]

Once elected, Nixon did shake up the War on Poverty bureaucracy, decentralizing in the name of the New Federalism. But he did not abandon the new post–War on Poverty reality—that the federal government had an important role to play in addressing the problems of the poor. Indeed, Nixon enhanced the federal government's capacity to intervene in those areas. He introduced a ground-changing proposal for the Family Assistance Plan, a guaranteed minimum income for all Americans that would have provided benefits to the working poor as well as those who did not work, to two-parent as well as single-mother families. The plan was killed by opposition from conservatives who believed it would disincline low-wage workers to seek jobs and from liberals who thought its benefits too small for anyone outside the rural South to live on.

Nixon subsequently tacked hard to the right, at least in terms of his public rhetoric. In 1971, he invited country artist Johnny Cash to sing the antiwelfare anthem "Welfare Cadillac" at the White House. Cash refused. The president vetoed a bill to create a national child nutrition program on the grounds that it was too expensive. And he publicly opposed new food and medical assistance programs proposed by Senate Democrats. Behind the scenes, however, Nixon continued the War on Poverty, with both energy and a lot of money.[2]

Federal spending on social programs nearly tripled during Nixon's time as president. Though control of some poverty programs shifted from the federal to the state and local levels, he dramatically expanded their reach. The number of public housing units doubled during his presidency. A new Section 8 housing voucher program enabled low-income tenants to choose rental housing outside public housing projects. Food stamps became a truly nationwide and permanent program. Nixon signed into law the Special Supplemental Nutrition Program for Women, and Infants, and Children (wic). Photographs of malnourished children supplied by the Memphis activists described in this volume helped generate the political support that enabled a Republican president to sign such a bill.[3]

If Nixon was simply a reluctant passenger in a car driven by Congress, his policy record does not show it. He approved substantial increases in health care spending for the poor, cost-of-living increases in old-age pensions, and the creation of Supplemental Security Income, which supported both the disabled and elderly immigrants who had never paid into the system. During his presidency, the Pell Grant program was created to help low-income students attend college. In 1973, Nixon signed into law the first public jobs program since the depression. The Comprehensive Education and Training Act (CETA) allowed community organizations to hire chronically underemployed neighborhood residents to work on needed local projects.[4]

Hundreds of millions of Americans have been helped by Johnson- and Nixon-era War on Poverty programs. Between 1965 and 1999, Medicaid brought medical care to more than two hundred million people, while seventy-nine million elderly received medical coverage through Medicare. The Community Health Center program, initiated by Johnson and expanded under Carter, became and still is the largest primary-care medical system in the country, serving more than fourteen million low-income patients a year. Seventy percent of these patients earn less than the federal poverty line; 66 percent are poor women and children. And even as he asked for cuts in other poverty programs, President George W. Bush requested increases in funding for community health centers.

Children's programs proved equally robust. Free breakfast programs served 100 million children by the turn of the twenty-first century, and 16 million children had graduated from Head Start programs. WIC remains a crucial source of protein and medical care for low-income pregnant and lactating women and their children. In 2009, it offered nutrition and medical aid to 9.3 million women and children every month.[5]

Community action agencies, products of the controversial Community Action Program, coordinate a wide range of community-specific services, including support for low-income families, education for youth and adults, substance abuse prevention, assistance to seniors, job training, dropout prevention, homeless shelters, housing development, and medical care. In 2010, eleven hundred community action agencies leveraged more than nine billion dollars in public and private funds to mount projects benefiting their communities. Federal funding still remains their lifeline, with the bulk coming from the Community Services Block Grant program, the descendant of the Community Action and Community Services Programs.

More than forty-five hundred community development corporations, (CDCs), products of the 1966 amendments to the Economic Opportunity Act, repair crumbling housing and decayed sewer and water delivery systems and build new homes in poor rural and urban communities. By 2006, CDCs had repaired or generated more than 1.25 million units of affordable housing for low-income tenants. They also provide assistance to small businesses and local economic development projects. CDCs have come to be seen as so vital in so many parts of the country that George W. Bush's repeated attempts to zero out funding for Community Development Block Grants in his second term met opposition from both sides of the aisle. Resistance by moderate Republicans kept the program alive.[6]

Other War on Poverty programs have proven similarly difficult to kill. Job Corps, Volunteers in Service to America, Foster Grandparents, and Upward Bound remain active in the twenty-first century. Even Legal Services, one of the most politically explosive of all the War on Poverty programs, survives to this day despite decades of political attacks and funding cuts. In 1974, Nixon tried to rein in the militancy of local Legal Services offices by creating a federal Legal Services Corporation controlled from Washington. He then barred staff attorneys from participating in political activities such as "strikes, boycotts, picketing and other forms of civil disturbance." These actions lowered the organization's profile politically and limited its capacity to file class-action suits on behalf of the poor but ultimately gave the program greater stability. Carter's pick to head the Legal Services Corporation, Hillary Rodham, consolidated those gains. Reagan tried energetically to abolish the program but found his efforts derailed by political resistance. In 2009, President Barack Obama celebrated forty-five years of Legal Services work, insisting that the program "every day . . . breathes life into the timeless ideal—equal justice under the law."[7]

To an even greater extent than any of these programs, two survivors of the War on Poverty era have become so fundamental to the American social safety net that killing them has now become out of the question. The food stamp program and the Earned Income Tax Credit (EITC) have expanded exponentially from their origins and continue to grow rapidly. That is not to say that they have been immune to attack. Food stamps have acquired a lasting stigma that has fueled periodic cuts, most significantly during the early Reagan years, and

justified such humiliating fraud-prevention measures as fingerprinting applicants. Still, food stamps remain an essential hedge against hunger in every city,
county, and state, while the EITC, a refundable tax credit for working families
with children, is the most successful federal income-transfer program outside
of Social Security.

The food stamp program has grown more rapidly in the twenty-first century than at any point since it was first created. In late 2008, Congress changed
the program's name to the Supplemental Nutrition Assistance Program (SNAP)
and expanded it considerably. Currency-like stamps were replaced by a debit
card to soften recipients' embarrassment at the cash register. Stigma lingered,
as did punitive antifraud measures in many states. Nevertheless, the number
of people receiving food assistance grew by 17.4 percent from 2008 to 2009.
By the 2009 holiday season, SNAP was feeding one in four American children.
Just a few months later, one in eight Americans of all ages was enrolled in the
program. Enrollment numbers hit new highs every month between December
2008 and May 2010, and the U.S. Department of Agriculture forecast continued growth, predicting that one in seven Americans would be receiving SNAP
benefits by 2011.[8]

The EITC has become equally crucial to the survival of tens of millions of
Americans. Originally conceived in the 1970s as part of a welfare reform proposal intended to reward work, EITC became and remains the largest federal
income-transfer program for the poor. In 2008, it provided cash benefits to
24 million families. In 2009, EITC raised an estimated 6.6 million Americans,
half of them children, above the poverty line. These benefits are augmented
in many parts of the country by similar state income tax credits. The effect is
greatest in the poorest sections of the country. A quarter of Louisiana and Mississippi taxpayers receive cash refunds through EITC.[9]

The idea for the program came from Louisiana senator Russell Long in 1971.
Then the powerful chair of the Senate Finance Committee, Long was a conservative Democrat infamous for his battles with welfare rights activists and for
calling welfare mothers "brood mares." Long believed that Nixon's proposal of a
national minimum income for all Americans would discourage recipients from
accepting low-wage work, so he asked his aides to create a plan that would reward those who worked for wages and filed federal taxes. In framing that plan,
he consulted with community activists who had come to know him while lobbying for poverty program allotments. In 1973, Long proposed a national public
jobs program and income tax credit. The jobs program failed in Congress, but

the tax credit was approved as a temporary program in 1975. EITC gave low-wage workers with children a refundable tax break equal to 10 percent of their income. That refund was made permanent under another southern Democrat, Jimmy Carter.[10]

Like Long, Carter was engaged with the ideas and the mission of the War on Poverty but sought to make federal assistance to the poor more palatable to conservatives by emphasizing a work requirement. Hoping to appease liberals who had criticized Johnson for failing to create more public jobs, Carter made two attempts to push through large public jobs programs, which he believed would help alleviate poverty and stimulate the economy. The 1977 Program for Better Jobs and Income was a guaranteed-income plan that promised to create up to one million minimum-wage public service jobs. Like Nixon's 1969 Family Assistance Plan, Carter's plan went down to defeat because conservatives worried that it would interfere with the workings of the free labor market, while liberals argued that work requirements were coercive. Leaders of poor mothers' community groups lobbied for the bill, however, arguing that creating jobs for the poor was a necessary step in the battle against poverty.

The public jobs idea came up again when Congress held hearings about CETA's reauthorization in 1978. Poor mothers and their advocates testified that job training and placement programs were crucial to getting women off welfare and into paid jobs. But mothers needed day care, medical coverage for their children, and access to decently paid work. The Carter administration worked more closely with poor mothers than had any previous president. In 1977, he appointed Graciela Olivarez to run the Community Services Administration. Olivarez had long advocated greater recognition of poverty as a women's issue and in particular as an issue for poor mothers of color. She and Women's Bureau director Alexis Herman worked with female community activists to help draft language for the 1978 CETA reauthorization and for the Youth Employment Training Act, which targeted jobs and job training for poor mothers and young people.[11]

One of the only job creation initiatives of the War on Poverty, CETA brought public service jobs into impoverished neighborhoods. It moved beyond the New Deal focus on construction jobs and beyond the male-breadwinner focus of the Johnson and Nixon years to create publicly funded service-delivery positions that hired women to do jobs their communities needed, including day care and translation services for immigrants. Carter's Labor Department also fashioned job training programs and placement quotas aimed at opening up well-paid and previously male-dominated trades to poor women. Together, these programs produced modest reductions in national unemployment rates. And Carter's focus on public jobs called attention to the problem of lack of demand for low-skilled labor as an obstacle to putting the poor back to work. Still, the programs would have had to have been much larger to have any significant impact in a time of recession. CETA came in for fierce criticism from many quarters.[12]

Two Carter antipoverty bills that were seen as more successful were the 1977 Community Reinvestment Act and the 1978 Urban Development Action Grant Program. The Community Reinvestment Act used federal regulatory power over banks to stop redlining—that is, the denial of loans and credit to poor communities. The Action Grant program provided federal loans to local governments for development projects in chronically distressed communities. Both ideas built on the community action and development premises of the 1960s but sought actively to reengage private capital and city governments in the revitalization of poor communities. Like CDCs, also public-private partnerships generated by War on Poverty legislation, these programs have proven extremely durable.[13]

RONALD REAGAN AND THE DECLARATION OF WAR ON THE WAR ON POVERTY

Reagan's election in 1980 marked the end of the period of policy innovation and structural transformation begun by the War on Poverty. Vowing to take away the influence of "special interests" in Washington, Reagan attacked two of Carter's key antipoverty institutions. The Community Services Administration was dissolved as part of the Omnibus Budget Reconciliation Act of 1981. Funds for community action agencies were cut, and more limited allotments were thereafter distributed through Community Services Block Grants to local governments. Second, at Reagan's request, Congress repealed CETA in 1982.

Several forces combined to undermine CETA. Employing only 750,000 people full time and 1,000,000 young people in summer jobs at its peak in 1979, it had a limited impact on overall unemployment rates. Under pressure to limit federal spending, Carter cut the program in half toward the end of his term. In part, CETA's political vulnerability arose from its emphasis on poor women, which tied it too closely in the public mind to the much-denigrated Aid to Families with Dependent Children public-assistance program. Because it was oriented toward service delivery, CETA created few lasting monuments on the order of the New Deal–era bridges and dams, hiking trails, and public murals that still generate positive feeling about Franklin Roosevelt's work programs. Finally, the late 1970s was a time of economic hardship for municipal governments. Too many public agencies used CETA monies to pay municipal workers already on the public payroll, limiting the program's impact on the number of chronically unemployed and giving it a reputation for encouraging corruption.

"We've spent billions on manpower programs for the last fifteen years and youth employment keeps going up," the Reagan White House said in 1981. Reagan pointed to newspaper want ads to prove his contention that the cause of unemployment was not a lack of jobs. "In the Sunday *New York Times*, there were 45–1/2 pages of help wanted ads," Reagan said in 1981, "and in the *Washington Post* Sunday there were 33–1/2 pages of help-wanted ads. . . . How does a person . . . justify calling themselves unemployed when there's a fellow spending money and saying . . . Come fill my job? . . . There are jobs waiting," concluded Reagan, "and people not trained for those jobs." The new president proposed paying local businesses to train people for unfilled jobs, replacing CETA with the Job Training Partnership Act, which permanently took the federal government out of the business of creating jobs. No president since, even in the depths of recession, has dared to propose a nationwide public jobs program.[14]

Reagan rode into office on a wave of popular discontentment with "big government" that he had been carefully stoking since Johnson was in the White House. The new president and his supporters cast the 1980 election as a "revolution," a resounding mandate to dismantle the War on Poverty state. Reagan's rhetoric both on the campaign trail and in the White House was uncompromising, and he enacted dramatic cuts in food stamps, Pell grants, housing subsidies, unemployment compensation, and student loans early in his presidency. The poor were hit hard: three million children were cut from the school lunch program, one million from food stamps, five hundred thousand from school breakfast programs, and an equal number from cash assistance. Three-quarters of a million children lost Medicaid benefits. More than three hundred thousand families were pushed out of public housing. Rates of homelessness soared.[15]

Reagan differentiated both rhetorically and practically between broad entitlements such as Social Security and means-tested poverty programs. Though programs serving poor and moderate-income Americans made up just 10 percent of the federal budget, they absorbed one-third of the cuts in Reagan's first budget. The bottom 20 percent of American earners lost income at seventy-five times the rate of the top 1 percent of earners. Such disparities were intentional.

During the campaign, despite pushback from some budget staff who wanted to completely dismantle the social safety net, Reagan had promised not to touch Social Security, Medicare, veterans' benefits, or disability assistance. When he talked about cutting "big government," he was focused on programs serving poor people and students. Middle-class entitlements were safe. Cutting those programs would have endangered his appeal with the white ethnic and blue-collar workers who made up a crucial constituency in the new Republican majority, the much-vaunted "Reagan Democrats."[16]

Yet even in the arena of federal poverty programs, Reagan's impact on policy was less dramatic than his influence on popular politics. That is not to underestimate the effects of his cuts. Millions of real people lost benefits, homes, and medical care during Reagan's time in office. The percentage of unemployed black youth skyrocketed, while the percentage attending college plummeted. Nevertheless, most federal poverty programs survived the presidencies of Reagan and his successor, George H. W. Bush, as well as that of George W. Bush. After an initial, highly visible round of cuts, Reagan increased spending for poverty programs, particularly in his second term. And in 1986, he called for and signed into law a significant expansion of the EITC.[17]

So how did Reagan's election affect the survival of the War on Poverty state? What changed, perhaps irrevocably, during the Reagan years was not the capacity of the federal government to address poverty but political support for an activist federal government, particularly with regard to aiding the poor. Reagan's career, more than any other in modern U.S. political history, helps to explain why American popular opinion regarding government antipoverty efforts in general and LBJ's War on Poverty in particular has been more or less in free-fall since 1964.

For more than twenty-five years, Reagan was chief spokesperson and standard-bearer for the conservative critique of the War on Poverty. In that time, buttressed by the popular writings of social scientists Charles Murray and Thomas Sowell, conservative politicians spun and embellished a politically usable history of federal poverty policy that rallied their base. This process began with Reagan's 1964 speeches on behalf of Barry Goldwater's campaign and continued through his years as California governor and into his presidency. Reagan's anti–War on Poverty rhetoric could be heard echoing at 2010 Tea Party rallies, but its popular influence has been far broader than the grassroots Right. It is in many ways the dominant view among Americans of all political stripes.

Reagan's rise to national political prominence was tied directly to the backlash against the War on Poverty that he helped to foment. He framed the fundamental populist critiques of federal poverty policy within months after the passage of the Economic Opportunity Act. First, he argued that the idea that government action could possibly ameliorate poverty was essentially softheaded and simpleminded. Speaking in support of Goldwater at the 1964 Republican National Convention, Reagan ridiculed the increasing national concern with poverty and exploitation of the poor: "We have so many people who can't see a fat man standing beside a thin one without coming to the conclusion the fat man got that way by taking advantage of the thin one," he said to resounding laughter. "So they're going to solve all the problems of human misery through government and government planning." But this solution was more than stupid, Reagan warned, it was fraught with danger.[18]

Evoking that sense of threat has been perhaps the most durable and effective method of rallying opposition to the War on Poverty. Expansion of the federal social safety net, Reagan argued, endangered core American values and eroded the freedom of every individual citizen. "Our natural, unalienable rights," Reagan said in 1964, "are now considered to be a dispensation of government, and freedom has never been so fragile, so close to slipping from our grasp as it is at this moment." Like many who came after him, he evoked the nation's revered founders to justify his position: "The Founding Fathers knew a government can't control the economy without controlling people. And they knew when a government sets out to do that, it must use force and coercion to achieve its purpose. So we have come to a time for choosing." This warning has resounded for decades, gaining volume and urgency each time a debate takes place about enhancing government-funded benefits programs.[19]

The final strand of the anti–War on Poverty narrative tapped into subliminal but potent race, sex, and class hostilities. It built on resentment of the civil rights movement, images of black single mothers as pathogens, and a long history of distrust of the poor to politicize the idea that government assistance promoted immorality. The soon-to-be-famous welfare queen, who would play a starring role in Reagan's 1980 campaign for the presidency, made her first cameo appearance in his 1964 speeches. "What are we doing to those we seek to help?" Reagan asked. "Not too long ago, a judge . . . told me of a young woman who'd come before him for a divorce. She had six children, was pregnant with her seventh. Under his questioning, she revealed her husband was a laborer earning 250 dollars a month. She wanted a divorce to get an eighty dollar raise. She's eligible for 330 dollars a month in the Aid to Dependent Children Program. She got the idea from two women in her neighborhood who'd already done that very thing."[20]

As he climbed toward the presidency over the next sixteen years, Reagan frequently tapped into these currents of prejudice and white working-class frustration. He attacked not only the Economic Opportunity Act but the Civil Rights Act of 1964 as an infringement of federal power on states' rights. He did not simply criticize cash assistance for poor mothers. He charged that food stamps and Medicaid benefited unemployed cheaters rather than the hardworking poor. In the winter of 1976, Reagan toured tiny all-white New Hampshire towns holding "citizen's press conferences" where he told stories of "a woman in Chicago" with "80 names, 30 addresses, 12 social security cards" and of New York City "slum dwellers" who lived in apartments "with 11 foot ceilings, with a 20 foot balcony, a swimming pool and a gymnasium." In 1980, he did something no previous presidential candidate had dared to do, launching his campaign with a paean to states' rights at the Neshoba County, Mississippi, fairgrounds where the bodies of three murdered civil rights workers had been buried in 1964 and where segregationist politicians had always kicked off their campaigns. In the months to come, Reagan repeatedly linked the War on Poverty in the public mind to inefficiency, corruption, and the undeserving poor.[21]

By the end of Reagan's first term, this linkage had become gospel for resurgent conservatives, codified in Charles Murray's best-selling 1984 study, *Losing Ground: American Social Policy, 1950–1980*. Murray's book bracketed the publication of Michael Harrington's *The Other America* twenty-two years earlier, arguing that the War on Poverty had been a dangerous turning point. "In only three years, from 1964 to 1967 . . . social policy went from the dream of ending the dole to the institution of permanent income transfers that embraced not only the recipients of the dole but large new segments of the population."[22]

Densely illustrated with imposing-looking charts and graphs, Murray's book recycled old arguments against government aid to the poor, warning that such aid undermined individual initiative and thus deepened rather than alleviated poverty. Murray built on Reagan's 1964 arguments that cash assistance programs undermined the two-parent family, promoting out-of-wedlock births and rising crime. Murray cited rising dropout, unemployment, and out-of-wedlock birth rates for African Americans as proof that federal poverty programs had poisoned precisely the people they were intended to help. Couched in the language of objective social science, *Losing Ground* was described by critics as "game changing." Since 1996, some observers have hailed the book as the spark that ultimately led to the end of welfare. Murray lent academic credibility to the idea that generous social welfare programs harmed the poor, affecting the policy vision of Democrats as well as Republicans.[23]

Bill Clinton campaigned for the presidency in 1992 as a "New Democrat" — code for, "I'm not like Lyndon Johnson, not tied to the verities of the civil rights past, not addicted to big government." In 1996, he made good on his campaign promise to "end welfare as we know it," signing the third version of a Republican-sponsored bill that ended the entitlement of the poorest Americans to cash assistance, which had been guaranteed in the Social Security Act of 1935. Though the 1996 bill was called the Personal Responsibility and Work Opportunity Reconciliation Act, caseload reduction replaced poverty reduction and work opportunity as the program's primary goal.[24]

Clinton's most important antipoverty effort was to double the number of people eligible for the EITC program. He also tripled the maximum benefit, reminding the public that the last president to expand the program had been Reagan. Clinton argued that his approach was a Republican-friendly strategy — improving economic well-being through tax cuts. The EITC was politically palatable for a New Democrat. It helped the working poor, a group overlooked by traditional poverty programs. It functioned as a substitute for a higher minimum wage, stretching the income of the working poor. And two-parent families were eligible.

"By expanding the refundable earned income tax credit, we will make history," Clinton promised in his first State of the Union address, delivered in February 1993. "We will reward the work of millions of working poor Americans by realizing the principle that if you work forty hours a week and you've got a child in the house, you will no longer be in poverty." The EITC did not end poverty any more than the Economic Opportunity Act did. Still, according to Census data, it has lifted more children out of poverty than any other government program. One estimate is that it reduced child poverty by 25 percent. By 1999, income of a single mother of two working half time at minimum wage plus EITC was greater than welfare benefits in most states.[25]

Clinton also doubled funding for federal child care subsidies, offered tax breaks to business to hire more than a million former welfare recipients, and nearly doubled the size of the Head Start preschool program. Analysts are very much split on the effectiveness of Clinton's antipoverty approach, but an analyst for the Progressive Policy Institute noted in 2009 that in an era of strong economic growth, poverty rates fell in every year of Clinton's presidency, reaching their lowest levels ever for African American children. In contrast, poverty rates rose steadily during the first decade of the twenty-first century, partly a result of Bush-era program cuts and shifts in the focus of poverty programs from job training and placement to strategies such as promoting marriage. Still, George W. Bush also made expansions that infuriated the most conservative members of his base, who accused him of betraying Reagan's legacy.[26]

THE WAR ON POVERTY: HISTORY AND MEMORY

Professional historians have until recently paid little attention to the transformation of the American welfare state between 1964 and 1980 or to its impact on political engagement by the poor. This omission resulted in part from left-wing and liberal ambivalence toward the War on Poverty. Progressives in politics and academe, some of whom had been community organizers in the 1960s and remembered their personal as well as political disappointments with federal anti-poverty programs, wrote little about those programs after the early 1970s. Most preferred to examine the grassroots social movements of that era as if they had operated completely independent of government aid.

Early in the twenty-first century, a new generation of historians began presenting research suggesting that the War on Poverty had wrought important and lasting changes, generating mixed responses from progressive historians. With an edge of irony but also palpable discomfort, one activist-historian quipped, "You mean I have to start saying nice things about the War on Poverty now?" Scholars old enough to remember the 1960s and 1970s had almost reflexively criticized the War on Poverty for its failure to engage in large-scale job creation, for the willful refusal of its planners and key officials to address the feminization of poverty, and for the willingness of Beltway-based officials to turn the administration of local poverty programs over to local elites. While such criticisms were wholly legitimate, progressives' widespread dissatisfaction with the cautiousness of the War on Poverty resulted in a gap in historical scholarship.

Important exceptions of course existed. Most notable was Michael B. Katz, whose decades of work on poverty history provided the foundation for most of the authors whose work appears in this volume. Nancy A. Naples offered important evidence of the key role played by poor mothers in community organizing. New work on the War on Poverty was also informed by Jacqueline Jones's pioneering analysis of dislocation and migration; by a rich feminist literature on the welfare state by, among others, Linda Gordon and Alice Kessler-Harris; by Jacqueline Dowd Hall's fruitful reframing of length and breadth of the civil rights movement; and by burgeoning literatures on the welfare rights struggles of the 1960s and 1970s, welfare policy, and civil rights activity in the urban North.[27]

Many of these works addressed the War on Poverty only indirectly, however. Historians' writings about the War on Poverty focused largely on its failures, as in the case of Allen J. Matusow's hefty *The Unraveling of America: A History of Liberalism in the 1960s*, first published in 1984. Matusow argued the importance of understanding local impacts of the federal effort to fight poverty and drew insights from local case studies, but his main point, as the title suggests, was that 1960s liberalism failed to deliver on its promises. Though Matusow may not have intended his book to be interpreted in this way, it became just more grist for the cresting conservative narrative.[28]

Criticism rained down from the left as well. Sociologist Jill Quadagno's 1998 *The Color of Welfare: How Racism Undermined the War on Poverty* powerfully illustrated the ways that racism and sexism undermined the potential of some of the most sweeping antipoverty proposals of the Johnson and Nixon years. Historian Frank Stricker's *Why America Lost the War on Poverty and How to Win It* recapitulated the main criticisms of the War on Poverty made during the 1960s, slamming the program for its failure to create significant numbers of public jobs and for its focus on individual solutions such as training and education rather than structural approaches to unemployment and underemployment. The War on Poverty, Stricker concluded grimly, was fought with "empty guns."[29]

While useful to students of poverty policy and politics, these nuanced scholarly examinations of the War on Poverty's failures reinforced the widespread belief that the War on Poverty had been a complete and abject failure. And they increased Democratic politicians' tendency to run away from any association with it. Joseph Califano, an official in both the Johnson and Carter administrations, noted in 1999, "In contemporary America politicians are paralyzed by fear of the label that comes with the heritage of Lyndon Johnson's Great Society. Democrats rest their hopes of regaining Congressional power on promises to preserve and expand Great Society programs like Medicare and aid to education, but they tremble at the thought of linking those programs to the liberal Lyndon. The irony is that they seek to distance themselves from the president who once said that the difference between liberals and cannibals is that cannibals eat only their enemies."[30]

Democratic politicians have long been ambivalent toward Johnson's War on

Poverty. The Community Action Program ran into trouble almost immediately with local politicians who felt that it represented too much federal meddling and too little oversight of militant local organizations. That viewpoint in part explains Democratic distaste for association with that program. But even more important, since the 1980s, Democrats have run in fear of being labeled *liberal*, in part because of the enthusiasm and relentlessness of the conservative campaign against the War on Poverty.

The fortieth anniversary of Johnson's declaration of War on Poverty and of the Economic Opportunity Act generated few observances, most of them scathingly negative. Conservative columnist Thomas Sowell marked this "painful anniversary" with a History Channel essay in which he argued that forty years of War on Poverty programs were directly responsible for the deterioration of American inner cities, teenage pregnancy, rising murder rates, and the tensions tearing apart poor black families. LBJ's poverty policy had also destroyed the last vestiges of American faith in liberalism, according to Sowell. "The War on Poverty," he wrote, "represented the crowning triumph of the liberal vision of society—and of government programs as the solution to social problems. The disastrous consequences that followed have made the word 'liberal' so much of a political liability that today even candidates with long left-wing track records have evaded or denied that designation."[31]

If Sowell's attempt to blame the miseries of the poor on government programs created to ease their suffering appeared to other scholars of poverty policy intellectually dishonest, he hit the nail on the head in his analysis of policymakers' and analysts' wariness regarding any association with the War on Poverty. In January 2004, former Republican House majority leader Dick Armey called on Congress to commemorate the fortieth anniversary of Johnson's declaration by putting an end to federal poverty programs because "welfare as LBJ conceived it . . . trapped several generations in a vicious cycle of lawlessness and dependency." A year later, Congress considered a proposal to cut or end funding for food stamps along with community development, social service, and community health programs. Heritage Foundation poverty policy analyst Robert Rector bemoaned the fact that few Republicans in Congress were willing to do so. The only strategy for reducing poverty, Rector insisted, was a campaign to reinforce traditional marriage.[32]

In September 2005, less than two weeks after the levees broke in New Orleans, George Will published a widely syndicated column in which he blamed the suffering of Katrina victims on forty years of failed poverty policy and the "cultural collapse" that it had caused. Responding to then-Senator Obama's charge that the government's failure to help those stranded in the flooded city was yet one more example of how little the Bush administration cared for this nation's poor—especially poor, black residents of a heavily Democratic city— Will argued that the real problem was too much federal attention to the poor. Trillions in federal dollars had been wasted on the poor over forty years, he wrote. His column was published while thousands sweltered in the Superdome. The only solution to entrenched poverty, he concluded, was for black girls to stay in school and avoid getting pregnant before marriage. "Women [with children] without husbands," Will wrote, "translates into chaos in neighborhoods and schools come rain or come shine."[33]

Though historians and others wrote to newspapers to challenge Will's arguments about the War on Poverty, these views received little publicity. When I suggested writing an essay for a major liberal daily about the successes of War on Poverty programs and how such programs might be deployed in the aftermath of Katrina, the publication's op-ed page editor politely declined, explaining that there had been too much sympathetic coverage of aid to the poor since the hurricane and suggesting that coverage of poverty required a fresh angle. So does national discussion of the War on Poverty. Without that rethinking, negative mischaracterizations of the War on Poverty continue to drive national politics and federal policy and continue to damage antipoverty programs run by the poor.

The destruction in 2009 of the Association of Community Organizations for Reform Now (ACORN), a national federation of poor people's community groups founded in the 1970s, illustrates the potency of this hostility. Since the War on Poverty years, ACORN had received a mix of public and private funds. In its early years, ACORN helped welfare recipients get onetime grants to purchase clothing and organized poor mothers to campaign for free and reduced-cost school breakfast and lunch programs. In later years, ACORN registered voters in poor neighborhoods, organized the poor to demand affordable housing, and improved schools and health care in their communities. ACORN advocated for repair of substandard buildings, helped veterans get their benefits, and fought discriminatory lending and insurance company redlining of poverty-stricken areas. That work received little or no press coverage for nearly thirty-eight years. During the 2008 election, however, ACORN became a household word after conservative talk show hosts and elected officials charged the group with voter registration fraud. The charges made headlines for the better part of two years, casting doubt on the integrity of all organizations receiving public funds to assist the poor.

The scandal revolved around the fact that Obama had once overseen an ACORN voter registration drive and that in 2008 his campaign paid ACORN to get out the vote in poor communities. ACORN workers in several locales were charged with padding the rolls of newly registered voters with fake names. The scandal called into question both Obama's integrity and that of campaigns to register more poor voters. After the election, Republican members of Congress continued to hold hearings on the group's alleged misdeeds, demanding that attorney general Eric Holder appoint a special prosecutor. In September 2009, two conservative activists masquerading as pimps entered an ACORN office, asked for help hiding profits from a brothel featuring underage illegal immigrants, filmed ACORN workers as they answered that damning question, and then aired the video on Fox News. Congress voted overwhelmingly—and in an unusually bipartisan manner—to cut off further federal funding for ACORN.[34]

ACORN's record was not without blemishes. A few scandals had erupted over the years, and ACORN officials in Nevada admitted to paying workers according to the number of voters they registered, a violation of state law, which considers that practice an inducement to fraud. In the main, however, idealistic ACORN staff who received only tiny salaries worked to help the poor and elderly, veterans and low-wage workers, children and single mothers receive the benefits to which they were entitled. Why were so few people in Washington willing to speak in defense of ACORN? Because the campaign against the group unleashed anew deep-seated hostilities toward federal poverty programs and reinforced the popular belief that they represented nothing more than federally funded corruption and subversion. One 2009 poll showed that 52 percent of Republicans and 26 percent of all American voters believed that ACORN had stolen the election for Obama. By November 2009, only 11 percent of Americans had a favorable view of the group.[35]

Although a federal district judge in New York ruled late in 2009 that Congress had violated the Constitution by imposing punishment on ACORN because of the group's political beliefs rather than evidence of criminal acts, ACORN dissolved as a national organization in March 2010. Two months earlier, the FBI arrested the same undercover filmmaker who had posed as a pimp to ACORN workers for trying to bug the telephone of a Democratic U.S. senator. His arrest generated far less media heat than the stories of ACORN's alleged improprieties. The political damage caused by the ACORN scandal was real and lasting.

By branding one of the country's longest-running poor people's organizations as corrupt, critics of federal poverty programs further weakened already atrophied public support for government aid to the poor. Many of us who study the War on Poverty felt a sense of déjà vu. We as a society had definitely been here before.[36]

During the 1970s and 1980s, political attacks on federal poverty programs intensified and scores of community-based antipoverty organizations across the country were investigated for fraud. The cases always began in the same way. A local or state or federal official charged the group with mismanagement of funds or with hiring a poor person for a job funded by public dollars that he or she was not qualified to fill. The local press jumped on the charges, and the scandal dragged on, in and out of court. More often than not, the fraud charges went unproven, but the clamor served both political and practical purposes. The staff or leaders of the clinic or school or community development corporation under investigation would spend energy, resources, and time rebutting those charges—in court, in the media, and in urgent meetings with officials who held the purse strings. While the investigations continued, these organizations became ineligible to receive federal funds. Meanwhile, negative publicity made private foundations leery of providing funding.[37]

As the authors in this volume make clear, this strategy was deployed across the United States in the 1970s and 1980s—against preschools and medical clinics, teen programs and community centers. The histories in this book give readers a sense of the devastating effectiveness of that strategy in undermining government funding and public support for antipoverty programs, especially those that employed poor people in jobs intended to benefit their communities. Readers may see in these histories echoes of twenty-first-century headlines.

Amid the euphoria surrounding Barack Obama's January 2009 presidential inauguration and the anxiety that accompanied the near-collapse of the American economy, it seemed strange to many of us who study the history of poverty policy that no one in the new administration could be heard calling for a renewed government campaign to improve standards of living for the nation's poor. The mainstream press reflected a bit about FDR and his programs. As the media ran story after story about foreclosures, there was some sense that, as in the Great Depression, poverty might have lost some of its stigma. Not so federal aid to the poor. Bank bailouts came first, road projects next, and finally some relief for struggling homeowners. But on the questions of hunger, job creation, and community renewal, an uncomfortable silence has persisted.

Ten days before the inauguration festivities began, the forty-fifth anniversary of Johnson's declaration of an unconditional War on Poverty came and went, unheralded. Politicians, the media, and average Americans might have taken advantage of the moment to reflect on the successes and failures of Johnson's attempt to grapple with widespread poverty in the richest of nations and to consider about what lessons that campaign might hold for policymakers in 2009. That such a discussion did not happen is telling.

When unemployment rates passed 10 percent nationally, a few liberal members of Congress talked about reviving the CETA community-based jobs program, dead since Congress repealed it in 1982 in a fury of accusations about corruption. Yet even this product of Nixon's New Federalism proved too politically explosive for the Obama administration. The idea simply carried too much negative baggage. "There is just a real allergic feeling in the White House and Congress toward this approach," the *Washington Post* noted in November 2009, "a worry that it smacks of socialism. Keynesianism has experienced a rebirth, but there's still enough Reaganism in the air that this is seen as a step too far."[38]

A cloud of negativity hangs over the sweeping federal initiative known as the War on Poverty, still coloring all of our perceptions about the feasibility and desirability of having the federal government spend taxpayer dollars to help poor people revitalize their communities. By gathering histories of many poor communities across the United States where such attempts took place forty years ago and where some programs continue to this day, this book dispels that cloud. We hope that honestly portraying such struggles in all of their complexity and difficulty will spark new conversations about what worked and what did not in America's War on Poverty and perhaps open up possibilities for fresh beginnings.

Notes

1. Richard M. Nixon, "Presidential Nomination Acceptance Speech," August 8, 1968, http://www.4president.org/speeches/nixon1968acceptance.htm.

2. Annelise Orleck, *Storming Caesars Palace: How Black Mothers Fought Their Own War on Poverty* (Boston: Beacon, 2005), chaps. 4–5; Arnold B. Sawislak, "Campaign Speeches Are No Clue as to How Nixon Will Act," *Hendersonville Times-News*, March 28, 1969; Charles Bartlett, "Backing into the Poverty Problem," *Spokesman-Review*, March 28, 1969; Edward Burke, "Job Corps Backer Sees Sharp Cutback," *New York Times* (hereafter *NYT*), March 29, 1969.

3. See U.S. Department of Housing and Urban Development, *HUD Historical Background*, http://www.hud.gov/offices/adm/about/admguide/history.cfm. See also Green, this volume; Orleck, *Storming Caesars Palace*, chaps. 6–7.

4. Peter Edelman, "The War on Poverty and Subsequent Federal Programs: What Worked, What Didn't and Why," *Clearinghouse Review Journal of Poverty Law and Policy*, May–June 2006, 17–18; Richard P. Nathan, "A Retrospective on Richard M. Nixon's Domestic Policies," *Presidential Studies Quarterly* 26:1 (Winter 1996): 155–64.

5. Sara Rosenbaum and Peter Shin, *Health Centers Reauthorization: An Overview of Achievements and Challenges* (Washington, D.C.: Kaiser Commission on Medicaid and the Uninsured 2006); Bonnie Lefkowitz, *Community Health Centers: A Movement and the People Who Made It Happen* (New Brunswick, N.J.: Rutgers University Press, 2007).

6. National Community Action Foundation, http://www.ncaf.org; CDBG Coalition, *Consequences for American Communities: A National Survey on the Impact of Recent Reductions in Community Development Block Grant Funding* (Washington, D.C.: National Association of Housing and Redevelopment Officials, 2006); Rachel Bratt, "Why CDCs Should Advocate for a Right to Housing," *Shelter Force*, Winter 2006, http://www.nhi.org/online/issues/148/whycdcs.html.

7. Linda Charlton, "Nixon Again Asks Legal Aid to Poor," *NYT*, May 12, 1973; Richard Nixon, *Statement about Proposed Legislation to Establish a Legal Services Corporation*, May 11, 1973, http://www.presidency.ucsb.edu/ws/index.php?pid=3840&st=&st1; *LSC Updates—35th Anniversary*, July 25, 2009, http://www.lsc.gov/press/updates_2009_detail_T246_R18.php.

8. Joseph Califano Jr., "What Was Really Great about the Great Society," *Washington Monthly*, October 1999; Mark Nord and Margaret Andrews, "Food Insecurity Up in Recessionary Times," *Amber Waves*, December 2009, http://www.ers.usda.gov/AmberWaves/december09/PDF/FoodInsecurity.pdf; Jason DeParle and Robert Gebeloff, "Food Stamp Use Soars and Stigma Fades," *NYT*, November 28, 2009; Charles Abbott, "Food Stamp Tally Nears 40 Million, Sets Record," *Reuters*, May 7, 2010; Rosenbaum and Shin, *Health Centers Reauthorization*.

9. Robert McIntyre, "A Payday Bonus," *American Prospect*, August 13, 2004.

10. "Information Brief Minnesota House of Representatives," *The Federal Earned Income Tax Credit*, December 2007, www.house.mn/hrd/hrd.htm; V. Joseph Hotz and John Karl Scholtz, *The Earned Income Tax Credit*, August 29, 2002, http://www.ssc.wisc.edu/~scholz/Research/EITC_Survey.pdf; Hilary Hoynes, *The Earned Income Tax Credit, Welfare Reform, and the Employment of Low-Skilled Single Mothers*, August 22, 2008, http://www.econ.ucdavis.edu/faculty/hoynes/working_papers/Chicago-Fed-Final.pdf.

11. See Bauman, this volume. See also Orleck, *Storming Caesars Palace*, chaps. 7–8.

12. Grace A. Franklin and Randall B. Ripley, *CETA: Politics and Policy, 1973–1982* (Knoxville: University of Tennessee Press, 1984); Katherine P. Dickinson and Terry R.

Johnson, "An Analysis of the Impact of CETA Programs on Participants' Earnings," *Journal of Human Resources* 21:1 (Winter 1986): 69–91.

13. Sheldon Danziger, "Welfare Reform from Nixon to Clinton: What Role for Social Science?" (paper presented at Social Sciences and Policy Making Conference, University of Michigan, March 13–14, 1998); Max O. Stephenson Jr., "The Policy and Premises of Urban Development Grant Program Implementation: A Comparative Analysis of the Carter and Reagan Presidencies," *Journal of Urban Affairs* 9:1 (June 2008): 19–35.

14. "Reagan Set to Replace CETA," *Associated Press*, December 19, 1981; "Little for Reagan in Want Ads," *Baltimore Evening Sun*, March 24, 1981; "Why Won't Obama Give You a Job?," *Washington Post*, November 9, 2009, http://www.washingtonpost.com/wpdyn/content/discussion/2009/11/06/DI2009110603214.html; Yvonne Liu, "Training for Green Jobs Is Pointless When There Are No Jobs," April 13, 2010, http://blogs.alternet.org/speakeasy/2010/04/13/trained-to-fail/; Gordon Lafer, *The Job Training Charade* (Ithaca: Cornell University Press, 2002).

15. See Orleck, *Storming Caesars Palace*, 268–70; *Congressional Quarterly Almanac* (1981), 32, 256, 490–91; R. Kent Weaver, *Ending Welfare as We Know it* (Washington, D.C.: Brookings Institution Press, 2000), 68–69; Center on Budget and Policy Priorities, "Falling Behind: A Report on How Blacks Have Fared Under Reagan," *Journal of Black Studies* 17:2 (December 1986): 148–72.

16. William Greider, *The Education of David Stockman and Other Americans* (New York: Dutton, 1981); David Stockman, *Triumph of Politics: Why the Reagan Revolution Failed* (New York: Avon, 1987). See also Marcus Gadson, "Ronald Reagan vs. FDR and LBJ: Inside the Conservative War on Welfare" (honors thesis, Dartmouth College, 2010).

17. Robert F. Durant, Teresa Kluesner, and Jerome S. Legge Jr., "Domestic Programs, Budget Outlays, and the Reagan Revolution: A Test of Competing Theories in Four Policy Arenas," *Journal of Public Administration Research and Theory* 2:4 (October 1992): 369–86; Raymond J. Struyk, "Administering Social Welfare: The Reagan Record," *Journal of Policy Analysis and Management* 4:4 (Summer 1985): 481–500; Robert Rector, "Means-Tested Welfare Spending: Past and Future Growth," March 7, 2001, http://www.heritage.org/Research/Testimony/Means-Tested- Welfare-Spending-Past-and-Future-Growth; Richard Viguerie, *Conservatives Betrayed: How George W. Bush and Other Big Government Republicans Hijacked the Conservative Cause* (Los Angeles: Bonus, 2006).

18. Ronald Reagan, *A Time for Choosing*, October 27, 1964, http://www.reagan.utexas.edu/archives/reference/timechoosing.html.

19. Ibid.

20. Ibid.; James Glaser, *Race, Campaign Politics, and the Realignment of the South* (New Haven: Yale University Press, 1996).

21. Bob Herbert, "Righting Reagan's Wrongs," *NYT*, November 13, 2007; Chris Kromm, "Why Rand Paul's Views Are No Surprise," *Facing South: The Online Maga-*

zine of the Institute for Southern Studies, May 20, 2010, http://www.southernstudies.org/2010/05/why-rand-pauls-views-on-civil-rights-shouldnt-be-surprising.html; "'Welfare Queen' Becomes Issue in Reagan Campaign," *NYT*, February 15, 1976.

22. Charles Murray, *Losing Ground: American Social Policy, 1950–1980* (New York: Basic Books, 1984), 24–25.

23. "California: No Business Like It," *Time*, September 19, 1966; Orleck, *Storming Caesars Palace*, 86; Murray, *Losing Ground*; Charles Murray, *In Our Hands: A Plan to Replace the Welfare State* (Washington, D.C.: American Enterprise Institute Press, 2006); Dalton Conley, "Charles Murray's New Plan," *Boston Review*, September–October 2006; Charlotte Allen, "Welfare Lines," *Washington Monthly*, December 1994.

24. For a fascinating examination of the evolution of welfare policy in the 1960s, 1970s, and 1980s, see Marissa Chappell, *The War on Welfare: Family, Poverty, and Politics in Modern America* (Chapel Hill: University of North Carolina Press, 2010).

25. Robert Greenstein and Isaac Shapiro, *Center for Budget Policy and Priorities, New Research Findings on the Effect of Earned Income Credit*, March 16, 1999, http://www.cbpp.org/research/index.cfm?fa=archive&id=30&year=1999; William Jefferson Clinton, State of the Union Address, February 17, 1993, http://en.wikisource.org/wiki/Bill_Clinton%27s_First_State_of_the_Union_Address; Bruce D. Meyer and Douglas Holtz-Eakin, eds., *Making Work Pay: The Earned Income Tax Credit and Its Impact on American Families* (New York: Sage, 2001).

26. Katie Campbell, "A Work Bonus for Men," Democratic Leadership Council, January 15, 2009, http://www.dlc.org/ndol_ci.cfm?contentid=254779&kaid=450020&subid=900201; Bill Clinton, "How We Ended Welfare Together," *NYT*, August 22, 2006.

27. See Michael B. Katz, *In the Shadow of the Poorhouse: A Social History of Welfare in America* (expanded ed., New York: Basic Books, 1996); Michael B. Katz, *The Undeserving Poor: From the War on Poverty to the War on Welfare* (New York: Pantheon, 1989); Michael B. Katz, *The "Underclass" Debate: Views from History* (Princeton: Princeton University Press, 1993); Michael B. Katz, *Improving Poor People: The Welfare State, the "Underclass" and Urban Schools as History* (Princeton: Princeton University Press, 1997); Nancy A. Naples, *Grassroots Warriors: Activist Mothering, Community Work, and the War on Poverty* (New York: Routledge, 1998). On the fallacy of value-neutral social science regarding poverty, see Alice O'Connor, *Poverty Knowledge: Social Science, Social Policy, and the Poor in Twentieth-Century U.S. History* (Princeton: Princeton University Press, 2001); Jacqueline Jones, *The Dispossessed: America's Underclasses from the Civil War to the Present* (New York: Basic Books, 1992); Jacqueline Jones, "Southern Diaspora: Origins of the Northern Underclass," in *Underclass Debate*, ed. Katz; Alice Kessler-Harris, *In Pursuit of Equity: Women, Men and the Quest for Economic Citizenship in Twentieth-Century America* (New York: Oxford University Press, 2001); Premilla Nadasen, *Welfare Warriors: The Welfare Rights Movement in the United States* (New York:

Routledge, 2005); Jacquelyn Dowd Hall, "The Long Civil Rights Movement and the Political Uses of the Past," *Journal of American History* 91:4 (March 2005): 1233–63; Felicia Kornbluh, *The Battle for Welfare Rights* (Philadelphia: University of Pennsylvania Press, 2007); Tom Sugrue, *Sweet Land of Liberty: The Forgotten Struggle for Civil Rights in the North* (New York: Random House, 2009); Jeanne Theoharis and Komozi Woodard, eds., *Groundwork: Local Black Freedom Movements in America* (New York: New York University Press, 2005); Chappell, *War on Welfare*.

28. Allen J. Matusow, *The Unraveling of America: A History of Liberalism in the 1960s* (New York: Harper and Row, 1984)

29. Jill Quadagno, *The Color of Welfare: How Racism Undermined the War on Poverty* (New York: Oxford University Press, 1994); Frank Stricker, *Why America Lost the War on Poverty and How to Win It* (Chapel Hill: University of North Carolina Press, 2007). See also Noel A. Cazenave, *Impossible Democracy: The Unlikely Success of the War on Poverty Community Action Programs* (Albany: State University of New York Press, 2007).

30. Califano, "What Was Really Great."

31. Thomas Sowell, "A Painful Anniversary: LBJ's War on Poverty" August 17, 2004, http://boards.history.com/topic/Is-The-Un/A-Painful-Anniversary/300021602.

32. Dick Armey, "The War on Poverty Turns 40," *Freedom Works*, January 9, 2004, http://www.freedomworks.org/publications/the-war-on-poverty-turns-40; Robert Rector, "How Not to Be Poor," *National Review*, October 13, 2005, http://www.heritage.org/research/commentary/2005/10/how-not-to-be-poor.

33. George Will, "River of Liberal Banalities Overflowing," *Valley News*, September 12, 2005; George Will, "A Poverty of Thought," *Washington Post*, September 13, 2005. The column also appeared under the titles "Poverty of Thought," "Race Obsession on the March," and "Misguided Mindsets Untouched by Katrina."

34. Claire Suddath, "ACORN," *Time Magazine*, October 12, 2008; Michael B. Farrell, "ACORN Scandal," *Christian Science Monitor*, September 19, 2009.

35. Public Policy Polling, November 19, 2009, http://publicpolicypolling.blogspot.com/2009/11/acorn.html; "ACORN Inquiry Finds No Illegal Acts," *Washington Post*, December 8, 2009.

36. Percentage derived from Public Policy poll. Relying *Lovett* (1946), which held unconstitutional a congressional act banning specified individuals from government employment based on the unadjudicated finding that they had "subversive beliefs" and "subversive associations," Judge Nina Gershon explained that under clear Supreme Court law, "the discretionary nature of government funding does not foreclose a finding that Congress has impermissibly singled out plaintiffs for punishment" (Glenn Greenwald, "Victory for ACORN," *Salon*, December 12, 2009, http://www.salon.com/news/acorn/index.html?story=/opinion/greenwald/2009/12/12/acorn; "ACORN Dis-

banding," *Huffington Post*, March 22, 2010, http://www.huffingtonpost.com/2010/03/22/ acorn-disbanding-embattle_n_508893.html.

37. For further information about fraud investigations of community antipoverty agencies, see Orleck, *Storming Caesar's Palace*; Christina Greene, *Our Separate Ways: Women and the Black Freedom Movement in Durham, North Carolina* (Chapel Hill: University of North Carolina Press, 2005); Rhonda Williams, *The Politics of Public Housing: Black Women's Struggles against Urban Inequality* (New York: Oxford University Press, 2005).

38. "Why Won't Obama Give You a Job?"

CONTRIBUTORS

SUSAN YOUNGBLOOD ASHMORE is associate professor of history at Oxford College of Emory University. She is the author of *Carry It On: The War on Poverty and the Civil Rights Movement in Alabama, 1964–1972* (University of Georgia Press, 2008).

ADINA BACK was a member of the editorial collective of the *Radical History Review* and an assistant professor of history at Brooklyn College. She was the author of numerous essays on the movement by African American, Jewish, and Puerto Rican women in New York City to desegregate public schools. She passed away in 2008.

ROBERT BAUMAN is associate professor of history at Washington State University, Tri-Cities. He is the author of *Race and the War on Poverty: From Watts to East L.A.* (University of Oklahoma Press, 2008).

WILLIAM CLAYSON is professor and lead faculty in history at the College of Southern Nevada. He is the author of *Freedom Is Not Enough: The War on Poverty and the Civil Rights Movement in Texas* (University of Texas Press, 2010).

DANIEL M. COBB is associate professor in the Department of American Studies at the University of North Carolina at Chapel Hill and has served as assistant director of the D'Arcy McNickle Center for American Indian History in Chicago. He is the coeditor of *Beyond Red Power: American Indian Politics and Activism since 1900* (School for Advanced Research Press, 2007) and author of *Native Activism in Cold War America: The Struggle for Sovereignty* (University Press of Kansas Press, 2008).

GRETA DE JONG is associate professor of African American history at the University of Nevada at Reno. She is the author of *A Different Day: African American Struggles for Justice in Rural Louisiana, 1900–1970* (University of North Carolina

Press, 2002) and *Invisible Enemy: The African American Freedom Struggle after 1965* (Wiley-Blackwell, 2010).

KENT B. GERMANY is associate professor of history at the University of South Carolina. He is the author of *New Orleans after the Promises: Poverty, Citizenship, and the Search for the Great Society* (University of Georgia Press, 2007), and coeditor of *The Kennedy Assassination and the Transfer of Power: The Presidential Recordings, Lyndon B. Johnson,* vol. 3, *January 1964* (Norton 2005), and *Toward the Great Society: The Presidential Recordings, Lyndon B. Johnson,* vol. 4, *February-March 8, 1964* (Norton, 2007).

LAURIE B. GREEN teaches in the history department and the Center for Women's and Gender Studies at the University of Texas at Austin. She is the author of *Battling the Plantation Mentality: Memphis and the Black Freedom Struggle* (University of North Carolina Press, 2007), winner of the 2008 Philip Taft Labor History Book Award.

CHRISTINA GREENE is associate professor in the Afro-American Studies Department at the University of Wisconsin at Madison. She is the author of *Our Separate Ways: Women and the Black Freedom Movement in Durham, North Carolina* (University of North Carolina Press, 2005), winner of the Julia Cherry Spruill Award for the best book in southern women's history (awarded by the Southern Association of Women Historians).

AMY JORDAN is associate professor of African American history at Hampshire College in Amherst, Massachusetts. She is the author of *From Rural Rehabilitation to Welfare Rights: Rural Relief, Land Ownership and Welfare Rights Activism in Mississippi* (forthcoming).

THOMAS KIFFMEYER is associate professor of history at Morehead State University in Morehead, Kentucky. He is the author of *Reformers to Radicals: Appalachian Volunteers and the War on Poverty* (University Press of Kentucky, 2008).

GUIAN A. MCKEE is associate professor at the Miller Center for Public Affairs at the University of Virginia. He is the author of *The Problem of Jobs: Liberalism, Race, and Deindustrialization in Philadelphia* (University of Chicago Press, 2008) and *Lyndon*

Johnson and the War on Poverty: How Policymakers Try to Deliver on Social Promises (Johns Hopkins University Press, forthcoming).

ANNELISE ORLECK is professor of history at Dartmouth College. She is the author of *Storming Caesars Palace: How Black Mothers Fought Their Own War on Poverty* (Beacon, 2005); *The Soviet Jewish Americans* (Greenwood, 1999) and *Common Sense and a Little Fire: Women and Working Class Politics in the United States* (University of North Carolina Press, 1995) and coeditor of *The Politics of Motherhood: Activist Voices from Left to Right* (University Press of New England, 1997).

WESLEY G. PHELPS received his PhD in history at Rice University. His dissertation is "A Grassroots War on Poverty: Community Action and Urban Politics in Houston, 1964–1976."

MARC S. RODRIGUEZ is assistant professor of history, law, and American studies as well as a fellow at the Institute for Latino Studies at the University of Notre Dame. He is the author of *Mexican Americanism: The Tejano Diaspora and Ethnic Politics in Texas and Wisconsin after 1950* (University of North Carolina Press, 2011).

KAREN M. TANI received her PhD in history at the University of Pennsylvania, where she has also earned a law degree and is Sharswood Fellow in Law and History. Her dissertation is "Securing a Right to Welfare: Public Assistance Administration and the Rule of Law, 1938–1960." She is an assistant professor at the University of California, Berkeley.

RHONDA Y. WILLIAMS is associate professor of history at Case Western Reserve University. She is the author of *The Politics of Public Housing: Black Women's Struggles against Urban Inequality* (Oxford University Press, 2004) and has coedited *Teaching the American Civil Rights Movement: Freedom's Bittersweet Song* (Routledge 2002) and the spring 2008 special issue of *Radical History Review.*

INDEX

Page numbers in italics refer to photographs.